TEST CRICKET
A HISTORY

Also by Tim Wigmore

Cricket 2.0: Inside the T20 Revolution
(with Freddie Wilde)

The Best: How Elite Athletes Are Made
(with Mark Williams)

Crickonomics: The Anatomy of Modern Cricket
(with Stefan Szymanski)

White Hot: The Inside Story of England Cricket's Double World Champions
(with Matt Roller)

Test Cricket
A History

Tim Wigmore

QUERCUS

To Dad, for inspiring my love of Test cricket

First published in Great Britain in 2025 by

QUERCUS

Quercus Editions Limited
Carmelite House
50 Victoria Embankment
London EC4Y 0DZ

An Hachette UK company

The authorised representative in the EEA is Hachette Ireland, 8 Castlecourt Centre, Dublin 15, D15 XTP3, Ireland (email: info@hbgi.ie)

Copyright © 2025 Tim Wigmore

The moral right of Tim Wigmore to be identified as the author of this work has been asserted in accordance with the Copyright, Designs and Patents Act, 1988.

All rights reserved. No part of this publication may be reproduced or transmitted in any form or by any means, electronic or mechanical, including photocopy, recording, or any information storage and retrieval system, without permission in writing from the publisher.

A CIP catalogue record for this book is available from the British Library

HB ISBN 978 1 52942 861 2
TPB ISBN 978 1 52942 862 9
EBOOK ISBN 978 1 52942 864 3

Quercus Editions Ltd hereby exclude all liability to the extent permitted by law for any errors or omissions in this book and for any loss, damage or expense (whether direct or indirect) suffered by a third party relying on any information contained in this book.

Typeset by Jouve (UK), Milton Keynes
Printed and bound in Great Britain by Clays Ltd, Elcograf S.p.A.

MIX
Paper | Supporting responsible forestry
FSC® C104740

Papers used by Quercus are from well-managed forests and other responsible sources.

CONTENTS

Note on the text — vii
Introduction: The cruellest game — ix

1. A mad idea — 1
2. Two become three: the emergence of South Africa — 17
3. The Golden Age – or Test cricket's great missed opportunity? — 28
4. The greatest opening pair — 45
5. Three become six: Test cricket opens up — 56
6. Bradman, Bodyline and the Invincibles — 77
7. No rations any more — 94
8. The emergence of Pakistan — 112
9. Cricket, lovely cricket — 126
10. Captaincy: a tale of class — 143
11. The South Africa question — 152
12. Tiger and the quartet — 166
13. The rise of West Indies — 179
14. Cricket's uncivil wars — 198
15. The impossible job — 213
16. The oracle: the story of reverse swing — 231
17. No longer just a whistlestop — 243
18. Shane Warne and the resurgence of leg spin — 253
19. The road less travelled — 262
20. How to buy a Test match — 279
21. The two ages of Tendulkar — 298

CONTENTS

22	The magic and mystery of Murali	319
23	The transformation of wicketkeeping	341
24	Expansionism and its discontents	354
25	England learns to expect	368
26	The great team hiding in plain sight	393
27	The slow rise of the Tigers	409
28	How umpires and technology changed Test cricket	423
29	Test cricket in exile	435
30	The parable of West Indies	445
31	Cricket's superpower	459
32	In the fast lane	478
33	New Zealand's moment	494
34	More than just a Commonwealth club	509
35	Bazball and beyond	522

Acknowledgements	541
Selected bibliography	543
Picture credits	560
Index	561

NOTE ON THE TEXT

PLACE NAMES
I have generally used place names as they were at the time – for instance Dacca before the city assumed its current name of Dhaka, and Bombay before Mumbai.

RACIAL TERMS
Throughout the book, I have chosen to use lower case when referring to the racialised constructs 'black', 'white' and 'coloured'. This includes South Africa and the apartheid era. In my chapters on South Africa, I have used the racial terms 'black African' and 'coloured' reflecting the categorisations that were used in the country historically. My decision to consistently use lower case for race determiners is a style preference, and in no way is intended to diminish the cultural and political significance embedded within them.

CRICKET TERMS
Below are a few helpful clarifications:
   The Marylebone Cricket Club ran English tours from 1903/04 to 1976/77, as I have reflected in the text.
   For batters, average is the number of runs scored on average per each dismissal. For bowlers, average is the number of runs conceded per wicket taken.
   For batters, strike rate refers to the number of runs scored per 100 balls. For bowlers, strike rate refers to the number of balls needed to take a wicket on average.

NOTE ON THE TEXT

A maiden over is an over in which the bowler does not concede a run.

The term first-class refers to multi-innings matches that are officially awarded this distinction – domestic games considered to be of high standard, as well as all Test matches.

Introduction

THE CRUELLEST GAME

Test cricket is the most brutal game.

Football is a low-scoring sport: to win, the weaker side might only need to score once in 90 minutes. Fifty and 20-over cricket limits the time for two teams to pull apart; one individual performance, even if it only lasts for a few overs, can bring victory.

While these games provide scope for underdogs to dream, Test cricket's format is the enemy of romance. To win, a country must better its opponent over not merely one innings each but two, in a match that can last up to five days; occasionally, even longer. A weaker team might thrive over one, two or even three innings of a match, yet gravity will probably get them in the end.

The notion of the second chance is wired into Test cricket. It is also why the game is so unforgiving. It is not sufficient to dismiss an opponent's star batters for few runs once, as in limited-overs cricket; in Tests, a team must do so twice. Those floundering, over a match or a series, are exposed repeatedly to opponents who have proved themselves too good.

Test cricket can make players who are exceptional, by almost every measure, appear technically and temperamentally lacking. The Test match pitch is sport's ultimate examination room. Football fans might argue over how, say, a central midfielder has played; when a cricketer is dismissed for nought, their complete failure to score a run is documented coldly and clinically. Every Test player's contribution, in every match, is immediately quantifiable, no matter that these numbers only tell part of the story.

And so there is no such thing as an undeserved Test win. Yet, despite the length of matches, luck is still at the heart of the game. A Test match's opening act is a matter of complete chance: the toss, determining which captain can choose whether to bat or bowl first. It is often a significant event: of Tests that end in a positive result, 53 per cent are won by the side who win the toss. Umpiring has often had a major bearing on results. Matches can hinge on such absurdities as when the clouds come in and so make batting harder.

From sharp bounce in Perth to lethal spin in scorching heat at Chennai or Galle to bountiful seam movement under sepulchral skies at Leeds: perhaps no sport offers such a rich tapestry of conditions for players to master. This heightens the difficulty of winning away from home. Home teams have a major advantage: throughout history, they win about 16 Tests for every ten they lose. Australia are the only nation who have won more Tests away than they lose.

The Matthew Effect states that small differences accrue and accumulate over time. So it is in Test cricket. A side with weaker openers, say, will then expose their middle order to the new ball, potentially making these players less effective. A team struggling in batting will in turn undermine their bowling strength: being bowled out cheaply will leave a side's bowlers with less time to rest between the first and second innings.

If Twenty20 minimises differences between opponents, Test cricket magnifies them. This unsparing logic comes at a cost: one-sided matches are common. In the first 2,573 Test matches, from 1877 to 2025, just 84 were won by a margin of fewer than 30 runs, or three wickets or fewer: 3 per cent, or barely a Test every two years. Great Tests are memorable partly because they are so rare: they require a confluence of teams playing at an equal level over several days and sheer serendipity. To produce a great series, these requirements must extend from days to weeks.

Sometimes, the best matches don't even have a winner. So it was with perhaps the most celebrated Test of all: the tie between

Australia and West Indies at Brisbane in 1960. Like many of the best Tests, this game was elevated by its wider significance. Throughout its history, Test cricket has reflected wider social and political forces. It has also helped to shape these forces.

A tie, requiring both teams to score exactly the same number of runs in the match, is a freak event; like Halley's Comet, a tied Test has only been seen about once every 75 years. But the tie's more mundane cousin, the draw, has been the result in nearly one-third of all Tests in history. The existence of a draw for a match lasting five days is among the game's peculiarities. Yet it is central to the format's DNA, offering the weaker side an escape route even when all hope of victory has been lost.

All these quirks add up to a maddening game, one so impervious to the demands of everyday life that the majority of play is scheduled during working hours. These idiosyncrasies are why, since its earliest years, there have been worries about Test cricket's future. But they are also why Test cricket has endured and will mark its sesquicentennial in 2027.

Test cricket's enduring appeal attests to its richness, complexity and capacity to generate simmering, slow-burning drama. The format also has an overlooked malleability. Since the first Test in 1877, matches have been scheduled to last three, four, five days or six – or even be 'timeless', played to a finish. Overs have comprised four, five, six or eight balls. Matches have been day or day-night, played with a red ball or pink. From two nations, the club has grown to 12. From the umpire's decision being final, in the days of the Decision Review System it has become merely a basis for negotiation.

Test cricket is derided as the most traditional game, oblivious of the changing world around it. Yet its adaptability has made it durable.

* * *

In writing this book I owe a debt of gratitude to dozens of people: the players and administrators – a full list is in the acknowledgements – who gave me their time, my employers at *The Daily Telegraph*, and those who read chapters as the project was developing. Scyld Berry, the doyen of cricket writing, looked over them all and is owed particular thanks.

Inevitably, too, a project of this nature stands on the shoulders of all the books, articles and broadcasts that have come before it. When they were especially helpful, I have endeavoured to reference such works within the main body of the text – though in a way that, I hope, does not bog down the general narrative. Books I consulted are listed in the bibliography. I have not included footnotes, to avoid slowing down the narrative and undermining the reading experience.

It is worth clarifying what this book is not. The focus is not on all cricket, but squarely on the men's Test game. The book is limited to men's Test cricket. The women's game, with its own tactics, personalities and history, deserves its own study.

The difficulty in writing a single-volume history of men's Test cricket lies in what to put in. There are dozens of players, matches and controversies to which I would have liked to devote far more attention. Within the space constraints, I have been led by a sense of Test cricket's overarching story, paying particular attention to players who helped to shape the game. This means that players with unremarkable statistics who emerged at a critical juncture in their country's development, like Abdul Kardar and Tiger Pataudi, get extensive coverage; titans in less successful or declining sides, like Graham Gooch or Shivnarine Chanderpaul, regrettably get much less. To have done all the finest cricketers in Test history justice would have been to write a volume several times longer. But I hope that readers have their curiosity sparked to seek out more literature on Test cricket.

How to structure this history was a profound challenge. There was merit in alternative approaches: by theme, say, or by country. But the intention of this project has been to emphasise the interconnectedness of players and teams from different nations in the sweeping history of the Test game. As such, I have adopted a hybrid approach – primarily driven by chronology, but also allowing for ample analysis and exploration of themes. The hope is that readers will learn how Test cricket has evolved – and, just as importantly, *why*.

Test Cricket: A History is intended to be read sequentially, as narrative history. By chronicling the game's tale from its inception to the modern day, I hope to give a sense of Test cricket's epic story over its near 150-year existence. Now, with the tale of a piqued Australian fast bowler, let us begin.

1

A MAD IDEA

'This thing can be done!' Fred Spofforth, Australia's moustached fast bowler cajoled his teammates in the changing room at The Oval. It was August 1882; Australia were playing a Test match, a two-innings-a-side game of international cricket, against England.

At the start of the final innings, on an unseasonably chilly afternoon in south London, England needed just 85 runs for victory. Spofforth – called 'The Demon' for both his appearance and cricketing attributes – was undeterred. He would not stop bowling until the thing was done.

As England reached 51–2, the 20,000 spectators, who had paid a shilling each, seemed to be getting their wish: a victory for the hosts. Bookmakers in the crowd were offering odds of 60–1 on an Australia win. Then, George Ulyett was caught pushing at a quicker ball from Spofforth; W.G. Grace, the greatest batter of his age, fell swiftly after, driving a slower ball from Harry Boyle to mid-off.

When they reached 65–4, just 20 runs away from their target, England were engulfed by fear. Alfred Lucas and Alfred Lyttelton, the fifth-wicket pair, played out 12 consecutive maiden overs; each over comprised four balls. The sequence only ended when Australia deliberately misfielded, allowing the bowlers a different target. Four overs later, Spofforth bowled Lyttelton middle stump, leaving England 66–5. In 17 overs, England had lost a wicket and added a solitary run.

'For the final half-hour you could have heard a pin drop,' Tom Horan, an Australian player, wrote. That was a match worth playing in, and I doubt whether there will ever be such another game for prolonged and terribly trying tension.'

All the while, Spofforth continued: he bowled 28 overs, a testament to his wiry fitness. He bowled at a good pace for the day, was 6 ft 3 in and had a venomous yorker, yet Spofforth's greatest asset was his mind: he contacted baseball pitchers to see what variations he could adapt for cricket. While his standard delivery amounted to a very fast off break, spinning in to right-handers, he brought the full force of his brain to the task of deceiving batters.

Spofforth varied his pace with no discernible change in his action. 'The sole object in variation is to make the batsman think the ball is faster or slower than it really is,' he wrote. He had a different grip for each of the three paces that he bowled and delighted in working batters out. 'Spofforth was no bowler,' England's allrounder Billy Barnes said. 'He were a hypnotist.' With his hair parted in the middle, creating the impression of horns, Spofforth was described as having the face of 'the Spirit of Evil in Faust'.

Spofforth's relentless accuracy suffocated England: he claimed seven of the first eight wickets, five clean bowled. Number 11 Ted Peate had been sipping a glass of champagne, his lips 'ashen grey' in trepidation of having to bat. At 75–9, Peate walked out to face Boyle, with England still ten runs shy. Peate made two; from his third ball, he swung for glory, and was bowled, silencing the crowd. Australia won by seven runs, bowling England out for 77. One of Test cricket's great traditions was already established: the England batting collapse. The last eight wickets fell for 26 runs. Spofforth took 14 wickets for 90 in the match, including 7–44 in the second innings. He was carried off by his teammates, and cheered off by spectators into the pavilion.

Nineteen years before winning independence from the United Kingdom, Australia had shown that they could best England on the sporting field. Even England's captain, W.G. Grace, accepted as much. 'The shouting and the cheering that followed Spofforth's performance I shall remember to my dying day, as I shall remember the quick, hearty recognition over the length and breadth of the land that the best of Australian cricket was worthy of the highest position in the game,' he wrote.

It was an extraordinary way for Australia to secure their first Test victory in England. In the following day's *Sporting Times*, the writer Reginald Shirley Brooks wrote a mock obituary.

> In affectionate Remembrance of English cricket, which died at The Oval on 29th August, 1882, deeply lamented by a large circle of sorrowing friends and acquaintances. R.I.P. N.B. – The body will be cremated and the ashes taken to Australia.

Before England left for the return tour to Australia, 12 days later, their touring captain, Ivo Bligh, pledged 'to beard the kangaroo in his den and try to recover those ashes'. When England won the series down under, Bligh was presented with a small terracotta urn. The Ashes were born.

* * *

The roots of cricket have been lost to history. Exactly why the game is called cricket, indeed, remains unclear. The name is thought to be an adaptation of the word *criquet*, which came to Britain around the time of the Norman Conquest.

Games with some resemblance to cricket – hitting a moving object with a wooden stick or bat – were played during the later Middle Ages. A more recognisable game developed in England over the 17th century: in 1668, the landlord of the Ram, at Smithfield, the premier sports ground in London, is recorded as paying for the use of a cricket field. But what was understood to be the game varied from town to town: around 1700, the historian Eric Midwinter wrote, 'it is likely that there were hundreds of versions of cricket being enjoyed.'

The year 1744 has a claim to marking the dawn of modern cricket. Kent's match against All-England, held at London's Artillery Ground, is the first major match for which a detailed scorecard remains. The game was attended by several thousand people, including the Prince of Wales, the Duke of Cumberland and the Duke of Richmond. In the last half of the 18th century, cricket grew in private schools and gained its first powerful private members' clubs. The most famous was Hambledon, in Hampshire, which developed many of the sport's early laws – often in the Bat and Ball pub opposite the ground – and became known as 'the cradle of cricket'. In 1787, Marylebone Cricket Club (MCC) was founded in north-west London; the club laid down a Code of Laws, including the requirement for wickets to be 22 yards apart. In theory – if not always in reality – matches would now be played according to uniform laws.

In the 1830s, matches between teams travelling significant distances, normally on railways between towns and cities, became more common; the inaugural North v South fixture in England was played in 1836. In turn, matches between sides from different regions encouraged the same laws to be adhered to throughout the country, rather than dozens of variants of the game. In 1838, it became mandatory to play with three stumps at each end, rather than two.

Around this time, bowling also moved towards its more modern version. Round-arm bowling – deliveries in which the bowler's arm was raised but did not go above the shoulder – had first been trialled in the 1780s but was subsequently largely barred. In 1835, MCC clarified the situation, amending the Laws of Cricket to make such balls legal. Later, after a close MCC vote in 1864, overarm bowling was fully legalised; deliveries released above the shoulder were no longer classed as no-balls. For the next decade or so, three types of bowling existed in tandem: underarm; round-arm; and the new method of overarm. But overarm decisively won out.

Cricket also gained its first figure of national significance: William Gilbert Grace, who made his first-class debut in 1865. Grace was from a cricket-loving family from Downend, a village four miles from Bristol. Every day from March to October, the five sons practised on a pitch in the orchard adjoining their home, often with their parents. EM, WG's elder brother, was a formidable player and is credited with popularising the pull shot, through the on side. WG delayed his qualification as a doctor while transforming the game.

Grace was one of England's first nationally recognisable figures: a product of not just his sporting excellence, but also his cartoonish beard, and his emergence when the printing press was thriving and the growth of railways made travel easier. When his testimonial, organised by *The Daily Telegraph*, raised £5,000 – over £500,000 in 2025 prices – Sir Edward Lawson, the editor, hailed cricket as 'the great national game', with Grace its 'most eminent, accepted and popular representative'.

So dominant was Grace that his first 50 first-class hundreds represented one-third of all those scored in England in the period, his biographer Simon Rae noted. In his first 200 first-class games, during a bowler-friendly age, Grace averaged 55.5 with the bat and 14.6 with the ball, predominantly bowling brisk medium pace with a round-arm action. In the 1870s and 1880s, he was simultaneously the best batter in England and a leading bowler. His first-class career garnered a monumental 54,211 runs, 2,809 wickets and 876 catches. The memorial to Grace at Lord's ground called him 'The Great Cricketer', using the definite article.

Ranjitsinhji – a great batter himself, as we shall see in chapter 3 – wrote in 1897:

> Before WG batsmen were of two kinds – a batsman played a forward game or he played a back game. Each player, too, seems to have made a speciality of some particular stroke . . . What WG did was to unite in his mighty self all the good points of all the good players, and to make utility the criterion of style. He founded the modern theory of batting by making forward and

back play of equal importance, relying neither on the one nor on the other, but on both.

To Spofforth, often his nemesis, 'W.G. Grace is like a master among pupils; there may arise pupils hereafter who will be no less skilful with bat and ball, but they will never command the permanent and worldwide reputation of the man who first taught us to play.'

But Grace's aura concealed that he prepared for matches rigorously. 'I cannot recollect many of my big innings that were not the results of strict obedience to the rules which govern the training for all important athletic contests,' he wrote. 'Temperance in food and drink, regular sleep and exercise, I have laid down as the golden rule from my earliest cricketing days.' If he did not always stick to his mantra – Grace, one of the fittest cricketers in his 20s, became distinctly rotund – he had remarkable longevity, playing his last Test aged 50, and last first-class game at 60.

Grace believed that 'going straight from the railway station to the wicket is often fatal', endeavouring to travel to games the day before. He practised on the morning of each match, batting in full kit. Grace distilled his unstinting focus thus: 'Begin as you mean to go on, playing good balls carefully, hitting loose ones, and bearing in mind that a large score is not made in half-a-dozen hits or overs. Do not be surprised and disappointed if the first few overs are maidens.'

A typical match price reflected Grace's appeal: 'Admission threepence. If W.G. Grace plays admission sixpence.' He used his popularity in two main ways. First, to make himself very rich. Notionally, Grace was classed as an amateur, meaning that, unlike professionals, he did not receive match payments. In reality, Grace was paid lavishly – touring Australia in 1873/74 and 1891/92, he earned ten times the fee paid to each professional, alongside generous expenses. The quintessential 'shamateur', the total he earned from his cricket career equates to over £10 million, when adjusting to modern wages. Such sums mocked MCC's proclamation in 1878 that

'No gentleman [as distinct from professionals] ought to make a profit by his service in the cricket field.'

On the pitch, Grace also exploited his appeal, intimidating umpires and opponents alike. On one occasion he was caught and bowled, but refused to accept the umpire's decision and made him change it. When Grace was given out lbw in one exhibition match, he declared, 'Play on – they came to see me bat, not you umpire,' and was reinstated. During the 1882 Oval Test, Grace ran out an Australian who had gone down the pitch after the ball had been bowled, with the ball seemingly dead. 'If you claim it, sir, it is out,' the umpire said. Spofforth branded Grace 'a bloody cheat' and channelled his rage into winning the Test.

Yet Grace was absent from what is now designated as the inaugural Test match, between 'All-England' and 'United Australia' – in reality a combined New South Wales–Victoria XI – at Melbourne Cricket Ground in March 1877. The teams were not genuine national XIs, but sides comprising players signed up by the tour; Grace did not agree a contract. James Lillywhite, a private entrepreneur, captained the side, which was often called James Lillywhite's XI.

'There'd be plenty of money in it,' Lillywhite said when discussing the prospects of a first representative – what would become Test – match between teams from Australia and England. Before countries had established national boards to oversee the sport, tours depended on private entrepreneurs. Players effectively formed companies, negotiating a share of the gate receipts with the promoters and those who would stage the games. To keep costs down – and maximise players' profits – touring parties were kept to a minimum. For a tour that saw players spend eight months away, including three on boats to Australia and back, Lillywhite's England squad in 1876/77 included just 12 players, forcing players to play while carrying injuries. By the Test, the number had dwindled to 11: Ted Pooley, the 12th member, lay in a New Zealand prison cell after being arrested for assault. Pooley had bet on the number of batters to make ducks in the match with a spectator. The fan refused to pay because Pooley, who was injured, umpired in the game.

Cricket's growth in England in the 18th and 19th centuries was inextricably linked to gambling. Bookmakers offered odds at the grounds for matches involving William Clarke's All-England Elevens. This itinerant side, purporting to feature the country's best players, launched in 1846. To make matches competitive, and enticing for gamblers, the All-England Eleven played local teams who were permitted to use as many as 22 players. The codification of cricket's laws, over the 1860s, was partly driven by pressure from gamblers, who wanted certainty about what they were betting on. Gambling created the opportunity for players to be paid to lose. 'Matches were bought and matches were sold,' the batter William Fennex, a prominent player around 1800, recalled. Lord Frederick Beauclerk, son of the Duke of St Albans, later admitted to making £600 per season – £60,000 today – from betting on games; he would serve as MCC president. It was said that 'he bought and sold matches as though they were lots at an auction'.

In 1817 William Lambert, a professional who was among the era's best batters, became the first cricketer to be banned for match-fixing. Notoriously, one match between England and Nottinghamshire was played between fixers on both sides: bowlers trying not to take wickets, against batters desperate to get out. The Green Man and Still pub, on a corner of Oxford Street, was a favoured spot for cricketers to discuss fixing. Reverend James Pycroft's book *The Cricket Field*, published in 1851, quotes an anonymous source detailing how players were convinced to fix: 'Your backers, my Lord this, and the Duke of that, sell matches and overrule all your good play, so why shouldn't you have a share of the plunder?'

Cricket, like several other sports, was exported from Britain. The first recorded match in Australia took place in Sydney in 1803, between the military and civilians. The first inter-colonial contest was in 1851, between sides representing Tasmania and Victoria. By the second half of the 19th century, the game was also vibrant in countries including Ireland, New Zealand, Canada and the United States. In 1844, over 10,000 in Manhattan saw the US play Canada in a three-day game: not just the first international cricket match, but believed to be the first international sports fixture of any sort. In the years that followed, tours between Australia and England were organised by opportunistic private promoters. An English team first visited North America in 1859. The first England tour to Australia was in 1861, landing on Christmas Eve after two months at sea; 10,000 greeted the party's arrival at Port Melbourne. The organisers, motivated by business rather than an altruistic desire to spread the game, were Felix Spiers and Christopher Pond, the owners of the Café de Paris in Melbourne; they offered the English cricketers a guaranteed £150 each, and are thought to have made £11,000 (over £1 million in 2025 prices) between them.

The first tour to England by a group of Australian cricketers came in 1868. A squad comprising 13 Indigenous Australians from the Western District of Victoria, captained by the tour organiser, the Englishman Charles Lawrence, travelled to Britain. Their first match, at The Oval, was watched by 20,000 people. The squad played 47 matches against county and local teams – winning 14, drawing 19 and losing 14. Crowds were strong, though some spectators seem to have been attracted partly by the players' other activities, like boomerang- and spear-throwing. The tour was marred by tragedy: one player, Bripumyarrimin – referred to as King Cole – contracted fatal tuberculosis. A year later, Victoria's authorities gained complete control over the residence, employment and marriage of Indigenous people, laws that would be mimicked in other Australian colonies, rendering similar future tours impossible.

* * *

At the Melbourne Cricket Ground on 15 March 1877, Australia won the toss, thereby winning the right to decide whether to bat or bowl, and chose to bat. A little after one o'clock, Charles Bannerman – who was born in Kent, but emigrated to Sydney aged two – faced the first ball in Test cricket. Off the second, he scored the first run. Later in the day Bannerman made Test cricket's inaugural century, increasing his score to 165 on the second day. These runs came out of a total of just 245. Bannerman's share of his team's total, 67.34 per cent, remains a record in any completed innings. The result – an Australia win by 45 runs – was exactly mirrored during the Centenary Test against England at the MCG 100 years later.

Only subsequently would the game that witnessed Bannerman's feat be designated as the inaugural 'Test match'. The term was initially used by opportunistic marketers, often to promote matches, including those between domestic teams, which are not now regarded as 'Tests'. Despite other nations playing cricket, such status was initially only conferred on England and Australia.

During the early years, matches were awarded Test status on an ad hoc basis, and often only retrospectively. In 1894 Clarence Moody, an Australian journalist, compiled a list of 'official' Test matches. His selection was a little arbitrary, yet became accepted. If Tests are considered to be contests between national sides comprising the strongest available teams, the bulk of 19th-century Tests miss this mark. Especially for English amateurs, who played Tests was governed by a player's availability, and whether the matches were sufficiently well paid. Grace played in just two of the first 13 Tests; on debut, though he wouldn't have known it at the time, he scored 152 in the first Test in England. Merely keeping up with the plethora of teams who claimed to represent Australia and England could be exhausting: in 1887/88, six different versions of an Australian XI met four different English sides. Only one of these matches would ultimately be considered a Test.

A tour by an Australia squad to England in 1878, while it did not feature any Test matches, was crucial in the development of international cricket. Australia initially floundered, losing their first match, against Nottinghamshire, by an innings. 'We all played in light silk shirts with no under-vests – the dress most comfortable in our own country – and also wore white felt hats, which, considering it was early spring, showed our refreshing ignorance of the English weather,' Spofforth recounted.

Australia then met a strong MCC side at Lord's and were expected to lose comprehensively. Instead, they only needed four and a half hours to rout MCC, bowling them out for 33 and 19 to win a surreal game by nine wickets. Spofforth took 10–20 in the match, bowling Grace for a duck in the second innings. The satirical magazine *Punch* marked the moment:

> The Australians came down like a wolf on the fold,
> The Mary'bone Cracks for a trifle were bowled;
> Our Grace before dinner was very soon done,
> And our Grace after dinner did not get a run.

This was a seminal match in Test cricket's development – even if, curiously, it did not later receive the seal of being considered an official Test. 'It is impossible to over-estimate the importance of this victory in its effect on the future matches and the destiny of Australian cricket,' Spofforth said.

Such wins had a galvanising effect. 'Cricket must, I suppose, take the first place amongst Australian sports, because all ages and classes are interested in it; and not to be interested in it amounts almost to a social crime,' Robert Twopeny observed in *Town Life in Australia*, published in 1883. Australia's coat of arms first appeared on the cricket team's blazer and cap in 1884, 17 years before Federation. In the 19th century, 'the cricket tour was perhaps the major popular cultural vehicle for bonding between England, the imperial parent, and Australia, the colonial child,' the academic Brian Stoddart has observed.

The Australians followed their 1878 tour with another in 1880, and returned again in 1882. These tours were lucrative. Very lucrative. The financial rewards – effectively forming a joint stock company, the £50 each cricketer contributed in 1878 turned into £750 – triggered what would become a familiar refrain: players had ceased to play for love, and were instead playing for money. Consider an editorial in *The Australasian* in October 1878:

> Cricket, unfortunately, is becoming now-a-days too profitable an investment of skill and muscle to be carried out in the same friendly spirit that characterised it fifteen or twenty years ago. Then the play was the thing, now it is £.s.d. also; and when the two come into collision the £.s.d. spirit is bound to carry the day.

A generation before what would be called cricket's Golden Age, here was a lament for how things used to be. Another one came in 1884, after the tourists to England earned £900 each – over £90,000 in 2025 prices. 'These Australian adventurous spirits have undertaken their enterprise less for honour than for filthy lucre,' *The Illustrated Sporting and Dramatic News* wrote. 'Win or lose, they accept their expenses all the same. The present generation of lovers of the once noble game must have seen enough of the Australians to last them for life, and their intrusion into the mother country will henceforth be regarded as a veritable nuisance.'

Too much money and too much cricket. Some things, at least, have remained the same.

While national pride motivated many players, others had a more transitory relationship with Test cricket. Billy Midwinter grew up in England before moving to Australia, and travelled between the countries; except when he was on a boat, he could play cricket almost all year round. In 1878, both Grace and Australia captain David Gregory sought his services; Grace reportedly kidnapped him from the Australian dressing room at The Oval to ensure that he played for Gloucestershire. Midwinter would do his best to please both masters: he played for Australia in the inaugural Test series in 1877, for

England against Australia in 1881/82, then for Australia against England from 1883 to 1887. He was one of five men to represent both Australia and England in Ashes cricket between 1877 and 1900.

England's team was divided between 'gentlemen' – so-called amateurs who were from privileged social backgrounds, held other jobs and tended to provide the bulk of the side's batters, including the captain – and 'players', professionals who did cricket for a living and tended to be bowlers. In Australia, there was no such distinction. All cricketers were, in English parlance, players; but as they juggled cricket and other sources of income, they were best understood as semi-professionals.

Money and class were the source of many tensions. Nottinghamshire's professionals went on strike in 1881, protesting against discrimination in favour of amateurs. During a match against Australia in 1882, Notts refused to allow the Australians into the dining room, on the grounds that their players were professionals. In 1896, five England professionals went on strike, demanding £20 as a Test match fee; the players backed down. Australia was just as susceptible to such skirmishes: there were player strikes in 1884/85 and 1886/87. In real terms, Malcolm Knox wrote in *Never a Gentlemen's Game*, it took a century for Australian cricketers to match what players had earned at the end of the 19th century. In the early 20th century, both MCC and the Australian Board of Control for International Cricket, formed in 1905, acquired control of tours, strengthening their positions and squeezing player salaries. The establishment character of MCC is hard to overstate. From 1825 to 1939, MCC had 111 Presidents; 95 of these were either knights or peers, Richard Holt has calculated.

Test cricket's development was shaped by the countries that initially played it. For Australia and England, it was only economically viable to arrange long series of matches, rather than annual regular multi-nation cup and league tournaments like those which became established in football and rugby.

While domestic matches became dominant in football, in cricket the appeal of multi-month tours criss-crossing the nations and the salience of the contest between mother country and colony helped the international game to be viewed as pre-eminent. 'The constant visits of Australians to England and of Englishmen to the colonies are proving disastrous to club cricket,' the New South Wales Cricket Association wrote in their report on an England tour in 1883/84.

* * *

Only in hindsight was the significance of Shirley Brooks's invention apparent. After Bligh regained the Ashes in 1882/83, the concept was forgotten about for a decade, with no reference to the urn being contested in future series. Matches were seldom keenly contested: Australia lost eight consecutive Ashes series from 1882/83 to 1890. One of the greatest reasons for England's dominance was the blond-haired George Lohmann, a bowler whose skills evoked Spofforth's: varying his angle and pace, while moving the ball both ways off the pitch, he took 112 Test wickets at an extraordinary average of 10.75.

The 1891/92 Ashes reinvigorated the Test game. Australia won the three-match series 2–1; a total of 140,000 spectators attended. Evidence of what Australia could do when they pulled together was the catalyst for the formation of the first national body to run the game: the Australasian Cricket Council, later replaced by the body known today as Cricket Australia.

The next series in Australia, in 1894/95, established the status of the Ashes as among the most hallowed contests in sport. Reflecting the contest's growing prestige, and the money that it could generate, five Tests were scheduled, for only the second time.

In the first Test in Sydney, Australia made 586 in their first innings; England were asked to follow on. Set 177 to win, Australia cruised to 113–2, needing only 64 more. England's players, certain that defeat beckoned, had a night on the town. While they drank, it rained on the uncovered pitch. The rain transformed the pitch's character, making the bounce far less predictable for batters.

Left-arm spinner Robert Peel, still feeling the effects of the night out, recognised that England now had a chance. He told the captain, Andrew Stoddart, 'Give me the ball, Mr Stoddart, and I'll get t'boogers out before loonch!' Revitalised by a cold shower, Peel did just that. Australia lost their last five wickets for eight runs, to tumble to a ten-run defeat.

After going 2–0 down in the series in Melbourne, Australia responded with a crushing victory in Adelaide. On debut, Albert Trott hit 38 not out and 72 not out and took 8–43; he developed into what could perhaps best be described as a fast mystery spinner, varying between off spin and occasional leg spin. Trott's most celebrated feat was hitting a delivery over the Lord's pavilion in 1899; no one has ever emulated his blow. He also embodied the itinerant careers typical of the day, later moving from Australia to England to qualify as a local player and then playing Test cricket for England against South Africa.

Another emphatic home victory in Sydney meant that the series was locked at 2–2. Over five days, 100,000 spectators crammed in to watch the final Test at the Melbourne Cricket Ground, about one-fifth of the city's population at the time. Australia won the toss and scored 414; England almost matched their total, hitting 385. Six wickets from Tom Richardson, whose pace, movement and physical durability made him the era's pre-eminent English fast bowler, meant that the tourists needed 297 to win, 98 runs more than any Test side had previously made to win in the final innings. England slipped to 28–2, after losing a wicket first ball on the fifth morning.

Out walked John Brown, a well-built Yorkshire professional renowned for chain-smoking and a sense of mischief. Fielding by the boundary edge during a tour match in Australia, he once got a spectator to change into whites, then let him take his place on the field while he relaxed in the refreshment tent. Brown's approach to

England's daunting target was to attack, especially with his favourite cut; like many short batters, he excelled playing the shot. Within 28 minutes he reached his half-century. In terms of time (the balls were not recorded), this remains the fastest Test 50 ever; his partner made five in the same period.

Brown continued to plunder Australia, reacting to his sole reprieve – a dropped catch at slip on 88 – by using his feet to attack the ball. His century took 95 balls; when he was out for 140, made at almost a run a minute, he had put on 210 for the third wicket with the more sedate Albert Ward. No matter their partisanship, the crowd gave Brown a standing ovation. His lone Test century underpinned a six-wicket victory that not only won England the urn, but also built the Ashes legend.

More than ever before, such feats could now be appreciated back home. In 1894/95, for the first time, London's *Pall Mall Gazette* published cabled reports within five hours of each day finishing. Brown's innings helped to lend the Ashes new mystique. While the next series, in 1896, consisted of only three Tests, from England's next visit, in 1897/98, the Ashes became established as a five-match affair. In 1903/04, England finally took what amounted to a first-choice squad down under. MCC now assumed control of English tours – preventing concurrent tours by different teams purporting to represent England and allowing for greater forward planning.

The length of series allowed the Ashes to take contests across Australia and England, develop heroes – and, just as importantly, villains – and gave players scope to redeem themselves over the course of a contest. F. Scott Fitzgerald wrote that there are no second acts in American lives; Test cricket has always allowed for second acts. From its inception, the idea of the second chance has been baked into the game.

2

TWO BECOME THREE: THE EMERGENCE OF SOUTH AFRICA

One day at Oxford University, probably in 1897, the Englishman Bernard Bosanquet was playing twisti-twosti. The game involved spinning a tennis ball from one end of a table to the other, aiming to elude an opponent at the opposite end.

'It soon occurred to me that if one could pitch a ball which broke in a certain direction and with more or less the same delivery make the next ball go in the opposite direction, one would mystify one's opponent,' Bosanquet wrote. 'After a little experimenting I managed to do this.'

Next, he practised the technique with a soft ball. Then, finally, with a cricket ball: the googly was born. While the wrist spinner's traditional delivery spins away from a right-hander after it pitches, the googly cunningly did the opposite – spinning *into* a right-hander. By introducing uncertainty about which way a ball would turn, the googly would be one of Test cricket's most significant innovations. But first, it would be a tool for Bosanquet to avoid bowling more physically arduous fast deliveries:

> The lot of an average fast-medium bowler on a county side was not a happy one. It generally meant being put on under a sweltering sun, on a plumb wicket, when the other bowlers had failed and the two batsmen were well set. If one was lucky enough to get a wicket, the original bowlers resumed, and unless the same conditions recurred one was not wanted again. If the

wicket was difficult, one was never thought of. As a result, partly from a natural disinclination to work hard on hot days (how much more pleasant to walk slowly up to the wicket and gently propel the ball into the air), and partly, I hope, from a sneaking ambition to achieve greater things, I persevered with the googly.

The delivery – which some called the 'Bosie' and Australians called the 'wrong 'un' – is thought to have been first glimpsed in a first-class match in July 1900, when Bosanquet bowled for Middlesex against Leicestershire at Lord's. Rather than merely bowl conventional leg spin, now Bosanquet could bend his wrist to spin the ball the other way too. The first first-class wicket with a googly was stumped after bouncing four times – simultaneously a testament to the disorientating effect of the ball on opposing batters and to how hard the delivery was for bowlers to master.

Bosanquet only played seven Test matches. While he could be erratic, he made a decisive contribution to two Ashes victories: taking 6–51 as England regained the urn in Sydney in 1903/04, and 8–107 in Nottingham in 1905, when most of his wickets came through orthodox leg breaks. The knowledge that he could spin the ball the other way was unnerving; some Australians chuntered that this subterfuge should not be allowed. The googly 'is not unfair', Bosanquet once said, 'only immoral'.

* * *

After playing their first Test in 1889, South Africa lost ten of their first 11 Tests and drew the other. The team needed a new tool to compete – so they borrowed, and perfected, Bosanquet's. Reggie Schwarz, who was educated in England and represented the country at rugby union before emigrating to South Africa, played with Bosanquet for Middlesex in 1901 and 1902, where he was taught the googly. Returning home to Transvaal, Schwarz passed his new trick on to three other

TWO BECOME THREE: THE EMERGENCE OF SOUTH AFRICA

South Africans: Aubrey Faulkner, Ernest Vogler and Gordon White. They became known as the quartet, and would become Test cricket revolutionaries.

When England began their series in Johannesburg in January 1906, they encountered four googly bowlers: Schwarz and the rest of the quartet, all making their Test debuts together. On the first morning, Schwarz and Faulkner opened the bowling; in the first Test, the quartet shared 14 wickets.

Though England were bowled out for 184 and 190, South Africa were skittled for 91 in their first innings, so needed to chase 284 to secure their maiden Test victory. At 105–6, the chase seemed futile. But the matting pitch did not deteriorate in the traditional vein of Test pitches. White and Arthur Nourse, who defended stoically and had a fierce square cut, added 121 for the seventh wicket. Three quick wickets left South Africa on 239–9, still 45 adrift of their target; Percy Sherwell, the captain and wicketkeeper, walked out to bat at number 11.

Sherwell's position belied his capabilities: he later scored a century at Lord's as an opener. With eight runs required, Sherwell edged a ball for four. He regained the strike with the scores level; a mid-pitch mix-up almost led to the first tie in Test history. Then, Sherwell received a full toss; he flicked it away to clinch South Africa's first Test win. Spectators ran onto the pitch, carrying Nourse, who finished undefeated on 93, and Sherwell to the pavilion.

South Africa's template in the series was established. The matting wickets – unique in the Test world, and used in the country until the 1930s when they were replaced by turf – offered appreciable grip and bounce, assisting spin. While the quartet all relied on Bosanquet's innovation, they also had different methods. Schwarz bowled the googly, which he spun prodigiously and at good pace, almost exclusively; he effectively functioned as an off-spinner, although he also used top-spinners, balls that did not turn. Faulkner used the googly along with his conventional leg-spinner but could spear in a fast yorker too. Vogler, deployed less prominently than those two in 1906, became the most dangerous, varying his pace and flight as well as the direction of turn without losing control. White was a dangerous auxiliary option and scored two centuries against England.

The quartet took 43 wickets between them in the series. Seamers Tip Snooke, with 24 wickets at 15.37, and Jimmy Sinclair were equally outstanding. South Africa triumphed 4–1, using the same 11 players throughout. The lower order averaged almost twice as many as the first five: 'Like a Manx cat, they had no tail,' said England captain Pelham 'Plum' Warner. While England's squad roughly equated to a second eleven, they would never dare send such an under-strength side to South Africa again.

The phalanx of spinners performed well in England in 1907, South Africa's first away series. In the second Test at Headingley, Faulkner's 6–17, turning the ball both ways, exploited the turn offered by a slow, treacherous wicket. But Colin Blythe, England's orthodox left-arm spinner, used his deceptive flight and control to expose South Africa's batting frailties: he recorded 15–99 in the match as South Africa lost by 53 runs in the only Test in the series that wasn't a draw.

When England returned in 1909/10, the quartet produced an encore: Vogler and Faulkner shared 65 wickets as South Africa won 3–2. In the first Test at Johannesburg, Faulkner showed off the qualities that made him the greatest allrounder of his day. England were not so much beaten by one team as one man. As a daring, counter-attacking number three, Faulkner hit 78 and 123; he also took 8–160 in the match, and was carried off the ground after South Africa's 19-run win. A year later, Faulkner's 56 and 115 at Adelaide secured South Africa's first away Test win; he made 732 runs in the series, the fourth highest ever made by a visiting player in Australia. The batter Clem Hill said that Faulkner had batted better than any other overseas player that he had seen in Australia before 1914.

As pitches changed and opponents deciphered the googly, the spin quartet's legacy did not endure: throughout Test history, no

TWO BECOME THREE: THE EMERGENCE OF SOUTH AFRICA

nation has bowled a lower percentage of overs with spin than South Africa. But for a brief and brilliant period, they were pioneers.

* * *

Cricket was brought to South Africa by the British military; it is first recorded being played in the Cape, during the occupation by British troops, in 1806. Cape Town was initially the sport's heartland; not until 1843 were the first organised club matches played elsewhere, in Port Elizabeth. Like other sports, cricket grew rapidly after 1875; Europeans, enticed by the discovery of the richest mineral deposits in the world, moved to Southern Africa in their thousands. 'South Africa's industrial revolution set the stage for the rise of sport as a modern phenomenon with mass appeal, in much the same way as the British Industrial Revolution had done,' André Odendaal wrote. Cricket particularly boomed in mining centres – nurtured by companies as an outlet for their workforce, who were largely white.

The sport also gained ground among the black African population. The first reference to cricket in an indigenous language newspaper was in 1859, Odendaal found; the first African cricket club was founded in Port Elizabeth in 1869. Cricket gained significant popularity among a group of Xhosa-speaking Africans, the academic Dean Allen documented; by the 1880s, the newspaper *Imvo Zabantsundu* carried regular reports of matches between black African teams.

These teams very seldom met sides who fielded players from other races. In South Africa, a game that purported to spread noble values was used to reinforce racial segregation. From its creation in 1890, black cricketers were excluded from the South African Cricket Association. Players not classed as white were forced to develop their own parallel cricketing structures: the South African Coloured Cricket Board was founded and organised the first interprovincial tournament for black cricketers in 1899.

The first English touring team arrived in South Africa in 1888/89. As in Australia 11 years earlier, they were brought there by private enterprise. The tour was devised by William 'Joey' Milton, an Englishman educated at Marlborough College who played rugby for England before emigrating to South Africa aged 24 to join the Cape Civil Service. Milton also worked as a salesman, and sensed the commercial possibilities of an English team touring South Africa. He raised a £3,000 guarantee to fund 13 English cricketers going on tour. Milton played in South Africa's first Test himself, and captained in their second. The players underwent gruelling travel to make the tour viable, sometimes travelling for two days by train.

While profit was the driving force behind the first English tour, it was also recognised as a way to strengthen ties between South Africa and Empire. Before England set sail for the inaugural Test tour in 1888 – leaving Dartmouth and arriving in Cape Town via Lisbon – Major Warton, England's tour manager, said that his main objective was to strengthen colonial cricket. During the tour, Sir Thomas Upington, recently prime minister of the Cape Colony, said, 'Nothing has greater effect of binding colonies together than visits by teams such as this. The future of England depended on her colonies.' The South African Cricket Association declared its duty to manage and encourage 'the visits of English teams to South Africa, and South African teams to England'.

England's 1888 tour squad was nothing like full-strength. To make games more competitive, England often pitted their 11 against teams of 22 players. All 22 men would field, making the pace of scoring, even against an inferior attack, funereal.

As an XI, South Africa played two matches that would later be recognised as Tests, losing both easily. On their first morning in Test cricket, South Africa had to wait for ten overs, and the loss of two wickets, before scoring their first run.

Yet the first steps had been made to give South African cricket a national identity; around 4,000 people watched each of the opening

TWO BECOME THREE: THE EMERGENCE OF SOUTH AFRICA

two days. Players wore olive-green caps with a yellow 'SA' monogram, stitched together by the wife of Owen Dunell, the captain.

England did not regard the match as a Test, only thinking of matches against Australia as 'Test caps'. As so often, the notion of what constituted a Test was unclear and dictated more by individual whim than any clear rules. In 1915, Maurice Luckin, the South African Cricket Association secretary, suggested a list of previous England–South Africa matches that should be classed as Tests. *Wisden Cricketers' Almanack* adopted the list in 1924, and it became accepted by governing bodies.

In 1891/92, England visited South Africa for the second time. England's professionals – no amateurs appeared in the game – played against a 'Malay' team, comprising players from the Cape coloured community. There, England encountered fast bowler William Henry – nicknamed Krom – Hendricks, born to a Dutch father and St Helenian mother. George Hearne, England's skipper in the match, described Hendricks as the 'fastest bowler in South Africa'. Tour captain Walter Read likened Hendricks to Fred 'the Demon' Spofforth, the great Australian pace bowler. During the tour, Read told local administrators contemplating a return tour, 'If you send a team, send Hendricks; he will be a drawcard and is to my mind the Spofforth of South Africa.'

Two years later, South Africa made their inaugural tour to England, although none of the games would be classed as Tests. On merit, Hendricks had an overwhelming case for selection. 'If "colour" is not an insuperable barrier, he can't be left out,' wrote the newspaper *Standard and Diggers News*. 'There is not a White man in the country who can be designated a really fast bowler.'

By now, William Milton was chairman of South Africa's selection committee. He was also private secretary to the British imperialist Cecil Rhodes, the prime minister of the Cape Colony. Rhodes and Milton discussed Hendricks's inclusion, as Richard Parry and Jonty Winch document. In the selection meeting, Milton said that it would be 'impolitic to include him in the team'. Hendricks – like several other players not classified as white who were potential contenders – was not selected. South Africa's team was not made up of all the country's talents.

Some attempts were made to ensure that Hendricks could still travel to England. The tour manager, Harry Cadwallader, floated a compromise: Hendricks would tour and could play, but his official role would be baggage master. Hendricks publicly rejected the degrading idea. Other South Africans found the suggestion that he should tour unpalatable for very different reasons.

'If he were to go on the same footing as the others, then I would not have him at any price,' said Bernard Tancred, one of the country's leading batters who played two Tests in 1889. 'To take him as an equal would, from a South African point of view, be impolitic, not to say intolerable.' Cadwallader was removed as tour manager by Milton for 'placing the Western Province Cricket Union in a very embarrassing situation' through his advocacy of Hendricks.

After the Hendricks affair, racial segregation increased: he was barred from playing representative matches. The match in which Hendricks made his name, in 1892, was the only official game played between a team whose players were not all classed as white and a touring side to South Africa until the end of apartheid.

Hendricks continued to try and play cricket within the Cape's white-run structures. In 1904, aged 47, Hendricks applied to play for Western Province Cricket Club, arguing that his bloodline made him European. Hendricks's request was denied; he played out his career in the coloured leagues. He embodied the tragedy of early South African cricket: while the game spread far beyond the Anglophile communities, administrators actively suppressed players who were not considered white.

Until 1992, it is believed that only one South African Test cricketer was not white: Charlie Llewellyn played 15 Tests between 1896 and 1912, when he was among the first left-arm wrist spinners in the international game. Llewellyn's skin complexion is thought to have indicated that he was of mixed race; he is believed to have been born in Natal to a Welsh father and mother from St Helena (though his family have said that he was born to two British parents). Because of his fair skin colour, Llewellyn appears to have been considered white by the South African Cricket Association.

* * *

The partnership between MCC and South Africa was one of 'mines, empire and cricket', write Richard Parry and André Odendaal. Three members of the first South Africa Test XI were born in England; Dunell, the captain, was not, but was educated at Eton and Oxford University.

Lord Hawke, an incessant tourist who captained England trips in 1895/96 and 1898/99, wrote in his autobiography:

> On the cricket grounds of the Empire is fostered the spirit of never knowing when you are beaten, of playing for your side and not for yourself, and of never giving up a game as lost. This is as invaluable in Imperial matters as in cricket.

From 1899 to 1902 the South African War was fought between the British Empire and the two Boer republics. During the war, a South African team – including one Afrikaner, with everyone else of British origin – toured England. They did not play any Tests, but recorded the first victory in a match designated as first-class by a South African side away from home. Before the war, cricket in South Africa – though most popular among players with an English background – had significant pockets of support among the Afrikaner community: two Afrikaners played in South Africa's first Test. After the war ended in 1902, cricket became increasingly identified as an English sport; it would be 25 years until the next Afrikaner played Test cricket. When South Africa defeated England for the first time, in 1906, England's captain Warner said that the victory could be explained by 'that grit and courage which we are so proud of saying are inherent in the British race'.

In 1910, the Cape, Natal, Transvaal and Orange River colonies were unified in the Union of South Africa, which signalled the formation of the South African nation as a self-governing dominion of the British Empire. This was said to unite the 'two races' in the country: the English-speakers and the Afrikaners. The Union furthered the oppression of other races, including the majority black population.

The Anglophile element in South Africa became more entrenched after the Union. In cricket, South Africa mimicked the English concept of amateur players. As in England, the side brimmed with 'shamateurs': notionally unpaid, but with jobs arranged for them by administrators.

In 1896, the Western Province Cricket Union passed Bye-law 10 – known as the Hendricks Law – which prevented professionals classed as black from either representing the province or even playing for white clubs: the first racially discriminatory legislation in any South African sport. As Jonty Winch and Richard Parry noted, Hendricks was probably the first cricketer in the world to be formally barred from playing because of his skin colour.

Administrators – invariably amateurs too – saw their role as being to promote not just a sport, but a whole way of life. 'Many of my most cherished recollections are connected with the world of cricket,' G. Allsop, a long-time administrator of Transvaal cricket, wrote in 1915. 'I will gladly render whatever assistance I can to the promotion of the game which has for so long retained its proud position in the British Empire.'

No figure embodied the intimate relationship between South African cricket and the Empire more than Abe Bailey. After watching a Johannesburg XXII thrashed by an English XI during the 1888/89 tour, Bailey remarked, 'We must set ourselves to beat the Englishmen on equal terms.'

TWO BECOME THREE: THE EMERGENCE OF SOUTH AFRICA

Bailey became President of the South African Cricket Association and set about trying to beat the Englishmen. Using his money earned from Consolidated Goldfields, a British gold-mining company in South Africa, he gave players cricket-related jobs or sinecures, which helped to establish Johannesburg as the country's leading producer of international players. Two of the googly quartet – Schwarz and Vogler – were Bailey employees. After South Africa's series win in 1905/06, he cabled England to arrange a three-Test tour by South Africa there in 1907.

To Bailey, South African cricket reflected, and nurtured, the nation itself. 'Our cricket has grown with our country,' he declared. Bailey, born in the Cape Colony but then educated in England, earned the sobriquet 'Rhodes the second'; he named his daughter Cecil. In England, where he spent several months a year, Bailey befriended Winston Churchill; one of his sons married Churchill's daughter Diana.

Bailey sought to strengthen ties between the three Test nations. He funded Australia's tour of South Africa in 1902; this included the first ever Test not involving England. The shipping route between England and Australia meant that touring parties from the two countries could extend their journeys and stop over en route. South Africa's first 16 Tests were all at home.

In November 1907 Bailey wrote a letter to F.E. Lacey, the MCC secretary. Bailey proposed the creation of an 'Imperial Cricket Board' – the first global governing body in the sport. The body Bailey envisaged would formulate rules for matches involving England, Australia and South Africa. In June 1909, representatives from the three countries met at Lord's. Together they created the Imperial Cricket Conference, international cricket's first governing body. The first meeting discussed eligibility rules for players and Test scheduling: issues that would become all too familiar to administrators down the ages.

3

THE GOLDEN AGE – OR TEST CRICKET'S GREAT MISSED OPPORTUNITY?

On a damp and miserable morning at Old Trafford in 1902, Victor Trumper, Australia's dashing opener, walked out to bat. 'If we keep Victor quiet, lads, we'll bowl the rest out,' England captain Archie MacLaren said. Australia were 1–0 up in the Ashes, needing to protect their lead over the final two Tests. With the matches scheduled over only three days, conventional wisdom would have been to bat cautiously.

Trumper was never the sort to pay heed to conventional wisdom. Instead, he spied an opportunity. With the pitch soft when play began, he deduced that the first morning would be the best time to plunder runs. And so he attacked. Trumper straight-drove over the infield, and repeatedly pulled deliveries through the on side; his range of shots was such that he could cut balls from middle stump. 'His whole bent is aggressive, and he plays a defensive stroke only as a very last resort,' wrote C.B. Fry, who played and captained against Trumper. 'He had no fixed canonical method of play, he defied all orthodox rules, yet every stroke he played satisfied the ultimate criterion of style – the minimum of effort, the maximum of effect.'

In 105 minutes before lunch at Old Trafford, Trumper secured his legend. He was the first man ever to score a century in the opening session of a Test match; in over 2,500 Tests since, only five men have emulated him.

By lunch on the opening day, Australia had gallivanted to 173–1. England fought back tenaciously, led by Bill Lockwood. One of the great fast bowlers to hail from Nottinghamshire, Lockwood combined pace with a deceptive slower ball to take 11 wickets in the match. In pursuit of 124, at various points – 44–0, 68–1, 92–3 and 107–5 – England were on course for an Ashes-levelling win. But Australia's spin twins, off-spinner Hugh Trumble and left-arm spinner Jack Saunders, exploited the pitch's grip and bounce. With eight runs needed, England were nine wickets down; their final pair, Wilfred Rhodes and Fred Tate, had to endure an excruciating 40-minute delay for rain. When they returned, Tate clipped a four through the leg side off Saunders. Three balls later, a delivery kept low: Tate was bowled, giving Australia a three-run victory. Tate, in his first and only Test, had earlier dropped a crucial catch off Australia skipper Joe Darling; many came to refer to the game as 'Tate's match'. A generation after the collapse at The Oval that had given birth to the Ashes, here was an encore.

Yet Australia's victory has come to be almost incidental set against Trumper's innings: the signature achievement of a cricketer who defined his era. The period up to 1914 is acclaimed as Test cricket's Golden Age. Trumper was the Golden Age incarnate.

Over 48 Tests Trumper's average, 39.04, was very good for the era but not extraordinary. His allure lay not in his statistics but in his style. This was captured in one of the most revered cricket photographs: Trumper, batting at The Oval in 1905, advancing down the pitch, with his bat almost perpendicular, about to play a trademark straight drive. The sight encapsulates the athleticism and buccaneering spirit of a player renowned for embracing any challenge. George Beldam's photograph was named 'Jumping out for a straight drive'. It was the defining image of a cricketer and even an age – no matter that the moment was set up by the photographer, rather than taken during a match, or that Trumper averaged 17.85 in the 1905 Ashes.

The 'Champagne of Cricket', Jack Hobbs, an Ashes opponent for England who averaged 18 runs more in Tests, hailed Trumper. 'He is the most perfect batsman in his scoring methods I have ever seen. He makes every orthodox stroke quite after the best models, and in addition he has several strokes of his own which it is quite hopeless for other batsmen to attempt.'

Others might need half a day to change the feel of a Test; with Trumper, an hour normally sufficed. His strike rate of 67, combined with the period's fast over rates, mean that Trumper averaged 40 runs per hour's batting: the fastest of any top-order batter in Test history, statistician Charles Davis has calculated.

Trumper's romantic appeal lay in his cavalier nature, and the sense that his best work came when it was most needed. His two highest scores – 214 not out against South Africa at Adelaide in 1911 and 185 not out against England in Sydney in 1903 – both came in defeat.

Until 1979 in England, and the mid-1950s elsewhere, Test pitches were not covered after each day's play. Before, pitches were uncovered while the heavens opened. After rain, pitches softened, initially making it easier to bat. But as the ground began to dry, especially under a hot sun, pitches became treacherous, spinning and bouncing viciously and unreliably. These 'sticky wickets' were considered the very hardest conditions for batters. Trumper was often their master. It is said that he paid the New South Wales groundsman to prepare a wet wicket especially for him to practise on after he had netted on a good pitch.

After Trumper scored his first Test century, at Lord's in 1899, W.G. Grace – whose last Test, Trumper's debut, was earlier that summer – approached him. Grace came with a bat inscribed 'From the past champion to the future champion'. Where Grace was a very English figure, Trumper – though his dad hailed from New Zealand – was an archetypal Australian, emerging as the nation gained independence from the United Kingdom. The Federation of Australia took place in January 1901; 18 months later, Trumper scored his Test century before lunch.

THE GOLDEN AGE?

In the 1920s, Jack Fingleton, a future Test batter, asked Hanson Carter, a former Australian Test cricketer, whether a player reminded him of Trumper. Carter retorted, 'You must never compare Vic with any batsman. He was up there, all on his own.' Trumper was, historian Gideon Haigh wrote, the first Australian to be hailed as the best in the world at anything. National pride was an inextricable part of Trumper's appeal: he was the first Australian to popularise wearing his same national cap in every Test. The lore of the baggy green cap, then, is also the lore of Trumper.

* * *

The notion of the Golden Age was popularised by Neville Cardus, one of the most celebrated cricket writers. Cardus, whose real name was John Frederick Newsham, grew up in Manchester. He never knew his father, was the son of a prostitute and left school aged 13. Cardus was essentially self-educated, devouring library books. He had two loves: classical music and cricket, both of which he wrote about with nostalgic, lyrical prose. What he considered the Golden Age perfectly coincided with his own youth – 'that distant and indeed lost world of the early 1900s', Cardus called it. 'Cricket more than any other game is inclined towards sentimentalism and cant. The players of cricket have been arranged and displayed in a white and shining hagiology.' He turned 26 in 1914, the year that marked the end of cricket's Golden Age.

There is an apparent paradox within these years. It is remembered largely as a Golden Age for batters; yet it ranks among the worst periods in Test history for batting.

From 1900 to 1910, Test teams scored 24.85 per wicket, comfortably lower than in any decade since. But the figure still marked a significant increase on the first years of Test cricket; until 1893, the average runs per wicket in the game was just 18.50, equating to an average team score of 185. Improvements in pitches – notably the growing use of the heavy roller, which smoothed out indentations, making the bounce more predictable – enabled batting to flourish as never before. The sense of precariousness in batting which remained, allied to three-day Tests, still encouraged attacking play. Pitches were not so benign as to create the feel of sterile, industrialised run-scoring: a common later critique, especially in the 1930s.

Table 1. Average Test runs per wicket by decade

	Average
1870s	18.18
1880s	19.25
1890s	25.19
1900s	24.85
1910s	26.90
1920s	33.25
1930s	32.15
1940s	35.34
1950s	28.54
1960s	32.10
1970s	31.90
1980s	32.09
1990s	31.51
2000s	34.10
2010s	32.45
2020s	30.10

To January 2025

In most cases, the celebrated Golden Age batters were amateur too; bowlers tended to be professionals. 'It was an age of so-called classical batsmanship inasmuch as style, fostered at the public schools, was upheld practically as an end in itself,' David Frith wrote. Amateurs were seen as being driven by more than mundane numbers, even if the reality was invariably more complex. 'The second line of defence – which is the pads – was known well enough to the batsmen of the Golden Age,' Cardus said. 'But it was a second and not a first line of defence.' He declared: 'Never since has such batsmanship been seen as this for opulence and prerogative; it was symbolical of the age's prestige.'

While Trumper embodied these values, he was not alone. The amateur Gilbert Jessop was nicknamed 'Croucher', for how low he bent in the crease. 'Jessop was on the short side, but he possessed long arms, had a barrel of a chest,' Pelham Warner recalled. Jessop batted with a chutzpah that few have ever matched, combining strength and imagination: 15 of his 53 first-class centuries came within an hour. 'The man who hits,' Jessop wrote in 1899, 'always possesses one consoling thought in success or failure, that with him goes the sympathy of the great majority of spectators.'

Jessop relished using his feet to advance down the pitch to drive pace bowlers and, crouching, playing what would now be called a slog sweep against spin and even seam. 'Length had no meaning for him,' wrote the former Surrey cricketer turned historian H.S. Altham. 'It was the length ball he hit best, and he hit it where the whim or the placing of the field suggested.'

These qualities came together when Jessop arrived at the crease with England 48–5 in pursuit of 263 on a green pitch at The Oval in 1902: a 50–1 shot, to the bookmakers at the ground. He attacked with gusto, using his feet and hitting three balls from Hugh Trumble, Australia's off-spinner, straight into the pavilion. These blows only counted as fours, with batters needing to hit the ball literally out of the ground to be awarded six; only after 1910 were sixes awarded for hitting the ball over the boundary. His century came in 76 balls and 75 minutes; during his 104, thousands more spectators entered The Oval. They saw England secure the first one-wicket victory in Test history.

A match earlier, Trumper had set up Australia's three-run win. These two Tests, within three weeks of each other in 1902, represented an apogee of the sport that, for those of a certain generation, could never be emulated: the golden summer of the Golden Age. Jessop's hundred, his lone Test century, was the golden hour, no matter that Australia won the series 2–1. 'The only man living who could beat us, beat us,' Trumble said.

Yet, to many, the most luminous figure of all during the Golden Age was Kumar Shri Ranjitsinhji: 'the *Midsummer Night's Dream* of cricket,' Cardus coined him. The son of a village farmer who was adopted as an heir by the Jam Sahib of an Indian statelet, Ranji moved to England to study at Trinity College, Cambridge, beginning in 1889. There, he scored bountiful runs. And he scored them with a distinctive style.

Grace is regarded as batting's first pioneer, mastering not just playing off the front foot or the back but *both*. Ranji represented the next evolution of batsmanship. While also driving adeptly through the off side, he popularised scoring on the leg side, which – especially to professionals – had been considered almost taboo. As a schoolboy, C.B. Fry, Ranji's long-time batting partner at Sussex, was told, 'If one hit the ball in an unexpected direction on the on side, intentionally or otherwise, one apologised to the bowler . . . The opposing captain never, by any chance, put a fieldsman there; he expected you to drive on the off side like a gentleman.'

Ranji took a very different approach. He developed the leg glance, flicking the ball off his pads to the on side, normally behind square leg. In the process, he reimagined the geography of a cricket field – opening up new areas of scoring, and forcing opponents to adjust their fields accordingly. Previously, teams had seldom placed more than two fielders on the entire on side. 'The stroke was a revelation of an entirely new technique only possible to a player with a quickness of eye, a nicety of poise, a surety of foot and a control of hand far superior to the best English practice,' Fry observed. Ranji's methods were rapidly replicated. 'We had got into a groove out of which the daring of a revolutionary alone could move us,' England batter Tom Hayward wrote in 1907.

The invention is remembered for its style, yet its roots were utilitarian. Facing fast bowling, Ranji tended to back away. In intensive training sessions at Cambridge, Ranji's right leg was pegged to the ground, preventing him from moving away from the ball and now opening up hitting straight balls to the on side. For all the shot's beauty, flicking balls to the leg side was simply a pragmatic way to score. Ranji was driven by efficacy, not aesthetics. The leg glance 'has the advantage of not wasting the batsman's strength and energy' and 'is a very safe stroke, because the ball can easily be kept down', he explained in *The Jubilee Book of Cricket*, his 1897 book. 'There is a certain class of batsmen nowadays who sacrifice effectiveness in order to attain what is called a pretty style. But a style which is not so effective as it might be can hardly claim to be either good or beautiful.' Ranji also developed formidable drives and is considered the inventor of the late cut – hitting the ball 'at the last possible instant', after it had passed the bat, with 'a quick sharp flick of the wrists'.

On his England debut, Ranji scored 62 and 154 not out at Old Trafford in 1896: 'Absolutely the finest innings I have seen,' declared Australia allrounder George Giffen. 'Ranji is the batting wonder of the age.' For several years, Ranji was perhaps the world's best batter. In 1896, he broke Grace's record for most runs in a first-class season, and scored 175 in his first Test in Australia in 1897/98. Between 1895 and 1904, Ranji scored 21,576 first-class runs at an average of 60.94, seven runs higher than anyone else who scored 1,000 runs in the period. His career was curtailed by princely duties: he became the Maharajah Jam Sahib of Nawanagar in 1907.

Alongside its romance, the Golden Age also significantly accelerated cricket's evolution. The sport developed a coherent domestic structure: England's County Championship, the national first-class competition, became an official title in 1890; Australia's equivalent, the Sheffield Shield, launched in 1892. National governing bodies were created in England and Australia in 1898 and 1905; the MCC assumed responsibility for assembling English teams overseas. In

England, overs – four balls in the 1880s and five balls in the 1890s – were standardised at six balls from 1900.

For all the difficulties in generalising about an era, the claim that batters in the Golden Age possessed more audacity than later players broadly stacks up. In matches for which balls faced were recorded, the data available suggests that Test batters scored more quickly during the 1900s – 2.7 runs per six balls – than in any decade in the format's first 100 years.

Bowling, too, made significant advances. As we have seen, Bernard Bosanquet invented the googly, the leg break which turned the other way, just before 1900. As pitches improved, more pace bowlers focused on beating batters in the air – using swing, by holding the seam upright, to move the ball late in its trajectory towards where the seam on the ball is angled. This was subtly different to swerve, which was effectively bowling spin at a fast pace, relying on drift in the air and then deviation after the ball had bounced. Swing was popularised around 1900, with England's George Hirst a leading exponent of the technique. It became notably more prominent after a rule change in 1907. Bowling teams were allowed to claim a second new ball – initially, after the batting side had reached 200 runs – thereby creating a second chance of new-ball swing in an innings.

England's Sydney Barnes was expert at obtaining swerve, but he could do much besides. Barnes was among the most skilful bowlers of all time, defying easy categorisation. Over six feet tall and with a high arm action, Barnes combined new-ball swing and quick leg spin with swerve – fast off breaks – while varying his pace and where he released the ball from on the crease. He was a unique bowler who swerved the ball both ways at speeds that could reach perhaps 65–70 mph, bowling by turns rapid off breaks and leg breaks. Barnes deliberately varied his pace, and could also seam the ball. Whether bowling to right- or left-handers, his speciality was to get deliveries to drift in, then spin away to off stump after they had pitched. 'The ball pitched outside my leg stump,' Australia's left-hander Clem Hill recalled of a characteristic Barnes dismissal in the 1911/12 Ashes. 'Before I could "pick up" my bat, my off stump was knocked silly.'

Barnes combined these qualities with a shrewd mind. 'I never bowled at the wickets; I bowled at the stroke,' he explained. 'I intended the batsman to make a stroke, then I tried to beat it. I tried to make the batsman move. The time a batsman makes mistakes is when he has to move his feet.' Barnes's 189 Test wickets cost 16.43 apiece; he took seven wickets a game. 'There's only one captain of a side when I'm bowling – me,' he declared.

The Test cricket played at the end of the Golden Age was of an altogether higher plane than that of the start. By 1914, Test cricket more closely resembled the 21st-century game than the format in 1890.

Yet perhaps the greatest reason for the nostalgia for the Golden Age lies less in the Age itself than in the idea of the era as a belle époque. Among the nine million killed in World War I were 275 first-class cricketers, including 12 who had played Test cricket. Both Grace and Trumper – perhaps the two most revered figures in cricket's history until that point – died in their homes within four months of each other in 1915; Trumper was 37 when he perished from kidney disease. Even amid the horrors of the Great War, his death, and the sense of a lost world, dominated front pages. Special trams had to be arranged for mourners in Sydney; about 20,000 lined the funeral route.

Charlie Macartney, his friend and former Australia teammate, tried to draw solace. 'I have one great satisfaction regarding Victor Trumper – I never saw him grow old as a cricketer.' Trumper, we can be sure, would have been proud when, in 1926, Macartney became the second man to score a Test hundred before lunch on the first day.

* * *

As with any gilded age, the more it is scrutinised, the more it turns sepia. The era's cricket was occasionally funereal; in the 1905 Trent

Bridge Test, Australia leg-spinner Warwick Armstrong bowled 52 overs for 67 runs, bowling negatively outside leg stump to slow the game down. In the 1911 *Wisden*, editor Sydney Pardon lamented that 'a good many people have come to the conclusion that first-class cricket is losing its hold on the public'. Before World War I, many English county sides struggled to stay solvent, the academics Keith Sandiford and Wray Vamplew documented. Counties had to save as best they could: scrapping second elevens, cutting the number of ground staff or not providing lunch for young players. Many relied on public appeals and patronage to stay afloat. Essex literally flogged a dead horse – sold for 7s 6d. Worcestershire and Gloucestershire called members' meetings to discuss withdrawing from the County Championship owing to their financial peril.

For all that Trumper is romanticised, he also represented the eternal cricketers' wish: to be paid what they were worth. As a working-class boy from Sydney, he needed to be. He considered signing for Worcestershire, which would have ended his Test career. In 1912, Trumper was one of the 'Big Six' who went on strike and refused to tour England out of dissatisfaction with the terms being offered by the Australian Cricket Board – both less money than they had wanted, and taking the power to name the manager away from the players. Trumper explained: 'What are we to do? Go down on our knees and ask the Board to let us go to England on any terms they like? No, they have got the thing down to bedrock, and it can stay there.'

Perhaps the best embodiment of the tensions between players and administrators was Sydney Barnes. He gave up his county contract aged 30, instead signing with a Lancashire League team, who paid more. England continued to pick him – at least, when money did not get in the way. After taking 49 wickets in the first four Tests, still a record in any series, Barnes missed the final Test in South Africa in 1913/14. South Africa's board had failed to reimburse him for bringing his wife on tour, as previously agreed.

The nostalgic appeal of the Golden Age also ignores the realities lurking beneath: who could play Test cricket was inextricably linked to race. In the 172 Test matches played until 1928, just three cricketers were not white.

Ranji suffered continued racism. During his first two years at Cambridge, he 'was not given a trial at the University ground, Fenner's, on account only of the colour of his skin', historian Ramachandra Guha wrote. At university, he was called 'Mr Smith'. Even as Ranji rose, his race remained an obstacle to gaining international recognition. MCC president Lord Harris, who had just finished a stint as governor of Bombay, opposed picking what he called a 'bird of passage' cricketer. Yet Ranji had far more connection to England than Billy Murdoch and J.J. Ferris, who were both picked to play Tests for the country after previously playing for Australia; Murdoch captained Australia 16 times. Harris himself was born in Trinidad.

'Some cricketers were, on principle, against the inclusion of Ranjitsinhji,' *The Times* reported. 'The Marylebone Club committee thoroughly weighed the matter, and, while recognising the wonderful ability of that cricketer, thought it scarcely right to play him for England against Australia.' Ranji only got his chance in the second Test in 1896, against MCC's wishes, because a representative from the hosting ground – Lancashire, in this case – got a casting vote on the side. Despite his stellar record, Ranji was not selected to tour South Africa in either 1898 or 1902; South Africa appear to have pressurised England not to pick him.

A generation later, Ranji's nephew Duleepsinhji faced similar discrimination. In 1929, aged 24, Duleepsinhji made his debut against South Africa, scoring 12 and one, before immediately being dropped. By England's next series against South Africa, their 1930/31 tour, Duleepsinhji was one of England's leading Test batters: his average was 60.53, and he made a magisterial 173 against Australia at Lord's. Yet Duleepsinhji was 'apparently not considered for selection for the South Africa tour as MCC did not challenge South Africa's racist requirements', historians Richard Parry and André Odendaal wrote.

Duleepsinhji finished with a Test average of 58.52 in a career truncated by his premature retirement aged 27 because of pulmonary disease. His appearance against South Africa in 1929 would be the only occasion in the country's first 172 Tests, until their Test return in 1992, that South Africa played against someone not of white skin.

The first black Test cricketer was Australia's Sam Morris, who played one Test in 1885, taking two wickets, during a player dispute about money. Morris's family hailed from the Caribbean; he was frequently referred to using racial tropes in contemporary newspaper reports.

For other Australians, race was also a barrier to winning selection. In 1902, Jack Marsh, an Indigenous quick bowler from New South Wales, was dropped from a state match against England. Archie MacLaren, the England captain, is said to have refused to play against him, alleging that he had an illegal action. Marsh was among the world's fastest bowlers.

His career was stymied both by racist laws that limited his movement and the stigma of being called a 'chucker'. In one first-class match, Marsh was no-balled for throwing 17 times by one umpire; the other umpire considered his bowling fair. To disprove the slur, Marsh visited a doctor. His arm was put in a splint, and he was given a certificate declaring that, with the splint, it would be physically impossible to throw. It made no difference. Marsh only played six first-class matches; 34 wickets at 21.47 apiece attest to his talent.

To England's Albert Knight, who played in a tour game against him, Marsh was 'quite the best bowler in the Commonwealth'; his action was 'not, one thinks, a throw or even essentially doubtful'. Monty Noble, the New South Wales and Australia captain, refused to pick Marsh, stating that he 'didn't have class enough'. Test opener Warren Bardsley, a state teammate, observed: 'The reason Marsh was kept out of big cricket was his colour.'

* * *

Abraham Lincoln once watched a cricket match between Chicago and Milwaukee. This was not unusual: cricket was played in at least 22 states, and 125 cities and towns, before the American Civil War. The USA and Canada hosted the first foreign tour by an English cricket team, in 1859. During the Civil War, baseball – easier to play in army camps, and shrewdly reinventing itself as an American, rather than English, creation – became the country's most popular sport. Yet cricket still remained vibrant in pockets; in Philadelphia, there were over 100 clubs around 1900.

At this time, one of the game's outstanding bowlers was an American: Bart King, who swung the ball both ways. Touring England with the Gentlemen of Philadelphia, King took 237 first-class wickets at 16.62 across his three tours to England, in 1897, 1903 and 1908 – when, aged 35, he came top of the English first-class bowling averages. 'One who, at the top of his power and speed, was at least the equal of the greatest of them all,' gushed Plum Warner, who played frequently against King. Across King's three tours to England, Philadelphia defeated ten first-class counties, including Surrey and Lancashire. Philadelphia even boasted one man who would play Test cricket: Ranji Hordern, who studied at the University of Pennsylvania, where it is said he learned the googly before returning to Australia.

In both 1893 and 1912, the Gentlemen of Philadelphia defeated the Australians – sides on their way back from England. Both Australia teams included nine players with Test caps; the two remaining players in the 1893 side would soon win international selection too. Yet Philadelphia defeated them by an innings. In this era, the US were almost certainly among the four strongest cricket nations.

Cricket was also developing further south. The first recorded game at Buenos Aires Cricket Club was in 1831. The early story of cricket in Argentina is typical of cricket's origin story in many countries: the game was initially played by British expats, then expanded into other communities. By the early 1900s, cricket was played in

Spanish-language schools in Buenos Aires. Scorecards of major matches include a notable number of Spanish names; the sport was covered in Spanish-speaking newspapers.

In 1911/12, Argentina and MCC played a series that both called Tests: three-day matches in Buenos Aires, the first two at the Hurlingham Club. Argentina won the first game by four wickets. MCC only sealed the series with a two-wicket victory in the third match thanks to 40-year-old Archie MacLaren, until recently one of England's best batters. If MCC's party was not as strong as the Australians defeated in the USA – it included six Test players, but only two in their prime – the series illustrated Argentina's potential. In 1926/27, when MCC next toured, with three future England Test captains, the result was the same: a 2–1 victory to the tourists.

Argentina's most renowned player, Clem Gibson, was the son of a British-Argentinian landowner; he learned the game at the Hurlingham Club in Buenos Aires, before being educated at Eton College. While at Cambridge University in 1921, Gibson was picked for an all-amateur England XI to play the Australians; he took 6–64 in victory. Three years later, in his office in Buenos Aires, Gibson received a telegram telling him that he had been picked for the 1924/25 Ashes tour. He declined, preferring to remain at home.

Rather than a national game, cricket retrenched into being an Anglophile sport. In 1947, the old pavilion on the Buenos Aires Cricket Club ground was burned down, seemingly at the behest of Eva Perón, piqued that her request to use the grounds for a charity social-aid event had been declined.

The Golden Age was cricket's great missed opportunity. By its very name, the Imperial Cricket Conference locked out nations outside the British Empire, barring them from Test status. Administrators prioritised the 'Imperial' over the 'Cricket'. Multi-day 'Test' matches involving Argentina and the United States could retrospectively have been classed as official Tests, just as happened with early South Africa matches. Based on their quality, both Argentina and the USA in the early 20th century had at least as strong a claim to gaining Test status as South Africa a generation earlier.

Even with this exclusionary attitude to status, the enduring confusion over what could constitute an official Test remained. Not until 1907, 30 years after the first Test, did the first match occur between a team that was both from a sovereign state and selected by the national governing body for cricket, Eric Midwinter wrote in *The Cricketer's Progress*.

When it came to determining which countries were allowed to play Test matches, cricketing quality was merely one factor. Politics was just as significant. Through a mixture of neglect and deliberate exclusion, the chance to develop a bigger and more geographically diverse game was lost.

* * *

Perhaps the period before 1914 wasn't a Golden Age or a missed opportunity, but both. The first, indeed, directly gave way to the second, as complacency about cricket in the early 1900s prevented the sport evolving – a failing that *Wisden*'s editor and other contemporaries lamented at the time.

The lone area in which ICC administrators gave a hint of more creative thinking was fated to fail. In 1912, largely at the behest of South Africa's Abe Bailey, South Africa and Australia toured England, where they played a triangular series. All three nations played six Tests each as part of a league, with an overall winner crowned.

The triangular tournament suffered from four essential problems. South Africa's team were falling away, early in a 16-Test winless streak; their batters and leg-spinners were ill-suited to English turf pitches. Second, Australia, missing their 'Big Six' players, were themselves far less attractive than in previous years; they had just lost the Ashes 4–1 at home. Third, attendances for matches not involving England were poor. The fourth problem was the weather. It was one of the wettest summers since records began in 1776 – particularly unfortunate because only three days were allocated for each of the nine Tests.

Even England's victory in the last match, over Australia – the game was timeless, to ensure an overall tournament winner – did not create any appetite to continue the concept. Instead, Test cricket evolved through bilateral series, rather than multi-team tournaments as in other sports. It would take another 87 years, with the launch of the Asian Test Championship in 1999, for another Test competition to involve more than two nations.

4

THE GREATEST OPENING PAIR

In July 1917, Lord's staged a charity match between an English Army XI and the Australian Imperial Forces. Among those playing was left-arm spinner Colin Blythe, celebrated for his Ashes deeds for England. Four months later, Blythe perished at Passchendaele.

As the Great War was ending, the English cricket establishment turned its thoughts to what the game would look like in 1919, hoping to mark the occasion with another visit from Australia. Plans were swiftly made for a series of 'Victory' Test matches. Instead, with not enough Australian players available for matches that could be classed as Tests, an Australian Imperial Forces team, comprising players who had served in the war, toured England. Their 28 first-class games, ending the war-induced hiatus in first-class cricket, were warmly received by a public yearning for any sense of normality. As the team set sail from Plymouth in September 1919, the captain sent a telegram 'to convey to the cricketing public of England their sincere thanks for the generous support given them'. The Imperial Forces side then played in South Africa before ending their tour against New South Wales.

First-class cricket had been abandoned at the outset of war; recreational, charity and exhibition matches continued. The aim was to keep 'the lesser game just alive while the greater game is being played', Donald Mackinnon, the president of the Victorian Cricket Association, said in September 1916.

Yet when Test cricket returned in 1920, after a hiatus of almost seven years, it had a very different feel. Adjusting for population,

England suffered about twice as many casualties as Australia in World War I. This was one factor behind a dramatic change in Ashes fortunes when Test cricket resumed. Until 1914, England had won 40 Tests against Australia and lost 35. Beginning with a 5–0 whitewash in 1920/21 before the return series a few months later in England, Australia won eight consecutive Ashes Tests. On the ship back between the two series, Australia found a new sport to beat England at: deck quoits, a game entailing throwing rings over a spike.

Australia's captain throughout this sequence was Warwick Armstrong. He towered above post-World War I cricket, and not only because he was 6 ft 3 in and weighed 22 stone. Over these ten Tests, he averaged 56.00 with the bat while chipping in with 17 wickets at 24.47 apiece. He was a pioneering leader too.

'Armstrong seemed to divide his bowling into two very distinct groups, attacking and defending,' wrote Percy Fender, an Ashes rival turned journalist. 'Directly a batsman came in, he was attacked along whatever line previous experience seemed to have shown him most vulnerable. If this did not succeed after a time, the attack changed and the batsman was made to go after the ball if he wanted to score.'

Pragmatism also marked Armstrong's leadership, as Gideon Haigh details in *The Big Ship*. To preserve Australia's undefeated run on the 1921 tour of the British Isles – which lasted until the 35th out of 39 first-class games – Armstrong sometimes allowed an opponent's defensive batters to remain at the crease. He explained, 'I directed my bowlers to let them stay there knowing the players would not force the pace.'

Previous Test sides had been limited to one bowler of express speed; in Jack Gregory and Ted McDonald, Australia had two. They took advantage of a significant change, first initiated just before World War I: tarpaulins to cover a bowler's run-up when it rained, allowing bowlers to run in without fear of the soggy ground giving way beneath their feet. Crucially, the 22-yard pitch itself remained uncovered; after a rain delay, bowlers could still benefit from a damp pitch. The pair harassed England from both ends with the new ball; they were then rotated, so one would almost invariably be operating. Gregory, in particular, relished bowling short; he often bowled from wide of the crease, spearing deliveries awkwardly into batters. The sense of physical threat was heightened because gloves were flimsy, and some players still did not wear them; there was nothing at all to protect a batter's thighs.

'Never before have English batsmen been so demoralised by great pace,' *Wisden* editor Sydney Pardon observed. 'I am sure that some of our batsmen, knowing they would have to face Gregory, were out before they went in.' Frank Foster, a former Ashes rival turned journalist, called Armstrong 'the man who had the confounded cheek to commence his attack with *two* fast bowlers! No wonder England gasped and quailed, shuddered and fell, and then expired.'

At Trent Bridge in the first Test of the 1921 series, Gregory and McDonald encountered a damp pitch, creating extra bounce. They shared 16 wickets for 177 in a crushing victory. Yet the pair would damage much more than just England's averages. In the second innings, Gregory first hit Ernest Tyldesley's elbow then his jaw, knocking him unconscious; the ball diverted onto his stumps. Tyldesley required assistance to go to the pavilion; the crowd heckled Gregory. England batters would be struck 11 times by Australia's fast-bowling pair that Test summer. Overall, R.H. Campbell calculated in *Cricket Casualties*, Gregory hit 20 English batters on the body, above the waist, in his 21 Tests – comfortably a record at the time. England were so discombobulated that they selected 30 players in the 1921 series, still a record in any series.

The tactics were the start of a recurring trend in Test history. Whenever fast bowling has been taken to new heights, it has had two consequences: a lot of wickets, and a lot of controversy.

To go with high pace, Australia had the classic complement: high-class leg spin, from Arthur Mailey, who particularly excelled against the tail. By comparison, England's attack was staid. Australia were also markedly superior in fitness and fielding; no matter his bulk, Armstrong was a fine slip fielder.

So great was Australia's dominance that their 4–1 victory in the 1924/25 Ashes was seen as a cause for English optimism. 'The dark days are coming to an end,' *Wisden*'s editor observed. England were markedly more competitive – and their wait of 14 Tests and 13 years for victory over Australia ended in Melbourne. There, Maurice Tate took seven wickets with his swing and bounce, part of his 38 in the series. He married skill with stamina: in the first Test in Sydney, where he took 11–228 in the match, he bowled 89 eight-ball overs – 712 deliveries. Over his career, Tate also avenged his father, Fred, who had suffered an ill-fated first, and only, Test against Australia in 1902. After he was last man out in England's three-run defeat, Tate told a teammate about his seven-year-old son, 'I have got a boy, at home, who will put it all right for me.'

The 1926 Ashes was contested against the backdrop of Great Britain's first, and still only, General Strike. The lorry containing Australia's kit for a tour match against Essex was held up at a picket line.

Armstrong's retirement helped to give England hope that they could win the Ashes for the first time since 1912. Victory was made harder because of the contrast in how Tests were organised in the two countries. In Australia, virtually all Tests until 1945 were timeless, played until one side won. In England, where counties wanted to minimise time without their players, three-day Tests remained the norm until 1930 against Australia, and 1947 against other opponents. One letter to *The Times* in 1926 even asked if there was 'a respectable body of opinion in favour of the abolition of Tests altogether'.

Late negotiations ensured that with the series 0–0, the fifth and final Test at The Oval in 1926 was timeless. English anxiety about not missing the chance to regain the urn led to captain Arthur Carr being sacked and replaced by Percy Chapman, another amateur. Carr fell ill during the previous Test, when he was part of 11; Jack Hobbs temporarily stood in as captain, becoming the first professional to captain England at home.

THE GREATEST OPENING PAIR

After England made 280, Australia scrambled a 22-run first innings lead. Opening pair Hobbs and Herbert Sutcliffe steered England to 49–0 after day two, the Test in the balance. At two o'clock the next morning, Hobbs was woken up at his house in Clapham by thunder and lightning. Sutcliffe too was 'awakened by peals of thunder': 'My thoughts turned to the Oval wicket and I wondered if fortune had once again ruined our chances of victory.' Overnight rain created a 'sticky wicket' with uneven bounce: one delivery might bounce up towards a batter's head; the next could scuttle along the turf.

This was the challenge that Hobbs and Sutcliffe faced as they resumed on day three. Steam rose from the pitch as the rain dried out under the cloudy skies. If the pitch dried too quickly, cracks would form, rendering batting even harder. After the first over in the morning, Hobbs told his partner, 'Jolly bad luck that rain; it has cooked our chances.' Frank Chester, the umpire, would call conditions 'the worst sticky I have seen. I did not give England a chance.'

The morning would be the turning point in the decade's balance of power in Ashes cricket. While Hobbs played at his usual tempo, Sutcliffe initially stonewalled; during the first 40 minutes of day three, Hobbs scored 26, Sutcliffe not a run. As the sun poked through the clouds, the ball started to spin more. Hobbs took a guard outside leg stump, getting his pads out the way, and played out eight consecutive maidens against off-spinner Arthur Richardson. Leg-spinner Mailey at one stage had Hobbs plumb lbw – but, bewilderingly, Australia did not appeal. In between austere defence, Hobbs drove with panache, reaching his century shortly after Sutcliffe had got to his 50. Both Australia's captain, Herbie Collins, and the umpire Chester called Hobbs's innings the best they had ever witnessed. When Hobbs was out for a round hundred, Sutcliffe accelerated, driving with confidence through the covers, to reach 161. Besides the openers, no other Englishman passed 50 in the match; Sutcliffe had scored 76 in the first innings too. Their partnership set up England's 289-run victory. England won the Ashes for the first time in 14 years.

As a pair, Hobbs and Sutcliffe were English batting in excelsis. They played for Surrey and Yorkshire respectively: the two most successful counties, one from the south, and one from the north.

Hobbs – 'The Master' – was the oldest of 12 children. Like many great cricketers of the day, Hobbs spent formative years at Cambridge University: not because he was studying there, but because his father was a groundsman at Jesus College. Hobbs went to his first cricket match aged 18 months; he played against the College servants with 'a tennis ball, a cricket stump for a bat and a tennis post for a wicket on a gravel pitch', *Wisden* recounted. Uneven bounce in the nets and on the pitch at Parker's Piece, the local park in Cambridge, 'honed his unique skill for playing on bad wickets', observed his biographer Leo McKinstry. Playing the ball very late, enabling him to make late adjustments, was a Hobbs hallmark: 'You should always play back if you can because you can watch the ball right onto the bat.' Distilling his batting philosophy, Hobbs said, 'The secret of power and hitting is not so much muscular force as ease of swing and perfect timing.'

After leaving school aged 12, Hobbs became a servant at Jesus College, helping to put up the nets and transfer cricket equipment. Perhaps because of class snobbery, and partly because he was a relatively late developer – he was 18 before he scored his first century in any cricket – Hobbs was turned down by Essex before signing for Surrey. With his classical technique, stylish driving and range of shots, Hobbs shattered one of the game's great divides; to the grandee Pelham Warner, he was 'a professional who bats exactly like an amateur'. No one has ever scored more than his 199 first-class centuries: a record surely safe for all time. His England record of 12 Ashes hundreds appears almost as impregnable. Fitness and anticipation made Hobbs an outstanding fielder too; *The Cricket Statistician* credits him with the most run-outs by a Test fielder, 18, which normally came when prowling at cover.

Sutcliffe grew up in Pudsey, a market town halfway between Leeds and Bradford. Aged nine, he became an orphan, and was raised by his aunts. Through prolific scoring in league cricket, he broke into Yorkshire's side. He combined fierce concentration with immense physical courage, best shown in his hooking behind square leg, a shot that reflected his self-assurance. 'Cricket is a game which calls for courage, skill, strategy and, above everything else, self-control,' Sutcliffe wrote; he was a man unfazed by the previous delivery or the situation. His judgement of when to leave the ball was as immaculate as his sense of how to dress. He once reprimanded a teammate for not wearing a blazer to lunch, telling Bill Bowes, 'We must do everything better than the amateurs. Your manners must be better, and if possible you must speak and dress better too.' Sutcliffe was also brave: he was hit on the body 18 times in Ashes Tests, comfortably a record in England–Australia matches from 1877 to 1933, R.H. Campbell finds. 'I love a dog fight,' he said after his century at The Oval in 1926.

Individually, a strong case can be made for either Hobbs or Sutcliffe to be England's best opener of all time. Sutcliffe averaged 60.73 overall in Test cricket; in Australia, he made six centuries and averaged 63.70. Hobbs's Test average was fractionally less, a still towering 56.94, but he flourished in two distinct eras.

Before World War I, bowlers held sway. From 1900 to 1914, the overall batting average in Tests was just 24.70, with spinners particularly thriving. Between the world wars, conditions were more fertile for batting, as the quality of pitches improved: the overall average rose by six runs, to 31.40. These two eras necessitated different approaches – attacking more in the first, when batters could not trust the wicket; and being more restrained in the second, when batters did not need to take calculated risks in the same way. The artist became an accountant. 'There were two Jacks, the Pre and the Post-War Jack,' wrote Frank Woolley, his long-time Test teammate. 'The real one was the Pre-War.'

Hobbs distilled his different approach before and after 1914: 'You could play cheeky shots and make 50 or 60 and feel life was worth living. Then came the exasperation when they started counting your hundreds, publishing averages, and it was all figures.' The wonder of Hobbs was that he could excel in both periods, against spin – he was described as the best player against South Africa's googly quartet and relished using his feet – swing, seam and pace alike. He made a hundred aged 46, in Australia in 1928/29, setting a record that endures for the oldest Test centurion. For how he embodied the English school of openers, and the undemonstrative way in which he challenged cricket's class barrier, Hobbs was named one of *Wisden's* Five Cricketers of the Century in 2000.

Yet, for all their individual qualities, together Hobbs and Sutcliffe were most imperious. Their start was precarious: Sutcliffe was almost run out in the first over of his debut, against South Africa in 1924. It was the first of 38 occasions that the pair opened together in Tests; 15 times, they added a century. Their average partnership was 87.81; this figure remains 17 runs clear of any opening pair to make 1,000 runs.

Table 2. Highest partnerships by opening pairs (top five)

		Innings	Runs	Average
J.B. Hobbs, H. Sutcliffe (ENG)	1924–1930	38	3,249	87.81
A.F. Rae, J.B. Stollmeyer (WI)	1948–1953	21	1,349	71.00
N.D. McKenzie, G.C. Smith (SA)	2008–2009	27	1,664	66.56
W.A. Brown, J.H.W. Fingleton (AUS)	1935–1938	16	1,020	63.75
J.B. Hobbs, W. Rhodes (ENG)	1910–1921	36	2,146	61.31

Most importantly, Hobbs and Sutcliffe had a penchant for delivering their best when the Ashes were at stake. In 1926, they added 156 when England had to follow on at Leeds, securing a draw, before their famous alliance at The Oval. In the third Test of the 1928/29 Ashes, in Melbourne, England needed 332 to win with the pitch at its most treacherous after a bout of rain. As the pitch dried out, deliveries reared up unexpectedly, leaving both batters with painful marks on their body. 'Our friends came to the pavilion to commiserate with us, saying what a pity it was the rain came,' Hobbs later recalled. In his diary he wrote, 'We did not think we had an earthly.'

But, channelling their performance at The Oval, the two added 105. Sutcliffe endured 462 balls for his 135, making good on his dictum that, on sticky wickets, 'all defensive strokes we make must be made with a dead bat and with the bat handle well forward at an angle of 45 degrees'. The pull shot was his sole indulgence. Many players batted on sticky wickets 'with an inferiority complex', Sutcliffe wrote:

> They are not prepared to fight. What a great mistake this is, for there is no wicket quite so interesting and thrilling to play on as a 'glue pot' . . .
>
> Those players who have specialised in sticky wicket displays and who have been highly successful, are the ones who have been able to concentrate very deeply on the task of cutting out certain strokes, thereby reducing risks to a minimum. That is the secret of all successful sticky wicket play.
>
> The best method as soon as one sees that popping, turning ball, is either to get clear of its course altogether or take the blow on the chest. It doesn't hurt much and a slight chest or rib tickler is much better than losing a wicket. That is one of the finer points of batsmanship. On a glue pot, with nearly all the fielders concentrated within a few yards of the bat, the main point is to be sure the ball goes almost straight down.

For days afterwards, Sutcliffe wore the bruises he sustained from balls that reared up; the afterglow of England's three-wicket victory, which retained the urn and set up a 4–1 series win, made up for the pain. When Sutcliffe gave his first son a middle name, he chose Hobbs.

* * *

Wally Hammond arrived in Australia in 1928 as a stylish 25-year-old batter; like W.G. Grace before him, he represented Gloucestershire. Like Hobbs and Sutcliffe, Hammond was a professional. Where the Golden Age in England had been characterised by amateur batters, by the 1920s, the best batters tended to be professionals.

Before the 1928/29 Ashes, Hammond had not scored a century in eight Tests. Yet in Australia Hammond scored 905 runs, vaulting past Sutcliffe's record for most runs in a single series. In the middle three Tests, he peeled off double hundreds at Sydney and Melbourne, then 119 not out and 177 in Adelaide. In each of these three Tests, Hammond batted for over six hours, the equivalent of a full day's play, attesting to his concentration and fitness.

The 1928/29 side came closer than any, before or since, to achieving English Test cricket utopia: a series whitewash in Australia. England thrashed Australia in the first two Tests, before their Ashes-clinching chase in Melbourne. In Adelaide, England had to defend 348 in roasting heat; they did so by 12 runs, thanks to left-arm spinner Jack White's indefatigable command of line and length. White bowled 749 deliveries in the Test. With his last, he bowled slightly shorter, inducing number 11 Don Blackie to try and clear square leg, giving the bowler his 13th wicket of the match. Australia needed 286 in the fifth Test, back in Melbourne, to deprive England of a 5–0 victory. Captain Jack Ryder was considered fortunate to survive a run-out appeal, and secured a five-wicket win.

Hammond's signature was the cover drive, which showed his quick footwork and precise placement; he could play the back-foot drive equally effectively. His height and burly build meant that Hammond combined style with unusual power. In 1933, he broke the record for the Test highest score by hitting 336 not out in Auckland, thumping ten sixes – eight over the off side – and scoring at faster than a run a minute. 'His method of batting is an almost unique combination of ease, grace, majesty and power, and above all of correctness,' the former cricketer R.C. Robertson-Glasgow wrote.

'He has it all and with double the strength of most players; strength scientifically applied.' The force of Hammond's shots was such that to 'field to him at cover point was a sort of ordeal by fire'.

He also brought a calculating mind to the crease, future England captain Len Hutton noted. 'Often he would make a shot that would cause the opposing captain to move a fielder to a particular spot to cut off the next stroke there. While the bowler walked back to his mark, Wally would look round to find a gap somewhere else. Having found it, he would send the ball clean through.'

Hammond's gifts extended beyond his batting. With a smooth rhythmical action he swung the ball at pace, once taking 7–87 in the match in a Test in Australia. As a slip fielder, Hutton observed, 'He was second to none – no diving to left or right, collecting green marks on his immaculate flannels.'

Not all were as enamoured with Hammond off the field. Captaining England during the 1946/47 Ashes, he travelled between matches by Jaguar as the squad travelled by train. To teammate Denis Compton, 'He tended to be individualistic and uncommunicative; worse still, he didn't seem to be part of the side.'

Hammond emphatically made good on his talents, averaging 58.45 in 85 Tests. His versatility was such that he performed markedly better away than at home, with bat and ball alike, both against Australia and overall.

'Everything he did, he did with the touch of a master,' Australia's Stan McCabe, a long-time opponent, observed. 'One could refer to him as the perfect cricketer.' But in the Ashes contests of the 1930s, Hammond would be eclipsed by someone even more perfect.

5

THREE BECOME SIX: TEST CRICKET OPENS UP

In Bridgetown on 11 January 1930, Frederick Calthorpe walked out to toss for England in a Test match. Arthur Gilligan had done exactly the same thing the previous day, 8,700 miles away.

England were playing two different Tests at the same time. In the winter of 1929/30, two teams – West Indies and New Zealand – were eager to mark their new-found Test status by hosting England. Before 1930, West Indies had played just three Tests, all in England in 1928; New Zealand had not played any.

A year earlier, England had enjoyed a gruelling but triumphant Ashes tour, winning 4–1. Most of England's squad did not want to tour the following winter. These absences forced England to be creative in their selection – especially when they had not one but two squads to pick. Both captains, Calthorpe and Gilligan, had never played for England before and would never do so again after the winter tours.

For almost two hours – 21 February in Guyana, and 22 February in Auckland – both England sides were on the field simultaneously. This remains the lone occasion in history that one country has played two Tests at the same time. England's decision to prioritise the squad for the Caribbean was vindicated: the four-match series was drawn 1–1. In the final Test, scheduled as timeless, West Indies were set 836 runs to win. George Headley's double century led West Indies to 408–5 at the end of day seven; the next two days in Jamaica were rained off, leaving the Test a draw. England had their boat home to catch.

THREE BECOME SIX: TEST CRICKET OPENS UP

The tale of the two England teams highlights how the notion of Test status was arbitrary; indeed, England continued to pay players more for Ashes Tests until the 1950s, indicating that they did not regard all internationals as of equal importance. If a Test team is meant to represent the very best of a nation's talents, it is axiomatically impossible for one country to field two such sides simultaneously. England's squad in the Caribbean was stronger than that which met New Zealand, yet the West Indies matches were only given Test status retrospectively. These games, taking place in unison, embodied how much Test cricket had changed over the 1920s, the only decade in which the game has welcomed three new members.

* * *

While the late 1920s was a period of classic Ashes contests, in Test cricket, something altogether more significant was happening in the committee rooms. In May 1926, the Imperial Cricket Conference admitted West Indies and New Zealand to Test cricket. They also effectively agreed to admit India, who merely needed to establish a national organising board, which they did in 1928.

During Charles Darwin's voyage on HMS *Beagle* in 1835, he stopped at the Bay of Islands. There, he watched a game of cricket played by Māori and Pākehā (of white European descent) people. The first recorded game in New Zealand was three years earlier. Cricket 'was encouraged in New Zealand as an important means of replicating English social customs and ideals', wrote the academic Greg Ryan. But 'a strong sense of imperial and inter-colonial symbolism' was associated with the game. Social elitism was less detectable in rugby, which overtook cricket in popularity over the 1890s. Scant attempts were made by European settlers to spread cricket to the Māori population: before 1920, only six Māori people played first-class cricket, Ryan has found.

New Zealand first welcomed a foreign tour in 1863/64, when George Parr's All-England XI played a series to break up a tour of Australia; the home sides fielded 22 players. The New Zealand Cricket Council was formed in 1894, helping to organise more inbound tours from teams from England or Australia. In 1906, William Plunket, the governor-general, donated a trophy to be awarded to the best regional side: the Plunket Shield, the national first-class competition, was born. The tournament was initially dominated by Auckland and Canterbury. By the late 19th century, these were established as the strongholds of New Zealand cricket, though for different reasons. In Auckland, cricket thrived through military garrisons. In Christchurch, the capital of Canterbury, cricket grew through the vast network of British public school and Oxbridge graduates, and was particularly prominent in elite schools.

Standards in New Zealand improved, helped by English and Australian professionals coming to play and coach. After gaining Test status, New Zealand made their first visit to England in 1927; MCC called it 'something of a sporting and educational trip'. There were no Tests, but New Zealand acquitted themselves admirably, winning five matches against counties and losing only four. Effectively, this team confirmed New Zealand's Test status: soon after, MCC agreed to tour in 1929/30.

New Zealand had already produced an outstanding Test cricketer: Clarrie Grimmett, who was born in Dunedin in 1891. Grimmett honed his leg spin on a backyard pitch; he trained his fox terrier to fetch his eight balls at the end of every over, before bowling another eight. He knew that New Zealand would not allow him to explore his full potential; in 1914, aged 22, after nine first-class matches for Wellington, Grimmett moved to Australia. He popularised the top-spinner – a leg-spinner's variation that goes straight on, quickly. When he retired, with 216 wickets in 37 games, he was the leading wicket-taker in Test history.

After New Zealand gained Test status, they remained blighted by losing their best players. Five players who toured England in

THREE BECOME SIX: TEST CRICKET OPENS UP

1927 – Ces Dacre, Stewie Dempster, Roger Blunt, Ken James and Bill Merritt – would move to England to play professionally. They signed deals to play either in county cricket or the lucrative Lancashire League, or for Sir Julien Cahn's XI, a wandering team of stars. Dempster, who averaged 65.72 in his ten Tests, including two centuries against England, played his last Test aged 29. New Zealand's board had a poor hand but they played it terribly, seeking to bar players from professional contracts abroad. The policy meant that New Zealand's overseas band couldn't even play Tests on the rare occasions when they were available.

In 1931, after the leg-spinner Merritt was signed to the Lancashire League, ending his promising Test career aged 22, Pelham Warner wrote in an editorial for *The Cricketer*:

> England is not showing up in a good light when they cast covetous eyes on players from other lands. Surely a great and powerful country like this should stand on its own; attempts to attract cricketers from outside should be taboo.

The talent drain continued. In 1949, Martin Donnelly hit a double century against England at Lord's, an innings which led C.B. Fry, a former England Test captain, to call Donnelly as good a left-hander as any he had seen. His displays helped a strong side draw all four Tests in the series; had the matches not been limited to three days, New Zealand could conceivably have won a couple. Donnelly never played another Test after the tour, ending his seven-Test career with an average of 52.90. Just 13 of his 131 first-class games were in New Zealand.

For the players who remained at home, cricket fitted in around the demands of work. Walter Hadlee, who was born in 1915 and went on to be New Zealand captain and later selector, manager and chairman, recalled that net practice was held in the early morning and evenings. This minimised clashes with work – in Hadlee's case, at the Christchurch Gas Company.

Deprived of their best talent, New Zealand struggled both on the pitch and financially. Provincial teams, which depended on patronage, could only afford to run a modest first-class programme. Australian sides showed little inclination to tour: 19 of New Zealand's first 22 Tests were against England. 'Marylebone Cricket Club has done more for cricket in New Zealand from a distance of 10,000 miles than the Australian Board of Control for International Cricket has done from 1,500,' wrote Vic Richardson, the former Australia captain.

In the 42 years after their inaugural Test, in 1930, big brother Australia played New Zealand just once. When they did, in 1946 – a match only afforded Test status two years later – New Zealand were bowled out for 42 and 54.

* * *

'Cricket is an Indian game, accidentally discovered by the English,' Ashis Nandy wrote in *The Tao of Cricket*. 'Cricket is a cultural import which has met a vital need of India.' The first game of cricket in India is thought to have been played by British merchant sailors along the beachfront in Cambay, a trading centre in Gujarat, in 1721. 'When my boat was lying for a fortnight in one of the channels,' a British sailor wrote, 'We every day diverted ourselves with playing Cricket.'

Even before direct British rule began in 1858, cricket was developing in India – but it was initially conceived of as a sport for Europeans only. The Calcutta Cricket Club – outside England, the oldest club in the world – was established in 1792; its membership, like that of many other leading clubs, was restricted to Europeans until after independence. The first recorded instance of a formal cricket match in India, in 1804, was in Calcutta between Old Etonian Civil Servants and Other Civil Servants – both teams comprising exclusively British people. 'The British saw cricket as a way of keeping their own community together, with little or no place there for the Indians,' wrote the historian Mihir Bose.

Centuries before cricket came to India, gilli-danda – a game involving a stick and ball – was played in the region. After observing British elites playing cricket, Indian communities came to embrace the sport too. 'The game was vigorously pursued by Indian middle-class youth residing in towns and cities,' Prashant Kidambi wrote in *Cricket Country*. 'Acquiring proficiency in the imperial game afforded Indian men an opportunity to savour its kinaesthetic pleasures and assert their masculinity in a context where it was constantly questioned by their colonisers.'

The Parsi community in Bombay initially popularised cricket in India. After leaving Persia, the Parsis first arrived in India before AD 1000. Parsis were often successful merchants; many developed links with some of the British in India, through whom they learned the game. The first Parsi club, the Oriental Cricket Club, was formed in Bombay in 1848; a string of others followed in the decades to come. In 1877, Parsis challenged the Bombay Gymkhana, a British-only club on the city's maidan, to a match: the first official game between the British and Indians. To their surprise, Bombay Gymkhana only managed a draw. Matches between the two became regular from 1884; the following year, the Parsis requested that each side provide one umpire. 'They will be gentlemen, members of the Club,' the Bombay Gymkhana secretary wrote in response. 'It is our rule to appoint the umpires on our own ground.'

In 1892, Lord Harris – the governor of Bombay and future MCC president – sanctioned matches between the Parsis and a team representing the 'Europeans'. The contest gained in popularity and was evenly matched: until 1906, the Parsis had won 11 games, and the Europeans ten. The match's appeal and cricket's development in other communities led to the concept expanding. From 1907, a Hindu team were invited; from 1912, a Muslim side played too, making the contest an annual 'Quadrangular' tournament in Bombay. This became a 'Pentangular' in 1937, when 'The Rest' – largely comprising Sikhs and Indian Christians – were invited. Vijay Hazare, an Indian Christian, wrote that scoring a century in the Pentangular against the Europeans was 'as if to punish them for keeping us out of the tournament so long'. While the Pentangular, and its earlier incarnations, was staged only in Bombay, it was increasingly conceived of as an all-India tournament, with players travelling for days to take part. Lahore, Karachi and Nagpur all developed tournaments structured along similar lines over the 1910s and 1920s; these were well-supported but lacked the original's pulling power.

The Bombay Pentangular was played until 1946, the year before independence and partition. Its continued existence was deeply contentious: Gandhi urged 'the public of Bombay to revise their sporting code and erase from it communal matches'. Yet the contests were largely – though not completely – free of acrimony. On the pitch, 'We cricketers personified secularism,' Syed Mushtaq Ali, a Muslim and one of India's finest allrounders, later said; Muhammad Ali Jinnah, the founder of Pakistan, lauded relations between Hindus and Muslims in the Pentangular. When the Muslims defeated the Hindus in a spectacular final at Brabourne Stadium in 1944, an eyewitness recounted that 'Communalism was nowhere in evidence and everyone, including the Hindus, cheered the Muslim team.'

The best cricketers, from all faiths – seven Parsis, five Hindus and three Muslims – came together for the first All-India tour, to England in 1911, which followed two previous tours by Parsis. Palwankar Baloo was their star player. A Dalit, the lowest Hindu caste, he found work as a groundsman at the Poona Club, one of Poona's leading European clubs, aged 17. Baloo would bowl his left-arm spin for hours to club members, eager for extra practice; yet, Ramachandra Guha has found, Baloo was never given the chance to bat at the club. After moving to Bombay, Baloo broke into the club scene and then the Hindu side at the Bombay tournaments – though, Guha wrote, 'caste was certainly the main reason why Baloo was not made captain of the Hindus'. In England, he took 114 wickets at an average of 18.84. Baloo's performance was even more remarkable because he was suffering from a sore shoulder and, aged 35, was considered past his peak. With a captain who was a prince and travelled with five servants, India's side spanned the country's full social spectrum. Baloo became a prominent campaigner for Dalit rights.

The Ranji Trophy launched in 1934. This was a first-class competition that, as elsewhere in the world, pitted domestic sides against each other on a regional basis. It recognised the need for Indian cricketers to play more, and sought to develop the game's appeal beyond the country's main centres. Yet some were slow to grasp the possibilities for Indian cricket. 'Notwithstanding their multitudes, I doubt if they are going to turn out a team of all India as good as the best of our county clubs,' Lord Harris declared in 1921.

* * *

In 1926/27, Arthur Gilligan, who had captained England in an Ashes series two years earlier, led an MCC tour to India. MCC initially thrived. Then, in front of 25,000 at the Bombay Gymkhana, Cottari Nayudu hit a rapid century for the Hindus against MCC. A representative Indian team later dominated MCC in an unofficial three-day match, the nearest to a Test on the tour. When Gilligan returned home, he recommended that India gain Test status. The Board of Control for Cricket in India was formed in 1928, a governing body to lead India to join the Imperial Cricket Conference the following year.

A Test debut had been planned for 1930/31, when India were due to host MCC; the tour was cancelled because of a national civil disobedience campaign. Instead, India's first Test came in 1932 in England.

India were not only concerned about how to field the most competitive team possible. They also wondered how to make their side socially acceptable: just as England felt compelled to select an amateur captain, so India felt compelled to pick a captain from the nobility. The local elite, who were often princes, paid to bring stars to the country, and delighted in playing with them. In 1930/31, Maharajkumar of Vizianagram – better described as a very rich landlord rather than a prince – lured Jack Hobbs and Herbert Sutcliffe, England's opening pair, to tour. They played for his team, the Maharajkumar of Vizianagram's XI. Vizianagram himself, who averaged 18.60 from 47 first-class games in his career, and was rumoured to bribe opposition bowlers to bowl full tosses to him, batted at three.

Two alternative options for captain had the background deemed preferable, and cricketing pedigree too: Nawab of Pataudi and Duleepsinhji, the nephew of Ranjitsinhji. Duleepsinhji had already played for England; Nawab of Pataudi would make his debut the following year. No other potential captaincy candidates from the nobility were good enough to command a place; whoever India picked would compromise the quality of the side, who were already major underdogs. 'We took to Test cricket,' wrote Anthony de Mello, the first secretary of the BCCI, 'with the knowledge that victories were not, for some years, to come to us very often.'

For months, the question of who would lead dominated India's preparations. Initially, the Maharajah of Patiala – who offered to underwrite the tour, and organised pre-tour trials for 50 players – was appointed, but pulled out because of ill health. Maharajkumar of Vizianagram, who was appointed his vice-captain and donated 50,000 rupees to help bankroll the tour, had already pulled out. And so a third candidate emerged: the Maharajah of Porbandar, a cricket enthusiast but inept player.

Porbandar had some awareness of his limitations. Just before India's inaugural Test, at Lord's, Porbandar told his side that Nayudu, India's best player – but an army officer, rather than a prince – should captain instead. Several teammates woke Porbandar in the middle of the night to say that they would refuse to play under Nayudu. He was adamant that they must.

THREE BECOME SIX: TEST CRICKET OPENS UP

Within ten minutes of the start of their first Test, Mohammad Nissar, India's leading pace bowler, dismissed Herbert Sutcliffe and his opening partner, Percy Holmes. India lost by 158 runs, yet it was a respectable enough debut.

In four first-class matches on tour, Porbandar, who didn't bowl at all, scored just two runs, both with a leg glance against Glamorgan. Porbandar bought three Rolls-Royces on the tour: he left with more new cars than runs.

When India hosted England in 1933/34, 50,000 packed into the Bombay Gymkhana to witness India's first day of Test cricket at home. Near the end of day three, Lala Amarnath – a Hindu farmer's son, who was employed in the railway workshops in Lahore – scored India's first Test century. Returning to the pavilion, escorted by police to protect him from spectators, Amarnath 'was unable to move an inch as hundreds of hands reached out to me with gifts'. Amarnath returned to the Taj Mahal hotel to a collection of gold Rolex watches.

While Nayudu captained during their 2–0 defeat to England in 1933/34, when India played their next series, in England in 1936, they were again lumbered with a princely captain. To England, Vizianagram brought two servants and 36 items of personal luggage. Unlike Porbandar three years earlier, Vizianagram insisted on playing: as a specialist number nine, he averaged 8.25 in three Tests. Vizianagram was also instrumental in sending Amarnath home early from the tour. After being demoted down the order during a tour match, Amarnath is said to have thrown some of his kit and sworn at Vizianagram.

In 1946, India yet again selected a captain based more on social standing than cricketing ability. Nawab of Pataudi, educated at the elite Aitchison College in Lahore, then at Oxford University, had played for England, scoring a century on debut against Australia in 1932. By 1946, Pataudi was 36, and had played just eight first-class games in the last 12 years. He performed impressively against the counties but averaged 11.00 in the three Tests.

India were nothing like strong enough to handicap themselves in this way. Amarnath was appointed captain for the tour of Australia in 1947/48: a sign of more meritocratic selection. In Adelaide, Vijay Hazare became the first Indian to hit twin centuries in a Test, though India still lost by an innings. 'This was a thrilling moment for me,' Hazare wrote of facing the quick bowlers Ray Lindwall and Keith Miller, 'both in their prime and on the kill . . . In India we hardly had any practice against real pace.'

Hazare, the son of a schoolteacher from Sangli, 390 kilometres away from Bombay, was one of two great Indian batters of his day. The other was Vijay Merchant, who grew up in a wealthy family of factory owners; he combined Hazare's powers of concentration with brilliant late cutting, an imperious hook and a classical technique.

Merchant – to Hazare, a 'perfectionist' and 'a model for batting' – had a first-class average of 71.64, the second best in history. He was among the first in the rich lineage of classical batters from Bombay. The hallmarks of the Bombay School of Batsmanship, Guha wrote, are 'immense concentration, resolute defence, rare courage, sharp cricketing acumen, nerves of steel and – undergirding it all – a fierce pride in their cricketing heritage. Like all great traditions, however, this one too has allowed for considerable innovation: many subtle individual variations in style, built on a shared set of learned techniques.'

Merchant did not only devote his attentions to cricket: he was one of three players to withdraw from the tour of England in 1932, in protest at the imprisonment of Mahatma Gandhi and other campaigners for independence. Later injuries and a sparse schedule limited Merchant to ten Tests, all against England. He scored three centuries, including hitting 154 in his final Test aged 40. In that Test at Delhi, Merchant shared a double-century partnership with Hazare, who he acclaimed as the man who 'played with the straightest of bats'.

That series ended with Hazare leading India to their maiden Test victory, when they thrashed England – admittedly, not at full

THREE BECOME SIX: TEST CRICKET OPENS UP

strength – in Madras in February 1952. Hazare was indebted to Vinoo Mankad, who took 12 wickets in the match with his left-arm spin. Mankad was the first Test bowler to dismiss a batter at the non-striker's end for backing up too far, though the dismissal had a long history in first-class cricket. The batter, Bill Brown, later said, 'By backing up despite his warnings, I deserved it.' Yet Mankad is better remembered as an outstanding Test allrounder, hitting five centuries alongside his cunning spin. In England in 1952, Mankad was not released by Haslingden, his Lancashire League club, for the first Test; they relented in the second Test, when Mankad scored 72 and 184 and took five wickets, though India still lost.

The name of Mankad, and the great Indian cricketers who followed, could have been lost to Test history but for a decision taken by Jawaharlal Nehru, the country's first prime minister. After independence, there was a major debate in national politics over whether to leave the Commonwealth; under the Imperial Cricket Conference rules of the day, doing so would have disqualified India from Test status. But Nehru agreed that, when India became a republic in 1950, after three years as a dominion, it would do so as a member of the Commonwealth, leading to India remaining a full member of the ICC.

* * *

The first known reference to cricket in the Caribbean was on 11 June 1778. 'In the evening Mr. Beckford and Mr. John Lewis etc, played at cricket,' Thomas Thistlewood, a Jamaican slaveholder, wrote in his diary entry. The sport was first mentioned in a newspaper in the *Barbados Mercury & Bridgetown Gazette* in 1806; in the years ahead, matches were covered in the same pages as reports of slaves being sold. In Barbados, and elsewhere, cricket gained a hold through military garrisons: during the Napoleonic Wars, the game was played by British officers in the Caribbean. St Ann's Garrison Cricket Club, in Barbados, was formed by 1807.

In 1841, the British army ordered that cricket grounds be established in every barrack in the island. Over the remainder of the 19th century, British army teams regularly played against Bajan sides. The Garrison Savannah, now a beautiful horse-racing venue, hosted a match between Barbados and British Guiana in 1865, the first intercolonial match played in the West Indies. All players in the match were white.

After the Slavery Abolition Act 1833 was passed by the UK Parliament, cricket was increasingly played by black people in the Caribbean. 'The inhabitants of the English-speaking islands of the West Indies play cricket because the English brought the game with them,' wrote Michael Manley, the former Jamaican prime minister. Slaves, and then indentured labourers, were required to bowl at the sons of British plantation owners; after slavery was abolished, cricket offered a route for black men to gain prestige.

A paradox ran through the game. 'Cricket in the West Indies functioned as an agency of colonial oppression and at the same time provided an area in which the socially oppressed majority ventilated endemic, antisystemic attitudes and ideals,' the historian Hilary Beckles wrote. The sport combined 'elite origins, and subsequent social democratisation'. Over the 19th century, 'the desire of the coloured and black communities to play cricket their own way seemed to have grown in direct proportion to the white elite's determination to establish it as the exclusive sport of the propertied, the educated, and the "well bred".' Cricket became 'the region's first expression of popular mass culture'.

When it came to taking on teams from beyond the Caribbean, the idea took hold that different territories were better together. The West Indies team has grown to represent a total of 16 island nations and territories. The most prominent are Barbados, Jamaica, Trinidad & Tobago and Guyana, situated in South America and the sole part of West Indies that is not an island. A West Indies team first played in 1886 when an all-white squad toured Canada and the United States.

THREE BECOME SIX: TEST CRICKET OPENS UP

Caribbean geography has always made inter-island competition expensive, and logistically complicated. In 1891 Barbados hosted two other colonies, Trinidad and British Guiana, as Guyana was then known, for the first inter-colonial tournament; 80 firms closed for the afternoons on all four days when Barbados played, to allow their workers to watch. Jamaica existed on the edge of the hub of Caribbean cricket because of its geography: it is 1,000 miles from Barbados, Trinidad and Guyana.

From its very earliest days, Caribbean cricket was inextricably linked to race. In Trinidad in the early 20th century, different clubs 'represented the different social strata in the island within clearly defined boundaries', C.L.R. James wrote in *Beyond a Boundary*. Queen's Park Club – 'the boss of the island's cricket relations with other islands and visiting international teams' – was for the white and wealthy, with black men 'rare and usually anonymous'. Shamrock was for the non-elite whites, principally Catholics. Maple – James's club, to his later regret – was for the 'brown-skinned middle class', who 'had founded themselves on the principle that they didn't want any dark people in their club'. Shannon was 'the club of the black lower-middle class'. Stingo's members were 'totally black', with 'no social status'. The game flourished across these social divides: every village with 50 houses in Trinidad had its own recreation ground.

Divisions between clubs were similarly pronounced elsewhere in the Caribbean. 'Cricket had plunged me into politics long before I was aware of it,' James wrote. 'I haven't the slightest doubt that the clash of race, caste and class did not retard but stimulated West Indies cricket.' In a separate article, he distilled what he considered the reasons for cricket's appeal:

> All the inhabitants of the British West Indian territories are expatriates: the islands are so small that it was not difficult for the early invaders to exterminate the native Amerindian populations. Thus language, labour and economic processes, arts and sciences

are moulded on the European pattern. Cricket has proved itself one of the most easily assimilated, most penetrating and most enduring...

Cricket was therefore a means of national consolidation. In a society very conscious of class and social differentiation, a heritage of slavery, it provided a common meeting ground of all classes without coercion or exhortation from above...

Cricket was a field where the social passions of the colonials, suppressed politically, found vigorous if diluted expression. On the cricket field all men, whatever their colour or status, were theoretically equal.

The first English tour to the Caribbean arrived in 1895. The quality of the hosts, and the region's attractions, meant that such tours became regular. In February 1911, MCC toured the West Indies for the first time.

Trinidad were the first nation to select black players in the intercolonial tournament, partly at the urging of Pelham Warner, an English Test cricketer who was born in Trinidad, the son of the Attorney General. When West Indies toured England in 1900, their squad included five black players; by their next tour, in 1906, the squad included seven, compared to eight white players. Tommie Burton, a leading black bowler, was sent home from the tour early for refusing to carry the luggage of his white teammates. Burton was subsequently banned for life from cricket in Barbados.

In 1923, West Indies returned for their third tour of England. This was their most successful yet, with six first-class victories, including a ten-wicket win over Surrey, to go with seven losses. These performances made West Indies' Test debut, in England in 1928, all the more disappointing. Facing a side about to win the Ashes 4–1 away, West Indies lost all three Tests by an innings; their pace bowlers troubled England, but the batting was flimsy. 'The playing of Test Matches between England and West Indies was a mistake,' *Wisden* judged. The historian Beckles believes that the side was weaker than in 1923.

THREE BECOME SIX: TEST CRICKET OPENS UP

On the brink of Test status, the West Indies Cricket Board of Control was formed in 1926. This was essentially controlled by the same families who enjoyed the bulk of economic power in the Caribbean: the board was initially all-white, and ensured that the captain should be white too.

Arguments about selection were heightened by players from different nations vying against each other for berths. Hosting England in 1929/30, West Indies teams were picked by the local association staging each match. West Indies selected 28 players over the four Tests and had four different captains – each time, a man from the association hosting the Test.

In the third Test, in Guyana, West Indies secured their maiden victory, two years after becoming a Test nation; New Zealand had to wait 26 years, and India 20. The 289-run victory over England was built on West Indies' twin totems: fast-bowling allrounder Learie Constantine, who took 9–122 in the match; and George Headley, who scored two centuries at number three. The team were 'dissatisfied' with a 1–1 series draw, Constantine wrote. 'We had the players to have pulled off the rubber fairly easily, I think; but the West Indies weakness has always been organising its strength to the best possible result.'

Cricket was in Constantine's blood: his father, Lebrun, had been a crucial player on West Indies' 1900 and 1906 tours to England. Learie grew up on a cocoa plantation in rural Trinidad; his grandfather was a slave. Learie performed well on the 1923 tour, when he was largely a bowler; by 1928, he had become an allrounder, capable of winning matches with his explosive hitting, pace bowling or fielding in the covers or slips.

At Lord's, during a tour match against Middlesex, Learie arrived at the crease with West Indies 79–5, trailing Middlesex by 273 runs on first innings. Constantine slammed 86 in under an hour, restricting Middlesex's advantage to 122 runs. In Middlesex's second innings, Constantine took 7–57, ending with a spell of 6–11. West Indies needed 259 to win; they were 121–5 when he walked out. 'I did not care where they put me in,' Constantine wrote. 'My star was in the skies.' He scored a century in exactly 60 minutes, walking off to a standing ovation; West Indies had toppled a side featuring several Test players.

Such performances led to Constantine signing for Nelson, in the Lancashire League, where each side was permitted one paid professional. His gifts were ideally suited to league cricket: single-innings matches played on Saturdays, with crowds often clearing 10,000. The format – matches were timed, and could be drawn – required dynamic, unselfish cricketers. In 225 matches for Nelson, Constantine averaged 37.21 with the bat, often thrashing a quick 50 to set up a declaration, and took 799 wickets at 9.90. Constantine and his wife lived on Meredith Street for 20 years; he won the Lancashire League seven times and was awarded the Freedom of the Borough of Nelson. In Nelson, he found no 'colour bar. A cricketer is just a cricketer and nothing else.' Between matches, Constantine studied for a law degree and gave anti-racism lectures, preparing him for his career after cricket. During the Second World War, he worked as a Ministry of Labour welfare officer for Caribbean workers; he won a historic case against racial prejudice from the Imperial Hotel in London, who refused to lodge him. Constantine was elected as an MP in Trinidad's first democratic parliament, serving as Minister of Works in the government, and then became High Commissioner to Great Britain in 1961. In 1969, he became the UK's first black peer.

In 1931, Constantine was approached by Lancashire to play county cricket. But, his biographer Harry Pearson detailed, Lancashire's 'pros let it be known they would oppose his appointment. "It would have seemed wrong seeing a black man sitting where an Englishman should have been," one later commented.'

Before gaining Test status, West Indies had already lost talent. In 1900, Charles Ollivierre, a black batter from St Vincent who played first-class cricket for Trinidad, thrived on West Indies' inaugural tour of England. He signed with Derbyshire, becoming the first black West Indian to play county cricket. On the next tour, in 1906, Ollivierre scored 64 not out to help his county beat West Indies. On the 1906 tour, the allrounder and left-arm spinner Sydney Smith, a white Trinidadian, excelled. Like Ollivierre after the previous tour, Smith signed with a county and emigrated. Smith became one of Northamptonshire's finest players, averaging 32.46 with the bat and taking 502 wickets at 17.41.

Constantine's brilliance was the catalyst for other clubs, especially in Lancashire, to sign West Indians. Playing as professionals in England helped cricketers develop and gave them secure livelihoods. Yet the benefits for Caribbean cricket were less clear. With Ollivierre and Smith, West Indies lost their talents altogether; Constantine's availability became limited. During West Indies' 1933 tour of England, Constantine played only one Test, scoring 64. For the other two Tests, he wrote, 'Nelson had key games and wouldn't release me; I should have gone fast enough if I could.' For the third and final Test, Nelson agreed to release Constantine if Stan Nichols, an Essex player, could replace him. Douglas Jardine, England's captain, is believed to have heard of the plan – and then selected Nichols for England, thereby preventing Constantine playing.

In 1946, Constantine advocated 'a rule that a Test selection committee's call for a player should override *every* other tie', highlighting how 'the effects of poverty which prevents us sending our best men to represent us abroad' damaged West Indies:

> A trip to Australia is worth about £650 and all expenses to an English professional cricketer; the Australians make even more when they come to England. The Englishman going to South Africa gets about £300 for the tour, and a free winter out of the English climate, which is worth a great deal more. If the West Indian makes from £30 to £50 for a tour he feels he has done well...

It does explain many things, doesn't it? . . .

On every tour so far, leading West Indian players have had to stay behind because they 'could not afford' to travel. Until that situation is altered, we are not likely to win many rubbers abroad.

C.L.R. James lamented that 'undermining of West Indies cricket by English money which has continued into our own day and done so much to prevent us developing to our fullest extent'. By the next tour to England, in 1939, Headley and Manny Martindale – a Bajan fast bowler who thrived against England in 1933 and 1934/35 – had joined Constantine in the Lancashire League. For over a year before the tour, the trio underwent fraught negotiations with the West Indies Cricket Board of Control, Richard Bentley detailed in the cricket quarterly *The Nightwatchman*. Eventually, all three agreed to play for West Indies: still receiving less than they would have done playing in Lancashire, but earning significantly more than for previous Tests. Such pragmatism ensured that West Indies made greater use of their talents in their early Test years than New Zealand.

* * *

West Indies' first Test line-up, who played at Lord's in 1928, had white players from one to four in the batting order; all other players were black. It embodied how leading batters in the region tended to be white, and leading bowlers black. West Indies' two most prominent players on the 1928 tour were George Challenor, a white Bajan, and Constantine. 'It was symbolic, if not quite socially inevitable, that Constantine would be a bowler and Challenor a batsman,' Michael Manley wrote.

George Headley's route to cricketing greatness was unique. His father, De Coursey, a Bajan, emigrated to work in the Panama Canal Zone. In Panama, De Coursey met Irene Roberts, a Jamaican. In 1909, she gave birth to George, who became accomplished in the

THREE BECOME SIX: TEST CRICKET OPENS UP

local bat-and-ball game of choice: baseball. Aged ten, Irene returned to Jamaica, taking George; De Coursey continued to work overseas. Headley took up cricket at Calabar Elementary School in Kingston, finding that his baseball skills transferred. Indeed, as a cricket bat is markedly bigger than a baseball bat, Headley considered his baseball grounding an advantage, developing his hand–eye coordination.

Aged 18, Headley planned to move to the US, where his parents had settled, to study dentistry. A delay in his immigration forms arriving helped to change cricket history. This allowed Headley to make his first-class debut for Jamaica against Lord Tennyson's touring side in 1927/28. At number three, he scored 71 in the first match, then 211 in the second. Dentistry could wait. As a 20-year-old debutant, Headley hit 176 against England in 1929/30. He ended the four-Test series with 703 runs at 87.87, helping West Indies secure a 1–1 draw.

West Indies' next series was a daunting trip to Australia in 1930/31. Initially Australia bowled on Headley's legs to stop him playing through the off side. Over the series, Headley opened up his stance to access the leg side; leg-spinner Clarrie Grimmett would hail Headley as the best on-side player he ever bowled against. In the final Test, Headley's second century of the series helped West Indies end a torrid tour with a 30-run victory, sealed by pace bowling.

Headley's approach was to see the ball early but play it late; England's captain Len Hutton said that no one played the ball later. This method won Headley acclaim for his batting on treacherous wet pitches. 'You have got to watch the ball and you can't make any mistakes,' Headley once said. 'When I am walking down the pavilion steps, going in to bat, if I met my father I wouldn't recognise him. And once I am at the wicket I am concerned with nothing else but seeing the ball from the bowler's hand.' The night before Tests, Headley planned his innings in his head. How would the bowler try to get him out? How would he react? Then, what would the bowler do in response? Headley was renowned for his strategic thinking: he often hit a spinner's fast ball hard back to them, hurting their fingers, which in turn could damage their control; identifying the weakest fielders, he deliberately hit the ball towards them.

Over the 1930s, Headley's monumental run-scoring was a constant. In his home island of Jamaica, an undefeated 270 in 1934/35 against England sealed West Indies' first series victory. At Lord's in 1939, he hit twin tons. By the end of the decade, Headley had played 19 Tests, scoring ten centuries – double all his teammates combined – at an average of 66.71. For the way that he carried West Indies, journalists took to calling Headley Atlas. Only one other Test cricketer in history has scored a greater proportion of his team's runs.

Table 3. Highest percentage of team runs by a single batsman (top ten)

		Matches	*Average*	*% of team runs*
D.G. Bradman	Australia	52	99.94	24.28
G.A. Headley	West Indies	22	60.83	21.38
B.C. Lara	West Indies	131	52.88	18.87
L. Hutton	England	79	56.67	18.13
J.B. Hobbs	England	61	56.94	17.90
A.D. Nourse	South Africa	34	53.81	17.76
E.D. Weekes	West Indies	48	58.61	17.35
B. Mitchell	South Africa	42	48.88	17.20
H. Sutcliffe	England	54	60.73	17.12
K.C. Sangakkara	Sri Lanka	134	57.40	17.03

In the process, Headley shattered the racist trope that black people could not be leading batters. Manley called him a 'revolutionary' figure who carried 'the hopes of the black, English-speaking Caribbean man'. The Bajan writer George Lamming's 1953 novel, *In the Castle of My Skin*, describes how:

> Jamaica cricket had captured the Barbadians' imagination. Every boy who felt his worth as a batsman called himself George Headley.

6

BRADMAN, BODYLINE AND THE INVINCIBLES

99.94: four indelible numbers in cricket's tapestry. Together they make up Donald Bradman's Test batting average, a figure that still shines like a sapphire in the sun. Most sporting records are ephemeral; Bradman's average, 38 runs higher than anyone else to play 20 Test matches, is an unmatchable figure. In very few areas of life, sporting or otherwise, is the best so far clear of the rest of the field.

Bradman's origin tale lies in Bowral, a country town 120 kilometres south-west of Sydney, where his parents moved when he was two. For hour upon hour, Bradman hit a golf ball with a cricket stump against the brick base of a water tank at his home, 52 Shepherd Street. 'It must have developed the co-ordination of eye, brain and muscle that served me so well,' Bradman wrote. Playing against Victor, his older brother by four years – they were the youngest two of the five Bradman siblings, with the first three girls – the young Donald could not compete through power. Instead, he had to find other means.

While Bradman was a keen young cricketer, and scored a century for his school aged 12, he was not unstinting in his devotion. In the summers of 1923/24 and 1924/25, between the ages of 15 and 17, Bradman played little cricket, preferring tennis. In December 1925, he played his first great innings in a match for Bowral, hitting 234 against Wingello, who included Test leg-spinner Bill O'Reilly. His ascent now was rapid: within two years, Bradman made his New South Wales debut; within another, his Test debut, in the 1928/29 Ashes series. He scored 18 and one on Australia debut and was dropped; former captain Warwick Armstrong declared that Bradman 'will probably be a good player later but, I think, is not a Test player at present'. After one Test out of the side, Bradman scored 79 and 112 on his Test return.

Bradman was essentially self-taught, learning to bat on concrete wickets covered with matting. He did not bat on a grass pitch until he was 18. His homespun method and the light bats of the age – his bat weighed only 2 lb 2 oz – forged an unusual technique. Bradman defied the little advice he received from coaches, who told him that his grip was unsuitable, as he recalled in *Farewell to Cricket*:

> I experimented – worked out the pros and cons – and eventually decided not to change my natural grip. Throughout a long career my grip caused many arguments, but I think it is sufficient to prove that any young player should be allowed to develop his own natural style, providing he is not revealing an obvious error. A player is not necessarily wrong just because he is different.

Where traditional batting technique emphasised the importance of meeting the ball straight, Bradman used the 'rotary method': bringing his bat down from gully, an angle of 45 degrees from the flight of the ball, with an open grip. Tony Shillinglaw, a former English minor counties player who spent decades analysing Bradman's method, said that it was his unorthodoxy that made such prodigious run-scoring possible:

> Bradman learned to control a fast, erratic, moving ball better than anyone else has ever done, and all I've discovered is you can't do it from an orthodox style. The only way you can do it is through rotation.

'Better to hit the ball with an apparently unorthodox style than miss it with a correct one,' Bradman said. It evoked Ranji's logic a generation earlier: 'A style which is not so effective as it might be can hardly claim to be either good or beautiful.'

Curiously, Bradman's success did not lead to any re-evaluation of what was considered optimal batting technique. Shillinglaw argued that Steve Smith, whose run-scoring in the 2010s had shades of Bradman, comes closest to replicating his style.

On strike, Bradman was entirely still, not even tapping his bat; he did not have what is now called a trigger movement. As the bowler delivered, Bradman moved forward to greet the ball, or back to give himself more time before meeting it. Bowling to Bradman 'was like trying to trap a wild duck, his movements were so swift', England pace bowler Harold Larwood observed.

As *Wisden Cricketers' Almanack* noted in 1931, Bradman predominantly played either 'half-way or entirely back'. From this position, Bradman could drive as well as cut through the off side and flick anything on his pads to the leg side.

'Us little fellows can hit 'em harder than the big ones,' legendary baseball hitter Babe Ruth told Bradman when the two met at Yankee Stadium in 1932. Bradman's height was 5 ft 7 in, about average for the time; he also had notably small hands. This unremarkable physique was probably an advantage. As of January 2025, 28 Test batters have scored 5,000 runs at an average of 50 or more, a good approximation for greatness. Of this rarefied group, only four are six feet or taller; about three-quarters are 5 ft 10 in or shorter. Tall batters have often found their height a problem at the very top level; they have to play at a greater range of lengths than shorter ones, including deliveries on and around off stump, and have generally not been as adept at playing square of the wicket as shorter batters.

'He had very small feet, that was one of the secrets of his success,' observed Len Hutton, one of this elite group himself. 'Very light on his feet and quick moving.' Bradman combined these gifts with unwavering professionalism and a preternatural determination. 'Stripped to the truth, he was a solitary man with a solitary aim,' wrote the former cricketer R.C. Robertson-Glasgow. 'There are no funny stories about the Don. No one ever laughed about Bradman. He was no laughing matter.'

Many cricketers of the day drank like fish; Bradman was teetotal and didn't smoke. After he scored the first triple century in Ashes history, at Leeds in 1930, Bradman went to the hotel reception requesting a pot of tea to his room. So much for the opinion of one bowler when England first encountered Bradman, in a tour match in 1928, who told him, 'You'll have to keep that bat a bit straighter when you come to England, or you won't have much luck.'

Bradman's 974 runs at an average of 139.14 in the 1930 Ashes, underpinning Australia's 2–1 victory, elevated him from being a mere cricketer. He was the most recognisable Australian, the 'boy from the bush', a standard-bearer for national self-confidence and identity during the depression era. 'No Australian had written *Paradise Lost*, but Bradman had made 100 before lunch at Lord's,' novelist Thomas Keneally wrote. In England, Bradman was 'something between an Emperor and an Ambassador', Robertson-Glasgow observed.

Bradman's life, whether he wanted to or not, balanced cricket and celebrity. At Headingley in 1934, Bradman walked out to 'a silence of suspense; a murmur of "He's here," swelling to a roar of welcome', J.M. Kilburn wrote. Bradman scored 304, matching his triple century in the Headingley Test four years earlier.

For most players, such feats would have created suffocating, impossible expectations. Bradman lived up to his legend for 18 years.

* * *

Bradman was a cricketer who genuinely changed the game – yet this was in response to him, rather than in imitation. At The Oval in 1930, Bradman scored 232. But England noticed a scintilla of weakness: an aversion to short deliveries.

'I've got it, he's yellow,' cried Douglas Jardine, England's captain, as he perused footage that showed Bradman stepping outside the line of balls aimed at his body at The Oval. Percy Fender, a Surrey teammate of Jardine who also worked as a journalist, received letters from friends down under suggesting that Australians could be vulnerable to short deliveries on the leg side; Fender passed the information on to Jardine. The two would have learned that, in 1931, the Queensland quick bowler Eddie Gilbert bowled a brilliant spell of five balls to Bradman. It culminated in a bouncer, top-edged to the wicketkeeper; Bradman was dismissed for a duck, and later declared that the five balls were 'unhesitatingly faster' than anything else he faced in his life.

The spell to Bradman is the centrepiece of the Gilbert legend. Gilbert also took 5–65 for Queensland against West Indies in 1930/31, and snared 87 wickets in 23 first-class games. Yet, like Jack Marsh, the leading Aboriginal pace bowler of a generation earlier, Gilbert would never be picked for Australia. In 1936, aged 30, Gilbert played his last first-class game for Queensland, taking six wickets in the match. That year, the academic Anthony Condon documented, a Queensland selector wrote to Gilbert's protector, a figure who had to sanction all movement of Indigenous people in the state. The selector declared that 'as it was considered unlikely that he would be chosen for any Representative team this season, it was decided with your concurrence, to arrange for Gilbert to return to the settlement early next week.' Removed from his family as a child, now Gilbert was forced to return to the settlement that housed Aboriginal people in Queensland. He lived out his years in a psychiatric ward. Not until Jason Gillespie, in 1996, did the Australia men's Test team field a player with indigenous heritage.

* * *

In the grill-room at the Piccadilly Hotel in August 1932, Jardine and Arthur Carr, the Nottinghamshire captain, met Harold Larwood and Bill Voce, the two Notts and England quick bowlers. Jardine asked Larwood if he could bowl into the batter's body on a leg-stump line. 'Yes, I think that can be done,' Larwood replied, unconsciously echoing Fred Spofforth's words 50 years earlier, in the game that gave birth to the Ashes. The ploy was to bowl short, fast balls bowled around leg stump, often bouncing to chest and head height; the leg side was packed, with a ring of fielders so close to the bat that they were known as the 'suicide squad'. Only 5 ft 7 in tall, Larwood was broad-shouldered and strong; lacking extra height, his bouncer tended to spear into the ribs, making it harder to evade.

'Something had to be done to curb Bradman,' Larwood later said. 'Bodyline was a plot and I was involved in it having been given the job of spearheading the attack to put the brakes on Bradman.' In Jardine, England had a man who would stop at nothing to find those brakes. His air during the 1928/29 Ashes had led Australia former captain Monty Noble to term Jardine 'this self-possessed aristocrat of the cricket field'.

Bodyline – Jardine preferred 'leg theory' – was not completely new. After World War I, 'unrest among bowlers, because of the difficulties and injustices of their job, had been simmering', Jack Fingleton, Australia's opener in 1932/33, wrote in *Cricket Crisis*. Bowling inswingers to a packed leg-side field was occasionally used as a tactic in the early 20th century. English fast bowlers Frank Foster and Fred Root had both bowled spells of short-pitched bowling to such a field in first-class or Test cricket; so, before 1932/33, had Larwood himself. Jardine first encountered 'leg theory' facing Ted McDonald, who moved to Lancashire from Australia after playing his last Test in 1921.

The difference with Bodyline lay in how relentless it was – and that, with both Larwood and Bill Voce, England had a pair who combined pace with what Jardine termed 'almost miraculous' accuracy. They also had a captain with no qualms about the tactic's physical threat. 'Well, we shall win the Ashes – but we may lose a Dominion,' an old schoolmaster at Winchester College, Jardine's alma mater, remarked when learning of his appointment as captain. If Jardine's upbringing was classically amateur, his views were not. Faced with two players of equal ability, 'I would unhesitatingly choose the

Northerner in preference to the Southerner for the exacting business of an Australian Tour,' he wrote in *In Quest of the Ashes*. 'There is far more attention paid to cricket education and tactics in the North than in the South of England. Up North they are not content with bowling you out; they think you out as well.'

Bradman himself had a sense of what was coming after England arrived from four weeks of travel aboard the *Orontes*. 'I promptly forecast that we would see an avalanche of bumpers because the team was loaded with fast bowlers. But what I did not foresee was the use of them in association with a packed leg-side field.'

Jardine originally hoped that Bodyline would be 'a profitable variation when two batsmen were well set'. Its potency became clear during the first Test at Sydney, which Bradman missed through illness. Larwood took ten wickets; England won by ten wickets, despite Stan McCabe hitting 187 not out, one of the great counter-attacking innings. 'The only shot to play against Bodyline was the hook,' McCabe said. 'With the crowd yelling and clapping and my blood up, my reaction was to hit Larwood and Voce with everything I had.'

Australian feelings were encapsulated by a verse written by Cyril Ritchard, a popular vocalist. 'After kissing their wives, And insuring their lives ...' Ritchard sang, 'Undertakers look on with broad grins ... When Larwood, the wrecker, begins.'

England doubled down on their tactics when Bradman – 'the little bastard' Jardine told his players to call him – returned for the second Test. When MCC had experimented with Bodyline during an earlier tour match, Bob Wyatt, standing in as skipper, noted that Bradman was 'decidedly uncomfortable when he played this type of bowling from Larwood'. Before the second Test, Jardine declared, 'We hope to go on being successful with the same methods.'

He did so against objections within his own side. On the first morning of the series, when asked if he could bowl more bouncers, Gubby Allen said, 'Douglas, I have never done that, and it's not the way I want to play cricket.' During the Tests, the Nawab of Pataudi refused to take up a Bodyline fielding position, prompting Jardine's icy observation: 'I see His Highness is a conscientious objector today.' Both Allen and Pataudi were amateurs: they did not depend on the game for their livelihoods. While Allen would not bowl Bodyline, he fielded in Bodyline positions.

Bradman only lasted a ball on his return in Melbourne: bowled off an inside edge, attempting a pull. In the second innings, he encountered Bodyline for the first time; he moved away to the leg stump to open up the vacant off side, which he peppered with square drives and cuts. It was a radical shift in approach; Bradman's undefeated 103, an innings of altogether less order and more chaos than those gargantuan knocks in 1930, set up a series-levelling victory.

On the second day of the third Test, Bill Woodfull, Australia's captain, was hit above the heart by Larwood. As Woodfull reeled away in agony, Jardine called out to his bowler, 'Well bowled, Harold.' For the 50,000 fans at Adelaide Oval, here was proof of England's disreputable tactics. The delivery to Woodfull was not bowled to a Bodyline field, but this was in place for Larwood's next ball to him. After the day's play, England's manager, Pelham Warner, asked Woodfull how he was. The captain's reply, leaked to the media anonymously – no one is sure by whom, as David Frith recounts in *Bodyline Autopsy* – distilled Australia's anger: 'I don't want to see you, Mr Warner. There are two teams out there. One is trying to play cricket and the other is not.'

The following day, Bert Oldfield suffered a broken skull after top-edging a Larwood delivery into his head. This ball, too, was not to a Bodyline field. The thud of ball against skull was heard resoundingly at the ground and on radio; Oldfield bled, and could have been killed. Oldfield placed no blame on the bowler: 'It wasn't your fault, Harold,' he said after being hit.

England won by 338 runs, to go 2–1 up. Yet whether the last two Tests would be played at all was unclear. Larwood visited a theatre, where a young girl pointed to him: 'Why, Mummy, he doesn't look like a murderer!' Australia escalated the situation by officially protesting. The Australian board sent a terse telegram to MCC at Lord's on day five of the Adelaide Test. It read:

> Bodyline bowling assumed such proportions as to menace best interests of game, making protection of body by batsmen the main consideration. Causing intensely bitter feeling between players as well as injury. In our opinion is unsportsmanlike. Unless stopped at once likely to upset friendly relations existing between Australia and England.

To MCC, this message made the gravest charge: of being unsportsmanlike. Over the next three weeks, the fallout put the tour in jeopardy. The fourth Test was only confirmed when, after several more cables were exchanged, the Australian board sent another message to MCC, which included the phrase: 'We do not regard the sportsmanship of your team as being in question.' In selection meetings, Jardine repeated his proposal made before the third Test: that he himself should be dropped, because '(a) I was out of form with the bat, and (b) I fancied that the team would get a better deal from the crowd if I was not in the field.' The committee did not agree.

England freely continued with their methods. 'My constant dread,' said George Hele, who umpired in the series, 'was that a batsman would be killed.' Mercifully, there were no blows to follow those suffered by Woodfull and Oldfield. Larwood took seven more wickets in the match in Brisbane; England's six-wicket win regained the Ashes.

Even after the urn was secured, Jardine ignored Larwood's request to miss the final Test: 'We've got the bastards down there, and we'll keep them there.' As nightwatchman, Larwood scored 98, receiving a standing ovation from the Sydney crowd. With five more wickets in the Test, he extended his series tally to 33 at 19.51, a haul that no Englishman in an away Ashes has since matched. Eighteen of Larwood's dismissals were either bowled or lbw, showing that he attacked the stumps regularly. Yet the physical danger during the series was of a different magnitude to anything previously seen in Test cricket. In Ashes matches before 1932, Australian batters suffered just under one major blow to the body per Test from English bowlers, R.H. Campbell has established. In 1932/33 Australian batters suffered 35 major blows, seven per Test; Larwood himself was responsible for 22 of these.

For Australia, there was one compensation to England's 4–1 victory: Bodyline was good for business. Compared to the 1928/29 Ashes, average daily attendances increased from 26,000 to 30,000. The next Ashes, in 1934, would earn England three times more in gate receipts than for their series with South Africa in 1935.

Jardine's ruthlessness should not be mistaken for animosity towards Australia. 'Where hospitality is concerned,' he wrote, Australians 'must surely have inherited the spirit of the ancient Greeks, for whom the entertainment of guests was a religious observance.' It was also ironic that Bradman should be at the centre of a rift with England, where his grandfather hailed from. 'Nothing in the world ever appealed to me more than England as nature made her,' Bradman wrote in 1934, after an extended stay in the English countryside with his wife. In 1948, he was photographed with his hands in his pockets, walking with the King.

Australia resisted selecting their own quickest bowlers to mimic Bodyline. Bill Woodfull, the captain and the son of a Methodist minister, seems partly to have been motivated by a desire to keep the moral high ground. Some thought that he was even driven by broader concerns for Anglo-Australian relations. Australia's Bill O'Reilly called Woodfull 'heroic' for tempering the hosts' anger, saying that his continued batting after being struck in the chest was 'the stuff that Empires were made of'.

In 1932/33, when he was supposedly cut down to size, Bradman still averaged 56.57. Larwood dismissed Bradman four times in the series, at a cost of 28.75; taking advantage of gaps on the off side,

Bradman scored at 4.5 runs per six balls against him, but lacked his usual sense of impregnability.

England's Bodyline tactics were used against them in Manchester in 1933. *Wisden* lauded West Indies for showing 'what an objectionable form of attack this kind of bowling can be'.

Administrators, in England and beyond, sought to prevent Bodyline from being seen again. This took several forms, including a gentleman's agreement between county captains; tweaks to the lbw law, allowing batters to be dismissed by balls pitching outside off stump, thereby increasing bowlers' chances of taking wickets without resorting to Bodyline; and the Laws being changed to allow umpires to intervene in the event of 'direct attack' by a bowler against a batter. In 1957, the Laws were changed to bar more than two fielders standing behind square on the leg side; this outlawed both Bodyline fields and, now more pressingly, negative tactics by off-spinners and inswing bowlers.

Jardine initially played on for England, scoring a century against West Indies and their Bodyline tactics in 1933, but retired before the 1934 Ashes. Both Larwood and Voce, England's two chief Bodyline practitioners, were absent from the series.

Larwood was instructed to apologise to Australia if he wanted to play for England again. 'I've nothing to apologise for,' Larwood said; he played his last Test in Sydney in 1933, aged 28. In Larwood's fate, it was not hard to see a parable of the English working class being made scapegoats for decisions made by the ruling class. In an unlikely Bodyline postscript, Larwood settled happily in Sydney. He became close friends with Oldfield, the man he hit at Adelaide, acting as a pallbearer at his funeral.

Bradman's run-scoring resumed unabated. In England in 1934, he almost matched his tally of four years earlier; Australia regained the Ashes, 2–1. Opener Bill Ponsford hit consecutive scores of 181 and 266, yet still couldn't match Bradman's run haul for the series; leg-spinners Bill O'Reilly and Clarrie Grimmett shared 53 wickets.

In 1936/37, England crushed Australia in the first two Tests, even while eschewing Bodyline methods. Bill Voce, shunned in 1934, took 17 wickets in these two games bowling conventionally; Wally Hammond hit 231 not out in the second. In his first two Tests as captain, Bradman made two ducks. He hit just 13 in the first innings of the third Test, at Melbourne. On the second day, after overnight rain, Bradman took the unusual decision to declare, on 200–9 – even though the match was timeless – to exploit the conditions. After England reached 76–9, Gubby Allen declared too. To stop Australia collapsing again, before the pitch dried out and became easier for batting, Bradman hatched a plan: the normal bottom three occupied the top three positions. Bradman arrived at number seven, with Australia 97–5. In conditions that were now sumptuous for batting, he scored 270, ensuring a crushing victory. He followed up with another double century in Adelaide, and 169 in the last Test, back in Melbourne. For the first, and still only, time a country won a Test series after being 2–0 down. Bradman had his revenge.

* * *

Cricketers had begun to recognise their commercial potential long before Bradman: Australia endorsed Perrier water on their 1909 Ashes tour. Bradman's run-scoring opened up new possibilities for enrichment; he published his first autobiography in 1930, aged 21. After the 1930 Ashes, Bradman docked at Perth – arriving in Adelaide, Melbourne and finally Sydney by plane – while his teammates remained on the boat. The itinerary was arranged by Bradman's employers, the Sydney sports-goods firm Mick Simmons, and caused resentment among some players.

Bradman almost didn't play in the Bodyline series at all. In late 1931, Accrington, a Lancashire League powerhouse, offered Bradman a lucrative, multi-year deal; this would have breached the terms of his contract with the Australian board, thereby placing his international career in jeopardy. He seriously considered accepting. Bradman only remained in Australia after a consortium of businesses – sporting-goods manufacturer F.J. Palmer & Sons, Associated Newspapers and radio station 2UE – put together a series of offers of sponsorship and work. Over his career, Bradman had several rows with the Australian Cricket Board over how he topped up his cricket earnings; he was docked a portion of the 'good conduct' bonus, no matter his 974 Test runs, for writing newspaper articles on the 1930 Ashes tour. Before the 1932/33 summer, the board challenged Bradman's right to write; Bradman was released from his *Sydney Sun* contract, freeing him to play against England. In 1934, Bradman moved state teams, from New South Wales to South Australia, to work as a stockbroker in Adelaide.

As a celebrity, Bradman benefited from wider forces. In Australia and the United Kingdom alike, radio broadcasting boomed during the 1920s and 1930s, creating a new thirst for heroes; 1932/33 was the first Australia series in which every ball was broadcast live – a factor, Frith has argued, in the outcry over Bodyline. Print audiences were also soaring.

If Bradman felt that he wasn't being paid his due, he was right. Between 1930 and 1948, Australian Test crowds were 25 per cent higher on average during days when Bradman batted: an extra 7,200 fans per day. As the academics Julian Blackham and Bruce Chapman show, Bradman generated an extra A$1 million per season in revenue to Australian cricket. Yet his annual playing salary was under A$10,000.

Perhaps Bradman's financial considerations were also motivated by an awareness of life's fragility. He almost died of peritonitis in 1934 in England. His wife dashed from Sydney to reach him, which took a month; obituaries were readied. It would be two years until Bradman played another Test. Fears about Bradman's health were heightened by the fate of Archie Jackson, a year his junior. As a 19-year-old on debut against England in 1929, Jackson scored 164; some suggested that he could be even better than Bradman. Jackson played just eight Tests before dying from tuberculosis, aged 23, during the Bodyline series.

* * *

Bradman, only 31 when World War II started, volunteered for the Royal Australian Air Force; he was barred from serving because of muscular trouble and bad eyesight. The war meant that Bradman did not play a single Test between the ages of 30 and 38. Yet, both times surviving vociferous early appeals for being out caught, he scored 187 and 234 in his first two Tests back, in the 1946/47 Ashes; Australia won 3–0.

In 1948, Bradman led Australia on their first tour to England after World War II. Over five months in England, Australia played 34 matches, won 25 – including 17 by an innings – and drew nine: the Invincibles. Bradman's determination to become the first Australia team in England to remain unbeaten underpinned his ruthlessness against counties. 'When you get in front,' he told his team, 'nail 'em to the ground.'

Uniquely, all five *Wisden* Cricketers of the Year were from Australia: the opener Arthur Morris; the middle-order stroke-maker Lindsay Hassett; the adroit wicketkeeper Don Tallon; Bill Johnston, a sharp left-armer who could also bowl orthodox spin; and Ray Lindwall, a menacing, metronomic pace bowler.

This list didn't even include the precocious Neil Harvey, who was 19 at the time. 'I just sat in the corner, said nothing, and listened to all these experienced guys,' Harvey recalled. 'That's how I learned to play.' It also didn't include Keith Miller, a bon vivant and effervescent allrounder talented enough both to bat at three in Test cricket and to take the new ball. In 1948, Australia exploited a trial that gave bowling teams a fresh ball after 55 overs: attacking initially with Miller, Lindwall and Johnston, then containing England before unleashing the quicks again with the second new ball. To Bradman, his 1948 side was the finest Test team of all. Yet he was emphatically the star.

'His appearances throughout the country were like one continuous farewell matinée,' Robertson-Glasgow wrote. Bradman still averaged 72.57. When Australia were set 404 to win in under a day at Headingley, on a pitch showing signs of turn, Bradman hit 173 not out, taking his tally at the ground to 963 runs at 192.60; the team record run chase endured for 55 years.

Bradman's captaincy showcased his extraordinary memory. Arthur Morris, top scorer on the 1948 tour, recalled,

> Compton came in and Lindwall bowled him a short one. Compton hooked him with all his force, and I had just been moved by Bradman five metres near the umpire. After I took the catch, and if I hadn't I'd have been in hospital, I said, 'Why did you move me?' He said, 'I remember in 1938, Compton hooked down that line from Ernie McCormick.'

Even a duck added to his legend. When Bradman walked out at The Oval in the final Test, he did so to three cheers from the England team. With Australia already well ahead, and nine wickets in hand, this loomed as Bradman's probable final Test innings; he arrived at the crease with an average of 101.39, needing, though few realised it, just four to end with an average of 100. He was bowled second ball by a googly from Eric Hollies.

When Bradman returned to the dressing room, Harvey recalled, 'He took his pads off and said, "Fancy doing a thing like that." That was all he said.'

John Arlott was commentating on BBC radio:

> I wonder if you see a ball very clearly in your last Test in England, on a ground where you've played out some of the biggest cricket of your life and where the opposing team have just stood round you and given you three cheers, and the crowd

has clapped you all the way to the wicket... I wonder if you really see the ball at all.

A cricket statistician later claimed to find evidence of four missing Bradman runs from a Test in 1929, which would have given him an average of exactly 100. Yet 99.94 is better: perfect in its imperfection.

Bradman returned home to retirement, and the first knighthood ever given to a playing cricketer. He called it 'the medium through which England's appreciation of what Australian cricket had meant to the British Empire' could be expressed. While enjoying a long retirement – he had two spells as Australian Cricket Board chairman, and was married to his childhood sweetheart for 65 years – Bradman replied with handwritten, personal letters to all who wrote to him.

Time has only made his feats seem more incredible. One explanation for Bradman's average is that standards in professional sport rise over time, so past titans stand out more against their competitors than recent stars. The tendency was observed by Stephen Jay Gould, analysing why no one would ever emulate the baseball player Ted Williams's batting average of .406 in the 1941 season. 'When we contrast these numbers of past and present, we encounter the well-known and curious phenomenon that inspired this article: great players of the past often stand further apart from their teammates,' Gould wrote. 'The "myth" of ancient heroes – the greater distance between average and best in the past – actually records the improvement of play through time. Declining variation becomes the key to our puzzle.'

In Bradman's case, this explanation only goes so far. Compared with the best batters of his era and earlier, Bradman averaged at least two-thirds as many again. He scored 29 hundreds in 52 Tests; 36 per cent of his innings were centuries, 15 per cent of them double centuries. When Bradman died, aged 92, it was the first time that he had been dismissed in the 90s.

Analysing the best performers across sport and how far away from the competition they were, a paper from Tony Aitken even asserts that it is 'reasonable to conclude that, on the basis of statistical analysis, Bradman is the greatest ever sportsman'. If that claim can never be verified, Bradman's status as Test batting's outlier will never be challenged.

Bradman remains for ever the gold, unattainable standard in Test cricket – a byword for perfection in a maddening game.

7

NO RATIONS ANY MORE

In 2000, *The Guardian* sportswriter Frank Keating chose his summer of the century for *Wisden*. His answer was unequivocal:

> It just has to be, doesn't it? 1947. The sun shone, the pitches were uncovered, it was the innocent year before the beastly new and faraway government of those nice chaps in green caps espoused apartheid, and from May to September, it seemed, Compton and Edrich were batting.

'Bill Edrich and I used to challenge each other saying, "First one out buys the first round,"' Denis Compton recalled. 'We got very thirsty that summer with all the running we did.'

The pair, christened The Terrible Twins for what they did to opposing bowling attacks and their off-field antics, were in a race to break the previous record for most runs in an English summer – 3,518, by Tom Hayward in 1906. Both men would beat Hayward's tally: Compton scored 3,816 first-class runs at 90.85, Edrich 3,539 runs at 80.43. These remain the two highest run totals in any first-class summer; like Compton's 18 first-class centuries in the season, a record. The tallies included Compton's four Test centuries, and Edrich's two – while averaging over 100 – as England defeated South Africa 3–0. The pair shared a third-wicket stand of 370 in the second Test at Lord's, then 228 in the third Test at Old Trafford.

Compton's gifts were not confined to cricket. One of the last great multi-sport cricketers, he also played for Arsenal, making 14 appearances as a left winger as the club won the 1947/48 league title. Compton played in Arsenal's 1950 FA Cup final victory against Liverpool; he also won wartime and victory football caps for England.

Debonair and handsome, Compton's appeal extended far beyond sport. During England's tour of South Africa in 1948/49, Compton handed his friend, the sports journalist Reg Hayter, a suitcase full of unopened mail. First, Hayter found a letter from the *News of the World*, offering Compton £2,000 a year to write a column. Second, Hayter found another letter, withdrawing the offer because Compton hadn't replied. 'Denis, you want looking after,' Hayter said. He became cricket's first agent, helping Compton to realise his commercial worth. Compton was sponsored by Brylcreem, the hair-styling product. 'That's the style' and 'Keeps you right on top', proclaimed Compton in promotional posters.

Such advertisements reflected Compton's elan. 'My style of play was soon discovered to be "unorthodox",' Compton wrote. 'On the days when things go well and every shot you attempt is a winner, I have been carefree and spontaneous and even seemingly effortless.' He thought of 1947 as 'a freak season, a phenomenal season: once I had got started everything seemed to go right for me, every kind of shot even if weird and unheard of was a surprising success'.

To open up gaps, Compton advanced down the pitch, even to fast bowlers, and moved across his stumps to flick balls to the on side. One captain, John Warr, said that Compton had 'read the textbook upside down'. Don Bradman said that he 'does things that are unexpected and which no one else can copy . . . you notice that he is so different and superior, perhaps, to his contemporaries.'

The winter of 1946/47 was among Britain's coldest of the century; there were power cuts, rations and a lack of fuel. In August 1947, Prime Minister Clement Attlee announced further cuts to petrol and food. Compton and Edrich were an antidote to the country's wider struggles. Neville Cardus captured Compton's spirit:

Never have I been so deeply touched on a cricket ground as I was in this heavenly summer, when I went to Lord's to see a pale-faced crowd, existing on rations, the rocket bomb still in the ears of most folk – see this worn, dowdy crowd watching Compton. The strain of long years of anxiety and affliction passed from all hearts and shoulders at the sight of Compton in full sail, sending the ball here, there and everywhere, each stroke a flick of delight, a propulsion of happy sane healthy life. There were no rations in an innings by Compton.

On 22 August 1939, West Indies played the final Test of their tour of England. On the last day, Learie Constantine hit 79 in 50 minutes before Len Hutton and Wally Hammond scored centuries to secure a draw, and a 1–0 series win. The team left The Oval, Constantine recalled, 'with newspapers in our hands and the match already forgotten, and the great silver balloons catching the last sunlit rays as the world beneath darkened steadily into chaos and war'. With the global crisis intensifying, and fears that U-boats would stop them reaching home safely, West Indies cancelled their other tour matches and returned home. They got the train to Scotland and then a boat to Montreal, arriving on 3 September, when war had already begun. Had they left a day later, the West Indies players might well have been killed. After the SS *Montrose*, which West Indies safely boarded, the next boat to Canada was the first ship sunk in the war.

Hedley Verity, who played against West Indies in 1939, was among the finest slow-left-arm bowlers in history, with immaculate control and a venomous quicker ball, sometimes delivered as a yorker. He took 15 wickets when England won the 1934 Ashes Test at Lord's. Verity dismissed Don Bradman eight times in Tests, at an average of 49.75, half Bradman's average against other bowlers. On 1 September 1939, the day that war was declared, Verity took 7–9 at Hove to bowl Yorkshire to victory. Four years later, as a captain during the Allied invasion of Sicily, Verity was killed; eight other Test cricketers were killed in action during the war. 'Keep going,' Verity told his men in the seconds before he died. 'Keep going and get them out of that farmhouse.'

As during World War I, first-class cricket was largely suspended during World War II; an exception was in India. Compton, posted to India with the army, played in the Ranji Trophy during the war. Elsewhere, the idea of cricket still remained alive. Lord's continued to host friendly matches, normally played over a single day. In one game, players were made to take cover during an air raid; the Luftwaffe bomb exploded 200 yards away.

After Benito Mussolini was dismissed by the Italian king in 1943, leaving Adolf Hitler as Britain's sole enemy in Europe, a Conservative MP remarked, 'We've got Ponsford out cheaply, but Bradman is still batting.' In a speech at Lord's in 1944, Australia's prime minister John Curtin declared, 'Australians will always fight for these 22 yards. Lord's and its traditions belong to Australia just as much as to England.'

Eleven days after Victory in Europe Day, on 19 May 1945, Australian Services XI played their first match against England, commencing a five-match series of Victory Tests. Curtin, battling the illness that would kill him six weeks later, sent his good wishes to MCC and hoped that no England–Australia series would ever be interrupted again. At Lord's, spectators – not only English, but also Australian soldiers – began queuing at 6 a.m., five and a half hours before the first ball; unusually, admission was a flat 1s (five pence) anywhere in the ground.

Crowds came not just for the love of the game, but also for what it represented. 'I thought it would be like the old days,' G.A. King, a retired building surveyor who was the first in the queue, told the *Evening Standard,* Mark Rowe recounts in *The Victory Tests.* Lord's turned away thousands. Australia's Graham Williams, who had been released from a German prisoner-of-war camp only a month earlier, received a standing ovation when he came out to bat. After four years in captivity, Williams hit 53.

The matches pitted an England side of Test quality against the best Australia players who were on military service in Europe. While England's side in the first match featured eight players with Test experience, the first Australian XI included only one, Lindsay Hassett. As such, the games were not awarded official Test status. But the 367,000 people who attended the three three-day matches at Lord's alone were enthralled.

The series announced Keith Miller's luminous talent. Emerging from his stint as a pilot officer in the Royal Australian Air Force, Miller scored a century in the first Victory Test and drove the Australian Services XI to an unexpected 2–2 series draw. It was the prelude to a brilliant career in official Tests. Whether attacking in the middle order – classically, but with a penchant for straight sixes – generating rapid pace from a small run-up, with what Len Hutton hailed as 'the perfect action', or snaffling catches acrobatically in the slips, Miller was captivating. 'A cavalier in a world of roundheads', England's John Warr called Miller, who hated arriving at a ground more than 15 minutes before play began. Tom Graveney, an Ashes opponent in the 1950s, observed, 'How could you play against him with any confidence when you never knew what was going to inspire him to an outburst of controlled violence? At one moment the match might be cruising gently along, the next it was in flames.'

Miller's Test figures – averaging 36.97 with the bat, with seven centuries in 55 matches; and taking 170 wickets at 22.97 – were terrific. They were even more remarkable considering that he could be guilty of a 'failure to concentrate', Bradman wrote; Miller was prone to giving his wicket away when Australia were dominant. 'I'll tell you what pressure is,' Miller famously said. 'Pressure is a Messerschmitt up your arse. Playing cricket is not.'

After the very first Victory Test in May 1945, Edrich recalled 'the first sharp lesson that we have not got a real Test match-quality attack'. He was right. In the 15 Ashes Tests from 1946, when official

Test cricket resumed, until 1951, Australia averaged 41.24 per wicket lost, England just 26.28.

Australia were undefeated in their first 25 Tests after World War II, winning 20. Even after Don Bradman retired, Australia remained ascendant: Arthur Morris, Hassett, Neil Harvey and Miller provided reliable runs. The bowling was at least as well stocked: quicks Ray Lindwall, Miller and Bill Johnston dovetailed superbly. These men ensured that Australia were victorious 4–1 in the 1950/51 Ashes. But a win in the final match marked the start of England's best period in Test history.

* * *

Just like after World War I, England were thrashed in the first three post-war Ashes series – losing 3–0, 4–0 and then 4–1, following 5–0, 3–0 and 4–1 defeats in the three Ashes series after 1918. Eight years after World War I, England drew the first four Tests of the home Ashes series before regaining the urn at The Oval. Eight years after World War II, the pattern would repeat itself.

The first four Tests in 1953 were drawn, not helped by rain and matches being only four days. At Lord's, Trevor Bailey and Willie Watson shared a five-hour partnership on the final day to salvage a draw. In the fourth Test at Headingley, Australia ended 30 shy of their target of 177 with six wickets remaining. England deployed Bailey to bowl down the leg side, and bowled their overs slowly – 12 in the last 45 minutes, around three fewer than the norm – to deny Australia time to complete a win. The teams arrived at The Oval for the final Test all square at 0–0: six days were allocated. The *Daily Express* called it 'the most thrilling Test in 20 years to decide world cricket supremacy'. The bulk of England's team played County Championship matches the day before the Test, only arriving in London late in the evening.

If Australia had dipped from their last tour of England, they still brimmed with storied names: the openers Arthur Morris and captain Lindsay Hassett; Neil Harvey, an attractive stroke-maker; the fearsome Ray Lindwall; and Miller. To see if England could regain the Ashes lost 19 years earlier, 550,000 watched the five Tests.

At The Oval, Hassett won the toss and chose to bat. But he had already made his first, perhaps decisive, mistake: omitting a specialist spinner. After making 275, Australia threatened to get a first innings lead but allrounder Trevor Bailey, batting in the style befitting his nickname of Barnacle Bailey, helped England score 69 runs for the last two wickets, getting a 31-run lead. In the second innings, Surrey spin twins, off-spinner Jim Laker and left-arm spinner Tony Lock, were whisked on after five overs, reducing Australia to 61–5; the pair shared 11 wickets in the Test.

As Len Hutton and Bill Edrich walked out to open the innings on the third evening, England needed 132 runs to win and regain the Ashes. England's run scoring was frozen like a mammoth in the permafrost. They advanced at barely two runs an over. Bailey had 'never experienced more tension in a dressing-room, because the objective for which we had fought so hard throughout that summer was within our grasp'.

When England arrived for the fourth day, 94 short of victory and with seven wickets in hand, newspaper placards outside the ground had drawings of the urn surrounded by the words: 'THEY ARE OURS!' A few hours later, they were. At 2.55 p.m. on 28 August 1953, Compton pulled the winning runs. BBC TV commentator Brian Johnston yelled, 'Is it the Ashes? Yes! England have won the Ashes!'

The BBC first broadcast a cricket match live on radio in 1927, and a Test in 1934, though not every ball. Teddy Wakelam, one of the BBC's leading sports commentators, initially said that cricket was too slow for radio. Instead, Australia led the way: the first live broadcast on a Test was in 1924. For the 1930 Ashes, Australian broadcasters deciphered cables sent in code from England. They used these to broadcast ball by ball: accurately recording the runs from each delivery but often using creative licence about where the ball had been hit, as Adam Collins and Daniel Norcross detail in the *Calling the Shots* podcast.

The rhythms of Test cricket were ideally suited to radio, doubling as the background noise to a working day. The BBC increased their output, broadcasting ball-by-ball commentary of more Tests. In 1957, *Test Match Special* launched, offering full commentary on every home Test. Especially after Brian Johnston moved to radio full-time in 1970, they discussed much else – dinners, holidays and cakes sent in by listeners – too. Johnston termed *Test Match Special* 'a bunch of friends going to a match and talking about it'; he noted that 'some people write in to say that they like the chit-chat more than the commentary!'

None of these friends was better-loved than the lyrical John Arlott, whose fruity Hampshire vowels and turn of phrase could make the banal seem riveting: 'The umpire signals a bye with the air of a weary stalk.' For Test cricket around the world, radio became integral not just to reaching existing fans but to gaining new ones: Ravi Chaturvedi and Jasdev Singh, among the first Hindi commentators, helped Indian cricket grow beyond the English-speaking population.

The first Test shown live on BBC television was the Ashes Test at Lord's in 1938. Viewing numbers for the 1953 Ashes surged after many people bought sets to watch the Queen's coronation in June. By 1960, nearly three-quarters of the UK population had a TV; Australia was close behind. After playing his last Test in 1964, Richie Benaud, Australia's former captain, was cherished as the sound of summer both down under and in England. Laconic and astute, he advised, 'Don't take yourself too seriously, and have fun.' Benaud believed that 'silence is your greatest weapon,' declaring, 'Don't speak unless you can add to the picture.'

* * *

To English fans of a certain generation, the identity of the 11 who won the 1953 Ashes would become as ingrained as any times table: Len Hutton (c), Bill Edrich, Tom Graveney, Denis Compton, Peter May, Trevor Bailey, Godfrey Evans (wk), Jim Laker, Alec Bedser, Tony Lock and Fred Trueman.

The 1953 Ashes was Len Hutton's triumph. With 443 runs at 55.37, he outscored everyone else; in the final Test, Hutton top-scored with 82 in England's first innings.

Hutton and Compton, born two years apart, were England's two great batting stars after World War II. Both had made their debuts against New Zealand in 1937, and they would be a common thread in English batting for the next two decades. As with Herbert Sutcliffe and Jack Hobbs a generation earlier, their alliance combined a man from Yorkshire with one from a London county – though Compton represented Middlesex, rather than Surrey. Both Hutton and Compton had modest roots. Hutton was a builder's son from Pudsey, a market town in West Yorkshire. Compton, the son of a self-employed painter and decorator, hailed from Hendon, in north-west London, a few miles from Lord's. He termed his childhood 'poorish' and 'happy', enlivened by ample games of street football and cricket. Both players were self-taught, but the idiosyncrasy of his approach meant that Compton was more conspicuously so.

'Our lives were to run parallel,' Compton wrote. But they were a study in contrasts. If their differences could sometimes be a little overstated – 'It would be quite wrong to get the idea that Compton's attitude to cricket was always casual,' Laker said – they were also real. Where Hutton was renowned for his punctuality, Compton once arrived late for a Test, forgetting that the start time had been moved forward.

'I don't suppose Len ever considered cricket as a game,' teammate Tom Graveney wrote. 'He was a great player who might even have been the greatest had he been inspired by that little bit of devil that would have had him murdering attacks once he had subdued them.'

Hutton almost invariably opened; Compton occupied the number-four berth traditionally reserved for the side's most lavish stroke-maker. Compton had 'a gift for improvisation that amounts almost to genius', Hutton purred. Hutton scored 364 at The Oval in the Ashes Test of 1938, but, echoing Jack Hobbs a generation earlier, sacrificed flair at the altar of consistency when cricket resumed after World War II. These differences obscured that both men shared profound courage, often withstanding blows to the body.

Compton played 78 Tests and averaged 50.06; Hutton played 79 Tests and averaged 56.67. The figure is even more notable because Hutton lost his prime years to the war, and broke his left arm – it was nearly two inches shorter than his right, forcing changes in his technique. After the injury, Hutton wrote, 'Only in warmer climates than that of England have I been able to enjoy comparative freedom from pain.'

John Woodcock, *The Times*'s long-time cricket correspondent, considered Hutton to be Hobbs's successor as 'the master' of English batting; like Hobbs, Hutton was knighted. Journalist Alan Ross observed that Compton's 'genius is romantic and individual. Hutton has never made such an appeal; his art has existed within precise technical limits.'

These limits transferred happily to any clime: Hutton averaged 55.29 in away Tests, Compton only 36.88. To playwright Harold Pinter, 'Hutton was never dull. His bat was part of his nervous system. His play was sculptured. His forward defensive stroke was a complete statement.'

Character differences help explain why Hutton captained in Test cricket – England won four, and drew two, of his six series in charge – but Compton never did. Even when the pair departed, English batting remained strong: Tom Graveney and Colin Cowdrey both provided middle-order style. After being dropped soon after his debut in 1955, Ken Barrington later reinvented himself as an iron-willed accumulator; particularly proficient off the back foot, he ended up with a Test average of 58.67.

Peter May was England's highest scorer in the 1950s. May was, perhaps, English Test cricket's last genuine amateur: he earned the bulk of his income as an insurance broker at Lloyd's in the City of London, and played his last Test aged 31. Broad-shouldered and six foot tall, his style was distilled by his elegant on drive.

But May was deeply pragmatic too. He embodied a paradox of the age: how England were by turns, or even at the same time, brilliant and boring. For all the success during his captaincy, it featured regular calls for 'brighter cricket'. Compton lamented that England often played 'cricket in handcuffs'; Jim Swanton, cricket correspondent for *The Daily Telegraph*, wrote 'this Test cricket was a desperately tough, grim affair'. Throughout the 1950s, England scored at 2.23 runs per six-ball over: their slowest ever in a decade. In Barbados in 1953/54, England scored 128 from 114 overs in a day. Worldwide, runs during the decade were scored at just 2.20 per six balls: comfortably the lowest of any decade since the start of the 20th century.

May rarely hooked because it 'contains too great an element of risk'. One of the decade's most significant innings, May's 285 not out against West Indies in 1957, when he added 411 with Cowdrey to save the first Test and set up a 3–0 series victory, was founded on pad-play. The pair could not read Sonny Ramadhin's mystery spin; May constantly took a decisive stride forward, knowing that umpires would be loath to give him out lbw if he did so. *Wisden* said that May 'came to represent the beau idéal of English batsmanship and sportsmanship'. Yet he played to win, not to maintain a quaint amateur idea.

* * *

Frank Tyson lay unconscious on the floor. At Sydney in the second Test of the 1954/55 Ashes, Tyson received a lifting bouncer from Ray Lindwall; turning away, he was struck on the back of the skull. 'My

God, Lindy, you've killed him,' partner Bill Edrich cried out when Tyson collapsed.

'It was overcast and I lost the ball completely out of the sight-screen,' Tyson later said. 'He let me have a very fast, short-pitched delivery. It hit me on the back of the head. I went down like a sack of potatoes. I was in a vague mist, slipping in and out of consciousness.' Teammates helped Tyson off the field. Tyson was whisked to hospital for an X-ray, which revealed that he had been lucky; he returned to bat, briefly – then to open the bowling in the final innings of the match.

After being pummelled in Brisbane, England had to defend a target of 223 in Sydney to square the series and stop Australia from going 2–0 up. As Tyson emerged from his concussed state, his captain Hutton noticed 'a new light in his eyes as if a spark had been kindled deep down inside him'.

'I was very, very angry with Ray Lindwall,' Tyson wrote in his tour diary. Australia began day five needing 151 runs, with eight wickets in hand. Tyson had the wind behind his back.

For all his pace, Tyson generally bowled full, attacking the stumps. Early on day five, he bowled Jim Burke and Graeme Hole with a yorker and another delivery that wasn't quite as full. When Lindwall arrived at the crease, attention focused on whether Tyson would retaliate with bouncers of his own. 'Knowing this, I kept the ball up to him,' Tyson wrote. He bowled Lindwall, for eight, with another yorker. Only Neil Harvey, who made 92 not out, could withstand Tyson's pace. Instead, England went around Harvey. With Australia's last pair threatening a heist, Tyson summoned a short delivery on the hip; Evans's catch from Bill Johnston secured a 38-run win. Tyson's 6–85 levelled the series at 1–1.

It was a terrific riposte to England's ignominious start to the 1954/55 Ashes. Hutton had won the toss in Brisbane but bafflingly chose to bowl; Australia scored 601–8 declared, winning by an innings. Tyson took 1–160.

Between the first and second Tests, England and Tyson had both made critical choices. After several nights fretting over 'the hardest decision of my cricket career', Hutton dropped Bedser, who had taken 30 Test wickets down under four years earlier but was now 36. To Hutton, a new-ball attack of Tyson – just two Tests into his career – and Brian Statham represented 'the fulfilment of my biggest wish as captain, to begin England's attack with a pair of express bowlers as a counter to the blasts of Lindwall and Miller'.

Before the second Test, Tyson abandoned his 38-yard run-up, moving to one barely half as long that he had used before. 'It helped me use my body weight,' Tyson wrote. Compton remembered his 'economical run, and with all his devastating power and fire intact'.

The run-up brought Tyson 25 wickets in the middle three Tests – all won, to give England a 3–1 victory. Most thrilling was his 7–27 in the third Test in Melbourne. The last morning dawned with Australia needing 165 runs, with eight wickets in hand, a similar position to in the previous Test; 50,000 expectant fans packed into the MCG. In the second over, wicketkeeper Godfrey Evans dived at full stretch down the leg side to snare Harvey off Tyson. Soon after, Miller fended off a ball from his nose to the slips. Tyson's final-day spell of 6–16, devastating Australia by bowling just short of a length, with the occasional yorker, was 'the luckiest and happiest day of my life', he recalled. 'I was bowling in a euphoric daze.'

Australia were used to similar pace – just not as a weapon to be used against them. Compton 'had never thought I'd see an Australian team demoralised, but Frank had done it before my wondering eyes'. Allrounder Ron Archer later told the book *The Summer Game* that one Tyson delivery 'was so fast that the force of it turned the bat in my hand'. England bowled about a quarter fewer overs per hour than Australia – attracting boos for their tardiness – giving Tyson chance to rest even during his spells. Hutton had a penchant for talking to bowlers mid-over.

Tyson was supported by a fine, resilient team. Brian Statham, who was almost as quick and bowled with great control, moved the ball off the seam and bowled into the wind to allow Tyson to bowl with it; he took 18 wickets in the series. Johnny Wardle and Bob Appleyard, both brought in for the last four Tests, complemented the pace bowlers with their parsimony: Wardle with his left-arm spin, Appleyard with off-cutters delivered at medium pace. For the first time, MCC sent a masseur with the squad, to monitor bowlers' fitness.

Only five centuries were scored in a low-scoring series. With Hutton in his final act as a Test cricketer, England's new generation of batters made crucial contributions. May scored a pristine century to help England overhaul a first innings deficit of 74 in the second Test, a combination of his trademark driving and working the ball precisely into on-side gaps. As May hit the ball, Alan Ross wrote, 'the air is split with the crispness of the impact'. From 41–4 on the first morning of the third Test, Colin Cowdrey's counter-attacking 102 – to Ross, 'a blend of leisurely driving and secure back play, of power and propriety' – lifted England to 191.

Tyson's autobiography, written in prose befitting a Durham University graduate prone to quoting Shakespeare to opponents, captures the thrill of bowling pace:

> With a feeling of uncertainty, I scar the ground with a little shuffle, and then away, long and loping, counting mechanically, yet rhythmically, the nine strides of my approach. My body bows, head forward, preparing to rise, reaching, clawing for height before bringing the ball banging down on the batsman. I feel my legs tense, my head is on one side and the wickets are in my sights. There is a sudden shock, shaking me to the skull, as the stiff left leg crashes into unsympathetic turf, and my whole body flings itself after the ball, as if in malediction towards the batsman . . .
>
> To bowl quickly is to revel in the glad animal action; to thrill in physical prowess, and to enjoy a certain sneaking feeling of

superiority over the other mortals who play the game. No batsman likes quick bowling, and this knowledge gives one a sense of omnipotence.

Injury limited Tyson to 17 Tests, during which he averaged 18.56: the Typhoon. Like Australia's destroyer a generation earlier, Harold Larwood, Tyson settled happily down under; he met his future wife in 1954/55.

For the remainder of the decade, England's pace attack was led by a man overlooked in 1954/55: Fred Trueman. In his third Test, against India in 1952, Trueman took 8–31, bowling with pace and menace from a classical side-on action. Trueman's penchant for off-field drama – sometimes overblown, as when he pointed out to the Yorkshire committee that he was 200 miles away, playing for England, when he was alleged to have been involved in an incident – contributed to MCC's reluctance to pick him overseas. Just 20 of his 67 Tests were away. But as he aged, Trueman became shrewder. 'By bowling a bit slower I could move the ball more and also develop the off-cutter,' he explained; the delivery devastated Australia in a spell of 6–1 on his home ground, Headingley, in 1961. When he retired, no one had more than Trueman's 307 Test wickets. He was, John Arlott wrote,

> the kind of fast bowler he had created for himself; a larger-than-life-sized figure compounded in the imagination of a boy from the fancies, facts, loyalties, cricket, reading, traditions and all the other influences of a semi-rural, semi-industrial area of South Yorkshire in the nineteen-thirties.

From the final Ashes match in 1950/51 until the 1958/59 Ashes tour, England won 32 Tests and lost 11, a win–loss ratio twice that of any other nation. England were undefeated in 14 consecutive series. They won ten, including three Ashes victories and an impressive 3–2 win against South Africa in 1955; their four draws included coming from 2–0 down away to West Indies in a tempestuous series in 1953/54.

England have not enjoyed a remotely comparable run over such an extended period since.

Together with their formidable pace bowlers, England had the best spin pair in their history. Off-spinner Jim Laker's 193 wickets cost just 21.24, left-arm spinner Tony Lock's 174 only 25.58. England did not view picking two spinners only as a tactic of necessity abroad. Both Laker and Lock took over 100 wickets at home at an average under 20.

Laker, who spun the ball more sharply, turned the ball into right-handers; Lock, who was a little quicker during the mid-1950s, spun the ball away. Their personalities also differed. Laker was more reserved; he described Lock as a 'firebrand' who 'bowled with an aggression not normally associated with slow bowlers'. During their careers, they were often rivals, but later they became warm friends. In their 24 Tests in tandem, England won 12 and lost four.

With the series locked at 1–1, the penultimate Test of the 1956 Ashes was played at Old Trafford. Pre-match intrigue centred on the dusty pitch, especially given Australia's lack of experience against finger spin. The previous Test, at Headingley, Laker (11) and Lock (7) had shared 18 wickets in England's innings victory. When Don Bradman, now working in the media, saw Laker by the pitch the day before the Old Trafford Test, he said, 'Flat and slow, with plenty of runs.' The judgement was hard to dispute as England amassed a first innings 459.

Australia's openers added 48 for the first wicket. Then, Laker and Lock switched ends: after moving to the Stretford End, Laker promptly induced Colin McDonald to flick to Lock at leg slip. The wicket brought the great left-hander Neil Harvey to the crease. He received a delivery that drifted in, pitched on leg stump and kissed the top of off stump. 'I never faced a better ball,' Harvey said; archive footage suggests that he was not wrong.

Lock got the third wicket, but now Laker was into his rhythm. He moved to around the wicket, against right- and left-handers alike. In his last nine overs, Laker took 9–16. Australia tried different methods – after the top order favoured playing back, two players used their feet, falling caught in the deep and stumped – but to no avail. Laker's seven wickets after tea came in 21 balls, one every three deliveries; Australia grumbled about a doctored pitch.

In the second innings, Australia's resolve was notably better. After two rain-ruined days, Australia did not lose a wicket on the final morning. At lunch, Laker had a beer and a sandwich, and saw the sun come out, knowing this would 'bring another change in the conditions – and, of course, the match'. As the pitch dried out, the match 'started on sand and it finished up on mud', opener Colin McDonald recalled.

'He took his wickets by unrelenting accuracy, by varying flight, length and intention with such imaginative skill that the batsman was first hemmed in, then driven to surrender,' Alan Ross wrote. Miller was bowled for a duck by a delivery from around the wicket that pitched on off stump, then curved through the gap between bat and pad to dislodge his leg stump. After making 89, McDonald inside-edged a delivery to leg slip, giving Laker his seventh wicket of the innings, and opening up the possibility that he could become the first Test bowler to take a perfect ten.

The moment arrived with last man Len Maddocks on strike. Maddocks played back, and was struck on the back pad as the delivery spun into him. After a polite appeal, umpire Emrys Davies raised his finger. Laker shook his teammates' hands, took his jumper from Davies, slung it over his shoulder and jogged up the pavilion steps to a standing ovation. 'I have never been a demonstrative person,' Laker wrote, 'and have always tried to take whatever success has come my way just the same as I have accepted the innumerable failures.'

Laker had recorded second innings figures of 51.2–23–53–10; his match figures read 68–27–90–19. Never since has his match haul of 19–90 been threatened. Laker snared 46 wickets at 9.60 in the 1956

Ashes; only one man, Sydney Barnes in South Africa in 1913/14, has ever taken more in a series.

On the way home from Old Trafford, Laker stopped in a pub in Lichfield. He ordered a modest celebratory dinner: a sandwich, washed down with a bottle of beer. Laker 'sat in the corner of a crowded bar while everyone talked about the Test. No one spotted me.'

8

THE EMERGENCE OF PAKISTAN

Nearing the end of day four in the Oval Test in 1954, Fazal Mahmood, Pakistan's fast bowler, turned to Abdul Kardar. Fazal asked his captain, 'What if I get Compton out?'

'Then we win the match,' Kardar replied, also in Punjabi. Shortly afterwards, Denis Compton edged Fazal behind. Compton succumbed to Fazal's signature: the leg-cutter, shaping away from right-handers. England closed the fourth evening on 125–6, in pursuit of 168 for victory.

All series, Pakistan's right to play Test cricket had been questioned. 'There were grave suggestions in certain quarters that Pakistan should not have been given Test status,' Kardar wrote. 'We were struggling desperately to guard it and, if possible, to confirm it once and for all.' The book's title is instructive: *Test Status on Trial*.

Pakistan arrived at The Oval, for the final Test, only trailing England 1–0 largely thanks to the weather. Pakistan had been bowled out for 87 in the opening Test, but there was no play until the fourth day and the match was drawn; they lost the second by an innings. In the third, at Old Trafford, Pakistan were bowled out for 90; they were 25–4 in their second innings when rain washed out the final two days. The side 'had no idea of fielding', which was 'of club standard', Kardar wrote. Late-lower-order resistance at The Oval – hauling Pakistan from 82–8 to 164 all out – gave the attack a defendable target.

When England reached 109–2 in their run chase, it did not seem as if Pakistan had enough. At this point, Kardar told Fazal that he was coming off. 'Do you want to lose the match?' Fazal asked his captain.

Peter May was suckered by a slower ball. Fazal then clean bowled Godfrey Evans, who had been promoted up the order with England seemingly trying to wrap up victory that evening.

Fazal was a bowler of consummate skill, combining accurate, full bowling with an array of variations; his methods resembled Sydney Barnes before World War I, but he could probably reach 75 mph or so. In his autobiography, he wrote about his strategy at The Oval:

> I would bowl the leg-cutter from the return crease which was a wicket-taking ball. There was also a hidden in-swinger from the return crease, an in-swinger from the middle of the crease and an in-swinger from close to the stumps.

Fazal also had profound self-belief. Before the Oval Test, with Pakistan being lambasted by the English press, Fazal advocated that the team release a statement declaring that they would win the final Test. At The Oval, 'Even though we were bowled out for 133, I did not think for a second we would lose,' he later said.

On the fifth morning, with England needing 43 more for victory, Kardar turned to pace once again: Fazal and Mahmood Hussain in tandem. After Fazal removed Frank Tyson caught behind, England's hopes rested upon Johnny Wardle, the number seven. When the left-hander came onto strike, Osman Samiuddin recounts in *The Unquiet Ones*, deep midwicket moved to a short square leg. Fazal told Shujauddin Butt, the fielder, 'You put your right foot here, left foot there, unfold your hands and stand ready for a catch. The ball will come right into your hands and you just grab it.' Wardle duly flicked the leg-cutter to Shujauddin.

Peter Loader, England's number nine, skied Fazal to cover, bringing the last pair together on 138–9, 30 runs shy of victory. Jim McConnon, the number ten, tried to farm the strike. From the last ball of Fazal's 30th over, McConnon attempted a sharp single to extra cover. Hanif Mohammad picked the ball up one-handed; McConnon, running towards the non-striker's end, was struggling to make his ground, but only a direct hit would suffice. Hanif had a stump-and-a-half to aim at: it was enough. Pakistan won by 24 runs, securing a 1–1 series draw. Fazal 'ran towards Hanif in frenzy, took him in my arms and started dancing. My dreams had been fulfilled.' When the team assembled on the balcony, they greeted fans chanting 'Pakistan Zindabad!' At home, millions of supporters listened live on Radio Pakistan's relay of the BBC commentary.

In 60 overs at The Oval, Fazal took 12–99 – including dismissing Len Hutton, Peter May and Denis Compton in both innings. In the second innings, Fazal took 6–46 from 30 overs: he had only four overs off during the entire chase.

The win, Kardar wrote, was 'a product of perseverance, courage, patience and a final stroke of luck which sometimes favours the adventurous and almost always the brave'. No country, before or since, has ever won a Test during their maiden tour of England. Pakistan's Test status would never be on trial again.

*   *   *

Seven years before the Oval Test of 1954, Fazal could have been killed.

In February 1947, the British government announced that they would grant India independence, setting the exit date as June 1948. The news was the catalyst for a rise in communal tensions, and attacks, across India.

Fazal, who was 20 at the time, was focused upon a different date: November 1947, when India would play their first Test in Australia. He wanted to win selection for the squad, which had never discriminated on the basis of religion. On 15 March, Fazal appeared in a game in Delhi that was effectively a Test trial, taking 5–45. He was picked for India's tour.

Partition along religious lines was agreed in June 1947. All touring players were required to meet at Poona on 15 August. This was the same date that, at the stroke of midnight, the independent nation of India would come into being, after Britain accelerated their plans to leave the country; at midnight on 14 August, 24 hours earlier, the independent state of Pakistan was created. The full boundaries of the two new sovereign nations weren't revealed until 17 August, allowing the British to leave before the migrations began. Millions of people thought they were in one country but learned that they were in another.

Fazal's home was in Lahore, just 25 kilometres from a border with India. He began 14 August here, before making the arduous 1,000-kilometre trip to the training camp: through Punjab to Karachi, then to Bombay by air and finally by train to Poona. 'Millions of Muslims were making the same journey, by whatever means they could find – but in the opposite direction,' Peter Oborne wrote in *Wounded Tiger*. 'It was an insanely dangerous journey for a 20-year-old Muslim male.'

When the team assembled in Poona, as Oborne documented, cricket was far from their minds. Lala Amarnath, who was appointed as the first captain of independent India, learned that fellow Hindus in his native Lahore were being massacred. Monsoon rains also rendered practice impossible. Fazal had to retrace his journey.

The first leg of Fazal's trip home almost led to his death. On the train from Poona to Bombay, Hindu fanatics tried to lynch Fazal. He was, in his account, kept alive only by the Indian cricketer (and Hindu) Cottari Nayudu, who defended Fazal with a cricket bat on the train. From Bombay, Fazal flew safely back to Lahore. His parents had feared that he was dead, and urged him not to go back to India. Reluctantly, Fazal agreed: he sent a telegram to Amarnath saying that he would be unable to tour Australia.

To fulfil his Test dreams, Fazal would have to play for Pakistan. But Pakistan lacked both Test status and a clear road map of how to attain it. Fazal was so disheartened that he 'wanted to leave the game altogether, because at that time the future of the game in Pakistan looked to be totally dark'.

Some even suggested that, while India and Pakistan were two nations, they could remain one team in cricket, a notion supported by powerful figures at MCC. The plight of Pakistani cricket, which lacked infrastructure and structure, partly reflected how new the idea of Pakistan was. The name was first coined in 1933; the notion of an independent Muslim state was only endorsed by the Muslim League in 1940.

Undeterred, the Board of Control for Cricket in Pakistan was created in May 1948. The three most prominent figures in the organisation were K.R. Collector, the secretary; Justice Cornelius, a vice-president; and Nawab Iftikhar Hussain Khan of Mamdot, the first president. So a Parsi, a Catholic and a Muslim together ran the first years of cricket in independent Pakistan.

Their overwhelming aim was to get Pakistan playing Test cricket. The exclusionary attitudes to Test status by global administrators meant that Test cricket was seen as a privilege that countries had to earn. Test status would be critical for the future of cricket in Pakistan, and a wider symbol of the nation's acceptance on the international stage.

For Pakistan cricket, there were major risks if they did not acquire Test status. In the cases of Argentina and the USA, as we have seen, the Imperial Cricket Conference guarded membership like a snooty London club. Those locked outside the club eventually gravitated to sports whose governing elite were more welcoming. Had they not acquired Test status, Oborne argued, Pakistan might have become a satellite cricket nation: producing Test players, but for India, just as Ireland long did for England.

Pakistan's new board immediately got to work organising matches, piggybacking onto teams touring India. West Indies, in November 1948, were the first visitors, drawing a four-day match in Lahore.

In November and December 1951, MCC took a break from their Test tour of India. In Lahore and Karachi, MCC – comprising the same players who were playing five Tests over the border – played representative Pakistan teams in two four-day matches. Many in the national press called these games Tests, although, as Pakistan were not members of the Imperial Cricket Conference, they lacked such status. Based on the seriousness with which they were taken by both sides, the matches have a better claim to Test status than some earlier games with the designation, notably many involving South Africa in the late 19th century.

In Lahore, Pakistan secured a 174-run first innings lead before England batted out a draw; *Wisden* noted that MCC 'found the standard of cricket higher than expected'. In Karachi, Pakistan were set a challenging 288 runs to win. As their chase developed, a crowd of 20,000 – including Khawaja Nazimuddin, the country's prime minister, packed into the Gymkhana Ground. Aptly, Fazal and Kardar were together at the end to clinch a four-wicket victory: Fazal took 6–40 in the first innings, Kardar scored an undefeated 50 in the chase. The win effectively sealed Pakistan's status as the seventh Test nation. In July 1952, India proposed that Pakistan be elected to the Imperial Cricket Conference; MCC seconded the motion, which was waved through. Fazal and his teammates had won Test status for Pakistan, five years after the nation was created.

* * *

Cricket in what would become Pakistan was a significantly younger game than in India. Whereas cricket was played from at least 1721 in India, with the Calcutta Cricket Club formed in 1792, the game only reached the areas that would make up Pakistan from the 1840s. In the territories of future Pakistan, British soldiers, as opposed to merchants, were the driving force in cricket spreading. The first tour by an English team to what became Pakistan was in 1889/90. Before partition, such visits tended to be concentrated upon Lahore and Karachi; Peshawar and Rawalpindi later became common destinations too. The Sind Quadrangular – which evolved into the

Pentangular, with teams divided along ethnic and religious lines in the same way as in the Bombay Pentangular – was launched in 1916 in Karachi. It became a focal point for cricket's growth in the city and beyond.

When Pakistan acquired Test status, cricket was not a genuinely national game. The national board had no representation from East Pakistan (future Bangladesh), who had about half of the country's total population.

Cricket was concentrated in two urban centres: Lahore, which produced six players who appeared for India before partition, and Karachi. Even here, cricket was a middle-class game. As Osman Samiuddin wrote, of the 18 players who toured England in 1954, ten studied at either Islamia College or Government College in Lahore, whose contests could attract crowds of over 6,000. Islamia College alone provided six of the 11 at The Oval, including both Fazal and Kardar. Happily, the two regions developed distinct strengths: Lahore specialised in producing pace bowlers, Karachi in batters.

Cornelius appointed Kardar as Pakistan captain before the two matches against MCC because, he wrote in a letter, 'you have a wider experience of English county players and their tactics than perhaps any cricketer from the subcontinent since Pataudi.'

Kardar's English experience took three forms. He was Oxford-educated, and very proud of the fact, earning a Blue at the university; always looking the part, he bought his suits from Jermyn Street in London. He had represented Warwickshire for two seasons in the County Championship. Most significantly, he had already played three Tests in England for India in 1946. Kardar was a limited Test cricketer, but his combination of doughty lower-middle-order batting and left-arm spin helped to balance the side. As well as captain, Kardar was by turns selector, coach, manager and even an organiser, instigating long camps to help Pakistan prepare for overseas series. 'Kardar was in charge of everything,' Hanif Mohammad, who played

THE EMERGENCE OF PAKISTAN

in every Test that Kardar captained, recalled. Deeply patriotic – he would work in politics and as ambassador to Switzerland – Kardar saw competing in sport as a wider extension of Pakistan's arrival as a sovereign nation.

When the first Pakistan Test squad was selected in September 1952, the *Dawn* newspaper called them 'ambassadors of goodwill'. In 1947/48, India and Pakistan had already fought their first war, over Kashmir.

Pakistan's inaugural journey into India could scarcely have been simpler: a two-hour bus ride from Lahore to Amritsar, where four of the Pakistan squad originally hailed from. At a welcome reception, Kardar was greeted by Amarnath. The two had much in common. Both had grown up in Lahore, only streets apart; they spoke the same language and played at the same grounds. While Amarnath was 14 years older, they had played against each other in club cricket. They had then played together in Test cricket, for India in 1946. Now, they were on opposing sides.

Wider political tensions were an undercurrent of the tour. The day that Pakistan arrived in Amritsar, the Muslim League announced an 'all-out struggle for the liberation of Occupied Kashmir'. Yet the overwhelming feeling during the tour was of warmth. Jawaharlal Nehru, India's prime minister, greeted the visitors before the first Test in Delhi; across India, Pakistan players were inundated with autograph requests.

Pakistan had claimed that they were ready to meet India, and other Test nations, on equal terms. After being defeated in their opening Test, they thrashed India by an innings and 43 runs in their second, in Lucknow, a city with a large Muslim population; exploiting a matting wicket, Fazal took 12–94 in the Test. Pakistan's inaugural series would be seen as a success, even though India fought back to win 2–1.

Off the field, Fazal was Pakistan's equivalent of Denis Compton – right down to endorsing Brylcreem. Tall, handsome and with blue eyes, Fazal combined cricket with working as a policeman: by the 1954 tour to England, he was a deputy superintendent.

On the field, Fazal was a common thread in the seminal victories of Pakistan's early years, despite a tempestuous relationship with his captain. Kardar was 'not very friendly' with Fazal, Hanif Mohammad said in *Wounded Tiger*. Even so, 'he used to get the best out of him.' Hanif Mohammad observed that Fazal 'was the doyen of Pakistan bowlers in the formative years' and 'All our wins since we started playing Test cricket were indebted to him.'

All but one, anyway. In the 1950s, Pakistan won eight Test matches; Fazal missed one through injury. In the seven victories that he played in, Fazal snared 65 wickets at 10.79 apiece, moving the ball both ways in the air and off the pitch while maintaining his pace through gruelling spells. From his schooldays he had developed his fitness doing daily ten-mile jogs, as well as 500 jumps with his skipping rope. At Karachi in 1956, Fazal took 13–114 from 75 overs against Australia, bringing Pakistan victory in the one-off Test. Three years later, in Dacca – in East Pakistan, the area that would become Bangladesh – Fazal took 12–100 against a fine West Indies side, clinching Pakistan the three-match series with a game to spare.

Across the 1950s, Fazal claimed 125 wickets at an average of 22.12. After beginning his career hoping to play for India, Fazal became the first great Pakistan Test bowler: the founding member of an illustrious club.

When India first toured Pakistan in 1954/55, the Wagah border crossing was left open; 10,000 Indian fans travelled to watch a Test match in Lahore, wrote historian Ramachandra Guha. But this series was marred by stultifying, conservative cricket that prioritised avoiding defeat: 'Match Saved But Cricket Killed', read a report after the fourth draw in the five-match series. What Kardar would write of the 1954/55 matches – 'the series without a counter-challenge to the challenge of negative tactics' – could be said of many others to come.

THE EMERGENCE OF PAKISTAN

After the first three Tests between the sides yielded positive results, the next 13 were all draws.

Perhaps the nadir was Pakistan's tour in 1960/61: on only 11 of the 25 days in the series were over 200 runs scored. Matches continued to emphasise what India and Pakistan had in common; 'India is not a foreign country to me,' Fazal declared before that 1960/61 series. Yet some political forces also sought to use games for their own ends. In 1960, Abbas Ali Baig, an Indian Muslim, received letters and phone calls telling him to stop throwing his wicket away against Pakistan.

As political tensions escalated, including the wars of 1965 and 1971, there would be no series for 17 years. When cricketing contact resumed, victories initially became more common. Batting audaciously in run chases, Pakistan secured their first series victory over India in 1978/79, following it up in 1982/83; India won a home series in between. But the pattern of turgid cricket soon returned. From 1983 to 1989, India and Pakistan met in 16 Tests; 15 were drawn. Losing an India–Pakistan series was the easiest way to get fired. After four of their first five tours to Pakistan – twice after defeats, and twice after 0–0 draws – India's captains were sacked. Asif Iqbal, who played nine Tests against India between 1978 and 1980, observed that 'avoiding defeat becomes the primary and overwhelming objective. The result is that both teams play at a level considerably below their full potential and in an atmosphere where fear of defeat is such a major component that often dull draws are the only outcome.'

Sixty-four per cent of Tests between the countries have been drawn, double the overall rate in Test history. The American writer Mike Marqusee considered India and Pakistan cricket matches the fiercest rivalry across any sport. For vast swathes of Test history, no fixture has promised so much but delivered so little.

* * *

India and New Zealand both had to wait over 20 years for their first Test victory; Pakistan had to wait 11 days. Over the 1950s, Pakistan played 29 Tests: they won eight, lost nine and drew 12. Pakistan can be said to have performed better than any other new Test side since England and Australia launched the format in 1877. These achievements are even more notable considering Pakistan's dearth of funding: during the 1957/58 tour to West Indies, for instance, players got a £1-a-day allowance to cover their expenses, and no separate tour fee.

New Test nations have generally struggled to produce fast bowlers adept at taking 20 wickets in all conditions. Led by Fazal and well supported by Khan Mohammad – who would have played more Test cricket, including in England in 1954, but for his Lancashire League commitments – and Mahmood Hussain, Pakistan had a pace attack to threaten the world's best. Only later would their spinners be equally incisive.

Fazal and the side were backed up by a system that helped Pakistan to compete from their earliest years. Their first Test team included two cricketers who had already played Test cricket for India, including Kardar.

The rest of the side also had a good grounding in first-class cricket. Representing the region that would become part of Pakistan, Northern India played in the Ranji Trophy from its inception in 1934 until 1947. Ranji teams were regional – meaning that different faiths and ethnicities played alongside, not against, each other. Northern India enjoyed considerable success, reaching the final in the first season of the Ranji Trophy. While Pakistan's Quaid-e-Azam Trophy, the first-class competition, was only launched in 1953, Pakistan sent an Eaglets side – a prototype for future A teams – to England every year from 1952 to 1959.

Yet perhaps the best experience for Pakistan cricketers was not from playing abroad or in first-class cricket; instead, it was playing among themselves. In many ways, the triumph of Pakistan cricket in their early years was the triumph of a few families.

Fazal was the son-in-law of Mian Saeed, who captained Pakistan before Test status. Kardar's brother-in-law was Zulfiqar Ahmed, an off-spinning allrounder who excelled in his brief Test career. Waqar Hasan, a batter who played 21 Tests, including Pakistan's inaugural Test, had a younger brother, Pervez Sajjad, who also enjoyed a fine Test career. Nazar Mohammad, the first man to face a delivery for Pakistan in Test cricket, was the father of Mudassar Nazar, who played 76 Tests as a batting allrounder. The Burkis of Lahore have produced over 40 first-class cricketers – including three Test captains, Javed Burki, Majid Khan and Imran Khan.

Most remarkable of all were the Mohammad family. Between 1932 and 1945, Ameer Bee and Sheikh Islam had five boys together. The family lived a comfortable existence in Junagadh in Gujarat. This was devastated by partition; the Nawab of Junagadh initially decided that the district should become part of Pakistan, even though the population was 90 per cent Hindu and didn't border the rest of Pakistan. As the city became increasingly unsafe for Muslims – it would eventually join India, in 1948 – Indian troops entered the city. 'There were tanks and soldiers with guns, marching in front of our house,' Hanif Mohammad, one of the boys, told Peter Oborne:

> We left the house in the middle of the night to avoid being seen and boarded a ship at a small port called Veraval on the southwest coast of the Arabian Sea . . .
>
> Leaving most of our possessions behind, we stepped onto the little ship and sailed to the unknown . . . Karachi! As the ship left the port, there was a feeling of great relief that nobody could now catch and kill us.

In Karachi, the Mohammads settled in a vacant hall that had previously been used as a Hindu temple. They remained there for seven years. Cricket was one of the few constants between their old lives and their new. Of the five Mohammad boys, four played for Pakistan;

a fifth, Raees, was once 12th man. One of the quintet, Hanif, became Pakistan's first great Test batter.

As a boy in Junagadh, Hanif and his brothers played 'Tests' on Sundays from 10 a.m. till sunset. 'The rules we played by were that if the ball was hit in the air and the batsman was caught off a rebound from the trees, he was out,' Hanif said. 'All of us tried to keep the ball down.'

Hanif brought these qualities to Test cricket. He both opened and kept wicket in Pakistan's first Test, just before turning 18, scoring his country's maiden half-century. Hanif had a range of shots, and is considered one of the first architects of the reverse sweep, following his younger brother Mushtaq – himself a terrific Test cricketer, combining an average of 39.17 with dangerous leg spin.

Recognising his country's needs, Hanif played in an ascetic spirit. His powers of concentration showed themselves most when Pakistan followed on against West Indies at Barbados in 1958, 473 runs behind. There was an hour to go on day three; to survive, Pakistan effectively had to bat for three full days of this six-day Test. After Hanif survived the end of the third day, undefeated on 61, he received a handwritten note from Kardar, urging him to keep going. Throughout the fourth day, 'a look at the scoreboard, which is so natural for a batsman, created pessimism', Hanif recalled in *Green Shadows*, Kardar's tour diary. He had entered what athletes call the zone: a state of unyielding focus. He described using cues from the bowler to sense what they were about to do. 'I felt that I was playing each ball automatically. Before the bowler had delivered the ball I knew what it was going to do.'

After day four, when Hanif added exactly 100 to his tally, Kardar slipped another note under his door. He slipped another note under his door the following night too. 'When I got back there was always a message from [Abdul] Hafeez Kardar waiting in my room: "You can save us" or "They can't get you out" or "You are our last hope",' Hanif recalled. This time, Kardar's message told him, 'If you can play until tea-time we will be safe.'

Hanif did. He endured for 970 minutes and over 300 overs to score 337, only being dismissed in the final session, when the Test was saved. That night, Hanif slept in his cricket whites.

The following year, Hanif defied West Indies again, scoring 103 in Karachi to set up a ten-wicket victory. With another win in the second Test – Fazal took 12–100 in the game – Pakistan secured a series triumph over a side who had just thrashed India 3–0. The contrast encapsulated how, despite having only one-ninth of India's population as of 1960, Pakistan were performing far better in the Test arena.

Hanif was Test cricket's original Little Master. He was the most celebrated member of an incredible clan: in Pakistan's first 101 Tests, spread over 27 years, there was a solitary Test in which no members of the Mohammad family played. Soon after, Hanif's son, Shoaib, would pick up the mantle, playing 45 Tests and averaging even more than his father.

9

CRICKET, LOVELY CRICKET

At four minutes to six in Brisbane, on 14 December 1960, Wes Hall, West Indies' tall Bajan quick bowler, was given the ball by Frank Worrell. He was about to bowl perhaps the most famous over in Test history.

Whatever happened when Australia hosted West Indies in 1960/61, the series' significance was assured. Worrell was the first black man to lead West Indies full-time.

Before the first Test, Worrell had two notable conversations. The first was with his team. Worrell urged his players, Vaneisa Baksh wrote in *Son of Grace*, to break free of racial and national divisions. 'Gentlemen, on previous tours I have noted we easily segregate into little cliques within the team. I want none of that on this tour. I want us to play as a team on the field and live as a family off the field.'

Worrell's other essential chat was with Australia's captain, Richie Benaud. When they met before the opening Test, the two resolved to play attacking cricket. Benaud said, 'Let's have a good series.' 'Yeah, it should be a lot of fun,' Worrell replied.

The public had grown weary of attritional fare. Benaud's side were addressed by Don Bradman, by now chairman of the Australian board, the day before the opening Test. 'He told us he felt this could be a wonderful year,' Benaud wrote. 'He hoped this season that cricket would come back into its own, and some of the play-at-all-costs-for-a-draw attitudes would be forgotten.'

Over the first four days, the teams delivered on these hopes. A sparkling 132 from Garry Sobers led West Indies to 453 in their first innings. 'Although I knew exactly where I was going to pitch each ball, I had no idea where he was going to hit it,' Benaud wrote of bowling his leg spin. 'Bad balls he hit for four, and good ones went the same way, sometimes faster than those of lesser quality.'

Led by Norman O'Neill's 181, Australia secured a first innings lead of 52 runs. Then Alan Davidson, swinging the ball at appreciable pace from his left-arm angle, took six wickets, to add to his haul of five in the first innings; Worrell's second score of 65 in the match hauled West Indies up to 284. When they were bowled out early on day five, Australia were set 233 runs to win in 310 minutes, simultaneously battling both West Indies and the clock.

Hall's ferocious new-ball bowling reduced Australia to 92–6, when Benaud walked out to join Davidson. At tea Australia were 110–6, needing another 123 runs to win. Bradman joined the two not-out players at tea, asking, 'What are you going for, Richie – a win or a draw?' Benaud replied, 'We're going for a win, of course.'

Benaud and Davidson combined brisk singles with thrashing the few deliveries that offered width. As Australia neared their target, the pair heard Worrell tell his side, 'Relax, fellas, and concentrate . . . come on now, concentrate.'

The two batters believed that West Indies could 'crack' under pressure. Needing seven more from the last 13 balls, the pair tried one quick single too many: after responding to Benaud's call, Davidson was run out by a direct hit from 25 yards from Joe Solomon at midwicket. Solomon's aim was honed as a boy in Guyana, throwing stones at a mango tree to knock off the fruit to eat. Davidson's aggressive 80 had taken Australia to the brink of victory. His fall brought in number nine Wally Grout, who had been chain-smoking on the balcony while watching the seventh-wicket partnership of 134.

Australia needed six runs from the final eight-ball over; Hall, renowned for his long run-up and pace, would bowl it. They still had three wickets in hand, but the second new ball, taken shortly before, was zipping off the pitch.

A leg bye from the first ball reduced the target to five runs from seven balls. Then, as he recounted in his front room in Barbados 63 years later, Hall had a chat with Worrell:

> He said, 'Look, he's going to try to hit you. I don't want you to bowl a bouncer at all.' I said, 'Oh no, not at all, I wouldn't do that. I won't do what you tell me not to.'

Hall ignored his captain's advice. 'Somehow the surge of energy came about me in the run-up,' he told me. 'The ball flew, good pace and good height.' Attempting a hook for four to bring the scores level, Benaud top-edged the bouncer to keeper Gerry Alexander; he fell for 52.

Hall turned to Worrell: 'Skipper, we got him.' Worrell replied, icily, 'What did I tell you? If that ball had gone maybe half of an inch up, it would have gone higher, do you know what would have happened?' Hall said, 'Well, he would have got four or six.' Worrell then called Hall and said, 'Let us forget that, we have a match to win, or not to lose anyhow.'

'It was a bumper delivered with every bit of speed and power the big fella could muster,' Benaud wrote. 'Have you ever tried so hard to do something ... concentrated so desperately that everything else was pushed out from your mind ... and then seen it disappear in a fraction of a second? Then you'll have some idea of how I felt as I passed Grout at the other end and said: "All yours, Wal."'

New man Ian Meckiff blocked his first ball, leaving Australia needing five from five balls. When the next ball went to Alexander, the batters tried to scrambled a bye; the ball was thrown to Hall. 'I should have steadied myself and thrown,' he recalled. 'I should have bowled it and I reckon I would have hit the middle stump.' Instead, Hall's hasty throw missed a simple chance to run out Meckiff, reducing Australia's target to four runs from four balls.

Next delivery, Hall sensed that Grout was anticipating a bouncer.

I pitched the ball right up. He sort of scooped the ball, that's the only word I can use, right up in the air. I've often wondered how could you field that, nobody was there. It was about 20 yards to midwicket. I didn't see anybody. I ran to the thing and got there, I was pretty quick. As I caught the ball, I hit [Rohan] Kanhai – a very short man – my elbow hit his head and I was in real trouble. I turned and said, 'The good Lord has left us.' He said to me words that were not complimentary to my mother and father. I said, 'What you said to me is true, I feel that way!' He realised how mournful I was that he actually came up and helped me. 'Don't worry about it, let's go again.'

Instead of being caught, Grout ran a single, leaving Australia requiring three from three balls.

Meckiff forced Hall's next delivery through the on side; the pair ran two, then turned back for the winning run. Instead, a rapid, precise throw from the deep by Conrad Hunte ran out Grout, who was returning to the non-striker's end. With the scores level and Australia nine wickets down, Lindsay Kline arrived at the crease with two balls remaining. Meckiff, the non-striker, told Kline, 'We'll run for anything.'

Before the final ball, Hall was summoned by his captain, Worrell: 'Do not bowl a no-ball, because if you do, you cannot go back to Barbados.'

Just to be sure, Hall planted his back foot several yards behind the popping crease when he bowled the final ball. 'The ball was fast but not as fast as I would like it,' Hall told me. 'It was on the leg stump, he clipped it.' Meckiff, backing up a long way, immediately raced down the wicket. Fifteen yards away and from side on, with only one stump to aim at, Solomon again hit the stumps; photographer Ron Lovitt's timing was as perfect too. 'You don't think about it,' Solomon recalled. 'You just go and pick it up and . . .'

In the pandemonium, and with the Brisbane scoreboard unable to keep up, both sides proclaimed themselves winners. In the changing room, West Indies' Gerry Gomez shouted, 'We've won.' Australia's Norman O'Neill replied, 'Wait a minute, I think we've won.' At 4 a.m. in Barbados, the radio station announcer initially told listeners that West Indies had won. The truth was even more remarkable: after 83 years and 498 Tests, a Test match was tied. To Hall, 'The best thing was both teams ate together, got the food from the hotel. We were there to ten o'clock.'

The two sides each won one of the next two matches, leaving the series locked at 1–1 heading into the final two Tests. Guyanese off-spinner Lance Gibbs, whose height and accuracy transferred easily to all climes, took a hat-trick in Adelaide; West Indies set Australia 460 to win in the final innings. With an hour and 50 minutes left, Australia were 207–9. Helped by a confident appeal for a catch by Sobers off Worrell being turned down – Worrell 'thought it was plainly a catch' – allrounder Ken Mackay and number 11 Kline salvaged a draw.

The final Test was at Melbourne: a world-record 90,800 crammed in to watch the second day's play on the Saturday, and 274,000 in total attended the game. The series got the finale it deserved: a winner-takes-all final day, with Australia needing 258 to win. Opener Bob Simpson's 92 put Australia on course; West Indies – this time through their spinners, Alf Valentine and Gibbs – fought back. When the eighth wicket fell, Australia were still two runs short of their target; could the series end in another tie? West Indies dropped a catch; instead, Johnny Martin, the number ten, ran a single to level the scores. Left-arm spinner Valentine then spun a delivery past both Ken Mackay and Gerry Alexander, the wicketkeeper. The batters hared through for a bye; Australia had won an intoxicating series 2–1.

Shortly before West Indies returned home, the side drove around Melbourne on their way to a civic reception. Half a million fans lined Collins Street to bid them farewell. 'The statement which was quite frequently made and which brought a lump to my throat and tears to my eyes, was: "Come back soon,"' Worrell remembered. The series, wrote the former Australian opener Jack Fingleton, had taken 'the corpse of international cricket out of its winding sheet'. Though most Test cricket during the decade was far less enterprising, the average runs per six-ball over rose from 2.2 in the 1950s to 2.4 in the 1960s. A new trophy was inaugurated for each Australia–West Indies series: the Frank Worrell Trophy.

* * *

Three great Bajan cricketers were all born in the space of 18 months from 1924 to 1926, reputedly delivered by the same midwife. The three Ws – Frank Worrell, Everton Weekes and Clyde Walcott – grew up within a mile of each other in the parish of St Michael. They averaged a combined 54.81 in Tests, scoring 39 centuries between them, and formed one of the greatest middle orders of all time. While all were aggressive players, they also differed. Worrell was the most stylish, admired for his economical movement and late cuts. Weekes, who had an unusually wide bat, had the largest array of shots and best technique; as a boy in his yard, he kept the ball down to avoid losing his tape ball. Walcott, standing at 6 ft 1 in, was the most powerful, combining fierce driving with a robust technique. Benaud wrote, 'Could anyone be brutally elegant? If the answer is yes, that was Walcott.'

When batting together, 'We have always let one another know if a bowler has been giving us trouble,' Worrell explained. 'The batsman who was in trouble would play for a quick single, and his partner would back him to the hilt. That is why there have been a lot of quick singles when we three have been in various partnerships.'

The three Ws are among the most celebrated talent to emerge from Barbados's 166 square miles and 300,000 people: a smaller land mass than the Isle of Man, and a smaller population than Coventry. It has been this way ever since West Indies' first Test tour, to England in 1928: Bajans bowled the first Test ball for West Indies, scored the first Test run and made up seven of the squad. As of September 2024, there had been 340 West Indies Test cricketers; 91 – 27 per cent – were born in Barbados, which only has about 5 per cent of the region's population.

Perhaps more than anywhere else in the Caribbean, the history of Barbados is intertwined with cricket. Cricket had been played formally in Barbados since at least 1806. While Bajan society was deeply stratified, cricket expanded across classes. The first club for black players, Spartan, was formed in 1893.

Worrell and Walcott, part of the black middle class, emerged through the Barbados Cricket Association system, the structure created by the white ruling classes, which was long seen as racially and socially elitist. Weekes left school aged 14 with no qualifications, emerging through the Barbados Cricket League: a more inclusive structure. Created in 1937, the league was 'built on the principle of equality and justice for all', Weekes wrote. 'This meant a great deal to young men who were daily degraded by the drudgery of the cane fields.' Growing up, Sobers said, 'A coloured player had to be three times as good as a white player to play for the island.'

The two parallel structures have created multiple pathways for talented cricketers to advance. There are 80 cricket clubs in the island – 54 in the BCA and 26 in the BCL – including many with several teams. Leading schools are involved in the Barbados Cricket Association, competing alongside leading adult teams; in sport, 'playing up' has been found to accelerate skill development.

The island's geography and climate are also ideally suited to developing talent. Beaches are open to all, encouraging children to enjoy an active lifestyle and play a variety of sports freely, away from the prying eyes of coaches. Ample sunshine and an average temperature of 26–28 Celsius in every month, with a sea breeze, ensures that players can play 12 months a year. Unlike most other Caribbean islands,

Barbados is mostly made up of coral limestone – which is ideally suited to providing wickets with true bounce. The pitches encourage fast bowling: over Test history, the single most important attribute for successful teams.

Barbados's small size is better understood as an advantage. The ease of getting around the island means that the best young players are always within easy reach of other players who can challenge and test them, and don't need to waste hours travelling around. Add in Barbados's cricket culture, and a certain magic, and you have the most fecund area for Test talent in the game's history.

The three Ws all made their Test debuts within three weeks of each other in 1947/48. Two years later, they formed the middle order in England. While West Indies had enjoyed success at home to England, partly because of facing sides below full strength, they hadn't come close to winning a Test on their three previous tours there. In 1950, England expected the pattern to continue. At a function for the visiting side, a speaker said that the series was 'a good chance to try out some of the young English players for the tour of Australia in the winter', Walcott recounted. There seemed little need to revise the judgement after England's 202-run victory in the first Test at Old Trafford.

At Lord's, each of the three Ws showed their qualities. Worrell, batting at number three, hit 52 and 45; at number four, Weekes hit a brace of 63s. After securing a first innings lead of 175, Walcott's 168 not out crushed England.

To win, West Indies now had to take the last 10 wickets. Their solution was to trust in spin. In the first Test, West Indies picked two new spinners: Jamaica's unerringly accurate and brisk left-arm spinner Alf Valentine, who was only 20; and Trinidad's off-spinner Sonny Ramadhin, who was 21. Ramadhin's grandparents had been among the Indian indentured labourers who worked in the Caribbean; the first ships of Indian labourers arrived in 1838; he was the first Indo-Caribbean cricketer to represent West Indies. 'I felt very proud, because Indians didn't have much chance in those days,' Ramadhin said in 2020. 'It was only white or black players, but I opened the doors.'

Rather than an off-spinner, Ramadhin is better understood as a mystery spinner. He first learned his method bowling with a rubber ball on a road in a village in central Trinidad. Ramadhin was only 5 ft 4 in, but his lack of bounce and unusually fast action – he bowled with his long sleeves buttoned, later admitting that he didn't bowl with a straight arm – threatened the pads and stumps relentlessly. His fingers could flick the ball to spin in either direction, varying the flight, length and speed craftily.

At Lord's, it was a lethal combination. Ramadhin took 11 wickets in the Test, Valentine seven. Together, they bowled West Indies to a 326-run victory: a seismic result, whose wider significance was immediately recognised. Two years after *Empire Windrush* completed its journey from Jamaica to Tilbury, near London, West Indians packed into Lord's on the fifth day. Among them were the Trinidadian calypsonians, Lord Kitchener and Lord Beginner; as victory approached, Beginner devised a song. After West Indies won, supporters danced on the ground and sang Beginner's new song, 'Victory Calypso', celebrating how John Goddard's West Indies had defeated Norman Yardley's England:

> Cricket, lovely cricket,
> At Lord's where I saw it.
> Yardley tried his best,
> Goddard won the Test.
> They gave the crowd plenty fun,
> The second Test and West Indies won.
>   With those little pals of mine,
>   Ramadhin and Valentine.

The calypso finished:

When Washbrook's century had ended,
West Indies voices all blended.
Hats went in the air,
People shout and jump without fear.
So at Lord's was the scenery,
It's bound to go down in history.
After all was said and done,
Second Test and West Indies won!

Worrell hit centuries in the next two Tests, including 261 at Trent Bridge, to ensure that West Indies passed 500 in their first innings, setting the game up for their spin twins. In their debut series, Ramadhin and Valentine shared 59 wickets in four Tests as West Indies won 3–1. No matter the victories that followed, Lord's remained the most indelible memory. Hilary Beckles, a future West Indies historian, recalled his father's friend, who was based in England in 1950, later telling him, 'Winning the series 3–1, the first time we beat them wasn't the big thing. It was Lord's, son – going in to their own backyard and taking their chickens out of the coop and frying them on the front lawn. For me son, the empire collapse right there.'

* * *

Victory confirmed West Indies' arrival as a Test nation: only Australia and South Africa had previously won a series in England. The captain, Goddard, was one of nine white players on the 1950 tour; there were six black players and, in Ramadhin, one of Indian descent. Racial dynamics were inescapable. Weekes told Vaneisa Baksh, 'The team spirit was, um, certainly on the field it always looked good, but sometimes off the field it was not very good because the white and black thing would put its ugly face somewhere out there, somewhere along the lines . . . There was a lot of ignorance.' In 1955, when Australia toured, the hosts held a cocktail party for both sides; the three Ws were not invited.

Ever since their maiden Test, by convention, West Indies' captain was white. Jack Grant, who led in all 12 Tests he played in from 1930 to 1935, wrote:

> I was younger than all of the sixteen players, save three; and most of these sixteen had already played for the West Indies, while I had not. Yet I was the captain. It could not be disputed that my white colour was a major factor in my being given this post.

As we have seen, George Headley was West Indies' first great Test cricketer. Headley was a popular teammate with an astute cricketing mind; Jeffrey Stollmeyer, appointed West Indies captain in 1953, described Headley as having more tactical sense than any cricketer that he played with. Yet Headley was never made permanent Test captain. He led in one Test, against England in 1948, as a one-off. West Indies immediately reverted to having a white captain.

This was in keeping with wider prejudice in the Caribbean. 'The subterfuge the whites employed to keep a club for themselves was clear to me,' the protagonist observes in George Lamming's 1953 novel *In the Castle of My Skin*. Under British rule, the most prominent roles were the preserve of the white population. Cricket clubs were deeply stratified on racial and class lines. In Lamming's Barbados, Pickwick and Wanderers only admitted white members from the 1960s.

Throughout the 1950s, Worrell was, like Headley before him, the obvious choice to lead West Indies. He was an outstanding batter, useful left-arm medium-pacer, and a cricketer of great tactical acumen.

Yet Worrell was repeatedly ignored. 'What am I going to say to Frank Worrell?' Stollmeyer said when Worrell was replaced as his vice-captain by Denis Atkinson in 1954. The decision was 'preposterous', Stollmeyer wrote. Atkinson captained in Stollmeyer's absence, then succeeded him. Two other white players then followed: John Goddard, for another stint, and Gerry Alexander.

Sometimes, the decision to ignore Worrell was blamed on him missing series – he studied at Manchester University, handily for a captain getting his highest marks in social anthropology – or on his demands for players to be paid more. But West Indies also overlooked other eminently qualified black candidates. 'Frank Worrell's turn as captain was long overdue; in the same way as Everton Weekes would have been an ideal skipper,' Benaud observed.

Alexander's elevation to the captaincy in 1958 was particularly revealing. While Alexander, as wicketkeeper-batter, would score five half-centuries and a hundred during the 1960/61 series in Australia, at the time of his appointment he had played two Tests, making 0 not out, 11, 0 and 0. In March 1960, according to *Son of Grace*, Alexander wrote to the board saying that he was not comfortable captaining when Worrell was available. Alexander was aware of the racial dynamics. 'I thought the great injustice of my appointment against Pakistan in 1959/60 was not primarily to Frank Worrell but to Clyde Walcott and Everton Weekes,' he later said.

In 1957, West Indies travelled to England by boat. White amateurs enjoyed luxury facilities. Black professionals were stuck 'like Jonah, in the bowels of the ship', Weekes recounted in David Woodhouse's book *Who Only Cricket Know*, lamenting the 'Race and class issues that got in the way of team unity'. Weekes once said, 'The Board was in the hands of the rich and powerful in the region and saw players such as myself in a way that estate owners saw field hands.'

As editor of *The Nation* in Trinidad, C.L.R. James campaigned for Worrell's appointment. The selectors' 'whole point was to continue to send to populations of white people, black or brown men under a white captain', James wrote in *Beyond a Boundary*. 'The more brilliantly the black men played, the more it would emphasise to millions of English people: "Yes, they are fine players, but, funny, isn't it, they cannot be responsible for themselves – they must always have a white man to lead them."' The captaincy, Learie Constantine asserted, was 'the most obvious and apparent, some would say glaring, example of the black man being kept in his place' and the refusal to appoint a white captain 'rots the heart out of our cricket'.

In 1960, Worrell was finally awarded the role, aged 36. Unlike Headley, Worrell was not appointed merely for a solitary match. For West Indies cricket, it was the 'grand historic moment', Beckles wrote. 'Worrell was the symbol of nationalist pride, anticolonial achievement, and sociopsychological liberation.'

The preference for selecting white players significantly weakened West Indies. In 1946, Constantine lamented that 'White captains have shown a marked preference for white players, and anyone who examines the statistics of West Indies teams during this century will see clearly that better coloured players have often been deliberately excluded.'

Subsequent analysis proves Constantine right. From their first Test, in 1928, until Worrell's first Test as skipper in 1960, all batters not classed as white had an average of 42.15 when batting in the top seven. White top-seven batters averaged just 28.04, an analysis by the sports economist Stefan Szymanski found.

Perhaps the most blatant instance of prejudice affected Andy Ganteaume. On Test debut in 1948, Ganteaume, a man of black and Indian descent, scored 112 against England in his home country, Trinidad. Ganteaume was dropped for the next Test, ostensibly for slow scoring, and never played again. 'The aristocracy had to be kept up and the establishment boys had to have a share of the pie,' Ganteaume wrote. 'The welfare of West Indies cricket was incidental.'

* * *

When he assumed the job, Worrell was the envy of every other captain: he could call upon the best player in the world, the greatest rival to Don Bradman for the mantle of finest Test cricketer ever.

If much of Test cricket was monochrome, Sobers played in glorious Technicolor. Most cricketers of the age were one-dimensional, or two-dimensional at best. Sobers had five dimensions: his left-handed batting, left-arm pace bowling, left-arm orthodox spin, left-arm wrist spin, and his effervescent fielding, principally as a close catcher.

As a boy in Barbados, Sobers played 'Lilliputian cricket', using a lump of tar as a ball and carving a piece of wood into the right shape for a bat. Every Sunday morning, Sobers played beach cricket with a tennis ball. Here, he developed his distinctive high backlift and relish for playing off the back foot.

'Throughout the West Indies you find that many play off the back foot and on the up because you cannot drive a tennis ball off the front foot – the bounce is too big,' he wrote. 'You either drive off the back foot or you play across the line of the ball because it was always bouncing above the height of the stumps.' These experiences informed Sobers's batting:

> My attitude was that if you played off the back foot, by the time the ball reached you it had gone so far you could leave it as you watched it move . . . No one told me or showed me what to do; I was completely self-taught. I watched and listened, took in what I thought would benefit me and rejected the rest.

Aged 21, Sobers announced himself with his maiden Test century: 365, a new world record, against Pakistan in Jamaica in 1958. It was the first of 26 Test hundreds, made with orthodoxy and sometimes breathtaking pace. 'I liked to attack,' Sobers wrote. 'Fear is the worst enemy of every cricketer. I decided from an early age that I could not afford to be scared of a bowler . . . They had the ball and I had the bat, and I was always determined that they were not going to dictate to me.'

Sobers's average of 57.78 would have been even greater had his performances for the Rest of the World in two unofficial Test series been included. This included 254 at the Melbourne Cricket Ground in 1971/72, an innings that Bradman considered 'probably the greatest exhibition of batting ever seen in Australia'. When Sobers powered a straight drive down the ground, it was said: 'Not a man move.'

Napping on the balcony in his pads, Sobers was only woken up when he was due in. 'That was the time for sleeping,' Sobers said; he had little time for sleeping after hours. In the 1973 Lord's Test, aged 36, Sobers was 31 not out overnight. He was out the entire night. 'We drank until about 9 o'clock, then I got a cold shower, walked up to Lord's, got my pads on and walked out as the umpires called play.' He hit a regal 150 not out.

It created an illusion of effortless genius, which Sobers was little inclined to play down. But in his 2003 autobiography, he outlines his method. Sobers generally batted with care in the first 20 minutes of an innings, especially in seaming English conditions:

> There are many things you have to weigh up when you go in to bat – the position of the game, what needs to be done for your team, what risks you should or shouldn't take, how you are going to plan your innings. It is not just natural ability that makes a batsman great; the planning in those early minutes is crucial . . .
>
> I would weigh everything up, decide the most likely way I was going to get out – and eliminate it. I may have thought that the only way I could give up my wicket on that particular day was by being caught in the slips, so everything outside the off stump I would leave well alone . . .
>
> Once you cover the stumps and the ball is outside your body, there is no way it can hit the woodwork.

Ian Chappell, who was later Australia's captain, was breaking into the first-class game when he played alongside Sobers for South Australia. 'Sobers is far and away the best cricketer I've ever seen,' Chappell says. 'Garry was a cricket genius, but importantly he knew how he did it. Not just batting. He knew how he bowled. He knew about fielding, he knew everything about cricket.

'I remember saying to Garry, "Mate, I've got a bit of a problem. Have you got any suggestions?" Garry said, "Son, go and get a bottle of beer." And he told me three things that I did for the rest of my career.' The first was 'Take a leg-stump guard rather than centre as your first move is back and across. That way you will still cover off stump but also know when the ball is on your pads.' The second was 'Bat just outside your crease to the pace bowlers because of your first move.' The third: 'Always have scoring runs as your priority.'

For most of his 93 Tests, Sobers's bowling alone would have commanded a place. New-ball swing was his most effective strand; he snared 235 wickets at 34.03. Sobers, the Australian writer Ray Robinson said, was 'evolution's ultimate specimen in cricketers'.

The judgement was particularly impossible to dispute in England in 1966. By now captain, after replacing Worrell, Sobers hit 161 in the first Test, 163 not out in the second, sharing a double-century stand with his cousin David Holford, and 94 in the third, helping West Indies go 2–0 up. At Headingley, Sobers first hit 174, square-cutting, pulling and driving imperiously. Then, after declaring on 500–9, Sobers switched between pace and wrist spin. His match haul of 8–80 bowled West Indies to an innings victory. In West Indies' 3–1 series win, Sobers scored 722 runs at 103.14 while taking 20 wickets at 27.25: the lone occasion a cricketer has both scored 700 runs and taken 20 wickets in a Test series.

'I seem to have spent a lot of time, this summer, sitting in front of the TV watching Garfield Sobers,' the English playwright J.B. Priestley wrote. 'Always I have stared at him out of a mixture of apprehension and admiration. He frightened me and enchanted me by turns. Batting, bowling, fielding, captaining his side, he seemed to be pronouncing, often with a grin, the doom of the England XI.'

Sobers was doing the work of several men: that was exactly the point. In 1959, Sobers and his friend, the Jamaican allrounder Collie Smith, were playing in the Lancashire League. Smith drove with Sobers and Tom Dewdney, a Jamaican pace bowler, to a charity game. On the A34 in Staffordshire, the car collided with a cattle truck. Three days later, Smith died from his injuries.

Smith, just 26, was the first man to score centuries in his first Test against both Australia and England. In 26 Tests, he scored four centuries, and took 48 wickets with his off spin. 'He had the heart of a giant, an unquenchable ecstasy of spirit, a joyous nature and unmatchable zest for living – and for cricket,' Sobers wrote. 'I played with him inside me. Trying perhaps to give him the innings that death had denied him.'

In 2007, *Wisden* retrospectively picked the leading cricketer in the world for every year going back to 1900; Sobers was awarded the accolade for eight separate years, second only to Bradman. 'Sobers was sent to Earth by God to play cricket,' said Hanif Mohammad, the Pakistan captain. 'All good players were rolled into one player and that was Sobers.'

After the 1960/61 Australian tour, West Indies defeated India 5–0 in the Caribbean. They beat England away in 1963 and 1966, either side of recording their maiden series win over Australia. From 1964 to 1968, according to the backdated world rankings, for the first time in history, West Indies were the world's best Test team.

Sobers was the centrepiece of a wonderful, balanced side. Rohan Kanhai brought style and substance at number three, followed by Basil Butcher, who hailed from the same Guyanese village, Port Mourant. The new-ball pair of Hall and Charlie Griffith, together with off-spinner Gibbs and Sobers's different forms of left-arm bowling, gave West Indies a varied attack.

Constantine saw his prophesy come true: he would live to 'see a West Indian team, chosen on its merits alone, captained by a black player, win a rubber against England'. When Worrell retired after the 3–1 win in England in 1963, he declared, 'My aim was always to see West Indies moulded from a rabble of brilliant island individuals into a real team – and I've done it.'

10

CAPTAINCY: A TALE OF CLASS

While prospective West Indies captains were seen through the prism of race, potential England skippers were viewed through the lens of class. English cricket was divided between amateur cricketers – notionally unpaid, almost exclusively public school-educated and from upper-class backgrounds – and professional 'players', who were paid to play. The stratification continued after World War II, even when other aspects of British society were becoming more meritocratic.

Amateur and professional cricketers stayed in different hotels, used different changing rooms, and even entered grounds through different gates. Butlers serving sherry would greet amateurs coming in for lunch, unbeknown to the professionals downstairs. Scoreboards reflected the discrimination, referring to gentlemen like P.B.H. May by their full initials and surnames, and professionals like Fred Trueman simply by their surnames.

In their very first Tests, England occasionally had professional captains. As the notion of a Test match became more clearly defined, the principle that the captain must be a gentleman hardened. From 1887 to 1952, all England's captains were amateurs. 'Pray God, no professional shall ever captain England,' said Lord Hawke, Yorkshire's captain and a prominent figure at MCC in the early 20th century, in 1925. 'I love and admire them all, but we have always had an amateur skipper and when the day comes when we shall have no more amateurs captaining England it will be a thousand pities.'

The unspoken convention that the team should be captained by an amateur often weakened England: many such amateurs were not worth their places in the side. This approach contravened Australia's principle that the captain should be selected only from those who would otherwise get into the team. Australia did not have the amateur–professional divide; until the 1980s, their players were effectively semi-professional – all playing for money, but almost invariably working in other jobs too.

During the early years of the Ashes, many considered Australia's different approach to captaincy a reason for their small, but enduring, edge. 'I have heard some English captains speak to their professionals like dogs,' said Joe Darling, who played for Australia against England from 1894 to 1905.

In England, the amateur captains – who were almost invariably batters – were expected to lead; the professionals did what they were told. Australia's captain 'receives the benefit of the opinions of his comrades as if he were chairman of a board of directors', observed Jim Phillips, who umpired 15 Ashes Tests during the 1890s. 'The average English captain is more of an autocrat. He rarely seeks advice from his men. If a consultation be held it is invariably confined to the amateurs and the batsmen, not the professionals and the bowlers.'

As standards improved, it became harder to be a genuine bon vivant amateur and play well enough. 'Shamateurism', first pioneered by W.G. Grace, became more common. Nominal amateurs were given additional work by counties – often in an administrative role like a secretary – or even received illicit payments so they could continue to afford to play for 'free'.

On England tours, gentlemen were 'compensated' for the costs of running their farms or estate, receiving far more than the professionals did in salaries. In 1958, the professional Jim Laker requested that he be given amateur status for an Ashes tour, because amateurs received a considerably greater allowance – and tax-free – than the professionals did in salary. Laker's request irked the English establishment and was turned down by the chairman of selectors, the former amateur Gubby Allen.

In 1938, Wally Hammond switched from professional to amateur to make him an acceptable choice as Test captain. Hammond joined the board of directors of a tyre company, who guaranteed that he could play as much cricket as he would like, letting him do so in exchange for the publicity. 'I was the same man as before, or perhaps I even had a declining skill,' Hammond wrote. 'But because I changed my label all was well . . . I submit this is illogical.'

After Hammond retired in 1947, England's next three captains appointed on a permanent basis – Norman Yardley, George Mann and Freddie Brown – all attended elite private schools and Cambridge University. None were players of the top rank. In 1951/52, Nigel Howard, an uncapped amateur batter who had averaged just 23.84 in first-class cricket the previous English summer, was named captain for the Test tour of India. Howard averaged 17.20 in his four Tests. It was an extreme example of a persistent trend: especially when touring, England's captain was often not worth his place in the side. In the first ten Ashes tours organised by MCC, from 1903/04 to 1950/51, all England captains were amateur. None made a century; in these 50 Tests, England captains averaged 22.36 with the bat and 34.11 with the ball.

In 1952, English cricket's class ceiling was broken by Len Hutton, who became the first professional captain for 65 years. Even Hutton was seen as a fairly conservative choice: he was a long-serving member of the side and had over 100 first-class centuries. 'When I'd put the phone down,' he later said, 'I wondered what I'd let myself in for.' Discussing selection with amateur administrators and selectors, Hutton 'felt rather like a head boy called to a meeting of house masters'. In his early Tests, he still unconsciously referred to Brown, the former captain, as 'skipper'.

Hutton's success was celebrated far beyond England. In 1954, six years before Frank Worrell's appointment as West Indies captain,

Learie Constantine said that Hutton's appointment 'in the most conservative of all English sports' held out the hope that the game could be run 'irrespective of colour' too.

Even Hutton's reign did not destroy class divisions. After Hutton, England's next four captains, until 1966, were all amateurs. In the 1946–61 period of Ashes cricket, 32.3 per cent of England players in the series had amateur status – more than in any previous era, David Horspool noted in *More Than a Game*. Typical of the different treatment of amateurs and professionals was England's trip across Sindh province in Pakistan in 1955/56. While amateurs travelled in an air-conditioned coach to protect them from oppressive heat, Simon Wilde detailed in *The Tour*, the professionals slummed it without air conditioning.

An MCC investigation into the gentleman–player divide in 1958 found that 'the distinctive status of the amateur cricketer was not obsolete, was of great value to the game and should be preserved'. On the 1958/59 Ashes tour, MCC tour manager Freddie Brown, the former England captain, insisted that professional players abide by the convention of addressing Peter May, an amateur who succeeded Hutton, as 'Mr' or 'skipper', and not use his forename. In the County Championship, 13 of the 17 regular first-class captains were amateurs as late as 1962. A spiky six-hour meeting at Lord's in November that year abolished the distinction between gentlemen and players for good. After 156 years, the division was over; the fixtures between the two, which some had once considered a highlight of summer, were immediately discontinued. Yet some divisions still remained. In Australia in 1962/63, weeks after the abolition of the amateur–player divide, the Duke of Norfolk was chosen as tour manager. 'None of the professionals were ever invited to dinner,' England's Ray Illingworth lamented. 'All the amateurs dined with the Duke of Norfolk and that created divisions.'

During the age of amateur captains and beyond, the England captaincy was dominated by graduates from Oxford or Cambridge

The very first Test match tour: England's squad in Australia in 1876/77.

'The Demon Bowler': Fred Spofforth, destroyer of England.

'The Croucher': Gilbert Jessop scored one of England's most celebrated Test centuries in 1902.

Left: 'The *Midsummer Night's Dream* of cricket': Kumar Shri Ranjitsinhji.

Below: The Golden Age incarnate: Australia's Victor Trumper.

Above: The greatest opening pair: Jack Hobbs (in cap) and Herbert Sutcliffe walking out to bat.

Below: Bodyline: a crowd of English fielders lie in wait during the 1932/33 Ashes.

Above: Don Bradman in his characteristic stance. Bradman's batting average, 99.94, remains Test cricket's most iconic number.

Left: 'Every boy who felt his worth as a batsman called himself George Headley.' West Indies' first great Test cricketer.

Below: The bon vivant Keith Miller during the Victory Tests in 1945, which marked cricket's resumption after World War II.

'There were grave suggestions in certain quarters that Pakistan should not have been given Test status': Pakistan answered this criticism with a stunning win on their maiden tour of England in 1954, sealed by Hanif Mohammad's run-out.

'We've won'.
'Wait a minute, I think we've won.'
Joe Solomon's direct hit produced one of Test cricket's greatest photos – and the first tied Test in history – when West Indies visited Brisbane in 1960.

Above: Garry Sobers in his prime: 1966.

Right: Basil D'Oliveira 158 at The Oval in 1968 – the most important innings in Test history?

Left: Richie Benaud: one of Test cricket's finest allrounders. Later he became even more famous as a commentator.

Below: Sunil Gavaskar, Indian cricket's first superstar.

The original West Indies pace quartet: Andy Roberts, Michael Holding, Colin Croft and Joel Garner.

University. Between December 1948 and 1966, eight out of England's ten captains attended Oxford or Cambridge. Between 1930 and 1977, 15 out of 28 England captains attended one of the two universities. This Oxbridge influence was also detectable elsewhere. Between 1930 and 1982, another 14 Oxbridge graduates captained Pakistan (four), West Indies (four), India (three), South Africa (two) or New Zealand (one).

For Pakistan's first 40 years as a Test team, there was a strong influence of what Javed Miandad, a captain who was not one of this group, called 'The Oxbridge Complex'. The captains Abdul Kardar, Javed Burki, Majid Khan and Imran Khan all attended Oxford or Cambridge University; several other captains attended elite Pakistani schools.

'English-speaking skills are an important consideration in appointing the Pakistani captain,' Miandad wrote. He lamented a 'tendency in Pakistan cricket in which players with an Oxford or Cambridge background have been overvalued, and players far removed from such a background have been undervalued. It is an injustice that was part of our cricket from the earliest days.'

* * *

Richie Benaud, Worrell's opponent in the 1960/61 Australia–West Indies series, was also a seminal figure in Test captaincy. While no other captain can match Worrell's social importance, there was still something notable about Benaud when he was appointed: he was a bowler.

The salience of class in determining who led sides was intertwined with a preference for batters to be captain. From cricket's earliest days, when landowners enlisted labourers to bowl to them, batting was seen as more glamorous than bowling. As Fred Spofforth, Australia's demon fast bowler in the late 19th century, observed: 'I may safely state that bowling is not nearly so popular with players as batting, for the reason that there is not the same amount of immediate pleasure to be derived from it, and a great deal more hard work is required in order to reach a standard of moderate proficiency.'

As of January 2025, 66 Test players have captained in 25 or more matches. The list comprises 51 batsmen, three wicketkeepers, and 12 players who were either allrounders – including Garry Sobers, Imran Khan and Kapil Dev, three of the best of all time – or bowlers. The default preference for batters as captain holds regardless of nation, or even whether the bowler is a quick or a spinner. Eighteen men have captained in 50 Tests; all bar India's keeper M.S. Dhoni have been specialist batters.

'I have great admiration for anybody who does a good job of captaining a side as a bowler,' says Ian Chappell, the former Australia captain. 'If you're walking back to bowl, you can't be thinking too much about who you're going to bowl next over – you've got to be thinking about what delivery you are going to bowl. It's easier for me as a batsman to stand at first slip, thinking about who I might be bowling next or where the field's got to be.'

When bowlers are captains too, it is often feared that it will hinder their performance. Unlike batters, bowlers must simultaneously juggle their primary playing skill and the tactical challenges of captaincy. Don Bradman believed that bowlers, especially quicks, 'should never be captains – they either under-bowl or over-bowl themselves'.

Yet there can be advantages for bowler-captains. Imran Khan, whose haul of 187 wickets while captaining is a Test record, wrote:

> I think that being a bowler helped my captaincy a great deal. Having bowled in different conditions, I felt confident of handling my attack, and capable of advising the younger bowlers in the side. It was easy for me to advise and encourage them, because I understood what they were trying to do.
>
> When I was younger, I always resented a batsman telling me how to bowl; it was much easier to accept criticism from a fellow bowler.

The standard captain's remark – just bowl a line and length – is useless: every fool knows that you should be bowling a line and length, but what matters is why you are not doing so. I used to study a bowler's run-up and delivery, and suggest what he might be doing wrong, or slight alterations which might improve his bowling.

The records of the few players to combine leadership with front-line bowling responsibilities suggests that the personal form of bowler-captains need not suffer. Of the 12 bowlers or allrounders to captain in at least 25 Tests up to January 2025, eight have better bowling averages when captaining. And, of the 12 batters to captain the most, nine average more when captaining. Both batters and bowlers who are appointed captain tend to be in their playing prime, and perform better than overall in their careers.

Benaud is one such example. After being appointed Australia captain in 1958, he adopted a consultative leadership style, explaining 'eleven heads are better than one'. Defying the era's stifling orthodoxy, Benaud's instinct was to attack, deploying close catchers and shuffling his field to create new challenges. He captained in seven series; Australia won five and drew two, losing just four of his 28 Tests in charge.

As captain, Benaud's individual contribution was outstanding: he took 138 wickets at an average of 25.78, three lower than his average in the ranks. His graceful leg spin claimed 31 wickets as England were beaten 4–0 in the 1958/59 Ashes, and 47 wickets in eight Tests as Australia won back-to-back series against Pakistan and India in 1959/60.

Never was Benaud's impact greater than in the 1961 Ashes Test at Old Trafford. The series was tied at 1–1 heading into the fourth Test; as reigning Ashes holders, Australia needed one more win to ensure that they would retain the urn.

After exploiting moisture in the wicket to bowl Australia out for 190, England dominated. On three occasions, Australia faced crushing defeat. First, England reached 358–6 in their first innings before losing their last four wickets for nine runs. Then, Australia were 334–9 in their second innings, a lead of just 157. Alan Davidson, who combined left-arm swing bowling with belligerent hitting from number seven or eight, thrashed 77 not out to add 98 for the last wicket. It lifted England's target to 256 in three hours and 50 minutes. 'We'll do these jokers, Rich,' Davidson told his captain in the changing room. But with the austere Raman Subba Row combining with Ted Dexter, driving with his usual elan, England reached 150–1 on the final afternoon. Australia, this time, seemed to have no escape route left.

On a fifth-day pitch, Benaud had loomed as Australia's greatest threat. He was struggling with a shoulder injury, which reduced how much spin he could generate. Benaud did not believe he could contain England enough to draw and sought wickets, he wrote in *A Tale of Two Tests*. He walked across to Neil Harvey, his vice-captain:

> 'We've had it as far as saving this, "Ninna". The only way we'll get out of it is to win.'
>
> He looked at me, and gave a bit of a grin.
>
> 'Get into it then,' he said. 'I'm with you.'

The night before, Benaud discussed with Ray Lindwall, who had recently retired, the idea of bowling around the wicket to right-handers. 'After a lot of thought he said that while it was unusual, he could see nothing against it – providing the bowler was accurate,' Benaud recalled. 'He could visualise the effect on batsmen going for runs with the ball jumping out of a line of footholes.'

Benaud started to bowl around the wicket to the right-handed Dexter, aiming to use the rough created outside the leg stump, which made up for his shoulder injury inhibiting his turn. Dexter cover-drove a four in Benaud's first over with his new tactic. But in Benaud's second over bowling around the wicket to him, Dexter could not score from the first five balls. The sixth delivery was a top-spinner; the ball kissed Dexter's outside edge and was well taken by Wally Grout, who had placed a bet on Australia to win.

CAPTAINCY: A TALE OF CLASS

In Benaud's next over, he bowled to Peter May, England's captain. The ball missed the rough, instead pitching on leg stump, causing May no alarm. Benaud told himself, 'Get it further out, you idiot.' The next ball, Benaud landed the ball into the footmarks outside leg stump. May shaped to sweep and was bowled around his legs, falling for a second-ball duck.

While Dexter was batting serenely, England had been on course for victory. After the two quick wickets, England now faced a dilemma: still strive to win, or try to bat out a draw? Number five, the left-hander Brian Close, thumped a six over long-on but continued trying to sweep Benaud from the footmarks outside his off stump: five times in ten balls. The fifth time, he top-edged to square leg: 'that grotesque stroke', John Arlott wrote.

Benaud had toiled for more than 50 overs during the Test without a wicket. Then, in the space of 25 balls either side of tea, he took 5–12. As captain, Benaud had one more trick left. Sensing that tailender Fred Trueman would be unable to resist a swipe, he brought on part-time leg-spinner Bob Simpson; Benaud himself took the catch at slip.

Twenty minutes from the close, Davidson bowled Brian Statham out of the rough, to seal a 54-run win; a draw in the final Test secured the series 2–1. Only twice before in Test cricket had a team overcome a bigger first innings deficit than Australia's 177 and won.

The captain celebrated with champagne on the balcony, chuckling about Australia's fortune: a sliver of an edge from Dexter had precipitated England losing their last nine wickets for 51 runs. To Benaud, it embodied the game's maddening nature:

> Have you ever stopped to think about the amount of luck necessary to win a Test match . . . or about the fine dividing line between success and failure. If that ball had spun another quarter of an inch or even landed on the seam it would have missed the edge of the bat and England would have been lionised in the National Press the next day, instead of being flayed.

11

THE SOUTH AFRICA QUESTION

The man lay in the middle of the road in agony. His leg was broken; he had been hit by a car while cycling. Yet when a policeman arrived at the scene, his focus was not on the cyclist's well-being. 'He was drunk, wasn't he?' the policeman asked one onlooker, referring to the injured cyclist. Then, he turned to another: 'He's always drunk, isn't he?' The men – who were black, and so had reason to fear the police – nodded. The case was closed.

An England Test cricketer, Alan Oakman, was driving the car that evening in Cape Town in 1956/57; Jim Laker, his teammate, was alongside him. While the man lay in pain, onlookers asked the England players for autographs: 'a particularly striking example of the general attitude to the coloured folk', Laker wrote. This, he observed, 'is what white men call justice'. Oakham visited the man in hospital the next day, giving him some money.

Cricketers who toured South Africa were expected to keep their focus on the field, with ample time for cocktail parties, tennis and swimming – and leave politics alone. Before the 1956/57 tour, Viscount Monckton, the MCC president, addressed the squad. 'He reminded us of South Africa's problems, and told us that colour, as a topic of conversation, was strictly out,' Laker recalled. 'It was something never to be mentioned.'

On board the *Edinburgh Castle*, the boat taking the team to South Africa in 1956, a parcel was delivered for the England team manager, Freddie Brown. It contained copies of a book – *Naught for Your Comfort* by the English clergyman Trevor Huddleston – which documented the inhumanity of apartheid. A few days later, Brown was told that the side would be 'in trouble at Cape Town if we tried to get the book through customs', England's Colin Cowdrey wrote. Brown threw the books into the Bay of Biscay.

* * *

'Today South Africa belongs to us once more,' D.F. Malan proclaimed when his National Party, an ultra-nationalist Afrikaner party, won the 1948 general election. The new government enacted the policies of apartheid – 'separateness' in Afrikaans – which would be maintained by over 300 laws. The best education, public spaces and jobs were reserved for white people; the remaining 80 per cent of the population, it has been calculated, could only access 13.5 per cent of the country's land. The entire population were registered according to their racial group, with the notorious 'pencil test for hair' one method used. This tore families apart; siblings could be classed as either white or coloured, depending on the classification of their skin. Marriage between racial groups was barred.

When South Africa left the Commonwealth in 1961, driven by opposition to apartheid, the team were technically ineligible to play Test matches. Australia, England and New Zealand simply ignored the Imperial Cricket Conference's own regulations: continuing to play against South Africa, and considering such games Tests. At Cape Town in 1964/65, H.F. Verwoerd, the prime minister, was a guest of honour and visited England's dressing room.

From their first Test in 1889, South Africa's selectors had only picked players classed as white. Before apartheid, South Africa did not play a single Test against India or West Indies, only playing Australia, England and New Zealand.

After the googly quartet's heyday in the 1900s, South Africa's fortunes declined notably, barring consecutive 1–0 series wins over England in 1930/31 and 1935. The first stirrings of a revival came at

Trent Bridge in 1951: captain Dudley Nourse's 208 set up the country's first Test victory in 16 years.

While South Africa's first successful Test era came through wrist spin, their second was underpinned by Hugh Tayfield's off spin. Tayfield went 137 consecutive deliveries without yielding a run against England at Durban in 1956/57; in more than 2,000 Test overs, he never bowled a wide or a no-ball. He combined unrelenting accuracy with height, often delivering the ball from around the wicket to right-handers to cramp batters. Against England at Johannesburg in 1956/57, Tayfield bowled unchanged on the last day, delivering 35 consecutive eight-ball overs, not ceasing until the match was won by 17 runs. *Wisden* ranked his 9–113 the greatest bowling performance of the 20th century.

During the mid-1950s, Tayfield was one of the world's best bowlers. His subtle changes of pace and shrewd deployment of his field – often using silly mid-on and silly mid-off and creating an enticing gap to drive through extra cover – made him unusually adaptable. Tayfield's 30 wickets in Australia in 1952/53, supported by dynamic fielding, secured a 2–2 draw, the first time that an opponent other than England had drawn a series down under.

* * *

It was a pernicious myth that cricket was not played among the non-white South African population. But the onset of formal apartheid devastated cricket. In the Western Cape, for instance, suburbs were designated as white group areas; clubs that black cricketers used were forced to relocate or disband altogether. In 1953, a South African 'Indian' team, comprising men of Indian heritage, was selected to tour India, replicating a similar trip in 1922. Just before the team boarded their ship in Durban, the Minister of the Interior revoked their passports.

THE SOUTH AFRICA QUESTION

Cricket carried on despite these challenges. In 1956/57, a South Africa side hosted Kenya for a series of unofficial Tests: players from all racial groups were eligible, but national laws barred white people from playing alongside other races. This side were the first ever non-racial South African international cricket team. The South African Cricket Board of Control, who ran the sport for non-white people, asked if they could join the Imperial Cricket Conference in 1955. They did not even get a response.

The non-racial South African team won six and drew one of their seven 'Tests' against sides from Kenya, Uganda and East Africa. These results made no difference to how many leading figures in white South African cricket regarded them. 'One excellent reason we are not ready for [mixed-race sport] is that there are no African, Indian or Cape Coloured rugby footballers, cricketers or athletes whose ability or exploits would justify their selection ahead of White candidates for South Africa,' John Waite, the side's Test wicketkeeper from 1951 to 1965, wrote. These words ignored the talent outside the confines of white cricket, including a man who could have lifted up South Africa's Test batting.

Basil D'Oliveira, who hailed from Cape Town, was not certain of his exact ancestry. He described it as 'a combination of either Indian and White or African and White' and was classed as coloured. He grew up playing at Green Point, a park in east Cape Town that overlooks Signal Hill, the segregated coloured area in which he lived. A star of the black leagues – in one game he hit 225, out of a total of 236, in 75 minutes – he captained St Augustine's, the premier Cape Town club, just as his father had done. D'Oliveira received little coaching, relying on familial advice, his own instincts and wisdom gleaned from Sir Donald Bradman's *Art of Cricket*, a cherished present from his aunt.

When Tests were played at Newlands, the spectacular ground in Cape Town that overlooks Table Mountain, D'Oliveira was only allowed to watch them from 'the cage', a small section of the ground for 'non-European' spectators. As a boy, D'Oliveira 'always supported the visiting country – after all, they weren't denying me the chance to play in such a magnificent stadium'.

D'Oliveira was appointed the inaugural captain of a non-racial South Africa side, in 1956. He thrived, averaging 55.87 with the bat and 15.86 with his medium pace over five 'Tests'. All the while, D'Oliveira earned a living at a printing works. Desperate to forge a professional cricket career, D'Oliveira wrote a letter in green ink to John Arlott, *The Guardian*'s cricket correspondent. When touring South Africa with England in 1948, Arlott had been horrified by racial stratification: 'human', he told a customs officer who asked him about his race. He vowed never to return while apartheid remained.

Others in English cricket took a very different view. After Arlott described the South African government as 'predominantly a Nazi one', noting the significant cabinet support for Germany in World War II, England keeper Godfrey Evans lamented that it was 'tactless and made it awkward for us with our friends over there'. Denis Compton, who had strong ties to South Africa, considered Arlott hypocritical, the historian David Rayvern Allen wrote.

In 1960, helped by Arlott's advocacy, D'Oliveira signed with Middleton as a professional in the Lancashire League; friends paid the airfares for Basil, his wife and their newborn son. In his first year, D'Oliveira outscored even Garry Sobers. D'Oliveira's dream was to play county cricket, qualifying through residency. Lancashire did not want to sign him. D'Oliveira was recruited by Worcestershire before the 1964 season; arcane qualification rules prevented him from playing in the County Championship until 1965. By now D'Oliveira was 33; shrewdly, he lied about his age, proclaiming to be born in 1934, rather than 1931 – though some suggest that he was actually born in 1928. In his first Championship season, D'Oliveira was one of only two players to score 1,500 runs; also contributing with his accurate swing bowling, he helped Worcestershire win the title. 'D'Oliveira did everything we hoped he might do and a lot more,' his captain, Don Kenyon, said.

Next summer, D'Oliveira made his Test debut for England at Lord's. 'This is a fairy tale come true,' he said. 'Six years ago, I was playing on mudheaps. Now I have played for England and met the Queen.' D'Oliveira scored three consecutive half-centuries against West Indies in his debut series, and was also a useful fourth seamer.

While D'Oliveira always preferred to speak of cricket, others recognised his wider significance. 'The whole of Africa was watching D'Oliveira's success and the majority, in South Africa, in particular rejoicing at this demonstration of the irrationality which prevents such a man from playing for the country of his birth,' C.L.R. James wrote in 1966. 'I am not African but I revelled in it.' D'Oliveira scored his maiden Test century against India the following year and was named one of *Wisden*'s Five Cricketers of the Year for 1967. His first blemish as a Test cricketer was in the Caribbean in 1967/68; not helped by a new penchant for late-night drinking, he averaged just 22.83 with the bat. 'I lived too well,' he admitted.

* * *

In March 1968, John Vorster, South Africa's prime minister, told Lord Cobham, England's senior viscount and a former MCC president, that England's tour at the end of the year would be cancelled if D'Oliveira was picked. Cobham then relayed the message to MCC grandees. But, Richard Parry and André Odendaal wrote in *Swallows and Hawke*, senior MCC figures, who included former prime minister Alec Douglas-Home, 'decided not to report Vorster's position and advised the committee to drop the request for assurances and wait until the party was selected'. Effectively, a wait-and-see strategy.

D'Oliveira later said that he was placed under pressure by senior MCC figures. In June, just before the second Ashes Test, D'Oliveira attended the customary pre-match dinner at Lord's. During the evening, Peter Oborne wrote in *Basil D'Oliveira: Cricket and Conspiracy*, MCC secretary Billy Griffith suggested to D'Oliveira that he declare that he wanted to represent South Africa, not England, saying that it was the only way in which the tour could be saved. 'Either you respect me as an England player or you don't,' D'Oliveira replied.

Together with external pressure on MCC not to pick D'Oliveira against South Africa, and the requests that he skip the tour, a third tactic was also deployed: offering a huge sum of money for an alternative winter engagement. With Vorster's encouragement, Oborne documented, Tienie Oosthuizen, from the tobacco company Carreras, offered D'Oliveira £4,000 a year, with a house and car thrown in, to coach for the South African Sports Federation, from 1968/69. D'Oliveira's work would be to coach coloured people; the offered salary was several times more than he was making as a professional cricketer.

The snag was that D'Oliveira would not be able to play for England that winter. Oosthuizen attempted to befriend D'Oliveira, who seemingly wanted to keep his offer in play should he not be selected. Oosthuizen pressurised D'Oliveira by setting a deadline before MCC's squad for the tour was picked. The offer looked particularly attractive when, in July, D'Oliveira did not receive one of the 30 letters MCC sent to potential tour candidates, enquiring about their winter availability. After his agent learned that he was being considered for the tour, D'Oliveira rejected the offer for good. D'Oliveira wanted, he later said, 'to prove that I could bat and that people from the Black and Coloured community, whatever you like to call it, know how to conduct themselves'.

Against this backdrop, D'Oliveira somehow had to perform in the 1968 Ashes. In the first Test, D'Oliveira, picked as an allrounder, made 87 not out, the lone English half-century. Yet he was dropped for the next Test; Colin Cowdrey said that England wanted a seam-bowling allrounder rather than one, like D'Oliveira, who bowled swing. The curiosity was that D'Oliveira was seemingly not considered as a specialist batter. It is very possible – especially when allied to his omission from the list of 30 tour probables – that

D'Oliveira was dropped on account of selectors' sympathies for South Africa.

In the weeks ahead, D'Oliveira struggled in county cricket. He regained his form just in time to be placed on stand-by for the fifth Test; two players then pulled out. When opener Roger Prideaux withdrew too, citing pleurisy, D'Oliveira was recalled. He would bat at number six.

Late on day one, D'Oliveira arrived at the crease with England 238–4. He produced the performance of a lifetime: a dominant 158, marked by powerful hooks, which helped to set up England's 226-run victory and a drawn series. The routine chance missed by wicketkeeper Barry Jarman, when D'Oliveira had 31, was the most consequential drop in Test history. 'Oh Christ, you've put the cat among the pigeons now,' umpire Charlie Elliott told D'Oliveira when he reached his century.

While England supporters willed him on, D'Oliveira's progress was greeted with horror by the National government: Oosthuizen was summoned to Vorster's office to follow the Test. Surrey's secretary, Geoffrey Howard, received a phone call swiftly after D'Oliveira was out with a message to pass on to Griffith, the MCC secretary: 'If today's centurion is picked, the tour is off.'

At 8 p.m. on 27 August, a few hours after England's victory across town at The Oval, the MCC squad to tour South Africa was picked in the committee room at Lord's. As well as the four selectors, half a dozen other English cricketing luminaries, including the tour manager, captain, MCC secretary and assistant secretary, MCC president and MCC treasurer, were all in the room. The meeting would last until 2 a.m.

When the squad was announced, D'Oliveira was not among the 16 names. 'No open mind will believe that he was left out for valid cricket reasons,' *The Guardian*'s John Arlott wrote. Jim Swanton, *The Daily Telegraph* cricket correspondent, mocked 'the paradoxical – some would even say ludicrous – theory [that] has been put forward that this cricketer, who learned the game under the shadow of Table Mountain, is essentially a man for English conditions'.

Exactly what was said in the meeting will never be known. Mike Brearley, a Middlesex player and MCC member at the time and future England captain, was later told that Doug Insole, the chairman of selectors, had originally picked D'Oliveira in the final squad. The likeliest explanation, Parry and Odendaal suggest, is that, in the early hours of 28 August, Gubby Allen, MCC treasurer and a former England captain, persuaded the selectors to deselect D'Oliveira.

In 2014, Insole said that Colin Cowdrey, the England captain, did not push for D'Oliveira's inclusion. 'He didn't say "I must have Dolly – he's key to my side,"' Insole told *The Nightwatchman*. Insole was adamant that cricketing matters alone dictated the squad selection. 'I was hoping very much that politics wouldn't intervene.' The issue of whether D'Oliveira would cope with the scrutiny that he would face in South Africa, Insole said, 'might have been in the back of people's minds, but it was never raised'.

Donald Carr, the MCC assistant secretary, told *The Nighwatchman*, 'People were aware of what might happen [politically]. It's a very difficult thing to say that it's purely on cricketing grounds when you're aware of what might be the final outcome.' Carr said that he was 'under the impression' that the D'Oliveira decision was made on sporting grounds alone, yet also said that Douglas-Home 'was very much involved' in the process.

D'Oliveira learned that he had not been picked while playing for Worcestershire. 'I was like a zombie,' he wrote. 'The stomach had been kicked out of me. I remember thinking, "You just can't beat the white South Africans."' D'Oliveira, his teammate Tom Graveney recalled, 'put his head in his hands and wept'.

Several Labour MPs demanded a government inquiry. 'MCC have never made a sadder, or potentially more damaging selection,' Arlott wrote, saying that the decision amounted to 'an apparent

British acceptance of apartheid'. Sir Learie Constantine, the former West Indies Test cricketer and prominent anti-racism campaigner, said, 'I am convinced that if Dolly was White he would be packing his bags.'

White South Africa's victory would prove ephemeral. Tom Cartwright, selected ahead of D'Oliveira, learned that playing while his shoulder had not fully recovered could mean never bowling again. Cartwright also read a news report saying that, when England's squad was announced, National Party MPs cheered. He withdrew from the tour. This time, D'Oliveira – a less effective bowler, but a far better batter – was picked at a swift selection meeting. 'It was the greatest moment I can remember,' D'Oliveira said of learning of his inclusion while having dinner with his wife and friends. 'I think I knew then in my heart, however, that the tour would probably not take place.'

Vorster denounced the party as 'not the team of MCC but the team of the Anti-Apartheid Movement', attacking the 'leftist and liberal politicians' who used sport to achieve their 'pink ideals' and 'to gain certain political objectives'. The man who refused to allow black and white cricketers on the same field was accusing MCC of mixing sport and politics. For these words, Vorster received a standing ovation at a National Party Congress in the Afrikaner heartland of Bloemfontein.

On 17 September, Carr wrote a letter to his counterpart at the South African Cricket Association with England's finalised squad. He said, 'I should be grateful if you would let me have your Board's assurance that all those on the above list are acceptable, and that every member of the touring party will be accorded the normal courtesies which are extended to touring teams.' South Africa, as they had always made clear, could not countenance playing an England side that included D'Oliveira. His contract from MCC to play in the tour would be left forever unsigned by the player; it now lies in the Lord's Museum.

SACA's stance on D'Oliveira led MCC to call off the tour on 24 September. South Africa were still due to tour England in 1970. After a coordinated campaign from anti-apartheid campaigners led by Peter Hain, later a Labour Cabinet minister, an official request from James Callaghan, the Home Secretary, led to that series being scrapped. D'Oliveira settled happily in Worcestershire; both his son and grandson represented the county with distinction too. When South Africa hosted England at Newlands in 1996, D'Oliveira was a guest of honour. In Test series against each other, England and South Africa now compete for the Basil D'Oliveira Trophy.

* * *

As Australia landed in 1970, a senior South African Cricket Association administrator was heard to remark, 'I wonder if we are not welcoming the last cricket touring team to South Africa for a long, long time.' The words were prophetic.

In the four Tests against Australia, South Africa suggested that they were among the most talented teams of all time. Australia were crushed 4–0, losing by margins of 170 runs, an innings and 129 runs, 307 runs and 323 runs. Together with another 4–0 loss, in India in 2013, it is one of only two whitewashes over series of four or more Tests that Australia have suffered in their history.

Perhaps one hour best embodied South Africa's dominance. In an hour after lunch on day one of the second Test at Durban, opener Barry Richards and number four Graeme Pollock added 103. Watching Richards's luminous stroke play, Keith Miller proclaimed him both the most exciting and the most technically correct opener in the world.

Pollock, a tall, languid left-hander, was even more dazzling. As a 19-year-old in Australia in 1963/64, Pollock had made two centuries. 'Next time you decide to play like that send me a telegram,' Don Bradman said after Pollock's 122 in Sydney. When Pollock joined

Richards that day in Durban, 'it felt like he said: "Well, you've seen the apprentice, now have a look at the master",' recalled Australia's Paul Sheahan. 'Richards did bat beautifully, but Pollock smashed us all over the shop.' Pollock's 274 was so majestic that, when pace bowler Graham McKenzie bowled with four men in the covers, he still pierced the ball between them. Bradman is the only man in Test history to score more than Pollock's 2,256 Test runs at a higher average than his 60.97.

South Africa's prowess extended well beyond the brilliant batting pair. Eddie Barlow and Mike Procter, a batting and a bowling all-rounder, ensured that the side always had an abundance of depth in both areas. Barlow scored three centuries opening during the drawn series in Australia in 1963/64; he averaged 45.74 with the bat to go with 34.05 with his swing bowling. Procter only played seven Tests, but was among his age's most effervescent talents. With his long run-up and an open-chested action, bending the ball back in to right-handers from around the wicket, he took 41 wickets at 15.02 to go with counter-attacking runs at number seven or eight. Gloucestershire, Procter's county, were nicknamed Proctershire. Graeme's older brother, Peter, provided venom with the ball, and useful lower-order runs. All South Africa lacked was a top-rank spinner. It wasn't merely modesty that led captain Ali Bacher, after being lifted off the ground by his players when the 4–0 triumph was complete, to say that the side's talents made the skipper redundant. Vanquishing Australia was a golden sunset: an emblem of what a team might have achieved without apartheid.

Until September 1971, Australia were due to host South Africa in 1971/72. Borrowing from anti-apartheid tactics used in England, campaigners urged people to boycott any work associated with the tour; airlines and hotels cancelled South Africa's bookings. In Adelaide, Bradman, the Australian Cricket Board chair, met Bob Hawke, the Australian Council of Trade Unions chief executive and future prime minister. Hawke recounted:

He said, 'Bob, I don't think politics should come into sport.' And I said, 'I couldn't agree with you more, Don. We haven't brought politics into sport; it is the government of South Africa which has brought politics into sport, because the government of South Africa has a policy that no person who isn't white is allowed to represent their country in sport. That's bringing politics into sport.' He looked at me for about 30 seconds and then he said, 'I've got no answer to that, Bob.'

Bradman then visited South Africa, meeting Vorster to discuss why black people were barred from representing their country. Vorster said that they were intellectually inferior and lacked feel for cricket. Bradman asked Vorster, 'Have you ever heard of Garry Sobers?'

Seven weeks before the tour was due to begin, Australia withdrew their invitation. Bradman declared, 'We will not play them until they choose a team on a non-racist basis.' During a match to celebrate the tenth anniversary of the Republic of South Africa, Richards and Procter organised a protest. Both their teams walked off after one ball, declaring that they 'subscribe to merit being the only criterion on the cricket field'. The South African Cricket Association did not agree. Faced with a choice between picking teams on merit and allowing their opponents to do so or not playing at all, SACA – compromised by their subservience to the government – preferred not to play official internationals.

Boycotts severely damaged the regime; they might even have shortened apartheid, argued Hassan Howa, of the South African Cricket Board of Control. Howa's mantra – 'No normal sport in an abnormal society' – became the basis for sporting boycotts the world over.

'I lost a Test career,' Procter said. 'But what is a Test career compared to the suffering of 40 million people? Lots of people lost a great deal more in those years, and if by missing out on a Test career we played a part in changing an unjust system, then that is fine by me.'

Richards's four Tests in 1970 were the sum total of his international career; later titans, like Clive Rice and Vintcent van der Bijl, never played a Test. For all the attention given to these players, the real lament is for those denied opportunity because of their skin colour. Krom Hendricks was prevented from playing Test cricket in the 1890s. Frank Roro, the 'W.G. Grace of African cricket', scored over 100 centuries in league cricket. Taliep Salie was hailed as a better allrounder than D'Oliveira: a leg-spinner known for his googly, he once took all ten wickets, including three South Africa Test players, for the Malay XI against a White XI. Allrounder Dik Abed enjoyed success to rank with any Test player in the Lancashire League, taking 855 wickets at an average of 10.27; his leg-cutter is said to have helped inspire another league professional, Dennis Lillee.

Even D'Oliveira's 44 Tests are tinged with sadness: he was 34, or perhaps even older, when his career began. Apartheid cost him another decade of Test cricket, and the chance to play in his prime; his batting average of 40.06 is even more extraordinary in this light. We will never know how many other South Africans could have enriched the Test game had they got the chance.

12

TIGER AND THE QUARTET

On 1 July 1961, 'Tiger' Pataudi – Nawab of Pataudi Jnr, to go by his hereditary title – got into a teammate's car in Hove. The Oxford University side that Pataudi led were playing Sussex, and were tired from being in the field all day. Robin Waters, an Oxford teammate, gave a group of players a lift back.

Three hundred yards from the team's hotel, the three other passengers got out. 'Come with us, Pat, a walk will do you good,' one told Pataudi. He replied, 'No thanks,' explaining that he preferred to stay in the car. Then, Pataudi wrote:

> As Robin started up again I clambered over into the front seat beside him. I had just settled down, when a big car suddenly pulled out into the middle of the road and into our path. We hit it straight on.
>
> There was just sufficient time for me to turn my right shoulder to take the impact, and when my shoulder hit the windscreen I must have broken it . . . As we were being carried into the ambulance I can remember saying to him: 'I've broken my hand. I doubt whether I'll be OK to play in the Varsity Match.' I had no idea then that I had injured my eye as well, because I felt no pain.
>
> When I awoke in hospital in Brighton I was told: 'You must have an operation on your right eye.' I was greatly surprised. Apparently a splinter had passed from the windscreen and entered my eye, and this splinter had to be extracted.

After his operation, Pataudi discovered that he 'had lost the lens of the eye, it having dissolved through injury, and that there was also a coat across the iris. The pupil of the eye had been stitched up, leaving me practically without vision.' An eye specialist told him, 'You will find it better to play cricket using only one eye.'

When lighting a cigarette in the weeks after his accident, Pataudi would miss the end of it by a quarter of an inch. He would also pour water from a jug onto the table, missing his glass. He couldn't read easily for several months.

'It took me a long time to realise that I had virtually lost the use of one eye, but even then, never for an instant did I consider I might not be able to play cricket again,' Pataudi wrote. Returning to the nets, Pataudi effectively had to retrain himself. Initially, he struggled to pick up the length and the flight of bowling. 'Gradually I learnt to judge pace by the amount of flight and the effort that the bowler was putting into it,' he explained. 'I found that I could no longer hook, because I couldn't follow the ball round.'

Pataudi was 20 when the car crashed, but was already being hailed as a batter of rare quality. In the summer of 1961, he scored 1,216 first-class runs for Oxford University, largely against first-class counties, at an average of 55.27.

In his first first-class game after the crash, Pataudi initially batted with a contact lens in his right eye, but found that he was seeing two balls. Next, he closed his right eye, relying on his left eye alone. 'It was a question of finding out my limitations and then playing strictly within them,' Pataudi recalled. 'To get over the fact that I could never be what I would have liked to be. To accept that I was, say, thirty or forty per cent below what I would like to have been.

'In the country of the blind, it has been said, the one-eyed man is king. But in the keen-eyed world of cricket, a fellow with just one good eye-and-a-bit has to settle for something less than the perfection he once sought. Lucky me, despite this, to have been able to play the game all over the world in the company of the giants.'

Five months after his crash, Pataudi made his Test debut. In his third Test, he made 103 against England. He had quickly learned 'to pull the peak of my cap right over my right eye to eliminate the blurred double image I otherwise saw'.

During a tour game in Barbados in 1961/62, India's captain, Nari Contractor, received a sickening injury of his own: a bouncer from Charlie Griffith hit him on the skull, threatening his life. After only six Tests, aged 21 and 77 days, Pataudi became India's new captain: at that point, the youngest in Test history.

His appointment might not have been unrelated to class. 'Cricket was still limited to a kind of background,' he said. The ninth Nawab of Pataudi, Tiger grew up in a palace with 150 rooms; the family employed over 100 servants, including seven or eight as his 'own personal attendants from childhood'. When Australian's captain Ian Chappell once asked him what he did for a living alongside cricket, Pataudi replied, 'Ian, I'm a bloody prince.' At Heathrow, Pataudi was once asked if anyone could vouch for him in the UK. 'Yes,' he said. 'The Queen.'

* * *

The India that Pataudi took over – following his father, who had led the Test tour to England in 1946, after previously playing for England – were stragglers. India had won just eight of their 79 Test matches, losing 31. When he was appointed midway through a series in the Caribbean, Pataudi's first three Tests – defeats by an innings, seven wickets and 123 runs – emphasised the enormity of his task. West Indies won the series 5–0.

Despite his physical handicap, Pataudi's batting was vital. His average, which dipped to 34.91 after a poor run late in his career, belied Pataudi's firefighting elegance, often marked by a willingness to use his feet against spin and hit over the infield. He scored 86 and 53 in a fraught two-wicket victory over Australia in 1964 – India's second victory over Australia, but first against what could be called a first-choice side – and 64 and 148 in defeat at Headingley in 1967. Pataudi was a dynamic cover fielder and the fastest runner in the team; India made notable improvements in the field under his leadership.

Pataudi claimed that he didn't enjoy being captain, calling the job 'something one doesn't refuse to do'. He was demanding, in an understated way. 'You wouldn't hear him shout and scream ever on the field, but he knew what he wanted from his players and expected us to deliver,' said left-arm spinner Bishan Bedi. Pataudi said that he 'always made a point never to betray emotion on the field', transmitting a sense of calm to his bowlers. 'When I bowled a bad over he never grimaced,' off-spinner Erapalli Prasanna wrote. 'Playing under him was no strain.'

Pataudi also fought against regional and factional divides. 'Our side was dominated by players from the west and south and it was difficult for a Punjabi like myself to be accepted,' said Bedi. He called Pataudi 'the first captain to give us a feeling of Indian-ness'. To Prasanna, 'Tiger had made a "team" out of us': 'He gave us back our self-confidence and our self-respect.'

Pataudi later said:

> Captaining any team is not easy but India is particularly difficult – different backgrounds, different languages, different food habits, all those different cultures. I think the best thing to do was to remain as fair as I could and ensure that people never felt you were being in any way biased or unfair, or that you were selecting on a personal basis.

Pataudi told his team, 'You are not playing for Delhi, Punjab, Madras, Calcutta or Bombay; you are playing for India. You are Indian.'

After his first home series as captain, five Tests against England in 1963/64, was drawn 0–0, Pataudi encouraged curators to prepare pitches that were more conducive to producing victories. 'He would attack every batsman, despite his reputation, and always give his bowlers a chance to get him out,' Prasanna wrote. 'He would tell us the strategy he had in mind and he expected us to bowl accordingly.'

Most importantly, Pataudi sought a solution to India's lack of quality fast bowlers. In their first decade in Test cricket, the pace pair Amar Singh and Mohammad Nissar were India's best bowlers; the country struggled to produce worthy successors. 'When selecting our team we were fully aware of starting with one particular disadvantage – complete lack of genuine pace bowlers,' Pataudi observed. Rather than continue to pick substandard seamers, Pataudi advocated a radically different approach, embracing the one area in which India did have abundant talent: spin bowling. This policy was pragmatic, not ideological: Pataudi always maintained that an optimal Test attack would include pace. For India, 'to find a couple of world-class fast bowlers is top priority', he wrote, urging administrators to prepare 'livelier wickets'. But his spinners 'were good enough to play to the kind of plan envisaged. We did basically shift the emphasis from defence to attack for a spinner.'

At Edgbaston in 1967, Pataudi's strategy reached its apogee. Pataudi picked four specialist spinners – the off-spinners Prasanna and Srinivas Venkataraghavan, the leg-spinner B.S. Chandrasekhar and the left-arm spinner Bedi. These four, who all made their debuts aged 21 or earlier, became known as the quartet.

Without any specialist seamers in Birmingham, Pataudi shared the new ball between Venkataraman Subramanya, who got three wickets at 67.00 in his Test career, and Budhi Kunderan, the reserve keeper. Before he took the new ball, Kunderan was asked by Pataudi what he would bowl. He replied, 'We will find out soon, Tiger, won't we?' The spinners shared 18 England wickets, as India bowled out the hosts for 298 and 203, only to be let down by their batting. Pataudi's embrace of spin changed the very character of Indian cricket. Kapil Dev, the country's finest pace-bowling allrounder, wrote, 'The strategy had an unintended consequence. At all levels of the game, youngsters wanted to emulate the great Indian spinners.'

Pataudi fought against a system not set up to thrive. In England in 1967, historian Mihir Bose noted, India's players only earned an allowance of £1 a day (£15 in today's money). This did not include equipment: one player had to save his allowance to buy a new bat.

Under Pataudi, results ticked up. In 1964/65 India drew with Australia 1–1, then beat New Zealand 1–0. In 1967/68, India came within 40 runs of winning down under for the first time, when Pataudi hit 74 and 48 at Brisbane. A month later, India won their first away Test – which came during their first away series victory, when New Zealand were defeated 3–1. Even in Dunedin, the world's southernmost Test venue, spin thrived: 54 of India's 69 wickets in the series were taken with spin. 'Many of us had never played such sustained and good spin bowling,' said Bruce Murray, New Zealand's opener.

Pataudi was 'India's most romantic cricketer', Bose wrote. The moniker reflects Pataudi's personal courage, glamour – he was happily married to the Bollywood film star Sharmila Tagore, a Muslim–Hindu union that was relatively rare at the time – and belief in spin.

* * *

In January 1971, Ajit Wadekar received 'a bolt from the blue': he controversially replaced Pataudi as captain. While Pataudi was no longer there, India remained faithful to his method. In the second Test in the Caribbean, at the Queen's Park Oval in Trinidad, India picked four spinners. Along with Venkataraghavan, Prasanna and Bedi, Wadekar also picked the allrounder Salim Durani – who had taken 18 wickets in the final two Tests against England in 1961/62 – to bowl India to a 2–0 series win.

In Trinidad in 1971, India's four spinners shared 17 wickets between them; West Indies mustered only 214 and 261 and fell to a seven-wicket loss. It was India's first win in 25 Tests between the two countries. India drew the last three Tests relatively easily; their spinners almost helped to win the final Test, back at the Queen's Park Oval, before West Indies held out for a draw. 'After that victory a new kind of enthusiasm infused Indian cricket,' Durani said. While West Indies' pace bowling was in a lull, this was still India's greatest achievement in 39 years of Test cricket.

It would only remain so for four months. The tour to West Indies was followed by a visit to England, who had just won the Ashes down under. At Lord's in the opening Test, the spin trio shared 17 wickets to set up a chase of 183; India reached 145–8 at tea on the final day, 38 runs from victory when rain rendered the match a draw. England dominated the second Test at Old Trafford; India were 65–3 in their fourth-innings chase when rain washed out the final day. The last Test at The Oval loomed with the series 0–0. India were playing their 22nd Test in England, and still hunting their first victory.

On the fourth morning, India were bowled out for 284, a deficit of 71. Syed Abid Ali and Eknath Solkar, the two medium-pacers, were whisked off after three overs apiece; England reached 23–0, a lead of 94 runs. In Chandrasekhar's first over, from the Vauxhall End, Brian Luckhurst hit a firm straight drive; the bowler got his fingers on the ball, deflecting it onto the non-striker's stumps to run out John Jameson. This fortune was the catalyst for one of Indian cricket's most remarkable afternoons.

In his next over, Chandrasekhar bowled to John Edrich, England's number three, for the first time. At mid-off, Dilip Sardesai told Chandrasekhar to 'bowl the Mill Reef' – the name of the Derby-winning thoroughbred, code for his quicker delivery. Chandrasekhar beat Edrich for pace and uprooted his middle stump. Next ball, Chandrasekhar delivered a googly; new batter Keith Fletcher was caught by Solkar at short leg, fielding so close that he was said to be in the batter's back pocket. England went to lunch at a precarious 24–3, the Test's possibilities newly tantalising.

After lunch Venkataraghavan operated in tandem with Chandrasekhar. Venkataraghavan, asked to bowl tightly, snared Basil D'Oliveira, caught at mid-on after trying to hit over the top, then Alan Knott – caught by Solkar diving at full stretch, with his legs pointing skywards, from short leg. Chandrasekhar dismantled the tail, finding bounce to go with pace and deceiving Ray Illingworth, England's captain and doughty number seven, with a slower ball. When he trapped number 11 John Price lbw with a top-spinner, England were all out for 101, their lowest innings at home for 23 years; Chandrasekhar's figures were 18.1–3–38–6.

'That was just one of those days,' Chandrasekhar told the book *Eleven Gods and a Billion Indians*. 'Most of the time, I bowled whatever I liked, without giving much importance to the conditions or who I was bowling to. I always believed that if I bowled well, I could trouble most batsmen because I could get extra bounce from a placid pitch and get some nip off it. That afternoon everything just fell into place.'

India had to chase 173 to seal both a maiden victory in England and a maiden series triumph. Wadekar, a tall and aggressive left-hander, and Dilip Sardesai made carefully compiled 40s; Gundappa Viswanath played with unusual restraint, taking three hours to score 33. On the fifth day, with sixth-wicket pair Viswanath and Farokh Engineer approaching their target, Wadekar felt so confident that he allowed himself a nap. After Syed Abid Ali hit his first ball for four, Wadekar was woken up by Ken Barrington, England's former player who was working with the team. Barrington 'told me that we had won', Wadekar recalled. 'I always knew we'd win.' Among those who watched the victory was Bella, an elephant who had been brought to The Oval from Chessington Zoo by a group of Indian supporters to mark the festival of Ganesh Chaturthi, honouring the elephant-headed god of good fortune. In India, Arunabha Sengupta wrote in *Elephant in the Stadium*, buses stopped as fans came onboard to tell passengers the result. Several Pakistan cricketers playing in England joined India's celebrations.

India's spinners thrived beyond home shores: in the eight Tests in West Indies and England, pace accounted for 28 wickets, but spin 88. Chandrasekhar overcame childhood polio, which weakened his right arm – in the field he threw with his left hand – but gave his action more flexibility. He came back from four years out of the side to befuddle England with his leg breaks, googlies and top-spinners; his quickest deliveries reached a pace in the region of 65 mph. When England visited 18 months later, Chandrasekhar's 35 wickets secured a 2–1 win; he also bowled India to victories in Australia, New Zealand and West Indies. 'His arm is like a sling, unpredictable,' Prasanna wrote. 'I don't think that Chandra really knows the speed at which the ball catapults out of his right hand.'

While Chandrasekhar took 242 Test wickets, Bedi claimed 266. Bedi's control, slow pace, which he varied subtly, and his flight made him the left-arm spinner in excelsis. Bedi attributed his prodigious turn to the strength of his index finger, developed playing the game of marbles as a boy in Amritsar. 'A lot of bowling is done in the mind,' he said. 'The greatest thrill in bowling is to have a batsman stumped. If you've achieved that you've really beaten him twice, in the air and off the wicket.' When he was hit for six, Bedi applauded, as if to suggest that it was all part of his ploy.

The off-spinners, Venkataraghavan and Prasanna, were also contrasting. Venkataraghavan, who was the better batter, was taller and quicker; Prasanna relied more on loop and spin. 'I come through slow enough for the batsman to come down the pitch,' Prasanna explained. 'To survive, I have to resort to variations.' He brought his engineer's mind to bowling. Prasanna sometimes released the ball from a foot further back than normal; with batters often deceived by a ball a few inches shorter than expected, he got an uncommon number of caught-and-bowled dismissals. When using his feet, Australia captain Ian Chappell said, 'my estimated time of arrival never coincided with Pras's appointed destination.'

The twin victories in 1971 were 'Indian cricket's coming of age', historian Ramachandra Guha wrote. Many at the time also grasped the significance. Keith Miller, the former Australian great, observed, 'India, once looked upon as in the Little League of Cricket, are in the Big League. And strong contenders for the best team in the world.' The team's plane back from England was diverted so that the team could meet Indira Gandhi, the prime minister. Hockey had been the source of India's greatest sporting triumphs; now, India had the cricket success that they craved too. When India returned from the Caribbean to Bombay, a crowd of 150,000 lined the road from Santa Cruz airport to City Hall. Never again would cricket's status as India's favourite game be challenged.

* * *

Before India departed for West Indies in February 1971, an uncapped batter named Sunil Gavaskar had acute pain in the middle finger of his left hand, which he put in a bandage during the team's long journey, via London and New York. On the flight to the US, Gavaskar's finger swelled up. While other players spent their day in New York visiting the city, Gavaskar was taken to hospital. When a doctor saw his finger, he said, 'Thank God, you've come now. If you had delayed even by 24 hours, gangrene would have set in, and the finger would have had to be chopped off.' Gavaskar then had a minor operation.

Early on the tour of the Caribbean, India's squad attended a function. One West Indies player pointed out Gavaskar, a shy 21-year-old who favoured soft drinks and talked little. Batter Dilip Sardesai responded, 'Before the tour is over our boy will have hit a double century.'

Gavaskar had to wait until the second Test to make his debut; he hit 65 and 67 not out, including the winning runs. Over the next three Tests he scored four centuries, including the double hundred that Sardesai had foretold, ending the series with 774 runs at 154.80.

Gavaskar scored the winning runs in Port-of-Spain, to secure India's inaugural victory over West Indies. A Trinidadian singer, Lord Relator, composed a calypso in tribute:

> It was Gavaskar,
> The real master,
> Just like a wall.
> We couldn't out Gavaskar at all, not at all.
> You know the West Indies couldn't out Gavaskar at all.

Gavaskar was another member of the Bombay School of Batsmanship; when India won in England in 1971, six of the top seven hailed from the city. He learned the game playing on a 15-foot balcony outside the family flat; Gavaskar played matches in the building's courtyard alongside several other future first-class cricketers. As Mihir Bose noted, any shot hit higher than four feet was liable to break windowpanes; players had to hit the ball down.

Living in Bombay gave Gavaskar access to the coaching, facilities and high-quality opponents that he needed to develop his talents; he went to St Xavier's, an elite Jesuit private school. 'Whatever I am in the game today is due, in a very large measure, to the fact that I have been nursed in the cradle of cricket, that is Bombay,' he wrote in his 1976 autobiography. Bombay won 15 consecutive Ranji Trophies from 1959 to 1973.

When Gavaskar was growing up, his father – who had been a good club player – promised his son ten rupees for every hundred that he scored. 'Often, when he returned home in the evening, he would take out his wallet and ask me if I had scored a century and would be most disappointed if I said "no",' Gavaskar wrote. 'I hated losing my wicket.' Sometimes, if he got out during street games, Gavaskar would take the bat and ball home; if he couldn't bat, no one could.

Opening was, traditionally, an area that India struggled in, often roping in middle-order batters. Before Gavaskar's debut, the overall average for Indian openers, despite Vijay Merchant's record, was

31.60, with 23 centuries in 434 innings. Gavaskar hit 34 hundreds in 214 innings, averaging 51.12; he fared even better away than at home. When he retired, in 1987, he had the most runs, hundreds and appearances of any Test cricketer.

A classical technique and consummate balance were the foundations of Gavaskar's batsmanship. 'Before I go out to bat, I find a wall and position into my stance with my right ear hard up against the wall,' he explained. 'I feel my head and eyes level, my balance perfect, my feet light and ready to move. The wall is ensuring that I stay still. In the middle I pretend the wall is still there. Head position and balance. From there my eyes are in the best position to see the ball and to stay watching it until the shot is played.'

Only 5 ft 4 in, Gavaskar realised that he needed to be proficient off the back foot: 'If I had gone looking to play forward, I would have been hit on the head all of the time.' Self-denial led Gavaskar to put away the hook – preferring to sway instead – for vast swathes of his career. Whether played off the front foot or back, Gavaskar's defensive stroke anaesthetised the ball.

These qualities earned him the tag the 'Indian Boycott' – a nod to England's supremely unyielding Geoffrey Boycott, who played 108 Tests and underpinned England's Ashes win in 1970/71. Boycott could 'play near-perfect against all kinds of bowling and on all kinds of wickets', Gavaskar wrote. 'There cannot be a better technician.' Except, perhaps, Gavaskar himself. As captain, Gavaskar was particularly obdurate; so were his team – losing eight, winning nine and drawing 30 of his 47 Tests in charge.

Gavaskar benefited from India's most robust top order yet. Mohinder Amarnath morphed into an outstanding player of short bowling, thriving overseas; Dilip Vengsarkar was a smooth driver with a rounded game. Gundappa Viswanath was perhaps Gavaskar's most reliable support. Gavaskar's claim that Viswanath was India's best batter wasn't merely a nod to family relations: Viswanath married Gavaskar's sister. A slight man, Viswanath developed a dashing square cut, using his wrists to manipulate the ball either side of fielders guarding against the shot; he averaged over 50 against both Australia and West Indies.

Gavaskar could also cast off his cloak of inhibition when the circumstances demanded. 'He is prepared to take calculated risks in his batting and thus able to score more often and faster than I did,' said Merchant, who hailed his 'rare ability of making strokes from the very first over'.

At The Oval in 1979, India were set 438 to win, more than any side had ever made to win a Test. Gavaskar's 221 brought India to the cusp of victory; they ended on 429–8 in a pulsating draw. Against West Indies at Delhi in 1983/84, his 94-ball century on the first morning was laced with on drives off the front foot, fierce square cuts and unshackled hooks. Against Australia in 1977/78, Gavaskar hit three consecutive second-innings centuries, often driving the ferocious quick Jeff Thomson down the ground.

'These big blokes have the power, but we little ones have the footwork,' Don Bradman said when he met Gavaskar. Like Bradman, Gavaskar opened up new commercial opportunities for his country's cricketers; his first autobiography, published five years into his career, was a best-seller. But where Bradman was deeply Anglophile, Gavaskar criticised what he saw as English hypocrisy over matters like umpiring.

When he landed in the Caribbean in 1976, a customs officer asked Gavaskar if he was going to score as many runs as five years earlier. This time, Gavaskar had to settle for two centuries. In five Tests in Trinidad, he scored four hundreds and averaged 99.12.

The last of these centuries helped India make a record chase of 406 in 1976; India began the final innings batting for a draw, yet reached their target with six wickets to spare. The result would go a long way towards shaping Test cricket for the next two decades.

13

THE RISE OF WEST INDIES

Floods are a part of life in Guyana. In April 1976, they changed the course of cricket history.

West Indies were hosting India in a four-match series in the Caribbean; they led 1–0 after two Tests. The third Test was scheduled for Georgetown. Floods forced the match to be moved to Port-of-Spain in Trinidad; the ground had just hosted the second Test, a draw dominated by India's spinners.

The pitch for the third Test was docile and slow, leading West Indies to pick three spinners – Imtiaz Ali, Albert Padmore and Raphick Jumadeen. West Indies dominated, declaring to set India 403 for victory. Only one side, Don Bradman's Australia in 1948, had ever chased more to win a Test.

With the pitch not breaking up, Sunil Gavaskar and Gundappa Viswanath both scored centuries. In 105 overs in India's second innings, the spin trio recorded combined figures of 2–220. When Brijesh Patel pulled the winning runs off Jumadeen, clinching victory with six overs to spare on day five, India sealed their moment of history. They also put West Indies onto a path towards making history of their own.

'Gentlemen, I gave you 400 runs to bowl at and you failed to bowl out the opposition – how many runs must I give you in future to make sure that you get the wickets?' Clive Lloyd asked his spinners afterwards. Ali never played again; Padmore played one more Test, Jumadeen seven.

No longer able to call upon his cousin, off-spinner Lance Gibbs, who took 309 Test wickets, Lloyd often didn't pick a spinner during the rest of his captaincy. It would be another 25 years until West Indies next selected two specialist spinners in a Test.

'We didn't have a spinner who was going to win us a game,' Lloyd said in David Tossell's book *Grovel*. 'I decided from then on to play the extra fast bowler.' It was, India's former captain Tiger Pataudi said, 'the most radical tactical innovation when he decided to use four fast bowlers'.

The next Test illustrated how dramatic the shift was. Jamaica hosted the deciding final Test, with the series locked at 1–1. Lloyd selected a four-pronged pace attack, retaining only one of the spinners picked in Trinidad.

Sabina Park's pitch had just been relaid; it had variable bounce, and a ridge at the northern end. On the opening day, India reached 175–1; overnight rain changed the wicket's character. The bowling was so venomous that West Indies didn't even need to take ten wickets; six would suffice. With players not yet protected by helmets, Anshuman Gaekwad was hit on the left ear, needing to spend two nights in hospital; Brijesh Patel had stitches after being hit in the mouth. Both retired hurt; Gundappa Viswanath broke his left hand when he was dismissed. Skipper Bishan Bedi declared at 306–6, reasoning that it would be too dangerous for the tailenders to bat.

In their second innings, with Gaekwad, Patel and Viswanath all unable to bat, India's innings stopped at five wickets down, setting West Indies a paltry 13 runs to win. The hosts, Bedi complained, were conducting 'a war'; he refused to take the field in their run chase. Gavaskar called the tactics, cheered on by a vociferous crowd, 'barbarism'. After the Test, pace bowler Michael Holding said, 'On that surface, it was inevitable that some batsmen would be hit against such a pace-based attack as ours, especially as we adopted the tactic of bowling round the wicket, aiming the ball at their bodies.'

To Lloyd, victory emphasised the lesson of his side's preceding series, a harrowing 5–1 defeat in Australia. Potent fast bowlers were the best way to win Test matches.

* * *

Against West Indies in 1975/76, Dennis Lillee and Jeff Thomson shared 56 wickets. It continued the devastating partnership that they had formed the previous home summer, when Australia won the Ashes 4–1.

'Ashes to Ashes, dust to dust, if Lillee doesn't get ya, Thommo must,' sang feral crowds. Then, they broke into chants of 'Kill, Kill, Kill'. The bowlers used the media to ramp up the sense of danger. 'I enjoy hitting a batsman more than getting him out,' Thomson declared before the series. 'I like to see blood on the pitch.' After their plane left Australia in early 1975, England captain Mike Denness recalled, 'Some of the lads said they were glad to get out alive, even if some of them didn't exactly get out all in one piece.' Three Tests into the series, Denness dropped himself.

Captaining the pair 'was pretty bloody easy', recalls Ian Chappell, Australia's skipper from 1971 to 1975. 'Thommo, you didn't really have to motivate him too much because he liked bowling fast. Dennis was pretty simple. If you said to him, for instance, "No Western Australian's taken five wickets at the Sydney Cricket Ground on a Friday," Dennis would say, "Well, we'll f***ing see about that." He'd immediately go out there and try to do it.'

The Lillee–Thomson partnership was forged the evening before the first Test against England at Brisbane in 1974. Lillee was returning from injury, after a dispute with the Australian board, whom he had finally persuaded to pay his medical bills. Thomson was playing his second Test, two years after going wicketless on debut. After the pre-Test dinner in Brisbane, Lillee saw Thomson drinking at the bar; he assumed it was water. 'That's straight scotch,' Thomson said. 'When I go out to bowl I want a hangover from hell. I bowl real well when I have a headache. It makes me just want to get in there.' Lillee wrote, 'I needed sleep and a good, solid meal. He could keep his headache; that was no sort of motivation to me. It showed what an unusual character the man was.'

Lillee, a Western Australian, was initially a tearaway; a severe back injury early in his career turned him into a craftsman, though his snarl remained. By 1974, Lillee combined pace with immaculate control generated from his grooved, rhythmical action. He was a master of swing and seam, and also developed both off- and leg-cutters.

Injury, Lillee believed, made him a better bowler. 'Maybe I bowled less quickly than before but I was a lot more accurate,' he explained. 'I was certainly thinking about my bowling more than I had ever done before. I guess that was because I could no longer simply blast batsmen out; I had to have a better worked out plan than that.'

Obsessive in his desire for an edge, he sometimes asked whether his action could be filmed front-on by broadcasters, to check his technique. Lillee, Ian Chappell recalls, never asked for the field to be changed to add another run-saving position. 'If he asked me for a change, it was to have another slip or a bat pad – he was asking for attacking fielders. That was very important with Dennis. He was trying to get wickets all the time.' No seamer with 200 wickets can match Lillee's average of 5.07 wickets per Test.

Thomson, a son of the Sydney suburbs, was a bowler sui generis. About to release the ball, he swayed wide of the crease, then started to swing his arm from behind his right knee. Watching the ball in Thomson's delivery stride, 'you lose it, it's gone,' remembers England's David Lloyd, who played in the 1974/75 Ashes. 'You're taught "keep your eye on the ball". Well, if you can't see it, you've got to pick it up again. You're losing a split second.' There was a visceral, primal quality to Thomson's bowling. 'The only way I can bowl is flat out,' he explained. 'I'm not one of those guys who could slow down and use all manner of cut and swing to suit the conditions. I come in and let you know, "Hey, this is my turf... get out."'

Whether aiming at the stumps or getting balls to rear up at throat height from just short of a length – he rarely had need to bowl shorter – the effect was devastating. For two years until his shoulder injury, Thomson was a ferocious sight. Against West Indies in Perth in 1975/76, high-sonic cameras tracked Thomson bowling at 160 kph: 100 mph. No Test bowler had ever been so quick before; for all the advancements in sports science, very few, if any, have been so rapid since.

* * *

If West Indies could bemoan some dubious umpiring down under in 1975/76, they could not shirk the truth: that they had been defeated by pace. Over a beer with Viv Richards during the tour, *Grovel* recounts, Clive Lloyd said, 'If we can get two more fast bowlers, we could really do something.'

Even in defeat in Australia, Lloyd found the first two men who would become his pace quartet. Aged 24, Andy Roberts announced himself as the new attack leader; at great pace, Roberts could both swing and seam the ball. After opener Roy Fredericks thrashed 169 in 145 balls, hooking Lillee and Thomson with impunity on a typically swift Perth pitch, Roberts's 7–54 sealed West Indies' sole Test win of the tour.

While Roberts averaged 26.36 in Australia, Michael Holding, his opening partner, averaged 61.40 in his debut series. But Holding was timed at 97 mph, giving notice of the pace that he generated from his 6 ft 4 in height and a smooth action. He left with a better sense of how to succeed. 'That Australia tour opened a lot of eyes,' he reflects.

Two days before their first Test against West Indies in 1976, England captain Tony Greig gave a pre-series interview. He declared that he intended 'to make them grovel'.

'It was just one ridiculous comment that he made, one foolish comment,' Holding recalls. 'That was enough to stir us up.'

To Holding, Greig's words were more incendiary because he had been raised in South Africa until moving to England. 'I thought this guy was this racist South African who thought, "Oh, these black guys, I'm going to show them." But later on in life, I got to meet the man, and I recognised that it was not a racist comment – well, it could have been interpreted as a racist comment, but that didn't mean that he was racist.' The two later became good friends.

The first two Tests were hard-fought draws. In the third Test, Old Trafford contained inviting cracks for pace bowlers. After West Indies chose to bat, with the wicket expected to worsen, only two men passed ten. One of those was Gordon Greenidge, whose dazzling 134 led the tourists to 211 all out.

Holding and Roberts exploited the variable bounce to skittle out England for 71. In West Indies' second innings, Greenidge scored his second century of the match; England were set a notional target of 552. In a chilling passage on the third evening, openers John Edrich and Brian Close, who had a combined age of 84, were repeatedly struck by deliveries. Clive Lloyd said, 'People are going to be hit; you hope it is not going to be fatal.' Roberts and Holding shared combined match figures of 16 wickets for 100; England were crushed by 425 runs.

By the final Test at The Oval, played in scorching heat during the hottest English summer in over 350 years, West Indies were leading 2–0. Batting first, West Indies were 5–1 when Viv Richards arrived at the crease with characteristic swagger: in his maroon cap, chewing gum and not so much walking out as sauntering. Over the next eight hours, Richards combined control, power and a preternatural ability to flick balls from off stump, or even wider, into the on side.

After ending day one on 200 not out, Richards wanted to keep his gum for the next day. He put it under his seat in the dressing room, then put it back in his mouth the following morning. He finally disposed of the gum after scoring 291; Richards scored 1,710 Test runs in 1976, more than anyone had previously scored in a year.

The Oval was characteristically flat, the heat rendering conditions even more unforgiving for bowlers; the outfield was parched and brown. After West Indies' 687–8 declared, Holding's unrelenting pace and accuracy effectively took the pitch out of the equation. His run-up scarcely made a sound as he approached the stumps.

The legend of Whispering Death was born. In a match in which all other bowlers returned combined match figures of 14–1,254, Holding took 14–149 from 53.4 overs. Targeting the stumps, and deploying reverse swing – though it wasn't yet called this – 12 of his wickets were either bowled or lbw, including clean bowling Greig cheaply twice. Holding 'wasn't fast, really, until I was probably about 17, 18 years old', he says. By the Oval Test, he was still only 22, living at home with his parents and combining cricket with working as a government computer programmer in Jamaica:

> I was relaxed. Everything just happened for me in that Test match. It wasn't a matter of planning out opposition batsmen – I didn't know enough at 22 years old to say, 'I'm going to bowl two out and then an inswinger.'
>
> I just ran in and bowled fast, and was bowling full because of the nature of the pitch. The ball wasn't bouncing above waist high, so I was getting the ball to in-duck a little bit because I was bowling that full.
>
> I don't think one ball left the right-handed batsman, but because of the conditions, the ball was just dipping in a bit. The fuller you bowled, the more opportunity it had to do something in the air. I just kept on running in and bowling fast.

As England walked off the field for the final time, after West Indies declared in their second innings at The Oval to set up their 3–0 win, Greig got onto his knees. He grovelled.

* * *

From 1980, when they lost an ill-tempered series in New Zealand, until 1995, West Indies were undefeated in 29 consecutive series. In this time they played 115 Tests, won 59 and lost just 15. Their apogee came in 1984: 11 consecutive victories against Australia, England and finally Australia again. West Indies were also the first great one-day international side, winning the first two World Cups, in 1975 and 1979, and reaching the 1983 final.

These feats amounted to one of the finest eras that any side has ever enjoyed in international sport. The achievements were even more astounding given the region's small population – typically, around five to six million – and lack of resources.

Previous teams had been renowned for 'calypso cricket'. 'It was patronising,' Lloyd said in the book *Fire in Babylon*. 'The suggestion was that we had always been slap-happy, unthinking – players who only hoped for the best. There was a lazy way of looking at the West Indies and West Indian cricket in those days. And "calypso cricket" was a big part of it.'

Lloyd effectively reinvented the traditions of bowling in the Caribbean. Until 1976, spin bowlers had delivered 51 per cent of all West Indies' overs in Test cricket, second only to India among the seven nations who had played Tests. But in the next 19 years, spinners bowled 12 per cent of West Indies' overs. Seldom has one sports team changed character so dramatically, and so successfully.

Test cricket had known pace-bowling pairs before. It had not known pace quartets. West Indies omitted fast bowlers who would have waltzed into any other team. Sylvester Clarke, who took 591 wickets at 18.99 for Surrey, was proclaimed the scariest of all Caribbean quicks, yet only played 11 Tests; Wayne Daniel took 685 wickets at 22.02 for Middlesex but played just ten Tests.

Each West Indies pace bowler posed a subtly different threat. The Antiguan Roberts, the godfather of this generation of West Indies quicks, was a fast-bowling chameleon. 'I used to watch a lot of cricket,

I used to imitate a lot,' he told me. 'I learned from watching anybody who bowled.'

Roberts was a pioneer in developing two types of bouncers. He used a slightly slower bouncer, which batters could often play untroubled, to lull opponents into attempting a repeat from a quick bouncer. Roberts would hold the ball more tightly for slightly slower balls, and looser for faster balls, so that he would turn his arm over at the same speed:

> If I can bowl at 100 miles an hour and then I bowl at 90 miles an hour – the batsman now will have to start thinking. But if everything is coming at 100 miles, he doesn't have to think because he knows what's coming. So that is something that I teach myself to do.
>
> It wasn't in the run-up. It wasn't in the effort that you see – most of it comes from the grip.
>
> That's why people had problems with the bouncers. Everybody's looking at the effort that you make, but the effort was the same.

From ball to ball, Roberts varied his release point. His cunning also led him to change his run-up: sometimes, deliberately chipping at the ground with his feet. 'One of the best ways to get the batsman out is to get him out of his comfort zone, because once you start he's focusing on your approach . . . You have to be ahead of the batsman.'

The original quartet was led by Roberts and Holding. First change was normally Colin Croft, from Guyana. From wide of the crease with an open-chested action, Croft bowled with fierce intensity: 'The most physically aggressive one,' Roberts told me. Second change was initially Joel Garner, a Bajan who combined the bounce from his 6 ft 8 in height and immaculate control with a lethal yorker – qualities that did not depend on bowling with the new ball.

Those who succeeded the original quartet maintained the same menace. Malcolm Marshall, another Bajan, was widely heralded as the finest of all, combining seam, swing – both in and away – and cutters with pace; his threat was undimmed with the old ball. He turned the apparent disadvantage of being 5 ft 10 in into an asset; he had an 'unusual skidding bouncer, which does not get up much but keeps coming at the batsman', wrote former Pakistan captain Imran Khan.

The Jamaican Patrick Patterson was unerringly hostile. Ian Bishop, from Trinidad, swung the ball prodigiously at pace approaching 90 mph; Viv Richards believed that he would have been the best West Indies bowler of all without injury.

Curtly Ambrose and Courtney Walsh formed one of Test cricket's finest new-ball pairs, extending their partnership until 2000. As a boy, Ambrose, from Antigua, 'didn't want to play cricket'. He dreamed of playing basketball, and only seriously pursued cricket when he was 20, encouraged by his mother, a fanatical fan. 'Everything took off just like that, so within four years of not wanting to play cricket, I suddenly became an international cricketer.'

Ambrose combined metronomic accuracy and bounce from his 6 ft 8 in height with seam movement – and the sense of when was the right time to ramp up his speed. In 1993, in the series decider against Australia in Perth, on the first morning Ambrose wasted the new ball on a pitch offering pace and bounce. 'I was bowling a little bit too short,' he told me. At lunch, with Australia 59–2, Ambrose didn't eat anything. 'I just sat there and said to myself, "You messed up."'

As West Indies returned to the field, captain Richie Richardson asked Ambrose how he was feeling. 'I said, "Ready to go." And I made the adjustment, bowling a little bit fuller: not half-volley length, but a length where the batters looked like they could drive.'

The difference, Ambrose believes, was under a metre: enough to force batsmen camping on the back foot to grope forwards instead. His spell of 7–1 in 32 deliveries, with a series of batters prodding to the keeper or slips, eviscerated Australia. 'That's what fast bowling is all about – the surface you're playing on and making adjustments accordingly.'

Facing Ambrose, Australia's batter Steve Waugh wrote, the challenge 'came in two guises: firstly the technical examination of a batsman's technique upon being confronted by a beautifully balanced yet seemingly jet-propelled rhythmic action that delivered the ball from a perfect wrist position.' Secondly, 'You then had to confront the physicality of the man... his towering height, deathly stare and imposing body language.' Among bowlers to play 40 Tests, no one averages fewer than Ambrose against top-six batters. Walsh, from Jamaica, had an open-chested action; he used the width of the crease adroitly and had extraordinary stamina, taking 77 wickets in Asia at just 20.53.

It highlighted the adaptability of West Indies' quicks. Through the prism of modern analysis, a *slight* weakness of the group was that they averaged five runs more against left-handers than right-handers. Yet any such flaws are relative. The nine leading West Indies quicks, who all debuted between 1974 and 1989, shared 2,389 Test wickets at 23.13.

Table 4. When West Indies fast bowlers dominated the world

		Matches	Balls	Runs	Wickets	Average
A.M.E. Roberts	1974–1983	47	11,135	5,174	202	25.61
M.A. Holding	1975–1987	60	12,680	5,898	249	23.68
C.E.H. Croft	1977–1982	27	6,165	2,913	125	23.30
J. Garner	1977–1987	58	13,169	5,433	259	20.97
M.D. Marshall	1978–1991	81	17,584	7,876	376	20.94
C.A. Walsh	1984–2001	132	30,019	12,688	519	24.44
B.P. Patterson	1986–1992	28	4,829	2,874	93	30.90
C.E.L. Ambrose	1988–2000	98	22,103	8,501	405	20.99
I.R. Bishop	1989–1998	43	8,407	3,909	161	24.27

Operating together enhanced the individual effectiveness of West Indies' quicks. 'If you have a good bunch of fast bowlers, the pressure is always on the batsman, so it makes everyone's job easier,' Holding says. Bowling with a spinner at the other end in Australia in 1975/76,

Holding only got 'two and a half, three minutes' between overs, which were eight balls each in the series. 'Bowling with another fast bowler, you get a bigger break between overs, so it's a lot easier physically.' During that tour to Australia, West Indies bowled 94 balls per hour; by the 1980 tour of England, they bowled only 75, helping to ensure that their fast bowlers remained fresh and at their best.

So did the presence of fellow fast bowlers at mid-on and mid-off. Initially through talking to Roberts, 'You learn how to assess batsmen,' Holding recalls. 'We always shared whatever knowledge we had with each other. We walked past each other in the field and made quick suggestions.'

Ambrose, Garner and Marshall were the first three bowlers in history to take over 200 Test wickets at an average of under 21. They focused less on swing and embraced seam, which relies less on conditions, in tandem with their bounce and pace.

'I don't remember any West Indian fast bowler in my time who swung the ball a lot,' Holding explains. 'You couldn't swing the ball in the Caribbean, so you had to find other means of getting batsmen out.' In a six-Test series in India in 1983, West Indies took just three wickets with spin; thanks to Marshall and Holding, they still won 3–0.

Characteristic of the group, Ambrose told me, 'My mantra is you want to drive, you buy a car. I've developed that short-of-a-length delivery where batters aren't sure to come forward or go back – an "in-between" length. The guys couldn't leave on length. They had to look to play.

'I was never a swing bowler. I relied on hitting the pitch and getting the ball to seam away or nip back or go straight on.'

The threat was to limbs as well as wickets. In 20 years until 1994, Simon Wilde calculated, 40 Test batters retired hurt against West Indies, almost the same as against all other Test teams combined. 'The beautiful game,' warned the former Sussex captain turned journalist Robin Marlar in *The Sunday Times* in 1984, 'will die of such brutality.'

Like many great teams, West Indies also changed their sport. From 1920 until 1976, spinners bowled 47 per cent of total overs in Test cricket. During the 1980s, as other countries tried to imitate West Indies, the proportion of spin bowled fell to 34 per cent.

Unable to beat West Indies, other nations tried to stop them in committee rooms instead. Ideas floated around including clamping down on slow over rates, thereby forcing teams to bowl more spin; a white line drawn halfway between the stumps, with bowlers barred from bowling shorter than the line; and even lengthening the pitch from 22 yards. In 1991, the ICC introduced a limit of one bouncer per over, the first restriction on the number of bouncers permitted; this was tweaked to two bouncers an over in 1994. The complaints and law changes were, Joel Garner said, 'jealousy'.

* * *

West Indies have always transcended the narrow confines of the field. Touring England, players understood the racism that Caribbean emigrants had experienced. 'The significance of West Indies cricket and winning is in England,' Roberts told me. 'I had brothers and sisters who lived in England, and who told me that the only thing that they have to shout about is when West Indies win a Test match.'

When he first played in England, in 1976, Holding 'really appreciated exactly what these people were going through and why they wanted us to be successful because they could then walk around feeling proud'. A chat with Greenidge distilled the team's importance:

> He said, 'These guys living here in England feel as if they are not appreciated as human beings, and they want to show the Englishmen that they are from the same place as the guys who are beating you. So if you can respect them and their ability, why can't you respect me?'

That's when I understood what these guys were going through living in this foreign country.

After Greig's 'grovel' comments it would be 14 years until England won another Test against West Indies. From 1976 to 1990, the score between West Indies and England read 20–0.

While fast bowling defined West Indies, the side's batters could be almost as intimidating. During their undefeated era, West Indies scored at 2.97 an over; other Test sides scored at 2.61 an over. Clive Lloyd, Viv Richards's predecessor as captain, was a languid, graceful and powerful left-hander, reshaping Tests from number five or six. Gordon Greenidge and Desmond Haynes were among the finest opening pairs. 'You have to be technically able to withstand the pressure and know when to apply pressure,' Greenidge said. 'I believe when I take the fight to you, I make you change your game plan.'

At Lord's in 1984, England set West Indies 342 runs to win in under a day. Often facing England's quickest bowlers only in a cap, eschewing a helmet, Greenidge square-cut with his characteristic authority; his off drives and on-side flicks were equally imperious. Greenidge's 214 not out, off only 242 balls, was supported by Larry Gomes, normally considered the side's insurance policy. West Indies won by nine wickets, chasing the target in 66.1 overs. The 1984 vintage became the first ever touring side to win 5–0 in England.

West Indies' jubilation could only be fully understood in the wider sociopolitical context. In 1962, Jamaica and Trinidad & Tobago became the first nations once part of the British West Indies to gain independence; Barbados and Guyana followed in 1966, and Antigua in 1981. At his home ground, the intimate Antigua Recreation Ground, five years later, Richards thrashed a century in 56 balls to seal West Indies' second consecutive 5–0 'blackwash' of England.

As a boy, Richards boxed for his neighbourhood. He brought this pugnacity to batting. Richards's slow strut to the wicket turned his entrance into an intimidatory act. 'I want them to know that I am confident and that I am not going to allow them to gain any early psychological advantage,' Richards wrote in his autobiography. He used to sleep in the dressing room while waiting to bat. 'My mind is clear of gremlins because I did not see the last wicket fall and, apart from the first couple of balls bowled, I have seen none of the cricket. This is now my war. Me and my chewing gum against the world.'

Richards preferred playing on the front foot, whipping balls from well outside off stump through midwicket or thrashing the delivery through extra cover. He also ignored the move towards wearing helmets:

> Helmet? Forget it. I tried one once in a dressing-room and felt trapped. I like to be free, to live on my nerves and be able to react in a fraction of a second against the bully at the other end who is trying to rip off my head...
>
> There was no more exciting shot to play than the hook off a rising fast ball. Facing bouncers was as much about technique as any part of batting.

Cricket is 'not some irrelevant, eccentric sport played by a handful of countries, but a game that gets right to the root of the societies involved', wrote Richards, who succeeded Lloyd as captain in 1985. 'I believe very strongly in the black man asserting himself in this world and over the years I have leaned towards many movements that followed this basic cause. It was perfectly natural for me to identify, for example, with the Black Power movement in America and, to a certain extent, with Rastafarians.' Richards wore Rastafarian colours on the field; Bob Marley was his 'battlefield music'.

While, for players like Richards, West Indies' rise was intertwined with black empowerment, the side have never only represented the region's black population. Richards learned as much on the one occasion that he received major criticism in the Caribbean, after calling West Indies 'the only sporting team of African descent that has been able to win repeatedly against all international opposition'. The comments enraged the Indo-Caribbean population.

Ever since Sonny Ramadhin's debut, in 1950, West Indies have been well served by the Indo-Caribbean population, especially in Guyana and Trinidad & Tobago. Larry Gomes, who played from 1976 to 1987 and averaged over 50 in both Australia and England, is part of another significant community: Portuguese-Caribbean people, the descendants of labourers from Madeira who came to the region in the 19th century. Holding observes, 'We always had all these cultures mixed together in the West Indies team.'

* * *

For all their gifts, West Indies players benefited from a system that enabled them to make good on their talents. Beyond the pitch, four pillars supported West Indies' dynasty.

The first pillar was expanding the player pool. The early story of West Indies cricket was the story of their 'big four' – Barbados, Guyana, Jamaica and Trinidad & Tobago. Until 1954, the selection panel comprised a selector from each; they often pushed for players from their nation to be picked, ignoring talent elsewhere. 'Some of the bigger islands sometimes have more than a reasonable number' of international players, Learie Constantine observed in 1946.

Only the big four territories had their own first-class sides; players from elsewhere needed to move to these territories, then hope to win regional selection. Over the 1960s and 1970s, West Indies became conscious of the need to supplement their talent pool. In 1965, Combined Islands, comprising the territories that made up the Windward Islands and Leewards Islands, were invited to the new Shell Shield first-class competition, giving players from these islands a chance to show their talents against Caribbean cricket's big four. Windward and Leewards then played in the competition individually from 1980.

West Indies also tweaked their selection method to reduce the big four's say. Horse-trading between different islands became less common, and the process more meritocratic. In 1973, Nevis's Elquemedo Willett became the first man from outside the big four to represent West Indies.

The following year, Andy Roberts became Antigua's first Test cricketer. 'We had better players than myself who never played,' he told me. 'They didn't look to the smaller islands.' Alongside Roberts, three other Antiguans – Ambrose, Richards and the batter Richie Richardson – underpinned West Indies' undefeated run. In 1981, Antigua became the fifth Caribbean nation, and first from beyond the big four, to host a Test.

West Indies' second pillar was English cricket. From 1968, West Indies players had a new avenue to develop their skills: county cricket. Each county was now permitted one overseas player, who no longer needed to fulfil a residency qualification. Caribbean players had once forgone the chance to play for West Indies by taking up a county contract – as Charles Ollivierre did when, after the tour to England in 1900, he emigrated to play for Derbyshire. Now, the skills that players gained in England could benefit West Indies.

Garry Sobers was among the first batch of overseas players, lured to Nottinghamshire by a salary of £7,000, an apartment and a car. In August 1968 at Swansea, Sobers hit six sixes in an over in a County Championship match. 'Having made themselves into a sine qua non in league cricket, West Indian cricketers are now embarked on what could be a comparable establishment in county cricket,' C.L.R. James wrote. Of West Indies' 17-man squad in England in 1976, only four had not already played county cricket. Twenty-seven of the 49 overseas players in 1977 were Caribbean. Caribbean. 'County cricket was a major source of development,' Roberts told me. 'Playing on uncovered pitches taught me to keep the ball up to the bat.'

For Ambrose, the unrelenting county schedule gave him a sense of how to bring his intensity up and down. He told me:

It would be crazy, stupid even, to run in and try to bowl 90 miles an hour every single day for five months. You will fall apart. So I choose my time when to step it up and when to pull back.

I did pace myself. But even though I pulled back a bit, doesn't mean I give away runs. I can pull it back to maybe 80, 85 or whatever but I'm still bowling with enough pace to have batters cautious. So it's not like I'm fooling around.

World Series Cricket was the third pillar behind West Indies' rise. As we will see in Chapter 14, Kerry Packer's breakaway cricket league caused ruptures in the world game. But, for West Indies, it enabled players to train and play together with unprecedented intensity and earn a proper living. 'After Packer, it was like a door had been shut on the past,' Lloyd said. In all World Series matches against Australia, the West Indies WSC team won 26 games and lost only 11.

'Packer demanded excellence and professionalism,' Holding explains. 'You might be a professional cricketer because you get paid, but you don't have a professional attitude. Kerry Packer changed that as far as a lot of West Indian cricketers were concerned.'

The fourth pillar was easily overlooked, except by the players themselves: backroom support. Richards credits Rudi Webster, the team psychologist, with helping his step up in 1975/76. 'We discovered through discussion that I wasn't concentrating in the way that I should have been when I reached a certain stage of my innings,' Richards said. 'Then it was a question of discovering how I could do so and taking it on to another level, going forward step by step.'

Dennis Waight, an Australian rugby league trainer, was enlisted as the team's physiotherapist during World Series Cricket; he then worked with West Indies until 2000. 'He made that West Indies team so fit – the discipline and professionalism and the fitness came together,' Holding recalls. 'It was a perfect storm because the ability was always there.'

Waight even encouraged bowlers to practise their run-ups at full speed while blindfolded, to harness their rhythm. Especially as West Indies lacked a leading allrounder, the strategy of four fast bowlers depended on the quartet sustaining a high workload. Waight's work, and bowlers' dedication, ensured that the strategy was sustainable even in debilitating heat. It embodied a broader truth: being genuinely professional cricketers empowered West Indies to make good on their talents. In training, fast bowlers 'gave no quarter', Greenidge recalled. 'It primed you for whatever you were going to receive out in the middle.'

These magnificent players and the wider forces of the age combined to produce one of the most storied Test teams of all time. The title of Frank Keating's account of England's 1980/81 tour encapsulated what awaited teams visiting the Caribbean: *Another Bloody Day in Paradise*.

14

CRICKET'S UNCIVIL WARS

'It's the easiest sport in the world to take over. Nobody bothered to pay the players what they were worth.'

So the Australian tycoon Kerry Packer declared in May 1977. He had recruited 35 leading players for his breakaway private tournament, World Series Cricket.

Packer's plan was simple, yet stunning in its audacity. He recognised the surge in interest in watching cricket on TV, and how – partly through borrowing from the way American sports were promoted – the game could be monetised. In a meeting in 1976, Packer greeted the Australian Cricket Board's chairman and treasurer with the words 'Gentlemen, we're all whores, what's your price?' When the board refused to give him a figure to show Australia's home fixtures, because of their partnership with the Australian Broadcasting Corporation, Packer vowed to get the players on Channel Nine anyway. His cricket league would pay players about three times their previous annual wages.

At the time England's players were paid £210 per Test match – £1,600 in today's money; Australia's earned A$400 (£230 at the time), after salaries had more than doubled in 1975. New sponsorship in 1976/77 meant that players stood to earn A$2,000 (£1,150 at the time) if they won a Test, yet players remained resentful of their treatment. During the 1974/75 Ashes, when pace bowlers Dennis Lillee and Jeff Thomson tormented England, players earned just 2 per cent of gate receipts. In American sports, players earned (and still do) nearly 50 per cent of all revenue a sport generates, as the economist David Berri has shown. Cricketers were chronically underpaid.

Worldwide, most Test players at the time were best described as semi-professional, needing extra earnings alongside their cricket. With no national central contracts, incomes were vulnerable to the vicissitudes of injury, form and selectors' whims. Before anything was known of Packer's plans, players were already rebelling. Six Pakistanis refused to play against New Zealand in 1976 until being offered better terms by the board. When Australian players had threatened to strike about salaries in 1975, the ACB's secretary, Alan Barnes, said, 'These are not professionals . . . they were all invited to play, and if they don't like the conditions there are 500,000 other cricketers in Australia who would love to take their places.'

Perhaps the surprise was not Packer's emergence, but that it took so long for an entrepreneur to organise an unsanctioned competition. Packer offered not just more money but also, by offering three-year contracts, security.

A meeting between England captain Tony Greig, one of the first recruits, and Packer at the time highlighted the appeal for cricketers of being able to plan beyond merely the next season. Greig told Packer:

> Kerry, money is not my major concern. I'm nearly 31 and probably two or three Test failures from being dropped by England. Ian Botham is going to be a great player and there won't be room in the side for both of us. England captains such as Brian Close, Ray Illingworth and Colin Cowdrey lost the captaincy before they expected. I don't want to finish up in a mundane job when they drop me. I'm not trained to do anything. I went straight from school to playing for Sussex. My family's future is more important than anything else. If you guarantee me a job for life working for your organisation, I will sign.

Greig, together with Australia's former captain Ian Chappell, doubled as Packer agents in early 1977, identifying potential recruits. Astutely, Packer also signed Richie Benaud, the former Australian captain turned commentator, as an adviser and broadcaster for the matches.

By May 1977, Packer had signed 13 of Australia's 17-man squad in England for the Ashes at the time, the bulk of the West Indies team and a phalanx of England and Pakistan stars. A month later, Packer met representatives from the International Cricket Conference. The acrimonious meeting merely confirmed that a seismic split in cricket was imminent. 'Had I got those TV rights I was prepared to withdraw from the scene and leave the running of cricket to the board,' Packer said after the meeting. 'I will take no steps now to help anyone. It's every man for himself and the devil take the hindmost.'

When asked if, given how underpaid cricketers were, his motives could be described as 'half-philanthropic', Packer mocked the notion. 'Half-philanthropic?' he said. 'That makes me sound more generous than I am.'

With WSC unable to use the term 'Test matches', the games were branded 'Supertests'. While Packer said that his players were free to continue playing in official internationals that didn't clash with WSC, national boards banned players who signed up. Greig was sacked as England captain two days after news of WSC broke.

Australia's board challenged Packer in court. On 25 November, while World Series players were undertaking trial matches, Justice Slade ruled that to ban WSC cricketers from county or Test cricket would be an unreasonable restraint of trade. He observed, 'A professional cricketer needs to make his living as much as any other professional man.' It was a verdict in keeping with the history of cricketers playing in leagues in Lancashire and elsewhere.

Jim Swanton, the doyen of establishment writers, denounced Packer as 'a ruthless tycoon'; Packer might have regarded this as a compliment. Swanton considered the venture nothing less than 'evil' and declared that he couldn't imagine cricketers of previous generations 'defecting in such numbers from Test cricket – and certainly not in such secrecy.' He also doubted whether Australians 'will prefer exhibition games with no official status to the real thing'.

Initially, it seemed that Swanton was right. On 2 December 1977, Australia's opening Test against India, and the first Supertest, between Australian and West Indian teams, began in tandem. The official Test, at the Gabba, attracted 32,000 fans over the match; the Supertest was watched by a total of 13,000. With Australia's board preventing cricket stadiums from hosting WSC, the Supertest was played at Melbourne's VFL Park, an Australian Rules football stadium that had never previously hosted cricket. On day one, 2,847 came to a venue with a 79,000 capacity. Not playing on traditional grounds led WSC to innovate with drop-in pitches – grown in greenhouses, then brought into grounds on trucks.

In the first season, Packer largely mimicked the traditional international summer. He predominantly scheduled Supertests – between three alternating sides, Australia, West Indies and a World XI – rather than one-day games, taking fixtures to all major cities. In its second year, WSC made two significant shifts. The schedule prioritised one-day cricket; and matches were concentrated in Melbourne and Sydney, the largest population centres. Packer also negotiated agreements with the state governments in New South Wales and Queensland to use the Sydney Cricket Ground and the Gabba.

These changes came together on 28 November 1978 at the Sydney Cricket Ground. A crowd of 44,377 packed in to watch the WSC 50-over match between Australia and West Indies; with long queues outside, the gates were thrown open. For the establishment, the contrast in 1978/79 was distinctly uncomfortable. While WSC had brilliant fast bowlers, aggressive marketing and innovations – day-night matches and coloured clothing for one-day games – an understrength Australia were pummelled 5–1 in the Ashes.

As Australia collapsed to 26–6 on the morning of the opening Ashes Test, children chanted, 'C'mon, Aussie, C'mon': the WSC anthem. Just as players could be lured away from international cricket, so could fans – loyal to their own entertainment, rather than officially sanctioned cricket. More than 40,000 watched the final Supertest of the 1978/79 summer, between Australia and the World XI, even though it finished in three days. Australia's final official Test of the summer, against Pakistan, lasted four days, yet was watched by just 22,000 spectators.

Many players judged WSC tougher than any other cricket they played, owing to the heightened professionalism and fitness standards under Packer and, above all, the sheer concentration of elite fast bowlers. 'How do you get back into form?' Ian Chappell asks. 'It was the hardest cricket I ever played – no doubt.' With WSC matches not even granted first-class status, great performances have largely been lost to history, perhaps most gratingly for South Africa's Barry Richards, who hit 554 runs at 79.14 for the World XI in Supertests.

While Packer reshaped the game, there was an irony to his project. For all the marketing and courting of sponsors, WSC was a loss-leader, because of the salaries paid to players and operating costs. Packer spent A$12 million on WSC in two years, and made a net loss of around A$6 million, according to historian Richard Cashman. All the while, the Australian Cricket Board suffered financially too; tour profits from the 1978/79 Ashes were a quarter those of four years earlier.

In May 1979, after meeting with Sir Donald Bradman, Packer and the board hit upon a truce; really, a Packer victory. Packer's Channel Nine gained the rights to broadcast Australian cricket; he was also given a ten-year promotion and marketing contract. From Packer and the ACB both losing money, now they would make it together – though most of this went to Packer. As journalist Daniel Brettig documented in *Bradman & Packer*, John Rogers, an administrator for the Western Australian Cricket Association, produced a report in 1984 that sought to find out where the money had gone. Rogers estimated that Channel Nine/PBL had earned somewhere in the region of A$134 million in advertising revenue over the five years since the new broadcasting deal was done – yet the board had got a paltry A$2 million of that windfall. Four years before the *Deal of the Century* film, Packer had his.

WSC's 66 players were all free to resume playing official international cricket. Yet, for Australia, the legacy of WSC would be apparent for years to come. Before the 1981 Ashes, the appointment of Kim Hughes over the far more experienced Rod Marsh as Test skipper – which infuriated Marsh, Lillee and other senior players – was driven by the board's desire to have a captain untarnished by any association with the breakaway league.

Cricket's evolution was shaped by WSC, as Gideon Haigh detailed in *The Cricket War*. These two years gave the first glimpse of day-night one-day cricket, white balls and fielding circles; of drop-in pitches; and of a world in which limited-overs cricket was more lucrative, and more frequent, than Tests.

WSC accelerated the game's commercialisation, with administrators more gluttonous in arranging matches. With WSC gone, in 1979/80 Australia played concurrent series against both England and West Indies, playing each Test in turn. Australia twice had only a day between Tests, spent travelling between cities. England had 31 internal flights during their tour. For players, the increased pay was proportionately less than the increase in playing and travelling – contributing to Greg Chappell, who had replaced his brother Ian as captain, opting out of the 1981 Ashes. Bob Simpson, Test captain during the WSC years, observed, 'The Board got what they wanted, control of the game, Packer got what he wanted, some of the senior players got what they wanted. But there were a lot of other blokes down the line on both sides who suddenly were saying, "Hey, I thought we were going to be looked after."'

WSC markedly improved fans' experience watching on TV. The competition pioneered cameras at both ends, emphasising the game's gladiatorial aspect: above all, the clash between fast bowlers and batters. No longer did viewers watch half of balls from behind the bowler's arm and the other half from behind the wicketkeeper. Others envied cricket's modernisation: Garry Kasparov said that chess needed 'its own Kerry Packer'.

The abundance of fast bowlers led England opener Dennis Amiss to come to the first WSC season with a custom-made helmet, built by a motorcycle manufacturer; he became the first player to wear a helmet in a professional game. A month into WSC, David Hookes broke his jaw facing Andy Roberts. The sight of him crashing to the ground, dripping blood, added to the sense of sporting authenticity. It also led Packer to insist that players wore helmets, even those who did not want to.

'I didn't like helmets so I didn't want to wear one,' Ian Chappell recalls. He recounts his conversation with Packer:

> 'Put a f***ing helmet on, son.'
> 'Kerry, I don't need a helmet. I haven't been hit. I don't need a helmet.'
> 'Put a f***ing helmet on, son.'
> 'Mate, I don't need a helmet.'
> 'I'm not paying you to f***ing be in hospital for three months.'

Eventually, Chappell thought, 'Bugger it, it's easier to bloody put a helmet on than argue with Kerry.' He only wore the small ear-pieces to cover the temple, rather than a grille covering the front of his face.

Yet it is striking how little Packer tried to change. As the anthem 'C'mon, Aussie, C'mon' attested, his structure was still predicated on nation-v-nation cricket, just wrapped around the WSC banner. Packer does not seriously appear to have considered basing his tournament on domestic, rather than international, cricket – giving city-based teams a couple of West Indies quicks each and enticing fans to watch Sydney v Melbourne. It would be another 30 years until a major alternative to international cricket appeared.

In 2005, Packer's death showed how he had been embraced by the game's establishment: he received a commemorative minute's silence at the Boxing Day Test.

* * *

In March 1982, less than three years after World Series Cricket disbanded, the second major rebel competition of the age launched. It was even more divisive than WSC.

Sport was intimately linked to the apartheid regime, as we have seen. Trying to maintain the illusion that South Africa was still part of the international community, the governing National Party made huge efforts to encourage 'normal' sport to continue to be played. The 1977 Gleneagles Agreement, when Commonwealth nations agreed to discourage sporting links with the regime, only had limited effect.

Official rugby tours continued until 1984, when England toured. Prestigious golf and tennis events, structured around individuals rather than nations, continued throughout apartheid. But since vanquishing Australia 4–0 in 1970, South Africa had not played any official international cricket.

During the 1970s, it was relatively common for international cricketers to play and coach with South African domestic teams. Derrick Robins, an English sports promoter, organised four private tours to South Africa, comprising a motley collection of cricketers from different nations, during the decade. The South African Cricket Union (SACU), formed in 1976 to run the sport on multiracial grounds, were determined for the team to play matches that resembled nation-v-nation sport. SACU made major overtures to the ICC to be readmitted; an ICC delegation visited the country and came to believe that the sport had been integrated. India, Pakistan and West Indies made clear that they would not countenance apartheid South Africa being welcomed back, or accept other nations playing them.

Dr Ali Bacher, South Africa's captain before the side's banishment from Test cricket, told SACU's board that there was 'no way back through the front door'. Bacher led SACU's recruitment of players to conduct rebel international tours to the country. Players set up a bogus chess club as cover for their meetings, though no one bothered to bring a board or pieces. Communication with potential English players was in code: 'knights and castles meet in the bishop's room at nine'; 'the chess tournament will now include this many matches'.

As it had been for Packer, Bacher's biggest asset was the chequebook. Each England player earned £40–60,000 – about £115–170,000 in today's money – to tour. For a month's work, players would earn several times more than the £10,000 they would receive for a four-month Test tour of India. Notionally, the rebels' salaries were bankrolled by SACU's sponsors. The truth was very different. Sponsors received huge government subsidies, in the region of 90 per cent, so their cash effectively came from the regime.

In March 1982, the first rebel tour landed at Jan Smuts Airport in Johannesburg. The tourists were called 'the dirty dozen' by Neil Kinnock, the future Labour leader; the label was then adopted by the British tabloid newspapers.

SACU had hoped that they could unveil a team that represented the best of the English game. Instead, both Ian Botham and David Gower reportedly reneged on their in-principle agreements to tour. England's squad – officially called the South African Breweries English XI – included Graham Gooch, Alan Knott and Geoffrey Boycott, and five players who had returned from a Test tour to India and Sri Lanka only a week earlier.

The cricket was underwhelming; South Africa won the first match easily before a pair of dour draws ended the series. England's trip was a 'triumph for common sense', said John Vorster, the former prime minister, during the series. 'I haven't been to many cricket games in the past ten years but I am enjoying this one. It's one thing I did not want to miss.'

Most South Africans did not feel the same way. Allan Donald, a white fast bowler who played in the rebel tours, wrote, 'When South Africa was still in isolation, there was no black support for us when we played against "rebel" sides who came to our country. Not that we deserved to be supported by the black community – we were hardly playing these sides to improve their lives.'

South Africa's government liked to proclaim that sport and politics did not mix. This was never the attitude that they themselves took: the rebel tourists were there because the South African government was effectively paying for them. England's tour was the first of seven tours undertaken by rebels between 1982 and 1990. Australia and England came twice, Sri Lanka once and, most contentiously, West Indies twice.

* * *

For all the differences between World Series Cricket and the rebel tours, there were also striking similarities. The recruitment process followed the same template: furtive meetings, targeting both players with grievances against their national board or selectors and the very biggest names. The rebel tours and WSC were both a by-product of particular vulnerabilities in cricket; the greatest was still the chronic underpayment of players.

Whether for Packer or for South Africa, economically insecure players were attractive targets. It was a reality recognised by Clive Lloyd. West Indies' captain had been recruited by Packer; after the first rebel tour, Lloyd feared that Caribbean players would also be approached. The risk was particularly acute because of a combination of players being underpaid, the region's economic difficulties and the strength of Caribbean cricket, which left outstanding players on the international fringes. In a paper presented to regional governments in 1982, Lloyd wrote:

Several West Indies players... many who do not have a secure playing future when their playing days are over... may be tempted to respond favourably to these offers. If members of what might be considered the West Indies first and second elevens were to give in to the considerable temptations that could be offered, the implications for both West Indies and world cricket could be grave.

Lloyd advocated a stipend of US$20,000–$30,000 a year for the leading 20 or so West Indies players: effectively, central contracts. He was ignored. In January 1983, the first West Indies rebels landed in South Africa. It was the first West Indies cricket tour to South Africa. In 1959, a proposed tour by a West Indies team to play against black players – in adherence to the laws of the time – was cancelled after the African National Congress argued that the tour could bring the regime legitimacy.

As the flight descended on South Africa, 'There was total silence,' Lawrence Rowe, a Jamaican batter who made 302 in a Test against England in 1974, recalled. 'Everybody was more or less thinking the same thing. Whoever was thinking about a career for the West Indies again, it was now gone.'

The motivations of Caribbean rebels were generally uncomplicated. They wanted to provide for their families; with West Indies' side so hard to break into, rebel tours promised financial security. Malcolm Marshall and Desmond Haynes strongly considered going on the tours, but ultimately declined. Most tourists were on the periphery of the national side, or towards the end of their careers. 'It was, like, 60 times more than what you were getting paid,' Rowe said in 2004. 'People like Everton Mattis didn't own a car, didn't have a house, didn't have anything. How do you tell a man in a position like that not to accept $100,000 to go play five months of cricket?'

'All of the countries of the world were trading with South Africa,' Collis King said in Ashley Gray's book *The Unforgiven*. 'You tell me I'm a cricketer and you're trading but I can't play.'

In the documentary *Fire in Babylon*, Colin Croft said,

> Money is everybody's god... Let's be honest, you had to look after yourself.
> I'm a mercenary? When I went to World Series Cricket, was I not a mercenary then? I'm not sure I understand the difference. This is not a game. This is my livelihood. It's my job.

West Indies' strength was such that, during their second tour, they became the only rebel side to win in South Africa. They did so without their stars who had just put together a streak of 15 consecutive Test victories.

* * *

Even if they wanted to, proclaiming themselves mere sportsmen, players could not easily escape their actions' political consequences. West Indies tourists acquired 'honorary white' status in South Africa, using hotels and bars normally reserved for white people alone. In 1983, Croft unwittingly sat in a whites-only train carriage and was told by the conductor to move to a different carriage. The government apologised to Croft for any 'embarrassment'; it was no different to what black people suffered every day. 'I should have been reading the whites-only signs, but not being accustomed to that sort of stuff I didn't worry about it,' Croft said.

Australia's prime minister, Bob Hawke, called the 16 tourists to South Africa in 1985/86 'traitors', attacking 'the comfort [the players] would give to a racist regime'. Against a backdrop of chants of 'Shame, Kim, shame' in Perth, Kim Hughes declared that he was 'going to South Africa with an open and, I hope, intelligent mind', and 'I also believe I will be able to comment and suggest ways in which the situation can be improved.' Few agreed. The rebels 'should have the decency to speak the truth and say they have sold themselves', Bishop Desmond Tutu said. 'There is a state of emergency, when the army is being set on the civilian population, they want to come here when on the average four blacks are killed every day and it doesn't touch on their consciences at all.'

One exception was Mike Whitney, who visited South Africa after being sounded out to go on the tours. After witnessing a policeman whip black men for standing together on a street corner talking, Whitney withdrew from discussions. Rodney Hogg, the fast bowler who went on both Australia rebel tours, mocked the idea that players sought to help South Africa. 'Anyone who says that's why they went on the tour is kidding themselves,' Hogg told *The Cricket Monthly*. 'You've never thought about helping South African cricket before, so why would you do it now?'

'The golden rule about rebel tours is the only person who doesn't know about them is the England captain,' David Gower told me. In 1989, as England ended a humiliating Ashes summer, Gower learned of another rebel tour. 'Half your team, whether you wanted to drop them or not – f***ing useless though they were – are no longer available.' At Old Trafford, after news of the tour broke, Neil Foster bowled with tears in his eyes: he had signed to go to South Africa, and knew that he faced a ban from international cricket.

In January 1990, just as Nelson Mandela was on the cusp of being released from prison, Mike Gatting captained England's second rebel tour. 'I don't know much about how apartheid works but one way to find out is by going there,' Gatting said before the tour. He described one demonstration during the tour as 'just a bit of singing and dancing'. Black hotel staff refused to serve England's squad. In Pietermaritzburg, a crowd chanted, 'Gatting, go home!' He did: after Mandela's release from prison on 11 February, the tour was curtailed. To *The Guardian*'s Frank Keating, 'No more inglorious, downright disgraced and discredited team of sportsmen wearing the badge of "England" can ever have returned through customs with such nothingness to declare.'

* * *

Different rebels would have very different fates. 'The lepers who are surreptitiously worming their way to South Africa must understand that they are not playing fair by the coloured world,' declared Gamini Dissanayake, the Sri Lankan board's president and a prominent politician. All 14 Sri Lanka rebels, including five who had previously played Tests, received 25-year bans from the game. The bans were lifted in 1991, nine years later, but the rebels never escaped the tour's legacy. 'We lived it,' Bandula Warnapura, who captained the tour, recalled. After the tour Warnapura 'faced a struggle to even get electricity connected at his house', Nicholas Brookes wrote in *An Island's Eleven*. Arjuna Ranatunga, one of the country's most promising players, almost signed for the tour but was then advised to withdraw; he would go on to be a transformative Test captain.

West Indies rebels would become known as The Unforgiven. 'I would rather die than lay down my dignity,' declared Viv Richards, who refused a 'blank cheque', rumoured to be £250,000, to tour. Several rebels, including Richard Austin, Herbert Chang and David Murray, became destitute, suffering drug addiction and mental-health problems and even living on the streets. Others still felt like pariahs, often emigrating from the Caribbean. The West Indies board rescinded the life ban on the rebels in 1989; only one player, Barbados's Ezra Moseley, played Test cricket after the tours. Roy Fredericks, a former West Indies cricketer, who also played WSC, and then became Minister for Youth, Sport and Culture in Guyana, said, 'They should not cause further discomfort to the West Indian population by attempting to live among us.'

For Australian and English rebels, life was altogether more palatable. Australia's players originally received two-year bans from domestic cricket; these bans were deemed to apply to the seasons when players were in South Africa, so they were free to resume their domestic careers as soon as they returned. From a year later, September 1988, rebels were eligible for international selection; three won recalls. One of these, swing bowler Terry Alderman, bowled masterfully in the 4–0 Ashes victory in England in 1989; another, Trevor Hohns, went on to become chairman of selectors. English rebels were all free to play county cricket immediately, but were handed three-year international bans.

Of England's 30 rebel tourists across their two tours, 12 played Test cricket again. Gooch, who captained the first rebel tour, later led England, enjoying a magnificent period as a Test opener in the early 1990s. He was one of eight rebels who became an England selector or coach; at one point, the entire selection panel comprised rebels. John Emburey, the only Englishman to go on both rebel tours, was recalled to international cricket after both bans, and later became England assistant coach. While West Indies' rebels were ostracised, England's rebels became, just as much as Packer, part of the establishment.

15

THE IMPOSSIBLE JOB

What is a Test allrounder? The common retort is a player worthy of their place both as a specialist batter and bowler. A good yardstick for a Test specialist, it is widely agreed, is someone averaging over 40 with the bat or under 30 with the ball. Yet even Sir Garfield Sobers missed this mark. Only one man to score 1,000 Test runs and take 50 wickets has met this double mark of excellence: South Africa's Aubrey Faulkner, who played from 1906 to 1924.

Some cricketers can turn a Test match with either bat or ball; the rarefied group of elite allrounders can do so with bat *and* ball. Yet the better a side is, the harder it is for allrounders to be of sufficient quality to get into the best XI. This is one explanation for why the West Indies 1980–95 side and the Australia 1995–2007 team did not have an allrounder. Instead, they selected their four best bowlers, trusting in them to take 20 wickets a Test. It was hard enough getting into these teams for batting or bowling, never mind both.

In the 1980s, Test cricket had a glut of outstanding allrounders, of an ilk never quite seen before or since. Ian Botham, Kapil Dev, Richard Hadlee and Imran Khan were less cricketers than superheroes, their individual tussles doubling as fights for team supremacy. 'We wanted to outdo each other,' Botham told *Wisden Cricket Monthly* in 2020. 'I'd always check to see if Imran had done well, or if Kapil had done well, or Richard. You wanted that No. 1 position.' Kapil spoke for the quartet when he declared, 'My aim has always been to try and achieve the impossible.'

* * *

Botham provides the quintessential image of the Test allrounder as superhero. From his childhood in rural Somerset, Botham was imbued with a sense of his own destiny; aged seven, he took to practising his autograph, reasoning that fans would want it one day.

Even as it was playing out, the English summer of 1981, the tale that would become known as Botham's Ashes, instantly moved from mere sporting performance to national mythology. For England and Botham alike, the summer began with strife. Botham, who had made a spectacular Test entrance – combining audacious counter-attacking batting with swing bowling of great accuracy and pace – was weighed down by the twin challenges of captaincy and facing West Indies. In 12 Tests as skipper, Botham averaged 33.08 with the ball and 13.14 with the bat.

In the second Ashes Test of 1981, Botham registered a pair. As he walked off for his second duck of the game, he walked through the Lord's Long Room to stony silence. He resigned, 'bitter as I was at being effectively forced from the England captaincy', he wrote. Alec Bedser, the chairman of selectors, confirmed at a press conference that Botham would have been sacked if he hadn't resigned.

England didn't win any of Botham's 12 Tests in charge, losing home and away series against West Indies, and slipping 1–0 behind in the 1981 Ashes. The series was played against a backdrop of national strife: there were riots from Birmingham to Manchester, London to Leeds and Liverpool, as frustrations over inflation and unemployment spilled over. England was a country in need of a fairy tale.

After Botham resigned, Mike Brearley succeeded him. In many ways, it was a curious choice: Brearley was 39, a specialist batter who averaged in the low 20s and made it clear he wouldn't tour the following winter. But Brearley's rapport with bowlers was like a horse whisperer's with his stable. Botham said that Brearley 'could wind me up in ten seconds' to coax a performance out of him. In the last

Test of Brearley's previous reign, in Bombay in 1980, Botham took 13 wickets in the game, either side of hitting 114. Brearley learned that he was appointed to lead England again via a reverse-charge phone call: Bedser, the chairman of selectors, had run out of coins. At nets before the third Test, Brearley asked Botham, 'Beef, are you sure you want to play?' Botham replied, 'Of course I want to play.'

At Headingley, Australia batted first under cloudy skies and reached 401–9 declared. Botham initially struggled with the ball; after three overs, Brearley called him 'the sidestep queen', encouraging him to revert to his original action. His 6–95 hinted that he would fare better back in the ranks; a round 50 in England's first innings, his first in Tests for 21 innings, confirmed the impression. Botham stood out as a rose in a dungheap; England were all out for 174.

When Botham walked out in the second innings, borrowing Graham Gooch's bat, because it was heavier, he was still the only England player to have reached 50 in the match. Following on, at 105–5, an innings defeat beckoned. That seemed a certainty by the time that Dennis Lillee and Terry Alderman left England 135–7 – still trailing by 92 runs, with the crowd emptying. As Graham Dilley, England's number nine, joined him, Botham said, 'Right. Come on, let's give it some humpty.' Botham was among the England players to have already checked out of the hotel. When Lillee and Rodney Marsh saw that the odds on an England victory had reached 500–1, they enlisted the team bus driver to place bets, against their own side: Lillee £10, and Marsh £5.

'My centre is giving way, my right is retreating, situation excellent, I am attacking,' French general Ferdinand Foch said in 1914. Botham began his innings in the same spirit, interspersing buccaneering drives with top edges; mastery with a good dose of mayhem. 'It wasn't exactly the noble art of batsmanship,' he wrote: 'a series of wild slogs that came off.' It was all the more thrilling because Botham had reverted back to batting without a helmet.

Imperceptibly, Botham's hitting went from defiance in defeat to holding out the possibility of being something more; he delighted in seeing Australia 'fretting', with 'about three or four people telling fielders where to stand'. Australia, says their bowler Geoff Lawson, should have used Ray Bright, their spinner, more and placed more men on the ropes. 'We should have set the field more out and just let him get ones and try to hit over the top,' Lawson reflects. 'We thought he was gonna get out every ball. He swung hard, he hit miles, he lobbed them in the gaps. Every mishit seemed to fall in a gap: he was top-edging over third man. In between, he was smacking them. Fortune was favouring the brave and Beefy was always brave.'

Belying his position of number nine, Dilley drove exquisitely off the front foot, hitting 56 and getting England into the lead. When Botham glanced up at the balcony, he expected to see Brearley 'urging restraint, but instead he was miming even wilder and more extravagant strokes'. Botham's favourite was a square cut for four off Lillee: 'I don't think I ever hit a more perfectly timed and executed shot.' Chris Old and Bob Willis helped Botham add another 104 for the final two wickets. Photographed in the dressing room after the fourth day, Botham was draped in his pads with a cigar in his mouth; he headed out for fish and chips and a couple of pints. When Botham ran out of partners early on day five, he had hit 149 not out, from 148 balls.

Australia still looked like they would waltz towards their target of 130. Despite taking an early wicket, Botham admitted that 'in our more rational moments none of us really believed we could do it'. Willis, fearing that he was playing in his final Test and initially not picked because England thought he wasn't fit, was first change and incensed by bowling into the wind. Brearley then switched Willis to bowling down the hill, with the breeze, from the Kirkstall Lane End, telling him to forget about his troubles bowling no-balls: 'Just run up and bowl fast and straight.'

Just before lunch, with Australia 56–1, one of these fast, straight balls was bowled at the throat of Trevor Chappell, an unconvincing replacement for his older brother Greg; Chappell fended it behind to wicketkeeper Bob Taylor. In his following over, Willis snared Kim Hughes and Graham Yallop. On each occasion, Willis didn't celebrate, simply walking back to his mark. When Dilley looked into his eyes, he said, 'It was like there was nobody there.'

After lunch, Chris Old bowled Allan Border. Now, Willis laid waste to Australia, who collapsed to 75–8, still 55 runs from victory. As Lillee and Ray Bright slashed 35 in four overs, abetted by two drops by Old at third slip, romance seemed to have run into cold reality. But Willis dismissed both, bowling Bright to secure England's 18-run victory: in the 20th century, this was the lone Test won by a side who had been made to follow on. With the series 1–1 thanks to his 8–43, Willis finally celebrated. That afternoon, the champagne had been on ice – in Australia's dressing room. England's manager negotiated with his opposite number to buy some for the hosts.

Botham authored two worthy encores before summer was out. First, gently prodded by Brearley exhorting him to 'Keep things tight' for off-spinner John Emburey, Botham's spell of 5–1 in 28 deliveries, attacking the stumps, bowled Australia out for 121 in Birmingham, clinching a 29-run win. Next, he hit 118, including six sixes, at Old Trafford: an innings that combined the same power as Headingley – at one stage he looted 90 from 48 balls, targeting the second new ball – but with the edges left out. Botham judged this the best innings of his life. Three times Lillee bowled fierce bouncers directed towards his nose; each time Botham's hook cleared fine leg for six. The Ashes were regained, 3–1; Australia's captain Kim Hughes said that, but for Botham, his side could have won 4–0. In 26 Tests under Brearley, Botham averaged 41.36 with the bat, with seven centuries, and took 150 wickets – nearly six per game – at an average of 18.76. This underpinned Brearley's phenomenal record as England captain: 18 victories, and just four losses. Both were at their best with each other.

* * *

Aged 15, Kapil Dev attended an India Under-19 coaching camp. The young Kapil had a big appetite; besides, he thought, a cricketer needed to be well fed to bowl first. When he protested about only being offered two dry chapattis and a spoonful of vegetables for lunch, Kapil was mocked. 'There are no fast bowlers in India,' said Keki Tarapore, the board official at the camp.

India's fast-bowling tradition, as we have seen, had lain dormant since the 1930s. When Kapil made his Test debut in 1978, 'in all of Indian cricket, there were no fast bowlers,' he wrote. 'Not in university cricket, not in club cricket, and certainly not in the first-class game.

'Being a pace bowler in India should rank as one of the most hazardous occupations in the world. Primarily, it is the wickets which make your job so tough. It is easy to say "bend your back and produce more pace" but it is far too tough to keep it up in home conditions where the climate itself can break your back.'

Against Pakistan, on Test debut, Kapil bowled to Sadiq Mohammed, a fine opening batter. Sadiq wore a hat, expecting to be met by medium pace. After one bouncer from Kapil raced past his nose, Sadiq requested a helmet.

Kapil had a quick bouncer and an athletic physique, partly nurtured through his childhood love of football. His greatest asset was swing, normally curving the ball away from right-handers. Within 16 months of his debut, Kapil became the first Indian pace bowler to take 100 Test wickets. These feats changed the character of Indian cricket: no longer were pitches prepared exclusively with spin in mind. With left-armer Karsan Ghavri providing useful support, Kapil showed that seam could win matches too. At Madras in 1979, Kapil's seven wickets in the match set up victory over West Indies, who were still capable despite losing players to World Series Cricket. His 26 not out clinched a fraught run chase; it was the only game in the six-Test series to have a positive result.

At the same ground a year later, India faced Pakistan and were 1–0 up in the series with two Tests to play. Imran scored 34 and 29 and claimed five wickets in between, but was overshadowed by Kapil. First, Kapil took 4–90, showing the speed and swing to overcome a benign batting surface; then he thumped 84 from number eight to lift India's lead to 158 runs. With 7–56 in Pakistan's second innings, Kapil ensured India's first series victory over Pakistan since 1952/53 – and victory for him in his personal duel. Imran later declared him 'one of the most intelligent bowlers in world cricket, and someone who always seems to be bowling to a plan'.

The final Test of India's tour to Australia in 1980/81 loomed with the hosts 1–0 up: after an innings defeat at Sydney, India had clung on, eight wickets down, to salvage a draw in Adelaide. In Melbourne, Australia got a first innings lead of 182, before openers Sunil Gavaskar and Chetan Chauhan almost erased that themselves in response. After Gavaskar was controversially judged lbw, despite an apparent inside edge – he was so incandescent that he threatened to forfeit the Test – India collapsed.

When their run chase began with an hour left on day four, Australia needed just 143 runs to wrap up a 2–0 series victory. India's attack was threadbare; off-spinner Shivlal Yadav had a fractured toe and couldn't bowl. Kapil had strained a thigh muscle, which had forced him to bat with a runner in the tourists' second innings. With the pair off the field, Ghavri had opener John Dyson caught behind. When Greg Chappell, Australia's number three and star batter, arrived at the crease, Ghavri planned to bowl a bouncer. 'That bouncer never came up because the Melbourne pitch had big cracks,' Ghavri explained. 'Chappell must have thought that it's going to be a short delivery. And it was a short delivery, but it kept very low and his leg stump was exposed. He was clean bowled.' Australia closed at a nervy 24–3.

The next morning, Kapil patched up his thigh. He recognised that the cracks on the pitch created uneven bounce, and so bowled straighter than normal. With the aid of pain-killing injections he bowled unchanged, for 16.4 overs. When last man Jim Higgs was lbw, Kapil raised his arms in triumph: his 5–28 had skittled Australia for 83. Save for two wins against a side decimated by World Series Cricket, it was India's only Test victory down under until 2003, and their first drawn series there.

Bowling was always Kapil's primary role; this perception liberated his batting. With his high backlift, trademark 'Nataraja' shot – a pull with his front leg in the air – and penchant for taking a stride forward to meet pace bowling, no one attacked West Indies' quick bowlers in the 1980s as audaciously. Between 1976 and 1995, the years of West Indies dominance, only three players hit three centuries at faster than a run a ball against them. Kapil alone managed two of them – in Delhi in 1979, albeit against a side depleted by World Series Cricket, and at Trinidad in 1983. At Madras in 1988, Kapil's 109 off 124 balls, against an attack including Patrick Patterson and Courtney Walsh, helped India to victory and a squared series. Kapil distilled his batting mantra: 'Hit the ball, over the slips, over the ropes. Runs on the board count.'

Perhaps the best encapsulation of Kapil's batting came at Lord's in 1990. India were 430–9, 24 runs shy of saving the follow-on, when off-spinner Eddie Hemmings came on from the Nursery End. With Narendra Hirwani, a hapless number 11, for company, Kapil sensed that he might not get another chance to save the follow-on. He struck four consecutive sixes – all with a clean, smooth swing of the bat over long-on, into the building works – then looked to the balcony and pumped his fist. For moments like these, Gavaskar called Kapil the most natural cricketer in the world.

In the five-day game, it was Kapil's fate to toil in a struggling side. India won just 18 per cent of Tests that he played in, a percentage 8 per cent worse than any of the other 1980s quartet of allrounders. From 1981 to 1984, India went 31 consecutive Tests without victory. India were even less successful when Kapil captained, winning four out of 34 Tests, with 23 drawn. His greatest deeds were often in vain. At Lord's in 1982, he slammed 89 from 55 balls and took eight wickets in defeat. In Ahmedabad the following year, he took 9–83 against West Indies; India still lost easily.

In 2002, Kapil was voted India's Cricketer of the Century. It recognised that few cricketers have left such a legacy. Kapil performed spectacularly in the 1983 World Cup, when India recorded a stunning triumph. He also embodied, and accelerated, a growing meritocracy in Indian cricket. Historically, India had relied largely on university-educated players from the biggest cities for their Test talent. While Kapil enjoyed a perfectly comfortable childhood, he hailed from Chandigarh – by national standards, a small city, with a population then under one million – and did not attend university.

'All we youngsters needed was a crude bat, an old tennis ball and a set of stumps,' he wrote. Kapil illustrated the talent that existed outside Indian cricket's traditional centres. 'When I was a boy, cricket was very, very English,' he said. 'Anyone who spoke English and anyone from a big town could play. And that was it. Now anybody from a smaller town can play, too.'

* * *

For New Zealand's first 43 years as a Test nation, Australia only deigned to play a solitary Test against them. When New Zealand were finally granted their second Test against Australia, at Melbourne on Boxing Day 1973, they lost by an innings. In his third Test, Richard Hadlee – the son of Walter, the patriarch of New Zealand cricket, and younger brother of the Test seamer Dayle – took 0–104. From this inauspicious beginning, Richard would transform New Zealand's record against Australia, and their Test standing.

Three months later, New Zealand hosted Australia in a return series. Using his 6 ft 1 in height and accuracy to exploit the seam movement offered at Christchurch's Lancaster Park, Richard took seven wickets in the match, helping to bring New Zealand's maiden Test victory over their trans-Tasman foes. He took another seven in the match in New Zealand's second win over Australia, at Auckland in 1982.

In 1985/86, New Zealand toured Australia for three Tests, beginning at the Gabba, Australia's lair. Before the Test, Glenn Turner, New Zealand's coach, had noticed that Hadlee was bowling too wide of the crease, preventing him from getting lbws. Turner advocated that Hadlee practise bowling with a rubbish bin six feet behind the stumps, where an umpire would be during the match. Hadlee then tweaked his action, he explained, to 'get closer to the stumps, be more "side on" at delivery and bowl wicket to wicket'.

Brisbane was his first opportunity to showcase these changes in a Test. In overcast conditions, Hadlee surprised Andrew Hilditch – the 'happy hooker' – with a short ball in his first over. He seldom deviated from his conventional approach thereafter. Now 34, Hadlee had pared back seam bowling to its essential components, wising up as he slowed down. After Australia reached 146–4 on a truncated first day, Hadlee's tactic of bowling just back of a length, with remorseless accuracy, swing, seam and bounce, decimated the hosts. Suffocated, some batters played at balls they could have left; one, Kepler Wessels, was lbw when not playing a shot. After he had taken the first eight wickets, Hadlee had thoughts of a perfect ten. When Geoff Lawson launched an off break from the debutant Vaughan Brown towards midwicket, Hadlee caught it himself, dashing his own dreams. He had to be content with 9–52.

Australia were bowled out for 179. Martin Crowe, driving regally through the off side and hooking emphatically when the bowlers dropped short, made nine runs more himself. New Zealand didn't declare until they had reached 553–7. By the time that Hadlee was dismissed, for a brutal half-century, fielders 'were dotted like bait around the boundary', captain Jeremy Coney told me. 'Every player except the bowler and the keeper. We'd broken them. It was a real moment, because New Zealand had been such a poor cousin.'

Despite the reliable support from his new-ball partner Ewen Chatfield, it would largely fall upon Hadlee to prevent Australia from escaping with a draw. With Allan Border at his cussed best, batting for over eight hours, New Zealand had to go around him. After Greg Matthews made a century in a sixth-wicket rearguard that lasted almost four hours, Hadlee dismissed him to open up the tail. A characteristic dismissal – fractionally short of a good length, seaming in and uprooting the off stump – clean bowled number 11 Bob Holland to seal New Zealand's first victory down under; an innings win, like all those that Australia had enjoyed against them. Hadlee took 15 wickets for 123 in the Test match, with 54 runs in between. He later said,

> You strive for excellence and performance. Sometimes you never get there but that was the closest I came. I had bowled just as well in other games without anywhere near the statistical rewards, but it was a day when everything worked. The rhythm, timing and technique were there to control the ball and commit the batsmen into errors.

There was no question of Hadlee being sated. In the series decider, at Perth, Hadlee took 11 wickets; New Zealand were only the third nation to defeat Australia in a series down under. A return series began only three months later. Hadlee was instrumental in New Zealand's victory in that too. Across the six Tests in the two series, Hadlee took 49 wickets at an average of 16.08, while also hitting two half-centuries. If the style was very different to Botham's Ashes, the results were perhaps even more spectacular.

New Zealand's next series, the 1986 tour of England, began with Hadlee taking 6–80 during a draw. England's Graham Gooch said that facing New Zealand was 'like the World XI at one end, and Ilford second XI at the other'. The comment ignored New Zealand's wider quality and resourcefulness; peeved, players trained in T-shirts saying 'Ilford seconds'. By the summer's end, New Zealand had secured another series victory. For all Coney's shrewd captaincy, Crowe's style and John Wright's tenacious opening batting, the win also bore the undeniable imprint of individual greatness. In the lone Test of the series to have a positive result, at Trent Bridge, his home as Nottinghamshire's overseas player, Hadlee took 10–140 in the match and scored 68. It evoked another remarkable performance against England, at Christchurch in 1984, when Hadlee thrashed 99, more than the visitors made in either innings, and took 8–44 in the match.

Hadlee took 431 wickets in 86 Tests, an average of over five wickets per Test. Only one seamer with 300 wickets, Lillee, took so many per Test; not even he could match Hadlee's record of 36 per cent of dismissals that his side took in matches that he played, or taking five-wicket hauls in 42 per cent of Tests. Normally, being over-bowled dilutes a bowler's effectiveness – forcing them to bowl when tired, or when conditions are less favourable. The wonder of Hadlee was that he took on this burden while still averaging 22.29. His adaptability was such that he averaged even less in Asia, and took 10–88 in the victory in Bombay in November 1988.

'I regard an over as having six bullets in a gun,' Hadlee explained. 'I use those bullets strategically, to manipulate the batsman into a certain position or state of mind, so that I can eliminate him.'

Hadlee was an altogether more earnest character than the other leading 1980s allrounders; a moustache seemed to be his sole indulgence. 'Statistics always motivated me,' he wrote:

> I was criticised from time to time for being single-minded and, at times, selfish. But I make no apologies for playing the game the way I did. Cricket, more than any other team game, is an individual game.

With the occasional exception, Hadlee's individual needs worked in concert with his team's. New Zealand were undefeated in ten home series in the 1980s, even managing a victory and draw from two tussles with West Indies.

* * *

Imran Khan made his Test debut as an 18-year-old in 1971. As a stand-in for an injured player, Imran did little to suggest an enduring career: he made five and did not take a wicket in 28 overs of medium pace. Unimpressed, Pakistan did not pick him again for another three years. In 1971, Sunil Gavaskar played for India against Worcestershire, Imran's county. He remembered Imran as 'a skinny boy with an unruly mop of hair' and 'could not have believed that this man, in a matter of three or four years, would be troubling the best of the batsmen in the world'.

When Imran returned, his physique was transformed; inspired by watching Dennis Lillee, he morphed into a man who could bowl quickly. Initially erratic, he became more consistent and, as we shall see, learned the art of reverse swing around 1980. Thereafter he could swing the ball both ways – both new and old – at a pace that exceeded the rest of the quartet.

Imran had wanted to be a Test cricketer from the age of nine, when he watched his cousin Javed Burki score a century against England in Lahore. In his initial years, Imran was 'a frustrated opening bat', struggling with adjusting from opening – as he did at Aitchison College, the 'Eton of Pakistan' – to batting lower down. In his 30th Test, against West Indies in Lahore in 1980, Imran hit 123. It signalled Imran's transformation into one of the best cricketers in the world. In his first 29 Tests, he averaged 23.87 with the bat and 29.94 with the ball; then, over the last 12 years of his career, Imran averaged 47.13 and 19.36. It was a prolonged period of individual excellence to rank among the best of all time.

Most of it came while he was captain too; Imran's aggressive captaincy style was modelled on Australia's Ian Chappell. Whether in cricket or even more important matters, Imran was never happier than when leading, insisting on having 'complete control' in team selection. 'I am convinced that unless a captain can lead from the front, he cannot inspire his team to fight,' he wrote in 1988. The most glamorous of the quartet, surpassing even Kapil, Imran professed himself 'constantly amazed at the amount of fame I have attracted', but 'I'm not complaining about it either: there is no greater satisfaction for any sportsman or entertainer than to be appreciated.' His teammate Aaqib Javed observed that 'Once he is convinced about something he will never retreat. Never.'

In the 1980s, Pakistan were a terrific team. Javed Miandad was a Test batter of such completeness and versatility that his average never dropped below 50. Miandad was one of the first to turn the reverse sweep into a pragmatic run-scoring option; importing the skills that made him a pioneering one-day player, he was particularly adept at dinking the ball into unguarded pockets and then haring between the wickets. His batting was fused with an insatiable competitiveness, first nurtured in tape-ball cricket in Karachi. 'Cricket was war and I was at war whenever I played,' he wrote. Miandad readily captained in Imran's absence.

Whoever was captain could call upon a fine assortment of talent. Zaheer Abbas, who had an unusually high backlift and dexterous wrists, provided Miandad with middle-order support; Shoaib Mohammad was an adhesive opener; Wasim Raja combined stylish batting and useful leg breaks. Pakistan's most distinctive bowler throughout the 1980s was Abdul Qadir, a leg-spinner with a French beard and beguiling googly. 'I added up all the things I learnt to create some impression in the minds of batsmen,' Qadir later explained. 'I wanted to do miracles.'

Before he bowled the flipper – a variation that went straight on and low – Qadir would tell the umpire discreetly, alerting him to a possible lbw. He often operated in tandem with Iqbal Qasim's wily, parsimonious left-arm spin. The end of the decade, as we shall see, marked the emergence of Wasim Akram and Waqar Younis as one of the most devastating new- and old-ball pairs around.

For all this company, it was Imran who elevated Pakistan to being the decade's second-best side. Against India in Faisalabad in 1983, Imran became the second man, after Botham in Bombay in 1980, to score a hundred and take ten wickets in the same Test. Swinging the ball both ways at pace – and learning that his inswinger was most effective when bowled close to the stumps – his 40 wickets in the six-match series cost 13.95 apiece. In 1982, he led Pakistan to a 3–0 whitewash at home to Australia. In 1987, with 7–40 at Headingley and 118 at The Oval, Imran was crucial in Pakistan's first Test series victory in England.

Over the 1980s, Pakistan won 23 Tests and lost just 13. Imran and his team maintained their standards against the best side of the age. Pakistan met West Indies in three classic series from 1986 to 1990. These contests elevated Imran to the very top rank of Test cricketers.

Table 5. The Superheroes

	Batting average	Bowling average	Batting average v West Indies	Bowling average v West Indies
Ian Botham	33.54	28.40	21.40	35.18
Kapil Dev	31.05	29.64	30.82	24.89
Richard Hadlee	27.16	22.29	32.41	22.03
Imran Khan	37.69	22.81	27.67	21.18

In 1986, Pakistan welcomed Viv Richards's side for a first meeting in six years. West Indies' aura had never been greater; they had won 18 out of their past 22 Tests, all by crushing margins. That sequence looked to be extending in Faisalabad. Despite Imran's 61, Pakistan were bowled out for 159; Wasim Akram's 6–91, showing his penchant for eradicating the tail, restricted West Indies to 248, still an 89-run lead. At 19–2 in their second innings, Pakistan looked to be hurtling towards defeat against an attack so strong that a young Courtney Walsh was third change. Wicketkeeper Saleem Yousuf – promoted as a nightwatchman to number four – hit 61 to begin a recovery. From number nine, Wasim blitzed 66, lifting West Indies' target to 240.

Swinging the ball back into the right-handers, Imran snared both Gordon Greenidge and Desmond Haynes. Then, on a worn pitch taking turn, he tossed the ball to Qadir. With close-in fielders stalking the batters like incessant mosquitoes, his array of leg breaks and googlies befuddled West Indies; Qadir took 6–16. West Indies were all out for 53.

Piqued, in Lahore Malcolm Marshall and Walsh skittled Pakistan for 131 and 77, handing West Indies victory by an innings. In the series decider in Karachi, West Indies gained a one-run first innings lead, then set Pakistan 213 to win. At 95–7, number nine Tauseef Ahmed walked out to join Imran, showing the austere defence learned in his days as a top-order batter. The pair remained together for an hour and a half, scarcely giving thought to scoring runs, before bad light ensured that Pakistan escaped with a draw.

Two years later – after Imran had retired and then, at the urging of the nation's president, unretired – Pakistan toured the Caribbean. Imran initiated batting practice against wet tennis balls thrown from 18 yards away, in preparation for the short bowling that his team would face. In Guyana, Imran produced a totemic performance: battling a toe infection, he took 11–121 in the match, including four wickets in three overs on the opening day with what appears to have been reverse swing. Miandad's seven-hour 114, leaving short balls alone and absorbing blow after blow to his body, secured a hefty lead. West Indies conceded 38 no-balls – Pakistan believed that pace bowler Winston Benjamin was deliberately over-stepping to try and intimidate them – and a total of 71 extras. Imran and Qadir then combined to secure a crushing nine-wicket victory. A wildly oscillating second Test ended with Pakistan chasing 372 to win; Miandad hit another defiant century, this one even slower. After his dismissal, Pakistan downgraded their aim from victory to survival. Walking out at 341–9, Qadir, the number 11, survived the final five balls.

That left Pakistan 1–0 up going into the final Test in Barbados. Pakistan snuck a three-run first innings lead, then set West Indies 266 to win. When West Indies were 207–8, Pakistan were on the brink of a 2–0 triumph. But, abetted by Qadir having several vociferous lbw appeals rejected, wicketkeeper Jeff Dujon and number ten Benjamin, who took the lead in attacking, steered West Indies to a two-wicket victory to salvage a drawn series. In the dressing room, Viv Richards cried, overwhelmed by relief at maintaining his side's unbeaten run. Pakistan were the only side to avoid defeat in a series in the Caribbean between 1974 and 1995; Imran left wishing that it had been a five-Test contest.

At Karachi in 1990, for the third consecutive series between the sides, Pakistan began with an emphatic win. Bowling fast and straight, Waqar took nine wickets in the match; Wasim took another six. In between times, Shoaib Mohammad's adhesive 86 and Saleem Malik's more aggressive 102 hauled Pakistan up to 345. The two were supported by Imran, playing as a specialist batter; he hit 73 not out off 189 balls, indicating a player equally comfortable as consolidator or counter-attacker. As in 1986, West Indies responded emphatically in the next Test, winning by seven wickets. Just like in 1986, Imran ensured that West Indies would not convert their dominance on the final day of the deciding Test into victory; he survived 162 deliveries in the second innings to salvage a draw. It also protected Pakistan's own undefeated run: from 1980 to 1995, they didn't lose a series at home.

Pakistan did not quite topple West Indies. But all three of their series from 1986 to 1990 were drawn 1–1. To Imran, despite Pakistan's victory in the 1992 World Cup, 'my greatest achievement in my cricket career was that I was the only captain in the 1980s who played three series against the far superior West Indians and who did not lose.'

These three series against West Indies provided proof of Imran's greatness: across the nine Tests, he hit 356 runs at 32.36 and took 45 wickets at 14.87. Hadlee declared Imran 'the best of the allrounders'.

Both Hadlee, who took a five-wicket haul in his very last Test innings, and Imran played the longest format until they were 39. Kapil remained effective, performing solidly even if he could no longer bowl as extensively. His durability was such that, of the 132 Tests that India played during his career, he played 131.

Botham was different. In 1989, Hadlee wrote that Botham's cricket was 'fickle' and 'the good life caught up with him'. In 23 Tests after turning 30, Botham averaged 23.96 with the bat and 45.80 with the ball.

And so at times even a player as extraordinary as Botham illustrated the perils of selecting allrounders in Test cricket. It encapsulates the brutality of a Test allrounder's existence. If out of sorts, a cricketer picked to make a side feel as if they have an extra player can make them seem as if they have one *less*.

16

THE ORACLE: THE STORY OF REVERSE SWING

At 4.30 p.m. on the final day in Melbourne in March 1979, Australia were 305–3. They needed just 77 more runs to complete a chase of 382 and defeat Pakistan.

When Sarfraz Nawaz came on, Pakistan's hopes did not extend beyond a draw. Sarfraz recalls telling Mushtaq Mohammad, the captain, 'Give me the ball. I'll take a longer run-up than usual. And we will slow down the over rate.' By doing so, Pakistan could avoid defeat.

Sarfraz found a better way. Sticking with his normal run-up after all, in 33 balls, he took seven wickets for one run. Australia crashed from 305–3 to 310 all out, unable to contend with Sarfraz swinging the ball back in and attacking the stumps. His spell of 7–1 included three wickets bowled, one lbw and two caught behind. Sarfraz walked off with figures of 9–86.

Many consider this the first time that reverse swing – which entails the older ball swinging in the opposite way to usual – showed its impact in Test cricket. Sarfraz himself is not quite so sure. From his home in south London, he says, 'It was a little bit reverse swing,' but points out that the second new ball was taken when Australia were seven wickets down, so his last three wickets came with conventional swing.

Confusion about the most famous spell of reverse swing illustrates the art's broader mysteries. In the 2020s, even with video footage and data demystifying the sport, it can still be hard to identify reverse swing.

Even if Melbourne 1979 wasn't really a triumph for reverse swing, Sarfraz's status as the oracle of reverse is well earned. In September 1974, after a Test tour of England, Pakistan played a short series of unofficial friendly matches in the Caribbean. In Guyana, Imran Khan and Sarfraz bowled in tandem. Imran was confronted by a mystery: why his teammate was able to swing the old ball, while he could not. After Imran was hit for a six, Sarfraz recalls,

> He came to me – he said your ball is swinging and mine is not swinging. Tell me why. I said, 'Immy, look at me. I can't teach you it right now on the field. Tomorrow, I'll teach you everything.'
>
> After the match, he came to my room and said, 'Show me how you swing the ball.' So I showed him shine this side, do this. Next day, we went to the nets.

In domestic cricket, Sarfraz first used reverse swing in the mid-1960s. In the nets, he practised bowling with both new and old balls. 'In Pakistan, these are dry conditions,' he explains. 'The ball will get ruffled quickly. So, I used to shine with the sweat. And with spit. I was very expert on shining one side.

'I put the sweat on and shine it quite well. And it reversed a lot, you know. So then I did it the other way round – shine the outside and it went away.

'Later on, they named it reverse swing. At the time, I didn't know what to call it, I used to say, "The old ball is swinging."'

* * *

To understand reverse swing, it is necessary to first understand conventional swing: that is, how the new ball moves in the air before pitching.

With the new ball, both sides are shiny. As bowlers have known since the late 19th century, the new ball will swing towards where the seam on the ball is angled. A ball with the seam angled towards the slips will swing away from a right-hander, and a ball angled towards fine leg will swing into a right-hander. This is because an angled seam creates turbulence, explains Rabindra Mehta, a sports aerodynamics consultant and NASA scientist who has advised the England and Australia cricket boards. Speed in the region of 70–80 mph, Mehta believes, is optimal to swing the new ball.

Contrary to popular belief, there is no evidence that clouds or humidity help swing. 'The only thing that matters is the block of air which the ball travels through,' says Aaron Briggs, who has completed a PhD in swing bowling and consulted for England cricket. 'There's no direct way in which the clouds can influence the air flow around the ball.' But clouds might make the ball harder to pick up, and so still do make swing bowling more dangerous. Cloudy conditions also encourage bowlers to focus more on swing: 'Perception becomes reality.'

When conditions are very hot and still, the sunshine can heat the pitch and may create turbulence in the air which prevents swing, Briggs explains. 'Sometimes the clouds and swing are indirectly correlated, but it's not a one-to-one correlation. There are many factors that affect swing and you can often only visualise a part of one of them, the weather.'

For around the first century of Test cricket, conventional swing was the only type of swing bowling widely known. In 1980, while living in London, Mehta first heard about a new, deviant form of swing during a visit from his childhood friend Imran Khan. Normally an inswing bowler, Imran explained that, at certain points, he could now swing the ball away without any change in his method. Mehta then tested the idea using wind tunnels at Imperial College in London.

Essentially, Mehta explains, reverse swing is produced by creating an uneven surface on the dry, rough side of the ball. While outswing bowlers swing the new ball away from right-handers, this trajectory is inverted with reverse swing. With an identical action, outswing bowlers are transformed into inswing bowlers. Under reverse swing, an old cricket ball moves from being unresponsive to curving late – generally swinging in, dipping towards a right-hander's stumps and toes.

> **Conventional swing**: Ball swings in direction the seam is angled – so will be an outswinger if it is angled towards first slip. Both sides are shiny with the new ball. The shinier side faces the batter for outswingers, with the ball moving towards the rougher side.
>
> **Reverse swing**: Ball swings in the opposite direction to where seam is angled – so will be an inswinger if it is angled towards first slip. The shinier side is the side released from nearer the batter, with the rougher side facing towards the bowler; the ball then swings towards the shinier side.

This was like a new language; before understanding of reverse swing grew, teams would normally shine both sides of the ball vigorously. The ball is more liable to acquire a rough side earlier in an innings on the subcontinent due to the dry and rough pitch and outfield conditions, Mehta says. Yet myths – such as that it helped if one side of the ball weighed more than the other – also developed around reverse swing.

*   *   *

Well before Sarfraz, there was a secret prehistory of reverse swing. A fielding side can make reverse swing much more likely through their actions; they can also occasionally stumble upon reverse swing by accident, simply because of how the ball deteriorates and the conditions.

In Pakistan, some believe that what we would now call reverse swing was deployed in club matches from the 1940s, with outswing bowlers swinging the old ball into right-handers. Yet several bowlers who are considered early exponents of reverse swing never came close to the Test team: to be deployed effectively, reverse swing needs to be married with pace and accuracy.

While reverse swing came to be thought of as a Pakistani invention, Australia's Alan Connolly, who played 29 Tests from 1963 to 1971, was renowned for his capacity to move the old ball. 'I used to experiment in the nets,' he recalls. 'I'd be fiddling around with different funny deliveries and all that type of thing.'

A successful baseball pitcher in Australia, Connolly imported the technique of applying moisture to one side of the ball. Connolly first used the method in a state match for Victoria in Adelaide in 1966. Initially, he recalls, the wicketkeeper 'would see my bowling and say, "Here comes the outswinger." And he'd shift a little bit with his gloves ready for the outswinger, and it went the other way and went for four byes. He came up after a few and said, "What is going on here? That was supposed to be an outswinger." I said, "Yeah it was, but it went the other way."'

Connolly and his teammates called the phenomenon 'going Irish'. He found that it worked best when applying sweat and saliva to only one side of the ball – the shiny side – and letting the other side become rougher.

'When the ball was new, I'd work on the side of the ball which was holding up best,' he explains. 'My creams [cricket whites] would be covered in red all the way down the front.' The method worked successfully at the MCG and Adelaide Oval, two grounds with abrasive surfaces, and in Tests in India in 1969.

Connolly passed the art down to Max Walker, another Victoria and Australia pace bowler. Dennis Lillee was also thought to have learned reverse swing during the 1970s. Imran later said that he saw Lillee bowl reverse swing against Pakistan in January 1977: once again, at Melbourne. In the same Test, Imran later said, he used reverse swing himself for the first time, taking five wickets. 'Towards the middle of the match the pitch had gotten so hard it began to take lumps out of the ball, which then behaved like a boomerang,' Imran told his biographer Christopher Sandford.

During his Test career, from 1964 to 1980, Australia's Ian Chappell says that he regularly encountered what we would now call reverse swing: 'There were a hell of a lot of blokes that could swing the old ball.' As far back as the 1950s, West Indies were thought to be able to swing the old ball in a different direction to the new one. In 1958, Pakistan complained about West Indies bowler Eric Atkinson, who was noted for his capacity to move the old ball, applying hair cream to one side of the ball to help gain extra swing. Atkinson might not have realised that doing so was in service of obtaining reverse, rather than conventional, swing.

While the true origins of reverse swing will never be definitively known, Sarfraz passed down the art's secrets, like a family heirloom. First, he told Imran Khan; later, the skill was taught to Wasim Akram and Waqar Younis. Together, these bowlers made Pakistan the first kings of reverse swing.

* * *

Imran, four years younger than Sarfraz, produced his signature display of reverse swing against India in Karachi in 1982/83. In their second innings, India reached 102–1. Then, Imran located reverse swing, angling into the right-handers: first, he bowled Sunil Gavaskar through the gate with a delivery that veered in late. The moment that best encapsulated Imran's wizardry came when Gundappa Viswanath shouldered arms to a delivery well outside off stump. To Viswanath's astonishment, the ball curved late and uprooted his off stump, almost defying geometry: the majesty of reverse swing in microcosm.

'He didn't know what was happening; no one did,' India's Arun Lal later told ESPNcricinfo. 'There was a bit of cross-breeze, and once the shine was off the ball, Imran got into business. We were completely caught unawares by the huge amount of swing that he managed to get – both ways. We asked ourselves how he could do that when our own bowlers, including Kapil Dev, who was known for swinging it, couldn't.'

Imran took five wickets for three runs in a 25-ball spell, ending with 8–60. He took 40 wickets at 13.95 and scored a century too, as Pakistan won the six-match series 3–0. India would not be the last side caught unaware: the low-quality video footage of the era allowed Pakistan to guard their secret for years.

Reverse swing reached its apogee under two men Imran mentored: Wasim and Waqar. Wasim was a self-taught bowler who grew up playing tape-ball cricket – with a tennis ball wrapped in electrical tape – in Lahore. The skiddiness of a tape-ball lends itself to attacking the stumps, just as a bowler does when the ball reverse-swings. A diet of tape-ball, and how the parched turf roughs up the ball, help explain why Pakistan has been such a fertile land for reverse swing.

Both Wasim and Waqar were fast-tracked into the Test team in the quintessentially, albeit sometimes romanticised, Pakistan way. Wasim was spotted by Javed Miandad, who frequently captained Pakistan when Imran was unavailable, at an Under-19 net session. This led to his selection, for his first-class debut, for a Patron's XI against the touring New Zealand side in November 1984. Aged 18, after three first-class games, he made his Test debut in Auckland in January 1985. Waqar made his Test debut in November 1989, the day before his 18th birthday; after spending most of his childhood in Sharjah, where tape-ball cricket dominates, he was spotted by Imran while bowling in a televised domestic match.

Once in the Test side, the two Ws set about mastering reverse swing. 'We called it *sibar* – "the opposite way",' Wasim wrote in *Sultan*:

Polishing was still important, Imran explained, but the key was keeping the unpolished side as dry and rough as possible. Imran told me how to prepare a ball, how to cant my wrist, how to disguise my hand, and how optimally to deliver it – fast and full. In some ways it was easier than the orthodox variety. If you tried too hard with the new ball, swing could desert you; with the old ball, the quicker the better.

In this observation lies the reason for why Wasim and Waqar, who could both exceed 90 mph, thrived with reverse swing. Conventional swing is widely thought to be hard to obtain if a ball is delivered too quickly. With reverse swing, no such barrier exists.

Together with their fast yorkers, the two Ws both possessed vicious bouncers which deterred batters from getting onto the front foot. Their threat was amplified because of their different angles. A left-armer, Wasim could curve the ball into batters from either over or – his speciality – around the wicket; Waqar had a particularly low, slingy action.

While reverse swing is said to feel later than conventional swing, this is an illusion: it only feels later because it tends to come at higher speeds. For conventional and reverse swing alike, the ball moves half its distance sideways in the last third of its journey. 'The fuller the delivery, the larger the swing distance,' Briggs says. 'The longer the time in the air, the more time for the ball to swing, or reverse-swing.'

In Test cricket, averages for specialist batters are lowest against the new ball, then increase in every ten-over phase until the second new ball; the longer a team bat, then, the easier batting becomes. Against Wasim and Waqar, the rhythm of an innings was inverted. In Lahore in 1990, Wasim ended West Indies' innings with four wickets in five balls. In England in 1992, when Pakistan won a tempestuous series 2–1, the hosts collapsed from 197–3 to 255 all out at Lord's, 292–2 to 320 all out at Headingley, and 182–3 to 207 all out at The Oval. Pakistan delayed taking the second new ball, because the old ball was so lethal.

The best reverse-swing bowlers do not depend on the pitch. Waqar got 57 per cent of wickets bowled or lbw, and Wasim 53 per cent, compared to about a third for all Test seamers. The Waqar reverse-swinging yorker, hooping back from several inches outside off stump to crash into middle or leg stump, is among the most venomous deliveries in history. Batters knew exactly what was coming; doing anything about it was a different matter. The two Ws ended with almost identical Test averages – Wasim 23.62; Waqar 23.56, despite an injury-riddled second half of his career. To Curtly Ambrose, Wasim was 'possibly the greatest. He could swing the ball, he could seam the ball off the pitch, he could bowl at high pace when he wanted to. Akram had it all.'

* * *

If 1992 marked reverse swing's peak, it also marked the moment when the phenomenon went from little-understood curiosity to major controversy. Pakistan generated reverse swing, it was said, because players had illegally lifted the seam, scratching one side with fingernails, or roughed up one side with a bottle top, as Imran once admitted to doing in a county match. Micky Stewart, England's manager, muttered, 'I know how they do it, but I won't comment on whether it's fair or unfair.' In a one-day international at Lord's, the ball was replaced after the umpires detected tampering – though nobody was ever formally charged with an offence. England's Allan Lamb later accused Pakistan of tampering; the *Daily Mirror*'s front page was headlined 'How Pakistan Cheat at Cricket'.

Together with pace, the 'most important thing for reverse swing is the ball condition', says Briggs. This explains why several bowlers often generate reverse swing in the same innings. Teams who generate reverse swing have persistently been accused of crossing the line between managing the ball through legal and illegal means. Since reverse swing has been popularised, teams have continually tried to rough up one side of the ball: witness sides throwing the ball on the bounce to the wicketkeeper to make it more abrasive, which is legal.

Yet a number of methods that can help reverse swing are illegal. In the mid-1990s, Mehta was tasked with examining a series of balls, used in both Tests and first-class cricket in England: 'The samples they showed me were definitely tampered with.' He noticed markings 'with something like a bottle top' and attempts to lift the quarter-seam of the ball with fingernails. During Test cricket in the 1990s, one prominent player remembers, 'picking the seam was just a standard thing'.

Before the last Test of the 1992 series, one England player recalls, 'We basically said, "They're doing all sorts of shit with the ball, why don't we?" Stop being so British about this – as long as we don't get found out, let's give it a go. So surreptitious fingernails and who knows what else – working as hard as we knew from what little we'd learned about it.' When England bowled, the ball still went 'gun-barrel straight'. England made 207 and 174, collapsing against Wasim and Waqar once again; Pakistan scored 380 and won by ten wickets.

In the 1990s, Pakistan resented the accusations that they had tampered. Unlike rival nations, they were never sanctioned for tampering in a Test – though Sarfraz alleges that, after his retirement, some Pakistan players used illegal methods to rough up the ball, including sandpaper.

Imran despaired of how critics considered reverse swing 'some kind of black magic'. To Wasim, England 'showed no curiosity about the skill involved. They didn't observe, for instance, how we only ever had one man polish the ball, how we took care to hold the ball in our fingers but never in our palm.' The 1990s were uniquely conducive to reverse swing, Wasim wrote:

> Boundary ropes and cushions were almost unheard of. Balls hit fences and boundary hoardings. Balls rolled in concrete gutters and bounced on bitumen concourses. Balls bowled cross-seam

scuffed up readily. Keep the damaged side dry by holding it in your fingers rather than your palm and the effect was even more pronounced. It was also better to ballast the ball with sweat, this being oilier than saliva.

Pakistan also benefited from using the Readers brand of balls, which are no longer used in Tests. The balls were considered particularly conducive to reverse swing.

Long before 1992, there had been notorious cases of ball-tampering. In the Ashes series of 1920/21 and 1921, Australia's Arthur Mailey admitted, 'Although it was against the law, I must break down and confess that I always carried powdered resin in my pocket and when the umpire wasn't looking lifted the seam.' The ploy helped pace bowlers Jack Gregory and Ted McDonald find greater swing and bounce. In Sydney, England captain J.W.H.T. Douglas threatened to report Mailey. Then Mailey asked to see Douglas's right hand and saw that his thumbnail had been 'worn to the flesh' picking the seam for his own bowlers. Mailey allowed himself 'to break this law without compunction because in lifting the seam I was keeping the ball in its original shape'.

Keith Miller was also spotted lifting the seam, in the 1953 Ashes. In 1977, India captain Bishan Bedi complained about Vaseline-dipped gauzes that England's John Lever had applied to the ball, accusing the visitors of cheating. In 1990, against Pakistan – who they believed were adopting similar tactics themselves – New Zealand gouged the ball's seam with a bottle top. In 1994, England captain Michael Atherton was fined for keeping dirt in his pocket and applying it to the ball.

England's Test rejuvenation from 2003 to 2005 was abetted by reverse swing. To make the old ball more lethal, England even selected the darkest available ball to bowl with, rendering the seam harder for batters to make out. England were also indebted to Marcus Trescothick's penchant for Murray Mints; while sucking them, he applied moisture to the ball. Using such substances to polish the ball is prohibited; the International Cricket Council subsequently clarified that Trescothick's actions were illegal. He wrote:

> It was my job to keep the shine on the new ball for as long as possible with a bit of spit and a lot of polish. And through trial and error I had finally settled on the best type of spit for the task at hand. It had been common knowledge in county cricket for some time that certain sweets produced saliva which, when applied to the ball for cleaning purposes, enabled it to keep its shine for longer and therefore its swing.

In England in 2006, Pakistan were docked penalty runs for ball-tampering; in response, the side initially refused to take the field, leading to England being awarded the Oval Test on a forfeit. From 2013 to 2016, South Africa were found guilty of tampering three times – for, respectively, scuffing the ball against a trouser zip; scratching the ball with the fingers and thumb; and applying saliva onto the ball from a mint. When South Africa were accused of tampering against Australia in 2014, Ryan Harris, Australia's quick bowler, defended them: 'You've got to do something with the ball, everyone does it.'

In 2018, Australia's Cameron Bancroft applied sandpaper to the ball during a Test in Cape Town. The players involved initially received modest sanctions: a one-Test suspension for skipper Steve Smith, the maximum permitted under ICC rules on tampering at the time. The public outcry demanded much more. Smith and David Warner were both suspended by Cricket Australia for a year. There was a sense that, for all their stupidity violating the laws of the game, the men were being tried by a kangaroo court: across a plethora of different nations, tampering was considered an open secret. For all that administrators decry tampering, it has aided one of the most beguiling sights in Test cricket.

17

NO LONGER JUST A WHISTLESTOP

En route to Australia in 1882 – on a quest to 'recover those Ashes' – England's boat docked in Colombo. Colombo Cricket Club, then a team for European players only, learned of the route; they reached out to England, inviting them for a game. It offered the promise of entertainment for the local cricket community, and a useful chance for England's players to practise on the way to Australia.

The tourists would only be able to play for a day and a half. Colombo were allowed to field 18 men, yet scored just 92 in the first innings. They reached 16–7 in their second innings when the ship's captain sounded his whistle: MCC had to catch their boat. Hence the name of these matches: the whistlestops. Often, they were only a single day.

From 1890, the matches featured local players too, not merely Europeans in the country. The structure was idiosyncratic: until 1926, the games were two-innings matches played over a single day – and every match was drawn. Later games were often only one innings a side, creating a small chance of one team winning. Yet the games remained about exhibitionism – moments like C.I. Gunasekera hitting Lindsay Kline, Australia's left-arm wrist spinner, for 24 in an over during a whistlestop in 1961.

The games were a product of Sri Lanka's geography: the country – officially known as Ceylon until 1972 – was a natural stopping point between England and Australia or New Zealand. Such happenstance, and the slow development of commercial air travel, helped shape Sri Lanka's development as a cricket nation. Matches against an MCC side travelling to Australia, or an Australia side making the opposite trip, provided a focal point for the cricket community. The relatively regular, albeit brief, fixtures against leading sides nurtured interest in the sport. Countries which once had designs on Test status, like Argentina, Canada and the United States, all had cause to envy Sri Lanka's location.

Until 1965/66, England undertook the journey to the Antipodes by boat, stopping off in Sri Lanka. Virtually all of the great England and Australia cricketers played in the whistlestops. Don Bradman visited four times, before each of his Ashes tours. In 1930, Bradman played his first match overseas: he made 40. In 1948, before his final Test series, about 20,000 packed into the newly built Colombo Oval; those who couldn't get in watched from the trees overlooking the ground. There was an 'eerie silence' when Bradman was on strike; spectators were left disappointed that he made only 20. It is rumoured that Bradman had to contend with an unexpected obstacle: the distance between the two sets of stumps was two yards short – 20 instead of 22.

* * *

The first Britons to land on the island that would become known as Sri Lanka are believed to have arrived in 1796, with the East India Company. The first known instance of cricket being played on the land was in 1832. Mirroring the game's development in India, cricket was introduced in part by army officers; coffee and tea planters, who came to the island from the late 19th century, also popularised the game. Colombo Cricket Club was formed in 1832, then revitalised from 1863. The first club created by the Ceylonese population, the Malay Cricket Club, formed in 1872.

More than clubs, cricket in Ceylon was shaped by the island's schools. British colonialists and missionaries made cricket central to the schools that they created in the mid-19th century. These schools then faced each other in a 'Big Match', a multi-day game that doubled as a wider social occasion. The Big Match between the 'Royalists' of Royal College Colombo and 'Thomians' of S. Thomas' College has been played since 1879 – making it older than the Ashes.

Cricket was, in part, a 'conduit for Westernization', as the historian Michael Roberts has asserted. As elsewhere in the British Empire, cricket was intimately connected with social and racial elitism. From 1887 to 1933, the 'Ceylonese' as a team took on the local 'Europeans' in a multi-day match played most years; by the 1910s, the Ceylonese side normally won. Colombo Cricket Club did not admit non-European members until 1962, 14 years after independence. In the early years of Ceylon cricket, teams were often reliant on players of European descent; until the 1970s, the national side tended to contain such players.

The challenge for Ceylon cricket was to become more than just a whistlestop: a worthwhile touring destination in its own right, not merely a place to pass through. In 1927, Ceylon played their inaugural first-class game, losing to an MCC side – visiting during a tour of India – by an innings.

Ceylon's schedule still remained sparse, regularly going more than a year without a match. Those who wanted to devote themselves to the game had to leave the country. After World War II, a series of players from the island moved to England to play league and county cricket. The batter Laddie Outschoorn enjoyed 14 years at Worcestershire from 1946 to 1959; Stanley Jayasinghe and Clive Inman batted together for Leicestershire's middle order in the 1960s. Gamini Goonesena, a leg-spinner and handy batter, was the first Asian to captain Cambridge University and later excelled for Nottinghamshire; he also played for New South Wales. While these players highlighted the talent that existed on the island, their professional commitments reduced their ability to play for Ceylon.

* * *

Playing Test cricket would be the only way to stop the talent drain. After Pakistan gained Test status in 1952, the island's cricket administrators started to give thought to how Ceylon could do the same.

To build their case, Ceylon invited other countries for unofficial 'Tests'. These were multi-day first-class matches against full-strength sides, or teams missing only a couple of leading players: Ted Dexter captained an MCC side in Colombo in February 1962 while he was also England Test captain. In 1964, a strong Pakistan side lost there, in what was hailed as Ceylon's first Test triumph. A year later, in Ahmedabad, Ceylon won their first 'Test' overseas.

The win gave immediate impetus for Ceylon to become the eighth team to win Test status. At the post-match reception, the Indian Board of Control's president pledged to sponsor the country's bid for Test status. Pakistan seconded the proposal. While the proposal was discussed – as ever, England and Australia were reluctant to welcome new Test nations – administrators hampered Ceylon's cricketers. A tour to England in 1968 was cancelled by the board, because of lack of funds and administrative wrangling over issues including who would captain. A lack of funds also meant that some leading players were scarcely available, Nicholas Brookes documented in *An Island's Eleven*. Michael Tissera, one of the side's best batters during the 1960s and 1970s, recounted, 'I had a family – I had to earn a living and it was working in tea that allowed that, not cricket.'

Not all within the island were convinced that pursuing Test status was wise. After a grim tour of Pakistan in 1966, a columnist wrote, 'We haven't Test match temperament. Let's go back to old times – and enjoy cricket.'

While Ceylon were making their push, the game's global structure was changing. In 1965, Imperial Cricket Conference representatives met at Lord's. In a perfunctory nod to modernisation, world cricket's governing body removed the word 'Imperial' from its title and rebranded as the International Cricket Conference (later the International Cricket Council). For the first time, the organisation of

Test-playing nations now permitted 'Associate Members' – a group of countries not allowed to play Test cricket but considered as part of the game's family for having 'fully recognised and organised' cricket. Three countries were granted membership at the ICC's first meeting in 1965: the United States – over half a century after the game there had been stunted by the Test-playing world – Fiji and Ceylon.

On the final day of a rain-ruined Ashes Test in 1971, Australia and England staged the inaugural one-day international, adapting the version of the game introduced in county cricket in 1963. A crowd of 46,000 turned up for the match at the Melbourne Cricket Ground, giving a hint of the latent interest in such a game.

Four years later, in 1975, the inaugural men's Cricket World Cup – two years after the first women's competition – was organised by the ICC in England. At the time, with South Africa ostracised, there were only six Test-playing nations. With the need to bulk up the tournament to give it more of a global feel, the World Cup included eight nations. The ICC didn't even deign to hold a qualifying tournament, but plucked two Associates – East Africa and Sri Lanka, as the island was known after it had become a republic in 1972 – to play.

Sri Lanka recognised the opportunities that the World Cup provided. The national board organised a two-week, pre-tournament camp in Nuwara Eliya, in Central Province: the hill-country conditions helped with acclimatisation for England. In the World Cup, Sri Lanka lost all three games comfortably. Yet their performance against Australia showed a team of skill and bravery. Batting without helmets against the pace of Jeff Thomson, opener Sunil Wettimuny was hit in the chest, and number four Duleep Mendis on the head; both retired hurt and were hospitalised. The next day, an English policeman visited Mendis and asked him, 'Do you want to press charges against Mr Thomson?' A total of 276–4 in their 60 overs affirmed Sri Lanka's promise. The tour ended with six players winning contracts to play league cricket in England.

Test status still remained elusive. After Pakistan proposed Sri Lanka for full membership in 1974, England and Australia used their veto powers to reject the application, much to the consternation of Abdul Kardar, Pakistan's representative.

In 1979, in the second World Cup – once again in England – Sri Lanka met India in Manchester. Duleep Mendis scored a freewheeling 64, from 57 balls, lifting Sri Lanka to 238–5: a total they defended easily. It was the first Associate Member World Cup victory over a Full Member and would be the catalyst to Sri Lanka winning Test status two years later. Arguably, it came a little late: the side were ageing, and the fruits of Test status would largely be enjoyed by a new generation.

Sri Lanka had first taken on other countries in their own curious version of one-day cricket. Now, one-day cricket provided a platform for Sri Lanka to meet the world's best in the Test game too.

* * *

On 17 February 1982, 100 years after hosting their first whistlestop, Sri Lanka welcomed England for their inaugural Test match. A gold coin was made specifically for the toss at the P Sara Oval in Colombo. The day before the game, Keith Fletcher, England's captain, said that Sri Lanka weren't 'County Championship standard'. Yet after three days, Sri Lanka sensed a debut Test victory: on a wearing pitch, they were 147 ahead in their second innings, with seven wickets still in hand. Instead, they lost their last seven wickets for eight runs against spinners Derek Underwood and John Emburey. 'We were dominating the first three days,' Mendis recalled. 'We didn't know how to cope with it the last two days, and we crumbled.'

Seven months later, Sri Lanka played their first Test in India. In the Chepauk Stadium, Duleep Mendis produced Sri Lanka's first great Test performance, hitting rapid twin centuries in a draw. It was an indication of how Sri Lanka would import a batting approach learned in one-day cricket to the Test game.

'The boys started playing well in the one-day game; automatically the same thinking came into Test cricket,' Mendis told me. 'We were used to the short game right from the start, until 1981 when we got Test status. Most of the players – they are on the attacking side.'

While Mendis averaged an unremarkable 31.64 as a Test batter, he embodied Sri Lanka's buccaneering approach in their incipient years as a Test nation. In Sri Lanka's first Test in England, at Lord's in 1984, Mendis hit 111 from 143 balls in the first innings, three times pulling Ian Botham for six. He hit 94 from 97 balls in the second innings before falling attempting to hit Botham, by now bowling off breaks, for another six. A draw continued Sri Lanka's solid start to Test cricket; a year later, Mendis captained Sri Lanka to their first Test win. Mendis's stylish innings of 95 and 60 not out, and nine wickets from fast bowler Rumesh Ratnayake, set up victory over India at the P Sara Oval. Players from generations past celebrated with the team in the dressing room; this was a victory for their endeavours, just as much as the 11 on the field. J.R. Jayewardene, Sri Lanka's president, announced a national holiday to mark the nation's first Test victory. Though Sri Lanka only won two of their first 41 Tests, they drew another 19, establishing themselves as more competitive than most embryonic Test nations.

* * *

Besides one-day cricket, Sri Lanka's cricket was also shaped by the school system. There are over 10,000 schools in Sri Lanka; 66 schools are self-governing – either fee-paying or with government financial support. These 66 schools have produced nearly all of the country's Test cricketers. Such schools are especially common in Colombo: the capital and its suburbs account for only about 20 per cent of the country's 25 million population, but 60 per cent of Test players.

All elite schools have an annual 'Big Match'. These games are societal occasions as well as cricketing ones – annual events for friends to catch up while wearing the colours of their favourite side. When England played a Test in Sri Lanka in 1993, the Test crowd was dwarfed by the Big Match crowd watching Royal College Colombo and S. Thomas' College even though tickets were more expensive.

Despite their elitism, Big Matches have also contributed to the game's growth. In the 1960s, the Sri Lanka Broadcasting Corporation started doing Sinhala-language commentaries for the annual Big Match between Ananda and Nalanda. The first Sinhala training manual was released in 1987.

A Big Match is a two-innings, multi-day affair – normally two days but sometimes three, and generally played on excellent pitches. To win, sides need to give themselves enough time to take 20 wickets. 'From school days my batting was always on the aggressive side,' Mendis told me. 'Within two days we've got to finish the game. At that small age it was cultivated in you that you've got to go for runs.'

For batters, these aggressive impulses co-existed alongside the emphasis upon being technically correct. After his 190 at Lord's in 1984, Sidath Wettimuny recalled that, as a boy, he read C.B. Fry's *Batsmanship* – published in 1912 – so exhaustively that a typed copy of it had to be made. Garry Sobers, who coached the country in the 1980s, said, 'Sri Lanka seem to combine something of the Caribbean spirit of cricket coming from their own nature and at the same time are bound by a very traditional approach to the game.' Sri Lanka illustrate a trend in the Test game, observable across nations: more batters than bowlers tend to have privileged upbringings. Nature is relatively more important for bowlers. Nurture – including benefiting from the facilities and coaching at elite schools – is more important for batters.

Arjuna Ranatunga attended Ananda College in Colombo. This was one of the country's leading schools – but, while many elite schools in the capital are Anglican or secular, Ananda is Buddhist.

The elitism and snobbery at Sinhalese Sports Club, the city's most prestigious club, was such that Ranatunga felt looked down upon there. Aged 15, Ranatunga's background was dismissed by a senior member of SSC, who said, 'We don't want any "Sarong Johnnie's" in this club.'

Ranatunga was the first instance of a Test player fast-tracked from the school system. He made his debut in Sri Lanka's very first Test, aged 18 years, 78 days, hitting 54 in 96 balls after coming in at 34–4.

During the years when the civil war was at its most bloody, Ranatunga would become among the most transformative captains in Test history. He forged a new collectivist attitude, making players agree to split the proceeds of player-of-the-match awards equally between the whole team. His determination to nurture all the island's talents helped Sri Lanka discover players from outside traditional hotspots, including Muthiah Muralidaran. 'He knew who are the good players who have got the talent and he stuck with them even when they failed,' Murali recalls. 'The belief in youngsters that they could perform – that's what that team had with the leadership of Arjuna.'

Ranatunga refused to be quelled by the game's more established nations. He led Sri Lanka to a maiden victory over England in 1993; the country's first away win, in New Zealand in 1995, after which he cried joyfully in the changing room; and a come-from-behind 2–1 victory in Pakistan in the same year, ending Pakistan's 14-year undefeated home run.

The win in Pakistan was Ranatunga's first series working with Dav Whatmore, who was born in Sri Lanka before moving to Australia, whom he represented in Test cricket. In 1995, Sri Lanka required the Australian Cricket Board to double the fee that they would receive for touring to hire Whatmore; Australia advised them to use the extra cash to secure him. As head coach in two stints – from 1995 to 1996 and 1999 to 2003 – Whatmore introduced a new focus upon fitness and fielding. At his very first training session, it was raining and the players wanted to return home. Whatmore prevented them from leaving; the rain cleared up and they could practise after all.

For all his Test achievements, the defining moment of the Ranatunga years came in one-day internationals. At the 1996 World Cup, Sri Lanka unveiled a new batting approach – attacking with abandon during the 15 overs of the fielding restrictions, led by Sanath Jayasuriya, then controlling the game thereafter. The strategy would take the side all the way to the World Cup final – where, after losing both openers early in pursuit of 242, Aravinda de Silva's magisterial century toppled Australia in Lahore. Ranatunga hit the winning runs. In 15 years, Sri Lanka had risen from Associate nation to world champions.

18

SHANE WARNE AND THE RESURGENCE OF LEG SPIN

I'm nervous and there's suddenly a hush that goes around the ground.

I take a step, I bowl and I let go of the ball and it's all like it happened in slow motion.

Gatting tried to turn it. It drifted and he followed the drift. It pitched, just missed his bat and just clipped the top of off stump.

First ball in an Ashes series and it felt pretty bloody good.

So Shane Warne recalled the delivery that made his legend. There never was a 'Ball of the Century', the term coined by *The Sunday Times*'s Robin Marlar, before Warne bowled at Old Trafford on 4 June 1993, in the first Test of the Ashes series.

At five past three on the second day, this 23-year-old with a cherubic face, peroxide-blond hair and a gold chain told himself, 'Pull the trigger, let's rip this.' He unfurled his first Ashes delivery: a sumptuous leg-spinner that first drifted to outside leg stump, then pitched, spun sharply past Mike Gatting's groping defensive stroke and kissed the top of his off stump. This was the consummate leg break; it instantly became Test cricket's most famous delivery.

'My thought process was to bowl the ball and spin the ball as far as you possibly can and send a message to the England guys that this guy can spin it,' Warne later said. 'Let them see it drift, curve and just rip it.' None who saw it would ever forget.

* * *

'The shame about Test cricket over the last decade has been the virtual disappearance of spinners, especially leg spinners,' Richard Hadlee, New Zealand's fast-bowling allrounder, wrote in 1989. Hadlee was not alone in his concerns.

England's left-arm spinner Derek Underwood, who speared the ball into the pitch and was lethal on uncovered pitches, played his last Test in 1982. A year later, with the end of uncovered wickets damaging spinners, he lamented, 'The high standard of fast bowling means they think: "We'd better get after the spinner now that the quicks are resting."' Ashley Mallett, a wily off-spinner who played 38 Tests for Australia from 1968 to 1980, said that by the end of his career, spinners 'became support staff, useful for keeping things tight while the quicks were rotated', and 'had to double as batsmen, or field like Trojans, or both'. The attempts to copy West Indies created a less varied game.

Leg spin was particularly embattled. Dependent on the wrist, leg spin (and rarely spotted left-arm wrist spin) is more volatile than off spin and left-arm orthodox spin, which depend on the fingers. With all spinners marginalised, leg-spinners were especially ignored. Abdul Qadir was an exception, but he averaged 47.58 outside Pakistan. India's Narendra Hirwani began his career with a stunning 16–136 in the match against West Indies in Chennai in 1988 but faded.

Before Warne, no country had as deep a tradition of leg spin as Australia. In the Golden Age, Herbert Hordern was a beguiling googly bowler. After World War I, the mantle passed to Arthur Mailey. In between Tests on the 1930 Ashes tour, Mailey shared tips with England's leg-spinner Ian Peebles on how to disguise his googly. Asked why he had helped an opponent during a series, Mailey replied, 'Spin bowling is an art. And art is international.'

Later in the 1930s, Australia often fielded two leg-spinners in tandem: Clarrie Grimmett, famed for his top-spinner, and Bill O'Reilly. Don Bradman described O'Reilly as the greatest bowler he had ever seen. O'Reilly combined unusual pace for a leg-spinner with accuracy, variations – of pace and flight as well as spin – and bounce from his 6 ft 2 in height, which contrasted with Grimmett's much smaller frame. Their nicknames encapsulated their characters and approaches: the aggressive O'Reilly was The Tiger, the wily Grimmett The Fox. In the 1950s and 1960s, Australia's leg-spin tradition was kept alive by Richie Benaud, who was to relish commentating on Warne.

* * *

As a boy in Black Rock, in the Melbourne suburbs, Shane and his younger brother Jason 'had a lot of fun picking our world XI teams, and having to imitate them', Jason told me. Shane would pick Qadir, 'just so he could bowl leg spin'.

Warne was fortunate to emerge in a country that understood leg spin. After bowling out Mentone Grammar in a school game, Warne was offered a scholarship there. Cricket won out over Warne's original sporting love, Australian Rules, after he was released from St Kilda reserves. 'Cricket found me,' he liked to say.

In 1990, before he had made his first-class debut, Warne was selected for the Australian cricket academy in Adelaide. He was sent home for ill-discipline. But Warne returned with a new knowledge of how to bowl the flipper and the slider – both deliveries moving straight, rather than turning, with the flipper skidding on quicker and the slider bowled with backspin. At the academy Warne also first encountered an essential confidant. Terry Jenner played nine Tests as a leg-spinner in the 1970s, and was then imprisoned for embezzling cash from his employee. He imparted cricketing and life wisdom to Warne, who was often reluctant to listen to others. Warne wrote in *No Spin*:

> He is a great listener and more often than not, you might just want to get something off your chest, or just lean on those ample

shoulders of his. Other times, though, he will say you're not quite doing this or that, and then his ability to show you really does make a difference. His coaching philosophy is to keep it simple.

In 1991, as he always did, Shane attended the Boxing Day Test with Jason. Shane had played only four Sheffield Shield matches. Over beers and pies in the stands, he told his brother, 'I could be playing the next Test.' Jason 'laughed and said, "Sure, mate, whatever."'

Shane was right. His introduction to Test cricket, in New Year 1992, was inauspicious: he took 1–150 against India in Sydney. He had conceded 346 runs, and taken a solitary wicket, by the time that Sri Lanka threatened to win a tense Test in Colombo. Warne polished off the last three wickets, handing Australia a 16-run victory: 'The greatest heist since the Great Train Robbery,' captain Allan Border declared. It would be the first Test bearing Warne's imprint. Warne marked his first Boxing Day Test by taking a match-winning 7–52 against West Indies.

From being cricket's most capricious art, in Warne's hands leg spin was the outlet for everyday excellence. Leg-spinners were thought to need favourable conditions, their inaccuracies rendering them liabilities before the pitch offered assistance. Warne was so dependable that, in the first of the four innings of a match, he averaged 27.63; he averaged fewer abroad than at home.

England often witnessed his very best. Gatting was the first of 129 Test wickets that Warne took in England; Warne's 195 wickets against England are more than anyone has ever got against any opponent. As the Barmy Army sang, 'We wish you were English'.

* * *

Warne's greatness is best understood in three parts.

First, he spun the ball – a lot. 'Spinning the ball is number one,' Warne told children who asked for advice. He brought the physicality of Australian Rules to spin bowling. The power in Warne's shoulders and upper body meant that he generated prodigious flight and drift, posing a huge challenge to opposing batsmen, even before the ball pitched and turned. The drift on Warne's first Ashes delivery meant that the ball pitched outside Mike Gatting's leg stump. After the drift through the air, there was then the bountiful turn off the pitch. Modern ball-tracking from the analytics company CricViz only began in 2005, after Warne had suffered shoulder injuries – but the average turn on each Warne ball was still significantly higher than the amount generated by any other leg-spinner.

Generating so much turn opened up new geometric possibilities. Warne was adept bowling around the wicket to right-handers; for leg-spinners, this had generally been seen as a method of containment. Under Warne, it became a new angle of attack.

Warne's second hallmark was more mundane: his consistency. For all the focus upon his variations, his whole craft was underpinned by the excellence of his stock leg break. 'His best delivery,' England's Mark Ramprakash wrote, 'would drift in towards leg stump before spinning away from the right-hander – it was his stock ball, and a bloody great one.'

The third mark of Warne's greatness was his tactical acuity:

> When I attacked with the ball, and by that I mean used more variations – which in turn meant the possibility of some bad balls – I would defend more with the field. When conditions were in my favour, I wouldn't worry about the variations but instead aim at leg-break after leg-break that gave nothing away to the batsman. I could then afford to attack more with the field placements.

Warne also brought his personality to bear. There was even a theatrical quality to how he shuffled his fielders between balls. Sometimes, these changes were for a specific tactical reason. Just as often, they were for show: he was an illusionist, who used his wiles to induce doubt. 'Part of the art of bowling spin is to make the batsman think something special is happening when it isn't,' he explained. Leg spin, Warne believed, 'is a magic trick, surrounded by mystery, aura and fear'.

Sometimes, he got into a verbal fight with opponents to get himself into the contest. 'Daryll, I've waited so long for this moment and I'm going to send you straight back to that leather couch.' So Warne greeted South Africa's Daryll Cullinan, who averaged 44.21 in 70 Tests, at Melbourne in 1997 after learning that Cullinan had sought out a sports psychologist to help with facing his leg spin. Cullinan was bowled for a duck.

Even by the standards of professional athletes, Warne was unusual for his competitiveness, which extended to Monopoly and cut-throat card games; he later became a professional poker player. His sense that no game was unwinnable turned perception into reality – perhaps most memorably at Adelaide in 2006/07. On a bland pitch that had yielded just 17 wickets in four days, Warne ignited a stunning England collapse. For Shane, his brother Jason told me, the sense of deciding the game's biggest moments was 'addictive':

> Anyone who plays sport goes to bed dreaming of being the one in control of a big game at that big moment and delivering and the adulation. And it's probably only once you start to get it a couple of times it is a little bit addictive too. He loved that. But I think in a perfect world he'd say, 'I love it on the ground, but not when I'm living my private life.'

Warne led an art feared to be nearing extinction into a brief golden age. Mushtaq Ahmed and Anil Kumble both made their Test debuts in 1990. Both were swiftly dropped, but returned after Warne's debut. Mushtaq, with a particularly delectable googly, bettered Qadir in winning matches for Pakistan abroad: he took nine wickets in the match in wins in Australia and South Africa, and eight in victories in New Zealand and England.

Kumble's height made him an unusual leg-spinner: he relied less on flight, instead combining accuracy with sharp speed and bounce. Perhaps his defining trait was his spirit: Kumble once bowled with a broken jaw, defying bandages around his face to dismiss Brian Lara. From being a destroyer at home, Kumble learned how to win Tests anywhere. After turning 30, he bowled India to some of their most famous victories – taking seven wickets in the match in Leeds, six in Adelaide, eight in Multan and seven in Kingston. But, of his 619 wickets, perhaps the most treasured haul came in Delhi in 1999. Pakistan raced to 101–0 in pursuit of an arduous 420 to win. Bowling wicket-to-wicket, fizzing the ball off the surface and exploiting some uneven bounce, Kumble induced Shahid Afridi to edge behind; the very next ball, Ijaz Ahmed was lbw to a quicker delivery. Now, Kumble happily bowled unchanged. From the Pavilion End, he bowled 20.3 overs in a row to claim all ten wickets, to end up with 10–74 in the innings and 14–149 in the match. 'All I had to do was pitch in the right area, mix up my pace and spin, and trap the batsmen,' he explained, understated as ever.

If Warne, supported by Mushtaq and Kumble, showed how leg spin could win Test matches, they also showed how difficult the craft was. There was no leg-spin revival after Warne. 'So this is life without Warnie,' captain Ricky Ponting remarked wryly to the slips as India were amassing over 500 at Sydney in January 2008, a year after Warne's retirement.

Stuart MacGill, 17 months younger than Warne, would have been the world's leading leg-spinner in many previous generations: he turned the ball prodigiously and had a fine googly, but bowled more loose deliveries. After MacGill retired, Australia reverted away from leg spin too.

This retreat was affirmation of how hard leg spin is. While wrist spinners have thrived in T20, where unpredictability can be an asset, leg spin remains Test cricket's most precarious art. As of January 2025, 71 spinners had taken 100 Test wickets; just 13 were leg-spinners.

More than anywhere else in Test cricket, the flame of leg spin was kept alive by Pakistan, home to five of these 13. The country's placid batting conditions often lend themselves to the classic cocktail: high pace from one end, wrist spin from the other.

* * *

In 2000, Warne was named as one of *Wisden*'s Five Cricketers of the Century. It was recognition that Warne had reinvigorated leg spin with breathtaking skill and showmanship.

Yet, in the 21st century, Warne took more wickets – 357, compared to 351 in the 1990s – at a slightly lower average, 25.17 to 25.66. He went from snaring a wicket every 64 balls to every 51. In the 2000s, Warne performed better outside Australia than at home. Warne also became more effective against left-handers: from averaging 33.17 against southpaws in the 1990s, Warne averaged 28.48 against them in the 2000s.

A year's ban in 2003, for taking a banned diuretic – given to him by his mum to try and help him lose weight, he said – was a typical controversy. Yet it might well have extended his career. Warne listened to his brother's advice: go months without touching a ball and let his body heal.

While other leg-spinners obsessed over variations, Warne pared back his craft. After a shoulder operation in 1998, he struggled to bowl the flipper and largely eschewed the googly. Instead, Warne depended mainly on his cricketing acumen and leg break. Opponents did not merely face his deliveries; they also faced his entire legend. When striding in, Warne focused, he said, not on where he wanted to bowl but on what shot he wanted the batter to play:

> Do I want him to go back and defend? Do I want him to come forward and drive? Do I want him to sweep?

That allows me to bowl exactly where I want, rather than focusing in on a spot. I've got my plan, and then I just have to execute it to get the batsman out.

Twelve years after his Ball of the Century, Warne produced an encore for the 21st century. Against Andrew Strauss at Edgbaston in 2005 he delivered a mirror image of the Gatting ball: bowled to a left-hander rather than a right-hander, uprooting the leg stump rather than the off. Except, if anything, it spun even more.

19

THE ROAD LESS TRAVELLED

Allan Border, who had led Australia out of the worst years in their Test history, was playing in his eighth series against West Indies. Six of those had been lost and one drawn. Now, at Adelaide in January 1993, Border was within sight of finally realising his dream.

Australia began the fourth Test of the series 1–0 up, bidding to become the first side to defeat West Indies in a series since 1980. West Indies retained an outstanding four-man pace attack, but, without Viv Richards, their batting line-up now had a scintilla of vulnerability. In Adelaide, Australia bowled out West Indies for 252 and then a paltry 146; off-spinner Tim May, playing his first Test in four years, took 5–9. Australia needed 186 runs to take an unassailable 2–0 lead in the series.

The only certainty was that it would not be easy; West Indies' potency was such that Courtney Walsh was second-change. Curtly Ambrose promptly trapped opener David Boon lbw for a duck. When Shane Warne – who braved 60 balls for nine measly runs – was lbw to Ian Bishop, Australia were 102–8.

Assisted by some edges landing fortuitously, May supported debutant Justin Langer to invite the prospect of a remarkable victory. But when Langer got a bottom edge attempting to pull Bishop, Australia were 144–9, still needing 42 more to win.

What began as a defiant last-wicket stand rapidly took on the hope of being something else: history-making and, as if preordained, on Australia Day too. To add to the sense of serendipity, it was May's home ground and his birthday. In the middle, May constantly told himself, 'It's Australia Day, it's my birthday; of course we're going to win.'

Edges continually evaded fielders; one drive narrowly eluded mid-off. Balls were clipped efficiently off the pads. May drove gloriously through the off side. All the while, supporters rushed to the Adelaide Oval, a ground nestled in the middle of the city. Border could occasionally be glimpsed sitting in the dressing room, nervously juggling a cricket ball; teammates called it his 'worry ball'.

When May flicked Walsh behind square leg, some urged him to scamper back for a risky second run that would have levelled the scores, guaranteeing Australia at least a tie. He thought better of it.

That left Craig McDermott, Australia's number 11, on strike. Walsh bowled short; McDermott flicked it off his hips, seemingly for the runs that would make good on Border's lifetime quest. Desmond Haynes, at leg slip, stopped the ball with his shins. Walsh speared the next ball into McDermott from his awkward angle wide of the crease. McDermott shaped to evade the ball, but turned himself around 90 degrees. As he moved his bat away, turning his back to the bowler, the ball kissed his glove – though not all agree – en route to wicket-keeper Junior Murray. For the first time in Test history, a match was lost by one run. When the umpire raised his finger, and West Indies' team engulfed Walsh, Border hurled his ball to the ground.

On a Perth wicket that could have been tailor-made for him, Ambrose's spell of 7–1 consigned Australia to an innings defeat in the decider. Border scored a pair. After 27 centuries in 156 Tests, during which he had broken every finger, and one thumb, batting for his country, Border retired the following year. He never won a series against West Indies.

* * *

In Test cricket, fights for world supremacy are rare. The international schedule is generally agreed years in advance; one team might rise while another is falling, without the two meeting on the pitch. The narratives beloved in sport – of one match marking the moment when one side dethrones another – seldom occur.

But in 1995, when West Indies hosted Australia, it was a tussle for the right to be considered world number one. While developing a formidable side, Australia's chief problem was a tendency to lose close matches. The year after the one-run Adelaide defeat, Australia lost by five runs to South Africa at Sydney in 1994, when chasing only 117; then by one wicket to Pakistan in Karachi, when Inzamam-ul-Haq and Mushtaq Ahmed added 57 for the last wicket, and keeper Ian Healy missed a stumping.

In the Caribbean, skipper Mark Taylor forced the side to practise against bouncers more. He also vowed to bounce the tailenders. 'If we were going to cop it, we may as well dish it out as well,' Taylor said.

The 1994/95 series was the first time that Glenn McGrath showcased his full talents, combining height and bounce with seam movement and metronomic control. Paul Reiffel stepped into the void created by the injured new-ball pair Craig McDermott and Damien Fleming. With Shane Warne complementing the pace bowlers, Australia persisted with the same XI all series. West Indies tinkered with their openers, hampered by a refusal to pick Desmond Haynes, who had not played enough domestic games to meet the selectors' criteria.

Just like in 1993, the final Test in 1995 loomed with the series at 1–1. While the 1992/93 series had been settled by Ambrose, the 1995 tussle was decided by Steve Waugh. He arrived at Sabina Park with Australia 73–3 in response to 265; the game, series and West Indies' unbeaten run were in the balance. In a low-scoring series, no Australian had yet hit a century. Over the series, a feud developed between Ambrose and Waugh, who took blows to the body after vowing that he wouldn't play the hook, because 'the odds aren't in your favour'. He joined his twin, Mark, who played with characteristic counter-attacking elan and initially dominated the run-scoring. The twins' double-century stand, helped by Steve being dropped by wicket-keeper Courtney Browne on 42, effectively sealed the series.

'All those years in the backyard, Mark and I, playing imaginary Test matches, and here was the biggest moment of our careers batting together,' Steve recalled. 'The best opposition, the toughest circumstances, the most on the line. That was why you wanted to play Test match cricket. Going into that, we knew this was a huge Test match and, for quite a few of us, the last opportunity to beat the West Indies at home. We knew if we didn't do it, some other team would probably come along and do it. We wanted to be the team that broke the stranglehold.'

For all their tussles on the pitch, Ambrose admired Waugh's cussedness. He told me,

> He's the kind of player that doesn't show emotions. Some players you bowl at and you get a bit aggressive with them. You can see when you look in their eyes, they're not that comfortable and it's only a matter of time before you get them out.
>
> Steve Waugh is one of those guys that you have to literally knock him out. It doesn't matter what you do to him. Sometimes he looks out of sorts, but he's never going to surrender. So he really fired me up a lot. And I want to believe that I fired him up as well.

By the time that Steve was dismissed, for a round 200, he had ushered in a new era. West Indies' innings defeat in Jamaica marked the end of one dynasty – Ambrose wrote that the team 'felt we had destroyed a legacy' – and the birth of another. History showed that this was a clash between one of the best Test sides ever, just after their peak, and one about to embark on a run of similar dominance. Australia made good on Taylor's words when the side returned home: 'make them suffer like we did'.

The 1950s marked the time when Test cricket became a multination international sport, rather than merely revolving around bilateral matches involving England. In the years since, two teams stand alone as recording win–loss ratios of more than three over at least 50 Tests. First, West Indies from 1980 to 1995, who won 59 Tests and lost just 15 – a win–loss ratio of 3.93. Then, Australia from their Caribbean tour in 1995 until McGrath and Warne retired in 2007, who recorded a win–loss ratio of 3.96.

* * *

Throughout Test history, the norm has been for Australia to be the best side. Such consistent success is a product of cricket's status as the country's sole genuinely national team sport, a vibrant sporting culture, an abundance of outdoor space and the climate.

'If you were a good athlete, you had that opportunity to go out and perform your skills 365 days of the year,' recalls Ian Chappell, the former Australia captain. Chappell believes that the strong club system has ensured the pipeline of talent to the national side. 'The club system has served us very well. Your better players were playing tough cricket pretty much all the time. If a Test player went back to club cricket, the club players were desperate to get him out. Then, Sheffield Shield cricket was bloody tough.' Pitches were generally similar to those seen in Test cricket, and tended to offer considerable bounce. When a player progressed to the Test team, 'you'd been well and truly tested, so you were pretty well prepared for whatever you were likely to run into.'

The English journalist John Arlott once described 'Australianism': 'It means that where the "impossible" is within the realm of what the human body can do, there are Australians who believe that they can do it – and who have succeeded often enough to make us wonder if anything is impossible to them.'

Overall, Australia win 1.75 Tests for every defeat they suffer; no other country wins even 1.25 Tests for every one they lose. Through myriad changes in the Test game, Australia have seldom been far from the gold standard. What was exceptional about the era from 1995 to 2007, then, was less the fact of Australia's dominance than the extent of it.

Like all great sides, Australia had an answer to the perennial problem of Test cricket: how to take 20 wickets? A large part of the answer lay in Shane Warne. His control enabled Australia to play a four-man attack almost invariably; even in conditions unconducive to spin, Warne could still threaten and contain. In 104 Tests playing together, Warne and Glenn McGrath shared 1,001 wickets.

McGrath's record is essentially devoid of any weakness. He averaged 20.70 against right-handers, 23.76 against left-handers. He averaged even less away than at home; in five continents, his *worst* average was 23.02 in Asia. He thrived against the very best: he dismissed Brian Lara 15 times, at a cost of 27.13 per wicket; and Sachin Tendulkar six, at a cost of 14.66 each. 'I never once felt as though I was the underdog,' McGrath wrote. 'I was always armed with a plan and I trusted the plan.'

Growing up in Narromine, in rural New South Wales, McGrath was self-taught, and not hailed as a future star. What became his template – using his economical action to pound out a good length, generally resisting the temptation to go too full – transferred readily to all climes. He aimed for 'that in-between length where they cannot really come forward or go back', he explained. 'If they go forward it is not quite there, if they go back it is not there and they nick. That length is a different length on every wicket. You have to assess the conditions, the bounce, the seam, and then you have to adjust accordingly.'

Some fast bowlers can be appreciated in isolation, through spectacular individual deliveries. McGrath's brilliance was cumulative; individual balls were rarely lethal, but his spells almost invariably were. 'If you bowled a persistent line and length, eventually it would be cricket's equivalent of water torture for some batsmen,' he wrote. 'No matter how good they were they'd eventually crack.' A relative lack of pace – he mostly bowled under 85 mph – and swing were no obstacle. The contours of McGrath's method mirrored the general approach of West Indies' quicks during their years of ascendancy: bowling back of a length, and focusing on seam over swing.

In his first Test in England, in 1997, McGrath struggled; he located a perfect length thereafter, and took 8–38 at Lord's in the next Test, seaming the ball back in from down the slope. Perhaps counterintuitively, data from late in his career shows that McGrath generally bowled slightly shorter in England than Australia. His focus rarely shifted from hitting the top of off stump. To do so in England, where there was less bounce, he did not need to bowl as full; in England, McGrath would extract seam movement throughout an innings, so did not need to strive for extra new-ball movement. In India, where bounce was less of an ally, McGrath bowled straight to attack the stumps while often generating reverse swing. The upshot was 563 wickets at 21.64: a consummate defensive and attacking bowler all in one.

* * *

One of the finest Test teams in history was born out of rubble. For Australian cricket, the early-to-mid-1980s was an era of turmoil. After World Series Cricket, rebel tours to South Africa provided more disruption, both robbing the national side of players and hollowing out the domestic game's depth. Three colossal figures, Greg Chappell, Rod Marsh and Dennis Lillee, retired together at Sydney in January 1984. Australia then won three, and lost 14, of their next 32 Tests: a sequence without rival as their worst since the 1890s. Malcolm Marshall described his five wickets to complete a ten-wicket victory in Jamaica in May 1984 as 'devalued by the lack of heart and courage shown' by Australia.

In 1986/87, when the Ashes had already been lost, Australia secured a consolation victory over England in Sydney. The year ended with Australia's win in the 1987 World Cup in India, belying pre-tournament odds of 16–1: another landmark on their slow ascent into being a Test side who could challenge West Indies and Pakistan for global supremacy.

The very abjectness of Australia in the mid-1980s was the catalyst for broader change. Rather than simply wait for talent to regenerate, Australia set about creating a better system.

The Australian Institute of Sport had opened in Canberra in 1981, marking an attempt to turn Australia into a sporting powerhouse and transform recent poor performances in the Olympic Games; it would come to be regarded as one of the leading such centres in the world. The institute's initial focus was largely on Olympic sports. Yet the wider focus upon sporting excellence, and knowledge-sharing in talent identification, sports science, coaching and beyond, came to benefit cricket too. The Test squad first visited the Institute in 1984.

In 1987, the institute established a cricket programme, with an academy for the best young players, in Adelaide: the first national cricket academy anywhere in the world. It would eventually house over 30 future international players, including seven who toppled West Indies in 1995. Ricky Ponting, who made his Test debut later that year, described his first stint there as 'two years' worth of tuition in those two weeks'. Rod Marsh oversaw the academy, and brought in experts to help with specific skills. Those at the academy 'picked up two or three pointers that accelerated your cricket education', recalls Damien Fleming, one of the graduates who played Test cricket. Fielding was a big focus; Fleming learned how to slide there.

Australia also became trendsetters in supporting the captain. In 1986, after home-and-away series defeats to New Zealand, captain Border sought more help. A head coach, similar to the position in football, would relieve day-to-day pressures on the captain, and allow more attention to tactical planning. Bob Simpson, the former captain, became 'cricket manager'. Effectively, Simpson was the first modern coach, influencing selection and preparation, including by using video footage.

When Simpson took over, 'the work ethic was non-existent,' he wrote in his autobiography. 'The whole training exercise [was seen] as a bit of a joke.' While Australia lacked batting and bowling quality, Simpson focused on other areas: fitness, fielding, and running between the wickets. Australia claimed 13 run-outs en route to winning the 1987 World Cup. By the early 1990s, an analogous position to coach existed in every Test side.

When Simpson took charge, Gideon Haigh noted, 44 current players had played international cricket. 'There has never been a period in history when Australia had 44 players good enough to play for their country,' Simpson lamented. Laurie Sawle, a national selector from 1982 to 1995, agreed; he developed a core of 16 players. As chair of the Australia Under-19s selection panel, Sawle nurtured players with unusual skills, notably wrist spinners. 'It was important for us to know what talent was coming through so that we could fast-track them,' Sawle said. After only six first-class games, Ian Healy was picked as Test keeper in Pakistan in 1988, aged 24; he retained his position for another 11 years.

Before the 1989 Ashes, the side were branded 'the worst team ever to leave Australia'. They returned celebrating a 4–0 victory. While England had used 29 players in the six Tests, the tourists had relied on 12. 'One of our big mistakes was not backing people,' England captain David Gower told me. Australia 'picked people not just on runs and wickets but on perceived character – they wanted the mongrel'. The series marked a shift in Australia's attitudes on the field; Border scarcely said a word to Gower until after the Ashes were won. At Trent Bridge, with the Ashes already regained, England's batter Robin Smith asked for a glass of water on the pitch, outside a scheduled drinks break. Border refused: 'No. What do you think this is, a f***ing tea party?'

In the first Test in 1989, Steve Waugh – who hitherto averaged 30.52, with no hundreds, in his first 26 Tests – scored his maiden century. After walking off, Waugh bumped into Sawle on the stairs and told him, 'Thanks for sticking by me.'

Like West Indies at the start of their own golden era, Australia could be described as more professional than any international cricket side to have come before. Advantages in youth development, talent identification, coaching and fitness augmented those with bat and ball.

A focus on lower-order batting illustrated Australia's commitment to self-improvement. In 1995, Australia introduced a 'buddy' system, pairing tailenders with top-order batters. McGrath took on Steve Waugh as a buddy. From averaging 2.23 with the bat in his first 20 Tests, McGrath averaged 8.61 thereafter, even scoring a half-century.

Opponents recognised that they were defeated by not just better players. 'The reasons for Australia's hegemony went deeper,' England captain Mike Atherton wrote in his 2002 autobiography. 'Their grade and state cricket produced tougher, hungrier cricketers than our system ... Good grade cricket in Sydney and Perth is of a better standard than county second-eleven cricket.'

Australia did not depend on players motivated by national pride alone. The model of 25 national contracts, introduced in 1986/87, allowed the country's best players to become genuine professionals and ensured that they remained sharp for Australia. McGrath played just 18 first-class games for New South Wales in the 14 years after his Test debut. By 1997, when the Australian Cricketers' Association was formed, leading players earned about $440,000 each (£220,000) – a five-fold increase on only three years earlier, the journalist Daniel Brettig noted. Financial rewards encouraged hyper-professionalisation.

The strength of domestic cricket was such that a striking number of cricketers during the era had better averages in Tests than the Sheffield Shield. Shield matches 'had Test match-like intensity', says Fleming, who averaged 25.89 in his 20 Tests from 1994 to 2001. 'Mates for Australia turned into enemies.'

The ultimate testament to Australia's system, perhaps, lay in the quality of those on the edge of the Test side. Paul Reiffel became the world's most overqualified reserve Test seamer: he averaged 26.96 with the ball, to go with 26.52 with the bat; then, the mantle passed to Damien Fleming and Andy Bichel. Leg-spinner Stuart MacGill averaged almost five wickets a game, yet was limited to 44 Tests by Warne. Colin Miller, who bowled medium pace with the new ball and off spin later in the innings, made his Test debut aged 34 and was later named Australia's Test player of the year.

The batting reserves were even more formidable. Damien Martyn, Matthew Hayden and Justin Langer all endured long periods out of the Test side – six years, for Martyn – before making their returns. During his time on the periphery, playing Sheffield Shield cricket, 'I had to be absolutely elite or I wasn't going to get opportunities,' Langer recalls. 'I was hungry and trying to take someone's place. That's the cut-throat competition we had.'

Where the most coveted county overseas players in the 1980s and early 1990s were West Indies fast bowlers, the most in-demand overseas players for the next 15 years were Australian batters. Australians on the Test fringes amassed staggering records in English domestic cricket. From 1995 to 2006, seven of the eight highest County Championship averages (of those who made 1,000 runs) were by Australians. Darren Lehmann had to wait until he turned 32 to become a Test regular; he averaged 44.95 in his 27 Tests, to go with an average of 68.76 for Yorkshire.

Lehmann was one of the lucky ones. Stuart Law made his Test debut in 1995. Trevor Hohns, the chairman of selectors, told Law, 'Make it hard for us to drop you.' Law hit 54 not out; he averaged 43.13 for Queensland and 56.52 in the County Championship, but was never picked again. Martin Love, Tom Moody, Michael Di Venuto and Brad Hodge all averaged over 45 in first-class cricket. None played more than Moody's eight Tests, which included two centuries.

* * *

For the first four years after toppling West Indies, Australia could be classed as very good, rather than great. Series victories in South Africa and Pakistan cemented Australia's status as the world's leading side. But Australia lost series in India in 1996 (a one-off Test) and 1998, and in Sri Lanka in 1999.

In this period, Australia occasionally failed to convert dominance into victory. On three occasions between 1997 and 1999, Australia secured first innings leads of over 100, but failed to take 20 wickets and drew. While on occasion the weather thwarted them, Australia suffered from their modest scoring rate. From their 1995 victory in West Indies to the 1999/2000 home season, Australia's scoring rate was joint fourth among the nine Test nations at the time.

In November 1999, Steve Waugh was beginning his first home summer as permanent full-time Test captain, after succeeding Mark Taylor. John Buchanan was about to oversee his first game as head coach. 'Waugh had the mantra of taking the road less travelled – he definitely wanted to play far more aggressively,' Buchanan told me.

Before his first home Test, against Pakistan, Buchanan addressed the squad about 'climbing Everest'. He discussed scoring more quickly – 'to be in a position to really advance the game on day one, if we batted first' – to create more time to take 20 wickets. He asked the group what legacy they sought to create; out of this came the idea of being 'the dominators', as a sequel to Australia's 1948 Invincibles. Before Buchanan's first Test at home, he stuck a piece of paper inside the changing-room door:

> Today is the first Test of our journey to the Invincibles.
> Let's make the ride enjoyable and attainable.

Previous generations had often worn the baggy green cap, but not revered it. 'I used to say it was a $10 piece of cloth,' says Ian Chappell. 'I can tell you about an Australian captain who wore the cap when he cleaned out the pigeon loft so he didn't get shit in his hair.'

Waugh continued wearing the baggy green cap that he was awarded on Test debut in 1985 for another 167 Tests; other players took to treating the cap with similar reverence. Seeking inspiration from beyond the field, he encouraged players to give talks about aspects of national life or history.

From his first tour as skipper, to West Indies in 1999, Waugh gave each player a single page outlining his expectations. Jason Gillespie was told to 'use your intimidating body language on the West Indies batsmen' and to 'set the tone for their tail-end batsmen – go for the jugular! – get personal, then get them out!'

In Buchanan's first game, Adam Gilchrist replaced Ian Healy as wicketkeeper. While Healy was an effervescent keeper and very handy batter, Gilchrist opened up new possibilities in front of the stumps. As we shall see in Chapter 23, Gilchrist accelerated the evolution of the Test wicketkeeper.

Gilchrist was merely the most extreme example of the aggression that Waugh preached. From scoring at 2.95 an over in their four years before Gilchrist's debut, Australia scored at 3.80 an over in the next four years: a difference of 76 runs a day. More assertive players – Hayden, a master of muscular crunching against the new ball, and the silky Martyn – were recalled.

While Waugh's strike rate only went up a little, even established batters were transformed: Langer's strike rate soared from 41 before November 1999 to 59 in the next four years. 'There was certainly a change in mindset,' Langer explains. 'Steve Waugh always encouraged me to back myself and be aggressive.' Under pressure early in Waugh's reign, Langer recalls their conversation: ' "I want you in the team, you're the best number three batsman in Australia. The coach wants you in the team, your mates love you and the selectors – show us what you've got." All of a sudden, I feel like Superman.' The next Test, Langer scored 59 and 127. 'If he made me feel like Superman there was times when he would have made everyone feel like Superman.'

From 2001, Langer formed a stellar opening partnership with Hayden. It was a mixture of the similar – they were left-handers and close friends born under a year apart – and the complementary. 'I'm very short, he's very tall – he smacked the ball down the ground, I hit the ball square of the wicket,' Langer explains.

'Their mindset in those days was ruthless,' says Shaun Pollock, who captained South Africa, Australia's nearest rivals, from 2000 to 2003. 'They didn't allow you to get up off the floor at any stage.'

Australia set a new record of 16 straight Test wins from 1999 to 2001. 'You feel like you're winning every single game – we're all individually going well, so we could be confident in ourselves, and now it was just like this wave,' Langer remembers. 'We didn't just have the talent and the experience by then, we had this sort of aura.'

Waugh's captaincy also witnessed Ricky Ponting's flourishing. From his childhood in Launceston, Tasmania's second city, greatness had been expected for Ponting; he got his first kit deal aged 12. Aged 16, he arrived at the Australian Cricket Academy's indoor school in Adelaide. Paul Wilson – who was ten inches taller than Ponting's 5 ft 8 in and would briefly play international cricket – greeted the new batter with a bouncer. Ponting pulled it disdainfully off the front foot in front of square leg: the shot became his signature. He credited the shot to a hallmark of the Australian system: how the best young players play club cricket against adults. 'I grew up as a ten- or eleven-year-old kid playing A grade cricket against some of the fastest bowlers in the state,' Ponting said. 'Playing against men, the ball was always bouncing up quite high . . . Probably as a kid maybe it was a defensive thing – get the ball away from me sort of thing.'

After seeing one Ponting pull, Rod Marsh, the former Test wicket-keeper who was now director of the academy, proclaimed, 'This bloke will play for Australia.' Aged 20, Ponting made his Test debut; he scored 96, given out by a dubious lbw decision.

His early years in international cricket were also marred by off-field difficulties; Ponting admitted to an alcohol problem and sustained a black eye after a night out in January 1999, when he was 24, and was suspended from the ODI side. He declared, 'It will be a huge turning point in both my life as a cricketer and as Ricky Ponting as well.' From a Test average of 36.63 at the time, Ponting averaged 62.92 in his next 100 Tests; he continued the national tradition that a side's most complete batter should occupy number three. His feats included consecutive double centuries against India in 2003; twin centuries in a match three times in eight Tests in 2005/06; and, perhaps best of all, a seven-hour 156 to secure a draw on the final day at Old Trafford during the 2005 Ashes.

Even more than his runs, Ponting's defining quality was his sheer tenacity. It was detectable in how he made himself one of the world's best fielders; in how, as captain, he steered Australia through the retirements of McGrath, Warne and Gilchrist; and in how he approached every practice session, let alone match. South Africa captain Graeme Smith called Ponting 'the most competitive man I've ever played against'. Aptly, Ponting is the only man to have played in 100 Test victories.

* * *

Where Border had been obsessed with defeating West Indies, Waugh craved victory in India, which he termed the 'final frontier'. Not since 1969 had Australia won there. They had spent the intervening years bemoaning Indian pitches, umpires and heat while performing poorly on the pitch. In 2001, after winning the first Test to extend their victorious run to 16 straight Tests, Australia were thwarted. 'We were all hell-bent on just going helter-skelter,' Gilchrist later reflected. 'We probably needed to learn how to put a handbrake on.'

Three years later, Australia returned to India. Since 2001, Australia had lost both Waugh twins; their replacements, Damien Martyn and Michael Clarke, were the two top scorers in the 2004 series, using their feet nimbly.

While Australia had floundered against India's magisterial middle order during their defeat in 2001 and a 1–1 draw down under in 2003/04, they brought a new approach in 2004. Building on research that Buchanan had done with Krishna Tunga, an Indian analyst, and advice from Vasoo Paranjape, a former Indian first-class player, Australia revised their bowling plans. They bowled markedly straighter than on previous tours, aiming to dismiss players lbw and clean bowled. Australia often deployed five fielders on the on side to avoid conceding easy boundaries. The plan was: 'rein in our natural instincts and play smart', Gilchrist said. 'The bowlers had to take a step back and run in with the new ball with one slip and a sweeper on the leg side.'

'They weren't going to let us score as quickly as we'd done in the past,' recalled India opener Virender Sehwag. From scoring 3.31 an over in the previous two series against Australia, India scored at only 2.76 an over.

Warne bowled straighter and in a more containing style than previously, enjoying his best series in India. Yet victory was built on Australia's pace attack, who combined off-cutters and other subtle variations with reverse swing. Gillespie was the premier threat, with McGrath typically frugal and Michael Kasprowicz bowling very straight with an occasional bouncer. With Australia 1–0 up, and players refreshed from a break between Tests – some went to Singapore, others fishing in southern India – Nagpur was an unexpectedly green surface. Martyn's century hauled Australia up to 398; Gillespie's nine wickets in the game clinched a crushing 342-run victory.

Buchanan had prepared for the series ever since 2001. Equipping his side with both new tactics and new kit, including ice-vests, he vowed that this time would be different. Many, especially Warne, regarded Buchanan, who only played seven first-class games, with suspicion. While saying that he could be 'inflexible', Waugh hailed Buchanan's 'vision and proactiveness' and 'thought-provoking' mind. 'He would always test us,' Langer recalls. 'You could see why that pissed some people off because when you're getting challenged all the time to get better – sometimes you're like "f***, let us be comfortable for a while". But his vision was extraordinary.'

Buchanan was a devotee of technology. From 2001, he enlisted Tunga to provide computer analysis. Coding each's ball line and length, and the batter's shot, in pursuit of tactical ideas, Tunga could be called the first modern analyst.

The successes in Asia in 2004 – the win in India was preceded by a 3–0 victory in Sri Lanka, overcoming first innings deficits each time – confirmed Australia's status among the Mount Rushmore of Test sides. Just as their bowlers were more economical than in 2001, so their batters scored more slowly too. 'If you are aggressive all the time you can become predictable without having a fall-back position,' Buchanan said. While India struggled to absorb Sachin Tendulkar's absence in the opening two Tests, vice-captain Gilchrist secured the series – the greatest moment of his career, he said – before captain Ponting returned for the last Test.

Perhaps there was an irony in the triumph too. Just as Border had been fuelled by desire to beat West Indies, only for Australia to do so a year after his retirement, so Waugh was consumed by winning in India, and saw Australia do so within a year of his own final Test. Yet both men were leading architects of the green-and-golden age.

20

HOW TO BUY A TEST MATCH

'Tell me Mr Fraser, is Don Bradman still alive?' So Nelson Mandela greeted Australia's former prime minister Malcolm Fraser at Cape Town's Pollsmoor Prison in 1986. Mandela's question reflected his love for cricket, reverence for Bradman and personal admiration for the Don's role in stopping South Africa from touring Australia in 1971/72, effectively confirming cricketing isolation for the rest of the apartheid years.

Four years later, when Mandela was released after 27 years in prison, Fraser presented him with a bat. It contained an inscription: *'To Nelson Mandela. In recognition of a great unfinished innings – Don Bradman.'*

In July 1991, with Mandela released and the road to democratisation under way, the Indian board proposed that South Africa become Full Members of the International Cricket Council. Four months later, South Africa toured India for three one-day internationals, ending their cricketing exile.

The format for the following year's World Cup was then tweaked to accommodate South Africa. Their squad betrayed the lack of investment in cricket beyond the white population during apartheid. Only one player, the 40-year-old left-arm spinner Omar Henry, was not white. (Henry was classed as 'coloured' – a person of mixed-race African, Asian and European descent. Under South African terminology, the term 'Indian' refers to players of South Asian descent; the term 'black' refers to black African players specifically.)

Growing up in Stellenbosch, Henry began his career playing in segregated teams, representing Western Province's non-white side.

Aged 23, in 1976, Henry was travelling with the squad; he saw that the white Western Province side were playing in Durban. Henry and some teammates sneaked in: 'We'd never been inside Kingsmead.' This led to the non-white Western Province team banning Henry. Players not classed as white had recently been offered the chance to play in the white system, the flagship of the South African Cricket Union's desegregation attempts. 'I was basically left with no other alternative but to move across and play with the whites,' he recalls. 'I wanted to see whether I could make it as a professional cricketer.'

For the remainder of his career, Henry played for provinces in this structure even while society remained racially stratified. When he travelled with the team, restaurants often refused to serve Henry, invoking the Liquor Act, which banned non-white people from being served alcohol in public; Henry, a Muslim, never ordered alcohol.

Reaction to his decision 'was mixed on both sides', he explains. 'You had friends who accepted you and some didn't. All my teammates that I played with accepted me. But you had either spectators or fans or citizens who disagreed.' Henry tried to convince teammates of the need to change the political system:

> I wanted to dismantle apartheid – whenever the white people spoke to me in the dressing room, then I would tell them about what is wrong in South Africa politically. Why should we go to separate schools? Why shouldn't we all be allowed to go to the same schools, travel on the same train? That was my discussions with them – and they agreed, but we didn't make the laws.

From 1982, Henry played in rebel Tests for South Africa. He received death threats from anti-apartheid groups, who resented his decision; armed guards were stationed outside his home.

'The rebel tours were sort of unlocking the door of international cricket – exposing the changes that needed to occur in South Africa,' he reflects. 'I knew they weren't going to be rapid changes.'

Henry was ill and missed South Africa's first Test back, in Barbados in April 1992. In his absence, South Africa fielded an all-white side, captained by Kepler Wessels, who had played 24 Tests for Australia after moving there aged 21. The Test was played only weeks after a referendum of the white population voted to continue negotiations to end apartheid. South Africa's team voted at the High Commission in Canberra, before the World Cup semi-finals – all bar Henry, because he was not allowed to vote. Wessels used his newspaper column to advocate a 'Yes' vote. One advertisement supporting the Yes campaign asked, 'Are you glad South African teams are participating in international events like World Cup cricket again?'

South Africa was not yet a non-racial democracy; not all West Indies countries supported their tour. It took a letter from Mandela himself to convince Jamaica's prime minister, Michael Manley.

Over the first four days at Kensington Oval, South Africa meticulously got into a dominant position: they needed 201 to win, and reached 122–2 at the close. West Indies had not lost a Test in Barbados since 1935.

On the final morning, a veteran fan wandered the ground with a warning to any South African supporters: 'Tell your boys,' he said, 'that the last day at Kensington Oval always belongs to us.' Curtly Ambrose and Courtney Walsh dragged their lengths back, denying South Africa the oxygen of runs while harassing the off stump and exploiting uneven bounce. The last eight wickets fell for 25 runs. Ambrose's match figures were characteristic: 60.4–26–81–8.

'A lot of lessons were learned,' recalls Allan Donald, who took six wickets in the Test. 'That's the way that Test cricket is played. And I want a lot of that because that was amazing to watch. Although it was hurtful, it was amazing to watch how those two guys went about their business.'

In November 1992, Henry became, in all probability, the second South African Test cricketer who was not white, following Charlie

Llewellyn, who played from 1896 to 1912. While he only played three Tests – 'I was past my sell-by-date' – Henry symbolised the transition to a non-racial society as the country moved towards fully democratic elections in 1994. So did the sight of Mandela as an honoured guest at South Africa's second home Test. Before readmission, black people had to watch Tests in Johannesburg in a cage.

* * *

Allan Donald, 'White Lightning', was South Africa's most thrilling sight when they returned to Test cricket. He combined an explosive action and 90 mph pace with insatiable competitiveness and a lethal yorker.

Like the bulk of the side, he had honed his game in the school system. Around a dozen schools, a mixture of private and state institutions that had been white-only during apartheid, produced the bulk of South Africa's players in their first 30 years back as a Test nation. Donald also played in the tough South African first-class system, which was boosted by strong overseas players after readmission, and in the rebel 'Tests'.

He signed for Warwickshire as an overseas player in 1987, aged 20. 'County cricket was absolutely brutal, with 20-odd three-day games,' Donald recalls. 'It was just ridiculous. So I learned very quickly.'

Donald feared that he would never be able to represent South Africa. In 1990, Robin Smith and Allan Lamb, who had both moved to England and enjoyed fine Test careers, asked Donald to consider playing for the country too. That year, Ali Bacher, the South African Cricket Union managing director, rang Donald 'to say that I must not make a rash decision, because South Africa will be back in 1991'. Had South Africa not returned, Donald would have played for England. 'If it was even three, four years down the line, post-1992 it would definitely have been in the England camp. I was desperate to play international cricket.' Donald learned of readmission when Bacher called him during a Warwickshire match: 'The moment was just surreal.'

South Africa reached the semi-finals of the 1992 World Cup, then established themselves as a hardy Test side. At the end of that year, they won their fourth Test after readmission, against India; Donald took 12 wickets. Led by Donald's opening partnership with Shaun Pollock, a tearaway quick when he debuted in 1995 who developed metronomic accuracy to go with swing and bounce, pace bowling would become the country's trademark.

In Sydney in January 1994, Australia were 63–4 after day four, needing another 54 runs to win. Donald recalls:

> I will never forget Mark Waugh's comment after the day's play – we went in for a little drink in their dressing room. And he was saying to Hansie Cronje, 'Why don't you guys just lob a few up and we get it done in less than an hour?' Cronje's response was: 'Make sure you bring the biggest hanky to the ground tomorrow because you're gonna need it.'

Wessels had a broken finger; he couldn't take the field next day. Cronje, who was only 24, captained instead. 'He handled that so calmly, so amazingly well,' says Donald. With the day's second ball, Donald bowled Allan Border. As the bounce got lower and more unpredictable, Australia collapsed to 75–8; Cronje ran out Shane Warne with a direct hit from extra cover. The usual roles of specialist batter and tailender were inverted: number ten Craig McDermott counter-attacked, Damien Martyn scarcely attempted a stroke. At 110–8, seven away from victory, Martyn's patience broke: he drove Donald to cover, ending his tortured 59-ball six. Next over, Fanie de Villiers had Glenn McGrath caught and bowled – his sixth wicket, sealing a five-run win.

The triumph was affirmation, says opener Gary Kirsten, that 'we'd arrived and we can compete with the best cricketers in the world.' While Australia clinched a 1–1 series draw, South Africa also drew the return series 1–1. Though South Africa didn't defeat Australia in their four series during the 1990s, over the decade their win–loss ratio was the best in Test cricket. This was testament to the partnership forged between Cronje and the head coach, Englishman Bob Woolmer, who was a pioneer in his use of video and data analysis. 'The communicator and the inventor', Donald calls the pair. 'Bob was an inventor. He was always smart; he became more scientific.' Woolmer identified small tweaks to techniques and urged South Africa to bat less conservatively, claiming that a side needed to score at 2.8 runs per over to win Tests regularly. 'When those two took charge, we had something to work with in terms of our culture, our values, and who we are as people – who we represent,' Donald believes. 'We had an identity.'

Growing up, like many Afrikaners, Cronje was sustained by two pillars: faith and sport. Hansie's sister once paid him and Frans, his older brother, to talk about something else over Sunday lunch. After two minutes, they spoke about sport again.

Tenacious, charismatic, with a bracelet inscribed with the letters WWJD – What Would Jesus Do – and young enough not to be tarnished by apartheid, Hansie became South Africa's standard-bearer. He met frequently with Mandela, who recognised his significance in building a new country. Cronje was 'a natural-born leader', Donald says. 'He had this enormous aura. When he spoke, he spoke sense – he wasn't overpowering. He knew how to give you confidence.'

Cronje and Woolmer led South Africa to notable success in Asia. With Donald developing off-cutters, the 'wobble seam' – a delivery that moves off the seam in an unpredictable way – and reverse swing, he thrived in all conditions. His haul of 330 Test wickets at 22.25 included 36 wickets at 20.33 in Asia. 'You need every ounce of your effort and skill and your imagination,' he explains. 'Once the ball starts reversing, it needs pace.'

In their first four series in Asia, South Africa secured series wins in Sri Lanka in 1993, Pakistan in 1997 and India in 2000; they were the first team to win in India for 13 years. The 2–0 victory was rooted in an abundance of allrounders, which simultaneously gave South Africa batting depth and ensured that they could keep their seamers fresh. It was perhaps South Africa's greatest achievement since readmission. A month later, South Africa faced one of the gravest crises that Test cricket has ever known.

* * *

'Hello, Hansie. I'm waiting in the lobby.'

'Hello, Sanjay. Come up to my room, I'm in 346.'

With these words on taped phone calls, the Delhi police first learned of Hansie Cronje's relationship with Sanjay Chawla, a businessman that they were tracking who was believed to be an illegal bookmaker. These conversations, on Chawla's phone and a mobile he had given Cronje, formed the basis for South Africa's captain being charged by Delhi police with match-fixing, which was revealed on 7 April 2000. South Africa's ODIs against India the previous month were under suspicion.

Cronje declared himself 'stunned'; Ali Bacher, the South African board's managing director, hailed his 'enormous integrity and honesty'. At 3 a.m. four days later, Cronje called Bacher, admitting that he had not been 'entirely honest'. Cronje initially claimed to have received cash for information – about the team, the conditions and when he would declare in a home Test against India in 1996/97 – but not fixing. He was sacked as captain. South Africa struggled to process his fall. At Grey College in Bloemfontein, his old school, 1,100 pupils stood in the main hall singing, 'Hansie is our hero, we shall not be moved!'

The King Commission, which began taking evidence two months later, overseen by Judge Edwin King, revealed rampant corruption in the game. Cronje's crimes went altogether deeper than he had admitted. Allrounder Pat Symcox said that Cronje had approached him about underperforming as early as 1995. Cronje claimed that his nefarious activities began in 1996, when India's Mohammad Azharuddin introduced him to Mukesh Kumar Gupta, a former bank clerk from Delhi, during a Test in Kanpur. South Africa were already on the brink of defeat; Gupta offered Cronje $30,000 (particularly attractive given the weak rand) to ensure that they lost. Cronje claimed that he did not have any conversations with his teammates to underperform but considered it 'easy money'; he left India with the cash hidden in his kitbag, then deposited it in a bank account in England. In the years ahead, Cronje provided Gupta with information about the team, conditions and tactics – such as when South Africa were planning to declare. He accepted money for throwing matches, but denied that he ever actually threw them. In an ODI series against India, Gupta claimed, Cronje apologised when he accepted money but South Africa won. Cronje allegedly told him that India played so badly that it wasn't his fault.

In December 1996, Cronje put to the entire national team an offer of $250,000 to deliberately lose an ODI against India, declaring that the side's decision had to be unanimous. 'We had heard that other teams had been approached and when we got this offer we thought, "We're one of the big boys at last,"' wicketkeeper David Richardson told journalist Simon Wilde in his book *Caught*, published in 2001. One player asked whether the money would be tax-free. After three team meetings, the offer was rejected; Cronje only told Gupta at 3 a.m. on the morning of the match. South Africa lost comfortably anyway; Cronje later admitted that he was 'very annoyed with myself' for not accepting the cash.

Woolmer claimed that he reported the 1996 approach. The press learned of the incident in 1998, but saw the side's rejection as proof of their integrity. The article revealing the approach was headlined, 'Proud South African Cricketers Hit Match-Fixers For Six'. The board's complacency remained. For all the rumours about other nations fixing, South Africa's attitude evoked the title of Sinclair Lewis's novel about fascism in the USA: *It Can't Happen Here*.

The shock of the revelations was compounded by the racial context. Cronje had approached cricketers designated as players of colour, who tended to be both from poorer backgrounds and less secure of their place. In ODIs in India in 2000, both Herschelle Gibbs (considered a Cape coloured player) and the black bowler Henry Williams had been sought out by Cronje and offered money – via a bookmaker, with Cronje taking a $10,000 cut per player – to underperform. The players both told Cronje they would accept. Neither underperformed in the manner they had promised. Gibbs was offered the cash to score under 20; he actually made 74. Williams was bribed to concede over 50 runs; he was injured after 11 balls. Neither Gibbs nor Williams received their cash. Cronje admitted to receiving $140,000, largely into offshore accounts, from Gupta and other bookmakers between 1996 and 2000.

In January 2000, the final Test of South Africa's series with England was drifting to a rain-ruined draw in Centurion: just 45 overs were possible over the first four days. With South Africa 2–0 up in the series, a day of futility loomed. On the fourth evening, Cronje received a call on his mobile. It was from Marlon Aronstam, a South African gambler, asking to meet. At ten o'clock in his hotel room, Cronje was asked whether he would declare the first innings, persuade England to forfeit their first innings and forfeit South Africa's second innings, thereby setting up a final innings run chase.

Aronstam said he did not care who won – only that there was a winner, which would enable him to back both sides at long odds, with bookmakers assuming that a draw was inevitable. In return, Aronstam gave Cronje 53,000 rand and a leather jacket for his wife. Aronstam also promised Cronje that he would give several hundred thousand rand to a charity of his choice. Cronje told Judge King that he was like an abstaining alcoholic, relapsing when offered a drink. He claimed that he had not engaged in corruption between around the end of 1997, when he ceased contact with Gupta, and January 2000.

Before day five, Cronje let England know of his intentions to set up a chase. As South Africa's first innings continued, with England keen to see how the pitch played after rain, captain Nasser Hussain sent a message to Cronje, suggesting a target in the expectation that Cronje would haggle. Instead, Cronje immediately agreed to Hussain's proposed target of 245 in 76 overs – 'I couldn't believe it,' Hussain wrote – which became 249 when Paul Adams accidentally hit four from the last ball of South Africa's innings. Cronje met with Barry Jarman, the match referee, to discuss whether it was legal to forfeit two innings; Jarman agreed that doing so was within the spirit of the game. No Test had ever featured two forfeited innings. But, to many English eyes, it seemed merely a more extreme version of the final-day deals common in the County Championship.

England slipped to 102–4 when Michael Vaughan joined Alec Stewart at the crease. Curiously, Cronje now brought on part-time bowler Pieter Strydom. 'A couple of boundaries off him kept the game open,' England's Mike Atherton wrote. 'South Africa were trying to win the game, but it was clear that Cronje was after a result.' It remains the only Test proved to have been fixed.

As England neared their target, Cronje retained aggressive fields, out of character with his normal conservatism. A late collapse reduced England to 240–8, with tailenders Darren Gough and Chris Silverwood together and only 11 balls left. Cronje kept attacking; Gough scored the winning runs with five balls left. The ICC were nonplussed; others hailed Cronje's gambit. 'Hansie did the game the biggest favour imaginable at the dawn of the new century,' said Woolmer. Cronje nobly proclaimed, 'As Test cricketers we have a duty to entertain.' Amid the early uncertainty over whether England would agree to a deal, Aronstam waited too late to place his bets before bookmakers learned of the captains' deal. The promised donation to charity never materialised.

Cronje's fixing in 2000 would culminate in him being caught by the Indian police and banned from the game. Cronje's King Commission testimony blamed the Devil:

> In a moment of stupidity and weakness I allowed Satan and the world to dictate terms to me . . . The moment I took my eyes off Jesus, my whole world turned dark and it felt like someone had stuck a knife through my chest.

Frans, Hansie's older brother, told me that he believed that relentless international cricket – 'there was one year where he spent 28 days at home' – eroded Hansie's judgement. He was also 'an adventurous bloke – never scared of taking chances. And I think in the end the intrigue of the people speaking to him, the bookies speaking to him, might have got him interested.'

On the morning of 1 June 2002, Hansie boarded a cargo plane from Stellenbosch to his house in George. The plane crashed because of fierce wind and rain that forced it into the mountain range. By the time that Frans drove to George six hours later, 'it was beautiful sunshine'.

* * *

The roots of the match-fixing crisis were simultaneously very old and very new. Cricket has an ignoble history. There was betting on the first recorded match, in 1646 at Coxheath in Kent. The sport's structure, with atomised, isolated actions – rather than the fluidity of a game like football – is ideally suited to corruption. Rather than a whole team, corrupting one player will often suffice for fixers, allowing them to bet on a particular batter to make below a certain score.

For all these ancient roots, there were modern catalysts for the fixing crisis. The satellite TV boom meant that those who wanted could now watch any major international match, anytime, anywhere. If they could watch it, they could – legally or illegally – bet on it too.

There were also more internationals than before, with the number of ODIs mushrooming after India won the 1983 World Cup.

These matches were taken to new outposts, which often attracted corruptors – most notoriously in Sharjah, which started hosting ODIs in 1984. For players, the plethora of matches created the allure of a victimless crime: accepting money to underperform in a triangular tournament group match, say, when qualification for the final was already assured. The dizzying array of betting markets increased temptation. With bookmakers offering bets on the number of runs scored over five-over blocks in ODIs, a player could agree, say, to score very slowly over the first five overs yet still be free to score a century. Cricket's belief in the decency and unimpeachable propriety of players encouraged a blasé attitude. The sport was 'exceedingly naive – naive, blind and short-sighted', Ehsan Mani, who was Pakistan's representative at the ICC in the 1990s, told me.

In so far as it can be dated, the modern history of corruption can be traced back to 1988. As Mihir Bose wrote in his history of Indian cricket, that was when Gupta first made contact with Ajay Sharma, who played one Test and 31 ODIs for India, at a club tournament in Delhi. Sharma, Gupta alleged, began to provide information about the team and conditions in exchange for payment; then, he introduced him to other cricketers. (Sharma was initially banned for life for match-fixing, but subsequently cleared from all charges.) Over the 1990s Gupta flew around the world, from one ODI tournament and lavish hotel to the next, meeting players. His template appears to have been to shower them with gifts, then start paying for information; and, finally, to ramp up his offers in exchange for players agreeing to underperform.

Nine current or former international captains had allegedly taken money from bookmakers, a report by India's Central Bureau of Investigation outlined in 2000. In 1999, bookmakers tried to enlist England's Chris Lewis to fix a Test against New Zealand; he reported the approach immediately.

In October 1994, the night before day five of the Karachi Test, Shane Warne received a phone call. It was from Pakistan captain Saleem Malik, inviting him to his room. There, Malik declared that Pakistan 'cannot lose'. He offered Warne and Tim May, his roommate and fellow spin bowler, $200,000 to bowl badly. The pair rejected the approach. The following day, despite Warne's five wickets, Inzamam-ul-Haq's 58 not out sealed a one-wicket Pakistan win.

Four years later, it emerged that both Warne and his friend Mark Waugh had given a bookmaker named 'John' – thought to be Gupta – information about the weather and conditions in exchange for cash during an ODI series in Sri Lanka in September 1994. The Australian Cricket Board had fined the players in 1995, but discreetly.

Malik's distinguished 17-year Test career continued until 1999. But he faced growing concerns about his conduct. Pakistan's Qayyum Commission, which took evidence from September 1998, gave voice to the allegations about the team's propriety. Over 13 months, 33 current or former Pakistan players and officials were questioned about their potential involvement in fixing or their belief that others were deliberately underperforming. Fast bowler Sarfraz Nawaz alleged that players had begun fixing from the tour of India in 1979/80.

On a taped phone call presented by wicketkeeper Rashid Latif to the Qayyum inquiry, opening batter Saeed Anwar said *'Is waqt sab ko sab par shaq ho raha hai'*: 'At the moment everybody is suspecting everyone else.' From February 1994 to September 1998, Osman Samiuddin noted in *The Unquiet Ones*, Pakistan had seven different captains and changed leader 13 times. Such instability made Pakistan's achievements of the era all the more remarkable: they defeated England away in 1992 and 1996, and won two Tests in India in 1999.

Rashid Latif alleged that fixing was widespread. When the Qayyum Commission's report was finally published, in June 2000, it agreed. Sort of, anyway. The report asserted that corruption was endemic. Yet its evidence was overwhelmingly hearsay, some of it contradictory. Eight national players were punished to varying degrees. Malik and Ata-ur-Rehman, a seamer whose testimony seemed to sway with the wind, received life bans; Malik's life ban was later overturned. Wasim Akram was fined and it was recommended that he never captain Pakistan again; leg-spinner Mushtaq Ahmed received the same punishment. The report stated that 'Wasim Akram is not above board.' Another four players, including Waqar Younis and Inzamam-ul-Haq, were fined for not cooperating fully with the inquiry. The report's conclusion exonerated the team from fixing systematically, even while leaving the lingering sense that much would remain unknown: 'The allegation that the Pakistan team as a whole is involved in match-fixing is just based on allegation, conjectures and surmises without there being positive proof.'

Dawood Ibrahim, the notorious Mumbai mob boss, was reportedly involved in fixing for decades, Chandramohan Puppala detailed in *No Ball*. Under a different name, Ibrahim is said to have entered India's dressing room in 1987, promising players a Toyota each if they defeated Pakistan in an ODI the next day. Ibrahim is believed to have especially dealt with players from Bangladesh, India, Pakistan and Sri Lanka. 'All match-fixers are answerable to Dawood Ibrahim,' said a Pakistani bookmaker quoted by Puppala in 2019.

India's former captain Mohammad Azharuddin, who was renowned for his dazzling stroke play, admitted to being involved in fixing ODIs. But he denied Cronje's claims that he had introduced him to Gupta in 1996. In 2000, India's Central Bureau of Investigation estimated that Azharuddin had earned 90 lakh (100,000 rupees) from Gupta – but that he had repaid 30 lakh, largely in instalments from his locker at Taj Palace hotel, when some of his predictions proved incorrect. The CBI said,

> It is clear that Azharuddin contributed substantially towards the expanding bookie/player nexus in Indian cricket. The enquiry has disclosed that he received large sums of money from betting syndicates to 'fix' matches. There is also evidence which discloses

that he roped in other players also to fix matches, which resulted in this malaise making further inroads into Indian cricket.

Azharuddin's Test career ended on a strangely apt 99 matches; his final Test was also Cronje's last.

In *Wisden* in 2001, Mihir Bose wrote that Cronje's identity helped to ensure that concerted action was taken to addressing corruption:

> 'There was, is, a power struggle in international cricket,' one highly placed ICC source admitted, 'and the Asian countries are resentful of England, the old colonial power, but then the subcontinent has not helped matters by being very defensive about match-fixing. We have known for years that match-fixing goes on, helped by the fact that betting is illegal and in the hands of criminals there. But in the past, whenever the matter has been raised, they have said we are cricket administrators, not cops. Then a clean-cut white South African, Hansie Cronje, was caught in the net, the game changed and everyone has had to come clean.'

Whether everyone really did come clean remains contentious. The ICC belatedly created an Anti-Corruption Unit in 2000, initially headed by retired British police officer Sir Paul Condon. Condon's report in 2001 warned of a 'core of players and others who continue to manipulate the results of matches', detailing a 'climate of silence, apathy, ignorance and sometimes fear'.

When he succeeded Cronje as captain, Shaun Pollock tried to change South Africa's culture. 'The faith of the team had been burned a little bit by Hansie,' he recalls. 'The leader who commanded that you did things and had a certain approach. The players weren't overly keen to buy into that same management style again.' Compared to Cronje, it had to be 'more of a servant leadership', Pollock explains. 'You had to be more open to suggestions, engage more with everyone – less authoritative.'

While South Africa failed to usurp Australia as world number one, they thrived otherwise, winning 14 Tests under Pollock's captaincy and losing only five. He made good on his aim: 'to restore the faith that we were going out there to compete and do our best and try and win games for our country.'

* * *

When the Cronje scandal broke, the game's response had been disbelief; this time, the reaction was of grim belief. While commentating on the fourth Test between England and Pakistan at Lord's in 2010, seeing that Mohammad Amir had bowled a huge no-ball, Michael Holding's reaction – 'How far over was that? Wow' – betrayed a sense that something untoward *could* be happening. Cricket's innocence had been lost long ago.

Amir, an electric 18-year-old left-armer, had emerged from the small village of Changa Bangyaal. Like many Pakistan bowlers before him, he was self-taught and reared on tape-ball cricket. After being spotted in a tape-ball tournament, he was given a scholarship at an academy in Rawalpindi, sharing a dormitory with three other boys. Excelling in the Test game aged 17, Amir was hailed as his hero Wasim's heir.

Before day four at Lord's, the *News of the World* detailed why he had bowled such an egregious no-ball. An undercover reporter – Mazher Mahmood, the *News of the World*'s so-called 'Fake Sheikh', posing as an Anglo-Indian businessman called Mohsin Khan – offered Mazhar Majeed, captain Salman Butt's agent, £150,000. He received the money in a suitcase stuffed with £50 notes. In return, he would use Butt to enlist Amir and Mohammad Asif, a 27-year-old seamer of consummate skill, to bowl three no-balls at specific points. Majeed claimed that a plan to do so in the previous Test was derailed after Pakistan coach Waqar warned the side against bowling extras.

The first no-ball, just as Majeed had promised, was delivered by Amir from the first ball of the third over on a truncated opening day; his front foot was nine inches over the popping crease, the point which bowlers cannot overstep. The second no-ball, delivered from the last ball of the tenth over following a signal based on when the first wicket fell, was by Asif, only two inches over. The third no-ball, promised by Majeed after discussions with the three players during the first evening, was by Amir on day two. He had removed England's number four, five and six for ducks in a mesmerising spell of swing. Butt then had a brief chat with Amir. The third ball of the 19th over was delivered 12 inches past the popping crease, prompting Holding's astonishment.

As day three ended, Pakistan learned of the story about to break; police arrived at Lord's. After play, Butt, Amir and Asif were interviewed by police at the team hotel. Police found £2,500 in notes in Butt's room, and £1,500 in Amir's.

The fourth day was miserable, brevity its lone redeeming feature; when Asif and Amir batted, they were booed, and greeted with complete silence by England's fielders. While it was only alleged that the no-balls, rather than anything else, were fixed, Pakistan crashed to an innings and 225-run defeat.

The undercover reporter claimed to Majeed that his syndicate would bet on the no-balls to be bowled at specific times. But, Ed Hawkins wrote in *Bookie Gambler Fixer Spy*, even Indian illegal bookmakers didn't allow bets to be placed on the timing of no-balls: such a bet would naturally attract suspicion. Yet the players' actions highlighted Majeed's power – and suggested that they could be bought. The sport's skewed economics might have made Pakistanis particularly susceptible to fixing; at the time, England's players earned around £400,000 a year in central contracts and match fees, Pakistan's around £22,000.

Amir later told Mike Atherton that he was only given money after the first day at Lord's and said that he had agreed to bowl the no-balls under pressure from Butt and Majeed. Amir claimed that, in a car the day before the Test, the two told him that, if he bowled the no-balls, they would ensure that he was not punished for an interaction with 'Ali'.

Ali was a mysterious businessman who had made a payment to Amir's bank account the previous week; Amir initially didn't know his bank details, and had to contact his brother for them. Ali then repeatedly asked Amir to fix. Amir, phone records seen by Atherton showed, was approached about bowling no-balls; he replied, 'It would be too much, friend.' Next morning, Amir reported the approach to his captain, Butt. In that car on 25 August, Amir claimed that his conversation with Butt went as follows:

> He said to me, 'You're in big trouble, bro. You're trapped and your career is at stake.'
>
> I said, 'Bro, what exactly has happened?' He replied that my calls with Ali had been recorded by the ICC police. I told him that, in any case, I had not done anything with Ali, but he insisted that a friend of his knew that they had a file with my name on it. He said he could help me out of my difficulties but that I had to do a favour for him in return. I asked him: 'What favour?' That's when he mentioned the two no-balls.

The following February, the ICC tribunal against the players concluded. Butt was banned from cricket for ten years (five suspended), Asif for seven years (two suspended) and Amir for five years.

For the trio, the worst was yet to come: all faced trial in the UK, after the Crown Prosecution Service brought criminal charges. Amir pleaded guilty; the two older players denied the charges. After 22 days, the trial ended with Butt, Asif and Amir – 15 months earlier, Pakistan's Test captain and two opening bowlers – escorted out of Southwark Crown Court in handcuffs. They were bundled into a large white police van and driven to their fates: 30 months' imprisonment for Butt, 12 months for Asif and six for Amir.

In 2016, while playing cricket in Norway, Asif told me, 'Every human being can make mistakes. They've given us punishment and after the punishment everybody has a right to play. Cricket is my life.' Asif never played another Test, ending with an average of 24.36 from 23 Tests. Amir, 23 when he completed his ban, made his Test return at Lord's in 2016, sealing Pakistan's win; he only played another 21 Tests, his promise unfulfilled. Butt played professionally again, but never for Pakistan.

The tawdry scenes at Lord's are the last-known case of part of a Test match being fixed. While this is no proof of the Test game's probity, gamblers have now largely turned their attention to other formats. The amount of money bet on the 2023 Indian Premier League was over five times more than all Test matches in the year combined on the betting exchange Betfair.

It is likely that the Test game is now mostly corruption-free. But cricket match-fixing hasn't been eliminated, merely displaced. Short-format competitions, particularly in T20 leagues, have become the most fertile area for corruptors to make money.

21

THE TWO AGES OF TENDULKAR

Late in his life, Sir Donald Bradman identified the batter who played most like him. 'I was very, very struck by his technique,' Bradman said in 1996. 'I asked my wife to come and have a look at him. Because, I said, "I never saw myself play. But I feel this fellow is playing much the same as I used to."

'It was just his compactness, his stroke production, his technique. It all seemed to gel.'

The player's name was Sachin Tendulkar.

Bradman later invited Tendulkar to his 90th birthday. 'We discussed batting,' Tendulkar recalls. 'How good batters could read the ball by looking at the bowler's wrist position and also see which way the ball is spinning in the air and hence could read the delivery as soon as it was released.'

The man who would become the heaviest run-scorer in Test history was first glimpsed on the maidans in Mumbai in the mid-1980s. Most days, the young Tendulkar – his father was a poet and university professor; his mother worked for the Life Insurance Corporation of India – boarded bus number 315 from the suburb of Bandra East to Shivaji Park.

The maidans are a characteristic of Indian cricket; their prevalence helps to explain the abundance of Test players, especially batters, from Mumbai. Dozens of matches take place in parallel; the field in one game normally overlaps with the adjacent field, so that extra cover in one game might stand alongside midwicket in another. 'Your peripheral awareness increased,' Tendulkar reflects. 'After having played on these maidans, when I started playing in stadiums with only one match happening at a time, suddenly finding gaps became easier.'

Aged 11, Tendulkar first met the coach Ramakant Achrekar. Initially, Achrekar turned down Tendulkar for a place on his summer camp. Tendulkar's older brother asked him to give Sachin another chance; Achrekar pretended that he wasn't watching as he observed Sachin again. Achrekar took Tendulkar from one maidan to the next; he frequently played multiple games on the same day. The coach persuaded Tendulkar's parents to move him to a different school, which was better for cricket; Tendulkar relocated from his parents to his aunt's, to be closer to Shivaji Park.

The young Tendulkar's routine was relentless. During the summer, he batted for two hours in the nets from 7.30 a.m. Then, he went straight into a match at Shivaji Park, playing 55 games in 60 days one summer. Matches normally finished at 4.30 p.m.; by 5 p.m., Tendulkar was in the nets again for another two hours, each broken into five chunks. His practice would end with a final 15-minute session – this time on a wicket on the practice pitch. Achrekar placed a one-rupee coin above his middle stump. Tendulkar could keep it if he survived the session without being dismissed; facing up to 70 fielders, he had to keep each ball along the ground. After running two laps of Shivaji Park with his pads and gloves on, Tendulkar finally went home; he often spoke of cricket in his sleep.

'The maidans gave me exposure to playing on different surfaces at a very young age,' Tendulkar says. 'Achrekar Sir, my coach, made it a point that I got to play on different surfaces against different bowlers.

'A lot of these maidans were big grounds and had big boundary lines. Hence, one had to run quite a bit between the wickets to score runs, which can become tiring. And when you are tired, the first thing that happens is that you lose concentration. Playing in those maidans in my school days was a good way to train and develop the habit of concentrating and maintaining focus for long hours.'

At Azad Maidan, ten kilometres south of Shivaji, the Tendulkar name would first reverberate. In the Harris Shield, an annual interschool tournament named after Lord Harris, Tendulkar played for Shardashram Vidya Mandir. In a semi-final against St Xavier's in February 1988, when he was 14, Tendulkar walked out at 84–2, joining Vinod Kambli, a boy who was 15 months older and would play Test cricket alongside him. The two batted in unison until lunchtime on day two, when their team declared on 748–2; Kambli hit 349 not out, Tendulkar 326 not out. After the semi-final, Tendulkar was taken to the other end of the maidan and scored 178 not out in another game. Across the quarter-final, semi-final and final of the 1988 Harris Shield, Tendulkar's scores read: 207 not out, 326 not out and 346 not out. Aged 15, Tendulkar made his first-class debut for Bombay; batting at his favoured number four, he scored 100 not out.

'I have never seen so much concentration and stamina in one so young,' said Raj Singh, then chairman of the national selection committee, in April 1989. Aged 16, Tendulkar's international entrance could scarcely have been more onerous: a Test series in Pakistan – India's greatest rival, whose attack included Wasim Akram, Waqar Younis, Imran Khan and Abdul Qadir. On debut in Karachi, Tendulkar scored one run less than his age; next Test, he hit 59.

In his fourth Test, in Sialkot, a Younis delivery deflected from the peak of Tendulkar's helmet onto his nose. He had blood all over his shirt. The team doctor asked Tendulkar if he wanted to retire hurt. 'No, I will play,' Tendulkar declared. He batted on, ignoring signs that read 'Child go home, and drink milk'. He flicked Waqar's next ball to the boundary, and batted for over three hours for 57 to secure India a 0–0 drawn series. A year later, Tendulkar made his maiden Test century – only Pakistan's Mushtaq Mohammad had got there at a younger age – to secure a draw at Old Trafford. Named player of the match, he was awarded a bottle of champagne; too young to drink alcohol, Tendulkar kept the bottle for years. Next day Tendulkar asked the team manager whether he had made any mistakes during his innings.

Many Indian batters were accused of struggling to match their feats at home abroad. Like Sunil Gavaskar before him, Tendulkar showed himself to be very different. Before turning 19, Tendulkar made centuries in England, South Africa and two in Australia.

* * *

From his earliest days as a Test cricketer, Tendulkar invited comparisons with Gavaskar. Both were only 5 ft 5 in; Gavaskar's nickname of Little Master became Tendulkar's. Both developed their craft at Shivaji Park, and were products of the Bombay School of Batsmanship. Tendulkar combined orthodoxy and poise with an elan seldom associated with Gavaskar.

For all the similarities between the two, they emerged into very different countries. Gavaskar's feats on the 1971 tour to West Indies were recorded only in 26 minutes of highlights of the entire series on Doordarshan, the Indian state broadcaster; there was not even live radio commentary.

In 1991, the year that Tendulkar turned 18, India underwent momentous changes. Manmohan Singh, the finance minister, announced a series of measures to liberalise the economy: devaluing the rupee; relaxing licensing restrictions for most industries (the so-called 'Licence Raj'); and encouraging foreign investment. 'No power on Earth can stop an idea whose time has come,' Singh said, quoting Victor Hugo. Over the next 20 years, India's economy grew by about 7 per cent a year. In 1991, India had one TV channel, Doordarshan; by 1996, it had 50.

Until 1993, Doordarshan had a monopoly over televising home matches. The Board of Control for Cricket in India even paid Doordarshan for the privilege of its games being broadcast. When England toured in 1993, the BCCI made a $600,000 profit on selling broadcasting rights for the matches: the first indication that Indian cricket could be monetised.

Through promising Associate nations a greater share of cash from the competition, the subcontinental bid for the 1996 World Cup gazumped England's Test and County Cricket Board. 'The TCCB has not got over the Raj hangover,' said the BCCI president I.S. Bindra. The World Cup allowed Jagmohan Dalmiya, a BCCI power broker, to test his belief that cricket could now make serious money. The 1996 World Cup organising committee sold the global broadcasting rights to WorldTel for $10 million, ten times the sum for the 1992 World Cup. The tournament even had an official chewing gum.

In the 1990s, globalisation and hyper-commercialisation helped to create a star whose global reach, popularity and wealth was unlike any that cricket had previously seen. Tendulkar had the runs and panache on the field. Off it, his alliance with Mark Mascarenhas, who ran WorldTel and became his agent, led him to become far richer than any cricketer before. In 1996, Mascarenhas agreed a contract which guaranteed Tendulkar about $6 million over the next five years, though he would receive much more. Tendulkar's career, Sanjay Nagral wrote in *Economic and Political Weekly*, rode 'the wave of the post-liberalisation mutant of the game with its spectacle, big money and fusion with the entertainment industry'.

In India, Tendulkar became ubiquitous in a manner that not even Gavaskar had rivalled. Only when driving around Mumbai in the early hours could he roam freely.

* * *

'Batsmen walk out into the middle alone,' the Mumbai poet C.P. Surendran wrote in 1998. 'Not Tendulkar. Every time Tendulkar walks to the crease, a whole nation, tatters and all, marches with him to the battle arena. A pauper people pleading for relief, remission from the lifelong anxiety of being Indian, by joining in spirit their visored saviour.'

Tendulkar had no choice but to accept this burden. 'I was aware of the expectations but did not consciously think of it,' he reflects. 'I have always believed that people should expect something of you. I enjoyed the fact that people had some expectations of me. It was all about messaging – what message I gave myself.

'My family played a huge role in helping me maintain balance between my cricket and the rest of my life. They never treated me like a superstar. My family and friends would be honest with me and that helped. It was like Formula 1. You only get to see the driver on track but there is a huge team working with the driver in the background.'

Tendulkar developed a mantra: 'Let everyone speak about the last game while we focus on the next one.' He recalls, 'The next match always made me tense and that's how I prepared. That's how my body responded before a game and I embraced it.'

Overseas, Tendulkar thrived against fast bowling. 'I have always enjoyed batting on pitches that had pace and bounce,' he explains. 'I also used my height to my advantage as I focused a lot on picking the length of a delivery and I could get under the ball or leave the ball on length.' For all of Achrekar's training about keeping the ball on the ground, 'when the situation demanded, I did not mind being under the ball and playing the ball over the slips'; the uppercut became a trademark.

Away from home, Tendulkar batted with the grim knowledge that even his best would probably be in vain. Tendulkar's 114 on the quick Perth pitch in 1991/92, showing his strength and timing while punching and pulling from the back foot, came in a 300-run defeat. At Birmingham in 1996, he struck 122 from 177 balls in the second innings; the next top score in the innings was 18, and India lost by eight wickets.

At Cape Town in 1997, Tendulkar hit 169, sharing a double-century partnership with Mohammad Azharuddin. Tendulkar was actually outshone: Azharuddin, India's former captain, used his wrists to pierce the on side and thrashed the ball, with little foot movement, through the off. Their 222-run stand was among India's most celebrated partnerships. India's other batting was hapless; they lost by 282 runs.

Later in 1997, Tendulkar's 92 set India on course for victory in Barbados. After the third day, India were 2–0 in pursuit of 120 to win. In a plush restaurant Tendulkar, now captain, told a waiter to chill a bottle of champagne; he would return to drink it the following day. On four, Tendulkar edged an Ian Bishop outswinger. India's 81 all out was 'a dark day in the history of Indian cricket and definitely the worst of my captaincy', Tendulkar wrote in his autobiography. 'I shut myself in my room for two whole days.'

India won just one of Tendulkar's first 44 away Tests. 'Tendulkar has done what no other Indian has – ensured that in his fans' minds, there is a split between his performance and that of his country,' the journalist Suresh Menon observed in 1999. 'It is almost as if fans are saying: "The result doesn't matter, so long as Tendulkar makes his runs."'

Tendulkar's most gallant innings in defeat would be at home. In 1999, India hosted Pakistan. 'Hindus should rise up against the Pakistan cricket team,' said Bal Thackeray, the leader of the right-wing party Shiv Sena, before the tour. Shiv Sena supporters dug up the pitch in Delhi, forcing the Test to be moved to Chennai; 3,000 military and police guarded the ground.

The contest culminated in India needing 271 to win. Younis reduced India to 6–2: the trigger, unusually, for the home crowd to break out in delirium, for they would glimpse Tendulkar on the third evening. He ducked at the bouncer he received first ball, then unfurled an early cover drive.

The next day, Wasim Akram produced one of the most celebrated deliveries – an away swinger that pitched on leg and uprooted Rahul Dravid's off stump, after a series of in swingers. India slipped to 82–5.

At lunch, Shahryar Khan, Pakistan's manager, told Wasim, the captain, 'Always be humble in victory.'

Wicketkeeper Nayan Mongia provided Tendulkar with his first meaningful support. Pakistan's attack demanded that Tendulkar show all his range: steadfast defence, steady accumulation and a sense of when to attack. Deep in the afternoon, Tendulkar 'was in tremendous physical pain and I had hence told my teammates that I would start playing shots as I cannot continue for long'. After tea, Tendulkar hit off-spinner Saqlain Mushtaq for four fours in an over: a pull, two paddle sweeps and a smear through midwicket. Against Wasim and Waqar Younis with the second new ball, Tendulkar punched drives as India scored 33 runs in five overs.

Saqlain didn't bowl his doosra, a variation that turned like a leg break, for an hour and a half. 'I made a strategy that I'm not going to show any sort of variation for a good period of time,' Saqlain remembers. With 17 needed, India still had four wickets in hand: 'I decided he's now almost forgotten my variation.' Wasim told Saqlain to bowl his doosra slow and wide. Saqlain stuck to the plan but bowled on leg stump instead. Tendulkar tried to launch the ball over the on side; Wasim caught the leading edge.

'We got Sachin's wicket, we got the whole match,' Saqlain says. The tail disintegrated. When Javagal Srinath's prod ricocheted onto his stumps, to hand Pakistan a 12-run victory, Saqlain was engulfed by his teammates: relieved, overjoyed and simply exhausted. With his mesmerising variations, Saqlain took 10–187 in the match. Tendulkar cried in the dressing room; for the only time in his career, he didn't even collect his player-of-the-match award, such was his devastation. 'That near-miss versus Pakistan was extremely painful, both physically and mentally,' Tendulkar recalls. 'It was very difficult to digest.'

He hit 136; his ten teammates mustered 86 between them. Pakistan did a lap of honour; for several minutes, 40,000 Indian fans applauded their rivals. The moment remains immortalised in a mural at the M.A. Chidambaram Stadium.

Tendulkar would sooner remember another Chennai innings, a year earlier. After India trailed Australia by 71 runs on first innings, Anshuman Gaekwad, India's head coach, told Tendulkar, 'I want you to score.' 'I will get it for you, don't worry,' Tendulkar responded. In Shane Warne's first over to him, Tendulkar hit fours straight, over cover and then through midwicket. Warne told his captain, Mark Taylor, 'Tubs, we're stuffed.'

For a month before the series, Tendulkar had got leg-spinners to bowl outside his leg stump, opening up his stance and being more leg side of the ball to combat Warne's drift. Now, he repeatedly hit Warne out of the rough, especially through the off side: Tendulkar's ebullient 155 not out set up victory in the Test and, ultimately, the series. No matter that Warne had just had shoulder surgery, it embodied Tendulkar's mastery against him: Tendulkar averaged 107.33 against Warne in Tests, and 176 in ODIs.

'There were very few spinners in world cricket against whom hitting the ball on the rise consistently was not a wise option – Warnie was one of them,' Tendulkar explains. 'Hence my approach against him was to wait for the ball to spin and play as late as possible. I would also mostly go inside-out and play with the spin.' When Warne bowled around the wicket, into the rough, Tendulkar adapted his approach, taking 'calculated risks' and playing more into the on side, hitting against the spin.

* * *

If Australia witnessed the crowning glory of the first age of Tendulkar, they also saw the moment when his role evolved. At Kolkata in March 2001, Tendulkar only made ten in each innings. It marked the start of an age when Tendulkar moved from being everything to the Indian team, or so it often seemed, to being a part of something.

In 1999/2000, India had been whitewashed 3–0 in Australia, and had then lost both Tests at home to South Africa, the second by an innings. Tendulkar resigned from his second stint as Test captain; India had won only four of his 25 matches in charge. Mohammad Azharuddin, the former captain, was banned in 2000 for match-fixing.

This turmoil begat two significant changes. Sourav Ganguly – nicknamed the Prince of Calcutta – was appointed captain. Like Tiger Pataudi, another man born into great wealth, Ganguly was a transformative leader. His mantra, he declared after he retired, was that 'The team wouldn't take any crap from any opposition.'

Ganguly was joined by New Zealand's John Wright as head coach. Arriving in India in November 2000, Wright found that three baseball mitts, 30 fielding cones and three old plastic stumps were the extent of the squad's training equipment. Initially, he bought more out of his own pocket. The physio was Wright's only support staff; India had no fitness or specialist coaches and no sports drinks or heart-rate monitors. At nets, players not batting or bowling relaxed in cane chairs while waiters served them tea and biscuits.

'It took a while for word to get around that the new foreign coach didn't believe in tea and biscuits at practice,' Wright wrote in *Indian Summers*. 'When it came to batting practice, the challenge was getting them to stop; with physical fitness, it was getting them started.'

At the time, 'Basically, there was no fitness regime,' Wright recalled. 'Few of them had access to gyms and physios when they weren't on international duty.' It took Wright 18 months to persuade the board to hire a fitness trainer. In 2000, the board launched its National Cricket Academy, which helped to professionalise player development and introduce a new focus upon fitness and fielding.

In the 2001 series, Australia thrashed India by ten wickets in Mumbai, extending their winning streak to 16 consecutive Tests. In the second Test, at Eden Gardens, Steve Waugh's century led

Australia to 445; India responded with a meagre 171. With a first innings lead of 274, Waugh enforced the follow-on early on day three.

Amid the despair, V.V.S. Laxman hit a stylish, counter-attacking 59 from number six in the first innings. It was a welcome moment in a stagnating career: Laxman arrived in Kolkata averaging 27.06 in his 20 Tests. The purity of Laxman's stroke play, and India's plight, led to Wright walking towards him in the changing room, placing his hand on his shoulder and telling him to keep his pads on.

In India's second innings, Laxman was promoted to three, his favourite position. He emerged with India still 222 runs behind. When Rahul Dravid, who had swapped places with Laxman in the second innings, walked out to bat on the third evening, he was greeted by sledges of 'From three to six and six to 12' – meaning being dropped. Dravid laughed. Shortly after, Laxman reached a sumptuous century; Steve Waugh, Australia's captain, declared, 'The young man's mind must be busy thinking about endorsements.' India ended day three 254–4, still 20 shy of making Australia bat again.

Cheered on by almost 100,000 at Eden Gardens, Laxman and Dravid batted in concert throughout the fourth day, reminding each other between overs, 'Job not done.' Dravid was much more than supremely adhesive, cutting and driving with authority. Laxman was outlandish.

Against seam, Laxman pulled deliveries through midwicket; he flicked a Michael Kasprowicz slower ball through mid-on for four and punched boundaries through backward point. Early on day four, Laxman played a flat-batted pull through mid-off against McGrath. Laxman's shots off Warne were even more audacious – using his feet, hitting the ball out of the footmarks and whipping deliveries from outside leg stump through midwicket, and driving balls pitched in the same place through extra cover or straight down the ground. 'Whenever he tossed the ball up and got it to drift, I was down the track,' Laxman wrote in his autobiography. 'Occasionally, to deliveries of the same length, I would go deep into the crease and play the pull shot. The idea was to throw Warney off his rhythm.'

'It was a special innings,' Warne recalled. 'A lot of players came down the track and hit me inside-out once or twice, but not as consistently as VVS did for two days – or however many days, three days, I can't remember! There are a few players who tried to play shots like that, but if they tried it twice or thrice I generally got them out. The key was how consistently well he did it – inside-out or through midwicket against the spin on a track that was turning big.'

Laxman and Dravid had added 409 together in a domestic match only two months earlier. Dravid remembers:

> It almost felt a little like déjà vu – just batting and batting, of course, against different opposition and different quality of bowlers. But there was a kind of history there. We've done it before.
>
> I wasn't really thinking too far ahead. We were so far behind the game, following on against a great Australian side. We were just playing what was in front of us. I wanted to stay in the moment and keep batting.

Laxman was battling back pain so severe that it almost led him to miss the Test; his spine had to be straightened during breaks in play. Dravid was ill before the game and on antibiotics. At lunch and tea, Dravid and Laxman had ice baths; at drinks breaks, players ran on with handkerchiefs that had been put in ice.

'I was cramping up all over the place,' Dravid recalls. 'But I always kept thinking, "If it's hot for me imagine how hot it is for the Aussies and how they must be struggling." You could see that their intensity was dropping.' At the end of day four, both players went onto a drip, to fight dehydration. Their 376-run partnership, which extended into day five and stretched for 104 overs, ensured that India would not be beaten.

In the pantheon of Test innings, Laxman's 281 – chanceless off his bat, though Australia missed a run-out opportunity when he had 183 – is not easily beaten either. To generations of Indian fans, to hear the number 281 is to be transported back to this magisterial performance.

When Australia reached tea on day five 164–3 in pursuit of their notional target of 384, they still looked likely to salvage a draw. But Harbhajan Singh, who had taken India's first Test hat-trick in the first innings, found turn, bounce and brilliant support from close-in fielders to take four wickets. Tendulkar's part-time leg spin yielded three wickets, including Warne with a googly. After Harbhajan had McGrath lbw pushing forward to clinch just the third Test victory by a side following on in history, Wright took in the scene. A stand at Eden Gardens appeared to be on fire; fans were burning newspapers in celebration.

The final Test in Chennai, so often witness to Tendulkar's greatness, saw him score another smooth century, playing the ball late to combat reverse swing. Harbhajan took 15 wickets in the match. Adam Gilchrist, who left his pad exposed against Harbhajan's quicker deliveries, ended the series with a sequence of 0, 0, 1 and 1 after a century in Mumbai.

Harbhajan was only 20, recalled because of Anil Kumble's injury. In pre-series trials, Harbhajan 'turned the ball a mile and got more bounce than any spinner I'd ever seen', Wright wrote. 'Everything about him – personality, body language, the glint in his eye – said he was a real competitor.' Harbhajan took 32 wickets in three Tests at 17.03 apiece; India's other bowlers took 17, at an average of 63.24. No bowler has ever taken a higher proportion of wickets in a series of at least three Tests.

Harbhajan adopted a more attacking line in the series: instructed to bowl in a box on a good length outside off stump, rather than on the stumps. He was a particular menace for new batters, greeted by prowling close-in fielders. Three times in the last two Tests, Australia lost seven wickets in a session.

Coming from a land with a dearth of high-class off spin, Australians were bereft of ideas. Across the series, Ricky Ponting succumbed five times in 28 balls to Harbhajan. In his autobiography, Ponting rued that 'No one in our set-up was able to help me sort out my problems against an excellent off-spinner on these types of wickets,' and that he 'certainly wasn't being helped when the captain and coach told me to back myself and to stick to what had worked for me in the past'.

In the series' final innings, India needed 155 to win. Laxman, once again, batted as if on a higher plane. While no one else topped 25, he made 66 from 82 balls, greeting Warne by late-cutting his first ball for four. Yet Australia threatened to pull off a heist: 101–2 became 135–7, then 151–8.

Aptly, Harbhajan – benefiting from Laxman's wisdom, after Wright introduced batting buddies for all bowlers – hit the winning runs in Chennai. When he squirted McGrath away for two, initially pausing to double-check the score before celebrating, it ended one of the most extraordinary series.

It was also among the most significant. Had India lost, Dravid believes, Wright could have been sacked, with many distrustful of having a foreign coach. 'I don't know whether that experiment would have lasted more than the series,' he says. 'There were far-reaching consequences to that day in Eden Gardens. To win the series meant that John and Sourav were able to stick with that same theme for the next few years. To beat Australia from that position changed a lot for Indian cricket.'

* * *

In the 1990s, India 'had the mindset that it was beyond us to win overseas, and even a draw was an acceptable result,' Ganguly said in the book *Eleven Gods and a Billion Indians*. After toppling Australia, India set about improving their dreadful away record. The years after

Kolkata witnessed a series of seminal Test victories. On the first day at Headingley in 2002, Dravid's stoic 148 led India through treacherous conditions, with the ball hooping in both directions. As the pitch flattened, Tendulkar and Ganguly scored centuries too to set up an innings victory; the series was squared 1–1.

A little short of three years after their Kolkata partnership, Dravid and Laxman were reunited against Australia. The situation in Adelaide rivalled Kolkata for hopelessness. India were 85–4 in their first innings – Dravid had just been involved in a run-out with Ganguly – in response to Australia's 556. Once again, they summoned a triple-century stand in response. 'You're not thinking, "Oh, I want to bat the whole day." But you know you've done this before, you can do this,' Dravid says. 'We played a lot of junior cricket together. So we can read each other's games well. We could pick up when we were losing concentration and remind each other about what the cues were and what we needed to focus on.'

In Kolkata, Dravid supported Laxman through his defining innings. Now, Laxman – who prepared for batting at six by sleeping and listening to music on his headphones in the changing room – supported Dravid through his. While Laxman's stroke-making was resplendent, this time Dravid scored at the same rate. Where a Laxman first innings half-century preceded his double hundred in Kolkata, Dravid's second innings half-century in Adelaide followed his own double century. When Dravid hit the winning runs, after navigating a chase of 230, Steve Waugh retrieved the ball from the gutter, then handed it to him. To Dravid, the gesture 'was special – I always looked up to him'. Waugh signed the ball; Dravid still has it at home.

Dravid made 305 runs for once out in the match and batted for 835 minutes. Such durability earned Dravid his nickname, The Wall: he faced more deliveries than anyone else in Test history. He made good on the dictum of Keki Tarapore, a coach who first worked with Dravid when he was 11: players were told not to hit any balls in the air.

I knew that I probably needed to bat a long time if I wanted to score a lot of runs. So I figured that I was going to have to concentrate and bat – a lot of it was drilled into me, in those early days.

Because of the competition and with so many kids playing, when you score, you have to make a lot of runs. I think it's somewhere in the back of your mind: you realise that you want to make big hundreds. It was never about only scoring hundreds because a lot of people scored hundreds. Maybe it just got ingrained.

It's a habit – the more you do it, the better you get at it. You figure out the way to do it, you figure out your routines. It's like a confidence thing – once you've done it once or twice, you know you could do it again.

From 1993 to 2008, only two sides left Australia undefeated after a Test series. In 2001, with an innovative approach orchestrated by captain Stephen Fleming – often packing the field in an opponent's strong areas, as when placing two gullies to Damien Martyn, a renowned cutter – New Zealand squared a three-match series 0–0, almost winning on the final evening. Over four Tests in 2003/04, India nearly triumphed. Anil Kumble took 24 wickets in three Tests; but for dropped catches and some debatable umpiring decisions on the final day in Sydney, he might well have secured a series victory. An honourable 1–1 draw affirmed India's progress.

In the final Test, Tendulkar eliminated the cover drive, and hit 241 not out; 188 of his runs were on the on side, attesting to his adaptability. 'I faced many different bowlers at different stages of my career and they had different styles and ideas,' he reflects. 'I had to have the flexibility to accept it and play accordingly.'

No Test pair in history have added more runs in tandem than Dravid and Tendulkar: 6,920 in their partnerships together. 'He was incredibly tough mentally, and had a great desire,' Dravid explains. 'He never let anything get in the way of him scoring runs, and truly loved the game.

'He was technically very, very strong – very good judgement of length and line. At his best, he was always fully forward or fully back. It almost felt like he was born to bat.'

* * *

Before they left for Pakistan in March 2004, Indian players were provided with $500,000 insurance cover against a terrorist attack, such were the safety concerns; hordes of security personnel were ubiquitous in grounds and hotels alike. The cricket was highly charged, but good-spirited; relations between supporters, with visiting fans warmly welcomed, led to the matches being called the 'goodwill series'. The Indian High Commissioner Shivshankar Menon remarked, 'Twenty thousand Indian fans had gone back to India acting as Pakistan's ambassadors.'

Not that Ganguly, India's captain, agreed, saying: 'I don't really agree with this goodwill issue – it's a cricket match and both teams are competing to win.' An oscillating ODI series won 3–2 by India was the prelude to the three Tests. After 14 years without India playing a Test in Pakistan, there was a curiously low-key feel to the start of the series: only about 1,000 fans watched the first day in the out-of-town ground in Multan.

It was there that Virender Sehwag asserted his claim to being the most revolutionary opener since Victor Trumper. Sehwag had learned the game playing 'gully cricket' – street games – in Delhi; for his purity of shot, he was initially likened to Tendulkar. The comparison was deceptive. Rather than the orthodox V, straight behind the bowler, Sehwag devised his own V – 'between cover-point and third man', the journalist Rahul Bhattacharya wrote – and used the crease to create width. Sehwag's childhood coach tied his feet to the back of the net to discourage him from charging bowlers; this helped nurture the balance that made him devastating with minimal footwork.

On debut in South Africa in November 2001, batting at six, Sehwag scored a century. With a logjam in the middle order, Ganguly promoted him to open, no matter that Sehwag had only batted there in one first-class match. In his first Test innings as an opener, at Lord's in 2002, Sehwag hit 84 from 96 balls.

After an hour in Multan's 36 Celsius heat in 2004, Sehwag had rushed to 40, interspersing boundaries with sharp singles; his partner, Aakash Chopra, was on six. Sehwag even riled Shoaib Akhtar, Pakistan's express quick, at one point calling out, 'Is this guy bowling or begging?'

Sehwag sealed his century with a six, an uppercut over third man off Shoaib, then his 300 with another, striding down the pitch and heaving Saqlain Mushtaq into the concrete stand over long-on. The landmark made good on a promise that Sehwag, who had yet to make his Test debut, had made to Laxman, shortly after his 281: that he would score India's first triple century. It set up India's first Test victory in Pakistan, at the 20th attempt.

Multan 2004 was merely one indication of Sehwag's talents. 'Virender destroys all strategies,' Matthew Hayden observed. Sehwag inverted the traditional logic of the new ball. From being a tool for bowlers to attack batters, it became a tool for batters to attack bowlers, viewing the ball's hardness and attacking fields as a way to score at haste. The apparent simplicity of Sehwag's approach created the illusion of unthinking genius.

'I beg to differ,' Laxman wrote. 'He understood his game . . . If the ball was pitched in areas where he wasn't comfortable, he would look for a single. If it was in an area of his strength, his first thought was a four or a six.'

Not even Trumper scored as quickly as Sehwag. No other man to score as many Test runs had a strike rate above 61; his strike rate was 82, to go with his average of 49.34.

Sehwag didn't only score quickly; he scored big, too – 319 off 304 balls against South Africa, 293 off 254 balls against Sri Lanka and 195 off 233 balls at Melbourne. Most extraordinary of all was an undefeated 201, out of 329 all out, against Sri Lanka in Galle in 2008; no other man made a century in the match. Fourteen of Sehwag's centuries were over 150, six over 200 and three 290 or more.

After India's innings victory in Multan in 2004, sealed by Anil Kumble's eight wickets in the match, Pakistan levelled the series 1–1 in Lahore. In the deciding Test, in Rawalpindi, Pakistan made 224. Squared up by Shoaib, Sehwag was caught first ball.

Out walked Dravid. Initially scratchy, he reached the close on day one undefeated on ten. That evening, he left dinner early, declaring that he needed to bat throughout the following day. He did so – and batted deep into the third too, only ceasing when he had made 270 in 12 hours and 20 minutes. A small measure of how India's ambitions had been recalibrated was that Gavaskar's national record for top Test score – 236 not out, against West Indies – had lasted 18 years. Between 2001 and 2009, nine Indian innings surpassed Gavaskar's 236; four were by Sehwag.

Dravid's gargantuan effort underpinned an innings and 131-run victory, sealing India's first Test series win in Pakistan. 'It was lovely to be a part of,' Dravid recalls. 'There was a lot of focus on the series and a lot of hype. But the cricket was great fun, and to be able to travel around was also really nice.'

Pakistan was perhaps India's most celebrated triumph of a momentous era. Until November 2000, India had won 13 out of their 156 away Tests. In their next 66 away Tests, until 2011, India won 24; discounting Tests in Bangladesh and Zimbabwe, India won 15 while losing 19, including drawing series in Australia and South Africa and winning in England, New Zealand and twice in West Indies. No longer did India need favourable conditions to be formidable.

When India and Pakistan played series in 2005 and 2006 – the first drawn, the second a 1–0 Pakistan home victory – it seemed that they would meet regularly. Instead, a collapse in relations between the countries mean that the teams have not played a Test against each other since December 2007.

* * *

On 26 November 2008, a horrendous wave of terrorist attacks began in Mumbai. Over the next four days, Islamist terrorists, who had crossed the border from Pakistan, orchestrated a series of lethal attacks.

The atrocities took place midway through India's ODI series against England, which preceded a two-Test series. One Test was due to be in Mumbai. After the attacks, England initially decamped to the UAE, but then returned for the Tests in a rearranged schedule.

Two weeks after the attacks, India met England in Chennai. A fine Test reached its final act when England set India 387 to win – at the time, the fourth-highest successful chase in history – in 126 overs. Standing up on his toes, Sehwag square-cut boundaries through point against the new ball, including lifting Steve Harmison over the slips for six. Spin was treated with equal disdain: Monty Panesar's first ball was slog-swept for six. Sehwag's 83 from 68 balls set up the game for his idol.

Early on day five, India were 141–2 when Tendulkar entered at number four, the same place from which he had made history as a 14-year-old. A wearing pitch presented diverse challenges: spin twins Panesar and Graeme Swann; Harmison's bounce; Andrew Flintoff's reverse swing. Tendulkar withstood them all – showing his range of sweeps and swift judgement of length against spin, matching Sehwag in uppercutting over the slips and placing the ball with finesse. Where Sehwag took the steep ascent up the mountain, Tendulkar preferred the steady incline.

As India neared victory, supporters cheered dot balls: an incongruous sight, explained by their fervent wish that Tendulkar would reach his century. India's twin moments of glory – victory and Tendulkar's hundred – arrived in tandem with a paddle sweep past fine leg.

On a cricketing level, it was a defining hundred: Tendulkar's first in a victorious fourth innings chase, an encore of his masterpiece against Pakistan on the same ground – only, this time, completing the job. Memories of the 1999 Test were 'there with me when we were chasing that big total against England', Tendulkar recalls. After Yuvraj Singh attempted a reverse sweep, 'I told him then that we should not take anything lightly and look to finish the game together.' Yet the true greatness of Tendulkar's innings lay in its wider context: Mumbai's favourite son providing solace in one of the city's darkest hours. 'It was an emotional one for all of us,' Tendulkar says. 'That moment remains very special.'

This was one of Tendulkar's most cherished centuries. In all international cricket, he made one hundred: 49 in ODIs, and 51 in Tests, including seven in 2010, when he turned 37. Where Bradman has his unsurpassable average, Tendulkar's 100 centuries stand as his own immortal figure. This number, like his tally of 200 Tests, is unlikely to ever be beaten.

Through it all, 'I went by my comfort and gut feel on the day,' Tendulkar explains. 'Every day you think differently. For me, it was about what made me comfortable on that particular day and helped me prepare best for the next delivery.' Then, 'I would try to switch off in between overs and give myself a break of 20 to 25 seconds. It was important to time the peaking of your concentration levels.' Even as Tendulkar rested fleetingly, his country did not rest from watching him.

22

THE MAGIC AND MYSTERY OF MURALI

Sri Lanka were only worth one Test: such was England's belief. By 1998, Sri Lanka were world champions, and had beaten England in their last Test, in Colombo in 1993. Yet England remained the lone country who considered Sri Lanka worthy of only a one-off Test, not a multi-match series.

Determined to show England's folly, Sri Lanka acclimatised for seven weeks before their Test at The Oval. On a benign pitch, the sort that could have almost have passed for one in Sri Lanka, Arjuna Ranatunga won the toss and defied conventional wisdom by choosing to field first.

The logic was not immediately discernible: Sri Lanka took only four wickets on day one. But on the second day, Muthiah Muralidaran's unique off spin – spun with the wrists, like a leg-spinner, rather than the fingers – bewitched England. When number 11 Angus Fraser was bowled through the gate, Muralidaran finished with 7-155, though the hosts scored 445 all out.

With 20 overs left on the second evening, Sri Lanka were expected to bat with caution. That was never Sanath Jayasuriya's way. His audacity had been forged in soft-ball cricket in Matara on the south coast: Jayasuriya was the first player from rural Sri Lanka to become an international star. Initially a middle-order player, he was given a run as a Test opener aged 26. He was a proto-Sehwag as opener, averaging 41.48, with a strike rate of 66.

On the second evening, Jayasuriya raced to a 58-ball half-century. The following day, he soared to 213; unusually, Aravinda de Silva's stroke play wasn't the main act, even as he caressed 152. After their first innings, England had assumed that they couldn't lose. Sri Lanka batted for ten balls fewer than England's 158.3 overs – but, with 591, scored 146 more. It embodied how Sri Lanka had brought the skills that made them 1996 World Cup champions to the longer format. In the three years after their triumph Sri Lanka scored at 3.1 per over, quicker than any other Test nation.

Now, with the pitch drying out and bouncing more, Murali set to work. For all the mystery with which he became associated, his history-making at The Oval was founded upon a simple method: ripping his off break as much as he could. 'I was bowling really well, and England were not reading me properly,' Murali recalls. 'When the spin started, they panicked.'

England's opener, left-hander Mark Butcher, opted to use his feet. The first time, he successfully cleared extra cover; the next he was stumped, beaten by Murali's flight and turn. Two balls later, Graeme Hick attempted the opposite approach, staying back. The ball kept low; Hick was plumb lbw.

The fifth day loomed with Sri Lanka sensing history. So did their supporters: attracted by lower prices and the promise of victory, the final day was watched by notably more Sri Lankans than previous days. They needed eight more wickets. One came through a direct hit from substitute Upul Chandana.

Besides some close catching, that was all the help that Murali needed. His finest delivery came on the stroke of lunch. John Crawley, England's first innings centurion, was bowled by a consummate off-spinner: released wide of the crease, spinning sharply, luring the batter into a drive and then dipping to bisect the gap between bat and pad.

It was for moments like this that Ranatunga had chosen to bowl. The rationale, he later claimed, was that Sri Lanka's best chance of winning lay in giving Murali enough of a rest to bowl England out twice. 'When Arjuna gives me the ball, I just bowl,' Murali says. 'I never say no.'

Whether he bowled from over or around the wicket, the Vauxhall End or Pavilion End, Murali posed an unrelenting threat. At eight wickets down, Mark Ramprakash tried to take as much strike against Muralidaran as possible. Trying to flick a ball, he was caught sharply at short leg.

Darren Gough was bowled around his legs, Murali's only wicket with the doosra, which turned like a leg break: 'He didn't know where the ball was.' Murali rushed to umpire David Shepherd to request the match ball. No cricketer can have deserved a ball more. He had taken 9–65; only the run-out, surely, deprived him of a perfect ten. His match figures of 16 for 220 were the fifth best in Test history; everyone else to bowl in the Test had combined figures of 13 for 1,049. Muralidaran bowled 113.5 overs in the match: the equivalent of one player bowling from both ends for four sessions. No one has bowled more deliveries in a Test since 1962.

All that remained was for Jayasuriya to blaze Sri Lanka to their target of 36; one uppercut for six was hit with both feet jumping off the ground. Murali had done more than bowl Sri Lanka to a glorious win; he had highlighted the absurdity of their second-class status in English eyes. Never again would England insult Sri Lanka by agreeing to only a one-off Test.

* * *

To understand the enormity of Murali's achievement, it is necessary to go back to his cricketing nadir. Two years and eight months before the best day of his Test career, Murali had to endure the worst.

The Boxing Day Test in Melbourne is perhaps the most feted occasion in the game, no matter that it only became an annual event in 1980. Playing at the Melbourne Cricket Ground in 1995, watched by 55,000 – a record Test crowd to watch Sri Lanka – reflected the side's progress.

Muralidaran was 23 years old, playing in his 23rd Test. He found himself in the eye of the storm. After lunch on day one, Darrell Hair, the Australian umpire, called Murali for throwing – straightening his elbow as he bowled, thereby contravening the laws of the game. Initially, most assumed that Muralidaran had simply overstepped, and bowled a front-foot no-ball. As Hair called the bowler seven times in three overs, it became clear that Murali was being no-balled for what the umpire perceived to be an illegal action. In the public glare, Murali was effectively called a cheat. He switched ends to avoid bowling at Hair's end. Hair then told Ranatunga he was prepared to no-ball Murali from square leg too; indeed, the convention, which Hair had originally ignored, was that bowlers should be no-balled for bowling with a bent arm only by the square-leg umpire. Hordes of spectators chanted 'no-ball'. Murali remembers Ranatunga's support:

> When I got under pressure on Boxing Day, he took it all on himself. I was young, so I couldn't handle it. He handled it for me.
>
> He taught me a lot, how to be confident in yourself and not to think about what others say. Do what you think is right – an attitude that you have to have on the pitch, not be scared by anybody else.
>
> He believed that I am something and what I can achieve. And I am not doing anything wrong.

As Murali's ordeal played out, one spectator left the MCG in distress, seeing uncomfortable echoes of his own experience. Ian Meckiff, an Australia left-arm quick, took 6–38 in an Ashes Test in 1958/59, but faced regular whispers about his action: England manager Freddie Brown considered making an official complaint. Don Bradman, Australia's chairman of selectors, told Brown to focus on the actions of Tony Lock and Peter Loader before casting aspersions elsewhere; England's Fred Trueman later described the series as 'two top international teams chucking the ball at each other'.

Throwing was such a serious accusation because Test players had always been required to bowl with their elbows straight. Bowling with an initially bent elbow, and then straightening it, can provide bowlers with significant advantages: helping quicks to find extra pace; and spinners to generate extra revolutions on the ball.

In January 1963, Bradman hosted Australia's team at his house. There, Daniel Brettig wrote in *Bradman & Packer*, Bradman 'screened numerous films of fast bowling actions'. That night, captain Richie Benaud made Bradman a promise that 'should any bowler in his team be called for throwing, he would not recall him to the attack'.

Eleven months later, Meckiff was no-balled four times in his first over against South Africa in Brisbane. Meckiff didn't bowl again in the game or in professional cricket. 'I was told that I wouldn't even be able to play for Victoria,' he told Brydon Coverdale in *The Cricket Monthly*. Aged 28, Meckiff retired; his son, Coverdale wrote, 'had to change schools because of the teasing he received about his father being a chucker'.

In 1960, the Imperial Cricket Conference ruled that a delivery was illegal if 'the bowling arm having been bent at the elbow, whether the wrist is backward of the elbow or not, is suddenly straightened immediately prior to the instant of the delivery'. This emboldened umpires to act on suspect actions. In that summer's Lord's Test, South Africa's Geoff Griffin took a hat-trick, but was also no-balled for throwing 11 times. No-balled again in domestic cricket, he played his last professional match aged 23. Like Meckiff, no allowance was made for Griffin's physique. Meckiff had a semi-disjointed shoulder; Griffin suffered a childhood accident, rendering him unable to straighten his right arm fully. Other bowlers in the era – Lock, for his quicker ball; and West Indies pace bowler Charlie Griffith – were also no-balled in Tests, but recovered. From 1960 to 1964, Gideon Haigh detailed, 16 bowlers were called in first-class cricket, in Australia, England, Pakistan and West Indies.

These controversies played out against a febrile atmosphere. Sheffield Shield captains gave Bradman a list of bowlers who they suspected of having illegal actions; captains agreed not to pick the players. In the 1950s, David Frith has noted, bowlers were even filmed behind bushes to try and see if their actions were legal.

Throwing wasn't a new problem. Fred Spofforth, the great Australian bowler, so despaired of actions' legality that, in 1897, he suggested that, if all else failed, 'the best way is to legalise throwing, and in one season it would bring about its own cure'. In 1898, Australia's Ernie Jones became the first man no-balled for throwing in a Test. The umpire was Jim Phillips, an Australian who also worked in England. Phillips effectively ended the career of England fast bowler Arthur Mold by calling him 16 times in one county innings in 1901. County captains subsequently agreed not to use 14 bowlers under suspicion.

Phillips did not think that illegal actions could be eradicated easily. A cricketer he foresaw, 'will, in attempting an increase of pace, use his elbow, especially if he be a bowler whose arm is not quite straight'. The next century would prove Phillips right.

* * *

Under Murali, for the first time science was applied to whether a delivery was bowled legally. In 1996, Murali underwent biomechanical analysis at the University of Western Australia and at the University of Hong Kong. This formed the basis for the International Cricket Council's judgement that Muralidaran's action was fair – while acknowledging that his congenitally bent arm created the 'optical illusion of throwing'. The perception was rooted in Murali's physical characteristics. He was born with an abnormality of the elbow joint and a highly manoeuvrable shoulder and wrist; his action entailed rotating his shoulder rapidly.

The murmurs continued. After the 1998 Oval Test, England head coach David Lloyd said, 'I have my opinions that I have made known to the authorities.' The following year, Australian umpire Ross

THE MAGIC AND MYSTERY OF MURALI

Emerson called Murali for throwing in a one-day international. Ranatunga threatened to haul his side from the field; Murali's action was cleared by the ICC again.

During this period, Murali mastered the doosra – a delivery which spun like a leg-spinner, the off-spinner's equivalent of a googly, and had been popularised by Pakistan's Saqlain Mushtaq. After praying that he would acquire 'something special', Saqlain developed the delivery practising on the roof with a ping-pong ball or tape-ball. By locking his wrist, and using the index and ring fingers (rather than the index and middle fingers) he could spin the ball like a leg break. 'It took a few years to be able to get the right feeling, right mechanism and right grip,' Saqlain says. 'The doosra gave me a big edge.'

Saqlain used the doosra to claim his first Test wicket, against Sri Lanka in 1995. Murali soon asked Saqlain how he bowled the ball. 'We used to pass on knowledge,' Saqlain recalls. 'You can't be stingy or self-centred – we are here to entertain.'

Murali first unveiled his doosra in 1998. 'That creates a little bit of doubt for the batsman, about which way the ball is going,' he explains. 'I confused them and then I got a lot of wickets from off spin.'

The delivery simultaneously heightened Murali's effectiveness and the scrutiny that he received, leading him to be tested by the ICC for a third time. In 2004, his doosra was shown to involve an elbow extension of 14 degrees; remedial work reduced this to 10.2 degrees, which was still illegal at the time. Sri Lanka's board even declared that Murali would cease to bowl the ball.

The ICC had already commissioned biomechanical experts to conduct further research. An extension of 10 to 15 degrees was generally considered the point at which the arm ceased to appear straight to the naked eye. Anything less risked myriad bowlers being found to have illegal actions: tests from 2000 to 2002 at the Australian Institute of Sport found that 14 out of 21 elite fast bowlers analysed straightened their elbows by more than 10 degrees. These demonstrated that cricket had been operating under the false premise that bowlers deployed straight-arm actions. Virtually all bowlers – including men hailed for the purity of their bowling actions, like Glenn McGrath – extended their arms. Under a strict interpretation of the old laws, 'excluding leg-spinners, nearly all bowlers would be deemed to be "throwing" to some degree', says Professor Jacqueline Alderson, a biomechanics professor involved in the testing process.

In 2004, the ICC settled upon a 15-degree limit for arm straightening, with the same figure for all bowlers after spinners were shown to bowl with similar arm speed to pace bowlers. It is 'categorically false' that the law was adjusted to suit Murali, Alderson says. Instead, the law reflected the realities of bowling and recommendations made in 2003, before his doosra was reported. Most fast bowlers required more than 10 degrees to bowl any legal deliveries; Murali only needed this greater limit to bowl one particular variation.

Ever since, anything under 15 degrees has constituted a legal action; anything over is illegal. From a 38-degree flexion position as Murali's arm went above shoulder height in his delivery swing, his point-of-release measurement was 27 degrees: an extension of 11 degrees, comfortably within the laws. He came to regard his physical condition as a benefit, saying in 2014, 'When you really straighten your arm, according to science, the movement of the wrist is less. When you're bent, it's more. So I have an advantage with a bent arm.'

'Murali certainly benefited from his fixed-flexion abnormality,' Alderson explains. 'His elbow bony misalignment provided him with mechanical advantage.' For bowlers with more typical shoulder, elbow and wrist structures, Alderson says, it is 'extraordinarily difficult, if not impossible' to bowl the doosra legally.

By the revised laws, Murali's action was legal. Many still denied as much: in 2004, John Howard, Australia's prime minister, said that he considered Murali to be a chucker. 'He doesn't know the facts,' Murali declared in response, then opted out of touring Australia.

No bowler would ever again face the indignity of being called for throwing on the field; reports were now submitted discreetly after matches. Bowlers under suspicion underwent testing, when they had sensors attached to assess the legality of their actions.

A new focus on actions began in 2014. Saeed Ajmal, Pakistan's mystery off-spinner – like Murali, his doosra was particularly venomous – bowled 37 deliveries at a testing centre after being reported. Each ball was released with an elbow extension between 36 and 43 degrees, almost three times the legal limit. Ajmal was suspended from international cricket. He never played a Test again.

In a curious way, such incidents remain one of Murali's legacies. His brilliance was the catalyst for scientific rigour to police bowling actions. 'The old rule – that's changed now for the betterment of cricket,' Murali reflects. 'It started from me.'

* * *

Murali's treatment was so keenly felt in Sri Lanka not simply because of his sporting achievements. From 1983 to 2009, the civil war, fought between the Liberation Tigers of Tamil Eelam, a Tamil separatist group, and the government, killed over 100,000 people. Murali was often the lone Tamil cricketer in the side; the bulk of players were Sinhalese, who make up 75 per cent of the population. While the national team has been multi-ethnic and multi-faith – comprising Buddhists, Hindus, Muslims and Catholics – the geographical make-up has been less diverse. Players from Colombo have dominated. No one from the north, where the Tamil population is concentrated, has ever played Test cricket.

Around 1920, Murali's grandfather came from India to work on a tea plantation. While his grandfather returned to India, Murali's father built a biscuit factory. Murali grew up in Kandy: hill country, in Sri Lanka's centre, far from the north. In 1977, when Murali was five, his father was attacked by a machete-wielding mob; the family's biscuit business was burned down in an anti-Tamil pogrom. While the attackers were largely Sinhalese, 'We were saved by Sinhalese,'

Murali told Peter Roebuck in 2010. 'They came and stopped the crazy people before they killed us. We never forgot that.'

Murali tried to refrain from being seen as a political figure, instead aiming to be a unifying one. Never was this truer than after the tsunami in December 2004, which killed over 30,000 Sri Lankans. The squad were in New Zealand. Nursing an injury, Murali was at home. He and his family set off late from their home in Colombo to a charity function on the south-west coast. 'If I'd set off 20 minutes earlier, I would have been caught in the waves,' Murali later said. Working with his manager, Kushil Gunasekera, Murali's Foundation of Goodness charity built over 1,000 homes for tsunami victims across 24 different villages. He led convoys to see that aid was distributed to those most in need.

Kumar Sangakkara, Murali's nearest rival as Sri Lanka's most celebrated cricketer, distilled his significance:

> For Murali, caste, class, ethnicity or faith is irrelevant – we are all equals. His life – the exploits on the field, his resilience in the face of intense provocation, his natural kindness and generosity, his remarkable charity work with The Foundation of Goodness – evokes a powerful spirit of reconciliation for a polarised nation.
>
> He has taken much from the game of cricket, but he has given back so much to our society. More than any other public figure in Sri Lanka, he stands apart, a source of joy on the cricket field, an example to us all and an answer to the ethnic conundrum we face in Sri Lanka.

Like many spinners, Murali originally bowled pace. Aged 13, Sunil Fernando, Murali's coach at his school St Anthony's College, told him that the side had enough quick bowlers. 'I was not a big man,' Murali recalls. 'Then I bowled my first two overs – the ball was spinning a lot.' Fernando recognised his gifts. 'A coach cannot change a bowler like Murali,' he later said. 'If anyone tried to do that he will be lost.'

THE MAGIC AND MYSTERY OF MURALI

Fernando taught Murali 'spot bowling'. 'He marked out a spot, and made me hit the target every day for 30 to 40 minutes.' Murali retained this training method throughout his career. His late release point – delivering the ball in front of his face, at an angle of one o'clock – helped his accuracy. In his stride, Murali's eyes bulged, watching any movement from batters until his final release. His action was unique. 'I'm a wrist spinner like Shane Warne,' he says. 'I was using the wrist more than anything else. I'm not a finger spinner.'

On Murali's Test debut, in 1992, Australia's Allan Border walked out to bat. His partner, Mark Waugh, told him that Murali was bowling off breaks. Observing how Murali rotated his wrist, Border responded, 'You sure he's bowling off spin, mate?'

Off-spinners generally fare much better against left-handers, against whom they turn the ball away. As in so many ways, Murali was different. CricViz data shows that he averaged 19.77 against right-handers but 32.35 against left-handers. 'I loved to bowl to right-handers,' Murali explains. Teammates convinced him to go around the wicket when the ball was turning, to get more lbws. Against left-handers his turn meant 'they don't have to play. So the lbw option is gone.'

Yet his doosra forced left-handers to play at more balls. With this, aligned to umpires' greater willingness to award lbws, Murali averaged 23.89 against left-handers in his last five years.

Uniquely, he took ten-wicket hauls against all nine Test nations that he faced. His method changed relatively little wherever he was. Murali bowled his off break '80 to 90 per cent' of the time, with the doosra and a top-spinner as his two variations; he also made minor changes to his speed and release point. 'He didn't worry too much about the opposition,' observes Dav Whatmore. 'He was the complete off-spinner.'

There has probably never been a Test bowler so devastating at home as Murali: his 496 wickets in Sri Lanka cost 19.56 apiece. Murali's gifts also transferred to conditions less conducive to spin. In

England, New Zealand and South Africa combined, he averaged 21.52, taking more than six wickets a Test: 'I love the bounce.'

Australia was an exception. Following his turbulent 1995/96 tour, Murali only returned for two more Tests there. 'They scrutinise me and put a lot of pressure to me – like "no ball" and everything. So then the mind is not set for competition. It's difficult.'

Murali still enjoyed great days at home to Australia. In Kandy in September 1999, Murali's seven wickets in the match helped Sri Lanka to victory. The next two Tests were marred by rain – the hosts were on top in the first, the tourists in the second – leaving Sri Lanka victorious in a series against Australia for the first time. The significance of the achievement was emphasised by Australia winning their next 16 Tests.

When Australia next visited in 2004, the contest pitted Shane Warne, returning after a year's suspension, against Murali. The two tussled in their 'Great Race' to overhaul Courtney Walsh's 519 Test wickets; by the series' end, Warne was only two wickets off. Trading places as the second-highest wicket-taker of all time from innings to innings, Warne took 26 wickets in the three Tests, Murali 28 at a slightly higher average. Despite trailing on first innings three times, Australia won 3–0.

While Warne triumphed then, Murali sailed past his 708 Test wickets. When he became the first man to reach 300 Test wickets, in 1964, Fred Trueman was asked if anyone would break the record: 'If they do they'll be bloody tired.' Think, then, of the physical toll on Murali's shoulders and knees as he attempted to reach 800 Test wickets.

Ahead of India's three-Test tour in 2010 Murali, now 38, said that he would retire after the first Test. This left him a solitary game to leap from 792 Test wickets to 800. Galle's roads filled with banners acclaiming Murali; the *Nation on Sunday* released a 16-page commemorative supplement.

In their archetypal manner, Sri Lanka batted first at Galle and amassed a monumental score: their 520–8 declared included a Kumar

Sangakkara century. Murali's 67th Test five-wicket haul, which began by removing Sachin Tendulkar lbw, left India following on. His own Test tally had jumped to 797. Murali ended day four by inducing Yuvraj Singh to edge to Mahela Jayawardene's trusty hands at first slip; no fielder–bowler pair have ever combined for more wickets. Jayawardene reflects:

> You're always in the game. The biggest thing for me was that conversation to see how much turn he was going to get so that I could get the angles right.
>
> Some surfaces he'd get more turn, some he wouldn't. Depending on whether he was bowling with the newish ball or the older ball, especially with the straight one, the angles were the key. Sanga and I would always try and discuss the distance that I would want to stay and the angle that I needed to be at to be in a good position to take those catches.
>
> You can't drop a catch for Murali – his eyes go up and he just goes crazy. You don't want to face him after you drop a catch. So my thing was, bloody hell, make sure that you grab on to those chances.

Thousands arrived to watch Murali's final day; thousands more took their seats atop the fort overlooking the pitch. Murali's 15th ball of the day claimed number 799: Harbhajan Singh lbw, sweeping a doosra. Now, all it would take was one ball. Murali toiled while India resisted; teammates picked off wickets, including one run-out. For 23 overs, Murali was marooned on 799; even with India threatening to salvage a draw, the crowd celebrated not-out decisions off other bowlers. Star pace bowler Lasith Malinga was off injured.

After one sharp single, Murali's throw missed by inches; by this point, other fielders weren't even attempting run-outs, loath to stop history. Finally, at 1.55 p.m., number 11 Pragyan Ojha edged Murali to Jayawardene at slip. Murali's 800th wicket set a record that will surely remain unassailable. Teammates lifted him aloft. He had spent his whole career carrying them; now it was their turn. 'It's like a fairy tale,' he says. 'Something meant to happen.'

Occasionally, Murali was accused of embellishing his record by feasting on weaker opponents. But excluding matches against Bangladesh and Zimbabwe, he claimed 624 Test wickets at 24.87, a lower average than Warne against the same opponents. Against top-six batters from sides excluding Bangladesh and Zimbabwe, Warne averaged 34.07, Murali 33.38. Against India, the era's finest players of spin, Murali averaged 15 runs fewer.

There are scores of ways to measure Test greatness. One is to ask the counterfactual historian's question: what if? In this case, what would have happened if they had never played a Test?

Murali emerged at a pivotal time in his country's cricket history, transforming their record. Before Murali, Sri Lanka had won two and lost 20 Tests; with him, Sri Lanka won 54 Tests and lost 41. He combined longevity with adaptability across continents. While Warne had McGrath and West Indies' pace quartet had each other, Murali largely had himself. Though a fine left-arm seamer, Chaminda Vaas took 3.2 wickets per Test; Murali averaged six, more than anyone else to claim 200 Test wickets. Murali's 22 ten-wicket match hauls in his career dwarf all comers; the second most, by Warne, is ten.

Murali 'wanted the ball all the time', Jayawardene recalls. 'He's going to bowl 25 to 30 overs in a day. Then we could attack with all the other bowlers from the other end – that gave us a lot of room to manoeuvre around our combinations and how we set up tactically.

'He knew where the batsmen could hit him and he would come and tell me, "I need fielders in these places because this guy has the ability to hit me here and here. Let's cover that."'

Taking 20 wickets is necessary to win Test matches; no man helped his side do so more than Murali. Richard Hadlee might be Murali's nearest competitor; Murali played another 47 Tests, and took over a wicket more per match. When he played for Sri Lanka, Murali took 39 per cent of the side's wickets.

Table 6. Highest percentage of team's wickets (top ten)

	Country	Matches	% of team wickets
M. Muralidaran	Sri Lanka	133	38.64
S.F. Barnes	England	27	38.25
R.J. Hadlee	New Zealand	86	34.34
C.V. Grimmett	Australia	37	33.96
Fazal Mahmood	Pakistan	34	33.90
W.J. O'Reilly	Australia	27	32.28
S.P. Gupte	India	36	31.70
Saeed Ajmal	Pakistan	35	30.95
Yasir Shah	Pakistan	48	30.73
Mohammad Rafique	Bangladesh	33	30.48

There might have been better Test players than Murali. But no other man can claim to have given his nation more victories than they would have otherwise been denied. On this basis, he could be considered Test cricket's most impactful player.

* * *

Sri Lanka's success in the second half of Murali's career indicated the team's development. From before Test status, Sri Lanka had fine batters, but no one who scored with the reliability of Sangakkara or Jayawardene. Sri Lanka's fortune was that the pair were born within five months of each other, in 1977. They combined for 283 Tests, 24,214 runs, 72 centuries and an average of 53.45.

In 2006, they were united at 14–2 at the Sinhalese Sports Club against South Africa. Between overs, the pair spoke mostly about dinner plans; after batting throughout day two in tandem, they headed for a Thai.

Near tea on day three, the pair learned that they were on the cusp of the Test world record partnership. 'You can't let your partner down in that situation,' Jayawardene recalls. 'That was probably the most nerve-wracking 15 runs.' What began as a counter-attack ended as a partnership of 624 runs.

Over their careers, only one pair, Rahul Dravid and Sachin Tendulkar, added more runs batting together in Tests. Jayawardene and Sangakkara averaged 56 together, six runs more. Sangakkara was left-handed, Jayawardene right; this 'helped us quite a bit to put the bowlers off – we knew how to use that quite well against certain bowling attacks,' Jayawardene reflects.

From his teenage years Jayawardene, a product of Colombo – he attended Nalanda College, a leading Buddhist school – was identified as a future star: the purity of his timing, particularly his off drive and square cut, brooked no argument. He felt as if he was playing for more than himself; his younger brother died of cancer aged 16. 'Dhisal loved cricket,' Jayawardene told the journalist Andrew Fidel Fernando. 'It's something we loved doing together, so everything I have done in cricket is for him as well. When I play, I honestly feel like I have him with me.'

Two months after turning 20, Jayawardene became a Test cricketer. By the time that Sangakkara joined him, three years later, Jayawardene was already vice-captain. As a boy in Kandy, Sangakkara became accustomed to playing on pitches with more bounce than elsewhere in the country. Sangakkara's father mixed throwdowns in the garden with lectures on batting correctly; the emphasis was on balance, footwork and how to tweak his game for different situations. He paid almost equal attention to education: Sangakkara enrolled in a law degree at the University of Colombo. There, he joined Nondescripts Cricket Club, swiftly winning elevation to Sri Lanka A and then the national team.

'We would always question each other on issues and various other stuff which happened on and off the field,' Jayawardene explains. 'That helped us to grow into better cricketers, better thinkers.'

If Jayawardene was the batting artist, Sangakkara was the scientist. 'He was quite precise in the way he played and he worked hard towards that,' Jayawardene observes. 'I was quite natural and didn't want to tinker.' Together they helped Sri Lanka to nine consecutive victories in 2002; Sangakkara stroked 230 as Pakistan were thrashed in the Asian Test Championship final in Lahore.

Initially, Sangakkara kept wicket. Playing as a specialist batter unlocked new feats. In 86 Tests without the gloves, he averaged 66.78; excluding Bangladesh and Zimbabwe, Sangakkara's average as a specialist batter was 59.59. Batters, Sangakkara said, should 'project an image of dynamism, confidence and, sometimes, arrogance'. Sangakkara's hallmark, Fidel Fernando wrote, was *nidanam*: 'In simple Tamil, it means focus. In the milieu of Jaffna batsmanship, it is charged with much more. *Nidanam* is immunity from distraction, and tranquillity through duress.' These qualities came together in Sangakkara's fourth innings 192, only ended by an egregious umpiring decision, at Hobart in 2007. Left with only the tail for company, at one point Sangakkara backed away and launched Mitchell Johnson over extra cover for six.

Perhaps Jayawardene's best work was done in 2006. In May, he batted for over six hours at Lord's to clinch a draw after Sri Lanka followed on. In Colombo in August, the game after his record stand with Sangakkara, Jayawardene arrived at 94–2 in the fourth innings in pursuit of 352 – at the time, more than any team had made to win a Test in Asia. Against South Africa, Jayawardene was confronted by a slow, turning pitch. He resolved to attack the pace bowlers: 'I felt that I could get more runs off them rather than the spinners.'

Batting out of his crease against Shaun Pollock enabled Jayawardene to meet the ball early. 'The straighter it was, it was easier for me to keep clipping on the on side or hit straight and not take too many risks against them when they tried to shut me down.'

Jayawardene only lapsed when he had made 123 and Sri Lanka needed another 11. Medium-pacer Andrew Hall claimed two wickets to bring in last man Malinga, who drove his first ball calmly for one to clinch a one-wicket victory. Sri Lanka's achievement in winning 2–0 would only grow: South Africa wouldn't lose another away series for nine years.

As captain, Jayawardene harnessed Sri Lanka's finest ever attack. With a slingshot action developed on beaches, Lasith Malinga complemented Murali and Vaas. 'Our attitude, our mindset, our appearance, it had to be more aggressive,' Jayawardene recalls.

Late in their careers, perhaps all Jayawardene and Sangakkara lacked was a defining away series victory. By 2014, Sri Lanka had gone 16 years, going back to The Oval in 1998, since winning a series outside Asia or Zimbabwe. Few thought that this run would end in England; England had poached Paul Farbrace, Sri Lanka's head coach, before the series to be their assistant coach.

In the opening Test, England cruised to 575–9 declared. In response, Sangakkara clipped his first ball for four; he had missed the Indian Premier League to play county cricket to prepare for the series. Whether cover-driving, pulling off the front foot or using his feet to loft spin straight, his timing was supreme. When he drove a four to reach his maiden century at Lord's, Jayawardene, who had already written his name on the honours board twice before, gave his partner a bear hug. Needing to survive the last day, Sangakkara top-scored again, with 61. The final pair batted out five balls against Stuart Broad to clinch a draw; Nuwan Pradeep was given out lbw off the penultimate ball, but his review revealed an inside edge.

Headingley was the second, and decisive, match of the series. Sangakkara's twin half-centuries extended his sequence of 50-plus scores in Tests to seven consecutive innings. Jayawardene hit 79 in the second innings, sharing a crucial stand with Angelo Mathews, now skipper. Mathews's cussed 160, benefiting from defensive tactics while he batted with the tail, allowed Sri Lanka to set England 350 to win in 117 overs. Right-arm quick Dhammika Prasad enjoyed a magical fourth evening, claiming four wickets in 23 deliveries.

England fought tenaciously on the last day; last man James Anderson supported Moeen Ali for over 20 overs. Just like eight days earlier, the final man was given out off the penultimate ball; this time, there could be no review – Anderson had gloved a brutish short ball from Shaminda Eranga to backward short leg. Anderson crouched over his bat in despair; Sri Lankan players rushed to exchange hugs and take stumps as mementos before piling onto Eranga.

* * *

If Murali's achievement was to forge a record-breaking career as he defied all preconceptions about what spin bowling looked like, Rangana Herath's was to morph from everyman into exceptional. With his rotund frame, and the simplicity of his art – round-arm, classical left-arm spin with no great variations – Herath was the antithesis of what modern spinners were expected to be. Yet Herath ended up more than halfway to Murali's Mount Everest: 433 Test wickets, a record for any left-arm spinner.

Throughout his 20s, Herath was viewed as Murali's back-up, a role akin to being understudy to Laurence Olivier at the Old Vic. He played just 14 Tests in his first decade as an international cricketer; between domestic games and Sri Lanka A tours, Herath worked part-time at the card centre for Sampath Bank.

In July 2009, Herath was playing for Moddershall in the North Staffordshire and South Cheshire League. When Murali fell injured, Sangakkara called Herath to ask if he could fly to Galle; he arrived the day before the Test. Four days later, after taking 4–15 in Pakistan's second innings, Herath secured Sri Lanka's 50-run victory.

Aged 31, Herath finally ceased to be a back-up. Test commitments allowed him to stop being a regular bank employee, instead only doing occasional promotional work. Years on the fringes left Herath 'disappointed and emotional', he reflects. 'Whenever I got dropped from the national team, I always used to go back to my club team and perform.'

By 2016, Sri Lanka hadn't defeated Australia in 17 years. There was little indication of that changing as Sri Lanka succumbed to 117 all out in their first innings of the series. In roasting heat, Herath, by now 38, was entrusted with the new ball. 'I always try to challenge the batter's forward defence,' he explains. 'With a new ball, it can always either turn or go straight. But for it to happen, the accuracy should be 100 per cent.'

Nine wickets for Herath, either side of Kusal Mendis's dazzling 176, secured a come-from-behind victory in the first Test. In the next, at Galle, after taking wickets in consecutive balls, Herath trapped Mitchell Starc on his front pad; it was given not out. Herath told his captain, 'I am not sure whether the ball [would have] hit the stumps.' Angelo Mathews decided to review anyway. Herath had a Test hat-trick, which had even eluded Murali.

Herath took 28 wickets at 12.75 in a 3–0 triumph, only the fifth whitewash that Australia have suffered over three or more Tests. Each time Herath spun Sri Lanka to victory in the fourth innings. Using flight, dip, variations of pace and nous, he was the ultimate last-innings destroyer: in Test fourth innings, his 115 wickets cost 18.08 apiece.

'In the fourth innings, batters always expect the pitch to turn,' he explains, with a mischievous laugh. 'So I played a different game.' Herath would use his arm ball – going straight on – more; he estimates that half of his fourth innings wickets came with these deliveries. In a career of defying conventions, perhaps Herath's greatest triumph was to show how, on spinning tracks, the non-turning delivery could be the most effective ball of all.

* * *

For Sri Lanka, the years since the retirements of Murali, Sangakkara and Jayawardene have been troubled. In Shehan Karunatilaka's *The Seven Moons of Maali Almeida*, the narrator laments, 'Follow any turd upstream and it leads to a member of parliament.' Uniquely among Test nations, Sri Lanka have had to submit national squads to the minister of sport for approval.

Leading players, including Sangakkara and Jayawardene, have called for a streamlined domestic structure, with five or six first-class sides. Instead, Sri Lanka awarded first-class status to more and more clubs because, as Sangakkara said, 'Any elected cricket board that offended these clubs runs the risk of losing their votes come election time.' The number of first-class sides has mushroomed to 26 (though there are some separate matches in a four-team competition), creating a chasm between domestic and international cricket.

While being handicapped by administrators, Sri Lanka have retained the capacity to deliver intermittent Test brilliance. This was never better illustrated than in South Africa in 2019.

In the first Test at Kingsmead, Sri Lanka needed 304, comfortably the highest score of the match, to win. At 52–3 Kusal Perera, a left-hander playing the second Test since his recall, walked out to bat. From 110–5, Perera forged a 96-run stand with Dhananjaya de Silva sprinkled with square cuts. Yet reminders of the potency of South Africa's pace attack, which included Dale Steyn and Kagiso Rabada, remained: Perera suffered vicious blows to his left hand and helmet against short balls.

After left-arm spinner Keshav Maharaj induced a collapse, Sri Lanka slumped to 226–9, still 78 runs shy of victory. Perera was now 86 not out. 'You score the runs,' number 11 Vishwa Fernando told Perera as he arrived at the crease. 'I'll hit the ball with my body, if nothing else.'

Perera sought to maximise the number of deliveries that he faced, targeting boundaries before then taking a single off one of the last three balls each over. In 16 overs together, Fernando only faced the first ball twice. When South Africa took the second new ball, the target had been whittled down to 41; the tenth wicket added 37 in 10.1 overs.

Now, with Fernando unlikely to survive long against the second new ball, the bedlam began. With the field scattered, Perera noticed a gap on the on side and swivel-pulled Rabada for four. Fernando edged Steyn just short of the slips; while the fielders despaired, Perera scurried to the striker's end. Faf du Plessis's missed direct hit cost the side four overthrows, taking the target down to 29 more.

Two balls later, Perera flicked Steyn over square leg for six; he pushed a single the following delivery. In Rabada's next over, Perera top-edged a six over fine leg; when Steyn returned, Perera swatted another six over square leg. Sri Lanka now needed seven more runs. Rather than attempt to level the scores in one blow, Perera pushed another single off the final ball of Steyn's over. With four needed, Perera steered Rabada wide of the lone slip, sealing victory and taking his score to 153 not out. The tenth-wicket alliance of 78, of which Fernando contributed six, is the highest last-wicket stand ever to win a Test. Sri Lanka backed it up by clinching the series 2–0 in Gqeberha, where Kusal Mendis and Oshada Fernando added an unbroken 163 to seal the first series victory in South Africa by an Asian side.

Besides one century against Zimbabwe, in the rest of his Test career, Perera did not pass 70. Like Gilbert Jessop's celebrated fourth innings hundred at The Oval in 1902, the very improbability of the innings adds to its legend.

23

THE TRANSFORMATION OF WICKETKEEPING

'You never know.' So Justin Langer greeted Adam Gilchrist when he walked out to bat at Hobart in his second Test in November 1999. Australia were 126–5, needing 369 to win: a pursuit that seemed like the acme of futility.

Walking out with an hour left to bat on the fourth evening, Gilchrist raced to 45 not out. For Pakistan, whose attack included Wasim Akram, Waqar Younis, Shoaib Akhtar and Saqlain Mushtaq, the effect was disorientating.

The next day, Australia still needed 181 more to win. Rather than attack Gilchrist, Pakistan sought to contain him, ditching close catchers for fielders protecting the boundary. With the field spread, Gilchrist scored rapidly while eschewing risk: only 58 of his 149 not out, at almost a run a ball, came in boundaries. After Gilchrist led Australia to a stunning four-wicket win, captain Steve Waugh purred, 'He could be playing in his own backyard.'

That was exactly the point. Gilchrist's approach was reared in backyard sessions in New South Wales. Announcing the start of the last 20 balls, Gilchrist's dad would say, 'Just hit the ball, just whack it – have some fun and feel the thrill of the ball coming out of the middle.'

'Those words always remained with me,' Gilchrist told me. 'Then it becomes a test of your trust in that approach on the days when you miss out – both personally and also from the team.'

From the age of eight, when he went into a sports shop and stumbled upon wicketkeeping gloves, Gilchrist kept. Yet his batting quality was such that Gilchrist made his first-class debut as a specialist batter. He averaged only 22.64 in ten games before moving to Western Australia, lured by the promise of keeping. As a batter alone, Gilchrist felt that he 'needed to be a bit more technically correct and a bit more responsible'. Without the gloves, 'I felt like half a cricketer – and I put too much pressure on my batting.'

While an imperfect keeper, Gilchrist became a very dependable one; he holds the record for the most Test dismissals, by any Australian keeper. 'My job as keeper was my number one,' he explained. 'There's only one keeper in the team, but everyone bats.'

In 2001, during Gilchrist's first Ashes series, Duncan Fletcher, England's meticulous coach, developed plans to stymie Australia's batters. In the final Test at The Oval, Fletcher's clipboard was filled with summaries of how to bowl to each batter. Next to Gilchrist's name was only a question mark; it remained there for the bulk of his 96 Tests.

For years Gilchrist battled Prince Charles Syndrome, as he joked. Despite his buccaneering opening in one-day internationals, his Test debut did not come until just before his 28th birthday. In Brisbane, he was booed by fans incandescent that he had replaced local boy Ian Healy.

Gilchrist swiftly became one of Test cricket's revolutionaries. Even more than the 5,570 Test runs he amassed at an average of 47.60, Gilchrist's impact lay in how he scored them: his strike rate was 82. Among the left-hander's 17 Test centuries – a record for a keeper – seven came at faster than a run a ball.

Whether Australia were 100–5 or 350–5, opponents were greeted by Gilchrist's belligerence and imperious range of shots: the square cut, hit with crisp brutality, rivalled his straight drive as the signature. Traditionally, wicketkeepers had been shrewd batters with limitations; Gilchrist extended the cricket field's contours. In his maiden Ashes innings, he reached his century with an uppercut straight over the keeper's head.

THE TRANSFORMATION OF WICKETKEEPING

While batting, Gilchrist's self-doubt was seldom apparent. Sometimes, he told me, it could feel as if teams had stopped trying to get him out:

> I tried to portray a positive, comfortable image of certainty. But I think most players have a little bit more self-doubt than anyone would really know.
>
> Some of my better innings were when we were in a bit of trouble – so five for 100 or 120. As you're walking in the opposition have got their tails up: they had attacking fields. So if I was able to be positive and counterpunch that, you could quickly take them away from what they'd been doing so successfully to get themselves into that position. They end up putting sweepers out. Particularly batting with the tail, I was a beneficiary of having some fields out where I was allowed to get off strike pretty easily and get some momentum in my innings. And then that would give me confidence to start to play really aggressively – because they were trying to attack the 9, 10, 11.

Perhaps the greatest indication of Gilchrist's capabilities came when he volunteered to bat at three against Sri Lanka in Kandy in 2004. Facing Muthiah Muralidaran, Australia had subsided to 120 all out in their first innings; they slipped to 26–2, still trailing by 65 runs, in their second. Gilchrist's 144, which showed off his slog sweep, straight hitting and lightness on his feet against spin, underpinned a 27-run victory.

In Johannesburg in 2002, Gilchrist noticed an advertising hoarding beyond the deep-midwicket boundary: it promised a prize of a bar of gold worth 1.3 million rand to anyone who hit it. 'As we drove in on day two, I looked out to the pitch and it looked like a long way. I said to someone, "There's no way someone's going to hit that."'

Gilchrist just missed with one of his eight sixes; he had to be content with 204 not out. 'I nailed it right out of the middle and it was going straight at the sign. I thought, "Get up, get up, go on, be big enough." And then it actually flew over the top of the sign.'

* * *

'Give it up and take on bowling.' So advised Jack Blackham, Australia's keeper in the inaugural Test match in 1877.

In Test cricket's early years, wicketkeeping was the game's most unforgiving craft. 'Sticky wickets', when pitches dried out after being left uncovered while it rained, behaved erratically. Standing up to spinners, keepers needed dexterity both to take catches and stumpings and simply to protect themselves from physical harm from balls that reared spitefully, with no helmets or even adequate gloves to offer protection. The mental and physical toil of keeping meant that picking men partly for their batting risked jeopardising their primary skill. The abundance of allrounders also lessened the need to select keepers based on batting ability.

Conventional wisdom was that sides should pick the best wicketkeeper, then worry about where they batted. Herbert Strudwick, who played 28 Tests for England between 1910 and 1926, batted at number 11 in over half. With good reason too: Strudwick averaged 7.93. George Duckworth, England's next regular keeper, averaged 14.62; he batted at 11 more than anywhere else.

In September 1928, England set sail for Australia. On board the SS *Otranto*, Duckworth sought out Les Ames for a chat. Duckworth said,

> Well, Les, only one wicketkeeper can play in each of the Tests, and that means you or me. If you are the lucky one, it will make no difference to our friendship, and I am sure you'll act the same if I am chosen to play. It is up to the one not selected to help the other in every way you can.

For England, and ultimately all Test nations, this was the start of what would become an eternal question: pick the best pure selectors to covet more than glovework alone. Never again would Australia tolerate a keeper averaging in the teens.

* * *

In Zimbabwe's early Test years, Andy Flower combined keeping with voracious run-scoring. Flower retains the highest Test average – 53.70 – of anyone to keep in 25 Tests. He normally batted at number five, accumulating carefully in the classical manner of a top-order batter.

Flower was the most extreme example of the improvement in keepers' batting over the 1990s; wicketkeepers' averages increased by four runs compared to the 1980s. England's Jack Russell was among the victims of this trend. In Adelaide in 1991, the Test after making an astounding leg-side stumping standing up to seamer Gladstone Small, Russell was dropped; Alec Stewart, who preferred his original role as a specialist batter, was increasingly picked as keeper-batter. 'I felt so sorry for Jack,' Stewart wrote. 'If the specialist bowlers and batters had done their job as well as Jack, there would have been no need to hand me the gloves.'

Gilchrist, then, did not cause the improvement in the general quality of wicketkeepers' batting. But he accelerated the transformation. He was also the catalyst for changing *how* wicketkeepers batted. The history of Test keepers is the story of BG (Before Gilchrist) and AG (After Gilchrist).

BG, keepers essentially batted like batters – just much less effective ones. AG, keepers batted in a distinct, altogether more audacious, way. From the 1990s to the 2000s, wicketkeepers' strike rates soared from 44 to 53, far exceeding the general acceleration in scoring; keepers went from scoring at the same rate as specialist batters to markedly quicker. Keepers batting below seven went the way of the dodo.

Gilchrist imported his aggressive style as an ODI opener to batting lower down in Tests. Romesh Kaluwitharana, who opened in Sri

Lanka's 1996 World Cup victory and had a Test strike rate of 60, was the ODI pioneer. 'They can take a lot of credit for what they did with Kalu, throwing him up the top with great effect. And that was probably the opening for me to get into the one-day team,' Gilchrist told me. 'People say you changed the role of wicketkeeper-batsmen, but it wasn't me. I think it was one-day international cricket.'

In 2001, 11 years into his Test career, England started picking Stewart as a keeper-batter at number 7, mimicking Gilchrist's position. Matt Prior, Jos Buttler and Jonny Bairstow later performed a similar role for England. In the 2023 Ashes, Bairstow was picked over Ben Foakes, for the same reason that Ames was preferred to Duckworth 90 years earlier. The difference was that, at the time, Foakes averaged 32.20 in Tests, over twice as much as Duckworth.

New Zealand's Brendon McCullum, India's M.S. Dhoni and Rishabh Pant, Pakistan's Sarfaraz Ahmed, and South Africa's Quinton de Kock also emulated Gilchrist's method. Like Walcott over half a century earlier, A.B. de Villiers and Kumar Sangakkara were largely used as specialist batters, in an attempt to maximise their batting output. De Villiers averaged more with the gloves, though he only wore them in 24 of his 114 Tests. 'To play very long innings makes it quite hard to stand behind the stumps for 100 overs at a time,' he reflects. 'It can be quite intense.'

These men, as much as his own career, can be considered Gilchrist's legacy: a man who enriched his sport and, in the process, inspired dozens of others to try and play like him. 'He's done something very bad to the traditional wicketkeeper,' Sangakkara observed. 'He's ruined their careers.'

After Gilchrist retired, his impact remained. In the 1920s, keepers averaged 19 runs fewer than specialist batters in the top six, which had decreased to ten runs fewer by the 1990s. The gap between the averages of specialist batters and keepers fell to eight runs in the 2000s, then just four runs in the 2010s. So far in the 2020s, keepers are averaging only two runs less than specialist batters in the top six. This is the logical culmination of the Gilchrist effect: when a keeper walks out to bat, they can now be expected to score virtually as many runs as a specialist batter.

Table 7. Batting averages for wicketkeepers and specialist batters

	Wicketkeepers	Specialist batters*
1870s	11.54	20.05
1880s	15.96	21.90
1890s	19.72	29.74
1900s	17.05	28.47
1910s	13.06	32.53
1920s	19.61	38.71
1930s	25.67	39.46
1940s	23.64	43.46
1950s	20.60	34.37
1960s	23.59	38.52
1970s	27.29	38.26
1980s	23.63	36.94
1990s	27.28	36.81
2000s	31.81	39.63
2010s	33.49	37.90
2020s	32.66	34.95

NB: To January 2025

* Specialist batters defined as anyone batting in the top six who is not a wicketkeeper.

While there is no denying the revolution, aspects of it can be questioned. As the use of data in cricket has mushroomed, there has been uncertainty about how it applies to wicketkeepers. Certainly, there are occasions when teams have been seduced by the most obvious statistic – who scores more runs – and, in the process, ignored the more difficult question of who contributes more to a team, when keeping and batting are balanced alongside each other.

'If you've got a top keeper who averages 40-plus with the bat, then there's no contest,' Nathan Leamon, England's senior data scientist, told me. Otherwise, 'you've then got to weigh the difference between a keeper who bats and a batsman who keeps. Generally in that regard the cost of the chances missed is harder to quantify, and may well be underestimated.'

Consider Kamran Akmal, who once scored one of Pakistan's finest Test centuries: a belligerent 113 to orchestrate a recovery from 39–6 on the opening morning against India in Karachi in 2006, setting up victory. Such counter-attacking concealed Akmal's inconsistency with the bat (average 30.79) and his consistent drops. At Sydney in 2010, Akmal dropped four catches and missed a run-out; Australia overcame a 206-run deficit to win by 36 runs.

Despite such mishaps, modern Test keepers take more catches than their predecessors. Gradual improvements in equipment – beginning with Australia's keeper Bert Oldfield designing new gloves in the 1920s, with rubber coating on the palm – have made a keeper's job easier. From averaging 1.06 dismissals per Test innings before 1914, keepers averaged 1.82 dismissals per innings in the 2010s.

Much of a keeper's impact remains hard to quantify. It was said that Godfrey Evans encouraged Alec Bedser to bowl a more dangerous fuller length by standing up to the stumps. Keepers who can stand up to 80 mph bowling can unsettle batters and create new opportunities. When the number of specialist bowlers would otherwise be the same, 'selecting the best keeper is the attacking option – more wickets equals more wins,' Leamon explained. 'Picking the batsman-keeper is the defensive choice – more draws.'

Data has confirmed one long-observed truth: wicketkeeping is hardest against spinners. Test keepers take 95 per cent of all chances two first-class games in Rhodesia in 1972/73 for an International Wanderers team. Mike Procter, the former South Africa allrounder, thrived as overseas player for Rhodesia in the Currie Cup.

After the end of Rhodesia's civil war and independence in 1980, the country moved away from white minority rule. The new nation of Zimbabwe was born in 1980 and welcomed into the international mainstream. In 1981, the country became an Associate Member of what was then the International Cricket Conference.

Zimbabwe could now qualify for the World Cup; they did so at the first attempt. In their debut World Cup match, at Trent Bridge in 1983, Zimbabwe showed the qualities developed in the Currie Cup. Captain Duncan Fletcher scored 69 not out and took 4–42 in a 13-run victory over Australia. In the 1987 World Cup, Zimbabwe went winless but performed competitively again. Like Sri Lanka before, Zimbabwe hoped that the World Cup would be the catalyst to winning Full Member status, especially as they performed admirably against Test nations' A teams.

'I thought we should have got Test status,' Houghton recalls. 'The fact we didn't meant we lost a lot of good players.' Graeme Hick, a schoolboy prodigy who was part of the 1983 World Cup squad aged 17, was the greatest loss. Hick played 65 Tests for England, though his average of 31.32 didn't make good on the promise of his bountiful scoring in county cricket. Kevin Curran, Zimbabwe's star allrounder in the 1987 World Cup, retired from international cricket and used his Irish passport to play as a local in county cricket; pace bowler Peter Rawson also stopped playing for Zimbabwe after 1987.

'That basically cut us in half as a team,' Houghton reflects. 'We had to start again.' He considers the side in the mid-1980s to be the finest that Zimbabwe has ever had.

'The choice to actually be a cricketer professionally wasn't available in Zimbabwe. The guys who wanted to make cricket the number one sport and their income couldn't do it here. So they had no choice but to go somewhere else.'

Defeating England in the 1992 World Cup ensured that Zimbabwe could no longer be denied. This also prevented a further exodus of players. Andy Flower and his brother Grant had contemplated leaving to play domestic cricket in South Africa.

When Zimbabwe was awarded Test status – England abstained, but all other Full Members voted in favour – the side was 'at a low ebb' compared to a few years earlier, Houghton says. 'We were picking our national side from probably six club sides and then they gave us Test status. So you almost thought: one, we shouldn't be playing Test cricket now because we just don't have the numbers; and two, why has it taken so long?'

For Andy Flower, who was 24 when Zimbabwe played their first Test, the idea of Test status 'didn't come into my head at all in those early days'. When he learned the news, Flower 'felt it was an amazing achievement – it was wow. The second thought was, "I can't believe we've been given Test status. I don't really think we deserved it."

'My third thought was, "Oh shit, we've got to play against these teams – the best in the world, the people that I revere and I've watched on TV, on tape." There was a feeling of trepidation.'

Flower believed that Zimbabwe should have become more embedded in South Africa's domestic system, and only aim to become a Test nation in around another decade. 'I thought that was a much more sensible approach – grow our first-class experience against very strong provincial sides in South Africa and then perhaps take on Test cricket.' When he was appointed captain, in 1993, Flower berated an administrator for agreeing to play a three-match series in Pakistan. 'I thought that playing one Test away against these nations was draining enough. I remember trying to persuade him not to make us play three Tests. I know it sounds very defeatist.'

* * *

Test status prevented the Flower brothers, Andy and Grant, from leaving the country to pursue their cricketing dreams. The national contracts that the two received were predominantly to coach junior cricket, making them tantamount to semi-professional cricketers; aged 23, Andy was appointed Zimbabwe's director of coaching. Doing coaching-qualification courses in England, Andy found that they 'really got down into the basics of proper technique drilling. I remember thinking that's doing my game a lot of good as well.'

During weekdays, the national squad trained at lunchtimes; several lawyers would arrive in their suits, change and then get to the nets. The squad reassembled after the working day. 'We'd practise into the twilight,' Andy remembers. 'When it got dark, then we'd do our fitness training on the outfield.'

In February 1995, Pakistan came to the Harare Sports Club. Zimbabwe were 42–3 on the first morning when Andy walked out to join his younger brother Grant at the crease. Growing up in Harare, the brothers were two of five children, immersed in a range of sports. In Harare, they combined for a remarkable alliance. While Grant's undefeated 201 took 523 balls, Andy's 156 was brisker. The Flowers' partnership extended to 269 – overtaking the fraternal Test record, set by Greg and Ian Chappell in 1974. To Andy:

> It was the stuff of dreams. Grant was my best batting coach, he knew my game so well, and he and I did a lot of one-to-one training as kids. We played a lot of cricket in the garden.
>
> We used to have a very clear theory of over-training, making it harder than we would expect out in the middle. We put in a lot of hours throwing a ball at each other – getting hit, learning to avoid bouncers, going forward to heavy length balls straight after that.
>
> We coached each other throughout that period. To get together and put on the highest Test partnership for a pair of brothers – we're both really proud of that.

From the Flowers to the Strangs, the Rennies and the Whittalls, family was at the heart of Zimbabwe's early Test years. This illustrated not just how a love of cricket is often familial, but also how Zimbabwe relied on a tiny white population – 70,000 in 1995 – for the overwhelming bulk of their side.

'The cricket community was quite small,' Andy says. 'People like my brother and I, Dave Houghton, we were almost guaranteed a place, without sounding cocky. You didn't have selection pressure hanging over your shoulder all the time, like some players did for other nations. We avoided that – felt comfortable going into the games and doing our best.'

After Zimbabwe's gargantuan 544–4 declared against Pakistan in Harare, the task of taking 20 wickets in the match largely fell to Heath Streak. If Flower was Zimbabwe's mini-George Headley, then, from the moment of his Test debut aged 19, Streak was a mini-Richard Hadlee. A seam-bowling allrounder who combined outswing with bounce and formidable fitness developed in his upbringing on a farm near Nyathi, 100 kilometres north of Bulawayo, Streak led the Test attack for 12 years. His 9–105 in the match against Pakistan, from 50 overs, secured one of the most unlikely results in Test history. Zimbabwe's maiden victory came by a stunning margin of an innings and 64 runs.

'People were still saying, "They shouldn't have got Test status – it's ruining the records,"' Houghton recalls. 'We felt we had justified our Test status.'

There would be encores in Zimbabwe's brief golden age. In 1998, they won consecutive Tests against India, in Harare, and against Pakistan, in Peshawar. After their seamers exploited an unusually green Pakistani pitch, an undefeated 73 from Murray Goodwin, who had returned home after emigrating to Perth aged 13, secured Zimbabwe's first away victory. When rain marred the second Test, Zimbabwe secured the series 1–0.

'Those Test memories I really cherish because it really is the pinnacle,' reflects Andy Flower. 'To win a Test takes so much hard work, the ability to soak up pressure.

'I remember looking at the records of New Zealand and Sri Lanka when we were given Test status, and really being determined to try and do better than that at the start.

'A big driver for us was justifying the fact that we've been given Test status and fighting for the pride of the country. We didn't want to be embarrassed on the international stage and we knew that we were playing against opposition teams with resources that swamped ours in size and depth. So it was quite intimidating, but also exciting.'

Zimbabwe even briefly had the world's number one-ranked Test batter. After losing the captaincy for the second time, in 2000, following a player strike over salaries, Flower 'was very angry and bitter. I refocused my energy into playing as well as I could.'

Flower took a piece of paper and wrote the number one in the middle. Around the number, he wrote down what he needed to do to reach the goal: everything from technical adjustments to the amount that he was drinking. He divided the topics into a pie chart, ranking them by importance. Flower took the piece of paper around with him, constantly adding to it:

> I drew up a personal training plan, which covered all sorts of areas – psychological, emotional, physical, technical. I looked at my nutrition, looked at how many beers I was drinking. I looked at my skill levels. I thought maybe I could make up a bit of a difference by being mentally tougher than some of the other people that we play against.
>
> My definition of being mentally tough was to make good decisions under pressure and to think clearly under pressure. I tried to train myself up in that regard. And I worked extremely hard on my fitness and strength.
>
> Absolutely, there was more of a focus on myself. I always think that cricketers have enough time and energy to really have a strong self-focus. Because if you develop yourself and you focus on your own game and you do it well, it's the biggest gift to your team.

Flower's quest embraced unusual methods. Through reading *Winning Squash* by the squash champion Jahangir Khan, Flower learned how Khan had used self-hypnosis. He adapted the methods himself, re-recording Khan's tape but inserting his own cricket topics instead, 'trying to convince myself that I could slow the ball down in its flight – the perception of it. I was looking for the mental edge on other people.' Before going to sleep, to his wife's chagrin, Flower listened to his own self-hypnosis tape on a Walkman.

He also became a devotee of Dr Jim Loehr, a performance psychologist who specialised in tennis. Loehr's idea was that players simultaneously needed to develop their 'super-strengths' while cutting out their areas of exploitable weakness. For Flower, this meant becoming more resilient against fast bowling, developing his cut and off-side punches. Then he showcased his prowess against spin bowling, where he had an array of sweeps and reverse sweeps – in part, a product of his time spent playing hockey and squash. In Test cricket, Flower averaged a phenomenal 97.47 against spin bowling.

For Zimbabwe, Flower's superlative deeds were often not enough. In India in 2000, Flower scored 183 not out, 70, 55 and 232 not out in the two Tests – 540 runs at an average of 270, while keeping wicket too – yet Zimbabwe lost 1–0. Against South Africa in Harare in 2001, Flower made 142 and 199 not out, batting for 14 hours and 39 minutes. It is the only time a keeper has ever scored twin centuries in a match; Zimbabwe still lost by nine wickets.

The performance lifted Flower to number one in the Test batting rankings. In a 13-month period in 2000 and 2001, Flower scored 1,466 runs from 11 Tests at an average of 133.27. The process by which he got there was exhausting. 'To attempt to thrive in the international arena, I had to raise my intensity. And that was tiring.' Over an extended period of time, he says, 'I don't know whether I could have carried on at that intensity.'

Compared with many nations, Zimbabwe performed strikingly well in their early Tests. From their first Test in 1992 to the end of

1999, Zimbabwe lost only 19 of their 39 Tests, drawing 17 and winning three – two against Pakistan and one against India. After Bangladesh gained Test status in 2000, Zimbabwe bested them comfortably; they also defeated India by four wickets at Queens Sports Club in 2001. Fleetingly, Zimbabwe seemed to fit into the Test lower middle-class, a Southern African equivalent of New Zealand at the time.

* * *

The Test at Harare in 1995 was notable for much more than the victory over Pakistan. It was also historic in another way: when Henry Olonga received his cap, he became Zimbabwe's first black Test cricketer.

Growing up in the 1980s, 'We were the first lot of kids who were born just prior to independence who started playing cricket at a young age as a natural other sport,' Olonga told me. 'Until '95 when I made my debut, it was a white sport, it was exclusive, it was hard to break into clubs.'

Olonga's first Test was decidedly mixed. He began with four wides; his second legitimate delivery claimed a wicket caught down the leg side. The next day, Olonga became the first Test cricketer to be called for throwing for 32 years. Yet he fought back to form a fine, contrasting new-ball pair with Streak: 'My remit was very simple: go out there, and bowl as fast as you can.' Bowling full and targeting the stumps, while generating reverse swing, Olonga took six wickets in the match in the consecutive victories over India and Pakistan in 1998.

In 2000, repression was ramped up by the Robert Mugabe government: farms were seized and farmers killed by war veterans, while the regime clamped down upon political opposition. 'You can't help [but] sit up and pay attention,' Olonga told me. 'I'm aware of the fact that my fellow countrymen are being pummelled over the head by corrupt police and war veterans who are killing people on farms.'

This growing awareness led to an extraordinary partnership with Andy Flower. The two had never been particularly close – after Olonga had told a group of white players they 'needed to get off their high horses' in 2000, 'we had a strained relationship', he recalled.

But Flower had shown an acute awareness of injustice. While Test captain, he had moved from the Old Georgians, a white, elite cricket club, to Old Winstonians (later renamed Takashinga), a predominantly black club in Harare. No white Zimbabwean player had played for the club before. 'There was not enough integration of white and black cricketers,' Flower says. He and his father, Bill, raised funds for a new ground for Old Winstonians in Highfield, an area of Harare that is a hub of black cricket; the venue has since hosted international cricket.

'Back in the day, people felt intimidated to mix and mingle with the white guys,' Vusi Sibanda, who played 14 Tests, told the journalist Tristan Holme. 'Seeing him come through to that side of town had a major influence on us.'

In 2003, Zimbabwe co-hosted the ODI World Cup, along with South Africa and Namibia. As the country descended into increasing despotism, Flower's friend Nigel Huff, whose land had been devastated by the government's land reforms, suggested that he use the World Cup to stage a protest. Over coffee in Harare, Flower then put the idea to Olonga, recognising the symbolism of a protest involving a prominent white and black player. Olonga told me,

> He dropped this bombshell, that he'd spoken to a man who had said to him that Zimbabwe playing in the World Cup without showing a strong disagreement for what was going on in the country would be immoral.
>
> We found ourselves on the same side of a coin, of the idea of protesting against Mugabe. And so we found common ground, and then put our differences behind us.
>
> A couple of days after meeting with Andy, I said to him, 'Listen. I'm in. Let's do this.'

The pair asked David Coltart, a human rights lawyer and member of the opposition party Movement for Democratic Change, for advice. Coltart suggested wearing black armbands. Minutes before the first World Cup game in Zimbabwe, pitting the hosts against Namibia in Harare, the two released a statement. It declared that they were wearing black armbands to symbolise the 'death of democracy' in the country.

Teammates were shocked. So were the Zimbabwe board. After a subsequent World Cup game in South Africa, one board member kicked Olonga off the team bus. Olonga was dropped and received death threats; the Minister of Information called him an 'Uncle Tom'. 'There was,' Olonga recalled, 'a deeper sense of betrayal than they felt with Andy.'

Olonga fled the country immediately after the World Cup. He did not visit Zimbabwe for another 14 years, after the end of the Mugabe regime.

'I was aware of the fact that I could meet an ugly end,' Olonga told me. 'I was able to criticise what I perceived to be an unfair, dictatorial, tyrannical regime – stood up and said, "Come on, guys, you can do better than this."

'Do we hope that more could have been done? Absolutely, sure. We had hoped that it would galvanise the political will around the world a bit more by our small peaceful gesture.'

The protests meant that Olonga played his last international match aged 26, and Flower his last one aged 34. The pair joined the exodus of leading Zimbabwe players, caused by a combination of the political and economic climate. In 2000, both Murray Goodwin, who averaged 42.84 in 19 Tests, and the allrounder Neil Johnson retired to pursue county careers; such a path would become common.

It continued a recurring theme for Zimbabwe, with parallels to New Zealand and other countries in previous generations. What chance did one of Test cricket's least-resourced nations have if continually short of their best players?

* * *

In April 2004, Streak protested about selection policies that he believed to be unfair, for overlooking white players. In response, he was sacked as captain. Fifteen white players, including Streak, went on strike; all were sacked. Tatenda Taibu was appointed captain aged 20.

Zimbabwe were forced to assemble a new team essentially from scratch. The following month, Zimbabwe Cricket's chairman made an urgent call to his counterpart, urging him to make Sri Lanka declare in a Test in Bulawayo. Only when Sri Lanka had reached 713–3 did they finally oblige. Such humiliations, even after Streak returned, led Zimbabwe to suspend themselves from Test cricket in 2005. They were the first ever nation to voluntarily withdraw from the Test stage; the ICC privately pushed them to step back, fearing the damage done to the format's integrity. Zimbabwe remained in exile for six years.

Since returning, Zimbabwe have been a ghost Test team. In their first 13 years as a Full Member, Zimbabwe played 83 Tests, 6.5 a year. In their first 13 years since returning to Test cricket in 2011, Zimbabwe played only 34 Tests, 2.5 a year. Even if strife has not quite matched that of the 2000–2005 era, players and coaches have continually been let down – underpaid, and sometimes not paid at all, with international and domestic cricket alike frequently curtailed because of a lack of funds. How International Cricket Council payments have been spent has been a regular mystery. In 2014, a $6 million loan from the ICC was deposited in a non-interest-bearing account with Metbank, where three Zimbabwe board members also sat on the board – with the bank benefiting financially. Migration of some of the country's best talent has continued, though Zimbabwe's cricketing governance has improved since 2017.

If Zimbabwe victories have been rare, they have been savoured all the more. When Zimbabwe defeated Bangladesh in August 2011, on their Test return, the jubilant side ran a lap of honour at Harare Sports Club and then celebrated deep into the night at a hotel. The scenes reflected the sport's popularity among the black African population since independence; cricket has long ceased to be predominantly a white game. The national team has moved beyond selection issues being seen through the prism of race.

In 2013, Zimbabwe welcomed Pakistan to Harare. After losing the opening Test, Zimbabwe set the visitors 264 to win the second and final match. With Pakistan eight wickets down in their second innings and needing 25 runs to win, seamer Tendai Chatara found movement with the second new ball; number ten Junaid Khan edged to gully. Two balls later, Misbah-ul-Haq, Pakistan's number five and captain, pushed the ball into the covers; Rahat Ali, the number 11, tried to run a single but was sent back. It was too late. Rahat was run out; Zimbabwe won by 24 runs.

Yet the victory remains Zimbabwe's only win over a traditional 'top eight' opponent since 2001; the side still had to wait another 11 months until their next Test. Such is Test cricket's enduring challenge in Zimbabwe.

25

ENGLAND LEARNS TO EXPECT

I completely bottled it. I put too much pressure on myself and let that get to me. I think the first Test was a learning curve in how not to do it, how not to approach the game of cricket. It was built up too much but it was just a game.

These words could pass as an England cricketer's recollections of the first Test of any Ashes series from 1989 to 2002/03, except the victory at Edgbaston in 1997. England lost all eight Ashes series in this period.

In fact, the comments were from Andrew Flintoff, recalling the start of the 2005 Ashes. After five consecutive series wins, including triumphs in West Indies and South Africa, Michael Vaughan led England into the Ashes in a rare spirit of optimism. Such hope seemed vindicated by Steve Harmison's hostility on the first morning: he hit Justin Langer above the elbow second ball.

'That first session was the best session I've ever played in – just intense,' Langer recalls. 'The very first ball Harmison bowled to me whistled past my nose. You could just feel England were all walking at us and going "whoa".'

Harmison then drew blood when he hit Ricky Ponting under the eye; he took 5–43. Yet England were still thumped by 239 runs at Lord's. For all his swagger in the previous 18 months, Flintoff mustered a duck and three in his first Ashes Test. Glenn McGrath and Shane Warne, once again, exerted an iron hold over England.

In previous series, such a reverse would have induced English panic. Instead, under the captain–coach partnership of Vaughan and Duncan Fletcher, England remained unchanged.

After the first defeat in the 2002/03 Ashes, Fletcher had heard one senior player say, 'Here we go again.' In the 2005 Ashes, Vaughan sought to develop a fitter and fresher squad, picking just one man in his 30s, left-arm spinner Ashley Giles. This thinking was based on his earlier experience. Before the 2002/03 Ashes, a chat with Sachin Tendulkar convinced Vaughan that he should attack. 'Sachin said, "You need to have an aggressive approach,"' Vaughan recalls. 'You had to counter-punch; if you went over there with a mindset of survival, they'd eat you alive.' Consciously seeking to attack Glenn McGrath, who was used to being treated with deference – 'I tried to just think, "He's only a human being"' – Vaughan hit 633 runs in the 2002/03 series, even as England lost 4–1. It gave him a template for how to approach captaining against Australia.

Before the 2005 series, Vaughan told the team to aim to score at 3.7 runs an over, the rate that Australia had scored at over the previous four years. 'We realised that they had a good batting line-up and if we batted for 80 overs and scored at, say, 2.8 an over, they'd only have to bat for 65 overs. We had to score as quickly as them.'

In the first Test in 2005, Vaughan felt that England had been 'too timid' with the bat. Before the second Test at Edgbaston, England held a team meeting, reiterating the 3.7-an-over target. 'It was a gamble to say that we were going to try and whack Shane Warne,' Vaughan recalls. 'The mindset that week was to clear away all the baggage of failure and think about being positive and being aggressive.'

Some players were 'looking around the room going, "Are you for f***ing real?"' Harmison remembers. The message was 'we need to fight fire with fire,' recalls Kevin Pietersen; a flamboyant batter raised in South Africa, he was preferred to veteran Graham Thorpe and made his Test debut at Lord's. 'They said, "Come in and play the way you play, take it to them." I didn't know any other way. And I hadn't had any mental scarring from previous Ashes series.'

On the first morning at Edgbaston, McGrath trod on a cricket ball. When they saw him on the turf, England's players initially thought that McGrath was messing around. 'Then we saw the golf buggy,' Harmison recalls. 'It does give you a lift, as much as you don't want to see anybody get hurt. There was some relief at not facing Glenn.' On a flat wicket, Ricky Ponting won the toss and still chose to bowl first.

Trescothick slammed 90, attacking Warne and the seamers alike. Pietersen and Flintoff followed with audacious half-centuries of their own, egging each other on. 'We were just playing the way we were told,' Pietersen reflects. England scored 407 on the opening day, the most they had scored in any day since World War II.

England's pace quartet were not simply four terrific bowlers, born within two years of each other; they also had contrasting qualities. Matthew Hoggard combined new-ball swing and off-cutters when the ball was older with an undemonstrative willingness to 'brush up the debris of the shop floor', as he put it. Harmison, his new-ball partner, offered brawn and pace; his 7–12 in Jamaica in 2004 had evoked what England had long encountered in West Indies. He also showed how England had benefited from Durham's elevation to the County Championship, from 1992, opening up more opportunities for local players. 'Without Durham,' Harmison says, 'I wouldn't have played first-class cricket, let alone international cricket.'

Flintoff, generally first change, brought back-of-a-length hostility. Whisked into the attack with Australia 47–0 in pursuit of 282 to win in the second Test at Edgbaston, Flintoff immediately found reverse swing, even though it was only the 13th over. His opening over combined 93 mph pace with bounce and sharp movement to account for Langer and Ponting, who termed it the best over he ever faced. With a skiddy action and deceptive pace, Simon Jones extracted devastating reverse swing, hooping the ball both ways. 'Michael managed us brilliantly,' Harmison explains. 'For any given situation, Michael had something up his sleeve to say, "These two are the best."'

For all England's relentlessness with the ball, and their meticulous planning – Flintoff thrived bowling around the wicket to Adam Gilchrist, packing the gully region – their path back in the Ashes hinged upon fate. From 175–8 in pursuit of 282, Australia's last three hauled them to the edge of victory. With 15 to win, Simon Jones shelled Michael Kasprowicz at third man: 'I thought I'd dropped the Ashes,' he said. With three to win, Kasprowicz received a brutish ball from Harmison, which tickled his glove and was snaffled by wicketkeeper Geraint Jones. Kasprowicz's glove was not attached to his bat at the moment of contact; technically, he should have been not-out.

It was merely one sliding doors moment in a series of a quality and intensity that has scarcely been repeated. Over five Tests, perhaps the closest comparison was with Australia's series against West Indies in 1960/61.

At Old Trafford, Vaughan's silky 166 showed the benefits of several days of one-on-one training with Fletcher. Reverse swing from Flintoff and Jones, in between the showers, helped England set Australia 423 to win. A defiant final-day century from Ponting gave Australia a chance to salvage a draw; the last pair, Brett Lee and McGrath, survived the final 24 balls. Vaughan gathered his disconsolate team together, pointed to their opponent's balcony and said, 'For the first time ever we can see an Australian team celebrating the draw.'

At Trent Bridge, a clinical, chanceless century from Flintoff and Geraint Jones's 85 led England to 477, topping 400 for the third consecutive first innings of the series; Australia didn't reach 400 at all. Simon Jones's 5–44, swinging the new ball conventionally before generating reverse swing, secured a lead of 259. Jones's injury – he never played another Test – and cussed Australian resistance left England needing to chase 129. 'Don't even try and score off Warne,' Fletcher told Hoggard before he walked out at number nine, with England 13 shy of victory. Hoggard drove Lee for four before Giles flicked Warne away to clinch a three-wicket win that took England 2–1 up.

The Ashes would be decided at The Oval, the traditional venue for the final Test, for the first time since 1953. No England home Test since then had been more anticipated. 'It was different because of the build-up, and the nation had become very obsessed,' Vaughan recalls.

The contest befitted the hype. Benefiting from Fletcher's advice to play Warne more off the front foot and focus on hitting him with a straight bat through the off side, Andrew Strauss's second hundred of the series lifted England to 373, considered to be just under par. From 323–3, though their progress was delayed by rain, Australia collapsed to 367 all out against swing from Hoggard and Flintoff, armed with the second new ball on a gloomy fourth morning.

At lunch on day five, England were 127–5, a lead of 133; Pietersen, who had already been dropped twice, was 35 not out, and had survived a torrid spell from Lee. Pietersen 'didn't eat anything. I had these almighty bruised ribs. So I iced my ribs for a while. And I was like, "Oh my gosh, what am I going to do here?"' Vaughan told him to 'keep swinging'. He thought England would be bowled out, and needed to set Australia a target of over 200 to win.

Lee unfurled a spell of bouncers after lunch to try and break the game open. They did, just not in the way that Australia hoped. Pietersen, sporting a blond mohican and using the power from his 6 ft 4 in height, smashed 37 in three overs, hooking a series of deliveries off his nose into the stands.

Facing bowling of such pace 'gets you going', Pietersen explains. Amid the enormity of the occasion, he retained his unstinting focus upon the next ball:

> I was never a batter that thought too much about results. I was always in the moment, in the game. I played my whole career like that. I never played the man, I played the ball. I was able to simplify stuff – really bring the hype down.
>
> I wasn't creating this drama of 'Oh my god, I've got to bat here. This is the biggest match in Test cricket history.' I didn't walk out

there thinking about the next day. I walked out there as a youngster going, 'Hey, this is pretty cool. It's a good wicket. Let's bat.'

When you're pulling well, the game becomes a lot easier. Being able to pull the ball and score off the back foot also limits the opportunities for the bowler to get you out. It takes away a lot from him that he's not able to rock your foundations.

I drove him down the ground. I pulled him. I didn't feel it was calculated – it was just playing on instinct.

Without the clarity to attack – and the courage to hook Lee in the air – the result would have been very different, Pietersen believes. 'I probably would have missed it and got clumped on my head.'

Pietersen's swagger secured England the Ashes for the first time in 18 years. His 158 echoed one of the most significant Test innings of all time, by another South African-raised England player in an Ashes Test at The Oval: Basil D'Oliveira in 1968.

On 15, Pietersen was dropped at first slip by the man who had done more than any other to keep Australia in the series until the final day. After bowling 'crap' for Hampshire early in the season, Warne had called his mentor Terry Jenner and bowled in the nets for six hours a day for the last two days before the opening Test. 'I wasn't walking away from those nets till I was right,' Warne wrote in *No Spin*. 'TJ got my arm a little higher and had me spinning the ball "up" rather than firing it into the pitch.' So often the architect of victory, Warne delivered his finest performance in defeat: 40 wickets at 19.92, while looting 249 runs at 27.67 from number eight.

Warne's monumental contribution was not enough to overcome England's more rounded side. England were indebted to perhaps their lone traditional advantage over Australia: a great allrounder, batting in the top six while also doing the work of a front-line bowler. In 2005, Flintoff scored 402 runs to go with 24 wickets: the third top run-scorer on either side, and the second-highest wicket-taker. After years labouring under the 'new Botham' moniker, Flintoff produced his own defining performance against Australia.

The 2005 Ashes were naturally compared to the 1981 series. But for all the similarities – coming from behind to win; the excruciatingly tense finishes; a talismanic England allrounder – perhaps the differences were more important. The 1981 win was achieved in spite of the wider structure in English cricket. Regaining the Ashes in 2005 was, in part, thanks to a more enlightened system.

* * *

Six years before the stumps were removed ceremonially at The Oval, marking the return of the urn, England ended their summer booed at the same ground. With good reason: after losing 2–1 to New Zealand in 1999, England crashed to the bottom of *Wisden*'s unofficial Test rankings.

The series embodied England's worst tendencies. England picked 18 players over the four Tests, making five changes for the decider; Mark Butcher, captain in the third Test, was immediately dropped. Such was the instability of the age. In the 1989 Ashes, England had picked 29 players; in 1993, they selected 24.

Rattling through players at such a rate often left England weaker and unbalanced. At The Oval in 1999, Alan Mullally – Test average, 5.52 – batted at nine; their tail, it was said, was longer than a diplodocus. England's bottom three made a combined nine runs in the match. They lost their last seven wickets for 19 runs, tumbling to an 83-run defeat.

During the presentation, supporters gathered on the outfield and sang, 'We're shit and we know we are.' *The Sun*'s front page had a photo of stumps on fire, proclaiming the death of English cricket, parodying the obituary that had led to the Ashes being created.

In the decades after World War II, England had the most professional system in the world. 'By the 1990s, other countries had caught up – and gone past it,' says Mike Atherton, captain from 1993 to 1998. Belatedly, England recognised as much, and made two significant changes in 2000.

For the first time in history – 110 years after the idea was first proposed – the County Championship adopted two divisions. Higher standards helped players step up to Test cricket. Beginning with Andrew Strauss in 2004, six consecutive England players picked as top-order batters or keepers made at least 50 on debut. In county cricket, 'The competition was fantastic,' Pietersen recalls. 'You were playing against the best players in the world.'

The second structural change was central contracts: players were now contracted primarily to England, rather than their domestic teams, 14 years after Australia had done the same. As captain, Atherton advocated central contracts in 1996; they finally came into effect in 2000. 'Central contracts were the most important decision,' Atherton reflects. Before, bowlers 'were going back and playing county cricket and bowling a lot of overs – they were often turning up to Test matches either knackered or injured or both'.

In the 1989 Ashes, fast bowler Angus Fraser finished a three-day match in Weston-super-Mare on Tuesday afternoon. Then, he hitched a lift with a teammate to Cheltenham, where Middlesex were preparing for another match. Fraser had lent his car to Mark Ramprakash, another county teammate who had been playing for Young England. 'Ramps was late and we had a row in the hotel car park,' Fraser recalls. 'He threw my keys at me.' Fraser now drove 150 miles to Nottingham, arriving late on Tuesday evening; he was bowling for England on Thursday morning. Australia ended the first day on 301–0. 'You got on with it,' Fraser reflects. 'It would have been nice to have been managed a little more sympathetically. I would probably have got another 100 or so Test wickets.'

After England lost the fourth Test of the 1997 Ashes in Leeds, Darren Gough travelled to Cardiff to play a one-day match the next day. Two days later, he was back at Headingley playing a

Championship match. He was injured midway through, leaving England without their premier quick for the last two Ashes Tests and the tour of West Indies. David Lloyd, England's coach from 1996 to 1999, remembers that opposing fast bowlers maintained their speed better over the course of a day. 'Pace went down in the evening. They were knackered, running on empty.'

It amounted to a very English form of home disadvantage. Before England's final Test against Pakistan in 1996, Lloyd asked Wasim Akram what he had been doing between Tests; Wasim had been rested for a tour match. 'I've been waiting for you,' Wasim responded, with a glint in his eye. He bowled Pakistan to victory and a 2–0 series win.

'There was too much chopping and changing,' Atherton reflects. For players, 'loyalty was county first – you were just picked for England on an ad hoc basis. Central contracts helped give people a sense of security and belonging.' They also made selectors more inclined to back those already in the team. 'For economic reasons – above all – and for other reasons, you're going to use those players more.' The insecurity in the 1990s was such that, Graham Thorpe wrote, the dressing room could be 'an unpleasant, intimidating experience. And not everyone in the team was always happy for you when you did well.' With contracts, Harmison explains, 'you could be the best version of yourself and not the safest, negative version of yourself,' merely aiming to stay in the team.

In 1993, after scoring 64 in his last innings and averaging 52.30 in his previous five Tests, Graeme Hick was dropped during the Ashes. Such treatment helps explain why Hick and Mark Ramprakash, the last two men to reach 100 first-class centuries, only averaged 31.32 and 27.32 in Test cricket. 'If those two had central contracts they would have absolutely flown,' Lloyd believes. ' "You're an England cricketer, you're in the team, you're in the squad, you're paid properly." Those two would have come out of the bubble they were in.' Damien Fleming, an Ashes rival in the 1990s, says, 'You wonder what they would have done in the Australian set-up – they were unbelievable players.'

To go with the introduction of two divisions and central contracts, England entered the new century with a new captain–coach partnership. Nasser Hussain was appointed for the New Zealand series; he was joined by head coach Duncan Fletcher on the subsequent South Africa tour.

Hussain had not long been marked as a leadership candidate. He had a penchant for hurling his kit after a cheap dismissal; he had 'a big fear of failure', he says. But he was a cricketer of rare tenacity: a fine teenage leg-spinner, he suffered the 'yips' aged 15, and transformed himself into a gritty batter. Through the demands he made of his side, tactical acumen and recognition of the need for continuity in selection – he sought to 'take that fear of failure away by saying "you're gonna play for a long time"' – Hussain helped to transform English cricket.

Fletcher was an even more surprising choice: England had never had a foreign head coach. He hadn't played Test cricket, though he captained Zimbabwe in the 1983 World Cup. Fletcher used his lack of ties to the English game as an advantage, pushing back against counties. He was 'staggered', he wrote in *Behind the Shades*, 'that so many people were more interested in the welfare of their own county than that of the national team'. Inscrutable behind his sunglasses, when England collapsed to 2–4 in Johannesburg, in Fletcher's first Test, he 'didn't really bat an eyelid', Atherton recalls.

To show players the attitude that he expected, Fletcher handed each one a copy of the poem 'The Guy in the Glass', by Dale Wimbrow, which ends:

> You can fool the whole world down the pathway of years,
> And get pats on the back as you pass,
> But your final reward will be heartaches and tears
> If you've cheated the guy in the glass.

The poem embodied a Fletcher mantra: players must be able to 'look in the mirror' and accept their responsibilities. 'Dunc was not for moving,' Hussain recalls. 'Others would be "what are the papers saying, who shall we pick?" You're so busy trying to save your job, you're not actually doing your job.'

Fletcher had a forensic knowledge of opponents and an astute sense that Tests demanded different qualities to the County Championship. He elevated Vaughan and Trescothick, despite middling first-class averages: when they made their Test debuts, Vaughan averaged under 35, Trescothick under 30. Fletcher also picked Harmison and Jones ahead of slower seamers with better domestic records. 'I was constantly trying to win the next game,' Hussain recalls. 'Dunc would have one eye on the future. In selection meetings, whenever any fast bowler's name came up, he would immediately go, "What pace is he?"'

In the summer of 2000, England lost the first Test at home to West Indies by an innings. At Lord's in the next Test, West Indies made 267; Curtly Ambrose and Courtney Walsh, a combined 73 years old but still consummate fast bowlers, took four wickets apiece to skittle England for 134. England's 31-year wait for a series victory over West Indies was in danger of being extended.

Under the new regime, Andy Caddick was free from forever fretting over his place. After a fine catch at third man by his opening partner Darren Gough, Caddick settled into a nasty short length; even Brian Lara, squared up and edging to gully, had no riposte. In 13 overs unchanged on a gloomy Friday afternoon at Lord's, Caddick took 5–16 to bowl West Indies out for a pitiful 54. England needed to chase 188 to square the series 1–1.

There was only one certainty: Ambrose and Walsh would make them fight for every run, treating each single they conceded like a personal affront. Atherton took 27 balls to get off the mark; Vaughan, who arrived at 3–1, needed 29. The two added 92 before Walsh, spearing the ball in from a wide angle using the slope, reduced England to 140–6, then 160–8.

Number eight Dominic Cork, recalled to the side, approached the situation with chutzpah. He lofted Walsh over mid-off for an all-run four; then, exploiting the relief provided by the support bowlers, he pulled Franklyn Rose for six. When Cork punched Walsh through the covers to seal a two-wicket win, it heralded a new age: West Indies' horizons would be shrunk, England's expanded.

After defeating West Indies 3–1, the apotheosis of the Hussain–Fletcher partnership came in their second winter together, 2000/01. Since losing all four Tests they played in India and Sri Lanka in 1993, England had avoided similar embarrassment by not playing in Asia at all. 'We just weren't very knowledgeable about subcontinental-style cricket or conditions,' Atherton recalls. 'Even though it was my last winter touring, I still felt it was a learning curve.'

In Pakistan, Hussain's first aim was to ensure that England didn't lose. 'It was like going to Man City: you're parking the bus – in the last minute, you could nick it,' Hussain remembers. 'You've got to stay in games long enough. Cricket, like anything in life, is pressure.'

After 14 attritional days, England found an opening on the 15th. Ashley Giles's left-arm spin, combined with cutters and reverse swing from Darren Gough and Craig White, produced the first collapse of the series in Karachi; Pakistan were all out for 158, setting England 176 to win the series 1–0. In theory, England had 44 overs to get the runs; Pakistan drew out their overs, hoping to be reprieved by bad light. Steve Bucknor, the neutral umpire in the game, was adamant that play should carry on until the overs were bowled, even as fielders sometimes failed to pick up the ball. When Thorpe inside-edged a ball past his stumps he and Hussain scrambled the final two runs, then roared in delight. By the presentation 15 minutes later, it was pitch-black. This was England's first victory in a

Test in Pakistan for 38 years; Pakistan had never before lost at the National Stadium.

In Sri Lanka, England were thrashed by an innings in the first Test in Galle, scoring at a funereal 1.8 an over. 'We parked the idea of just holding an end and playing time,' Thorpe recalled. In two spiky games marred by woeful umpiring – Hussain joked that he was out '12 times' during a restorative hundred – England ground out wins by three and then four wickets. Of non-Asian sides, only Australia, in 1959/60, and South Africa, in 2007/08, have also won two series in the subcontinent in the same winter.

A coterie of 30-somethings underpinned England's consecutive series wins against Zimbabwe, West Indies, Pakistan and Sri Lanka. Hussain resisted media calls to discard the generation associated with the troubled 1990s. Caddick and Gough shared 100 wickets at 23.07 apiece in 13 Tests during the four consecutive series victories; Hussain cannily harnessed their rivalry. Atherton made stoic centuries in the final Tests against both West Indies and Pakistan, using his technical prowess and concentration to defy seam and spin alike. Thorpe exposed the folly of attempts to discard him prematurely. 'What else does [Graham] Thorpe bring except runs?' Mike Gatting, one selector, asked early in Hussain's reign. Hussain was aghast: 'What does he bring? Well, he averages 40 in Test cricket.'

In the 2000/01 winter in Pakistan and Sri Lanka, Thorpe averaged 61.44, combining playing the ball extremely late with lightness on his feet. Thorpe adapted his tempo to the game's demands – scoring sedately in the first innings, when he could trust the bounce, but rapidly during England's three victorious run chases. In the final Test in Sri Lanka, defying oppressive heat and vicious turn in Colombo, Thorpe scored 113 not out and 32 not out, steering England to a four-wicket win in a fraught chase of 74. No other Englishman passed 26 in either innings.

Rather than hit Murali 'with the spin', as was customary thinking, on Fletcher's advice Thorpe generally hit him against the spin, with a straighter bat. 'Batting has much in common with geometry,' Fletcher wrote. 'Angles, angles.' The coach also taught several players the 'forward press'. Batters, Fletcher believed, should move their weight gently onto the front foot as spinners were bowling. This motion would enable them to react more quickly and dead-bat the ball when playing defensively, avoiding close-in catchers, yet still rock back if needed. Fletcher also advocated using the sweep extensively. 'Duncan would say, "If you sweep the spin early on, they've got nowhere to go because their best ball is going for runs,"' Hussain says. 'The biggest thrill for Duncan would be someone taking on board what he said and making himself better. He could see your problem. He knew how to correct it – it might be just a subtle change in grip. And he knew *when* to tinker.'

Fletcher's technical eye spotted that Brian Lara's backlift made him susceptible to early yorkers; White clean bowled him first ball at The Oval in 2000. Under Fletcher, fielding also became sharper, and the tail more resilient: in the three wins in the subcontinent in 2000/01, the tenth wicket contributed stands of 39, 41 and 26.

But, meeting Australia at their peak under Steve Waugh, England had no riposte. For all the improvements under his captaincy, Hussain believes that it had to fall to a new generation to topple Australia.

'Even I had mental scarring and baggage against Australia,' he reflects. 'It needed that fresh group. Even when we lost in Australia, Vaughan was belting them so he didn't have any kind of mental baggage or scarring and the 2005 team definitely didn't. I don't think we were ready as a team two years earlier. I had had too many Australian moments under pressure.

'We had to learn to stop losing and stay in games long enough that in the end you can nick them. Then Vaughan comes in when we've done that bit, now you've got to try and attack. It was just the progression of a team.'

* * *

Hussain was widely credited with taking England out of the 1990s. Yet perhaps the 1990s have been misunderstood. England's overall record in the decade was an improvement on the 1980s. Even with allrounder Ian Botham and the contrasting batting pair of Graham Gooch, who trained with ascetic zeal, and David Gower, whose languid elegance reflected his personality, England lost 17 Tests, and won none, against West Indies in the 1980s. In the 1990s, they lost 16 Tests to Australia, now the world's pre-eminent side, but won five. The 2–1 victory over South Africa in 1998, sealed by Angus Fraser and Darren Gough bowling England to a 23-run win in the decider, came against better opponents than any series triumph that England secured in the 1980s.

For all the humiliation of 1999, England's real nadir was a decade earlier. From 1987 to 1989, England played 25 Tests and won only one, while picking 41 players. England's Ashes preoccupation meant their woes were somewhat concealed by winning three series out of four against a modest Australia between 1981 and 1987, until ending the decade with a chastening 4–0 home defeat.

Beginning with a shock victory in Jamaica, the 1990s marked a modest uplift from the hapless late 1980s. They also heralded the start of lasting improvements in the English game: improved fitness, beginning with Gooch's regime; slightly less haphazard selection; and the end of three-day County Championship matches. The creation of the England and Wales Cricket Board, in 1997, replacing the Test and County Cricket Board, was the catalyst for crucial changes. Lord MacLaurin, then the ECB chairman, was adamant that the national team was the sport's 'shop window'. Yet the side's best interests were still often ignored: captain Alec Stewart spent the afternoon before the first Ashes Test in 1998/99 in a long meeting with the board about player salaries.

Table 8. England decade by decade in Test cricket

	Matches	Won	Lost	Drawn	Win–loss ratio
1870s	3	1	2	0	0.5
1880s	29	17	8	4	2.13
1890s	32	16	10	6	1.60
1900s	38	11	18	9	0.61
1910s	21	14	4	3	3.50
1920s	48	18	16	14	1.13
1930s	72	23	14	35	1.64
1940s	32	6	9	17	0.66
1950s	83	39	22	22	1.77
1960s	100	32	15	53	2.13
1970s	95	33	21	41	1.57
1980s	104	20	39	45	0.51
1990s	107	26	43	38	0.60
2000s	129	55	37	37	1.49
2010s	126	57	46	23	1.24
2020s	64	32	24	8	1.33

NB: To January 2025

In the new century, England's talent ceased to be let down by the system. While structural changes helped to bring Ashes victory, 2005 was an ending, not a beginning. As with other England teams after peaks – the 1966 Football World Cup; the 2003 Rugby World Cup – deliverance was followed by swift disintegration. In England's next series, in Pakistan at the end of 2005, Vaughan observed that players now talked far more about money and commercial deals. Facing Shoaib Akhtar's electric pace, and bowling to Inzamam-ul-Haq and Mohammad Yousuf, would have been arduous enough without such distractions; England lost 2–0. Sixteen months after the open-bus parade, England were whitewashed 5–0 in Australia.

But the broader transformation in the support that administrators provided the side ensured that England fared far better after 2000 than before. After a long malaise, England came to perform roughly at a level that could be expected from one of the three wealthiest and best-resourced Test nations. From 1980 to 2000, England won 46 Tests and lost 82 – a win–loss ratio of 0.56, the seventh best in the world. From 2000 to 2020, England won 112 Tests and lost 83 – a win–loss ratio of 1.35, over twice as good as from 1980 to 2000.

* * *

Ten years after being ranked bottom of the world, England again confronted crisis. At the start of 2009, Pietersen, captain for just three Tests, and head coach Peter Moores were sacked simultaneously after Pietersen told the board that he could not work with Moores. In the first Test in West Indies, under stand-in coach Andy Flower and new captain Strauss, England were skittled for 51 all out and lost by an innings.

Before the second Test, Flower gathered the squad in a room in Antigua for two hours. No subject was taboo. Flower criticised the players' lack of responsibility for their performance, the way they were practising, the amount that they were drinking, and their shot selection. He recalls,

> Strauss and I thought, 'Listen, there's nothing to lose, 51 all out. What the hell else are we going to do?'
>
> It gave us the opportunity we needed to really get down to brass tacks. And get into depths, things that these guys weren't used to. It was a very tricky meeting to run. Some players spoke with tears in their eyes, which was great to see – that depth of feeling.
>
> We needed to change the way that we were training. We needed to change the way that we were looking after ourselves

physically and emotionally. We needed to change the way that we were briefing and debriefing practices and matches and our own performances. Strauss and I thought there wasn't the level of openness that we needed if we were going to move forward. We had to honestly assess our skill levels, our fitness levels, our mental and emotional consistency.

Under Moores, Strauss thought, players felt overwhelmed by information from coaches. Influenced by Justin Langer – the two had lockers next to each other at Middlesex – Strauss sought to emulate the culture of Australia in the early 2000s. Flower and Strauss – 'The Andocracy', as Scyld Berry called them – shared a belief in personal responsibility and self-reliance.

Training became more specific, focused and intense, but also shorter. Their slogan encapsulated how they wanted players to treat the side's values with respect: 'The team is not a hire car.'

While England lost 1–0 in West Indies, despite Strauss's three centuries, the tour signalled the onset of a new team in their captain's image. Strauss's debut in 2004, when he hit 112 and 83 against New Zealand at Lord's before enjoying a stunning series in England's 2–1 win in South Africa, indicated a cricketer of understated self-assurance.

England regained the Ashes in 2009, clinching a series in which they were largely outplayed by winning at The Oval. After asking the groundsman to prepare a pitch to help spin, off-spinner Graeme Swann took eight wickets in the match; just as in the 1953 Oval Test, Australia rued not picking a specialist spinner. The captain's controlled batting and Stuart Broad's 5–37 at The Oval could not conceal that, unlike 2005, this was a mid-table clash. Strauss's comments after winning 2–1 indicated that his ambitions were unsated: 'When we were bad, we were very bad; when we were good, we were good enough.'

Several months later, Flower assembled the squad at Loughborough, England's performance centre. There, Nathan Leamon,

England's analyst, did a presentation about what it would require to get to number one in Test cricket. It mirrored Flower's earlier journey as a player to reach world number one. 'That's where it came from,' Flower explains. 'I thought we needed a goal, some sort of focus.'

Leamon showed how the squad were performing compared to the best sides in the world. While the fast bowlers were performing well by global standards, the batters were not. Flower told the batters, 'I don't know what it is, but let's put our heads together. With group wisdom, we will find solutions.'

On Boxing Day 2010 at the Melbourne Cricket Ground, in front of 84,000 at the ground, English Test cricket delivered perhaps its most perfect day. Under cloudy skies, Strauss chose to bowl; James Anderson and Chris Tremlett took four wickets each. Australia were bowled out for 98. As thousands of aghast spectators left early, Strauss and Alastair Cook steered England to 157–0 at the close.

It set up an innings victory to retain the urn. When England backed it up at Sydney, they won the Ashes 3–1, securing their first overseas Ashes win since 1986/87. They became the first ever side touring Australia to win three Tests by an innings; no one else had ever done so twice. Australia got one thing right: the board's pre-series slogan that 'History will be made'.

While allrounders had been at the heart of many English Ashes triumphs, for the first time since 1911/12, England won a series in Australia with only four front-line bowlers. After Flintoff's retirement, at the end of the 2009 Ashes, England conducted research on the success of teams with four and five bowlers. The findings revealed that sides with five front-line bowling options tended to win no more games than those with four main bowlers – but also lose more. Essentially, many teams sacrificed an extra front-line batter for an allrounder who contributed little with either bat or ball. Rather than seek a new Flintoff in vain, Strauss's England trusted their best four bowlers.

They were indebted to Swann, whose control enabled them to pick a four-man attack. An orthodox off-spinner, his nous and drift were such that his average in the first innings, 31.62, was almost as low as his overall average, 29.96 in 60 Tests. 'If you only have four bowlers, sometimes the bowler has to bowl when things aren't in his favour,' Strauss told me. 'Swann was able to do that – especially against left-handers, he always caused a threat. He complemented the other bowlers well in terms of keeping a lid on the run rate.'

Swann also benefited from the regime's flexibility: for all the attention on increased professionalism, the captain accommodated his individualism. 'You should allow people to be themselves, but if they overstep the mark it's important they know that it's not a free ticket,' Strauss once said.

The summer before the Ashes, Strauss held dinners with three or four players at a time, helping them to shape the tour – including the focus on winning warm-up matches before the first Test, rather than merely treat them like glorified practice. This helped to forge an intensity in the field: England effected four run-outs in the series, Australia none.

In 2010/11, England's bowlers were a little lucky too: it was one of Australia's coolest and wettest summers, reducing the strain on the front-line bowlers. But England's greatest fortune was that Anderson led their Ashes attack. Pitching the new ball up, to maximise the few overs of conventional swing, Anderson then pulled his length back to contain: part of England's mantra of 'bowling dry'. When England found reverse swing, Anderson could turn attacker once again. Anderson also used the 'wobble seam', which he had seen Pakistan's Mohammad Asif bowl the previous summer. Delivered with the fingers wider of the seam, the ball wobbles in the air and moves unpredictably after pitching, generating natural variation: 'I could nip it off the seam rather than just rely on swing,' Anderson explained.

Anderson's 24 wickets in the series are the most by any England bowler in an away Ashes since John Snow in 1970/71. Even after

Broad was injured and Steve Finn was dropped – he took 13 wickets in three Tests but was expensive – England's threat was undimmed. The beanpole Tremlett settled into a nagging length, removing Ricky Ponting on Boxing Day with a brutish lifter; Tim Bresnan joined Anderson in generating reverse swing.

To go with their attack, England had one of their most robust batting line-ups, founded on a classical idea. The top three blunted the new ball before the stroke-makers, Pietersen and Ian Bell, who followed.

'The ethos,' Strauss told me, 'was much more around playing smart cricket, and when we got on top, being ruthless. So it was much more about containment, building pressure, bowling maidens. It was about getting a big first innings on the board. It was more traditional old-school cricket.

'That was putting the strategy around the players, rather than the players around the strategy. For myself, Cook and Trott, that was a natural approach. Then KP, Bell and others were going to attack more. It's easier to attack when the ball's older.'

Down under in 2010/11, England averaged 51.14 per wicket: their highest ever figure in an Ashes series. Six players made centuries. Three got there in the opening Test at Brisbane; Strauss, opening partner Alastair Cook and number three Jonathan Trott all hit hundreds as England reached 517–1 declared when batting to secure a draw after conceding a first innings deficit of 221. Five men averaged over 50, including wicketkeeper Matt Prior from number seven.

Pietersen hit an imperious double century in Adelaide; Trott, also reared in South Africa, scored a monumental 168 not out in Melbourne. Their presence illustrated the enduring influence of South African-raised players in English cricket. These have tended to be batters, with England benefiting from their prowess against pace. 'You face a lot of fast bowling and a lot of aggressive stuff,' Pietersen explains of growing up in South Africa. 'If you're not good at it, you're going to drown.'

Before arriving down under, Alastair Cook's place as opener had been in doubt. Summer anxiety was the prelude to a winter of content. Retaining his trademark steadfast defence and using his height to cut and pull, Cook batted for almost 36 hours throughout the series, beginning with 235 not out in the second innings at Brisbane. His 766 runs, at 127.66 apiece, are the second most by an Englishman in any Test series, after Wally Hammond in the 1928/29 Ashes. No one else more deeply imbibed the mantra of batting coach Graham Gooch: make 'daddy hundreds'.

England's attention to detail extended to analysis; both Flower and Strauss were influenced by *Moneyball*, the 2003 book on statistics in baseball. 'Some of those cricketing conventions like winning the toss and batting first were disproved,' Strauss told me. 'You need to interpret those facts well, but often batting first was definitely not the right option.' Melbourne 2010 was the most spectacular example.

Nathan Leamon, England's analyst, broke down the pitch into 20 blocks, of 100 cm by 15 cm each, assessing how opposing batters fared in each block. He also isolated where batsmen scored runs in particular phases of their innings. Before England played India at home in 2011, Leamon showed that Sachin Tendulkar seldom scored on the off side early in his innings. England packed the off side at the start of his innings, hanging the ball outside the off stump; Tendulkar averaged only 34.12 as England won 4–0.

At The Oval, Strauss was presented with the Test mace. After winning 20 Tests, and losing just four, since May 2009, England were now top of the rankings. It was the first time that England had been number one since a brief period in 1979/80.

As after 2005, England's time at the summit was brief. England were whitewashed 3–0 by Pakistan in the UAE in early 2012, floundering against spin bowling while the team struggled to refocus. In 2013/14, the second of back-to-back Ashes series, England disintegrated, succumbing to a 5–0 defeat. Several retirements indicated an exhausted group.

The team's decline after reaching number one shows 'there's a limited lifespan to that sort of motivation,' Flower believes. 'Once you become number one, where do you go from that? We needed something greater than that – a more holistic goal, to sit alongside something that specific.'

Yet, in 2012/13, England produced a worthy encore to their win in Australia. Indeed, beating India 2–1 away was an altogether greater achievement; India won their next 18 home series. As in Australia, Cook – by now captain – made three centuries, here showcasing his judgement against spin and mastery of the sweep shot. Cook's defiant 176 in defeat in Ahmedabad showed the way. In Mumbai, in the second Test, his 122 supported an even greater innings: Pietersen's 186, in 233 balls, using his reach to slog-sweep spinners out of the footmarks and launching the ball down the ground. 'I played through the off side so well that there was an off-side field,' he recalls. 'Once that was set, I went over the leg side and once they strengthened the leg side, I was able to hit through the off side again.'

It was a triumphant return. Pietersen had been dropped against South Africa the previous summer for sending derogatory messages about Strauss to opposing players. 'I was under extreme pressure,' he reflects. 'When I was batting, I felt absolutely fine. I was really, really comfortable in my own space. It was just away from batting that I felt very, very uneasy.'

Both Pietersen and Cook sought to avoid playing spin in the 'danger zone': two to three metres after it pitched. Batters fare better against spin when they either meet the ball head on, smothering the turn, or go well back. 'Practice was all about picking length,' Pietersen explains. 'You have to be either far forward or back or use your feet. You've got to be decisive and you've got to take calculated risks. You can't just let the bowler bowl.'

Swann and Monty Panesar shared 19 wickets in Mumbai and outbowled India's spinners. Anderson, with a toolkit to thrive anywhere, was exemplary once again. On pitches designed to nullify pace, no other seamer on either side mustered more than four wickets in the series; Anderson snared 12.

Injury meant that Stuart Broad played only a peripheral role in these two seminal away victories. Yet he has a unique place in Ashes history: Broad is the only Englishman ever to win player of the match in three Ashes-clinching victories against Australia.

Most extraordinary was Broad's 8–15 on the first morning at Trent Bridge in 2015. At one point Broad covered his mouth in disbelief; so did a nation, as Australia were bundled out for 60 in 18.3 overs. England waltzed to an Ashes-regaining win.

In 138 Tests together, Anderson and Broad shared 1,039 wickets, usurping Glenn McGrath and Shane Warne as the most prolific bowling partnership of all time. After Moores dropped Harmison and Hoggard in Wellington in 2008, Anderson and Broad were virtually ever-present together for 15 years until Broad retired, typically, by taking the last wicket in an England victory over Australia.

For all their similarities as bowlers – their competitiveness; their gradual embrace of seam, especially wobble seam, over swing; their ability to withstand pain – they complemented each other too. Broad's extra height offered a distinct threat. Until 2019, Broad averaged 35.46 against left-handers. He then became one of the bowlers to thrive going around the wicket to southpaws, bringing the ball back into the batters before moving it away off the seam, making him harder to leave. Broad averaged 23.46 against left-handers in his last 43 Tests.

After struggling in his early Test years, suffering after attempts to change his action, Anderson reverted to his natural action. His roundedness and ceaseless evolution turned him from an erratic swing bowler into one who could excel in all climes. Sheer bloody-mindedness was an essential part of Anderson's game too: he suffered constant pain in his left shoulder, whether bowling or not. It hurt when he put a T-shirt on in the morning; it even hurt when he brushed his teeth.

The presence of Anderson and Broad together was the greatest reason why England lost just two out of 24 home series from 2009 to 2020. For all their bowling brilliance, most remarkable was their longevity: testament to central contracts, and England prudently curtailing their white-ball careers after 2015. Gough, England's standout quick in the 1990s, played 248 first-class matches; 69 per cent were in county cricket, and the remainder either Tests or for representative England sides. For Anderson and Broad, this figure was reversed: 30 per cent of Broad's 265 first-class games were for his county and, as of his international retirement, 32 per cent of Anderson's 298 first-class games. Where English bowlers of previous eras had been undermined by the system, Anderson and Broad were enabled.

Sometimes, Anderson and Broad were called once-in-a-generation bowlers. England ensured that they lasted for two generations.

26

THE GREAT TEAM HIDING IN PLAIN SIGHT

On a resplendent afternoon at Lord's in August 2012, Graeme Smith held the Test mace aloft. Twenty years since readmission, South Africa now stood atop the Test game.

South Africa arrived at Lord's, for the third and final Test, with a 1–0 series lead, needing to win the series to dethrone England as the world's top-ranked side. After South Africa conceded a six-run first innings lead, Hashim Amla's 121 left England needing 346 runs to win. The Lord's pitch remained true. As Matt Prior, England's pugnacious keeper-batter, counter-attacked, South Africa feared missing out on history.

Vernon Philander ended such notions. Generating swing and seam movement from the Lord's slope, Philander had dismissed Alastair Cook and Andrew Strauss within 11 deliveries with the new ball. With the second new ball, he needed just 11 balls to take the final two wickets: Prior, edging to Smith's reassuring pouch at slip, and Steve Finn, prodding to Jacques Kallis at second slip next ball, sealing South Africa's 51-run win.

The victory came with five men who, in South Africa's first 82 years as a Test nation, would not have been allowed to play. This list of cricketers considered in South African terminology to be either black, Indian (meaning of South Asian descent) or coloured included Philander, player of the match at Lord's, and Amla, player of the series. It seemed to represent deliverance on the hopes after apartheid: a team comprising all talents, becoming the world's best.

The notion was reinforced in Australia later that year, when South Africa took to the field as the number one Test team for the very first time. After a rain-ruined first Test, that crown appeared to be slipping in the second. In Adelaide, South Africa needed to bat for 148 overs to save the game; the final day began with the Proteas already four wickets down. But Faf du Plessis, a 28-year-old on debut, batted throughout the final day, salvaging a draw with the help of his old friend at Afrikaans High School for Boys in Pretoria, A.B. de Villiers. 'It was not the prettiest cricket to watch – but, for us as players, it felt like war,' de Villiers reflects. 'That's the beauty of Test cricket.' Du Plessis batted for 535 balls in the match – the equivalent of an entire day, batting at both ends – making 78 and 101 not out. South Africa escaped with a draw, eight wickets down.

'We were behind the eight-ball the whole time,' de Villiers recalls. 'Graeme and the senior players got the message across: "There will be a tipping point at some stage. Find a way to survive and to stay alive."

'If we could hang in there for long enough, they would break at some stage. We knew if we could somehow find a way to get through that Test match, we would be the team to take momentum into the final one. We really pushed our limits.'

With the series locked at 0–0, a spicy Perth pitch would determine the series winner. Against Australia's all-new pace attack – such was the toil of Adelaide – South Africa mustered a modest 225; it would have been far fewer without du Plessis's 78 not out, marshalling a recovery from 75–6. That evening, head coach Gary Kirsten called a meeting at the hotel, emphasising the commitment and character that would be needed in the days ahead. Next day, Dale Steyn's 4–40 restricted Australia to 163.

South Africa had a first innings lead of 62; it was still only midway through day two. Traditionally, South Africa were cautious. Now, with Australia's attack only afforded a short break before bowling in the second innings, and aggressive fields in place, 'we just went with the flow,' Amla recalls. 'Nothing suggested that we should stop. The

Australian mood and body language dropped as we scored and that increased our impetus.'

At the end of day two, after 38 overs, South Africa had reached 230–2, scoring at six runs an over. After Smith bludgeoned 84, Amla hit a second innings century in the series-clinching Test, matching his feat three and half month's earlier at Lord's. His scintillating 196, brimming with characteristic square cuts and drives bisecting the off-side field, took only 221 balls. South Africa's 569 in 111.5 overs was extraordinary, even before considering the stakes and the opposition.

Ricky Ponting, playing his final Test, observed, 'A lot of the other teams we have played against over the years that have been in a position like that have been too scared to do that and push the game forward. What they did the other day was a sign that they had total belief.'

When Steyn induced Nathan Lyon to edge – yet again, landing in Smith's bucket hands at first slip – it sealed a 309-run victory. Over six Tests in England and Australia in 2012, South Africa had remained undefeated and won three games.

Yet perhaps 2012 wasn't even South Africa's most memorable victory at Perth. That had come four years earlier.

Early on day four at Perth in December 2008, South Africa began their run chase needing 414 to win. After a cautious start, Smith approached the challenge with characteristic pugnacity: punching drives, shovelling flicks through midwicket and cutting firmly to make 108. Teammates showed similar intent. With 15 balls of the day remaining, Kallis scored 21 in a five-ball burst. 'Instead of closing up for the day, as I had been taught to do, I thought another 30 runs would change everything,' he recalled.

At 227–3 overnight, de Villiers, on 11 not out, 'was really nervous and shaking, and I thought, I've got a massive mountain to climb', he later said. De Villiers made the mountain into a molehill. Aged 24, making the leap from prodigy into perhaps the world's best all-format batter, de Villiers showed his repertoire. He uppercut Brett Lee, used his feet to attack Jason Krejza and reached his century with a pull off Mitchell Johnson. J.P. Duminy, who hit a fluent half-century on debut, punched the winning runs through the covers, then leapt in the air and embraced de Villiers. In one of the fortresses of Test cricket, South Africa had cruised to the second highest ever chase, scoring at 3.5 an over while losing only four wickets. A nine-wicket win in Melbourne then made South Africa the first side to win a series down under since 1993. Players bellowed out to the empty stands, 'You're not singing any more.'

In the years to come, South Africa travelled better than Bill Bryson. From 2006 to 2015, they were undefeated away from home; since World War II, only Australia, from 1956 to 1965, and West Indies, from 1980 to 1997, have matched this run. Two defeats at home to Australia, in 2009 and 2014, prevent South Africa from ranking among the very top group of Test sides. Yet from 2006 to 2015, South Arica played 30 series, winning 20 and drawing eight.

* * *

'Greg ... Graeme ... what's-his-name.' So Nasser Hussain, England's captain, referred to Smith before first meeting him in a Test; he opined that South Africa were 'there for the taking'.

Smith was 22, and had played just eight Tests, when appointed skipper. His untainted past – asked for an opinion on Hansie Cronje, Smith replied that he had 'never met him' – promised a new beginning. He succeeded Shaun Pollock, who was sacked after a dire home World Cup in 2003.

Aged 12, Smith's school asked students to write down their ambitions. On his family fridge, Smith had written down his ultimate aim: to captain South Africa. 'When he was a child, being captain was all he ever spoke about,' his father recalled. At King Edward's School in Johannesburg, an elite state school, Smith excelled in athletics and football too. He captained for much of his school and Under-19 career, but had never led in a first-class game before being appointed Test captain. In his interview, he was asked what he would be prepared to sacrifice to get the job. He replied, 'My youth. I've done that.'

Smith was unperturbed by captaining much older men. Gary Kirsten, who was 35 when Smith was appointed, recalls,

> Often it takes a bit of time for people to settle – but he settled very quickly into a team full of more senior players. You could see straight away that he had the confidence to have big discussions with senior players.
>
> He just commanded a lot of respect from his team because he led by example, he fronted up to the most pressure, he was a fantastic orator. He could really move and motivate people very quickly.

After two Tests in Bangladesh, Smith arrived in England for his first high-profile series as leader, in 2003. He won the toss at Edgbaston and decided to bat. Then, he added 338 for the opening wicket with Herschelle Gibbs. Smith reached 277, at the time his country's highest ever Test innings; after rain helped England scramble a draw, Hussain resigned. When Smith was on eight in the second Test at Lord's, Hussain shelled a catch at cover – then watched another double century, this time 259. Smith lived up to his mantra for the team on the tour: 'Never Satisfied'. While England salvaged a 2–2 draw, no one would doubt his suitability to captain again.

Over 11 years as captain, Smith guided South Africa from the maelstrom to their best Test era. Smith exuded self-confidence from his broad-shouldered 6 ft 4 in frame and was exacting in his demands, bringing forward the time when the team had to arrive at the ground. In a manner similar to Australia's Steve Waugh, he emphasised the pride of players representing their country.

Before the 2003 tour to England, Smith ensured that all players were given their cap in a green velvet bag; their name was inscribed in gold letters. During this year, the moniker the Proteas – a nickname free from racial connotations, unlike the rugby side's Springboks name, which had been associated with apartheid – became widely used. In 2010, Smith initiated a three-day culture camp. Thirty players were addressed by figures including sporting greats, a Robben Island political prisoner and a botanist, who explained the regenerative powers of the protea in the world of fauna. Here the notion of 'Protea Fire' was born; a protea flower is often the first to bloom after a bushfire. 'You feel like you're playing for something more important than yourself,' de Villiers explains. 'It gave us a bit of direction and a reason to play.'

After Gary Kirsten joined as coach in 2011, Smith's leadership became more adventurous. 'The team was very secure,' Kirsten reflects. 'There was an opportunity to add more risk – be a little bit more experimental, innovate more. We needed to unlock what we already had.'

Smith's muscular inelegance – the bottom-handed shovel through midwicket, closing the face of the bat even against balls on off stump, was his trademark – could obscure his quality. His average of 48.25 at home rose to 54.98 overseas, showing how his own returns suffered from the wickets that South Africa prepared to benefit their seamers. The very best of Smith was in run chases, when he attacked calculatedly: in the fourth innings, he averaged 51.96, with a strike rate of 63. Smith hit four centuries in victorious chases.

Best of all was 154 not out at Edgbaston in 2008. Battling a back injury which almost ruled him out of the Test, and tennis elbow too, Smith hauled South Africa from 93–4 to their target of 281 on a turning wicket. He batted outside off stump against left-arm spinner Monty Panesar, pushing him through midwicket, and hit Andrew Flintoff for seven fours, mainly driven through the off side. Flintoff presented the greatest challenge. 'The roar as he ran in . . . it made the hair on the back of my neck stand up,' Smith told the book *The Proteas*. 'I remember thinking, "This is what you dreamed of as a boy, Graeme – now you've got it."' After near-misses on their three tours since readmission, Smith sealed South Africa's first series victory in England for 43 years.

Smith dethroned England Test captains with the ruthlessness the 1922 Committee reserves for Conservative prime ministers. Just as Smith's runs had led to Hussain's resignation on South Africa's previous tour of England, now they prompted Michael Vaughan to step down. When Andrew Strauss resigned after South Africa's series victory in 2012, it completed the set.

No one has captained in more than Smith's 109 Tests. His side's achievements would come to seem more remarkable as, in part because of players prioritising more lucrative Twenty20 competitions, South Africa had slipped to the Test mid-table by 2020.

* * *

For most of Smith's captaincy, he led a magnificent array of fast bowlers. A common thread in South Africa since readmission has been abundant pace-bowling talent. Between 1992 and January 2025, 23 fast bowlers took 275 Test wickets; seven were South African. In this period, South African quicks averaged 26.4, a run less than Australia's; no other nation's quicks averaged under 30.

Sport's cultural status underpins South Africa's fast-bowling prowess. Many pace bowlers develop their physique through rugby and running; such multi-sport backgrounds help to improve movement skills, robustness and athleticism. 'We're quite athletic, quite strong and spend a lot of time outdoors,' explains Shaun Pollock, who took 421 Test wickets at 23.11. 'Most kids who go to school play a lot of sports – you kind of play everything.' Pace bowling fits easily within the macho environment: 'Sport in our country can be a little bit all-consuming.'

From the start of his career, Makhaya Ntini was a fast bowler who transcended the game. When he made his debut in 1998, he became the first black African picked in South Africa's 109 years as a Test nation.

Ntini grew up in Mdingi, a rural village in the Eastern Cape; his tribe, the Xhosa, have been playing cricket since the 19th century. As a boy he worked barefooted as a cattle herder. Ntini only had one pair of shoes, which he saved for school; to keep his feet warm in the winter, he and his friends 'would wait for freshly dropped cow dung and sink our feet in it'. Aged 14, Ntini was spotted by a talent development officer. He won a place at Dale College, a leading sports school; Ntini was swiftly picked for the provincial age-group side, and made his Test debut aged 20. Ntini vowed, 'I don't want to be remembered because of my skin. I want to be remembered as a bowler who earned his legacy.'

Much of that came at Lord's in 2003: Ntini became the first South African to take ten wickets in a Test at the ground, marking the moment by kissing the pitch. 'I thought of my children seeing their name on the wall one day, and then I thought of all the young black boys who would know that anything is possible,' he said. 'I wanted every South African to share my pride.' Ntini combined an awkward wide angle with legendary fitness. For 101 Tests, he was simultaneously an outstanding bowler and a flag-bearer for the new South Africa.

Yet of all South Africa's fast bowlers, one man stands pre-eminent: Dale Steyn. Lithe, with an explosive run-up that generated dazzling pace, eyes that bulged, a penchant for staring at batters and a primal scream when he got them out, to see Steyn was to see the essence of pace bowling. 'It was very natural,' he says. 'I always wanted things to sound good, wanted things to look good . . . I almost wanted to look poetic when I was running in.'

Steyn grew up in Phalaborwa, a small northern town, spending his early years on a skateboard; he was ten before he first played cricket. 'Skateboarding, you are falling all the time – you're scraping your legs, you're breaking your wrists and you're falling. It's not comfortable, I promise you, when you fall on concrete.

'I was taking everything that I learned in skateboarding and applying it to cricket: from visualisation to never giving up to constantly having fun.'

Steyn combined a focus on aesthetics with sheer bloody-mindedness. He explains:

> The mentality was always keep going, keep pushing, keep going faster and harder all the time. That's how you're going to get wickets.
>
> I didn't understand why somebody could start off with 145 kph in the morning, and then at the end of the day, bowling 130. I was like, 'I don't want to do that. I didn't sign up for that.'
>
> I always wanted people to go, 'Shit, this guy. He's gonna come at you all day. And if anything, it's going to be more difficult to face him at the end of the day.'

Steyn strove to marry Allan Donald's pace with Pollock's accuracy. He succeeded. Deep into his second and third spell, Steyn often still exceeded 90 mph. His explosive action generated prodigious swing – normally outswing – with the new ball, and reverse swing with the old ball, angling the ball into the stumps. He had a devastating yorker, a ferocious bouncer and slower balls too.

In 2008, Steyn ensured South Africa backed up their Perth victory. At Melbourne he produced one of the finest Test performances: ten wickets in the match, either side of making 76 in a 180-run partnership for the ninth wicket, which began when South Africa still trailed by 143 runs. Steyn's partner was J.P. Duminy, who batted exquisitely for 166 in his second Test – playing very late, cutting and driving with precision and exploiting the large unguarded pockets at the MCG.

The performance befitted South Africa's achievement. Australia's first home series defeat since 1993, after 25 series victories and three draws, confirmed the end of their golden age.

Steyn benefited from playing alongside a cadre of quicks: first Ntini, then Morne Morkel, who generated venomous bounce, and later Philander, who brought relentlessly accurate swing and seam. Yet Steyn was the single biggest factor in South Africa developing an attack to thrive in all conditions during boom years for Test batting.

No overseas pace bowler has taken more wickets in Asia than Steyn; his 92 there cost just 24.11 apiece. 'There was always a focus on understanding the pitches and bowling accordingly, so trying to get the ball slightly fuller because of the low bounce.

'I was skiddy enough that if I managed to get through a guy's defence, I hit the pegs or the front leg, and then he knew he was in big trouble because the line is pretty straight. That was the mentality when I was playing in Asia.'

Twice Steyn produced stellar performances to lead South Africa to victory in India. At Ahmedabad in April 2008, the first morning offered a scintilla of grass; Steyn exploited the seam movement, snaring 5–23 – including bowling Rahul Dravid with a delivery that moved away late to kiss his off stump – and bowling India out in exactly 20 overs. Another three wickets in the second innings secured an innings victory.

This performance was bettered two years later. Nagpur is among the most unforgiving venues for bowlers; Hashim Amla and Kallis showed as much by sharing a 340-run stand in South Africa's first innings. With the new ball Steyn dismissed Murali Vijay – set up by two away-swingers, then bowled, leaving the ball alone, by an inswinger – and Sachin Tendulkar, edging a delivery that swung viciously. Later in the innings, spinner Paul Harris was hit out of the ground, leading to the ball being changed.

'First ball I bowled with this ball, I thought it was gonna swing away. It just hooped in. [Subramaniam] Badrinath fell over, clipped it and got caught at midwicket. I remember going to Graeme and saying, "I was trying to swing it away but it reversed." He said, "Okay, cool, let's go with that."'

It was the start of an intoxicating spell of reverse swing: 5–3 in 22 balls, including three wickets clean bowled. With three second innings wickets, Steyn claimed a match-winning haul of 10–108. South Africa couldn't quite do justice to Steyn's performance: just as in 2008, India levelled the series in the final Test.

* * *

In one way, Smith's South Africa had an advantage over the West Indies and Australia dynasties. Those two teams relied upon four specialist bowlers; South Africa had a great allrounder, enabling them to pick a five-man attack.

For 18 years, from his debut in 1995, Jacques Kallis was a behemoth. During his career, only Sachin Tendulkar scored more Test runs; only 13 men took more wickets. There could never be a cricketer like Garfield Sobers; yet, numerically, here was a near-replica. In 93 Tests, Sobers averaged 57.78 with the bat and 34.03 with the ball. Over 166 Tests, Kallis averaged 55.37 and – though he was a more reluctant bowler than Sobers, taking 1.75 wickets a Test compared to 2.5 – 32.65 with the ball. Both were also supreme fielders: Sobers just about anywhere, Kallis normally at second slip.

The statistical similarities highlighted their stylistic contrasts. If Sobers's cricket was joyous, Kallis was derided as merely uberefficient. The description belied his skill, reliability and adaptability. Ricky Ponting spoke for many when he described Kallis as 'Australia's No 1 opponent'.

While Kallis was sometimes termed selfish, such cries were absent in his homeland. Kallis's approach reflected his teammates' limitations: for his first decade in Tests, South Africa's batting rarely approached their fast-bowling strength. Aptly, perhaps, Kallis's maiden Test century came to save a match: batting six hours for 101 on the last day in Melbourne in 1997, defying Glenn McGrath and Shane Warne.

Kallis's game was founded upon an orthodox technique. 'My dad taught me the basics,' he explained in *South Africa's Greatest Batsmen*. 'He had a philosophy he instilled in me: if you're behind the ball, you can control the ball. So I always try to get behind the ball, not play away from the ball.'

As a small boy – though he bulked out in his teens and grew to 6 ft – Kallis focused on the fundamentals. 'I tried to make sure I had a strong base, and then aimed to expand,' he said. 'If you haven't a good technique, it's difficult to get out of a bad trot.'

Not that Kallis got into many. He hit 45 Test centuries, the second most ever; his worst average against any opponent was 38.86 against Sri Lanka. Kallis almost maintained his average away, hitting three centuries in both Australia and India.

Paradoxically, given some critiques of his play, Kallis attributed his success to retaining childlike joy in the game. He scarcely watched any cricket. 'I do whatever I can to make the game feel fresh,' he explained. As South Africa's batting became sturdier, Kallis became more expansive: his strike rate soared from 43 before November 2007 to 53 after. Kallis hit 97 Test sixes, a number with his lofted extra-cover drive.

His adroit cricket mind showed itself against India in 2011 at Newlands, with the series locked at 1–1. India edged a two-run first innings lead. At 64–4 in their second innings, South Africa faced defeat. With off-spinner Harbhajan Singh thriving while bowling to a packed on-side field, Kallis saw the gaps on the off side and unfurled several reverse sweeps for four. This flurry led India to protect the off side too. Now, there were gaps for Kallis to play orthodoxly. His undefeated 109 backed up his first innings 161, all while battling a rib injury; the series was saved. Reverse-sweeping Harbhajan 'was no more risky than playing a forward defence. There was nobody there to catch it if I top-edged it, so why not?' Kallis told the journalist Neil

Manthorp. 'I made the decision and then, as I always do, committed to it 100 per cent.'

Throughout his career, Kallis was not merely South Africa's best batter. He was also a potent, versatile bowler – combining strength with a classical, strong sideways action that generated away swing. Kallis was capable by turns of swinging the new ball prodigiously, generating reverse swing at 85 mph, or bowling defensively. At Leeds in 2003, a teammate's injury forced Kallis into the role of front-line bowler. Bowling outswingers with the occasional bouncer, Kallis took 3–38 in the first innings and 6–54 in the second in South Africa's victory.

'He balanced so many of our sides,' Pollock reflects. 'We could have a fast-bowling option in the first innings and the spinner to step up in the second innings. Then you add the batting numbers – it was just sensational.'

During Kallis's career, South Africa won two Tests for every one that they lost. With him, South Africa seemed as if they were playing with more men than their opponents.

* * *

For all Kallis's qualities, de Villiers was the side's most captivating batter. 'AB had that streak of genius,' recalls Robin Peterson, a spin-bowling allrounder who played 15 Tests between 2003 and 2014. 'You'd always cast your eye to de Villiers when he was batting in training, because you didn't want to miss anything.' A renowned schoolboy athlete, de Villiers excelled in rugby and golf and was the national age-group tennis number one.

Like many teammates, de Villiers's best was seen in Australia. At Adelaide in 2012, he survived 220 balls for 33 runs to help save the Test. A week later, in Perth, de Villiers thrashed 169 off 184 balls. In consecutive matches, he had painted the full canvas of Test batting. Even more remarkably, de Villiers had done so while keeping wicket too, after Mark Boucher was forced to retire before the series against England earlier in the year. He explains:

> After 2008, I felt like my technique was starting to find a rhythm where I could play any kind of innings. I could knuckle down and build slowly or I could be more attacking. I really trusted my technique. That's a really good feeling when you know you've got different gears.

In Adelaide, 'I stayed in first gear,' de Villiers reflects. 'When I decide to play a certain way, I've always had the ability to be really disciplined in that. I almost took it all the way to a different level, completely forgetting about runs and trusting my technique to survive.

'I developed a way to really play the ball late. That was one of the keys that day: to play under the eyes, almost finding pleasure in letting the ball just drop around your feet.'

When de Villiers arrived at the crease in the second innings in Perth, 'The situation told me, "It's time to express yourself." I played a completely different style.

'I really played with the moves the captain made. I realised the different ways that they were trying to get me out and countered that with attacking cricket. On other wickets, you would have a different approach. But because Perth had so many scoring opportunities, because there's pace on the ball, you can really manipulate the field.'

Perth 2012 was also Amla's apogee. His rapid second innings century was the culmination of an astounding run: 859 runs in six Tests, at an average of 85.90, during the twin series victories in England and Australia.

In his stance, Amla's bat pointed towards gully. This trait came 'from my days playing in our small courtyard. The door was the stumps and because it was a short distance to the bowler I would stand as close as possible to the door. Naturally, I would have to pick the bat up to the side instead of straight.' The quirk helped him glide the ball through the off side or whip it through the on. Only Kallis has scored more Test runs for South Africa.

Yet, when he struggled early in his Test career, it was said that Amla was only picked to make the side more representative. A devout Muslim – he refused to wear the logo of Castle, the lager company that sponsored the team, on his kit – Amla was the first man of Indian descent to play for South Africa's Test team. 'I am incredibly grateful for all the good my Indian culture has taught me,' he reflects. When he batted, this significance 'was the furthest from my mind. All I could concentrate on was scoring runs.'

In 2014, Amla became the first person of colour to be South Africa's full-time Test captain; Ashwell Prince had done the job as stand-in in 2006. After apartheid, opportunities opened up for other races that were previously reserved for the white population: Amla attended Durban High School, which has produced more than 25 Test cricketers. He was the first who wasn't white.

While South Africa have had a succession of fine black African bowlers – Kagiso Rabada could yet be viewed as the country's greatest ever quick – there has been a dearth of black batters. It took until January 2016, 24 years after readmission, for the first century by a black African, by Temba Bavuma against England in Cape Town. Seven years later, Bavuma scored the second.

Where bowling depends relatively more on nature – a player's physical gifts – batting depends more on nurture: the equipment, coaching, facilities and practice time available to children. The dearth of black batters, then, has reflected the wider socio-economic environment in South Africa: a few dozen elite schools, which remain disproportionately white, produce the vast majority of leading batters. The best black players tend to either be from the middle-class or win scholarships to elite schools at a young age. The reliance on a few dozen schools to produce talent is a microcosm of the nation: according to the World Bank, South Africa has the most unequal distribution of wealth of any country. 'I certainly benefited from the fact that I wasn't really competing with 50 per cent of the population,' Jonty Rhodes, a white batter who played 52 Tests, said in 2020. 'You talk about white privilege and it raises a lot of heat and debate on social media but it is the case.'

Government frustration about the continued dominance of white players, who account for about 20 per cent of the population, has been a continual source of tension. After an all-white side played West Indies in 1998/99, Ali Bacher, then the board president, declared that South Africa 'cannot have an all-white team'. In 2002, a subsequent board president pushed for Justin Ontong, a coloured player, to be selected ahead of the white batter Jacques Rudolph. Graeme Smith said that he only had his ideal squad for 20 per cent of his captaincy. From 2015, South Africa had a target to select an average of six players of colour, including two black Africans, in the national team over each season.

Ntini's story has come to be reassessed. His career 'might have made us complacent', Haroon Lorgat, then chief executive of the board, said in 2015. In 2020, with global attention on the Black Lives Matter movement, players described their experiences of racism. Ntini recalled being 'forever lonely' playing for South Africa, which drove him to run between the team hotel and grounds: 'I'm running away from that loneliness.' In 2021, a social justice committee set up by Cricket South Africa revealed endemic racism. Paul Adams, a left-arm wrist spinner who made his Test debut in 1995, was called 'brown s***' in a song sung by international teammates.

'We didn't transform properly,' reflects Omar Henry, who played three Tests in 1992/93. During apartheid, his school played cricket; now, they don't. 'That leaves a huge question mark around what has actually happened.' For all South Africa's achievements since returning to the Test arena, only fleetingly have the side been able to escape the country's divisions.

27

THE SLOW RISE OF THE TIGERS

Bangladesh was forged in the shadow of war. After a catastrophic conflict, East Pakistan gained liberation from West Pakistan in December 1971. The independent nation of Bangladesh was born. This new country had 70 million people, yet inherited a land ravaged by famine, the tragic impact of the Bhola cyclone and the destruction of the Liberation War; estimates of the deaths in the conflict stretch as high as three million.

When Pakistan gained independence in 1947, a slight majority of the population resided in the east, in eastern Bengal, but political power was concentrated in the west. East Pakistan, 2,000 kilometres away and separated from West Pakistan by India, received only around one-third of government spending. Cricket was a microcosm of West Pakistan's neglect of East Pakistan.

While Dacca's first cricket club was founded in 1867 and a vibrant local league developed, East Pakistan teams played only spasmodically in Pakistani first-class cricket because of a lack of funds. Though Pakistan played Tests in Dacca, including their first home Test against India in January 1955, the board focused on developing the game in the west. During the 24 years when East Pakistan and West Pakistan were part of the same country, all the national selectors hailed from the west. Only one East Pakistan player – fast bowler Niaz Ahmed, who made his debut in 1967 – was ever selected for Pakistan. He hailed from West Pakistan, and was working in Dacca.

Cricket both reflected the growing independence movement in East Pakistan and played a role in it. President Ayub Khan, ruling over a country on the brink of collapse, sought to use England's tour in 1969 to prop up his regime. 'We were no longer cricketers, it seemed, but ambassadors being paid a tour fee to keep the peace,' wrote England's Keith Fletcher.

Pakistan's government tried to use the national team to quell secessionist feeling. The regime pushed for the board to select Ahmed, for his second and final Test, against England in Dacca in February 1969. The government are also thought to have encouraged this Test to be played in the East, which was in the hands of secessionist rioters, with the Pakistan state losing all control over the area. Before agreeing to play in Dacca, England received assurances from student leaders that the Test would pass without incident. Players feared for their lives.

In Dacca, England arrived to find 'the entire place in the hands of the rioting students', fast bowler John Snow recalled. He described the Test as 'probably the most nerve-wracking of my life. Day and night we could hear gunfire – some of it only yards from our hotel.' The Test ended in a draw, in part because Ayub Khan had insisted on matches in the series being reduced to four days, thereby reducing the risk of disruption. The third Test, in Karachi, was still abandoned on the third morning because of student rioting.

In February 1971, Dacca hosted a Pakistanis XI against a Commonwealth XI, against a fraught backdrop of a nation about to split and Yahya Khan, Ayub Khan's successor as Pakistan president, postponing the next National Assembly session. The East Pakistani Raqibul Hasan was picked to play, seemingly to ensure local support for the game. During the match, Hasan had a map of what would become Bangladesh painted on his face, declaring that, next time they came to East Pakistan, they would need a visa. On the fourth and final day, following urges by Sheikh Mujibur Rahman, later Bangladesh's first president, to protest, students set fire to the stadium. The game was abandoned. Three weeks later, war broke out. Hasan spent much of the rest of the year in India, playing matches for a Bangladesh side in exile to promote the independence cause. After the war, he captained the nascent Bangladesh side.

* * *

Attempts to run cricket in the new nation began when the Bangladesh Cricket Control Board was created in 1972, just months after independence. The new board possessed 'nothing, not even a dollar', Ahmed Sajjadul Alam Bobby, a long-time director and prominent figure in Bangladesh cricket, told me. In the early years, the board's telephone line never worked. When the national team practised, there were no refreshments.

The suggestion from Abdul Kardar, Pakistan's former captain, that Bangladesh immediately be elevated to Test cricket was ignored. Indeed, Bangladesh were not invited to the inaugural men's World Cup in 1975.

In 1976 Robin Marlar used his *Sunday Times* column to highlight Bangladesh's plight:

> Bangladesh is not a member of the International Cricket Conference. She should be. Bengali cricket is numerically strong. Dacca is a Test match ground fit to rank with any in the world, and if the attraction to Pakistan for playing there in the 50s and 60s was as much concerned with revenue at the gate as encouraging local stars, that in itself was a reflection of the passionate interest in the game. And there have been talented players there, too. Something has to be done to restore the people of the seventh-largest democracy in the world to the international family of cricket.

MCC toured Bangladesh for the first time in 1976/77, sending a team of solid county players; a crowd of 30,000 a day saw MCC's draw with Bangladesh in a first-class game in Dacca. This helped Bangladesh gain associate membership of the ICC in 1977, making them eligible to qualify for the World Cup. Bangladesh lost to Canada and Denmark: the first in a string of World Cup qualification failures. But the country was paying more attention to sport; from 1977, an annual sports week was launched by the new National Sports Control Board. Other sides, beginning with Sri Lanka in 1978, also visited.

Bangladesh benefited from a new avenue to showcase their talents. In 1984, the Asian Cricket Council created the Asia Cup, a biennial ODI tournament. Two years later, Bangladesh featured in the Cup for the first time. If their first appearances highlighted the gulf that existed between Bangladesh and the continent's Test nations, regular participation in the Asia Cup helped to generate greater interest and revenue. Membership of the Asian Cricket Council – the most proactive continental member association – gave Bangladesh access to youth tournaments, coaching and facilities that emerging nations in other regions lacked. In 1988, Bangladesh hosted the Asia Cup, the first top-level international cricket in the land since independence. Wasim Akram and Sanath Jayasuriya were among the international stars to feature in the Dhaka league, with some crowds exceeding 10,000. Such games helped cricket spread beyond the middle and upper classes.

Yet Bangladesh still awaited their breakthrough. Even when the World Cup expanded to 12 teams, in 1996, Bangladesh failed to qualify. In Malaysia in 1997, thousands of migrant workers – 'We felt like we were playing at home,' recalls batter Aminul Islam – watched Bangladesh qualify for the 1999 World Cup. Returning from Kuala Lumpur, the squad were given a red-carpet reception at the airport. Thousands lined Dhaka's Manik Mia Avenue to celebrate; the government declared a national holiday. Reaching the World Cup was Bangladesh's finest sporting achievement yet, a seminal moment in cricket usurping football as the nation's most popular sport.

The growing excitement about the nation's potential was reflected by Bangladesh hosting the inaugural ICC KnockOut – a mini World Cup, which came to be called the Champions Trophy – in 1998, shortly after terrible floods had covered over 60 per cent of the country. The tournament, instigated by Jagmohan Dalmiya, the ICC's chairman from 1997 to 2000, indicated a new commitment to expansionism from cricket's ruling elite: it was explicitly designed to raise funds for Associate nations. The surge of broadcasting revenue in the 1990s encouraged the ICC to expand its horizons. Dalmiya was especially aware of the sport's potential in Asia; as a Kolkatan, he grasped cricket's appeal over the border.

In 1999, the seventh World Cup, Bangladesh marked their first appearance in the tournament by recording a maiden win, scraping victory over Scotland after recovering from 26–5 in Edinburgh. Bangladesh ended their campaign in Northampton against Pakistan, who had already progressed to the next stage. In front of a crowd dominated by Tigers supporters, Bangladesh reached 223, abetted by 28 wides. Pakistan imploded, succumbing to 42–5 against Khaled Mahmud's wicket-to-wicket swing and seam bowling. Bangladesh, who were 33–1 to win, secured a 62-run victory when, amid rumours of match-fixing, Saqlain Mushtaq became the third player run out.

'Beating Pakistan, one of the best teams in the world, will help us attain Test status,' captain Aminul Islam declared after the match. The calls for Bangladesh's elevation recognised the country's love for cricket. But they ignored Bangladesh's wider challenges: the lack of investment in grounds and training facilities; the slow pitches; the initial overdependence on Dhaka for talent; and, above all, the absence of any multi-day domestic competition until 1999/2000.

These obstacles are not only discernible in hindsight. 'People are forcing it to happen a lot sooner than it should,' Gordon Greenidge, who was sacked as Bangladesh coach on the morning of the victory over Pakistan, said of Test status the following year. Reviewing Bangladesh's application, an ICC inspection team recommended 'a concentrated diet of overseas experience' and noted that 'the game is being run from Dhaka with Dhaka interests as their paramount concern'.

No matter. At Lord's in June 2000 Saber Hossain Chowdhury, the president of the Bangladesh Cricket Board, made a presentation to the ICC, arguing for Test status. Bangladesh's bid needed support from seven of the existing nine Full Members; bar England, who abstained, every other country voted in favour. 'I knew that our on-field performances alone wouldn't get us Test status,' Chowdhury later recalled. 'Our off-field diplomacy compensated for our lack of playing standards.'

At the time Bangladesh were not even the strongest team beyond the Test world. By 2000, Bangladesh had played six ODIs against Kenya, all in the last three years; they had lost five.

Kenya defeated West Indies in the 1996 World Cup, then beat Sri Lanka, Bangladesh again and Zimbabwe in 2003. With the help of New Zealand forfeiting a game for security reasons, they progressed to the semi-final. Kenya's victory over Sri Lanka was cheered on by a raucous crowd at Nairobi Gymkhana Club. This highlighted both cricket's traditional strength among the country's South Asian diaspora and its growing popularity among the black African population.

In 2000, Kenya applied for Test status; their case was proposed by the West Indies and seconded by Zimbabwe. But reticence to opening up Test cricket remained. Performance, after all, was not the ICC's only criteria. When one Kenyan board member made their case to an ICC official, they were told: 'You do not have 100 million people.'

The 2003 World Cup campaign ought to have been Kenya's breakthrough. Yet Test teams became newly reluctant to play Kenya, seemingly because they feared defeat; in 35 months after the World Cup, Kenya played a paltry five ODIs. All the while, rumours of insidious corruption at the Kenyan Cricket Association grew; the governing body was eventually replaced by an entirely new entity. Through poor administration at home and in the global game, Kenya became, like the United States and Argentina a century earlier, a lost Test nation.

THE SLOW RISE OF THE TIGERS

* * *

Bangladesh's first Test, against India in Dhaka in November 2000, initially provided little indication of the strife that was to come. In front of a heaving, expectant crowd, which included the prime minister, captain Naimur Rahman won the toss and chose to bat. Number four Islam made 145, batting for almost nine hours; Islam reached a century with his favoured paddle sweep shot. A round 400, second only to Zimbabwe among scores made by teams in their first Test innings, was a fine achievement for a side who had not won any of the ten previous first-class matches in their history. India recovered to secure a 29-run lead.

By day three, with dignitaries congratulating players, 'our dressing room was like a bazaar,' Islam recalls. 'We started thinking that the match is finished – we never thought that there was still 180 overs to go. The second innings was a disaster because there was no experience of playing five-day cricket. I'd never played more than three-day matches.' Bangladesh were all out for 91, and thrashed by nine wickets.

This collapse, not the first three days, was a harbinger of what was to come. In their first throes as a Test nation, Bangladesh became – to borrow an Americanism – one of the losingest teams in sports history. From 1999 to 2004, excluding matches abandoned, Bangladesh lost 71 of 72 matches across Test and one-day internationals; during this period Bangladesh lost 26 of their 27 Tests and were on course to be thrashed in the other too, but rain allowed them a draw against Zimbabwe. By the end of 2004, Bangladesh had played 34 Tests and lost 31 – 20 by an innings.

The embodiment of Bangladesh cricket in these years was Mohammad Ashraful. A batter of rare panache against spin, Ashraful struck a sublime hundred against Sri Lanka on debut in 2001, becoming the youngest ever Test centurion. Using his feet adroitly, he played Muthiah Muralidaran without inhibition; Ashraful scored five Test hundreds against Sri Lanka. Yet, hampered by early vulnerability at the crease and without a robust defence against pace, Ashraful averaged a meagre 24.00 in 61 Tests; his international career ended after a corruption scandal.

No side had ever suffered such a chastening start to Test cricket. It reflected the folly of asking Bangladesh to try and turn players from the Dhaka Premier League into Test cricketers without extensive experience in multi-day matches, especially overseas.

'It was a bit early,' Islam says of Test status. 'We could have played more competitive cricket against A teams.' Facilities were notably less advanced than elsewhere in the subcontinent; the country's biggest cities lacked the culture of maidans in Mumbai and elsewhere. The monsoon season prevents Bangladesh playing outside from June to October, exposing the paucity of high-quality indoor facilities. In 2007, as his stint as head coach was ending, Dav Whatmore said, 'The lack of basic knowledge is a bit staggering, really. When these young cricketers were growing up in youth cricket, they weren't told about the basics.' A preponderance of slow and low wickets also impeded the development of quick bowlers and denied batters experience against pace. Such pitches rewarded accuracy, meaning that Bangladesh produced orthodox finger spinners rather than wrist spinners.

Bangladesh were also victims of a structure that stratified nations, as if they were children passing or failing their 11-plus exams. Playing first-class games, even Tests, against similarly matched opponents like Kenya, Scotland and Ireland would have given Bangladesh a better understanding of multi-day cricket. In 2015, a senior figure at the ICC told me that Bangladesh and Zimbabwe were 'scared' to play Associates, seemingly fearing that losing would call into question their Full Member status and their extra funding.

Instead, Bangladesh's most competitive rivalry was with Zimbabwe. How much of this owed to Bangladesh's improvement, and how much to Zimbabwe's strife, was not always clear. But at Chittagong on 10 January 2005, in their 35th Test, Enamul Haque Jnr – yet another slow left-armer – had Zimbabwe's number 11 Christopher Mpofu caught at silly point. Bangladesh had won a Test match; players rushed to claim stumps as mementos, before captain Habibul Bashar was given a national flag and led his team on a victory lap. Bashar called it 'the best day of my life'. To observers it was tainted by their opponents' plight: Zimbabwe withdrew from Test cricket later that year.

Amid the thrashings, Bangladesh had occasional glimpses of a breakthrough win against a top-tier side. Inzamam-ul-Haq's fourth innings 138 not out gave Pakistan a one-wicket win in Multan in 2003; Ricky Ponting's fourth innings 118 not out, helped by a dropped catch, ensured Australia escaped Dhaka with a three-wicket victory in 2006, despite Mohammad Rafique's nine wickets in the Test.

Victory would have been a fitting testament to Rafique's indefatigability. Growing up in a shantytown on Dhaka's Buriganga river, he used to hitch a lift on a boat across the water to get to cricket practice. Rafique had planned to retire after the 1999 World Cup. Instead, he became the first Bangladeshi to take 100 Test wickets, albeit at an average of 40.76, with a style that became his country's hallmark: left-arm spin, with subtle changes of pace and angle and a dangerous arm ball. From 2000 to 2021, in their first 20 years as a Test nation, journalist Mohammad Isam noted, Bangladesh took 42 per cent of wickets with left-arm orthodox spin; no other country took more than 20 per cent. In their early Test years, whatever Bangladesh's plight, the answer was the same, captain Habibul Bashar recalled: 'When I needed wickets, let's try Rafique. If I needed to contain the runs, let's try Rafique.'

* * *

As Bangladesh entered their second decade as a Test nation, helped by a more robust youth programme and improved cultivation of players from beyond Dhaka, the thrashings became less common. On some lifeless home tracks, Bangladesh could even escape defeat. 'The mindset was to draw against big teams – try to play five days,'

Shakib Al Hasan, Bangladesh's greatest cricketer yet and captain in several stints, told me. After 16 years, Bangladesh's only Test victories were against Zimbabwe or, in 2009, a West Indies side decimated by player strikes.

England's tour, in October 2016, marked a shift in Bangladeshi thinking. In Adelaide the previous year, Bangladesh had knocked England out of the World Cup. Now, they aimed to topple them in Test cricket too. 'A big decision was taken at that time, and we took the right decision. And we played fearless cricket,' Shakib explained. 'We started thinking, "Let's try to win."' The wickets prepared changed accordingly.

In Chittagong, in the first of the two Tests, Bangladesh's plan almost worked. Their spinners shared 18 wickets in the Test, setting up a run chase of 286. At 227–5, Bangladesh were on course; the dismissal of captain Mushfiqur Rahim, the impish keeper-batter, triggered collapse and a 22-run defeat.

In Dhaka, needing to win to square the series, Bangladesh doubled down on their approach. They opened with spin – 19-year-old Mehidy Hasan Miraz's off breaks and Shakib's classical left-armers – from both ends in both innings.

Opener Tamim Iqbal, whose penchant for lofting the ball over the off side had been forged in rooftop cricket as a boy in Chittagong, was the lone man to master a pitch dusting up. Tamim's 104 and 40 left England needing 273 runs to win when their chase began shortly after lunch on day three. By tea, openers Alastair Cook and Ben Duckett had led England to 100–0. Once again, Bangladesh faced having their destiny denied.

Not this time. The first ball after tea, from Mehidy, kept low and uprooted Duckett's middle stump. In the next over, Shakib got a delivery to grip and straighten to dismiss next man Joe Root. Now, with signs of uneven bounce, fielders crowded the bat. So much for any questions about self-belief; England lost all ten wickets in a session, the first time they had done so for 78 years. It was a victory in

Right: Caught Rodney Marsh, bowled Dennis Lillee – Test cricket's most common dismissal.

Below: Wasim Akram shattering stumps with reverse swing.

Three of the great quartet of 1980s allrounders: Imran Khan (*left*), Richard Hadlee (*right*) and Kapil Dev (*below*).

Left: Viv Richards batting – characteristically wearing his maroon cap instead of a helmet – against England in Barbados in 1981.

Below: Brian Lara celebrating beating Australia by one wicket in 1999, after scoring 153 not out in the fourth innings.

Pakistan celebrate a magnificent victory in Chennai in 1999, after Saqlain Mushtaq (*centre*) clinched a 12-run win. India's fans applauded as Pakistan did a lap of honour.

Rahul Dravid and VVS Laxman walking off after batting all day in partnership at Kolkata against Australia in 2001. The two added 376 runs together to transform the match and series.

Test cricket's two greatest spinners, Shane Warne and Muthiah Muralidaran, both made spectacular first appearances in England.

Warne (*above, centre*) delivered the 'ball of the century' with his first ball in Ashes cricket in 1993. Five years later, Muralidaran (*below, arms aloft*) took 16 wickets at The Oval in Sri Lanka's victory.

Left: 'He could be playing in his own backyard': Adam Gilchrist hitting his first Test century, at Hobart in 1999. Gilchrist would score 17 Test centuries, a record for any wicketkeeper.

Below: Sachin Tendulkar celebrates his first Test century, at Old Trafford in 1990. He would score another 48.

Kevin Pietersen saluting The Oval crowd in 2005 after scoring 158: the innings that secured England the Ashes after 18 years.

In the age of the Decision Review System, the umpire's decision is no longer final. Here, England's Joe Root signals to review an umpiring decision.

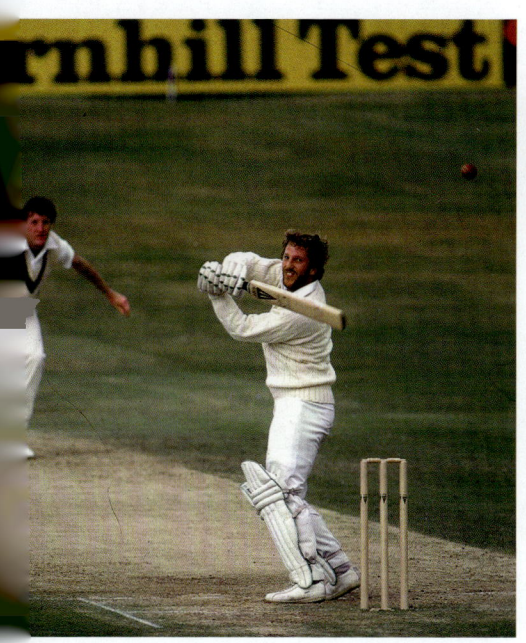

Two Headingly miracles: Ian Botham (*left*) during his 149 not out at Leeds in 1981, and Ben Stokes (*right*) celebrating England's one-wicket win after his 135 not out in 2019.

Above: South Africa at Lords 2012, celebrating becoming the Test world number one side. Captain Graeme Smith is holding the Test mace.

Right: The Tigers roar: Bangladesh celebrating beating England at Dhaka in 2016, their first major victory after a torrid start to Test cricket.

Above: Rishabh Pant celebrating at the Gabba in 2021, after India overcame being bowled out for 36 in the first Test, and the loss of virtually an entire squad to injury, to win the series 2-1.

Above: New Zealand winning the inaugural World Test Championship in 2021. The trophy is held by captain Kane Williamson.

keeping with the underlying character of Bangladesh cricket: they took all 20 wickets in the Test with spin. Mehidy, who took 12 wickets, symbolised the promise of Bangladeshi cricket; Shakib's five wickets in the match, alongside a vital second innings 41, attested to his continued importance.

Forty-five years after independence, 16 years since winning Test status, 90 minutes of bedlam secured Bangladesh's first flagship victory. Mehidy bellowed a successful lbw appeal off last man Steven Finn; the heady jubilation, on the pitch and among the fans dressed as tigers, recognised a historic moment: Dhaka 2016 rivalled India's maiden Test victory in Madras in 1952 or Pakistan's win at The Oval in 1954. Cricket's most exclusive club had become a little bigger.

Bangladesh, and Shakib, confirmed this truth in the months that followed. With 116 and six wickets in the match, he clinched a series-levelling victory in Sri Lanka in March 2017. 'There is no shortage of self-belief,' he told me shortly afterwards. 'Now we feel that we are very much unbeatable at home – doesn't matter who we are playing against.'

Finally playing Bangladesh for the first time in 11 years, Australia would learn as much too that August. First, Shakib's 84, showing his lightness on his feet against spin and dexterity sweeping, lifted Bangladesh to 260 on another pitch turning markedly from day one. Then, combining easy rhythm and flight with bounce and bite off the surface, he took 5–68 to secure a first innings lead of 43. Tamim's 78, defying off-spinner Nathan Lyon, left Australia needing 265 to win.

David Warner, Australia's buccaneering opener, slammed 112. After he fell lbw to Shakib, sweeping a delivery that skidded on, Australia's frailties against spin resurfaced. They also encountered a new and more combative Bangladesh: 'Australians are very good at it; we are learning from them,' Shakib said after the Test about his side's sledging.

When number 11 Josh Hazlewood succumbed lbw to Taijul Islam, Bangladesh had another affirming victory; this time, by 20 runs. With 10–153 in the match alongside his 84, Bangladesh's finest five-day player yet had produced his defining Test moment, even if Australia levelled the series 1–1.

Such performances made Shakib one of Bangladesh's most recognisable figures. 'They used to say that you can't go out regularly when you play for the national team – your life will be different,' he told me. 'I have had that in my mind, that that will be my life.'

It was not a burden that he always relished. Shakib faced several disciplinary problems, including kicking down the stumps in anger after not being given an lbw decision in a domestic match. In 2019, he was banned for a year for failing to report approaches made to him by bookmakers.

Whatever the wider questions, Shakib rose from being a football-loving child, who only played his first game with a hard ball aged 13, to being a great allrounder. Across his 17-year Test career, Shakib averaged 37.77 with the bat and had taken 242 wickets at 31.72. He was Bangladesh's totem, simultaneously fulfilling the role of front-line batter and bowler with a reliability that few in Test history have matched. At times, Shakib was both Bangladesh's leading batter and bowler. In ten Tests, Shakib both scored a 50 and took a five-wicket haul; only Ian Botham managed the feat more often.

Table 9. Number of times players scored a 50 and took a five-wicket haul in the same Test

I.T. Botham	11
S. Al Hasan	10
R. Ashwin	7
R.A. Jadeja	7
R.J. Hadlee	6
M.D. Marshall	5

Only a dearth of Tests – just 71 from 2007 to 2024 – prevented Shakib from acquiring career run and wicket tallies similar to the vaunted

1980s allrounders. He was a good enough batter to hit two centuries in New Zealand, including a 217; and a good enough bowler to take 6–99 in South Africa. Bangladesh still lost all these three Tests.

When the World Test Championship launched in 2019, Bangladesh were among the nine participating teams, recognition that they had leapfrogged Zimbabwe, their predecessors to win Test status. While Bangladesh finished last in the first two editions of the Test Championship, victory in New Zealand, in January 2022, hinted at a side who could now be more competitive beyond Asia.

In August 2024, Bangladesh toured Pakistan. Shortly before the team left for a two-Test series, Bangladesh's prime minister, Sheikh Hasina, resigned and fled the country following a series of violent protests, especially by students, against her regime. Unable to train at home, Bangladesh's team left for Pakistan early.

In the first Test, in Rawalpindi, Pakistan cruised to 448–6. Conscious of the need to leave enough time in the game to take 20 wickets, and remembering Bangladesh's past frailties, Pakistan declared. But the impish Mushfiqur Rahim, just 5 ft 3 in tall, hit 191 – his 11th Test hundred, brimming with his usual forceful square cuts – to secure a 117-run first innings lead. Unexpectedly needing to save the game, Pakistan succumbed to Mehidy Hasan Miraz, who took four wickets, and crashed to a ten-wicket defeat.

Still, Pakistan expected to regain their habitual dominance over Bangladesh in the second and final Test, once again in Rawalpindi. After Pakistan had scored 274, Bangladesh collapsed to a desolate 26–6. Yet, with Mehidy at number eight, Bangladesh had lower-order depth. He combined with Litton Das – now keeper, with Rahim a specialist batsman – for one of Bangladesh's most significant partnerships: 165 runs for the seventh wicket, reducing the first innings deficit to a meagre 12 runs.

Bangladesh's rare Test successes had come with spin. This time would be different. With the Rawalpindi pitch offering unusual assistance, Bangladesh's triumph would be set up by pace. The seamer

Hasan Mahmud and Nahid Rana, whose pace cleared 90 mph – both playing their third Tests – shared nine wickets in Pakistan's second innings; only four years earlier, Nahid had played with a hard ball for the first time. Aptly, Rahim and Shakib were there together at the end of the fourth innings chase of 185 to seal a six-wicket win, clinching the series 2–0. Barring the 2009 win over a West Indies side decimated by strikes, this was Bangladesh's first away series victory against one of the traditional top-eight nations.

Coming against the nation that Bangladesh used to be part of, at a time of political strife and after early tumult in both Tests – turning facing 448–6 declared into a ten-wicket win and a first innings 26–6 into a six-wicket win – elevated the achievement further still. Mehidy dedicated the feat to the student protestors killed.

The ascent has been rickety; given the country's demographics and passion for cricket, the sense of unfulfilled potential in Bangladeshi cricket remains. But, from a nation unable to reach the World Cup, the triumph in Pakistan confirmed Bangladesh's elevation to being an established Test side.

28

HOW UMPIRES AND TECHNOLOGY CHANGED TEST CRICKET

The sight was unmistakable: the batter kicking over his own stumps. In Brisbane in November 1984 Australia's Geoff Lawson trod on his stumps while playing a shot against West Indies' Michael Holding.

Under the laws of the game, players are out 'hit wicket' if they dislodge their own stumps either in the course of playing, or trying to play, a shot or in setting off for their first run. To West Indies' bewilderment, Lawson was given not out. The only possible reason would have been if the bails had been dislodged naturally, by the wind.

In Holding's next over, he bowled a delivery on Lawson's stumps. The batter went back to defend the ball and, in the process, kicked his off stump and knocked off a bail. 'I went a long way back and across,' Lawson says. 'I did feel my heel go on it.' Once again, the umpire reattached the bail yet didn't give Holding out: another blatant decision to go against West Indies.

It crystallised West Indies' frustrations about the umpiring. 'Growing up, you hear all the ideals of Test cricket and you figure that once somebody's out they're just out – that never happened in Australia,' Holding says. 'It was horrible.'

As well as whether batters were given out or not, West Indies sides were also continually distressed by what they perceived as the leniency of umpires to Australians bowling no-balls. 'It's the distance that the Australian bowlers were overstepping that weren't called that opened your eyes to it,' Andy Roberts told me of the 1975/76 tour. 'It was very unfair.' After the tour, captain Clive Lloyd said that umpire Jack Collins 'made too many errors' and 'didn't know the rules'.

Complaining about Australian umpiring was not a new lament. Learie Constantine wrote of West Indies' inaugural tour down under, in 1930/31:

> We suffered badly from umpiring during that tour. I do not think that it is an unfair comment. Our appeals against light were disregarded, but once or twice when things were running our way on a wet wicket, play ended rather suddenly before time. There were some queer decisions about catches; when we got them something was wrong with them, but it was not so the other way round. The English side which toured just before us made the same comments on the umpiring.

It was a view shared by India's Kapil Dev. 'Any team touring Australia has come away convinced the umpiring there inevitably favours the home side,' Dev wrote. He said about one umpire, 'We would have had to entertain some doubt over whether his vision was all right if not for the fact that the vision became suspect only when an Australian batter's dismissal was concerned.' In the 1970/71 Ashes, even as they won 2–0, England did not get a single wicket lbw; the hosts got five.

What was said of the umpiring in Australia could be said of any Test country. Javed Miandad was so convinced of bias during the 1979/80 tour of India that he took to practising against spin without pads – reasoning that, if his legs were hit during a Test, he would be given out lbw.

'I was given out leg-before to a ball from [John] Snow, which clearly pitched outside the leg-stump,' India's Sunil Gavaskar wrote, scathingly, of a decision in the 1971 Oval Test. 'But then you don't question an English umpire's decision, do you? They are supposed to be the best in the world.'

HOW UMPIRES AND TECHNOLOGY CHANGED TEST CRICKET

In Pakistan in 1988, Australia captain Allan Border threatened to pull out of the tour after the first Test in protest at the umpiring:

> What are you going to do if you feel you don't have a chance? It is a conspiracy from the word go. The team will do some rethinking and decide about the future of the tour. If the management insist on completing the tour then we will play under protest.

Imran Khan, Pakistan's captain, claimed that home umpires were biased in Sri Lanka because of political pressure. He believed that Pakistan suffered dubious decisions during their tour in 1986 because the government pressurised umpires to help the hosts, desperate for a victory as a distraction from the country's civil war. That series, Pakistan lost 14 wickets lbw, Sri Lanka only two.

The perception of umpires cheating created bitter feuding. Incandescent after a batter gloved the ball behind yet was ruled not out, Holding kicked down the stumps in New Zealand in 1980. In 1987, Pakistan umpire Shakoor Rana accused England's captain Mike Gatting of cheating by moving the field as the bowler was running in. Gatting then wagged his fingers at Rana, who responded in kind. Rana refused to resume the next day until Gatting apologised; he didn't, so the day's play was abandoned. The Test only resumed when Gatting gave a handwritten apology the next day; the acrimony between two stubborn men remained. 'In Pakistan many men have been killed for the sort of insults he threw at me,' Rana said. 'He's lucky I didn't beat him.'

* * *

In a sense, both Gatting and Rana were victims. Other major sports had long recognised how having officials associated with one team could create bias – or the perception of bias, which could be just as damaging. Test cricket did not consider umpires important enough to haul around the world, instead trusting home boards to select the match officials.

Pakistan were the first nation to advocate a system in line with other sports, with neutral officials. Hosting West Indies in 1986, Pakistan enlisted two Indians to serve in two Tests. Advocating neutral umpires in 1988, Imran Khan observed, 'The modern umpire is caught between two opposing forces – the domestic pressures which encourage error and the technology which reveals them.'

While Pakistan continued to experiment with neutral umpires, the idea was resisted by Australia and England, who thought that standards would suffer if umpires from their own countries were not allowed to officiate at home. In 1992, the International Cricket Council began an experiment with one neutral umpire per Test, which was implemented worldwide from 1994. From the end of 2001, barring a period during the Covid-19 pandemic, both standing umpires in a Test have been neutral, coming from the ICC's Elite Panel of umpires. Officials are promoted to, or relegated from, this group based on assessment of their performances.

The moves to neutral umpires have allowed a question to be answered: what was the impact of using home umpires? Home teams across the world benefited, but more in some countries than others.

Analysing Test matches from 1986 to 2012, a Royal Statistical Society paper found that, with two home umpires, visiting teams were 16 per cent more likely to be given out lbw. With one neutral umpire and one home umpire, visiting teams were 10 per cent more likely to be given out lbw. But with two neutral umpires, visiting teams were now under 1 per cent more likely to be given out lbw.

Which countries benefited the most from home umpires? The answer is unambiguous: Sri Lanka, where away batters were 2.8 times more likely to be out lbw than home batters. In India and Pakistan, away batters were about 1.5 times more likely to be given out lbw, showed research in *The Cricket Statistician* analysing Tests after 1946. In other countries, including Australia, there was little difference in the proportion of lbw dismissals for home and away teams; in England and New Zealand, away players were actually less likely to be given out lbw than home players. Before neutral umpires, captains were less likely to be lbw than other players; since neutral umpires, they have had no such advantage.

During the Covid-19 pandemic, the ICC permitted home umpires once again. Interestingly, the result was home *disadvantage*. Compared to before the pandemic, home teams now got fewer marginal decisions, with decisions that were 'umpire's call' disproportionately favouring away teams, the academics Subhasish M. Chowdhury, Sarah Jewell and Carl Singleton documented. When umpiring on their own sides, the authors wrote, 'Home umpires show evidence of a "reverse" or "overcompensating" bias against the home team for crucial judgment decisions.'

* * *

As neutral umpires were adopted, the ICC also began to use technology to improve decision-making. From 1992, on-field umpires could refer run-out decisions and stumpings; this soon broadened to whether a fielder had taken a catch cleanly. This subtly changed the game, believes Simon Taufel, a Test umpire from 2000 to 2012 and five-time winner of the ICC Umpire of the Year award. 'The big debate at that stage was batters were starting to be given out run out and stumped by millimetres. A lot of people thought that was a very strange way to play the game because it was always benefit of doubt to the batter. Now, you had batters being run out by the smallest of margins.'

The tentative embrace of technology created an odd paradox. Technology would determine relatively trivial matters: whether a fielder had flicked a ball back inside the boundary rope, and so whether the team scored three or four runs from that delivery. But it wouldn't be used in cases that were both more obvious and more important: like when a ball from New Zealand's Andre Adams passed three inches from the bat, yet Andrew Flintoff was given out in 2002. Or when, as he was giving Sri Lanka hope in their run chase, Kumar Sangakkara was given out when a ball deflected off his shoulder in Hobart in 2007. Umpire Rudi Koertzen apologised for the decision after the game.

In Sri Lanka in 2001, the on-field umpire checked whether Russel Arnold had been cleanly caught by Nasser Hussain at slip. He had been, so Arnold was out; the third umpire was not allowed to check whether the batter had actually hit the ball, which he had *not*. So the third umpire was forced to give Arnold out caught, even though replays showed that he shouldn't have been.

Beginning with India's series in Sri Lanka in 2008, a new system was trialled: the Decision Review System. The pressure to make more use of technology came largely from broadcasters, rather than administrators. On the ICC cricket committee, 'we were always of the view that technology needed to be accurate before it should be implemented,' Taufel recalls. 'But the game came under so much scrutiny – the ICC is very conscious and sensitive to public criticism. Once that public criticism became too loud, the decision was made that we're going to have a DRS system whether we like it or not.'

DRS shattered one of cricket's maxims: that the umpire's decision was final. Now, teams could challenge a decision immediately after it was made, by referring it to the third umpire.

Each team was awarded several reviews per innings; eventually the number settled on three per innings, with reviews lost for incorrect challenges. The system was used on an ad hoc series-by-series basis from 2008 to 2016. After 2016, India overcame their initial objections to the system and agreed to use the method too; during India's series against Sri Lanka in 2008, the first to trial DRS, only one of their 15 reviews had been successful.

For borderline lbw decisions, 'umpire's call' was introduced, under which the decision remained with the on-field umpire, but the team did not lose one of their reviews. Umpire's call was partly recognition that the predictive element of ball-tracking was not infallible. 'Opinion is not fact,' Taufel says. 'A predicted path by its own definition is predictive, it's not fact.'

After DRS was introduced, 'the captain of the team had to become a de facto umpire in his own right, trying to judge whether the umpire had got the original decision correct,' wrote England captain Andrew Strauss. His solution was that two out of the bowler, wicketkeeper Matt Prior and Strauss himself needed to be convinced that it was wise to review before the captain would do so; if height was a question, fielders at point or square leg would be consulted too. While bowlers, notably Stuart Broad, tended to be overenthusiastic about the prospects of a review leading to a wicket, Strauss 'was always grateful for the more measured and accurate responses' from Prior.

Technology did not eliminate shocking decisions, if teams had already used up their reviews. At Trent Bridge in the 2013 Ashes, Broad slashed a cut to first slip off Ashton Agar's left-arm spin, yet was not given out.

DRS was expected to increase the amount of accurate decisions, and it did: from 92.8 per cent of Test decisions being right before, 98.9 per cent of decisions have been correct since, according to the ICC. Altogether less anticipated was how DRS fundamentally changed the game.

Counter-intuitively, fast bowlers got a slightly lower proportion of wickets lbw after DRS was introduced than before. The likeliest explanation is that DRS has shown that some batters were previously given out lbw by balls that were bouncing above the stumps, to Taufel's initial surprise. 'The only time I've been caught short, which would constantly blow me away, was the ball would be going over the top and you think, "How is that possible?" A lot more batters are being found to be not out because the ball's going over the top.'

While seamers have slightly suffered, spin bowlers have thrived since DRS was introduced. Throughout most of cricket history, batters have routinely been given not out lbw when, according to modern ball-tracking, the ball would be hitting the stumps. Effectively, umpires used to adjudge lbws according to stumps that were less wide than the stumps actually are but also higher: this helps to explain why the proportion of wickets that seamers and spinners have got since DRS has gone in different directions.

Table 10. Percentage of lbw decisions among bowlers' total dismissals in Test cricket, just before and during DRS era

	Pace	*Spin*
2002–July 2008	17.8%	18.1%
2008–2023	14.4%	21.7%

Before DRS, spinners long bemoaned how, if opponents took a big stride forward, they were given not out lbw regardless of whether the ball was crashing into the stumps. They also loathed how batters played with their pads first, deliberately keeping their bats behind the ball but in such a way as to create the impression that they were playing a shot. Batters struck outside the line of off stump cannot be given out if they are deemed to have been playing a shot.

'If you put out your pad and look like you're a playing a stroke, umpires wouldn't give you out,' recalls Muthiah Muralidaran. Exploiting such umpiring was the basis of the 411-run partnership between Peter May and Colin Cowdrey against West Indies in 1957. In Chennai in 1967, Garry Sobers told the tailender Charlie Griffith to take a big stride forward to every delivery from India's spinners on the final afternoon; Griffith helped Sobers seal a draw.

Under DRS, spinners found umpires far more willing to give lbw decisions. Consider two Indian left-arm spinners: Bishan Bedi, who played from 1967 to 1979, got 6 per cent of his wickets lbw; Ravindra Jadeja, who debuted in 2012, has got 21 per cent lbw.

DRS didn't just lead to decisions being overturned in spin bowlers' favour by the third umpire. It also led to spinners getting more lbws from the on-field umpires, Taufel explains:

> Imagine my world as an umpire where I've got to give someone out lbw, and I reckon it's missing leg or the batter is too far forward for me to have a high degree of confidence that the ball is hitting the stumps, then the broadcaster overlays a ball path that shows that it's hitting. Automatically, people believe what they see. They're not standing where I'm standing, they're not seeing what I'm seeing, and then I've got to almost be in the position of trying to defend the original decision. They've got a piece of overlay illustration that tells people the technology's view that it's actually hitting the stumps.
>
> What you do as an umpire is you start to align your decision-making with what people are seeing on TV. We have to deliver what the game expects. If you've got a broadcast showing people that the ball is hitting the stumps, then what does the game expect?

Off-spinners bowling to left-handers have been perhaps the biggest beneficiaries: 35 per cent of Graeme Swann's dismissals of left-handers were lbw. With DRS, 'Bowling straight was a massive weapon for me,' he said. Swann, like most off-spinners, started to bowl around the wicket far more to left-handers, targeting the stumps. In turn, awareness of the danger of being given out lbw also compelled batters to try and play at more deliveries with their bats, rendering them more vulnerable to being caught by a close-in fielder.

'Umpiring has become a lot more positive,' observes India's off-spinner Ravichandran Ashwin, who played both with and without DRS. 'This in turn has impacted the way the batsman has gone about his business. If you do not have a great defence that is probably dictating you to take that extra aggressive option.' As well as using their bats more, Ashwin has seen batters aim 'to play a lot more front and back decisively than before because you can't get in "no man's land"'. Before DRS, a batter hit pushing forward on the front pad was rarely given out; since DRS, they have been given out far more often in this position.

Batters had to recalibrate their techniques accordingly: defending with their bats in front of their pads, rather than alongside or even behind, or playing back to smother the spin. One prominent example was England's Kevin Pietersen; he could no longer rely on his big stride to prevent him being given out lbw.

'DRS messed about with the way that my technique worked,' Pietersen explains. With umpires more prone to giving lbws, making being hit on the pad more perilous, Pietersen 'couldn't lunge and couldn't hit the ball as much through the leg side. I had to open up the off side and play more with the bat.' Pietersen tinkered with his technique and footwork, especially against left-arm spin, and hit a stunning 186 in Mumbai in 2012. Batters of a new generation effectively had to learn a different way of playing spin to their predecessors.

* * *

In Test cricket's early years, left-handed batters were rare, especially in England. Not until their 120th Test, at Sydney in 1912, did an English left-hander, Frank Woolley, score a century. In 1913, *The Times* even advocated banning left-handers.

While Australia produced some notable left-handers in Test cricket's first 50 years, including Joe Darling and Clem Hill, southpaws remained unusual. In all Test cricket until 1920, 10 per cent of players who batted in the top seven were left-handers, in line with the global average for the number of left-handers. Such rarity, indeed, might help to explain why left-handers came to be described as 'elegant' far more than their more mundane right-handed counterparts.

In sports with small reaction times, being left-handed is an advantage, the academic Florian Loffing documented. Essentially, playing in the opposite way to the majority of players provides an asymmetrical advantage. Left-handed batters will normally face right-arm bowlers, but right-arm bowlers will normally bowl to right-handers; at all levels of the sport, bowlers can struggle to be as accurate when bowling to left-handers.

There is another reason why left-handers fare better: many aren't really left-handers at all. A striking number of the finest Test left-handers, including Graeme Pollock, Brian Lara, Clive Lloyd, Adam Gilchrist, David Gower and Alastair Cook, are right-handers: they are top-hand dominant, batting with their right hand above their left. Such a method has been shown to provide better control of the bat swing. Professional cricketers are 7.1 times more likely to be top-hand dominant than amateur players, according to research in 2016. The advantage holds even when those who are left-handed switch to batting right-handed. Historically, the culture of batting top-hand dominant has been stronger in Australia than anywhere else, which might be a small factor in the country's cricket success. Nine of the 17 players to score 5,500 Test runs for Australia are top-hand dominant; eight of those are right-handers who switched to batting left-handed.

Over the 20th century, batting left-handed became more common, stabilising at just above 20 per cent of top-order left-handers. From the mid-1990s, the number leapt again: 29 per cent of all players who batted in the top seven in the 2000s were left-handers, and 33 per cent in the 2010s.

This increase was directly attributable to changes in umpiring and DRS, former England analyst Nathan Leamon and his co-author Ben Jones argue in *Hitting Against the Spin*. Better umpiring meant that left-handers became far less likely to be given out lbw when the ball pitched outside their leg stump: a typical angle, when right-handed bowlers bowled over the wicket against them. This particularly benefited left-handers facing right-arm seam. Between 2010 and 2024, the 20 highest-scoring opening batters in Tests included 11 left-handers, including six of the top seven. In this period, left-handed openers averaged three runs more than right-handed openers. Universally, the best advice for any aspiring Test opener was: bat left-handed.

Once again, Test cricket provided a neat case study in unintended consequences. Neutral umpires, and then DRS, were introduced to improve the quality of decision-making, and they did so. They also created two curious beneficiaries: spinners, especially finger spinners, and left-handed batters. Test cricket's umpiring revolution not only improved the quality of officiating; it also changed how the game was played.

29

TEST CRICKET IN EXILE

On 3 March 2009, Sri Lanka's players boarded the team bus in Lahore. It was the morning of the third day of their Test at the Gaddafi Stadium; after Sri Lanka had made 606 all out, Pakistan were 110–1 on a flat pitch. A dull draw awaited.

As the bus reached Liberty Roundabout, under a kilometre from the stadium, players heard a scream: 'Get down.' It was from Tillakaratne Dilshan, who had made 145 the previous day. Dilshan was sitting just behind the driver, Mohammad Khalil; he was the first player to see that the team were under attack. Twelve militant jihadist gunmen ambushed the team, using AK-47 assault rifles, grenades and rocket launchers.

As the gunmen approached, shooting bullets through the glass windows, players and team officials scrambled to the bus floor to evade the fire; several were soaked in blood. With a flat tyre, and helped by Dilshan sometimes popping his head up to give him directions, Khalil drove the final half-kilometre to the ground.

As the bus hurried away, Kumar Sangakkara observed Tharanga Paranavitana clutching at his bloody chest:

> I see him and I think: 'Oh my God, you were out first ball, run out the next innings and now you have been shot. What a terrible first tour.' It is strange how clear your thinking is. I did not see my life flash by. There was no insane panic. There was absolute clarity and awareness of what was happening at that moment.

After being shot at for several minutes, the bus reached the ground. Players were hastily taken to the physio room. Seven players, plus assistant coach Paul Farbrace, were injured by bullets or shrapnel. Ajantha Mendis had between 16 and 20 pieces of metal taken out of his head; Paranavitana, hit in the chest, and Thilan Samaraweera, shot in the thigh, suffered particularly dangerous injuries. Officials, who were travelling separately in a small white minivan, were even more exposed than the players: match referee Chris Broad had his white shirt covered in blood; Ahsan Raza, the fourth umpire, was shot in the back.

Six policemen, a driver escorting match officials and a traffic warden were killed in the attacks. Incredibly, none of the players or match officials died.

Refusing to get into a bus again, Sri Lanka's players remained at the Gaddafi Stadium for five hours, while emergency travel plans were finalised. The team were picked up by two helicopters, which landed on the pitch; they flew 15 minutes to an air force base, where they got a flight back to Colombo. Many players remained at hospital there for several days. The Test was abandoned.

Throughout its history, Test cricket has been played against a backdrop of political and security crises. On the day that England arrived in India in October 1984, Prime Minister Indira Gandhi was assassinated. After leaving for Sri Lanka during the two weeks of mourning, England returned. The tour was almost cancelled again after Percy Norris, the Deputy High Commissioner of Western India, was assassinated in Mumbai, only hours after taking the England team for a night out. England received safety guarantees and continued with the tour – losing the first Test in Mumbai but then recording an unlikely 2–1 victory. In England in 2005, Australia held a series of meetings about security following the 7/7 terror attacks in London. 'If another bomb did go off here in England, there would be serious questions asked about the tour,' Jason Gillespie said at the time. 'I know a lot of guys are quite nervous.'

Security concerns during the civil war meant that Sri Lanka didn't host a Test from 1987 to 1992. Before their second series back at home, a suicide bomb exploded 50 metres from the New Zealand team's hotel in Colombo; one Test was cancelled and five players withdrew, but the tour continued. In May 2002, another bomb exploding near New Zealand's hotel, in Karachi, led to the final Test of their series against Pakistan being cancelled. Later, in March 2019, Bangladesh's team were on their way to a mosque in Christchurch for Friday prayers, and ran back to the Hagley Oval as they heard shootings, by right-wing extremists, at the mosque. The team rushed home, with the final Test cancelled.

Yet, outside world wars, there was no precedent for Pakistan's fate after the 2009 attacks. It would be another decade before Pakistan played a Test at home again.

* * *

The landscape of Pakistan Test cricket swiftly became grimmer still. Already unable to play at home, Pakistan were hit by a new crisis during their series in England in 2010: the spot-fixing scandal, which led to bans for captain Salman Butt and fast bowlers Mohammad Amir and Mohammad Asif. The chaos of the era was such that Butt was one of four men to captain in the previous 13 Tests, a period of just 13 months. After losing in England, Pakistan had not won any of their last nine series. Amid rumours of further corruption, for several years after, players were subjected to curfews and tight monitoring. 'We lost the freedom of going out,' says Azhar Ali, who made his debut in 2010.

When the spot-fixing scandal broke at Lord's, Misbah-ul-Haq was at home. Not selected to tour England, Misbah's Test career looked at an end: he had played 19 matches, averaging 33.60, and was 36 years old. After being dropped earlier in the year, he contemplated retirement.

In a country in thrall to the idea of the young prodigy, Misbah's career was the antithesis. Hailing from Mianwali, a cricketing backwater in Punjab that is also the home to Imran Khan's ancestors, Misbah was a tape-ball cricket star and a district snooker champion. Rather than try and become a professional cricketer, Misbah studied for an MBA in Lahore. After getting a job at a textiles company, he made his first-class debut aged 24. Two years later, he made his Test debut, but played only spasmodically over his first nine years in international cricket. During this period, he honed his leadership skills in domestic cricket.

When Misbah was appointed, 'I was nervous,' he recalled. 'I hadn't proved myself at that level in international cricket. I'd been in and out of the team. Captaincy wasn't a big issue – first I had to prove myself as a player too. Those were the worries, but then I just thought: "This is an opportunity. Why don't I just take it and give it my best shot?"' The sight of Misbah fielding at short leg, traditionally the position reserved for junior players, encapsulated how his leadership style eschewed ego.

Misbah's first Test back, in November 2010, also saw Younis Khan recalled. Younis had been banned by the board for his alleged role in 'infighting' during the 2009/10 tour of Australia. The first Test of the Misbah era showed what Pakistan had been missing: he and Younis added an unbroken 186 on the final day to salvage a draw against South Africa in Dubai. Here were the first hints of something emerging from the debris of the worst 18 months in Pakistan Test history.

Pace bowlers have generally been Pakistan's heroes. Under Misbah, Pakistan embraced spin like never before. The spot-fixing scandal had deprived Pakistan of their two best seamers. The UAE, established as Pakistan's home-from-home, was the ideal location to adopt this new spin strategy. Misbah was content to focus on bowling economically, trusting that his spinners could still take regular wickets without attacking recklessly. The first indication of how lethal this tactic could be came when England visited in January 2012.

In the UAE, England arrived as the world's number one side. England stuck with three pace bowlers and one spinner, their normal balance. Pakistan adopted a very different approach, pairing the off-spinning mystery of Saeed Ajmal with classical slow left-armer Abdur Rehman; allrounder Mohammad Hafeez provided extra off spin.

On the first day in Dubai, Hafeez was whisked into the attack after five overs; from his third ball, Alastair Cook edged a cut behind. Now, Ajmal took over. At the time, Ajmal was the best spin bowler in the world, renowned for his doosra, which spun away from the right-hander with no discernible change in his action from his standard off break. It was an era when the ICC were lax on bowlers suspected of breaching the 15-degree limit; Ajmal was eventually found to extend his elbow by around 40 degrees. Bowlers from elsewhere also extended their elbows markedly, yet could not emulate Ajmal's results.

Often pausing as he was about to release the ball, Ajmal showed England his full repertoire. Within ten balls of coming on, he had dismissed Andrew Strauss, Ian Bell and Kevin Pietersen: a wicket apiece with his three main deliveries – first with a quicker arm ball that skidded on; next the doosra, which Bell prodded behind, utterly deceived; and then the off break, which spun past Pietersen's groping pad. There was little turn on offer on the opening morning, yet Ajmal still bewitched England; before the series, in a manner evoking Shane Warne, he pretended to have devised another variation – 'the teesra' – with teammates playing along with the ruse. He finished with 7–55 as England were bowled out for 192. After Pakistan secured a lead of 146, Ajmal snared another three wickets; Rehman took three too as England were thrashed by ten wickets inside three days.

The template for the series was set. England were bowled out for under 200 four times in six innings. Chasing 144 to win in the second Test, England crashed to 72 all out; Rehman took 6–25, with players often flummoxed by his arm ball while playing for turn. 'We don't have that extravagant spin you see in India,' Ajmal explained. 'We varied our pace slightly or spun it a little more. When England weren't scoring, then we knew they were ours.'

After England bowled Pakistan out for 99 in the final Test in Dubai, the spin pair shared another 14 wickets; in between, Azhar and Younis scored centuries to ensure a 3–0 whitewash. Ajmal and Rehman shared 43 wickets at a combined 15.60. It was a microcosm of why Pakistan became so formidable in their adopted home: under Misbah in the UAE, they claimed 61 per cent of wickets with spin.

Misbah led Pakistan in nine Test series in UAE. They were undefeated, and won five series; after he retired, in 2017, Pakistan lost two out of three series in the UAE.

'Dubai suited us very nicely,' says Azhar, a fixture in the top three throughout the Misbah years. 'I would have loved to bat more in Pakistan because the tracks here are more suited to batting. But for winning Test matches, those tracks suited our bowling attack more because we had good spinners.

'When you play against Australia and England, you want to have turning tracks. But you don't find them in Pakistan as easily as you get in Dubai or Abu Dhabi.' Pakistan settled into the tempo of UAE Test cricket. 'The run rates have always been on the slower side because of the slow nature of the pitches,' Azhar explains. 'You had to be patient.'

* * *

Pakistan has known many arduous tours down under over the years, yet seldom have they been gutted in quite the manner that Australia were in the UAE in 2014. Over the two Tests, Pakistan averaged 76.33 per wicket during the series, Australia just 25.65.

Early in their run chase in the second Test in Abu Dhabi, David Warner hit a boundary: 'Only 595 more to get,' he told the close-in fielders. To Azhar, 'What Australia does to us in Australia, we were doing there to them.'

The 2–0 victory highlighted Pakistan's regeneration. Without Ajmal, who was suspended while his action was investigated, Pakistan discovered leg-spinner Yasir Shah, who took 12 wickets in the series, showing off his wonderful googly.

More than anything, the win was secured through the bats of Younis and Misbah, with Azhar in support. In the first Test in Dubai, Younis's twin centuries set up the game; Misbah chipped in with 69 in his only innings. In the second Test in Abu Dhabi, Younis's 213 set up Pakistan's imperious 570–6 declared. Azhar and Misbah also scored centuries themselves. In the second innings, Azhar and Misbah scored their second hundreds in the match. While Azhar's was made at his customary sedate tempo, Misbah showed his range. Repeatedly launching spin and pace alike down the ground, he thrashed his second century in the match off only 56 balls; at the time, it was the equal fastest in Test history, tying with Viv Richards's record. The tuk-tuk had become a Ferrari.

For all the differences in their style – at number four, Younis tended to maintain the same breezy tempo; at number five, Misbah was more anarchic, comfortable in first gear or fifth, but rarely in between – they had an extraordinary record in tandem. Batting together in Tests, Younis and Misbah added 3,213 runs at an average of 68. Only two other pairs to add more together in partnership – Justin Langer and Ricky Ponting; and Jack Hobbs and Herbert Sutcliffe – average more.

During the Misbah years, both he and Younis were at their best with the bat. As captain, Misbah averaged 51.39, almost 20 more than when in the ranks. Younis, who turned 33 shortly after Misbah took over, and also feared that he was now considered too old for Test cricket, hit 18 centuries under the new skipper.

Like Misbah, Younis was born in an area with little cricket pedigree – Mardan, in Khyber Pakhtunkhwa, in the country's northwest. He moved to a major centre, Karachi, as a child. Unable to break into Karachi's first-class side, Younis returned to Mardan. He often practised on potholed tennis courts with a hard ball, training himself to cope with uneven bounce.

Younis converted his gifts into a record that gives him a strong case to pip Javed Miandad, Hanif Mohammad and Inzamam-ul-Haq for the tag of Pakistan's best Test batter. His final average, 52.05, is only decimal points below Miandad and Mohammad Yousuf; Younis's 10,099 Test runs is comfortably a national record. Younis's adaptability was such that he averaged over 50 in Australia, England and India; he scored centuries in all 11 countries that he played in, a record.

The greatest indication of his quality, perhaps, was Younis's relish for the final innings of the match. Younis was the first Test player to hit five centuries in the fourth innings. One came in defeat; three helped to clinch draws. His final effort was a classic. Arriving at 13–2 in Pallekele on a wicket offering unusual seam movement for Sri Lanka, Younis was confronted with a target of 377, comfortably the highest of the match, in the series decider in 2015. He responded with a clinical 171 not out, showcasing his prowess sweeping and using his feet against spin. Misbah, naturally, was with him when victory was sealed. The two even retired in tandem, after helping Pakistan win their first series in West Indies in 2017.

* * *

After the mid-1990s peaks of Wasim Akram and Waqar Younis, the next outstanding Pakistan Test team came under Inzamam-ul-Haq. This side was built around a middle order of Inzamam, Younis Khan and Mohammad Yousuf and the contrasting pace pair of the express Shoaib Akhtar and the canny Mohammad Asif, complemented by Danish Kaneria's leg spin. This group squared a series in India in 2005, then recorded stirring home victories over England and India in 2005/06. But ultimately, Inzamam returned 11 wins to go with 11 defeats as Test captain: an underwhelming return for a side of such talent.

Ostensibly, Misbah's side from 2010 to 2017 was far less impressive: Pakistan's best pace bowler in these years was left-armer Junaid Khan, who averaged an unremarkable 31.73. And yet Misbah, inscrutable and with a forensic eye for opponents' batting foibles, has the most Test wins of any Pakistan captain: the country won 26 and lost 19 of his Tests in charge. If Misbah's team is less celebrated than some with less impressive records, it is partly because its style ran counter to the romantic view of earlier Pakistan teams. His side's default batting tempo was more attritional; in the field, he relied far less on pace, and generally preferred control to chasing wickets. Leg spin was a shared feature with previous Pakistan sides: Yasir Shah took 116 wickets from just 17 Tests in the UAE, a rate of 6.8 per Test.

In 56 Tests, Misbah never led Pakistan at home. Playing in the UAE meant that Pakistan's cricketers spent virtually all of each year away from their home country. 'Living every day away from our country, without family and friends – it's really difficult,' Misbah once explained. 'I see my mother and sister only once a year.'

Exile was equally unwelcome for the Pakistan Cricket Board. Every time Pakistan played in the UAE, they had to pay $50,000 per day to rent the stadiums; at $200–250 per person a night, hotels were twice as expensive as at home – and Pakistan needed to pay for themselves too. Overall, staging cricket in the UAE is estimated to have cost the board over $100 million. Most importantly, it deprived the next generation of the chance to see Pakistan play Test cricket at home. Some days in the Emirates played out in front of crowds of under 100.

Yet, for all the joy of routing England and Australia in the UAE – to go with the twin whitewashes in 2012 and 2014, England were beaten 2–0 when they returned in 2015 – it was elsewhere that Misbah enjoyed his crowning glory.

In 2016, Misbah considered retirement once again. By now he was 42, the oldest Test cricketer in the world. Before their tour to England, Pakistan had no Tests for eight months. Rather than retire,

Misbah arranged a two-week army boot camp for the squad in Abbottabad. Here, players had to ask permission whenever they needed the toilet or to have a drink of water: they had to do push-ups before leaving, then another ten when they returned. In between their other exercise, players did about 400 push-ups a day. At the end of the camp, Azhar recalls, 'we promised them: whenever someone takes five wickets or someone scores 100, we will do ten push-ups.'

Misbah was the first to make good on this vow. At Lord's in the opening Test, he became the oldest Test centurion since 1934, celebrating with ten press-ups on the outfield, in homage to the fitness camp. The four-Test series ended back in London, with Pakistan now 2–1 down. At The Oval, Younis arrived at 127–3 in response to England's 328, with his form being questioned. His 218, marked by regal driving, underpinned a total of 542; Yasir's five wickets, zipping the ball off the pitch, sealed a ten-wicket win. It was Pakistan's sixth consecutive undefeated series.

On their previous tour to England, in 2010, Pakistan had left in disgrace. They ended the 2016 tour with a triumphant lap of honour; they clinched a 2–2 series draw on Independence Day. A week later, an International Cricket Council press release confirmed Pakistan's ascent to being the world's number one Test side. While the achievement was only fleeting, it was a testament to the side's consistency under Misbah.

Pakistan hadn't merely survived during their exile; they had thrived. In December 2019, a decade after the horrors of Lahore, Pakistan played a home Test once more. After 75 Tests, Azhar finally played in front of his own fans. 'I thought I'd never play a Test in Pakistan, so that was a moment – that was emotional, thanking God that at least I played one Test match at home.'

30

THE PARABLE OF WEST INDIES

Few cricketers have ever taken guard under as much pressure as Brian Lara on the evening of 13 March 1999.

The match situation in the second Test in Jamaica was onerous enough. Lara walked out with West Indies 5–2 in their first innings, in response to Australia's 256.

Yet Lara's challenge transcended the match. After a pay dispute followed by a 5–0 whitewash in South Africa, the board had put Lara's captaincy – which was always divisive – on probation for the first two Tests. West Indies' ignominious collapse to 51 all out in the first Test, crashing to a 312-run defeat, meant the second Test in Jamaica loomed as his last in charge. As he walked out to bat, Lara was greeted by boos: the crowd were furious that he, rather than the Jamaican Courtney Walsh, was captain.

Lara was weighed down by 'the embarrassment of South Africa, the embarrassment of the first Test match', he later told me. He hadn't scored a Test century for 21 months, or made one as captain; he was also battling a chipped bone in his right elbow. At the toss, Lara told his counterpart Steve Waugh, 'This could be the last time I'll be doing this.'

From his first years, Lara was used to defying the odds. Before becoming the Prince of Trinidad, Lara grew up as the tenth of 11 children. He is one example of the little-sibling effect: those with older siblings have significantly more chance of becoming elite athletes.

Younger and smaller than those he played with, Lara had to compete through other means. 'I was playing with my bigger brothers from a very early age and I felt that that was huge in my development.'

In street cricket, Lara learned his distinctive backlift: lifting his bat so high that it was vertical, in a manner similar to Garry Sobers. 'It might have been even more exaggerated when I was a teenager... It's just a part of how I played and happily no one actually tried to change that.'

When West Indies resumed on day two in Jamaica in 1999, they were a perilous 37–4, with Lara seven not out. Australia possessed an outstanding attack: pace bowlers Glenn McGrath and Jason Gillespie, and the leg-spinners Shane Warne and Stuart MacGill. Lara began solidly, and then unfurled a stunning counter-attack. Against both Warne and MacGill, Lara waltzed down the wicket, and launched sixes over long-on.

'You're lying if you say that you're not nervous,' he recalled. 'My batting was based around understanding that it was a period of survival. I did carry a nervous energy, as a lot of successful sportsmen will tell you – you have to be nervous.'

His 213 transformed a match that looked lost and ensured that he retained the captaincy. It also kept alive the very idea that West Indies could still defeat any Test team. 'The pressure that I was under, the state of mind that I was in and what that innings brought out of me showed me how strong I was as an individual,' Lara told me.

Tony Cozier, the voice of Caribbean cricket, wrote, 'In its context, with due deliberations and apologies to George Headley, Sir Garry Sobers and a host of other greats, I cannot identify a single innings by any West Indian batsman in our 71 years of Test cricket of such significance.'

Yet Lara surpassed the innings in the very next Test, in Barbados. After Australia scored 490 and reduced West Indies to 98–6 – Lara made eight – the hosts fought back. Opener Sherwin Campbell and wicketkeeper Ridley Jacobs helped West Indies recover to 329. It was still a deficit of 161, but Courtney Walsh's 5–39 led a stirring bowling performance. Australia were all out for 146 in their second innings, setting West Indies 308 to win: highly improbable, not quite impossible.

On the fifth morning at Kensington Oval, with West Indies 85–3 overnight, Lara was undefeated on two. He couldn't sleep. At 5 a.m., he called up an old school friend, Nicholas Gomez, who was in Barbados. Gomez was at a nightclub. But when he got Lara's call he knew to come.

A few weeks earlier, Gomez had talked Lara through his slump; now, he was needed again. In Lara's room, they watched footage of two of his most devastating innings against Australia: his double hundreds at Sydney in 1993, and in Jamaica a fortnight earlier. 'We watched the 277, we rewatched the 213 in Jamaica and worked out a plan of "How are we gonna score these runs? Who am I gonna attack and defend against?"'

Inspired by Michael Jordan – Gomez gave him a book detailing his preparation for basketball games before the series – Lara became a devotee of visualisation. 'If you do it, you can sort of feel it when you go out into the middle,' he recalled. 'The majority of the time it was a mental war, coming up against an Australian attack... A lot of young players don't understand how to put together an innings in your mind before you actually do it with the bat.'

In front of his mirror that morning in Barbados, Lara planned the innings before he played it. 'They were going to throw the fast bowlers against me in the first hour of play, but the minute that the spin came on I was going to attack. If it's Stuart MacGill, if it's Shane Warne, I was going to go on the attack because I wanted them to bring the fast bowlers back again while they were tired.'

On the fifth morning, Lara used his feet to hit MacGill for three fours in his first over. His assault on the two leg-spinners – pulling Warne for six over midwicket, onto the roof, launching him over long-on and playing several delectable late cuts – showcased why he was among the finest ever players of spin. He averaged 82.52 against spin in Tests – averaging similarly against even Warne and Muthiah Muralidaran – scoring at a strike rate of 65.

This prowess was first developed in soft-ball cricket, normally played with a tennis ball, in Trinidad; the island has a rich history of slow bowlers. 'You can chuck it into the pitch, turn it a mile . . . That was a huge part of understanding how to play spin from an early age.

'A lot of people try to read off the pitch – I think that's a bit too late. I'm trying to understand what's coming out of the bowler's hand.'

On the fifth day in Barbados, attacking MacGill and Warne forced Australia to give McGrath a gruelling workload: he bowled 44 overs, after delivering 33 in the first innings. Lara shared a 133-run stand with Jimmy Adams.

'I was very focused – very, very focused,' Lara told me. 'A little bit of panic seeped in when we lost Jimmy Adams and we lost two more wickets very quickly at that stage, and I was left with Curtly Ambrose.' West Indies had slipped from 238–5 to 248–8, still 60 shy of victory.

'You're ten boundaries away from winning. And if you can pick up a couple of boundaries every over, hopefully Ambrose could survive – we're going to put them under pressure again. So I did not lose the belief.'

With seven runs to win, Lara flashed Jason Gillespie behind; Ian Healy spilled the catch. One run later, Ambrose was dismissed, bringing out Walsh, a notorious rabbit. He walked out against Gillespie with three balls of the over still to face; this became four, as Gillespie bowled a no-ball. After each delivery Lara went down the pitch to confer with Walsh. Jamming his bat down on one Gillespie yorker, Walsh just about survived the over.

In the next over, from McGrath, Lara turned down a single from the fourth ball. The following ball, the fifth of the over, Lara levelled the scores with a hook for one. Walsh had one more ball to survive; the captains, past and present, had a long discussion and embraced. With three slips, a gully, a short leg and a leg gully prowling, Walsh left the ball safely alone.

Now, with the Barbados crowd chanting his name, Lara thrashed the first ball of Gillespie's next over through extra cover. He ran, with his arms aloft, as fans spilled onto Kensington Oval. His 153 not out, in an innings when no one else passed 38, clinched a one-wicket victory. In consecutive matches Lara had played two of the finest Test innings of all time. Even more than breaking the world-record score twice – 375 against England in Antigua in 1994, and 400 not out against the same opponents at the same ground a decade later – these two performances were Lara's signatures.

Yet they would come to take on a different meaning: as the last flickering of a great team. Lara's efforts to seal a 2–2 draw in 1999 – despite his blistering 82-ball century, Australia won the final Test in Antigua – suggested that West Indies could still compete with the best.

Over the 1990s, Australia and West Indies shared a captivating rivalry. Both sides won nine Tests against each other, with two series wins each before the drawn series in 1999. From 2000 until 2025, Australia won 24 Tests against West Indies and lost just two. It was a microcosm of West Indies' decline.

From Lord's 2000 until January 2025, West Indies won just 24 out of 189 Tests against other teams considered among the top eight Test sides – Australia, England, India, New Zealand, Pakistan, Sri Lanka and South Africa – and lost 117. Against these sides away, West Indies won five games, and lost 72, in 97 Tests.

* * *

'All of us are very clear, the issue of the governance and structure of West Indies cricket – this is the fundamental issue,' Grenada's prime minister, Dr Keith Mitchell, said in 2015, speaking as chair of the Caribbean Community's Cricket Governance Subcommittee. Caricom advocated the immediate dissolution of the 'antiquated' and 'anachronistic' West Indies Cricket Board, which has essentially been unreformed since 1927. The Cricket Governance Subcommittee detailed how both the WICB and its members, the six territorial boards of Trinidad & Tobago, Barbados, Jamaica, Guyana, Leeward Islands and Windward Islands, 'do not respect the basic tenets of good governance'. This was merely one of several reports to identify how bad governance has damaged West Indies and to advocate the creation of a wholly new governing body.

Rather than a streamlined board and independent directors, the WICB's six members have two votes each. These representatives have often been led by parochialism – what is best for their specific country – rather than the larger interests of Caribbean cricket.

Here lies the genesis for much of what has afflicted West Indies Test cricket: the short-termism. The lack of investment in infrastructure, detectable in how pitches have become anaemic. The often-toxic relations between players and board, which led to the side pulling out of a tour to India in 2014 midway through because of a contractual dispute. The failure to create a men's academy until 2022. The lack of pragmatism in adjusting to the T20 ecosystem. The uncertainty over what, exactly, happened to the $100m that West Indies received from the International Cricket Council for hosting the 2007 World Cup.

When the Test side dominated, 'West Indies and territorial boards didn't do enough to nurture the talent,' Curtly Ambrose told me. 'They sat back and believed that we will forever produce great cricketers. Other nations put things in place – academies, whatever they've got to do. So when guys leave the international scene, other guys can step up. We didn't do that.'

Even had West Indies been run better, the side would still have been unable to escape an unwanted reality. 'They could have thought about doing a few other things but they never had money to do some of the things that other countries did,' observes Michael Holding. 'So to a degree you could say, "Oh, they didn't forward-plan." You need money to plan. You need money to put things in place.'

THE PARABLE OF WEST INDIES

While West Indies' decline owes much to unique circumstances in the islands, in a broader sense their fate also doubles as a parable. Financial clout has become more important than ever in determining who wins in Test cricket.

In the 1990s, Test cricket possessed more strength than ever before or since. At various points in the decade, before official rankings were introduced, four sides – Australia, Pakistan, South Africa and West Indies – could mount a claim to being the world's number one side. Below them, India were outstanding at home; England enjoyed victories home and away against the best teams in the world; Sri Lanka had Muthiah Muralidaran to complement some dashing batters; New Zealand were characteristically doughty. Even Zimbabwe, the lowest-ranked of the nine Test nations at the time, had a nucleus of solid players.

Such competitiveness was not a coincidence. Inequalities between countries in how much they could invest in their teams were far smaller than in later decades, observes Mike Atherton, England captain from 1993 to 1998. Before the proliferation of T20 leagues, only a few players – generally from Zimbabwe – missed Tests to play in more lucrative domestic cricket overseas.

'Everybody's focus was playing Test cricket – you couldn't really make a good living as a cricketer unless you played Tests,' Atherton recalls. 'It was just a much simpler time where the focus was very much in one direction.'

As money surged into cricket from the 1990s, the wealthiest countries sought to divide it up less equitably. Until 2001, revenue for international fixtures was divided between the home board and visiting boards, who would also receive a fee for touring; the amount would be negotiated individually, as a fixed sum, but typically equated to about 20 per cent of the home board's earnings from the series. While West Indies lost money from most, if not all, home series, their cricket was effectively bankrolled by regular fees they earned to visit the game's wealthiest nations. From 1979 to 1997, West

Indies toured Australia, for Tests, one-day internationals or both, ten times in 18 years.

From 2001, the system changed. The new Future Tours Programme provided boards with more certainty of fixtures. But this was accompanied by a significant change that damaged poorer nations. Instead of a fee for away teams, hosts now got everything, but agreed to undertake a similar reciprocal tour in return. In theory, the new system was fair; in reality, it only was if the two nations were from similar-sized economies. West Indies complained about the new model and 'wanted to maintain the status quo of tour fees', recalls Malcolm Speed, who later become ICC chief executive.

The changes came into force just as the worth of broadcasting rights was exploding, fuelled by a boom in satellite-television revenue, principally in Australia, England and India. In practice, richer nations came to earn many times more than poorer teams from the reciprocal arrangement. From 2020 to 2024, England earned £220m a year from their broadcasting contract; West Indies earned just £20m. Effectively, when the two sides hosted each other for series of equal length, at home and away, England earned over ten times more revenue over the two series. With West Indies now much less attractive opponents, they played the richest nations less, further undermining their earning capacity. 'In the 1990s, the financial differences between West Indies and England and Australia would have been minimal,' Atherton reflects. 'Now they are very significant.'

From 2007 to 2008, Holding was on the ICC cricket committee. His suggestion that away teams once again receive fees was ignored, he told me:

> I said the West Indies' population has been five million for decades – it does not grow because there's constant migration. We have no international organisations or companies in the Caribbean that will sponsor West Indies cricket because every island has its own thing.

I explained that in the meeting. You know what the general manager of the ICC [David Richardson, the future chief executive] said?: 'Whose fault is that?' When he said that, I said, 'Well, we have no chance. They're not interested in helping West Indies cricket or helping the poorer nations.'

You always hear them saying, 'Oh, it's so sad West Indies are so weak.' You tell me one thing that the ICC has done to try and balance the equation. They have done absolutely nothing – they have talked.

By the early 2020s, Tests that did not feature any of Australia, England or India typically lost $500,000 net for the hosting board. In the Caribbean, the costs of moving teams around different islands meant that these losses could be far more. In 2018, West Indies hosted Sri Lanka for three Tests and Bangladesh for two Tests, three ODIs and three T20Is. With under $1m in broadcasting revenue for the two series, and scant gate receipts, Cricket West Indies lost $22m net from the two series.

While the amounts that boards earned from their home series diverged, the ICC divided their cash less equitably too. Until 2015, all ten Full Members received the same amount of central funding; this money was largely the proceeds generated by global events. This formula inhibited the game's global development: the ten Full Members shared 75 per cent of ICC profits, while the 90-or-so Associate Members shared 25 per cent. In 2012, the independent Woolf Report slammed the ICC as a body whose 'interest in enhancing the global development of the game is secondary'. It advocated reducing the dominance of larger countries on the board; adopting the principle of one board member, one vote; and revising the distribution model, with amounts distributed to members on a needs basis.

The Woolf Report's recommendations were not merely ignored. Instead, Australia, England and India, the three wealthiest cricket nations, did the exact opposite of what it advocated. They pushed through an even less egalitarian revenue-distribution model, which came into effect in 2015. Through a combination of threats – the prospect of the three nations abandoning the rest of the world game altogether – and promises of lucrative tours, other Full Members eventually acquiesced. Narayanaswami Srinivasan, who became BCCI president in 2011 and the inaugural ICC chairman in 2014, orchestrated the 'Big Three' takeover. One representative of another Test nation felt 'sick' voting through the changes. Another insider told me of Srinivasan:

> He, more than anyone, believes that cricket is a business, needs to be run as a business and that its outcomes are business-focused and India should have their due. The attitude is, 'We were kept down for decades so why should we not have our time in the sun?'

Rather than build a more equitable system than that which Australia and England oversaw until losing their ICC veto in 1993, India essentially reproduced the old order. The changes were denounced by Transparency International as antithetical to good governance.

The new revenue-distribution formula, nebulously calculated, gave the Big Three the most ICC cash, on the basis that they generated the most revenue. This was an act of reverse Robin Hood-ism – taking from the smaller Test nations, and especially the Associate countries, to give to those who were already the wealthiest. It also ran contrary to the example of FIFA which, for all its corruption, has helped to grow football around the world through giving all member nations, regardless of size, equal basic funding every year. While the ICC formula has been tweaked since, the principle has remained. From 2024 to 2027, India will receive around $230m a year from the ICC: 38.5 per cent of total profits. England receive the next most: $41m a year, 6.9 per cent. West Indies receive $27.5m, 4.6 per cent of profits. The 96 Associate Members earn just 11.2 per cent combined.

Such structural changes compounded the impact of the new cricket economy. The IPL, which launched in 2008, instantly transformed the sport's economics: players could earn more in two months than in a year of international cricket. Indian cricket now generated far more cash from domestic than international games. Media rights for the 2023–27 IPL fetched $6bn, making the sports league the second-most valuable on a per game basis after the American NFL. Rights for India's home matches in the corresponding five-year period fetched $750m – just one-eighth as much as those for the IPL.

Even compared to other members of Test cricket's middle class, West Indies were uniquely vulnerable to the sport's changing landscape. First, because of the array of T20 talent that the region produced: West Indies won the T20 World Cup in 2012 and 2016. Trinidad & Tobago, with a population of 1.5 million, developed players including Sunil Narine, Kieron Pollard, Dwayne Bravo, Samuel Badree and Nicholas Pooran. In previous generations, such talent would have pursued Test cricket; among those T20 giants, only Bravo played more than six Tests.

West Indies' other particular problem was bad luck. The IPL season clashed with the traditional Caribbean home summer. Until 2017, West Indies played home Tests during the IPL; in almost every case, players opted for the better-paid option. In previous generations, English league cricket and county cricket allowed Caribbean stars to earn amounts that West Indies could not provide. These commitments, barring a few exceptions, were generally compatible with playing Tests; representing half a dozen T20 franchises every year is not. National boards receive a payment from the IPL equating to 10 per cent of the player's salary per season; West Indies, and others, argued that this didn't reflect the cost of developing such cricketers. Even inbound tours from India were less lucrative than other sides. West Indies has the worst time zone for the Indian market out of all Test nations – another handicap for a penurious region.

Jason Holder, West Indies Test captain from 2015 until 2021, long argued for a minimum wage in Test cricket. 'The only way you can keep players from moving on to domestic leagues,' he told me in 2019, 'is if you pay them well in international cricket.'

Such a mechanism, guaranteeing players from all nations a certain sum per match, would require central management from the ICC: the sort of tool to protect competitive balance enshrined in US domestic sports. Instead, ironically, the only professional cricket competitions to pay heed to competitive balance are T20 leagues. Franchise competitions have salary caps and draft structures designed to ensure a relatively equitable distribution of talent, to maintain sporting uncertainty. Collectivist ideas – like a proposal to pool broadcasting rights for all countries' away series, selling them under one package – have continually been rejected.

Chris Gayle represented 25 different domestic teams in officially recognised T20s. This gallivanting image obscures that Gayle played 103 Tests for West Indies, scoring 7,214 runs at an average of 42.18. He is the unique holder of the '3–2–1': a Test match triple century (actually, two – one at home to South Africa and one in Galle); a one-day international double century; and a T20 international century (two, again). Gayle most cherishes 'the triple century, obviously', he told me. 'It's hard work to bat for a day and a half. It's not easy.' In T20, Gayle has often worn the shirt number 333, his highest Test score.

In 2022, Gayle told me of his fears for Test cricket. 'They're treating it as a business when India play against England, Australia, it's big bucks for them. But we – the lower-ranked teams – need to be looked after.'

Players from larger markets are aware of how financial inequality threatens the Test game. Australia's captain Pat Cummins observes:

> We're so lucky to have the professional system that we do. You can seek out the best coaches, amazing medical facilities – all those things. Ideally, you'd love every Test-playing nation to have those opportunities. How you do that is you've got to find money somewhere.

We've got to find a way to keep investing in the systems that create really good Test cricket teams.

Cummins suggests that players from richer nations could accept taking a pay cut for Test cricket if it was part of a broader attempt to help the format. 'We'd all be open to it, if it was a really good plan. You'd look at it and see how we go through. In Australia, we support all kinds of domestic cricket because we know how important that is to future generations and for our Australian team set-up. I think everyone's quite open-minded, because we are one of the lucky nations.'

* * *

West Indies' decline is often told through cliché. It is said that the best Caribbean sporting talent now gravitates to US sports. Yet cricket has never been unrivalled in the region. As a boy in Jamaica, Michael Holding (born in 1954) remembers cricket being 'a poor cousin' of football and athletics; he considers the idea that cricket has suffered from new interest in other games 'a myth'.

For a talented young Caribbean sportsman, there has never been a better time to become a professional cricketer. While international cricket might have had a more obvious political significance in previous generations, closer to independence, it is ludicrous to claim that recent cohorts do not care. During the Covid-19 pandemic, West Indies were the first side to undertake a tour – visiting England, which had far higher Covid-19 rates, and winning the first Test in 2020. In 2021, a depleted side endured another taxing quarantine period before their series in Bangladesh: they chased 395 in Chittagong, with Kyle Mayers hitting a double century on debut, then edged the second Test by 17 runs.

In the queue at the popcorn stall during the first Test against England in Antigua in 2022, a local told me that fans 'couldn't take time out for a Test match . . . T20 is faster and more popular.' The regular sell-outs in the Caribbean Premier League, benefiting from night games priced affordably to cater to the local audience, attests to this truth. Yet the fan was adamant that the lack of support at Tests should not be mistaken for a lack of interest in the team: 'The game is alive.'

Three weeks later, West Indies bowled England out for 204 and 120 in Grenada to win by ten wickets, sealing a 1–0 series win. Like so many before, this was a victory achieved through pace. From 2004 to 2022, West Indies hosted England in four series, winning three and drawing the other: the sequence contrasted sharply with the side's other results.

In the hyper-professionalised modern game, individual talent can only take a team so far. Asked about West Indies' plight, Lara had no laments about players not respecting the maroon cap. Instead, he had a more prosaic explanation: the inequality in facilities, a problem during his career that has become more pronounced since.

> It's simple, always infrastructure. When you come to Australia, of course it's a big island, they have huge investment in sports. That's something that's lacking in West Indies.
>
> Everyone is looking for the next superstar, if he's Usain Bolt or Viv Richards, to just come out of nowhere and be as brilliant as they were. I feel that to do that you need structure.
>
> The talent in the Caribbean is amazing. I just think that we take that talent and make it pretty ordinary. In some other countries, the talent could be ordinary, but then ordinary talent is turned into something special. So it really and truly has to do with the investment that they are not making in sports in the Caribbean.
>
> Maybe 50, 60 years ago talent was the number one thing. Today is much more about discipline. The technical side of sport, understanding injuries and understanding how to do all sorts of different things, it's now a whole different ball game. It's a business and we haven't caught up.

But nor has the structure of the sport allowed them to do so.

31

CRICKET'S SUPERPOWER

Thirty-six all out: the score alone conveyed a nation's ignominy. It was the lowest Test innings from any country for 75 years, and India's lowest ever.

After being humiliated in Adelaide, in the first Test of their tour of Australia in 2020/21, India faced widespread predictions that they would suffer a whitewash. Virat Kohli, India's captain, would miss the rest of the tour, because his wife was giving birth.

Kohli could not then return to Australia. As Covid-19 ravaged the world, tours had to be played under biosecure conditions. India's squad began the tour with a 14-day quarantine period, able to leave their hotel rooms only for training.

In the Adelaide Oval dressing room, Ajinkya Rahane, captain for the final three Tests after Kohli's return home, addressed the side. Unlike Kohli, Rahane was no icon: aged 31, he was a solid Test batter and undemonstrative character. Now, he took on the role of a lifetime.

He reminded the team of how they had played to get a first innings lead, before the second innings debacle, and sought to refocus them for the challenges ahead. Rahane told them, 'Whatever has happened, it's gone. Yes, we got out for 36, but in the Test match we played really good cricket. Because of one bad session we lost the Test match, and that can happen to any team.'

Rahane remembers:

Many people were saying India will lose 4–0. As a captain and player I wanted to stay in the moment and focus on the controllable things, which were enjoying our cricket and playing an aggressive brand of cricket. That was very important.

My message was clear. There's a three-Test match series from here on. Let's try and give our best, we've prepared ourselves really well, and most importantly, enjoy our cricket rather than focusing on the result or outcome. Whatever is going to happen, it will happen. We don't have to focus on that straight away. Let's play one game at a time.

I believe in giving responsibility to others. I wanted to create that healthy atmosphere inside the dressing room. Players can come up to me and tell me whatever they feel, they can open up to me anytime.

You cannot go too defensive or into your shell playing in Australia. If you show intent, you have a better chance.

Amid the frustration with himself for being involved in a run-out with Kohli in the first Test, India's turmoil and the huge complications caused by touring during a global pandemic, Rahane realised the stakes. He recalls thinking, 'This is an opportunity for you to stand up for your team, stand up and do something special for your country.'

In overcast conditions, Rahane walked out to bat early on day two at the MCG. He had scarcely slept the night before, because of a back spasm. After Australia's 195, Rahane, who had taken several painkillers, came out with India 61–2; he had promoted himself to four, Kohli's customary position. 'I was in pain, but I didn't want to show everyone that I was in pain. I just wanted to stay there, bat as long as possible and take my team forward.'

Taking 17 balls to score his first run, Rahane used soft hands to negate the swing and seam movement. He interspersed careful defence with some sumptuous drives and late cuts; defying his back pain, he was comfortable either ducking, hooking or cutting short balls and used his feet decisively against Nathan Lyon's off spin. His 112 was cathartic: 'That innings was really special.'

After India secured a 131-run lead, their attack ensured that Rahane's work was not wasted. Australia mustered only 200 in their second innings: for the first home Test in 32 years, no Australian made a half-century. Both India's pace bowlers and spinners adopted a 'leg trap' approach, especially against Steve Smith and Marnus Labuschagne – bowling very straight and packing the on side.

'The idea was to get them a little out of their comfort zone,' Rahane explains. 'When you're playing on the leg side, you are not in control. Most of the time we have seen there's only mid-on and square leg. When bowlers are bowling on the stumps, batsmen can score on the leg side and balls go in the air. So, I just wanted to see if I can play with that field.' In India's second innings, Rahane hit the winning runs to level the series 1–1.

Halfway through the final day of the third Test at Sydney, India were five wickets down and faced going 2–1 down in the series. The sixth wicket pair were Hanuma Vihari and Ravichandran Ashwin. Vihari had a torn hamstring; Ashwin had a back injury so debilitating that his wife and children had to help him out of bed in the morning. Their injuries forced India to abandon their plans to try and chase down their target of 407; instead, the best that they could manage was a draw.

Vihari was unable to stretch forward, so Ashwin tried to stay at Lyon's end when possible. Ashwin 'couldn't bend but I was okay to take blows if it was short', he recalls. 'I was leaning forward, trying to protect my stumps, because I was worried about fuller balls.

'Pain was the barrier I needed, just to clear my mind. That pain and the complete blankness to be able to respond to the ball enabled me to do this. I got into some sort of zone.'

Together, while barely able to run between the wickets, they survived 42.4 overs undefeated: one of Test cricket's bravest partnerships. Ashwin lasted 128 balls for 39 not out; Vihari endured 161 deliveries to reach 23 not out. Neither would be fit enough to play in the final Test – but they ensured that India arrived in Brisbane still level at 1–1.

India's greatest challenge was putting together a team. By the fourth Test, ten players who might otherwise have featured – including Kohli, the entire first-choice pace attack and first two quick bowling reserves, and Ashwin and Ravindra Jadeja, their pair of spin-bowling allrounders – were absent. Rahane and Cheteshwar Pujara were the only two men to feature in every Test in Australia. India's five-man attack at Brisbane contained a total of four Test caps; one of those, Navdeep Saini, went down injured, and could only bowl 12.5 overs in the match. Before the Gabba Test, India's team had taken the sum total of 13 Test wickets, Australia's 1,033. Rahane told his players, 'We are going to get an opportunity to represent India, so let's give our best. Just think that you're representing your state team.'

At 186–6 in their first innings, barely halfway to Australia's 369, Washington Sundar and Shardul Thakur – a 21-year-old debutant, playing his first first-class game for three years, and a man with a total of four runs in his Test career – shared a 123-run stand to lift India close to parity. Australia reached 89–0, a lead of 122 runs, in their second innings; then, pace bowler Mohammed Siraj took a five-wicket haul.

Siraj was originally only picked in the squad to provide injury cover. Early in the tour, Siraj's father died: he knew that if he left to attend the funeral, he would not be able to return down under. 'Your father's *dua* [blessing] is with you,' head coach Ravi Shastri told Siraj when he went to training after his father's death, recounted the book *The Miracle Makers*. 'You'll end up with a five-wicket haul in this Test series.' The prediction came true in Brisbane: both Smith and Labuschagne were undone by extra bounce. Siraj raised his hands aloft to salute his father.

While Australia slipped to 294 all out, India needed 328 in 100 overs; closing day four 4–0, they required 324 from the last day. Australia had not lost a Test in Brisbane for 33 years. They possessed one of the finest attacks of all time: quicks Pat Cummins, Josh Hazlewood and Mitchell Starc, together with off-spinner Lyon. Cold logic appeared to demand that India attempt to bat out the final day to secure a 1–1 series draw and retain the Border-Gavaskar Trophy.

Thunderstorms were predicted for the final day. 'Tomorrow,' Rahane told his team, 'the sun will come out.' He was right. Before play began, he addressed the side: 'If you play good cricket until lunch, we'll assess the situation.'

Pujara's approach was to safeguard against defeat: he took 97 balls to crawl into double figures. In over five hours at the crease, Pujara made 56; he was hit on the body – the head, shoulder, forearm, elbow and fingers – 11 times. Pujara had observed Australia being troubled by variable bounce. He reasoned that, as long as he got his gloves and bat out of the way, bouncers could hit him but they would not dismiss him. This was Test cricket at its most elemental.

'If the ball follows you, you just take the blow on your body – and that is how you survive,' Pujara told me. 'The first couple of blows didn't hurt much, because I'm used to getting hit on the body when I'm practising, even at home.

'You need to be fit enough, you need to be emotionally and mentally strong. There are so many ups and downs in those five days.'

Stylish opener Shubman Gill, who was 21, thrived as Australia became frustrated and dropped short: in three consecutive deliveries from Starc, he pulled a six over square leg, uppercut a four through third man and pulled another four in front of square. After he fell for 91 and Rahane hit 24, Rishabh Pant arrived at the crease at 167–3. India were 183–3 at tea, needing another 145 runs to win. Remarkably, India could now spy a series victory.

In the previous Test, Pant's audacious 97 on the final day in Sydney, defying elbow pain, had briefly opened up a chance of victory. By making Australia more defensive, it ultimately made it easier to salvage a draw.

In Brisbane, India's target was more attainable. The threat of Pant's boundaries allowed him to score briskly at low risk. Launching Lyon over long-on for six was a reminder of Pant's power, but his innings was marked by shrewd calculation.

When Cummins dismissed Pujara and Mayank Agarwal with the second new ball after tea on the final day in Brisbane, India slipped to 265–5. With a notably weak last three batters, the pragmatic option would have been to accept an honourable draw. Instead, with 49 needed from 44 balls, Sundar hooked Cummins for six over fine leg; next ball, he slashed past gully for another four. Pant, who had mostly treated Lyon with respect, now played an impudent scoop sweep for four, falling onto his shoulder as he hit the shot. Next ball, Pant slog-swept another four. Pant had begun the series dropped for being overweight. When he drove Hazlewood down the ground, with 18 balls remaining, it sealed one of Test cricket's greatest heists. While his teammates ran onto the pitch, Rahane sat motionless on the balcony, taking in the scene. He recalls:

> All the memories from Adelaide were playing in my head. How it started and the Melbourne Test match. What happened in Sydney, players getting injured.
>
> It was draining. You're putting in everything for your team, mentally. It was very special and very emotional.

Some Test series victories are, really, a triumph for a few players. Others are a triumph for a team. This victory was a triumph for a squad: all 20 men – the highest ever for any away team in a series – who represented India in Australia.

Exactly a century earlier, Lord Harris had claimed, 'Notwithstanding their multitudes, I doubt if they are going to turn out a team of all India as good as the best of our county clubs.' Now, India didn't just have one team who could take on the world; they had several. Until India's tour to Australia in 2018/19, no Asian side had ever won a series in Australia. Essentially with two completely different teams, India won twice down under in three years.

It seemed to make good on a prophecy made by the historian and former cricket administrator Ramachandra Guha in *The Commonwealth of Cricket*, published in 2020. 'With this demographic and financial base, India should always and perennially have been the top team in all formats of the game,' Guha wrote. In 1992, the Board of Control for Cricket in India had a deficit of $150,000. By 2023, the BCCI had a net worth of $2.25 billion; the next most by any national board was $79 million.

Table 11. India's transformation by decade

	Matches	Won	Lost	Drawn	Win–loss ratio
1930s	7	0	5	2	0
1940s	13	0	6	7	0
1950s	44	6	17	21	0.35
1960s	52	9	21	22	0.43
1970s	64	17	19	28	0.89
1980s	81	11	21	48 (+1 tied)	0.52
1990s	69	18	20	31	0.90
2000s	103	40	27	36	1.48
2010s	107	56	29	22	1.93
2020s	49	24	19	6	1.26

NB: To January 2025

Their team had transformed at a similar rate. In their first 69 years as a Test nation, India had won 63 Tests and lost 113 – a meagre win–loss ratio of 0.56. From the seminal Eden Gardens victory in 2001 until April 2025, India won 118 Tests and lost just 71 – a win-loss ratio of 1.66.

* * *

In 1952, Vijay Merchant lamented the cricketing impact of partition. 'Above all, the partition has deprived India of future fast bowlers,' he wrote. 'In the past, India often relied for fast bowling on the North Indian people, who because of their height and sturdy physique, are better equipped for this kind of bowling than the cricketers of Central India or the South. Now this source of supply has ceased and the gap has not yet been filled.'

Even while pursuing a strategy based around spin, Tiger Pataudi recognised how a dearth of fast bowlers held India back. Kapil Dev showed that occasionally fine fast bowlers could still emerge from India. But for Indian pace bowling to transform, the system that nurtured it had to do so too.

In 1987, Ravi Mammen, the managing director of the Madras Rubber Factory, was fed up. Why, he wondered, could India not replicate the fast-bowling talent produced elsewhere? Mammen believed that India needed a new centre focused upon bowling fast. So he created one himself: the MRF Pace Foundation in Chennai, the first pace foundation in India. He enlisted T.A. Sekhar, who had played two Tests, to be coach.

Even when India produced exciting pace bowlers, they were mistrusted. Selectors preferred 'some other fast bowler who can bat a bit', Sekhar told me. 'The guy getting picked would have been a bits-and-pieces player.' Such thinking had its own self-justifying logic: if seamers did not get wickets, it made a certain sense to select multi-faceted cricketers to perform the role. Or simply no fast bowlers at all. Sunil Gavaskar opened the bowling in Tests five times; his career included just a solitary wicket to go with his 10,122 runs.

The MRF Pace Foundation sought to give India what they had lacked since the 1930s: a battery of quicks. The foundation hired Dennis Lillee as director. When Lillee arrived at the foundation for the first time, Sekhar recalled, 'He said: "I want a running coach, I want a dietitian, I want a swimming pool and I want practice wickets which will be very similar to Australia. I want to do video analysis."' Lillee, and the foundation, got them all.

Mammen died of a heart attack in 1990, aged 39. His family ensured that the foundation realised his vision. By 2023, 17 Test bowlers had trained here. One of the first, Javagal Srinath, was India's leading quick in the 1990s: with pace and bounce, he took 6–21 against South Africa in Ahmedabad in 1996. Zaheer Khan, who didn't bowl with a hard ball until he was 17, was discovered after an MRF initiative to find a left-armer; he could not break into Mumbai's team, but Sekhar helped him secure a trial at Baroda. With conventional and reverse swing, he led India's pace attack in the 2000s.

In 2000, the National Cricket Academy – modelled on the Australia equivalent – was set up, creating a better structure to funnel young talent. By the 2020s, before each Under-19 World Cup, India would shortlist 150 potential players, before filtering them down. 'If you're really good, it's very hard to get missed,' says Rahul Dravid, who played for India from 1996 to 2012, and then worked as U-19 and national head coach.

'When I was playing, if you were trying to get selected in an U-19 India team you played one or two matches – if you had a bad game, you could just get lost. Now, some boys are playing 15 to 20 games before the selections. The aspiration is just to ensure that more and more opportunities are given. I think it's made it a lot fairer.'

In the first five editions of the U-19 World Cup, from 1988 to 2004, India reached one final. In the next ten editions, from 2006 to 2024, India reached eight finals, winning four. Players also benefited from a burgeoning A-team programme: before his Test debut in Australia, Siraj had played 16 first-class games for India A, touring England, New Zealand, South Africa and West Indies. India's A team attempted to model the roles and style of play in the Test side.

More investment in domestic pitches, including through the launch of a pitch curator's certification course in 2010, created wickets with more pace and bounce. 'It led to better wickets – so better fast bowlers,' Dravid reflects. 'We became very competitive because we could play good fast bowlers overseas. Then, playing in India, we can still play very good spinners.'

Economic incentives also encouraged more young Indians to bowl fast. With the country always possessing abundant spin-bowling talent, domestic quicks were particularly rare – and valuable – in the Indian Premier League. Some pace bowlers became dollar millionaires before they had won an international cap.

The heightened focus upon fast bowling and scouting talent – by state teams, private academies, IPL or copycat state T20 leagues – uncovered players who might have been lost in previous eras. Shardul Thakur grew up in Palgarh, a small town of 70,000; he used to lug his cricket kit on the 90-kilometre train journey to Mumbai. Navdeep Saini did not bowl with a hard ball until he was 19. Mohammed Siraj, the son of an auto-rickshaw driver, was a star in tennis-ball leagues in Hyderabad; he only started bowling with a hard ball aged 20. Thangarasu Natarajan, the son of a weaver, hails from the remote village of Chinnappampatti; he grew up in a shack. He also didn't bowl with a hard ball until he was 20, instead playing tennis-ball cricket – he was known as *Left-u* Mani [Left-arm Mani]. Together, this unlikely quartet toppled Australia at the Gabba.

These players illustrate a central reason for India's improvement: the democratisation of the national team. The six states of Bengal, Gujarat, Karnataka, Maharashtra, Punjab and Tamil Nadu – which have consistently made up around 35 per cent of the population – contributed 97 per cent of Test cricketers born from 1931 to 1941. This fell to 76 per cent of Test players born from 1951 to 1961, then 51 per cent of those born from 1991 to 2001. Far more players than ever before come from beyond the traditional centres. The bulk of these men, like Dhoni, are from urban areas outside Indian cricket's traditional hotbeds – benefiting from investment in better facilities and more professionalised, less parochial, selection. India's reliance upon a few large cities in a few states for its players has lessened.

The surge in money also meant that playing cricket professionally became financially aspirational, rather than something that many could not afford to do. In the 1960s, Indian players were paid 250 rupees a Test. After beating New Zealand in four days, players were docked one-fifth of this paltry fee, justified on a per diem basis, for winning too quickly.

'Cricketers cannot develop unless they are assured of a secure future when their playing days are over,' Erapalli Prasanna, who played Tests from 1962 to 1978, wrote in his 1977 autobiography. 'Parents of budding cricketers must be assured that proficiency in the game will assure the future of their children. Players of my generation have suffered; I don't want the next generation to suffer too.'

The creation of national central contracts in 2003 gave cricketers greater stability and wealth. Especially after the IPL launched in 2008, players could now make a good living without playing international cricket.

'The upper-caste and elite composition of Indian cricket until well into the 1960s was a direct consequence of who could afford to play,' the journalist Keshava Guha noted. 'Not only was cricket not a vehicle for social mobility; its paltry financial rewards ensured that the game was dominated by the educated middle and upper classes.' An all-time India Test side chosen by ESPNcricinfo in 2011 included seven players from the Brahmin caste, who account for 4 per cent of the population.

The Indian side has since become more of an engine of social mobility. The phenomenon was captured in Aravind Adiga's 2016 novel *Selection Day*, describing a chutney seller's attempts to train his two sons, including one who does not like cricket, to be professionals. Against a backdrop of rising Hindu nationalism, the team has continued to embody India's pluralistic traditions, with Muslim and Sikh players prominent.

'India never lacked passion or interest in the game,' Dravid reflects:

India lacked infrastructure, India lacked facilities. To succeed at Test cricket, you need coaching, you need infrastructure, you need cricket balls.

Suddenly more money came into the sport. That money was distributed to different associations, different cities. It allowed more and more kids to get access to better facilities and infrastructure. When television exploded, suddenly you were in a small town, but you were getting access to great players talking about cricket. Before, in many small towns, there were no coaches and then you couldn't even learn through watching someone.

From the 1990s, we were picking from a larger pool of talent, because the infrastructure was better. It still is not a 100 per cent inclusive game but it's become a lot more equal.

India is picking from a larger group of players so the depth is more. There's more A tours, there's more exposure to sports science and medicine.

M.S. Dhoni was a standard-bearer for India embracing talent from previously ignored areas. A product of Ranchi, in north-east India, Dhoni initially worked as a ticket inspector with Indian Railways. He was 'as cut off from the system as you can be in the context of Indian cricket', wrote his biographer Bharat Sundaresan.

While Ranchi had a modest cricket tradition, it was small only by Indian standards: the population reached one million in 2007. Such cities had little tradition of developing international players: Ranchi had only produced one Test cricketer.

In 2008, Dhoni became India's 31st Test captain. He had already made an indelible mark on Indian cricket, captaining a young side to victory in the inaugural T20 World Cup (then called the World T20) in 2007. In 2011, Dhoni lifted the ODI World Cup crown too. The white-ball game was always an obvious fit for a man with a ponytail, love of motorbikes and trademark helicopter shot, with Dhoni using his high backlift and the power of his wrists to whip balls to the on side. Dhoni's rise coincided with India's: he was the first cricketer picked as one of *Time* magazine's 100 most influential people in the world.

Dhoni was also a significant Test captain. He won, a lot: 27 times in 60 Tests, from 2008 to 2014, with 18 defeats. 'He had an incredible ability to get people to follow him because he just had a great feel for the game and people were inspired,' says Gary Kirsten, India's head coach from 2008 to 2011. Dhoni was the first man to take India to the top of the Test rankings, a summit they reached late in 2009 before losing eight consecutive away Tests to England and Australia in 2011–12. Yet no man in Test history has performed the triple role of captain, leading batter – his average was 38.09, and over 40 when captain – and wicketkeeper so well for so long.

* * *

Dhoni's successor as captain led the finest Indian Test team yet. Aged nine, Virat Kohli enrolled in West Delhi Cricket Academy; thereafter, he remained unstinting in his ambitions. When he was 18, Kohli was playing for Delhi. Overnight during a Ranji Trophy match, Kohli's father died at 3 a.m. 'I want to bat,' Kohli declared the next morning. He resumed, on 40 not out, and reached 90 when he was wrongly given out caught behind; then, he went to his father's cremation. 'We both had the same dream,' Kohli later said. 'He wanted me to play for India. After losing him, I just became more determined.'

Like his predecessors as standout Indian batters, Kohli had an essentially classical technique and a shrewd cricket brain. After an abject tour of England in 2014, four years later he returned with a new technique – pointing his back toe at point, rather than cover, and meeting the ball an average of half a metre further forward to negate swing movement. He hit a supreme 149 in his first innings in the 2018 series, when he averaged 59.30.

Kohli combined his stroke-making with an unusual physicality, generating awesome power for a man of 5 ft 9 in. He didn't merely aim to be the fittest cricketer in the world, but one of the fittest *athletes*. Even when he reduced his body-fat percentage to just 9 per cent, he was not content: '[Novak] Djokovic's is 7.5 per cent,' he said.

'He set an example,' fast bowler Ishant Sharma said. 'Take the case of fat percentage – before him I had never heard of it being spoken about in the Indian team.' Tellingly, Kohli's team often played their best cricket when coming from behind in matches.

Like Sachin Tendulkar, Kohli played many of his most cherished innings in Australia. Quick pitches suited Kohli's prowess against pace, especially his hook; the large grounds suited his placement and intense running between the wickets.

Australia was also the perfect outlet for Kohli's competitiveness. Norman Mailer wrote that Muhammad Ali fought the entirety of the other person when he was in the ring. The same could be said of Kohli, whose body language, the passion with which he celebrated wickets and his own centuries alike and willingness to engage opponents verbally always conveyed his relish for the contest.

Where others saw danger, he saw opportunity. In his first Test as captain, standing in for Dhoni in December 2014, Kohli hit 115 at Adelaide. On the final day, Australia set India 364 to win; Kohli resolved to go for the runs. The sweep, ordinarily a shot he rarely played, became a tool to attack Nathan Lyon; he also drove magisterially out of the rough, and pulled quick bowlers off the front foot. Kohli's stunning 141, off only 175 balls, put India on course to win before a late collapse; since 1961, no other away batter has scored twin hundreds in a Test in Australia.

Even in defeat, Kohli showed the sort of side that he wanted to lead. 'At no point did we not think about chasing the score down,' Kohli declared. 'No sort of negativity is welcome in this group.'

Such an attitude helped India become a side who could regularly best all comers anywhere. In 2018/19, Kohli captained India to their first series victory in Australia: a 2–1 win, which would probably have been 3–1 but for Sydney rain. As well as Kohli, this landmark was underpinned by Pujara's undemonstrative run-scoring – he scored three centuries and faced 1,258 balls in the series, almost twice as many as anyone else – and India's unrelenting seam attack.

Just one year into his Test career, Jasprit Bumrah produced one of the great away performances in a series in Australia. With conventional and reverse swing and seam, pace and his awkward angle – from wide of the crease, making him difficult to leave – Bumrah's 21 wickets came at 17.00 each, literally the stuff of nightmares. 'I'd wake up in the night thinking about getting out,' Australia opener Aaron Finch said in the documentary *The Test*, 'thinking I'm facing Bumrah again tomorrow.' Bumrah's 6–33 at Melbourne, the decisive spell in a series that had been 1–1 going into Boxing Day 2018, distilled his qualities. Batters were beaten on the inside and outside edge by balls moving in and out; stumps were shattered; opener Marcus Harris succumbed to a bouncer; number four Shaun Marsh, who had survived several yorker attempts, was too early on a slower yorker. Before the delivery, Rohit Sharma told Bumrah, 'You can try a slower ball like you bowl in one-day cricket.' Such deception embodied how the best modern players bring white-ball skills to the red-ball game.

From 14 steps – a slow trot, then a gallop – Bumrah unfurled his sling-arm action, hyper-extending his arm to generate extra pace. Generating 90 mph pace from such a small run-up was the product of playing backyard cricket as a boy in Ahmedabad. 'This was the longest run-up you could have while playing at the backyard,' he explained. 'I have tried the longer run-ups, and nothing changes, the speed is still the same.'

After taking 9–91 in the Test against England at Visakhapatnam in February 2024, defying a flat pitch, Bumrah became the first Indian quick bowler to be ranked number one in Test cricket. Ishant Sharma – whose late career profited from bowling fuller and going around the wicket to left-handers more – and Mohammed Shami, whose pace and relentless length generated sharp seam movement, could be almost as dangerous. Opposing batters had as much to fear from India on a pitch that seamed as one that turned.

Despite those two totemic triumphs down under, there was also a hint of missed opportunity overseas. Between 2018 and 2024, India lost four and drew two of their six series in England, New Zealand and South Africa; on three of these occasions, victory in the final match would have given India the series. Most gallingly, India lost the first two World Test Championship finals, in 2021 and 2023.

Yet India under Kohli remained an outstanding side. During the seven years when he was full-time captain, from 2015 to 2022, India won 44 of their 77 Tests, and lost just 17: the best record in the world.

At home, India eviscerated all comers with a reliability unmatched in history. From the start of 2013 until the end of 2022, India played 42 home Tests, won 34 and lost just two. Fourteen of their wins in this period – 33 per cent of their home Tests – were by an innings; West Indies' 1980–95 team won 10 per cent of home Tests by an innings, Australia's 1995–2007 side 23 per cent.

* * *

While Kohli's India had new strengths, in fast bowling and fitness, they were also sustained by a traditional trait: spin bowling. Ravichandran Ashwin and Ravindra Jadeja were born two years apart; Ashwin made his Test debut in 2011, Jadeja in 2012.

As a boy in Chennai, Ashwin was initially a batter who bowled medium pace. A hip injury in an Under-14 game led him to switch to off spin: an ideal fit for a supple, individualistic mind. Ashwin complemented school and club matches with an obsessive diet of gully cricket, with a tennis ball on roads. After playing official games all day, he would rush back for gully cricket, ignoring his father's concerns that the game would detract from the technique that he learned with a hard ball. 'I don't think he quite realised what gully cricket was giving me,' Ashwin reflects. 'My attitude, my zeal, my sharpness, even understanding cricket – a lot of it came from those gully games.' More than anything, Ashwin was imbued with an ability to problem-solve. 'I became game-smart, which has stuck with me for ever.' Whether with a hard ball or tennis ball, 'I used to bowl overs like a maniac.'

After making his Test debut aged 25, Ashwin thrived at home; but he took just 12 wickets in his first six away Tests. At Adelaide in December 2014, Ashwin was dropped. 'The way I used to play cricket until then was you spin the ball, you didn't get success – you try and spin it harder.'

While making a technical adjustment – tweaking his foot position to be straighter, to give him more balance and accuracy – Ashwin expanded his repertoire. 'You need to have the subtlety, you need to have the right speed to be able to push the batsman constantly in trouble. So it is more about subtleties – trying to find loading positions, trying to find good airspeed, get different rotations, side-spin, overspin, on occasions you can get top-spin in Australia.'

Ashwin increasingly used a 'carrom ball' (also called a *sodukku* ball), a delivery he first developed in gully cricket. The carrom ball is flicked out of the hand with the middle finger, turning like a leg break; he later even developed a reverse carrom, which turns like an off break but with backspin. Before returning down under in 2020/21, Ashwin perused footage of Steve Smith and Marnus Labuschagne. There, he hatched a plan: to bowl very straight and pack the on side, using his carrom ball as a surprise delivery; both Smith and Labuschagne duly fell to it.

Here was the analytical mind sharpened by Ashwin's engineering degree, a common thread with several other India spinners, applied to Test cricket. While Ashwin notionally bowled conventional off spin, no two deliveries were quite alike. He subtly varied his pace, flight and release point from ball to ball, and switched seamlessly between over and around the wicket. 'If you're searching, I believe you will find your answers.' After each day, from the age of 21, Ashwin recorded his feats in a diary; around the same age, he started coaching – he later founded an academy too – nurturing his obsessive thirst for cricketing knowledge.

> I write about how I feel, rather than how it looks. So when I write how it feels, I can always go back to the feeling of doing a certain thing before I start my action, my gather or something.
>
> The mindset is trying to constantly find answers, troubleshooting problems, because Test cricket will throw a lot of problems at you. You will have challenges that you have to encounter – the beauty about it is that it gives you time to correct it.
>
> I always slept poorly over success and slept better at failure. When I found solutions, I slept really well. I used to constantly search for newer terrains to conquer.
>
> It's like you're a chemist – they enjoy being with the chemicals and staying in the lab and doing the experiments. That's pretty much what I do. And so it is a competitive edge and I found when I've bowled and played against certain cricketers, and I've been able to get the better of them, I'd be quietly chuckling inside. You know what? I've been watching you for the last 15 years. What have you been doing?

No Test bowler has taken more wickets against left-handers than Ashwin. For all the threat posed by his off break, Ashwin's greatest weapon of all to left-handers is the ball that doesn't turn: the arm ball. Playing for the turn away from the bat, left-handers can be snared by the ball that doesn't spin and instead holds its line.

Ashwin's relish of bowling with the new ball, generating bounce from his 6 ft 2 in height, made him a threat at any time; no Test spinner has ever opened the bowling more. Of the nine men to take 500 Test wickets, only two – Muthiah Muralidaran and Glenn McGrath – average less.

Jadeja was the perfect complement: a left-arm spinner, whose orthodox delivery turned away from right-handers. If his tricks were not as bountiful as Ashwin's, Jadeja's unerring accuracy, and the bite he got from surfaces bowling at rapid speeds, gave him a suffocating quality. Australia were particularly bewitched: across three series victories in India in 2013, 2017 and 2023, Jadeja harvested 71 wickets at 18.28.

'He puts enough on the ball and still hits the bat at high speed and repeats it over after over and puts it on length – these are not ordinary traits,' says Ashwin. 'He's got such a lovely repeatable action, his alignment is so good. You wouldn't see him miss his line or length very often. And he's got the durability to go on for a very long time.'

India's fortune was not merely that these two brilliant, contrasting spinners were contemporaries. It was also that both were reliable batters. Jadeja's batting evolved so much that India happily picked him at number six. A cricketer that could sometimes be underestimated acquired a record that bore comparison with leading Test allrounders. In his first 80 Tests, up to mid-2025, Jadeja averaged 34.75 with the bat and 24.14 with the ball; his athleticism and pinpoint throwing also made Jadeja probably his country's best ever fielder.

Abroad, India often picked between the two, meaning that Ashwin, remarkably, was frequently squeezed out; at home, they didn't face such an unpalatable choice. Combining both was akin to a cheat code: giving India spinners who could turn the ball both ways, a batting line-up deep enough to have Ashwin, a man with five Test centuries, at number eight, and pick a five-man attack. Selecting a Test XI is normally an exercise in compromise; with Ashwin and Jadeja, India had no need.

32

IN THE FAST LANE

Test cricket is a hard game. Never more so than when a fast bowler stands atop their mark, ready to unleash hell. Batters through the ages have had to face the same fundamental question: how to confront pace.

Twenty-two yards away from their stumps, and only about 18 yards away from where the batter is standing, a bowler releases the ball at a speed approaching 100 mph. A batter only has 0.4 seconds between the ball leaving the hand and it reaching their bat.

This is Test cricket at its rawest. It is also central to the game's theatre. Outstanding, and often physically dangerous, fast bowling has been a common thread in every great Test side. Having the technique, temperament and sheer courage to withstand hostile spells of fast bowling unites the finest batters in Test history.

Every batting prodigy who emerges from first-class cricket inevitably encounters the same question: 'But can they play the short ball?' Unless a batter can answer in the affirmative then, no matter what their other qualities, they will not have a successful Test career. Perhaps the most brutal illustration of this truth is Graeme Hick. In 1991, Hick arrived in Test cricket, after completing his qualification period for England, with 57 first-class centuries and an average above 60. Exposed to Caribbean pace bowlers, Hick could not find a riposte to the short ball. After 75 runs in four Tests, Hick was dropped. For all his first-class records, he only averaged 31.32 in Test cricket.

* * *

IN THE FAST LANE

To bowl at 90 mph is a scientific miracle. Bowling at such speeds entails contorting the human body into a strange and often painful shape. Fast bowling is cricket's most perilous art: as a bowler's speed increases, so does the risk of injury.

Bowling fast is 'an unnatural thing to do', Rob Ahmun, the England and Wales Cricket Board's head of performance science and medicine, told me. Quick bowlers run in at speeds approaching 25 kph (15.5mph); a treadmill only goes up to 20 kph. 'You jump and then you come to a complete stop. Then you bowl something as fast as you possibly can, which creates a huge amount of force on the body.'

At the point of release, a bowler's front foot absorbs up to ten times their body weight. Physically, the most similar demand is throwing a javelin. Athletes only throw up to nine times in an entire javelin competition; fast bowlers might bowl over 300 deliveries in the course of a Test. In his celebrated 14-wicket performance at The Oval in 1976, Michael Holding bowled over 320 balls. Fast bowlers need extraordinary physiques to withstand these demands.

Stress fractures in the back are a quick bowler's perennial enemy. To cope with the peculiar demands of bowling fast, one long-time England quick came to rank in the top 0.01 per cent of the population for bone density in his back. Developing extra bone density 'is so extreme that if you stop bowling, it starts to decline extremely fast', observes Paul Felton, a biomechanics expert who has worked with England. Bowlers lose about 3 per cent of the adaptation in bone density in their lumbar spine per month of inaction, a rate only matched by astronauts in space. As such, quick bowlers are particularly susceptible to injury when returning from long breaks.

However smooth a pace bowler's action appears, they have to confront a constant foe. To bowl fast is to accept pain.

'Something is hurting all the time,' says Dale Steyn, who took 439 Test wickets between 2004 and 2019. 'You really develop this thick skin and way to handle it and you just get on with it.' He expands:

There's always something sore. You're going to have a little hamstring injury, there's going to be a little quad that's sore – you might land in a foothole where you've just tweaked your ankle a little bit. Or you've got a bruised heel or your toe's been bashing into your shoe all day long and now you've got a bleeding toe.

So you'll be strapping your toes in Vaseline and make sure that one shoe has got shorter spikes than the other. And you become very professional with managing the things that have hurt you.

The most committed pace bowlers have no choice.

'It's basically just "hold on for dear life",' explains Pat Cummins, one of Australia's greatest pace bowlers. 'You wake up in the middle of the night because one side of your body's sore. You turn on the other side and you wake up half an hour later and that's sore. So you keep switching over.

'We call it the niggle worm – if your ankle's feeling good one day, it probably means the elbow is going to start hurting. If the elbow feels better, it means the shoulder's gonna go. There's always something going on. It's part of the job. It makes winning a Test match or a series even more rewarding – the amount of toil that's gone into it.'

Whatever their style, bloody-mindedness is a non-negotiable for any fast bowler. 'I just had this passion that I'm going to do whatever I can ball by ball that you're not going to beat me,' recalls Allan Donald, who took 330 Test wickets for South Africa. 'Whatever it takes, and however much the body can take in a day, there is that mindset of I am not going to go away ever. Not this ball, not the 24th over and last ball of the day come five, six o'clock. That is the line that you draw in the sand.'

In return, fast bowlers gain the knowledge that they can inflict pain on opponents. Bowling fast is a feeling like no other. 'It's exhilarating,' explains Holding, who took 249 Test wickets between 1975 and 1987:

You feel powerful. You know you have this capacity to intimidate someone without even bowling a ball because you could see some batsmen walking out to the crease and not really wanting to.

When you can bowl fast enough to know that the batsman at the other end is in trepidation about this ball coming at him – it gives you goosebumps, to be honest. Because you know that you're intimidating someone, you don't even actually need to do anything intimidating. You just have the pace and you know that they are worried about it. I went through my career feeling that way most of the time.

If you know that you're intimidating somebody, you have that intimidatory factor without even bowling a ball. You make sure that you use that advantage.

For pace bowlers, 'the physical threat is always there, the fear,' Steyn explains. 'Fear is an amazing thing, it makes people do silly things.' Some bowlers have used sledging – verbal insults to batters – to augment their threat. Many do not bother.

This was England's experience facing Mitchell Johnson in the 2013/14 Ashes. In the first Test, Kevin Pietersen walked out to face Johnson, went up to the bowler and declared, 'I'm less scared of getting out than you are scared of giving me a lot of runs.' Johnson didn't bother to respond, instead staring at Pietersen and walking past him.

Johnson's career, oscillating between the magnificent and the maddening, embodied how exacting pace bowling is for bowler and batter alike. Despite his gifts – pace and bounce allied to a left-arm angle that speared into batters – Johnson struggled with self-belief. But, with an uncluttered mind, new rhythm and the liberation of being used in three- or four-over bursts, against England and South Africa in 2013/14, he looted 59 wickets at an average of 15.23. England tumbled to a 5–0 whitewash; then, in South Africa, the hosts – enjoying a prolonged run as the world's best Test side – were defeated 2–1.

Facing Johnson at Brisbane in the first Test of the 2013/14 Ashes, Jonathan Trott, England's normally dependable number three, felt 'I was being questioned as a man,' he wrote. 'I felt my dignity was being stripped away with every short ball I ducked or parried. It was degrading. It was agony.' While he batted, Trott could hear fielders 'circling like hyenas around a dying zebra'. When Trott was caught off Johnson fending at a short ball down the leg side, 'a shudder ran through the dressing room,' Pietersen wrote. 'I was sitting there, thinking: I could die here in the f***ing Gabbattoir.' All series long, the threat of Johnson 'was in our heads even when he wasn't bowling'.

* * *

For anyone facing 90 mph, 'If you don't see it out of the hand, you're in deep shit,' says Ian Chappell, the former Australia captain renowned as a fine player of pace. 'You're not going to pick it up later.'

In the 0.4 seconds that a batter has between a ball being bowled and reaching them, they have to make myriad decisions: where the ball will pitch; how it will bounce; whether it will swing in the air before pitching; and whether it will seam off the pitch after it lands. Then, batters either play their shot, leave the ball or, if the delivery is speared towards their body, sway out of the way. To make effective contact with the ball, the margin of error is infinitesimal: batsmen must judge the ball's position to within three centimetres and the time it reaches them to within three milliseconds.

Batters don't even get the full 0.4 seconds to decide what shot to play. David Mann, an associate professor at the University of Amsterdam who has conducted extensive research with Australian Test players, has found that batters must commit to their shot 0.15 seconds before the ball reaches them. For the last one-third of the ball's journey, batters are effectively blind: this is why a ball that moves late or bounces unpredictably is so devastating. Against the quickest bowlers, Chappell recalls, 'You never see the ball hit the bat.'

There is simply far too much to process in the time after the ball leaves the bowler's hand. As such, batters use cues to get a sense of what delivery they will face. Batters, Mann explained to me, use information 'before the ball is even released from the body cues of the bowler' – from their face, shoulder, arm and their instincts – to deduce where the ball is likely to be. Some bowlers will display more effort in the final moments of their run-up when about to deliver a bouncer. Bowlers tend to release the ball slightly earlier when they are about to bowl yorkers, and later when bowling a bouncer.

'You pick it up out of the hand and you get a lot of information about the delivery,' Chappell says. 'The best bowlers don't give you early-warning signs. If somebody gave you an early-warning sign, that was a big plus.'

After the ball is released, it travels too quickly for batters to follow it all the way onto the bat. Instead, they follow its first movement, identifying information about the ball's line, length, and whether it swings before pitching. Elite batters, Mann has shown, then perform two 'saccades', moving their eyes to where the ball is going to be: first to the point when it bounces; second, to the point when they make contact. This is why the best batters are said to have more time: their eyes get into place more quickly than other players, so they look less rushed at the crease.

Shaping up to play a shot, the latest time that any batter can make a minor adjustment – say to the angle of their bat, with it already too late to change what stroke they are playing – is about 100 milliseconds, the equivalent of seven yards before the ball reaches them. The only exception appears to be moving the head; survival instincts allow batters to move their head out of the line of the ball in the final yards as it travels towards them.

The best batters process the cues about what a ball is likely to do faster and more accurately. Then, they use their hand–eye coordination to get into position to play their shot. 'They're just like clockwork,' Mann told me. 'They're so well trained and so accurate with their predictions.'

Test batters that Mann studied 'tracked the ball perfectly with their head, essentially to the point where their nose would be pointing at the ball the whole way. We've got this funny thing in cricket, where we say, "Watch the ball and keep your head still." Most of the tracking is done with the head. The eyes do very little work.'

Of all Test batters since 2006, when CricViz's ball-tracking began, A.B. de Villiers has the best record against deliveries of 87 mph or faster, averaging over 60. De Villiers defied Mitchell Johnson at his most menacing, averaging 56.83 in the three-Test series against Australia in 2014.

'That was an opportunity to show people and my teammates that I'm prepared to fight it out,' de Villiers recalls. 'It's more a personality trait than anything else.'

Facing such speeds, 'It all happened in slow motion,' de Villiers explains. 'My biggest strength was to be exceptionally still at the crease at the point of delivery. As the ball was about to leave his hand, that's where things started for me. I was always dead still.

'It's just a matter of being still and seeing that first metre after the ball is released from the hand. From then on, all the information would flow in.

'The faster the bowlers, the more important that gets because you can't afford to miss out on that first metre when the ball comes to you. When you're moving around, you miss that first yard – that's when you get into trouble.'

Contrary to popular belief, elite batters' reaction times are not unusually quick; their eyesight also isn't exceptional. Batters' brilliance lies less in genetics than in how they refine their anticipation – identifying cues to make complex decisions in the blink of an eye.

* * *

To face 90 mph bowling is to accept the possibility of terrible consequences if you are hit. 'I hated facing it but I loved it,' says Australia opener Justin Langer, who played from 1993 to 2007. 'You knew you're alive. Fast bowling is probably the foundation of great, great Test cricket.'

At least since Australia paired Jack Gregory and Ted McDonald together in 1920/21, the physical threat of facing pace bowling has been an indelible part of Test cricket. Remarkably, no one has been killed in a Test when facing a short ball; perhaps the closest was New Zealand tailender Ewen Chatfield, who stopped breathing when he was hit on the temple by a bouncer from England's Peter Lever in 1975. But Test players have been killed in first-class cricket. In 2014, Phillip Hughes was struck on the back of the neck during a Sheffield Shield match; he died of the blow, aged 25.

It was a terrible reminder that helmets have not eliminated the risk of fatalities. Research by Peter Brukner, the former Australian team doctor, and Tom Gara, a historian at the South Australian Museum, has found that blows to the head sustained while playing – and therefore concussions – have risen markedly since the 1990s, especially since the 2010s. This spike since helmets were popularised suggests several potential causes: bowlers are bowling faster; bowlers are more willing to use the bouncer, especially against lower-order players; and batters' techniques have changed for the worse.

'I once got to the halfway stage, but out of the corner of my eye I could see the local hospital,' England's Len Hutton said of hooking Keith Miller and Ray Lindwall in the 1950s.

'There are more front-foot players around now than there were in my time,' believes Ian Chappell, who played Tests from 1964 to 1980. 'A lot of players were back-foot players – in playing back, you give yourself that extra metre to see the ball and play the ball. Being on the back foot, you can get inside the ball – so if you miss the hook shot, the ball misses you. That's how it should be. But if you're hooking off the front foot, how do you get inside the line of the ball? You cannot.

'If you get inside the ball and you know that if you miss it, it is going to miss you, then you're more likely to watch the ball closely onto the bat. To me, that's crucial in hooking – you've got to watch the ball closely. Blokes who are hooking off the front foot when the ball is coming straight at their face – they'll turn their head. I think it's the turning of the head and taking the eye off the ball that sees more players get hit.'

After helmets became common in World Series Cricket, and were popularised over the 1980s, the sport has become notably safer, Brukner and Gara have illustrated. In the 1970s in Australia, nine players died while playing cricket at any level; another five died in the 1980s. From 1990, when helmets became common at all levels of the game, until 2016, there were only five recorded deaths across all Australian cricket. In a happy tale of unintended consequences, World Series Cricket can be said to have saved lives.

Hughes's death in 2014 led to two other significant improvements in safety: neck guards were added to helmets; and concussion substitutes were adopted in Tests from 2019, with anyone deemed to have suffered a concussion now automatically replaced. Before, there was no replacement for concussed players, leading players with suspected concussion to bat on – putting them at risk of suffering a second concussion, which is especially dangerous. Justin Langer estimates that he suffered 'six or seven' concussions during his career, including from his very first ball on Test debut, against West Indies' Ian Bishop. 'I literally got the boxers' knees – when the boxer gets knocked down, they get the jelly legs,' Langer recalls. 'They were vicious blows.' Today, Langer would have been withdrawn from the game.

If the physical threat of facing pace bowling has become slightly less, in other ways the Test batter's challenge has become more difficult. Whether or not the pace of the very quickest deliveries has increased, it is likely that more bowlers regularly bowl at speeds of around 90 mph than ever before. One slight caveat is that, until 1963, no-balls were determined by whether a bowler's back foot landed behind the bowling crease. Bowlers, especially taller ones, could then drag their back foot forward, and deliver the ball with their front foot several inches beyond the popping crease, reducing the distance to the opposing batter. The no-ball law was then changed to mandate that some part of the front foot must be behind the popping crease.

Compared to the 1990s, modern quicks 'have to be consistently faster', believes Damien Fleming, a pace bowler for Australia from 1994 to 2001 who became a coach and analyst. 'They're fitter, they're stronger – they've got a lot taller as well.' Better strength and conditioning means that 'the modern fast bowler bowls more balls to the optimum of their speed than a generation or two ago,' Fleming says. 'They don't drop too much from day one to day five. Whereas 30 years ago, the drop-off on day five would be more significant.'

Initially, the speed gun was not always to bowlers' benefit. The speed gun was first used in Australia for the 1998 Boxing Day Test against England. Fleming and Glenn McGrath, Australia's new-ball pair, became preoccupied with the number that the speed gun would show after each delivery. 'We kept trying to bowl short and fast,' Fleming recalls. 'That was certainly the worst I bowled at Test level.'

Australia's Brett Lee and Pakistan's Shoaib Akhtar were among the bowlers who strove to break the 100 mph barrier: cricket's equivalent of the four-minute mile. Contrary to what Fleming and McGrath had assumed, bouncers are slower than fuller deliveries: the ball loses pace after it hits the pitch. Indeed, speed guns remain notoriously unreliable; insiders say that they prioritise producing bowling speeds quickly over reliability. But speed guns have contributed to monitoring pace bowlers more rigorously, thereby giving coaches a better sense of which bowlers maintain pace.

Improvements in sports science, strength and conditioning and the surge of money in cricket has kept players in the Test game who might have been lost in previous generations. Pat Cummins went six years between playing his first and second Test; after suffering a series of stress fractures, his workload was managed assiduously. From his return, in 2017, he became among the world's most robust bowlers.

During his long Test hiatus, Cummins 'definitely' thought he wouldn't play another five-day match:

> It wasn't until within a couple of weeks of playing my second Test did I genuinely think that I was a chance to play another Test.
>
> To get back to playing Test matches, you feel like you needed to go back about six steps – being able to bowl back-to-back days; being able to bowl 20 overs and back-up; string together a few months. I didn't tick off any of those things for five or six years. I felt a long way away.
>
> I was incredibly well looked after: I was always contracted, had amazing medical support, didn't have to go and find another job or any of those things. The support staff of Cricket Australia and New South Wales was so much more patient with me than I wanted to be with myself. They'd seen it before. The whole time they'd say, 'Once you get to 23, 24, you should be over the hump of injuries.'

While Cummins was frustrated to wait so long until making his comeback, he believes the attention to detail on modern quicks ultimately extended his career. 'Because I was patient and forced to take rests, my back's basically perfect,' he reflects. 'Your bone strength isn't fully developed till you're about 23, 24. So that's why you get more stress fractures. And obviously, around that build up some strength, hopefully some better technique. But the main thing is just your bones are not dense enough or fully mature until you're 23 or 24 – you can do some damage in that time.'

Better awareness of fast-bowling mechanics has encouraged bowlers to incorporate methods shown to increase speed. Bowling with a braced front leg is one such way. Another is hyper-extending the arm, in the manner of India's Jasprit Bumrah. This enables him both to generate extra pace – the hyper-extension acts like a recoiling spring – and to release the ball later, at the equivalent of three o'clock, rather than twelve o'clock. In turn, the motion further reduces the amount of time that the ball has to travel to reach the batter.

* * *

More consistent pace has contributed to a decline in batting averages: from 2001 to 2016, each Test wicket cost an average of 34.21 runs, which fell to 29.97 from the start of 2017 to January 2025. Attacks have become deeper, with sides less reliant upon their one or two best bowlers; pitches have generally become spicier, with greater attempts to exploit home advantage.

Home teams have a major advantage: throughout history, they win about 16 Tests for every ten that they lose. The advantage was stronger in the 2010s than in any previous decade in Test history, suggesting that home sides are becoming more ruthless in tailoring conditions to suit their strengths.

The best quick bowlers have always relied upon much more than speed. But modern pace bowling has ramped up the threat facing batters. Bowlers have become more adept at bowling around the wicket, especially to left-handers; data has shown that, in general, most southpaws are more vulnerable to this line of attack.

In the 2010s, pace bowlers also refined the most potent innovation in quick bowling since reverse swing. The 'wobble seam' is altogether less glamorous. The ball is delivered with the fingers wider of the seam, or held more loosely, so it is released with the seam somewhere between eleven and one o'clock; some bowlers move their fingers across the seam. The ball will 'wobble' in the air, then move off the pitch in either direction; unlike with swing, batters cannot look at a bowler's wrist position for clues about which way it will move. The unpredictability of the movement off the seam gives bowlers a tool when the ball is not swinging; the knowledge that the ball could move in either direction, or simply move straight on, compels batters to play at more deliveries to protect their stumps.

The wobble seam's popularity embodies the general move from swing to seam. While swing is more alluring, seam is even more dangerous: the ball moves later off the pitch, so batters have even less time to react and fare worse. Those 0.4 seconds or so are made even shorter. Swing depends upon the state of the ball, leaving some bowlers devoid of any way of generating movement if the ball is not in a condition to swing conventionally or to reverse swing. But wobble seam is a more reliable friend. Essentially, any ball, at any time, can wobble-seam if it is delivered in the right way.

Pakistan's Mohammad Asif and Australia's Stuart Clark first popularised the wobble seam in the late 2000s. 'He was unbelievable,' Kevin Pietersen says of facing Asif in 2006 and 2010. 'You had no idea which way it was going to go. It also felt like it accelerated off the wicket. He was an absolute joke.' Pietersen's experience showed why wobble seam is more lethal than conventional seam. This gives clues about which way the ball will move after pitching: bowled with a more upright seam, tilting towards where the ball will seam. But the wobble seam denies batters this essential information.

The wobble seam was then deployed by bowlers including England's James Anderson and Stuart Broad, New Zealand's Tim Southee, South Africa's Vernon Philander, Pakistan's Mohammad Abbas and Australia's Cummins, Josh Hazlewood and Mitchell Starc.

'When I was really young, swing was the only thing I was thinking about,' Cummins reflects. Yet he came to realise that while the wobble seam 'is not as sexy', it would be more effective. This intuition is backed up by data. As Ben Gardner noted for *Wisden Cricket Monthly*, CricViz have shown that balls that swing over 1.5 degrees average around 27 runs per wicket; balls that seam over 0.75 degrees – half as much – average 20.

Cummins took to bowling wobble seam 'basically 100 per cent of the time', he explains. 'I never really try and swing the ball. I'm always looking for nip and, particularly in Australia, trying to get some bounce.'

Like some of the most skilled wobble-seam bowlers, Cummins believes that he can generate some control of which way the ball moves with his action. 'If I want to seam it out, I'd seam it out 80 per cent of the time,' he explains. 'If I'm jumping out at the crease it is more likely I'm going to bowl that as an away-nipper.'

This method underpinned perhaps Cummins's most famous delivery. At Manchester in 2019, Cummins seamed a ball past Joe Root's groping bat and uprooted the top of his off stump first ball; the next day, Australia retained the Ashes. 'That's my version of the wobble ball,' he says. 'If I get the seam going like that it normally means that it leaves the batter just a little bit and bounces.'

What was hailed as an invention by Asif or Clark actually might have been a reinvention. In the 1990s, Allan Donald and Curtly Ambrose discussed how to bowl to Sachin Tendulkar. Ambrose, Donald recounted, said that he deployed what would become known as the wobble seam: 'It was an interesting discussion about having to make Tendulkar play every single ball.' But, with video footage relatively unsophisticated, the delivery appears to have been the preserve of a select few.

The use of video and data, analysed microscopically, means that bowling secrets spread faster than ever. While batters can learn from each other in a similar way, on balance modern technology probably benefits bowlers more. Bowlers, after all, set the terms of the contest. Both sides might know, say, that a particular left-hander is much more vulnerable to deliveries from around the wicket. But the bowling side are free to act upon this knowledge. Fielding sides have always thought about opponents in this way, as the tale of Bodyline in 1932/33 shows. Modern analysis allows teams to be far more precise in how they identify, and exploit, batters' weaknesses.

*　*　*

When a leading pace bowler and batter meet, they can produce sport at its most intoxicating. At times like these, a Test seems less like a fight between teams than a personal duel.

Mike Atherton's tussle with Allan Donald at Trent Bridge in 1998 encapsulates Test cricket at its most primal. On the fourth evening, England had progressed to 76–1, in pursuit of their target of 247, when Donald returned to bowl. He was, at the time, perhaps the world's leading pace bowler. And he knew the stakes: dismiss Atherton, and it could well precipitate a collapse, which would hand South Africa an unassailable 2–0 series lead.

Atherton, too, knew the stakes. Withstand Donald, and he would set England on course to level the series at 1–1, and the chance to clinch a series win in the final Test. The situation demanded all of his technical fortitude and bloody-mindedness. 'It was great fun – Sunday evening, full house, match on the line, a brilliant fast bowler bowling very fast.'

In the second over of his spell, Donald moved to bowling around the wicket: the angle from which fast bowlers are most physically imposing. In his next over Atherton gloved – or punched, as Donald says – a brutish delivery behind, taken by wicketkeeper Mark Boucher. Donald raised his arms aloft in triumph. In the days before the Decision Review System, all that mattered was that the umpire did not give Atherton out.

Now, having been denied the wicket that was his due, Donald was enraged. 'There was a lot said on that field,' he recalls; swearing in Afrikaans and English alike.

Atherton inside-edged Donald's next ball for four. He returned the bowler's many stares, knowing that the bowler would have to break eye contact first. As Donald's speed ratcheted up, well past 90 mph, deliveries slammed into the batter's gloves, thigh and chest; Atherton hooked a ball over square leg for two.

Nasser Hussain, England's number three, spent most of Donald's spell at the non-striker's end. With England 100–1, Hussain gloved another brutish delivery behind; this time, Boucher spilled it, leaving Donald enraged.

Somehow, Atherton endured Donald's 45-minute spell at the end of the day. On day five, Atherton's 98 not out clinched a deceptively simple-sounding eight-wicket win; England won a riveting final Test by 23 runs at Leeds to seal the series 2–1.

The contest transcended matters of victory and defeat. After the match, Atherton showed Donald the right glove that bore the palpable red mark of the delivery which had been caught yet not given out. Donald signed it.

'It was just the best bit of cricket I've ever been involved in,' Donald reflects. 'Me and this bloke Atherton just never blinked an eyelid – we just wanted to keep coming at each other. There were a lot of people screaming and shouting on the field, but the way he battled, the way he got out of that situation, was exemplary.'

Extended passages like this are an intrinsic part of the Test game. For all the skills showcased in the shorter formats, the prolonged duel is an essential part of Test cricket's allure.

33

NEW ZEALAND'S MOMENT

Mike Hesson, New Zealand's head coach, knocked on Brendon McCullum's hotel room in Cape Town. The captain had just grabbed a beer from his fridge, 'trying to find some answers at the bottom of the bottle'.

It was the evening of 2 January 2013. For McCullum, it ought to have been a time for celebration: his first day as Test captain. Instead, New Zealand were all out for 45, the lowest score in any Test for 39 years. South Africa had soared to 252–3 by the close.

A few minutes after Hesson got to McCullum's room, Bob Carter, the assistant coach, and Mike Sandle, the team manager, arrived too. The meeting was not preplanned; all had come to see the captain. Over a few drinks, they came to realise that 'the perception of the New Zealand cricket team was that we were overpaid, underdelivering, lazy prima donnas,' McCullum said. 'I was one of those prima donnas.'

The greatest problem, the quartet agreed, was of culture. With 'no real certainty over selection,' Hesson told me, 'there was a real self-preservation mode ... Players were basically just looking to do enough to stay in the team.'

Out of this recognition came a determination to find a better way. McCullum tried to channel the values learned as a boy in windswept south Dunedin. He explained to me:

> We had to be brutally honest with ourselves about how we were going to turn it around, and what we were going to do to try

and become more of a representation of our New Zealand people, because I think we weren't really playing with any type of soul.

We just wanted to be strong representations of our people. Our people are humble, we're hard-working, we can handle failure, but we just want to be known to be hard to beat.

After New Zealand lost by an innings on day three, players discussed the new vision. 'It was definitely a moment in time,' recalls Kane Williamson, then a young batter. 'People were quite quick to adopt that change in direction and commit to something more than ourselves. It was "Where can we try and take this team and how can we do it together and have a lot of fun doing it?"'

With the smallest population of any Test nation and many leading athletes gravitating to rugby, New Zealand had to maximise every iota of what they had. 'We decided that money can't be an excuse,' Sandle told me. 'A lot of the things that we can control will cost no money – that's fitness, working hard, attitude, giving to the team'.

The vision boiled down to being more authentic. Sledging – an imitation of Australia's approach but without the quality of players to back it up – was out, replaced by cricket with fewer histrionics. More stable selection encouraged selflessness. New Zealand doubled down on the attention that they gave fitness and fielding. The side aimed to combine toughness with enjoyment.

'Just because there's more at stake now doesn't mean you should lose the innocence of why you played the game in the first place,' McCullum explained. 'For a long time I had lost that, and I think our team had lost that.'

* * *

Seldom has the power of example been stronger. McCullum averaged 35.63 while scoring at a strike rate of 60 before he was made captain, albeit normally while keeping wicket too. As Test skipper, McCullum averaged 45.28 and scored at a strike rate of 74.

For New Zealand, the first Test of 2014 began almost as inauspiciously as their first of 2013. New Zealand were 30–3 against India in Auckland when McCullum walked out to bat. He responded with a rollicking 224, including five sixes. It set up New Zealand's first Test victory against India for 12 years.

But New Zealand faced a crushing defeat in the second and final Test in Wellington. All out for 192 on day one, New Zealand conceded a deficit of 246. When McCullum, nursing back pain, walked out in the second innings, early on day three, New Zealand were 52–3. They were soon 94–5, still trailing by 152 runs.

McCullum was joined by B.J. Watling. Where McCullum's natural approach – initially suppressed, as he took 146 balls to reach 50, before counter-attacking against the second new ball – was gallivanting, Watling's was stoic. Together, they combined for 352 runs across 123 overs, more than four sessions together unabated. James Neesham then hit a century too.

When he walked off after day four against India, on 281 not out, McCullum strode towards his seat in the changing rooms. He found an ice bucket with two cans of beer, and a packet of cigarettes.

Back in 1991 against Sri Lanka at the Basin Reserve, Martin Crowe had approached New Zealand's maiden Test triple century. On 299, he edged behind; Crowe likened the experience to climbing Everest and pulling a hamstring in the last stride.

The long queues outside Wellington – the scene of Crowe's near-miss – on day five reflected the expectation that McCullum could finally be the first Kiwi to score 300. Before walking out to bat, McCullum settled his nerves with a final cigarette in the changing room. When he cut a delivery between the slips and gully, a country rose to their feet: the ovation lasted for four minutes.

No one was happier than Crowe, by now battling terminal cancer. 'I have finally removed the one remaining stone in my shoe,' he wrote for ESPNcricinfo. 'Not a week would go by when I wouldn't be reminded of the one run I craved so much. It tore at me like a vulture pecking dead flesh.'

McCullum's history-making ensured a draw and a 1–0 series victory against India. It was part of a sequence of seven successive undefeated Test series, the longest in New Zealand history. Australia, not for the first time, ended their winning streak. But McCullum's farewell was still in keeping with his spirit: in Christchurch in February 2016, he slammed a century in 54 balls, a new Test record.

* * *

While New Zealand were recovering from the ignominy of being all out for 45 in 2013, the International Cricket Council were grappling with something even more onerous: how to bring structure to Test cricket.

Ever since what came to be classed as the first Test, in 1877, the format had bumbled on without an overarching structure. Other sports came to embrace World Cups. In the one-day format, so did cricket, with the women's World Cup launching in 1973 and the men's World Cup following in 1975.

Yet men's Test cricket continued to reflect its Victorian roots. Sides were invited to tour for multi-match series, as in the days of boat travel. Where they toured and when was governed partly by tradition – England and Australia generally hosted each other every four years – and mostly by administrators' whims, the result of short-term alliances and greed. Although the family of Test nations was small – just six active countries in the 1970s – sides could go unfathomably long periods without meeting. Pakistan didn't face West Indies between 1959 and 1975; England only met India in one series from 1993 to 2001. Series were of different length, lasting anything from one game to six.

The quaint structure of bilateral matches, meandering on without any final, was out of kilter with all other major sports. Until 2002, Test cricket didn't even bother with rankings. Even these had only limited relevance, with no symmetry in fixture lists. In August 2016 alone, three teams were ranked number one; that year, the ranking changed hands five times. The financial rewards offered for five-day excellence did not live up to administrators' platitudes about 'protecting the primacy of Test cricket'. In 2011, Gideon Haigh noted, the ICC executive board spent more on their own entertainment at the 2,000th Test than on annual prize money for the world's number one Test nation.

Towards the end of the 20th century, the International Cricket Council, as it was called from 1987, belatedly professionalised. From 1993, the ICC separated completely from the Marylebone Cricket Club, appointing a chief executive for the first time. In 2005, the ICC moved its headquarters from the Clock Tower at Lord's to Dubai, lured by a 50-year tax exemption; symbolically, this marked the end of English control of the game.

Administrators grappled with the need to create a more coherent global structure. The first step was the Future Tours Programme, which launched in 2001. All ten Test nations agreed to tour and host each other over a ten-year period, a commitment whittled down in subsequent editions.

As T20 grew, with leagues proliferating around the world, the structure of Tests came to seem more archaic. Essentially, there was no structure. Attempts to introduce more meritocracy and context repeatedly ran into short-termism and self-interest.

Simply to recount the number of failed plans for Test cricket is dizzying. In 2004, proposals for the top eight nations to play each other home and away over a four-year period were opposed by Bangladesh and Zimbabwe, who would largely have been limited to inbound tours. A plan for a World Test Championship in 2008, pushed by Australia, was rejected: teams wanted to retain more control over their schedule. A World Test Championship, featuring the top four sides, was originally agreed for 2013. Then it was postponed until 2017; it was cancelled altogether because broadcasters thought it worth less than the Champions Trophy ODI tournament. In 2014, two divisions were proposed, but with Australia, England and India, the 'Big Three', all exempt from relegation. In 2016, a model for two divisions, of seven and five, with promotion and relegation every two years, was championed by David Richardson, the ICC chief executive. Sri Lanka, Bangladesh and Zimbabwe, who all feared being in Division Two, helped to scupper this plan.

When an overarching structure for Test cricket was finally agreed, it was inevitably beset by compromises. The World Test Championship was essentially imposed upon an already agreed fixture list. This explains its curious form, with the nine competing nations only playing six opponents each, three at home and away over the two-year cycle. The complex points system, with teams ranked on percentage of points contested, reflects the difficulties of creating a table when series are of different length. Rather than semi-finals, the championship has only a final. For many in England, accustomed to long series against the best teams, the concept seems futile. But the championship gives more context to series that lack a historic rivalry, potentially driving greater interest. The second final, between Australia and India in 2023, was the most-watched Test of all time.

Test cricket has been a byword for conservatism. Yet this image conceals how much has actually been altered. Tests have gone from being played by two sides to 12. Matches have been scheduled over three, four, five, six or unlimited days, on uncovered or covered pitches. Overs have been four, five, six or eight balls long, delivered by cricketers bowling underarm or overarm with a red ball or – since 2015, when day-night games were introduced – sometimes a pink one. For all its flaws, the World Test Championship illustrates the game's eternal evolution.

* * *

After an excruciating defeat in the 2019 World Cup final at Lord's, New Zealand were in need of a new challenge. A month later, they began their inaugural World Test Championship campaign.

By now, McCullum had retired, replaced by Kane Williamson. In the Bay of Plenty, along the north coast, the young Williamson – an identical twin, following three girls – grew up in a sports-mad family. The family house backed onto Pillans Point, where Williamson went to school; when Kane was five or six, his dad, a keen club player, helped to raise money to build nets there.

Whether practising cricket or other sports, Williamson brought an unusual focus. His dad nurtured Kane's play off the back foot: a common New Zealand weakness, with pitches making it difficult to trust the bounce. Kane also trained to use his feet against spin.

'The idea was that you get to it on the full and wouldn't have as many problems,' Kane recalls. 'We'd do lots of throw-downs and practise different things. The whole "ten more" and an hour later you're still there.' Above all, he says, 'what really drew me to cricket from a young age was that idea of problem-solving.'

When he left school, Williamson had already made around 40 centuries. Aged 20, he made his Test debut in Ahmedabad: 'I remember thinking, "A lot of these players were on my backyard cricket team."' He made 131 in his maiden innings.

Williamson only averaged 31.47 in his first 25 Tests. But he gained a sense of what he needed to do to thrive in the format:

> You get exposed in certain areas that would shape where you need to go next. So whether it was your first experience in the subcontinent or playing against tall, quick bowling, there are a number of new experiences throughout the early years.
>
> You're always trying to adjust and adapt to what's in front of you, especially when you're having those experiences for the first time. And I tried to remind myself that I was just trying to be better.

But then realise that failure in the sport is there, and it's there often. And to be able to accept that you can go out and commit to a plan wholeheartedly – that you might get a good ball and be able to see it for what it is rather than be hypercritical. How can you use the experience to get better?

When Williamson was 24, and had already hit nine Test centuries, Crowe declared, 'We're seeing the dawn of probably our greatest ever batsman.' Williamson's undemonstrative nature made him 'David playing like Goliath,' Crowe wrote. 'Batting suited him from the minute he picked up his first bat; he had the perfect height, balance, fast-twitch muscles, electric feet, an inquisitive mind.'

* * *

New Zealand began the 2020/21 summer needing to win all four of their Tests, against West Indies and Pakistan, to have a chance of qualifying for the inaugural final. In the first game against West Indies, Williamson scored 251; in the second, he was on paternity leave, but New Zealand won by an innings again.

When Williamson returned for the Boxing Day Test at Mount Maunganui, his local ground, he encountered far more difficult opposition. He hit a serene 129, but Pakistan's batters resisted on a flat pitch. In the second innings, Williamson declared early, saying after the game that he was motivated by the 'carrot' of the World Test Championship. Pakistan were set 373 runs to win in 128 overs, a run rate of under three.

From 75–4 on the fifth morning, Fawad Alam and captain Mohammad Rizwan batted in tandem for 63.2 overs. With each one, New Zealand could see their dream slipping away.

By this point, left-arm quick Neil Wagner had two broken toes: the product of a yorker from Shaheen Shah Afridi earlier in the match. On the final morning, Wagner arrived at the ground unable to walk.

Williamson tried to time Wagner's spells around his painkilling injections. While Alam and Rizwan batted during the final session, Wagner said prayers at fine leg, imploring God to 'just give me one more over'; he bowled 11 straight in the final session. In the seventh over of his spell, Wagner's short ball strangled centurion Fawad Alam down the leg side. By the end of his 11-over spell, Wagner had added Faheem Ashraf – edging a rare fuller ball behind, after being pushed back by a short-ball barrage.

'To break two toes and try and run in just shows what it means to play for this team,' Wagner told me. Originally a new-ball swing bowler from Pretoria, Wagner had emigrated to New Zealand. Recognising the new-ball excellence of Tim Southee and Trent Boult, he 'tried to think about how I can actually complement them' and focused on developing old-ball skills. With ostensibly unremarkable gifts – on the small side for a fast bowler, normally bowling just above 80 mph – Wagner turned himself into a unique threat.

Most quicks have a bouncer or two; Wagner developed an entire collection. He had the stamina to bowl five short balls an over at different lengths, with most below shoulder height and so not counting towards the two bouncers permitted per over. Other bowlers have sought to follow this template to extract life from unresponsive flat pitches.

'I always had to rely on different things and that is just work ethic and banging the ball in as hard as I can,' Wagner told me. When bowling a gruelling spell, 'the sacrifices of everything that I've gone through to try and be where I am, all those things come to mind. It motivates you to play through every bit of pain.'

With five overs remaining, Williamson summoned left-arm spinner Mitchell Santner back into the attack. From his third ball, Santner deceived Naseem Shah in the air and plucked out a return catch, sealing victory with 4.3 overs remaining. When Williamson peeled off 238 in the next Test, and Australia stumbled – losing at home to India, before fears over Covid-19 led to their series in South

Africa being cancelled – it confirmed New Zealand's place in the final.

It was reward for eight years of unobtrusive excellence, stretching back to Cape Town 2013. Just before the 2021 World Test Championship final, New Zealand made six changes for the second and final Test against England at Edgbaston. They still won inside four days. It was New Zealand's 10th victory in 12 series; the sequence included beating England twice at home and once away and defeating India 2–0 in 2020. Perhaps most notably, New Zealand defeated Pakistan 2–1 in the UAE in 2018; Williamson made 89 and 139 in the decider. During Pakistan's eight years in the UAE, New Zealand were the sole side from outside Asia to defeat them in a series there.

* * *

New Zealand's success can be explained in two broad ways. The first is the great man theory of history. In this light, McCullum was the catalyst for New Zealand's ascent; the serendipity of Williamson, Southee and Boult all being born within 20 months of each other then ensured that the revival continued after he left.

But there is another interpretation, which could be called Whig history. This sees New Zealand's rise as an institutional triumph: a testament to a robust and nimble national cricket structure.

In 1995, with New Zealand in strife – three players admitted to smoking marijuana on tour in South Africa, with claims that over half the squad were involved – New Zealand Cricket set up a committee, chaired by John Hood, to review the game's structure. The Hood Report found a governing body unfit for purpose. The board had 13 members, all part-time. They were also all drawn from the six provincial associations, rendering them liable to act according to their province's interests. The organisation was too large, too unwieldy and too parochial. In this respect, of course, it was much like New Zealand's rivals. But, unusually, the board embraced the report's recommendations: the 13 members voted themselves out of existence. They were replaced by a seven-person board of professional administrators; their actions were dictated by what was best for the game in the country, not merely a particular province. The substance of the reforms was reinforced in 2013: New Zealand Cricket changed its constitution to ensure director independence and greater cricket expertise.

The first professional national contracts were introduced in 1995. The New Zealand Cricket Players Association was created in 2001; this negotiated a fixed proportion of revenue to be distributed to player contracts. Now, players were full-time professionals for seven months a year; coaches became professional too. Before, 'The characters you could pick were pretty much people who were in jobs that could afford to take two or three months off, so clearly you weren't always getting the best people,' said Mike Hesson. He began his coaching career in Otago in 1996, and was New Zealand coach from 2012 to 2018.

The Players Association pushed for radical changes to the domestic game. In 2002/03, domestic matches were played at 24 different grounds, in conditions that bore little resemblance to the flat pitches seen in Test cricket. In 2005, a 'warrant of fitness' – criteria for playing and practice facilities which any ground hosting domestic cricket had to meet – was introduced. Batting averages in first-class cricket rose. Conditions that better replicated the international game, and far more investment in the A team programme, helped players make the step up. Since 2018, leading cricketers can train outdoors all year round, after the High Performance Centre at Lincoln University opened all-weather facilities. As T20 transformed the game, New Zealand reacted nimbly. The board allowed players to miss low-key internationals to play in overseas leagues; such pragmatism helped prevent the premature international retirements that weakened many rivals.

New Zealand also benefited from a culture that put the national team's interests first. Similar to the model used in rugby, a portion of each domestic head coach's salary is directly paid by NZC; developing international players is part of each coach's key performance indicators. National coaches can make requests to domestic teams: Hesson asked that B.J. Watling move down from opening for Northern Districts, his province, to bat in the middle order and keep wicket. As keeper, Watling was at the heart of the team to reach the World Test Championship final.

* * *

And so when India and New Zealand arrived in Southampton in June 2021, it was the culmination of two remarkable journeys: Test cricket's, to have a winner-takes-all match decide the world champion for the first time in its 144-year existence; and New Zealand's. Compared to a normal Test, the final 'did feel different', Williamson recalls. 'It was intense.'

Rain marred the week. Under sepulchral skies between the showers, 'When you were batting out there, you never felt in,' Williamson explains. 'The ball was always going past the outside edge. And the challenge was from both ends.'

The teams balanced their attacks very differently. India picked three seamers and both of their spin-bowling allrounders, Ravindra Jadeja and Ravichandran Ashwin. New Zealand picked four front-line seamers; the metronomic Colin de Grandhomme provided auxiliary seam too.

The pace quartet were wonderfully complementary. Southee, who would retire second to Richard Hadlee as New Zealand's top Test wicket-taker, and Boult swung the new ball prodigiously, Boult from his left-arm angle. Both had also subtly refined their craft, learning the wobble-seam delivery; Southee snared Shubman Gill with this ball in the second innings, darting the ball back after a series of outswingers.

With India threatening to bat out a draw on the final afternoon, a typically ferocious Wagner spell extended into a 10th over. Then, his variation – a ball that wasn't short – elicited an edge from Jadeja.

The most valuable member of the quartet in the final was the newest. Kyle Jamieson showed his capacity to swing and seam the ball from his menacing 6 ft 8 in height, taking 5–31 from 22 overs in the first innings. On the sixth morning, his bounce and probing line just outside off stump led Virat Kohli and Cheteshwar Pujara to edge deliveries in consecutive overs.

The fourth innings, which began midway through day six, the reserve day, loomed with New Zealand requiring 139 to be champions. If it sounded easy, only one man – Devon Conway, with 54 – had made a half-century in the first three innings. Like Wagner, Conway had emigrated from South Africa – selling his house and car when he moved from Johannesburg to Wellington aged 26, with only a contract to play for a local club and coach in schools. 'It was basically the mindset of saying, "Right, we're going to do this and we're going to fully commit,"' he recalled.

When Conway fell lbw to Ashwin on the final afternoon, New Zealand were 44–2. With the pitch turning, India had hope of securing a win or slowing the scoring rate so much that the Test would be drawn, the title shared.

Ross Taylor joined Williamson. The son of a Samoan mother and a Pākehā (of white European descent) father, Taylor was only the second player of Samoan heritage to play Tests for New Zealand. Growing up, Taylor sometimes felt 'a brown face in a vanilla line-up', he wrote in his autobiography. His first name was Luteru, but schoolteachers started calling him Ross, his middle name, which he stuck to.

An aggressive driver, Taylor was adept at hoisting balls from off stump over the midwicket boundary; he honed the shot in *kilikiti*, a Samoan variant of cricket, played with a rubber ball and a bat shaped like a baseball bat. 'I played it a lot,' he explains. 'I was just trying to whack every ball. I got told off for blocking. You've got to try and smack it as far as you can.'

Back in 2011, aged 27, Taylor was appointed captain in all formats. After Hesson became head coach in 2012, he advocated making McCullum white-ball captain. On a tour of Sri Lanka, shocked after learning of his own coach pushing for his removal, Taylor survived 'two weeks on maybe an hour, two hours sleep a night'.

In the second and final Test, Taylor hit 142 and 74 in Colombo, top-scoring in both innings to square the series 1–1. Given the circumstances, conditions and opposition, Crowe rated it New Zealand's second finest Test performance, behind only Richard Hadlee's 15 wickets in the match against Australia in 1985.

'I have no idea how it happened – it shows the power of the mind,' Taylor says. 'A lot is made now about mental well-being – that wasn't around in 2012. It was made out to be a cricketing issue, whereas really it was a well-being issue.'

It was the last Test of his reign. Taylor declined to stay on as Test captain only, and opted out of the tour to South Africa in 2013. Back in the ranks, Taylor channelled his frustrations and used statistics as 'the driver when things weren't going well – it gives you a balance'. He averaged 49.10 under McCullum and 47.21 under Williamson.

Almost always with Williamson at three and Taylor four, the pair played for 11 years in tandem. Their defining moment came in the second innings of the final in Southampton.

The quality of India's attack was such that, for 31 balls early in their stand, New Zealand didn't score. Taylor's three boundaries in six balls – a steer through backward point from Shami, a whip over mid-on from Ashwin, and a drive through cover – put New Zealand on course once again. Williamson accumulated steadily, then punched a four through point off Shami. In the last throes of the game, New Zealand could savour the occasion. 'About 20 runs out,' Williamson recalls, 'it was "Right, let's try and be more positive and get this done."'

Williamson's scores of 49 and 52 not out were two of the three highest innings in the Test. He and Taylor had both endured consecutive defeats in the ODI World Cup final; before the Test, they had a dinner discussing how out-of-sorts they felt. They took it upon themselves to take New Zealand to their first world title.

Taylor had begun his first-class career in 2002, just as domestic cricket turned professional: he was the last link with New Zealand's semi-professional age. He observed how New Zealand shed their inferiority complex. 'I always felt the team was too busy watching Australia warm up – we were almost beaten before we turned up,' he reflects. Winning the Test Championship 'made us feel vindicated – it was just nice for that group of players to finally win a World Cup.'

In the age of the Big Three, New Zealand provided a counterpoint to the notion of financial determinism in international cricket. A nation of five million, where cricket will never be the national sport, had defeated one of 1.4 billion, where cricket's primacy is unchallenged. A board with annual revenue of £28 million – smaller than Surrey County Cricket Club, let alone major Indian Premier League franchises – had toppled one who brought in £380 million a year.

It took New Zealand 26 years to win a Test and 13 more to win a series. Another 52 years later, they finally stood atop the Test game. For the World Test Championship, the inaugural victors were apt: the format's vibrancy depends on the game continuing to captivate countries beyond the Big Three.

After Taylor clipped the winning runs on a glorious midsummer's evening, he turned to Williamson: 'Well, we're bloody world champions and no one can take that away.' Williamson put his right arm around Taylor and said, 'F***, yeah.' When Taylor woke up next morning, he was still in his whites.

34

MORE THAN JUST A COMMONWEALTH CLUB

Test cricket has not been a friend to new nations. United States, Argentina and Kenya all learned as much at various points in cricket's history. Administrators have protected the exclusivity of Test status, like members of a snooty Victorian members' club delighting in their elevated company. Aspiring members have been treated with distrust and suspicion.

The attitude to expansion stands in contrast to other sports. Over 200 countries have played full football internationals; more than 100 have played full rugby internationals. Yet the International Cricket Council has kept Test status the preserve of a select few nations: in part snobbery about the quality that exists outside the club; in part a lack of interest in growing the sport; and in part a belief that too many sides would undermine the sanctity of statistics.

Administrators have continually rejected ideas of creating a multi-tiered system with promotion and relegation between divisions. Full one-day international status has been awarded only a little more generously; Twenty20, first played at men's international level in 2005, has become seen as the game's globalisation tool.

All of this emphasises the achievement of Afghanistan and Ireland when, in June 2017, they became the 11th and 12th Full Member nations, winning the right to play Test matches. In the 17 years since Bangladesh's elevation, many had come to believe that the rarefied group of Test nations would never welcome another member again.

* * *

Jagmohan Dalmiya, the ICC president from 1997 to 2000, was the first global administrator to believe that cricket could significantly expand its footprint. Dalmiya was a critical figure in Bangladesh becoming the 10th Test nation in 2000 and believed that the game could develop more competitive teams.

In the new century, cricket became newly welcoming to emerging nations; the number of ICC member nations swelled by dozens. Even with Full Members still reserving 75 per cent of the ICC's cash for themselves, the burgeoning value of television rights trickled down. Associate nations (together with a lower category of Affiliate nations, which was later abolished) received about US$65 million from 1999 to 2007, which rose to $250 million from 2007 to 2015. During this time, leading Associates received over $1m a year each from the ICC. While this was barely 10 per cent as much as Test nations, for the first time Associates were able to make players professional, and hire full-time coaches and administrators to support them.

As well as extra cash, Associates also had greater opportunity to showcase their quality. The World Cup expanded from 12 to 14 nations in 2003, then to 16 in 2007; from 2005, ODI status expanded to allow leading Associates to play ODIs against Test nations outside world events. In 2001, the ICC hired Bob Woolmer, the former England Test cricketer and South Africa coach, as their first high-performance manager, charging him with improving global standards.

Woolmer pushed for the creation of the Intercontinental Cup in 2004, which saw Associates compete in regular first-class matches against each other for the first time. The competition aimed both to improve players' skills, with Woolmer convinced that playing first-class cricket would create better limited-overs players too, and create a pathway for eventual elevation to Test status. After the 2003 World

Cup, when Kenya reached the semi-finals and Canada beat Bangladesh, Woolmer advocated the Intercontinental Cup evolving into the second division of Test cricket, envisaging two Test leagues of eight teams each.

At the 2007 World Cup, on St Patrick's Day, Ireland played Pakistan. As they left their dressing room, they were mocked by a group of Pakistani fans: 'You should be back in the pub and you should be drinking Guinness celebrating St Patrick's Day. You don't play cricket.' By the day's end no one was mocking Ireland any more: on a green pitch, they won by three wickets, knocking Pakistan out of the World Cup. It represented the fulfilment of Woolmer's vision. But Woolmer could not enjoy being vindicated: he was now Pakistan coach. Even in defeat, he reaffirmed his global vision, supporting the enlarged World Cup. 'I'm fully in favour of 16 teams,' he said. With Bangladesh defeating India on the same day, Woolmer declared, 'March 17, 2007 will be a historic day for cricket.' Tragically, Woolmer died suddenly the following day.

Later in the tournament, Ireland beat Bangladesh, to add to victory over Pakistan and a tie with Zimbabwe. For a side that included a postal worker, an electrician, a van driver and a farmer, it was a spectacular performance. Ireland's first World Cup catapulted the game back into the nation's consciousness.

In the mid-to-late 19th century, cricket was Ireland's most popular sport, played by Catholics and Protestants alike and by different classes, the historian Paul Rouse wrote. In the 1870s, there were teams in all 32 counties, and perhaps 1,000 cricket teams actively playing in Ireland. As Rouse documented, an editorial in the *Irish Sportsman* in 1875 declared that cricket 'is one of the few English importations with which the most sincere "Nationalist" cannot find any cause of quarrel, and in which all ranks and classes may meet on equal terms'.

Kilkenny, later home to Ireland's best hurling team, was first a cricket stronghold. In the county and beyond, cricket was, in part, a victim of the break-up of the old landed estates. Kilkenny had drawn players from landlords, but also had sides comprising tenants and labourers who built pitches on the land, explains the historian Steve Dolan.

Perhaps more than anything, cricket suffered from growing Irish nationalism, attacked as an 'English' game. The Gaelic Athletic Association, founded in 1884, aimed to popularise Irish games like hurling and Gaelic football. In 1901, the GAA prohibited all members from playing, or even watching, 'foreign' sports like cricket. 'The Ban' lasted until 1971. In County Tipperary, for instance, the number of cricket teams fell from 117 in the 1870s to nine by World War I. The decline was accelerated by the lack of an overarching national governing body, Rouse noted; the Irish Cricket Union was not created until 1923.

Cricket remained a fringe sport in Northern Ireland, which was created in 1921 after partition; in the Republic, it was marginalised further after independence and confined to small, passionate pockets. James Joyce was a noted fan, playing at school in County Kildare; his books are peppered with cricket references. In his 1916 novel *A Portrait of the Artist as a Young Man,* Joyce wrote, 'In the soft grey silence he could hear the bump of the balls: and from here and from there through the quiet air the sound of the cricket bats: pick, pack, pock, puck: like drops of water in a fountain falling softly in the brimming bowl.' Samuel Beckett, the playwright, played at Dublin University, playing two first-class games; he is the only Nobel literature laureate to play first-class cricket.

Unlike in football, Ireland continued to play as an all-Ireland side featuring players from both sides of the border. They often played one- or two-day friendly matches against countries touring England; in a game in 1969, they bowled West Indies out for 25 at Sion Mills. Until 1993, Ireland did not even have an official national team or enter World Cup qualification, instead existing on the edge of the English structure, tantamount to a minor county. While floundering in the 2003 World Cup qualifiers, held in Canada in 2001, Ireland enlisted a journalist to act as a substitute fielder. The national team played 'mickey-mouse cricket', as Ed Joyce (no relation of James), then the side's most prominent player, later put it. When Adi Birrell arrived as coach in 2002, he was handed the keys to a car, and told that the boot doubled as the storeroom for Ireland's team kit.

As a boy, Ed Joyce hid his cricket equipment when travelling on trains in Dublin: the sport was perceived as a game for Anglophile 'West Brits'. Joyce became the first born-and-raised Irishman for half a century to enjoy an extensive county career. 'Coming from Ireland, there was a big inferiority complex,' Ed told me. 'We just assumed everyone from England was much better.'

After Joyce made his debut for Middlesex in 1999, counties became alert to Irish talent. Irish cricketers, from both the Republic of Ireland and Northern Ireland, did not count as overseas players, rendering them more attractive. The side who beat Pakistan in 2007 included six men who had played either for English counties or for MCC Young Cricketers. Ireland's team was supplemented by committed part-timers and migrants from Australia and South Africa, who moved to the country during the years of the 'Celtic Tiger'.

Joyce was not on the field for Ireland against Pakistan. During the World Cup he played for England, who could offer far greater cricketing and financial opportunities. Even after Cricket Ireland introduced professional contracts from 2008, players still left for England – Eoin Morgan, who would lead England to World Cup glory, in 2009 and Boyd Rankin in 2013.

Without Morgan, but with Joyce now back, Ireland toppled England in the 2011 World Cup. 'The biggest thing that broke down the idea of cricket being an English sport was the Irish people witnessing an Irish team beat England at what they call their own sport,' John Mooney, who struck the winning runs in Bangalore, later said.

World Cup successes also highlighted the barriers that Ireland faced, especially in two areas: funding and fixtures. When Ireland reached the Super Eights in the 2007 World Cup, they received US$56,000; Zimbabwe, knocked out in the first stage, earned US$11 million, because they were a Full Member. Between the 2011 and 2015 World Cups, Ireland played only nine ODIs against Test nations. All the while, they remained locked out of Test status, despite the board's protests that only this could develop the game and prevent players from leaving for England.

* * *

Where Irish cricket was influenced by the proximity to England, Afghanistan cricket was shaped by its border with Pakistan. The first recorded game of cricket in what is now Afghanistan took place in 1839, when British soldiers in Kabul played the game during the First Anglo-Afghan War. But the game was lost to the country. After the Soviet Union's invasion in 1979, millions of Afghans fled to Pakistan, principally to the Kacha Garhi refugee camp in Peshawar; the Taliban's rule in Afghanistan, from 1996 to 2001, led to a new exodus.

In baking-hot camps, where the temperature often exceeded 40 degrees Celsius, Afghan refugees first came across cricket. During the 1987 World Cup, and especially the 1992 tournament, which Pakistan won, thousands of Afghan refugees huddled around grainy television sets to watch. Where cricket fans in Ireland at the time largely watched Test cricket, on British terrestrial TV, for Afghanistan one-day cricket was the main attraction.

Pop-up cricket games were set-up using a stick and plastic bags wrapped up to make a ball or, if the players were more fortunate, a tennis ball. There was little flat land at Kacha Garhi, so games were played on slopes. In 1996, Taj Malik, who had been a refugee since the mid-1980s, formed the Afghan Cricket Club in Kacha Garhi; he went from tent to tent there and in nearby refugee camps to find players. The recruits, often children who played without telling their parents, pooled together money from working to buy a bat and tennis ball from a bazaar in Peshawar City, Nihar Suthar wrote in *The Corridor of Uncertainty*. At district cricket grounds in Peshawar, the team played together against local clubs, including ones with first-class cricketers. Here, the nucleus of the team that would take Afghanistan to their first World Cup learned the game.

Steps were already being taken to bring cricket to Afghanistan itself. In 1995, Allah Dad Noori formed the Afghan Cricket Federation in Kabul: the first organised cricket body in Afghanistan's history. It registered with the Afghan Olympic Committee as a national sport. Cricket was permitted by the Taliban regime. The game's conservative dress code was seen as a Pakistani one: cricket was Pakistan's national sport, and Pakistan was one of only three states to recognise the Taliban as Afghanistan's government. Cricket also had significant resemblances with the old Afghan game of gillidanda: both games involve a wooden bat hitting a spherical object. In June 2001 the ACF was registered with the ICC, who awarded Afghanistan Affiliate membership. Four months later, the war in Afghanistan began, after the 9/11 terror attacks in the USA.

Afghan cricket grew in spite of the country's tragedies. The two men who could claim to be the fathers of Afghan cricket tussled for control before settling upon a compromise: Taj would become national team coach; Noori would be board president. In 2004, Afghanistan played their first official match, at the Asian Cricket Council Trophy; all the side had first learned the game in Pakistan. An unlikely array of foreign governments and agencies, eager to support a social project in the country, supported Afghan cricket, including the Swedish Committee for Afghanistan, USAID and the German government.

'I might suggest,' US Secretary of State Hillary Clinton said in 2010, 'that if we are searching for a model of how to meet tough international challenges with skill, dedication and teamwork, we need only look to the Afghan national cricket team.' Earlier that year, Afghanistan featured in their first world tournament, the T20 World

Cup. In 2015, they played in their first ODI World Cup. Afghanistan also showed their red-ball qualities: they won the Intercontinental Cup in 2010 and 2017. Their successes were celebrated across political divides, by Taliban supporters and opponents alike; stories exist of Taliban commanders listening to matches on the radio. 'It's the main role of playing cricket in Afghanistan – it brings peace to every tribe,' explained Mohammad Nabi, who spent the first 16 years of his life as a refugee in Peshawar and later became a Test cricketer. For security reasons, Afghanistan have never played an official game at home.

Where Irish players relied upon county cricket to hone their skills, Afghanistan's team leaned on the global T20 circuit. The short-format prized the skills – power hitting, pace bowling and, especially, wrist spin – in which Afghanistan specialised. Leg-spinner Rashid Khan, who first signed with the Indian Premier League in 2017, became Afghanistan's flag-bearer.

Rashid was born in Jalalabad, a Taliban stronghold, in the 1990s. Shortly after the US attacks on Afghanistan in 2001, the family fled to Peshawar. It was here that Rashid learned cricket, watching on TV and playing with friends and family in the streets. Inspired by Shahid Afridi – who hailed from Khyber, along the border with Afghanistan – Rashid and his six brothers all bowled leg spin.

In Peshawar, Rashid followed the Pakistani tradition of playing cricket with a tape-ball – a tennis ball covered in electrical tape. The games he played were either in his yard or on cement. This was good training for the challenges ahead: turning a tape-ball on cement is reckoned to be tougher than turning a hard ball on a cricket pitch. 'It was really tough to spin the ball but still I was spinning the ball on any surface,' Rashid told me. It was not until the age of 14 that Rashid finally played cricket with a hard ball, in Peshawar. Only at the end of 2013, after over a decade away, did Rashid and his family return to live in Jalalabad.

For nearly ten years, Afghanistan and Ireland vied for Associate supremacy on the pitch. Yet, off it, they were allies, both pushing for greater ICC recognition. Geography helped their cause: with one country from Asia and the other from Europe, admitting Afghanistan and Ireland simultaneously as Full Members maintained the regional balance among Test nations. Afghanistan was the first Test nation who were not current or former members of the Commonwealth.

Afghanistan's bid ignored one stated ICC criterion: a functioning women's team, with a record of success. When Afghanistan gained Full Member status, the board pledged to develop the women's game, blaming cultural issues for the slow progress. In 2020 the Afghanistan Cricket Board announced the creation of 25 contracts for female cricketers. Before they could play an international match, the Taliban regained power the following year. The Taliban banned women from playing sport; the contracted players all fled, most to Australia.

It has been suggested that ICC funding intended for Afghanistan's women's programme – now non-existent – could be diverted to female cricketers who have fled, with the exiled players forming a team. 'We want the same opportunity,' Tuba Sangar, who was the women's cricket development manager for the Afghanistan Cricket Board and fled to Canada as the Taliban returned, told me in 2023. 'Cricket is the only thing that at least people talk about Afghanistan positively. But, as a woman, it's a hard feeling for me – I wish we have the same opportunity.'

* * *

In May 2018, Ireland became the 11th nation to play a Test match. They welcomed Pakistan to Malahide, a charming club ground in the north Dublin suburbs which was now encircled by temporary stands.

Growing up in Dublin, Kevin O'Brien and his older brother Niall used to play 'Test matches' in their garden. 'He was always Australia,

I was England,' Kevin recalls. 'To think that Ireland would play Test cricket was Roy of the Rovers stuff, a pipe dream.' Even after hitting 113 to help beat England in the 2011 ODI World Cup, 'the idea of playing Test cricket was never really there.'

Ireland's inaugural Test side at Malahide contained seven men aged 32 or older; several had prolonged their careers to realise their dream of playing a Test. For the team, the occasion felt like payback for 'the years of quiet games where it was two men and a dog', Kevin O'Brien reflects.

'The hype leading into our first Test was massive. You could definitely sense it. A few days out, it was very exciting to think that you'd be walking out as a Test cricketer.' That the first day was washed out only added to Irish anticipation.

Pakistan reached 310–9 before declaring, to allow a burst at Ireland before lunch on day three. In 6.1 overs, Ireland collapsed to 5–3, the latest nation to learn of Test cricket's brutality. After a slight recovery, to 130 all out, Ireland trailed by 180 runs, and were made to follow on.

Early on day four, Kevin O'Brien walked out at number six. At 95–4, Ireland were still at risk of an innings defeat. After scoring 40 in the first innings, 'I was extremely well focused,' O'Brien says. 'I was supremely confident in how I prepped before the game.'

O'Brien had sometimes been derided as explosive but unreliable. Yet he defied Pakistan for almost six hours, driving assertively through the off side in between his steady accumulation. 'Dad always told me, "If you keep the ball on the ground, you can't get caught." So that was my only game plan going into the Test: whatever you do, keep everything on the ground.'

As he neared a century, O'Brien grasped the enormity of scoring Ireland's first Test hundred. 'The only real passage where I got a little bit jittery was in the 90s. They had four men on the boundary, so I just kept taking what they were giving me. If it meant I got to 100 by taking ten singles, that was fine.'

On 99, O'Brien tried to flick a ball through the on side. His thick edge squirted away for two; Malahide could acclaim Ireland's history-maker. 'An edge through extra cover is as good as a cover drive so I'll take it,' he reflects. 'It was just relief. I was obviously hugely proud and excited – probably mentally fatiguing as well.'

While Ireland lost by five wickets, despite their comeback, O'Brien has come to regard his Malahide hundred as his most cherished innings. 'The history and the traditions of the game make that hundred stand a little bit higher than the hundred against England. A smaller percentage of international players get to play Test cricket – get to experience the nuts and bolts of Test cricket, the ups and downs, the technical battle, the tactical battle within an innings, within a spell, within an over. It's a special game.'

* * *

While Afghanistan fared far worse than Ireland in their first Test, when they were crushed by India in June 2018, they needed only one more match to record their first victory. That came against Ireland in India in March 2019, the long-time Associate foes now competing in the Test game. Later that year, Afghanistan secured a notable win in Bangladesh. Aptly, Rashid Khan underpinned the triumph: thrashing a quick 51 to lift Afghanistan to 342 in their first innings, then taking 11–104 in the match.

'To beat an established Test nation in an away Test match was a huge achievement,' Rashid recalls. 'It was a real team effort and one that made other teams aware that we aren't here to make up the numbers.'

Across Afghanistan's first four wins – two against Zimbabwe, and one apiece against Ireland and Bangladesh – Rashid took 40 wickets. His rapid leg spin, fizzing the ball at speeds approaching 65 mph, could succeed in Test cricket too.

With more venomous bowlers than Ireland, Afghanistan were better-equipped to take 20 wickets. For Ireland, the glorious exception was at Lord's in 2019. Ireland bowled out England for 85 in a surreal opening morning. Tim Murtagh took 5–13 in a masterful spell of swing and seam bowling on his home ground; after England tailender Jack Leach hit 92 in the second innings, Ireland still lost.

Table 12. Matches taken to register first Test win

Australia	1
England	2
Pakistan	2
Afghanistan	2
West Indies	6
Ireland	8
Zimbabwe	11
South Africa	12
Sri Lanka	14
India	25
Bangladesh	35
New Zealand	45

The contrasting early fortunes of Afghanistan and Ireland concealed that both occupied a similar place in the Test game. From 2017 to 2023, both boards received under half as much ICC funding as Zimbabwe. The lack of funds hampered their ability both to play matches and, as importantly, to develop the wider infrastructure to nurture five-day cricketers.

When the World Test Championship launched in 2019, Afghanistan and Ireland were not included. Instead, they joined Zimbabwe as part of Test cricket's 'small three': Test nations, yes, but at times in name only. In the seven years after being awarded Full Member status, in June 2017, Afghanistan played nine Tests and Ireland eight. Unlike World Test Championship games, these matches had no overarching context.

'One bad game and we don't have the chance to learn from our mistakes for another four, five, six months,' Rashid says. 'We want to play against the best. That's how you improve and leave your legacy on the format.'

For Afghanistan and Ireland alike, Test status would have been more significant a decade or so earlier, before franchise leagues were so established. Both Rashid and Ireland's star quick bowler Josh Little missed Tests to rest between appearances in the shorter format.

After losing their first seven games, Ireland became the 12th nation to register a Test victory when they defeated Afghanistan in 2024. It was simultaneously a momentous feat and a curiously underwhelming one: the game was moved from Abu Dhabi's main ground to a smaller adjacent one because of a clash with a school sports day, which was given precedence.

Ireland's first Test victory did not alleviate their financial problems. Unable to afford the costs of staging games, they went six years without playing a home Test until hosting Zimbabwe in 2024, and didn't play any domestic first-class cricket from 2020 to 2023.

It encapsulated the challenge facing the two newest members of the Test club. For Afghanistan and Ireland, competing in Test cricket was challenging enough. Simply being able to play matches often felt even harder.

35

BAZBALL AND BEYOND

'You don't want to play for England. You just want to piss it up the wall with your mates and have a good time.'

This was the message that Andy Flower, England's head coach, delivered to Ben Stokes in a hotel room in Hobart in February 2013. On tour with England Lions, the national second string, Stokes was sent home after a series of late nights.

Born in New Zealand, Stokes moved to England aged 12 after his father Ged, a rugby league coach, found a new job in Cumbria. Rising through club and youth cricket, Stokes was a thrilling, uninhibited allrounder, combining left-handed batting – aggressive, but underpinned by a classical technique – with swing and seam bowling. At Cockermouth Cricket Club, a mystery benefactor paid for private coaching, recognising his potential; Stokes later learned his identity and thanked him.

Ten months after being sent home in disgrace, Stokes returned down under with England's Test squad. In his second Test, aged 22, Stokes confronted a cracked Perth pitch and Mitchell Johnson at his most ferocious; hooking and pulling imperiously, he hit a defiant 120, England's sole century of the series. Even as England were whitewashed 5–0, Stokes showed a rare combination of combativeness and chutzpah. Stokes confirmed as much by taking 6–36 as England regained the Ashes at Trent Bridge in 2015. In January 2016, Stokes plundered 258 against South Africa at Cape Town, with 11 sixes.

In September 2017, Stokes's career faced another critical juncture. Involved in an altercation outside a Bristol nightclub, a few hours after a one-day international, Stokes faced trial and was ruled out of the ensuing Ashes tour. He feared that he would never play another Test; he was eventually found not guilty of affray.

When Stokes returned, in 2018, he was initially short of his best, averaging only 26.85 in ten Tests in the year. But the 2019 summer offered an unprecedented opportunity: a home ODI World Cup, followed by the Ashes. In the World Cup final at Lord's, Stokes's 84 not out hauled England level with New Zealand's total; he returned for the Super Over, when England won on an arcane tie-breaker: boundary countback.

Yet as Stokes walked out in the second innings at Headingley six weeks later, England faced Ashes ignominy. Already trailing 1–0 with three Tests remaining, one more England loss would guarantee that Australia retained the Ashes. England hurtled to 67 all out in their first innings; Stokes drove egregiously to succumb to a wide half-volley for eight. With the rest of the bowling attack fatigued, Stokes summoned all his bloody-mindedness – barring a four-ball break, until a teammate was injured, he bowled for 24.2 consecutive overs, taking 3–56.

Australia still set England 359 to win. In the chase, Stokes walked out at 141–3. His innings would show the full range of Test batting.

First, Stokes batted with the self-discipline of an ascetic monk, taking 73 balls over his first three runs. Exhausted from his bowling, 'the biggest thing for me on that evening of day three was just grinding it out,' he said.

With Jonny Bairstow counter-attacking, Stokes located a smooth tempo the next day, adding 58 in his next 101 balls. While Stokes found his groove, England lost theirs, losing five wickets for 41 to slide to 286–9. Australia were one ball away from retaining the urn; England needed 73 to keep the Ashes alive.

Now, the gradual crescendo of Stokes's innings gave way to chaos. With only number 11 Jack Leach for company, Stokes ransacked 74 off 45 balls. His eight sixes included ramping Pat Cummins over fine leg and, most outlandishly, a reverse slog sweep over point, falling over as he hit Nathan Lyon into the febrile Western Terrace. When Stokes reached his century, he did not even raise his bat: only victory was on his mind.

Many of Test cricket's best innings rely upon luck. So it was with Stokes at Headingley. First, he slashed to third man with 17 to win; Marcus Harris shelled the catch. Second, with two runs to win, Leach, at the non-striker's end, raced down the pitch; sent back, he would have been run out, but Lyon dropped the ball. Finally, the ball after Leach's reprieve, Stokes missed a slog sweep and was struck on the pads. Ball-tracking projected that the delivery would have hit middle and leg stump, but Australia had used all their allotted reviews.

After batting for an hour without scoring a run, Leach was on strike at the start of an over, for the first time in the partnership. He survived two Cummins bouncers, then tucked a ball off his hip: the most valuable one not out in Test history. With the scores level, Stokes scythed Cummins through point, raising his arms aloft in gladiatorial triumph. On the outfield hours later, the bespectacled Leach re-enacted his role in the match-winning partnership: he had contributed one, Stokes 74.

Headingley 2019 would take its place alongside Headingley 1981 in the pantheon of England's greatest Ashes victories. In both cases, stunning innings from allrounders levelled the series 1–1. Yet while Ian Botham's Leeds century was the prelude to England's series victory, Stokes's feat came in a summer in which the Ashes remained Australia's.

* * *

In the Ashes cricket of the 2010s, it was not only Stokes who forced early opinions to be reassessed.

When Australia toured New Zealand in early 2010, they took an uncapped young batter, Steve Smith. He was renowned for his idiosyncratic technique – initially lifting the bat out to gully, rather than straight, and then moving across his stumps to hit the ball to the leg side. In Wellington, Justin Langer, now Australia batting coach, gave his verdict on Smith. He told the captain, Ricky Ponting, 'This guy has got no chance of being a Test batsman.'

'I look back on it and laugh,' Langer reflects. 'I'd say, "Okay, we'll put some balls in, play some cover drives." He'd hit a few cover drives and then he'd smack them through midwicket. I was always taught when you play the pull shot, keep your head very still. He would swivel. Everything he did was out of the box.'

Primarily a batter in domestic cricket, Smith made his Test debut as a leg-spinning allrounder at number eight, miscast as Shane Warne's replacement. Picked for his first Ashes series, in 2010/11, Smith described his role as about 'having fun and making sure everyone else around is having fun, whether it be telling a joke or something'. Only England were laughing: Smith's insubstantial cameos came in a 3–1 Australia defeat.

While some mocked his quirks, Smith doubled down on them. He took to standing outside leg stump to prepare for deliveries before shuffling across his stumps. 'When my back foot goes back towards off stump, and sometimes even outside it, I know that anything outside my eyeline isn't hitting the stumps,' Smith explained. 'You shouldn't get out if the ball is not hitting the stumps. So that began to limit the way I could get out.'

Smith fits squarely within Australia's cricketing history. He is an autodidact, in keeping with the country's self-reliant traditions. Where Don Bradman trained by hitting a golf ball with a stump against a water tank, Smith developed playing in his back garden, with a soft ball on uneven paving which deviated unpredictably – honing his ability to play the ball late. Like Bradman, Ricky

Ponting, Greg Chappell and a series of other distinguished Australian batters, Smith was selected early – in his case, shortly after turning 21.

A second Test hundred, against England in Perth in December 2013, signalled that Smith had become a batter of the top rank. 'Everything just sort of clicked from then on,' he later said; against short balls during the innings, Smith tweaked his technique to step further across to the off side. In 52 Tests – the length of Bradman's career – from the start of 2014 until September 2019, Smith averaged 75.03, the second highest ever over such a streak.

Smith's zeal for self-improvement led him to ask his wife to feed balls into a bowling machine at home. But his obsession had a dark side. Smith blamed a lack of perspective for the events of 2018 in Cape Town. The furore over Cameron Bancroft applying sandpaper to the ball led to Smith being sacked as captain and banned by Cricket Australia for a year. The ban expired shortly before the 2019 Ashes; Smith faced a summer of being harangued by English crowds.

On the first morning of the Ashes, under overcast skies at Edgbaston, Smith walked out to boos at 17–2. After ten balls on nought, which included almost edging Stuart Broad, Smith's first Test runs in 16 months came in characteristic style – flicking a delivery on middle and off stump through the on side. Even as Australia collapsed to 122–8, Smith was serene. When he drove Stokes through the covers in the early evening, Smith enjoyed a moment of catharsis: a century in his first Test since his ban, celebrated with a smile that was part elation, even more relief. He followed up his 144 with a second innings 142, getting through more than 20 pairs of gloves during the match. Australia turned a first innings deficit of 90 runs into a crushing win.

Before the second Test at Lord's, the PA announcer at St John's Wood underground station issued an urgent request. 'Anyone who knows how to dismiss Steve Smith, please report to the England dressing room.'

On debut, fresh from a starring role in the World Cup win, the Barbados-born Jofra Archer was England's best answer. Bowling at over 90 mph and exploiting uneven bounce, Archer posed a threat to both stumps and body, hitting Smith on the gloves and arm. On 80, Smith was struck in the back of the head as he tried to duck an Archer bouncer, collapsing to the floor before retiring hurt. Smith became the first man to be substituted out of a Test after incurring concussion.

When Smith returned, for the fourth Test at Old Trafford, so did his sense of impregnability: his double century set up Australia's win. Smith's 774 runs in seven innings ensured that Australia retained the urn, even if defeat in the final Test tied the series at 2–2. With each innings, English boos were replaced by standing ovations, no longer able to deny Smith's majesty.

Had he been able to bat in all ten innings in England, Smith was on course to topple Bradman's record for the most runs in a Test series, 974. Following on from three centuries in four Tests when Australia toured India in 2017, Smith's haul invited the question: was he the best since Bradman?

* * *

In the 2021/22 Ashes, Travis Head blazed two centuries, benefiting from Adam Gilchrist's advice: 'Fight fire with fire, play your way.' Head was player of the series as Australia won 4–0 and extended their most dominant streak in home Ashes cricket. Over 15 Ashes Tests down under from 2013/14 to 2021/22, Australia won 13 games and lost none.

While Head thrashed through the off side, Stokes was in the field. 'He was so hard to bowl to,' Stokes later said. 'He threw counter-punches and was hard to set fields to.' When Stokes took over as Test captain, before the 2022 home summer, he wanted England to bat in the same way.

He took over a moribund team. As England crashed to a ten-wicket defeat against West Indies in March 2022, Grenadian locals playfully sang 'London Bridge is falling down'. England had won one of their previous 17 Test matches.

It wasn't just that England were losing. It was also *how* they were losing, playing timid and inhibited cricket. English cricket reflected the joylessness of the age of Covid-19, which forced players to travel from one biosecure bubble to the next.

At tea on the final day at Trent Bridge in June 2022, in the second Test of Stokes's reign, England were 139–4. They needed another 160 runs to win; with up to 38 overs left, that meant scoring at 4.2 runs an over. In the second of the three Tests against New Zealand, England were 1–0 up; a draw would guarantee that they could not lose the series. One hundred and forty-five years of Test history all pointed the same way: towards England batting for a draw.

Stokes did not agree. 'Don't even think about hitting one down, hit it into the stands,' he told Jonny Bairstow in the dressing room at Trent Bridge. At tea, in front of a mirror, Bairstow gave himself a pep talk. 'Jonathan Marc Bairstow!' he told himself, as documented by the book *Bazball*, 'This is your day, your chance to show what you can do.' Noticing a teammate was watching, Bairstow roared, 'That's Marc with a C!'

With a packed leg-side field, Matt Henry and Trent Boult attempted to bounce Bairstow out. Bairstow gave no thought to trying to duck and weave. Instead, he trusted in his timing, the true pitch and the short boundaries to do the rest. Bairstow thrashed five sixes – four over the leg side from short balls – in 11 balls. In an hour after tea, Bairstow pummelled 93 from 44 balls. England took 16 overs to score the last 160 runs.

The template for England's approach under Stokes and Brendon McCullum, who had previously overhauled New Zealand's culture while captain, was set. 'It was a great "this is what we're about" day,' Stokes later recalled.

Before the next Test, Bairstow asked McCullum how he should bat. McCullum told him, 'Whatever you did last week, go out and do it again.' Over three weeks, beginning with the second innings at Trent Bridge, Bairstow peeled off one of English cricket's finest sequences: 136 off 92 balls, 162 from 157 balls and 71 not out from 44 balls against New Zealand; then 106 from 140 balls and 114 not out from 145 balls against India. In these five innings, Bairstow was dismissed three times and scored 589 from 578 balls. His coruscating batting distilled the vision that Stokes and McCullum shared.

At the heart of their thinking was bringing back a sense of joy – liberating and emboldening players, rather than weighing them down. After taking a break from playing for several months to prioritise his mental well-being in 2021, Stokes sought to protect his team from pressure. 'I have gone through my career fearing failure,' Stokes said in the documentary *Phoenix from the Ashes*, released in 2022. 'Rather than fearing failure, embrace it.'

McCullum and Stokes decluttered the dressing room, paring back the role of support staff while encouraging players to take more ownership of their performance. Players were given more freedom over how to prepare and train, and what time to arrive on the morning of Test matches. McCullum wanted to create an 'amateur' spirit – not an unprofessional team, but connected to what had originally drawn players to the game. The idea, McCullum explained, 'is to ensure that we're always reminding ourselves that this job is meant to be the greatest time of our life'.

Between 2016 and 2022, England reached the semi-finals in five consecutive global white-ball tournaments, including winning the ODI World Cup in 2019 and the T20 World Cup in 2022. In the period before Stokes took over, England's selection between red- and white-ball cricket diverged, reasoning that the formats were becoming more different. Under Stokes, England inverted this logic, importing white-ball batting skills to red-ball cricket. In 50-over cricket, England had become masters of scoring at close to a run a ball; the Test side now aimed to do the same. England had been asking players to bat in the traditional mould of Test batters, even as defensive techniques declined; the new approach made better use of the country's talent pool. Bazball also fitted within a body of research across sport: teams tend to play more conservatively than optimal, seemingly out of fear of losing while playing unconventionally. For instance, where Test batters often slowed down nearing a break, England would continue attacking.

The most salient shift was in how England targeted particular bowlers. Teams generally sought to milk perceived weaker links – scoring at, say, three an over while minimising the chances of losing a wicket. England accepted a greater risk of dismissals against such bowlers, in the knowledge that they could score at haste. New Zealand off-spinner Michael Bracewell conceded 285 runs at six an over in the three Tests in England in 2022. Such calculated aggression didn't only bring runs; it also forced opponents to recall other bowlers to the attack before they were fully rested. One feature of the first summer of Bazball was the number of injuries that opposition bowlers suffered: in part luck, but England's tactics had made such blows more likely.

To show his side that they could attack without fear of the consequences, early in his tenure Stokes sometimes batted recklessly. 'I needed to demonstrate what I wanted the lads to do,' he told *The Daily Telegraph* in 2023. 'My teammates can say, "Oh, he actually means this. We can go out and play in this fearless way and we're not going to be told what a s*** shot we hit, because Stokesy's out there and he's just been caught at mid-off when we're four down."'

Free-spirited former players were envious. 'I got abused so much by the coaching staff for getting out caught on the boundary,' recalls Kevin Pietersen. 'It was almost playing with a hand tied behind your back. A lot of people say, "You would have loved playing under Brendon."'

England's openers became the side's standard-bearers. If they benefited from balls that offered less swing and seam than those in England from 2018 to 2021, they were also empowered by the new regime.

During his underwhelming start to Test cricket, Zak Crawley was told to 'chase moments' by McCullum. In Pakistan in December 2022, Crawley was joined by Ben Duckett. For all their differences – Crawley was a tall right-hander who favoured driving down the ground, Duckett a short left-hander who thrived hitting the ball square – they shared the same spirit. In the first Test of their partnership, at Rawalpindi, both made blistering centuries on the opening day – Duckett's from 105 balls, Crawley's from 86 – and added 233 at 6.5 an over. England ended the day on an absurd 506–4, even with 15 overs lost to bad light. Such haste, together with Stokes's creativity in shuffling his fields and sheer ambition on a flat pitch that many assumed was destined to end in a draw, helped England clinch victory in the fading light on day five.

* * *

A change in approach was even detectable in England's greatest modern batter, Joe Root. At the start of his international career, Root was given a thigh pad by Michael Vaughan, who played for the same club, Sheffield Collegiate, and same county. It extended a Yorkshire tradition of distinguished batters often passing down a small piece of kit to mark their successors.

Root made his Test debut as a cherubic 21-year-old in Nagpur in December 2012. Joining Kevin Pietersen at the crease, with England a precarious 119–4, Root greeted his partner with the words 'Ey up, lad, how's it going?' His assured 73 helped England to secure the draw that they needed to win the series.

Unusually for a player reared in northern England, Root's hallmark was his quality against spin. While touring Asia with England

Lions in 2011/12, Root worked extensively with Graham Thorpe – a terrific player of spin himself, who was now coaching the side. Root refined a method that involved making decisive movements against spin. Assessing each delivery's length swiftly, he then moved either well forward or well back. This method avoided the 'danger zone' of hitting the ball 2 to 3 metres after pitching – when players are neither so close to the ball as to smother the spin, nor sufficiently far away as to be able to react to it. Root combined such dexterity on his feet with a repertoire of shots. His array of sweeps and reverse sweeps were particularly significant, allowing him to disrupt length and score on both sides of the wicket. Supreme fitness, which he honed with the help of an exercise bike during the lockdown period, gave Root remarkable stamina too. From his debut until 2025, he only missed two Test matches: one when he was dropped in 2014 in Australia, one on paternity leave.

All these qualities came together early in 2021. Across three consecutive Tests – two in Galle and one in Chennai – Root amassed first innings scores of 228, 186 and 218. England won all three of these Tests, but then disintegrated over the next 12 months.

When his five years as Test captain ended in 2022, after 64 Tests, Root had a 'very unhealthy relationship' with the job, which had begun to 'take a bad toll on my own personal health'. Back in the ranks, Root ensured that Stokes won his first game as full-time skipper, marshalling a fraught chase against New Zealand at Lord's in 2022.

Under Stokes, Root played with a new panache. At Edgbaston on day four of the 2023 Ashes, with the Test finely poised, Root attempted a reverse scoop from the first ball of the day, from Pat Cummins. He missed and was almost clean bowled. Undeterred, Root unfurled two reverse scoops in the next over, from Scott Boland: the first was hit for six, the second for four. With a packed slip cordon indicating Australia's plans to bowl outside off stump, and no third man, Root saw the shot as a pragmatic way to score runs.

'The hardest thing to hone with that shot was being terrified of getting it wrong and looking stupid,' he later told ESPNcricinfo.

'Almost the bravery of just saying, "I've got to trust everything I've been practising and just give myself the best chance of doing it by staying in the shot."' His underlying rationale was simple: 'I average more with that than with the forward defence.'

Root's reverse-scooping embodied how England made good on their promise not to change their style of play because they were facing Australia. Bazball and a magnificent touring side came together to produce one of the most captivating Ashes summers, which ended 2–2.

Perversely, the only one-sided Test was the one without a result; nearly two days of Manchester rain prevented England from clinching victory in the fourth match. Until the rain came, England were on course to become the second team in history, after Don Bradman's Australia in 1936/37, to win a series after losing the opening two Tests.

Unusually, Australia were cast in the role of less adventurous side. 'They'd take the game on,' reflects Pat Cummins, Australia's captain in the 2023 Ashes. 'I liken it to some one-day cricket – where there's not a lot in the wicket and the batters are taking it on and they're doing it really well and you're left with fewer options.

'It was a different tempo. Things were moving faster, but in some ways, it felt like you were close to wickets the whole time as well. I've played in many Test matches in Australia where there's a big dip and you feel like you're two days away from taking a wicket. I quite enjoyed that aspect of it. It felt like the game just moved faster. The way that they approached the batting, it all felt like it happened a little bit quicker than normal.'

The Bazball story is ongoing. But, from the debris of one win in England's previous 17 Tests, Stokes and McCullum oversaw a run of 22 victories and 12 losses in the first 35 Tests of their partnership, until 2025. If the effectiveness of England's tactics against the best opponents remained a source of debate, especially after a 4–1 defeat in India in 2024, their intent was not.

'The approach was excellent – it challenged us,' reflects Ravichandran Ashwin, who took 26 wickets in the series. 'I saw a lot of rationale in a lot of situations in that series. At the same time, I saw a lot of risk being taken when it wasn't warranted, which is a balance that will take some time to master.' When England were in dominant positions, Ashwin says, 'I don't think they drove it home well enough.'

At times, the excitement around England's approach overlooked that Test cricket has always had audacious batting. Yet no side has embraced an attacking mindset with quite such gusto. In the first 35 Tests of Bazball, England scored at 4.47 an over. The 4.01 an over Australia scored at from 2001 to 2003 under Steve Waugh's captaincy is the next highest by any other side over such a long period, calculates the statistician Benedict Bermange. In terms of their batting approach, Stokes's England could justifiably be said to be the most revolutionary Test side since Waugh's Australia.

The knowledge of what England's batters could unleash led many opponents to deploy defensive fields – Cummins bowled the first ball of the 2023 Ashes with a deep point, yet Crawley still drove him for four. Conservative fields, in turn, created scope for England to score quickly while minimising risk. From a historical perspective, it is too early to say that England are changing Test cricket, but not too soon to say that they are trying to do so. Other countries have borrowed something of their approach. In 2023, the overall Test scoring rate was the highest for any year in history; in 2024, the figure increased again, even with England's own scoring rate slowing.

The greatest significance of Bazball, perhaps, is that almost 150 years after Test cricket was created, teams are still finding new ways in which to play it. Those watching, too, are still arguing about how it should be played.

* * *

'I do not know that Test cricket can be saved. I hope so but I am not convinced. People will no longer sit through five days of a match. Those days are long gone. People don't go to watch beautiful defensive shots or the battle of tactics any more. Unless something is done to change the rules and the manner in which it is played, then officials will have a hard time to make it attractive.'

These words, from Lynton Taylor, an executive for Australia's Channel Nine TV station, in 1978 illustrate that existential fears for Test cricket's future are nothing new. Indeed, as we have seen, worries about the viability of Test cricket are almost as old as the format itself. Yet the game has endured because, like the best novels and films, its qualities are discovered by every new generation afresh.

Such history does not mean that fears about Test cricket's future are misplaced. Administrators are even lax to address fundamental issues: over rates continue to become slower. Since their introduction in 2015, day-night Tests have increased viewing figures by around 20 per cent, compared to day Tests. Yet, as of the end of 2024, only 23 day-night Tests have been played.

All the while, the format risks being cannibalised by shorter forms, with the calendar saturated by domestic leagues. Increasingly, national boards are prioritising such competitions ahead of Test cricket. In early 2024, South Africa sent a depleted squad to New Zealand for a Test tour, with leading players appearing in the country's franchise T20 league, the SA20, instead. Cricket South Africa's unconvincing statement confirming the weakened squad proclaimed that they had 'the utmost respect for the Test format as the pinnacle of the game'.

The 1990s, the most competitive era of Test cricket on the pitch, was also a period of relative equality off the pitch. To give more penurious nations a chance to compete more regularly, administrators need to think more collectively. Under the ICC's distribution model, for 2024 to 2027, India receive 38.5 per cent of ICC earnings;

England earn 6.9 per cent, the next most; West Indies receive only 4.6 per cent, and the 96 Associate members a paltry 11.2 per cent between them.

Even without sharing the ICC's central income more equitably, other reforms could safeguard the Test game. The terms of bilateral series should be reformed, so that away teams are paid a share of income; in football's FA Cup, away teams earn 45 per cent of gate receipts. This would allow teams from poorer economies a chance to thrive: England currently earn ten times more from hosting West Indies than West Indies generate from hosting England in a series of equal length. It would also give touring sides a financial stake in away series: Cricket South Africa would have suffered monetarily from not sending their best players to New Zealand in 2024.

A Test Cricket Fund worthy of the name could ensure that players from outside the big three are paid enough to prevent them from prioritising more lucrative franchise tournaments. Windows for World Test Championship matches – periods without any franchise cricket – would give the tournament a better chance to thrive, especially if accompanied by a more coherent fixture list. Not since 2019, when South Africa met Pakistan, has a series not involving at least one of Australia, England or India been played over more than two Test matches. One potential solution would be for each Test Championship series to comprise three Tests of four days each – each game running from Thursday to Sunday, with a reserve day in case of rain. This would give more scope for narratives to develop than unsatisfactory two-match series, and reflect how the draw is rapidly becoming extinct. Series like the Ashes could continue to be played over more Tests, but with only the first three counting towards the Test Championship table.

Table 13. Percentage of Test draws, and run rates, by decade

	Matches	% Drawn	Run rate per six balls
1870s	3	0	2.31
1880s	29	13.79	2.18
1890s	32	18.75	2.52
1900s	41	24.39	2.68
1910s	29	13.79	2.84
1920s	51	31.37	2.54
1930s	89	40.45	2.58
1940s	45	48.89	2.51
1950s	164	31.10	2.20
1960s	186	47.31	2.38
1970s	198	42.42	2.52
1980s	266	45.86	2.71
1990s	347	35.73	2.75
2000s	464	24.57	3.09
2010s	433	19.40	3.11
2020s	196	13.26	3.21
Total	2573	30.70	2.90

NB: To January 2025

This would allow each game in the Test Championship to be worth the same number of points – creating a coherent league table and helping to build a narrative around the competition, similar to those for World Cups. It would be a rare case of looking at Test cricket through the needs of all competing nations, not merely the three wealthiest.

As Test cricket approaches its 150th birthday such thinking has never been more essential. The worst case for Test cricket in the decades ahead is a continuation of short-termist, myopic administration – and a game hollowed out beneath Australia, England and India. The scenario is far from inevitable. But, if it is to be stopped, administrators' platitudes about their esteem for Test cricket will not suffice.

* * *

For all the game's inequalities, Test cricket continues to provide reminders of why it has endured for so long. On 28 January 2024, the format enjoyed perhaps its greatest day.

In Hyderabad, England overcame a first innings deficit of 190 to secure one of their most unlikely victories. On the first evening, the debutant left-arm spinner Tom Hartley was hit for six first ball and thumped for 63 in his nine overs. On the fourth day, exploiting a pitch now offering appreciable turn, Hartley took 7–62 to secure a 28-run win. In the process, he provided a reminder of one of Test cricket's qualities: the in-built second chance.

Yet England's win was overshadowed by events 6,000 miles away. In Brisbane, West Indies arrived to expectations that they would suffer another thrashing, after a ten-wicket loss in the first game in the two-Test series. That result was wholly unsurprising: it extended West Indies' winless run against Australia to 20 Tests over 21 years.

Shamar Joseph grew up in Baracara, a remote village in Guyana only accessible by boat, and initially worked as a logger. While working one day, he was almost hit by a tree. 'It was a very narrow escape,' he told Cricbuzz. 'I said in that moment, as my life flashed before my eyes, that I can't do this any more.' Joseph became a security guard in New Amsterdam, 120 kilometres away; he initially played cricket only on Sundays before being spotted at a talent camp by Curtly Ambrose. In Brisbane, he played his second Test.

In the second innings, Joseph was struck on the boot by a Mitchell Starc yorker. With a badly injured toe, Joseph feared that he would be unable to bowl the next day; he initially didn't even bring his kit to the Gabba.

Australia began day four on 60–2, in pursuit of 216 to win and seal the series 2–0. Forty minutes into the day, with the help of painkillers, Joseph came on. His first 1.4 overs conceded 19 runs – bowling too full and, in pursuit of pace, twice bowling no-balls – as Australia soared to 113–2. The next delivery bounced sharply, thudded into Cameron Green's elbow and ricocheted onto the stumps; Travis Head was greeted by a pinpoint yorker, crashing into his off stump at 88 mph.

Joseph told Kraigg Brathwaite, West Indies' captain, that he would bowl until the last wicket fell. He was as good as his word. While hobbling between overs, he bowled ten overs straight until dinner, breaking open the game with six wickets. Joseph's stamina and determination, in defiance of his injury, were such that he was recorded at 93 mph in the eighth over of his spell.

The interval came with Australia 187–8 and the Test agonisingly poised: Australia needed 29 runs to win, West Indies two wickets. Alzarri Joseph (no relation of Shamar) snared the ninth wicket when Nathan Lyon edged behind. But Steve Smith remained at the crease; he had the temerity to scoop Alzarri Joseph for six. When Smith got a single from the fourth ball of Shamar Joseph's next over, it reduced Australia's target to nine runs. Joseph probably only had two balls left to get the last wicket before it was too late.

He only needed one. The next delivery was too full, too fast and too straight, and uprooted Josh Hazlewood's off stump. Joseph ran to the boundary rope in jubilation, engulfed by his entire side. Aged 24, in his second Test, Joseph's 7–68 had bowled West Indies to an eight-run win, one of the greatest upsets in Test history. For West Indies and the format alike, the result offered the fleeting promise of regeneration.

The brutality of Test cricket means that moments like this – close matches, let alone those where underdogs triumph – are rare. But, as Joseph hared across the Gabba outfield, he showed Test cricket's enduring capacity to mesmerise.

ACKNOWLEDGEMENTS

I would like to thank all my employers at *The Daily Telegraph* who allowed me to pursue this project and also helped me develop my journalism and knowledge of Test cricket over the years. In particular, I would like to thank my editors Julian Bennetts, Ben Clissitt, Andy Fifield, Jake Goodwill, Gary Payne and Adam Sills; and my colleagues on the cricket team, Scyld Berry, Nick Hoult and Will Macpherson. Previous editors and colleagues at other publications have also been invaluable, especially Rahul Bhattacharya, David Hopps, Leslie Mathew and Osman Samiuddin at ESPNcricinfo.

I am particularly indebted to Alan Rees and the staff at the Lord's library; Adam Sofroniou and the staff at The Oval library; and all those at the Bodleian Library, particularly Xanthe Malcolm.

I would also like to thank the players, coaches, umpires and administrators who did interviews specifically for this book: Jimmy Adams, Azhar Ali, Hashim Amla, Ravichandran Ashwin, Mike Atherton, Ian Chappell, Alan Connolly, Gary Crocker, Pat Cummins, A.B. de Villiers, Allan Donald, Rahul Dravid, Damien Fleming, Andy Flower, Angus Fraser, Daren Ganga, Steve Harmison, Omar Henry, Rangana Herath, Michael Holding, Dave Houghton, Nasser Hussain, Aminul Islam, Mahela Jayawardene, Rashid Khan, Gary Kirsten, Justin Langer, Geoff Lawson, David Lloyd, Duleep Mendis, Muthiah Muralidaran, Saqlain Mushtaq, Sarfraz Nawaz, Kevin O'Brien, Robin Peterson, Kevin Pietersen, Shaun Pollock, Ajinkya Rahane, Malcolm Speed, Dale Steyn, Simon Taufel, Ross Taylor,

ACKNOWLEDGEMENTS

Sachin Tendulkar, Michael Vaughan, Dav Whatmore and Kane Williamson.

A number of other figures involved in the game off the field in various ways, including as journalists, statisticians and academics, also kindly gave their time to help, including: Jacqueline Alderson, Benedict Bermange, David Berri, Aaron Briggs, Peter Brukner, Subhasish Modak Chowdhury, Anthony Condon, Paul Felton, Nathan Leamon, Paul McMahon, Rabindra Mehta, Timothy Noakes, John Orchard, David Paton, Paul Rouse, Clem Seecharan, Jonny Singer, Jonty Winch.

Others also spoke on the condition of anonymity – your contributions are equally appreciated.

I am also hugely indebted to all those who read parts of the manuscript and helped shape the final work. My wife Fay read the entire book, mostly while I did the washing up. I would like to pay particular thanks again to Scyld Berry, who also read the entire book. Matt Roller went above and beyond; Nathan Johns was particularly helpful too.

The following colleagues, friends and family read part of the manuscript: Ben Bloom, Mihir Bose, Nicholas Brookes, Adam Collins, James Coyne, Bertus de Jong, Andrew Fidel Fernando, David Frith, Dan Gallan, Ben Gardner, Keshava Guha, Tristan Holme, David Hopps, Nick Hoult, Brian Hurwitz, Andrew Leonard, Suresh Menon, Firdose Moonda, Daniel Norcross, Andre Odendaal, Richard Parry, Danyal Rasool, Greg Ryan, Rob Smyth, Ania Wigmore, Richard Wigmore, Simon Wilde, Jonty Winch and David Woodhouse.

Others kindly shared contacts with me, including Sambit Bal and Bharat Sundaresan.

SELECTED BIBLIOGRAPHY

A book such as this naturally stands on the shoulders of those who have gone before. I am indebted to all who have written on aspects of cricket history. The websites ESPNcricinfo, CricBuzz and Cricket Archive, old copies of *Wisden Cricketers' Almanack*, *The Cricket Statistician*, *The Cricketer*, *Wisden Cricket Monthly* and the archives of *The Daily Telegraph*, *The Times* and *The Guardian* were all essential resources. The *Double Century* podcast was also very useful. In the course of my research, I have used over 350 books, reports and journal articles.

In the interests of readability, I have not used footnotes in the main text. I have distinguished interviews I have personally done for this project by using the present tense (so 'says' for an interview I conducted myself, 'said' for one given elsewhere). A note on the bibliography style: I have cited the particular edition of the book I have used – in many cases not the first edition.

GENERAL

Altham, H.S., and E.W. Swanton, *A History of Cricket: From the First World War to the Present Day*, Allen & Unwin, 1962
Barker, Ralph, *Ten Great Bowlers*, Chatto & Windus, 1967
Bateman, Anthony, and Jeffrey Hill, *The Cambridge Companion to Cricket*, CUP, 2011
Berry, Scyld, *Beyond the Boundaries: Travels on England Cricket Tours*, Fairfield, 2021
Berry, Scyld, *Cricket: The Game of Life: Every Reason to Celebrate*, Hodder & Stoughton, 2016

SELECTED BIBLIOGRAPHY

Bose, Mihir, *The Spirit of the Game: How Sport Made the Modern World*, Constable, 2012

Bowen, Rowland, *Cricket: A History of its Growth and Development Throughout the World*, Eyre & Spottiswoode, 1970

Cardus, Neville, *Cardus on Cricket: A Selection from the Cricket Writings of Sir Neville Cardus*, Souvenir, 2012

Coward, Mike, *Champions: The World's Greatest Cricketers Speak*, Allen & Unwin, 2013

Ferriday, Patrick, and Dave Wilson, *Masterly Batting: 100 Great Test Centuries*, Von Krumm, 2013

Ferriday, Patrick, and Dave Wilson, *Supreme Bowling: 100 Great Test Performances*, Von Krumm, 2016

Fingleton, Jack, *Masters of Cricket: From Trumper to May*, Pavilion, 1990

Fraser-Sampson, Guy, *Cricket at the Crossroads: Class, Colour and Controversy from 1967 to 1977*, Elliott & Thompson, 2011

Frith, David, *Bodyline Autopsy: The Full Story of the Most Sensational Test Cricket Series: Australia v England 1932–33*, Aurum, 2002

Frith, David, *The Fast Men: A 200-Year Cavalcade of Speed Bowlers*, Corgi, 1984

Frith, David, *Frith on Cricket: Half a Century of Writing by David Frith*, Allen & Unwin, 2010

Green, Benny, *A History of Cricket*, Barrie & Jenkins, 1988

Guha, Ramachandra, ed., *The Picador Book of Cricket*, Picador, 2016

Gupta, Amit, 'The Globalization of Cricket: The Rise of the Non-West', *International Journal of the History of Sport*, 21/2 (2004), 257–76

Haigh, Gideon, *The Cricket War: The Story of Kerry Packer's World Series Cricket*, Wisden, 2017

Haigh, Gideon, *Game For Anything: Writings on Cricket*, Aurum, 2005

Haigh, Gideon, *Silent Revolutions: Writings on Cricket History*, Aurum, 2006

Haigh, Gideon, *Sphere of Influence: Writings on Cricket and its Discontents*, Simon & Schuster, 2011

Haigh, Gideon, *Uncertain Corridors: The Changing World of Cricket*, Simon & Schuster, 2014

Hopps, David, *A Century of Great Cricket Quotes*, Robson, 1998

Howat, Gerald, *Cricket's Second Golden Age: The Hammond-Bradman Years*, Hodder & Stoughton, 1989

Jakeman, Mike, *Saving the Test*, Ockley, 2013

James, C.L.R., *A Majestic Innings: Writings on Cricket*, Aurum, 2013

SELECTED BIBLIOGRAPHY

Keating, Frank, *The Highlights: The Best of Frank Keating*, Guardian Faber, 2014

Kimber, Jarrod, *Test Cricket: The Unauthorised Biography,* Hardie Grant, 2015

Leamon, Nathan, and Ben Jones, *Hitting Against the Spin: How Cricket Really Works*, Constable, 2021

Loffing, F., 'Left-handedness and time pressure in elite interactive ball games', *Biology Letters*, 13 (2017): 0446

Loffing, F., and Hagemann, N., 'Performance differences between left- and right-sided athletes in one-on-one interactive sports', in Loffing, F., Hagemann, N., and Strausse, B. (eds), *Laterality in Sports*, pp. 249–77. San Diego, CA: Academic Press, 2016

Mann, D.L., Loffing, F., and Allen, P.M., 'The success of sinister right-handers in baseball', *The New England Journal of Medicine*, 377 (2017): 1688–90

Marks, Vic, *Late Cuts: Musings on Cricket*, Allen & Unwin, 2021

Marqusee, Mike, *War Minus the Shooting: Journey Through South Asia During Cricket's World Cup*, Heinemann, 1996

Martin-Jenkins, Christopher, *The Top 100 Cricketers of All Time*, Corinthian, 2010

McCrery, Nigel, *The Coming Storm: Test and First-Class Cricketers Killed in World War Two*, Pen & Sword, 2017

Midwinter, Eric, *The Cricketer's Progress: Meadowland to Mumbai*, Third Age, 2010

Rajan, Amol, *Twirlymen: The Unlikely History of Cricket's Greatest Spin Bowlers*, Yellow Jersey, 2013

Roebuck, Peter, *Great Innings*, Anaya, 1990

Roebuck, Peter, *It Takes All Sorts: Celebrating Cricket's Colourful Characters*, Allen & Unwin, 2005

Roebuck, Peter, *Tangled Up in White*, Teach Yourself, 1992

Smyth, Rob, *The Spirit of Cricket: What Makes Cricket the Greatest Game on Earth*, Elliott & Thompson, 2011,

Speed, Malcolm, *Sticky Wicket*, HarperSports, 2011

Stoddart, Brian, and Keith Sandiford, eds, *The Imperial Game: Cricket, Culture and Society*, Manchester University Press, 1998

Szymanski, Stefan, and Tim Wigmore, *Crickonomics: The Anatomy of Modern Cricket*, Bloomsbury, 2022

Thomas, Richard, *Cricketing Lives: A Characterful History from Pitch to Page*, Reaktion, 2021

Wagg, Stephen, *Cricket: A Political History of the Global Game, 1945–2017*, Routledge, 2017

Walker, Peter, *Cricket Conversations*, Pelham, 1978
Williams, Jack, *Cricket and Broadcasting*, Manchester University Press, 2011
Williams, Jack, *Cricket and Race*, Berg, 2001
Williams, Marcus, *Double Century: 200 Years of Cricket in The Times*, Willow, 1985
Woolmer, Bob, and Tim Noakes, *Bob Woolmer's Art and Science of Cricket*, Struik, 2008

CRICKET BEFORE 1914

Grace, W.G., *How to Make a Big Score at Cricket*, Moduno, 2013
Haigh, Gideon, *Stroke of Genius: Victor Trumper and the Shot that Changed Cricket*, Simon & Schuster, 2016
Knox, Malcolm, *Never a Gentlemen's Game: The Scandal-filled Early Years of Test Cricket*, Hardie Grant, 2012
Kynaston, David, *WG's Birthday Party*, Bloomsbury, 2011
Major, John, *More Than a Game: The Story of Cricket's Early Years*, HarperPress, 2009
McCrery, Nigel, *Final Wicket: Test and First-Class Cricketers Killed in the Great War*, Pen & Sword, 2015
Morrah, Patrick, *The Golden Age of Cricket*, Eyre & Spottiswoode, 1967
Nicholls, J.L., *The Legendary Cricket Genius: Sydney F. Barnes (1873–1967)*, UK Book Publishing, 2018
Rae, Simon, *W.G. Grace: A Life*, Faber, 1998
Ranjitsinhji, K.S., *The Jubilee Book of Cricket*, Good Press, 2020
Sandiford, Keith, 'Cricket and the Victorian Society', *Journal of Social History*, 17/2 (1983), 303–17
Sandiford, Keith, and Wray Vamplew, 'The Peculiar Economics of English Cricket before 1914', *International Journal of the History of Sport*, 3/3 (1986), 311–26
Spofforth, Fred, *The Demon Speaks: Recollections and Reminiscences*, Amazon Digital, 2014

CORRUPTION

Greenslade, Nick, *The Thin White Line: The Inside Story of Cricket's Greatest Scandal*, Pitch, 2020
Hawkins, Ed, *Bookie Gambler Fixer Spy: A Journey to the Heart of Cricket's Underworld*, Bloomsbury, 2013

SELECTED BIBLIOGRAPHY

Puppala, Chandramohan, *No Ball*, Pan Macmillan India, 2019
Wilde, Simon, *Caught: The Full Story of Cricket's Match-fixing Scandal*, Aurum, 2001

OFFICIAL REPORTS

'ACB Player Conduct Inquiry Report', Rob O'Regan, February 1999
'Justice Qayyum's Report', Pakistan Cricket Board, 24 May 2000
'The CBI Report on Cricket Match Fixing and Related Malpractices', 1 November 2000
'Report on Corruption in International Cricket', Sir Paul Condon, May 2001
'Commission of Inquiry into Cricket Match-Fixing and Related Matters', Judge Edwin King, June 2001

UMPIRING/LAWS OF THE GAME

Chowdhury, Subhasish M., Sarah Jewell and Carl Singleton, 'Can Awareness Reduce (and Reverse) Identity-driven Bias in Judgement? Evidence from International Cricket', *Journal of Economic Behavior & Organization*, 226 (2024)
Crowe, S.M., and Jennifer Middeldorp, 'A Comparison of Leg Before Wicket Rates between Australians and their Visiting Teams for Test Cricket Series Played in Australia, 1977–94', *The Statistician*, 45/2 (1996), 255–62
Portus, Marc R., Charles D. Rosemond and David A. Rath, 'Cricket: Fast Bowling Arm Actions and the Illegal Delivery Law in Men's High Performance Cricket Matches', *Sports Biomechanics*, 5/2 (2006), 215–30
Ringrose, Trevor J., 'Neutral Umpires and Leg Before Wicket Decisions in Test Cricket', *Journal of the Royal Statistical Society, Series A (Statistics in Society)*, 169/4 (2006), 903–11
Sacheti, Abhinav, Ian Gregory-Smith and David Paton, 'Home Bias in Officiating: Evidence from International Cricket', *Journal of the Royal Statistical Society, Series A (Statistics in Society)*, 178/3 (2015), 741–55

COUNTRY-SPECIFIC LITERATURE

AFGHANISTAN

Albone, Tim, *Out of the Ashes: The Remarkable Rise and Rise of the Afghanistan Cricket Team*, Virgin, 2011
Breuer, C., and S. Feiler, 'Sports Clubs in Germany: Organisations and Internal Stakeholders', Sport Development Report for Germany, 2017

Breuer, C., S. Feiler and P. Wicker, 'Sport Clubs in Germany', in Breuer et al., eds, *Sport Clubs in Europe*, Springer, 2015, 187–208

Michelini, E., U. Burrmann, T. Nobis, J. Tuchel and T. Schlesinger, 'Sport Offers for Refugees in Germany. Promoting and Hindering Conditions in Voluntary Sport Clubs', *Society Register*, 2/1 (2018), 19–38

Suthar, Nihar, *The Corridor of Uncertainty: How Cricket Mended a Torn Nation*, Pitch, 2016

AUSTRALIA

Aitken, T., 'Statistical Analysis of Top Performers in Sport with Emphasis on the Relevance of Outliers', *Sports Engineering*, 7 (2004), 75–88

Benaud, Richie, *A Tale of Two Tests*, Hodder & Stoughton, 1962

Blackham, J., and B. Chapman, 'The Value of Don Bradman: Additional Revenue in Australian Ashes Tests', *Economic Papers: A journal of applied economics and policy*, 23/4 (2004), 369–85

Bradman, Don, *Farewell to Cricket*, Hodder & Stoughton, 1950

Brayshaw, Ian, *Lillee & Thommo: The Deadly Pair's Reign of Terror*, Hardie Grant, 2017

Brettig, Daniel, *Bradman & Packer: The Deal that Changed Cricket*, Slattery, 2019

Brettig, Daniel, *Whitewash to Whitewash: Australian Cricket's Years of Struggle and Summer of Riches*, Penguin, 2015

Campbell, R.H., *Cricket Casualties*, Australian Broadcasting Corporation, 1933

Condon, Anthony, 'The Positioning of Indigenous People in Australian History: A Historiography of the 1868 Aboriginal Cricket Tour of England', *International Journal of the History of Sport*, 35/5 (2018), 411–30

Coward, Mike, *Cricket Beyond the Bazaar: Australia on the Indian Subcontinent*, Allen & Unwin, 1990

Fingleton, Jack, *Cricket Crisis*, Pavilion, 1985

Gilchrist, Adam, *True Colours: My Life*, Macmillan, 2009

Gould, Stephen Jay, *Triumph and Tragedy in Mudville: A Lifelong Passion for Baseball*, Vintage, 2010

Haigh, Gideon, *The Big Ship*, Aurum, 2003

Haigh, Gideon, *Crossing the Line*, Slattery, 2018

Haigh, Gideon, *The Green & Golden Age: Writings on Cricket*, Aurum, 2008

Haigh, Gideon, *On the Ashes*, Allen & Unwin, 2023

Haigh, Gideon, *On Warne*, Simon & Schuster, 2012

SELECTED BIBLIOGRAPHY

Haigh, Gideon, *The Summer Game*, ABC, 2006
Hayden, Matthew, *Standing My Ground*, Aurum, 2011
Knox, Malcolm, *Bradman's War: How the 1948 Invincibles Turned the Cricket Pitch into a Battlefield*, Robson, 2013
Knox, Malcolm, *The Keepers: Australia's Wicketkeepers and the Heart of Australian Cricket*, Viking, 2017
Kynaston, David, *Richie Benaud's Blue Suede Shoes: The Story of an Ashes Classic*, Bloomsbury, 2024
Lillee, Dennis, *Menace*, Headline, 2004
Mailey, Arthur, *10 for 66 and All That*, Phoenix, 1958
McGrath, Glenn, *Test of Will: What I've Learned from Cricket and Life*, Allen & Unwin, 2015
Moyes, A.G., *Australian Cricket: A History*, Angus & Robertson, 1959
Osmond, Gary, and Murray G. Phillips. 'Viewed from All Sides: Statues, Sport and Eddie Gilbert', *Australian Aboriginal Studies*, 1 (2014), 16–32
Ponting, Ricky, *At the Close of Play*, HarperCollins, 2013
Roebuck, Peter, *In It to Win It: The Australian Cricket Supremacy*, Allen & Unwin, 2006
Rosenwater, Irving, *Sir Donald Bradman*, David & Charles Batsford, 1978
Ryan, Christian, *Australia: Story of a Cricket Country*, Hardie Grant, 2011
Ryan, Christian, *Golden Boy: Kim Hughes and the Bad Old Days of Australian Cricket*, Allen & Unwin, 2017
Smyth, Rob, *Benaud in Wisden*, Wisden, 2015
Tatz, Colin, 'The Sport of Racism', *Australian Quarterly*, 67/1 (1995), 38–48
Tatz, Colin, *Obstacle Race: Aborigines in Sport*, UNSW Press, 1996
Twopeny, Richard, *Town Life in Australia 1883*, Hard Press, 2006
Warne, Shane, *No Spin*, Ebury, 2019
Waugh, Steve, *Out of My Comfort Zone*, Penguin, 2005
Whimpress, Bernard, *Passport to Nowhere: Aborigines in Australian Cricket, 1850–1939*, Walla Walla Press, 1999

BANGLADESH

Bandyopadhyay, Kausik, *Bangladesh Playing: Sport, Culture, Nation*, Ahmed Mahfuzul Haque, 2012
Isam, Mohammad, *On the Tigers' Trail*, Mighty Press, 2023
Khondker, Habibul Haque, 'Cricket in Bangladesh', *India International Centre Quarterly*, 44/3–4 (2017), 31–43
Van Schendel, William, *A History of Bangladesh*, CUP, 2020

SELECTED BIBLIOGRAPHY

ENGLAND

Anderson, Jimmy, *Bowl. Sleep. Repeat.: Inside the World of England's Greatest-Ever Bowler*, Cassell, 2019

Arlott, John, *Concerning Cricket: Studies of Play and Players*, Longmans, 1949

Arlott, John, *Gone with the Cricketers*, Longmans, 1950

Arlott, John, *How to Watch Cricket*, Collins, 1984

Arlott, John, *Vintage Summer: 1947*, Eyre & Spottiswoode, 1967

Atherton, Mike, *Glorious Summers and Discontents: Looking Back on the Ups and Downs from a Dramatic Decade*, Simon & Schuster, 2011

Atherton, Mike, *Opening Up*, Hodder & Stoughton, 2002

Birley, Derek, *A Social History of English Cricket*, Aurum, 2013

Botham, Ian, *Botham's Book of the Ashes: A Lifetime Love Affair with Cricket's Greatest Rivalry*, Mainstream, 2010

Botham, Ian, *Head On*, Ebury, 2008

Brearley, Mike, *On Cricket*, Constable, 2018

Chalke, Stephen, *Summer's Crown: The Story of Cricket's County Championship*, Fairfield, 2015

Compton, Denis, *End of an Innings*, Oldbourne, 1958

Cook, Alastair, *Sir Alastair Cook: The Autobiography*, Michael Joseph, 2019

Cox, Peter, *Sixty Summers: English Cricket Since World War II*, Labatie, 2006

Easdale, Roderick, *Wally Hammond: Gentleman & Player*, Lume, 2012

English, Ross, *Cricket and England Through Five Matches: Class, War, Race & Empire 1900–1939*, self-published, 2018

Evans, Godfrey, *The Gloves are Off*, Hodder & Stoughton, 1960

Fay, Stephen, and David Kynaston, *Arlott, Swanton and the Soul of English Cricket*, Bloomsbury, 2019

Fletcher, Duncan, *Ashes Regained: The Coach's Story*, Simon & Schuster, 2005

Fletcher, Duncan, *Behind the Shades*, Simon & Schuster, 2008

Gibson, Alan, *The Cricket Captains of England*, Cassell, 1979

Gough, Darren, *Dazzler*, Michael Joseph, 2001

Gower, David, *An Endangered Species*, Simon & Schuster, 2013

Graveney, Tom, *On Cricket*, Frederick Muller, 1965

Haigh, Gideon, *Ashes 2005: The Full Story of the Test Series*, Aurum, 2005

Haigh, Gideon, *Ashes 2011: England's Record-Breaking Series Victory*, Aurum, 2011

SELECTED BIBLIOGRAPHY

Haigh, Gideon, *The Ultimate Test: The Story of the 2009 Ashes Series*, Aurum, 2009

Hammond, Walter, *Cricket: My Destiny*, Stanley Paul, 1946

Hill, Alan, *Herbert Sutcliffe: Cricket Maestro*, History Press, 2022

Hobbs, Jack, *My Life Story*, 'The Star' Publications, 1935

Holt, Richard, *Sport and the British: A Modern History*, OUP, 1989

Horspool, David, *More Than a Game: A History of How Sport Made Britain*, John Murray, 2023

Hoult, Nick, and Lawrence Booth, *Bazball: The Inside Story of a Test Cricket Revolution*, Bloomsbury, 2023

Hussain, Nasser, *Playing With Fire*, Michael Joseph, 2004

Hutton, Len, *Just My Story*, Hutchinson, 1956

James, Steve, *The Plan: How Fletcher and Flower Transformed English Cricket*, Transworld, 2012

Jardine, Douglas, *In Quest of the Ashes*, Orbis, 1984

John, Simon, '"A Different Kind of Test Match": Cricket, English Society and the First World War', *Sport in History*, 33/1 (2013), 19–48

Knott, Alan, *It's Knott Cricket*, Macmillan, 1985

Kynaston, David, *Austerity Britain, 1945–51*, Bloomsbury, 2008

Kynaston, David, *Family Britain, 1951–57*, Bloomsbury, 2010

Laker, Jim, *Cricket Contrasts*, Stanley Paul, 1985

Laker, Jim, *Over to Me*, Frederick Muller, 1960

Marqusee, Mike, *Anyone but England: Cricket, Race and Class*, Bloomsbury, 2016

McKinstry, Leo, *Jack Hobbs: England's Greatest Cricketer*, Yellow Jersey, 2012

Midwinter, Eric, *Class Peace: An Analysis of Social Status and English Cricket 1846–1962*, ACS, 2017

Peel, Mark, *Ambassadors of Goodwill: MCC Tours 1946/47–1970/71*, Pitch, 2018

Peel, Mark, *Never Surrender: The Life of Douglas Jardine*, Pitch, 2021

Pietersen, Kevin, *KP: The Autobiography*, Sphere, 2014

Pietersen, Kevin, *Kevin Pietersen on Cricket*, Sphere, 2015

Quelch, Tim, *Bent Arms and Dodgy Wickets: England's Troubled Reign as Test Match Kings during the Fifties*, Pitch, 2012

Ramprakash, Mark, *Strictly Me: My Life Under the Spotlight*, Mainstream, 2011

Rayvern Allen, David, ed., *The Essential Arlott on Cricket: Forty Years of Classic Writing on the Game*, Fontana Press, 1991

Ross, Alan, *Australia 55: A Journal of the MCC Tour*, Faber, 2012

Ross, Alan, *Cape Summer and the Australians in England*, Legend, 1986

SELECTED BIBLIOGRAPHY

Ross, Gordon, *The Testing Years: The Story of England's Rise to the Top in Post-war Cricket*, Stanley Paul, 1958

Rowe, Mark, *The Summer Field: A History of English Cricket Since 1840*, ACS, 2016

Rowe, Mark, *The Victory Tests: England v Australia 1945*, SportsBooks, 2010

Russell, Dave, ' "Ashes that Leave no Regrets". Anglo-Australian Cricket and English Society, c 1880–1939', *Sport in Society*, 15/8 (2012), 1038–54

Sandbrook, Dominic, *Never Had It So Good: A History of Britain from Suez to the Beatles*, Abacus, 2005

Sandbrook, Dominic, *White Heat: A History of Britain in the Swinging Sixties*, Abacus, 2006

Sandford, Christopher, *Laker and Lock*, Pitch, 2022

Scovell, Brian, *19–90: Jim Laker*, Tempus, 2006

Smith, Ed, *What Sport Tells Us About Life*, Penguin, 2008

Smyth, Rob, *Gentlemen and Sledgers*, Head of Zeus, 2015

Stewart, Alec, *Playing for Keeps*, BBC, 2003

Stone, Duncan, *Different Class: The Untold Story of English Cricket*, Repeater, 2022

Strauss, Andrew, *Driving Ambition*, Hodder & Stoughton, 2013

Sutcliffe, Herbert, *Batting*, Blackie, 1937

Swanton, E.W., *Cricket and the Clock: A Post-War Commentary*, Hodder & Stoughton, 1952

Synge, Allen, *Sins of Omission: The Story of the Test Selectors 1899–1990*, Michael Joseph, 1990

Thorpe, Graham, *Rising from the Ashes*, Willow, 2005

Trott, Jonathan, *Unguarded: My Autobiography*, Sphere, 2016

Turbervill, Huw, *The Toughest Tour: The Ashes Away Series*, Aurum, 2010

Tyson, Frank, *In the Eye of the Typhoon: The Inside Story of the MCC Tour of Australia and New Zealand 1954/55*, Parrs Wood, 2004

Warner, Pelham, *Cricket Between Two Wars*, Chatto & Windus, 1943

Wilde, Simon, *England: The Biography: The Story of English Cricket*, Simon & Schuster, 2018

Wilde, Simon, *Ian Botham: The Power and the Glory*, Simon & Schuster, 2011

Wilde, Simon, *The Tour*, Simon & Schuster, 2023

Williams, Charles, *Gentlemen & Players: The Death of Amateurism in Cricket*, Phoenix, 2013

Williams, Jack, *Cricket and England: A Cultural and Social History of the Inter-War Years*, Frank Cass, 1999

Williams, Jack, 'Cricket in Industrial Lancashire between the Wars – the Impact of Leagues', *British Society of Sports History Bulletin*, 9 (1989), 67–80

Williams, Jack, 'The Economics of League Cricket: Lancashire League Clubs and their Finances since the First World War', *British Society of Sports History Bulletin*, 9 (1990), ??–??

Williams, Jack, '"Fiery Fred": Fred Trueman and Cricket Celebrity in the 1950s and Early 1960s', *Sport in Society*, 12/4–5 (2009), 509–22

INDIA

Astill, James, *The Great Tamasha: Cricket, Corruption and the Turbulent Rise of Modern India*, Wisden, 2013

Bal, Sambit, et al., *Rahul Dravid: Timeless Steel*, ESPN EMEA, 2013

Bhattacharya, Rahul, *Pundits from Pakistan*, Picador, 2005

Bose, Mihir, *A History of Indian Cricket*, André Deutsch, 2002

Bose, Mihir, *The Magic of Indian Cricket: Cricket and Society in India*, Routledge, 2006

Bose, Mihir, *The Nine Waves: The Extraordinary Story of How India Took Over the Cricket World*, Pitch, 2022

Cashman, Richard, *Patrons, Players and the Crowd: The Phenomenon of Indian Cricket*, Orient Longman, 1980

Dev, Kapil, *Kapil*, Sidgwick & Jackson, 1987

Doshi, Anjali, *Tendulkar in Wisden: An Anthology*, Wisden, 2016

Dutta, Anindya, *Wizards: The Story of Indian Spin Bowling*, Westland Sport, 2019

Ezekiel, Gulu, *Sachin: The Story of the World's Greatest Batsman*, Penguin, 2002

Gavaskar, Sunil, *Idols*, Allen & Unwin, 1984

Gavaskar, Sunil, *Sunny Days*, Rupa, 1976

Giridhar, S., and V.J. Raghunath, *From Mumbai to Durban: India's Greatest Tests*, Juggernaut, 2016

Giridhar, S., and V.J. Raghunath, *Mid-wicket Tales: A Century and More of Cricket*, Speaking Tiger, 2023

Guha, Keshava, *The Story of Indian Cricket*, working documentary script, 2019

Guha, Ramachandra, *The Commonwealth of Cricket: A Lifelong Love Affair with the Most Subtle and Sophisticated Game Known to Humankind*, William Collins, 2020

Guha, Ramachandra, *A Corner of a Foreign Field: The Indian History of a British Sport*, Picador, 2002

Guha, Ramachandra, *Spin and Other Turns*, Penguin, 1994

Guruprasad, K.R., *Going Places: India's Small-Town Cricket Heroes*, Penguin, 2011

SELECTED BIBLIOGRAPHY

Hazare, Vijay, *Cricket Replayed*, Rupa, 1974
Hazare, Vijay, *A Long Innings*, Rupa, 1981
Kesavan, Mukul, *Men in White*, Motilal Penguin India, 2010
Kidambi, Prashant, *Cricket Country: An Indian Odyssey in the Age of Empire*, OUP, 2019
Laxman, V.V.S., with R. Kaushik, *281 and Beyond*, Westland, 2018
Majumdar, Boria, *Eleven Gods and a Billion Indians: The On and Off the Field Story of Cricket in India and Beyond*, Simon & Schuster, 2018
Majumdar, Boria, *Indian Cricket Through the Ages: A Reader*, OUP, 2005
Majumdar, Boria, *Twenty-two Yards to Freedom: A Social History of Indian Cricket*, Penguin, 2004
Mathur, Amrit, *Pitchside: My Life in Indian Cricket*, Westland, 2023
Menon, Suresh, *Pataudi: Nawab of Cricket*, Harper Sport, 2013
Mukherjee, Abhishek, and Arunabha Sengupta, *Sachin and Azhar at Cape Town: Indian and South African Cricket Through the Prism of a Partnership*, Pitch, 2021
Mukherjee, Sujit, *Playing for India*, Orient Blackswan, 2018
Nandy, Ashis, *The Tao of Cricket: On Games of Destiny and the Destiny of Games*, Penguin, 2000
Pataudi, Nawab of, *Tiger's Tale*, Stanley Paul, 1969
Prasanna, E.A.S, *One More Over*, Rupa, 1977
Raman, W.V., and R. Kaushik, *The Lords of Wankhede: Tales Between Two Titles*, Rupa, 2023
Samant, Nikhil D., *It Wasn't a Waste of Time*, Leadstart Inkstate, 2021
Sardesai, Rajdeep, *Kapil Dev: Superman from Haryana*, Juggernaut, 2021
Sen, Ronojoy, 'Introduction: The Landscape of Sport in South Asia', *India International Centre Quarterly*, 44/3–4 (2017), 1–13
Sengupta, Arunabha, *Elephant in the Stadium: The Myth and Magic of India's Epochal Win*, Pitch, 2022
Sundaram, Venkat, *Indian Cricket: Then and Now*, Harper Sport India, 2023
Sundaresan, Bharat, *The Dhoni Touch: Unravelling the Enigma that is Mahendra Singh Dhoni*, Ebury, 2018
Sundaresan, Bharat, with Gaurav Joshi, *The Miracle Makers: Indian Cricket's Greatest Epic*, Ebury, 2023
Tendulkar, Sachin, *Playing It My Way*, Hodder & Stoughton, 2014
Wadekar, Ajit, *My Cricketing Years*, Vikas, 1973
Wadhwaney, K.R., *Kapil Dev: The Prince of Allrounders*, Siddharth, 1996
Wright, John, with Sharda Ugra and Paul Thomas, *John Wright's Indian Summers*, Souvenir, 2006

SELECTED BIBLIOGRAPHY

IRELAND

Bairner, A., and D. Malcolm, 'Cricket and National Identities on the Celtic Fringe', in C. Rumford and S. Wagg, eds, *Cricket and Globalization*, Cambridge Scholars, 2010, 189–209

Gemmell, Jon, 'Naturally Played by Irishmen: A Social History of Irish Cricket', in D. Malcolm et al., eds, *The Changing Face of Cricket*, Routledge, 2013, 17–33

Joyce, James, *A Portrait of the Artist as a Young Man*, Diamond, 2021

O'Brien, Kevin and Siggins, Gerard, *Six After Six: Ireland's Cricket World Cup*, Brickfields, 2011

Reid, Sean, 'Identity and Cricket in Ireland in the Mid-nineteenth Century', *Sport in Society*, 15/2 (2012), 147–64

Rouse, Paul, *Sport and Ireland: A History*, Oxford University Press, 2015

NEW ZEALAND

Astle, A.M., 'Sport Development – Plan, Programme and Practice: A Case Study of the Planned Intervention by New Zealand Cricket into Cricket in New Zealand', PhD thesis, Massey University, New Zealand, 2014

Bradbury, T., and I. O'Boyle, 'Batting Above Average: Governance at New Zealand Cricket', *Corporate Ownership and Control*, 12/4 (2015), 352–63

Ferkins, L., D. Shilbury and G. McDonald, 'The Role of the Board in Building Strategic Capability: Towards an Integrated Model of Sport Governance Research', *Sport Management Review*, 8/3 (2005), 195–225

Hadlee, Richard, *Changing Pace*, Hodder Moa, 2009

Hadlee, Richard, *Rhythm and Swing*, Souvenir, 1989

McCullum, Brendon, with Greg McGee, *Declared*, Upstart, 2016

Ryan, Greg, 'Where the Game was Played by Decent Chaps: The Making of New Zealand Cricket 1832–1914', PhD thesis, University of Canterbury, 1996

Taylor, Ross, with Paul Thomas, *Black & White*, Upstart, 2023

PAKISTAN

Akram, Wasim, with Gideon Haigh, *Sultan: A Memoir*, Hardie Grant, 2022

Bandyopadhyay, Kausik, 'Pakistani Cricket at Crossroads: An Outsider's Perspective', *Sport in Society*, 10/1 (2007), 101–19

Beech, John, et al., 'Sport Tourism as a Means of Reconciliation? The Case of India–Pakistan Cricket', *Tourism Recreation Research*, 30/1 (2005), 83–91

Crace, John, *Wasim and Waqar: Imran's Inheritors*, Boxtree, 1992

Heller, Richard, and Peter Oborne, *White on Green*, Simon & Schuster, 2016
Kardar, Abdul, *Green Shadows*, Process Pakistan, 1958
Kardar, Abdul, *Test Status on Trial*, National Publications, 1954
Khan, Ali, 'The Mercurials: The Nature of Pakistani Cricket', *India International Centre Quarterly*, 44/3–4 (2017), 17–30
Khan, Imran, *All Round View*, Chatto & Windus, 1988
Khan, Imran, *Pakistan: A Personal History*, Bantam, 2011
Khan, Shaharyar, M. Khan and Ali Khan, *Cricket Cauldron: The Turbulent Politics of Sport in Pakistan*, I.B. Tauris, 2013
Mahmood, Fazal, with Asif Sohail, *From Dusk to Dawn: Autobiography of a Pakistan Cricket Legend*, OUP, 2003
Oborne, Peter, *Wounded Tiger*, Simon & Schuster, 2014
Samiuddin, Osman, *The Unquiet Ones: A History of Pakistan Cricket*, HarperCollins India, 2014
Sandford, Christopher, *Imran Khan*, HarperCollins, 2009

SOUTH AFRICA

Alfred, Luke, and Ian Hawkey, *Vuvuzela Dawn: 25 Sporting Stories that Shaped a New Nation*, Pan Macmillan SA, 2019
Allen, Dean, *Empire, War & Cricket in South Africa: Logan of Matjiesfontein*, Zebra, 2015
Allen, Dean, 'South African Cricket, Imperial Cricketers and Imperial Expansion, 1850–1910', *International Journal of the History of Sport*, 25/4 (2008), 443–71
Bacher, Ali, and David Williams, *Jacques Kallis and 12 Other Great South African All-rounders*, Penguin (South Africa), 2013
Bacher, Ali, and David Williams, *South Africa's Greatest Batsmen: Past and Present*, Penguin (South Africa), 2015
Bacher, Ali, and David Williams, *South Africa's Greatest Bowlers: Past and Present*, Penguin (South Africa), 2019
Booth, Douglas, 'Hitting Apartheid for Six? The Politics of the South African Sports Boycott', *Journal of Contemporary History*, 38/3 (2003), 477–93
Desai, Ashwin, *Reverse Sweep: A Story of South African Cricket Since Apartheid*, Jacana, 2016
Farred, Grant, 'The Nation in White: Cricket in a Post-Apartheid South Africa', *Social Text*, 50 (1997), 9–32
Gemmell, Jon, 'South African Cricket: "The Rainbow Nation Must Have a Rainbow Team"', *Sport in Society*, 10/1 (2007), 49–70

Guha, Ramachandra, 'Cricket, Caste, Community, Colonialism: The Politics of a Great Game', *International Journal of the History of Sport*, 14/1 (1997), 174–83

Jordaan, Maxwell Abraham, 'Race, Class and Place in Transforming Sport: A Case Study of Cricket South Africa, 1991–2020', MA thesis, University of Johannesburg, 2022

Manthorp, Neil, *The Proteas: 20 Years, 20 Landmark Matches*, Mercury, 2011

May, Peter, *The Rebel Tours: Cricket's Crisis of Conscience*, SportsBooks, 2009

Murray, Bruce, 'Abe Bailey and the Foundation of the Imperial Cricket Conference', *South African Historical Journal*, 60/3 (2008), 375–96

Oborne, Peter, *Basil D'Oliveira: Cricket and Conspiracy*, Sphere, 2005

Odendaal, André, 'South Africa's Black Victorians: Sport and Society in South Africa in the Nineteenth Century', in *Pleasure, Profit, Proselytism. British Culture and Sport at Home and Abroad 1700–1914*, edited by J.A. Mangan, 193–214, Frank Cass (London), 1988

Odendaal, André, *The Story of an African Game*, David Philip (Cape Town), 2003

Pakenham, Thomas, *The Scramble for Africa*, Abacus, 1992

Parry, Richard, and André Odendaal, *Swallows and Hawke: England's Cricket Tourists, the MCC and the Making of South Africa 1888–1968*, Pitch, 2022

Parry, Richard, and Jonty Winch, *Too Black to Wear Whites: The Remarkable Story of Krom Hendricks, a Cricket Hero Rejected by the Empire*, Pitch, 2021

Sengupta, Arunabha, *Apartheid: A Point to Cover: South African Cricket 1948–70 and the Stop The Seventy Tour Campaign*, CricketMASH, 2020

Steen, Robert, 'MCC, English Complicity and the D'Oliveira Affair', in *British Society of Sports History Annual Conference*, 2008

Swart, Kamilla, and David Maralack, 'Black Lives Matter: Perspectives from South African Cricket', *Sport in Society*, 24/5 (2021), 715–30

SRI LANKA

Brookes, Nicholas, *An Island's Eleven: The Story of Sri Lankan Cricket*, History Press, 2022

Fernando, Andrew Fidel, *Upon a Sleepless Isle*, Pan Macmillan India, 2019

Ismail, Qadri, 'Batting Against the Break: On Cricket, Nationalism, and the Swashbuckling Sri Lankans', *Social Text*, 50 (1997), 33–56

Karunatilaka, Shehan, *Chinaman*, Vintage, 2011

Karunatilaka, Shehan, *The Seven Moons of Maali Almeida*, Sort of Books, 2022

Roberts, Michael, *Essaying Cricket: Sri Lanka and Beyond*, Vijitha Yapa, 2006
Subramanian, Samanth, *This Divided Island: Stories from the Sri Lankan War*, Atlantic, 2015

WEST INDIES

Ambrose, Curtly, with Richard Sydenham, *Time to Talk*, Aurum, 2015
Baksh, Vaneisa, *Son of Grace: Frank Worrell – A Biography*, Fairfield, 2023
Beckles, Hilary, *The Development of West Indies Cricket*, i: *The Age of Nationalism*, Pluto, 1998
Beckles, Hilary, *The Development of West Indies Cricket*, ii: *The Age of Globalization*, Pluto Press, 1998
Beckles, Hilary, *A Nation Imagined: First West Indies Test Team*, Ian Randle, 2003
Beckles, Hilary, and Brian Stoddart, eds, *Liberation Cricket: West Indies Cricket Culture*, Manchester University Press, 1995
Birbalsingh, Frank, 'Learie Constantine the Writer', *Caribbean Quarterly*, 30/2 (1984), 60–75
Burton, Richard D.E., *Afro-Creole: Power, Opposition, and Play in the Caribbean*, Cornell University Press, 1997
Constantine, Learie, *Cricket in the Sun*, Stanley Paul, 1946
Constantine, Learie, and Denzil Batchelor, *The Changing Face of Cricket*, Eyre & Spottiswoode, 1966
Dabydeen, David, and Brinsley Samaroo, eds, *India in the Caribbean*, Hansib, 1987
Downes, Aviston, '"Flannelled Fools"? Cricket and the Political Economy of the West Indies c.1895–1906', *International Journal of the History of Sport*, 17/4 (2000), 59–80
Downes, Aviston, 'From Boys to Men: Colonial Education, Cricket and Masculinity in the Caribbean, 1870–c.1920', *International Journal of the History of Sport*, 22/1 (2005), 3–21
Ganteaume, Andy, *My Story: The Other Side of the Coin*, Medianet Limit, 2007
Gayle, Chris, *Six Machine: I Don't Like Cricket . . . I Love It*, Penguin, 2016
Gray, Ashley, *The Unforgiven: Mercenaries or Missionaries? The Untold Stories of the Rebel West Indian Cricketers Who Toured Apartheid South Africa*, Pitch, 2020
James, C.L.R., *Beyond a Boundary*, Duke University Press, 2013
Kincaid, Jamaica, *A Small Place*, Daunt, 2018
Lamming, George, *In the Castle of My Skin*, Penguin, 2017

Levett, Geoffrey, 'The "White Man's Game"? West Indian Cricket Tours of the 1900s', *International Journal of the History of Sport*, 34/7–8 (2017), 599–618
Lister, Simon, *Fire in Babylon*, Yellow Jersey, 2016
Naipaul, V.S., *A House for Mr Biswas*, Picador, 2016
Pearson, Harry, *Connie: The Marvellous Life of Learie Constantine*, Little, Brown, 2017
Richards, Viv, *Sir Vivian: The Definitive Autobiography*, Penguin, 2001
Ryan, Selwyn, 'East Indians, West Indians and the Quest for Caribbean Political Unity', *Social and Economic Studies*, 48/4 (1999), 151–84
Sobers, Garry, *Garry Sobers: My Autobiography*, Headline, 2003
Stollmeyer, Jeff, *Everything Under the Sun: My Life in West Indies Cricket*, Hutchinson, 1983
Tossell, David, *Grovel! The Story and Legacy of the Summer of 1976*, Pitch, 2012
Woodhouse, David, *Who Only Cricket Know: Hutton's Men in the West Indies 1953/54*, Fairfield, 2021
Worrell, Frank, *Cricket Punch*, Stanley Paul, 1959
Young, Greg, *From Lilliput to Lord's*, SilverWood, 2017

ZIMBABWE

Butcher, Alan, *The Good Murungu?: A Cricket Tale of the Unexpected*, Pitch, 2016
Olonga, Henry, *Blood, Sweat and Treason*, Vision Sports, 2015
Taibu, Tatenda, *Keeper of Faith: Cricket, Conflict and God in Zimbabwe's Age of Extremes*, deCoubertin, 2019
Winch, Jonty, ' "Rejects of the Sporting Whites of the Continent": African Cricket in Rhodesia', in Murray et al., eds, *Cricket and Society in South Africa, 1910–1971: From Union to Isolation*, 2018, 243–271
Winch, Jonty, ' "There Were a Fine Manly Lot of Fellows": Cricket, Rugby and Rhodesian Society during William Milton's Administration, 1896–1914', *Sport in History*, 28/4 (2008), 583–604

NON-TEST NATIONS

Abraham, Timothy, and James Coyne, *Evita Burned Down Our Pavilion: A Cricket Odyssey Through Latin America*, Constable, 2021
Brooks, Tim, *A Corner of Every Foreign Field: Cricket's Journey from English Game to Global Sport*, Pitch, 2020
Brooks, Tim, *Cricket on the Continent*, Pitch, 2016

Musk, Stephen, and Roger Mann, *Bart King of Philadelphia*, Troubador, 2022

Penman, Richard, 'The Failure of Cricket in Scotland', *International Journal of the History of Sport*, 9/2 (1992), 302–315

Potter, David W., *The Encyclopaedia of Scottish Cricket*, Empire, 1999

Wigmore, Tim, and Peter Miller, *Second XI: Cricket in its Outposts*, Pitch, 2015

PICTURE CREDITS

In order of appearance:

1 – Popperfoto; 2 – Hulton Archive; 3 – George Beldam/Popperfoto; 4 – George Beldam/Popperfoto; 5 – Hulton Archive; 6 – Topical Press Agency/Hulton Archive; 7 – Paul Popper/Popperfoto; 8 – Keystone/Hulton Archive; 9 – PA Images/Alamy Stock Photo; 10 – PA Images/Alamy Stock Photo; 11 – Hulton Archive; 12 – Central Press/Hulton Archive; 13 – PA Images/Alamy Stock Photo; 14 – Smith Archive/Alamy Stock Photo; 15 – PA Images/Alamy Stock Photo; 16 – Mark Leech/Offside; 17 – Adrien Murrell/Getty Images Sport Classic; 18 – Patrick Eagar/Popperfoto; 19 – David Munden/Popperfoto; 20 – Bob Thomas; 21 – Patrick Eagar/Popperfoto; 22 – David Munden/Popperfoto; 23 – Patrick Eagar/Popperfoto; 24 – Ben Radford/Getty Images Sport Classic; 25 – John MacDougall/AFP; 26 – Arko Datta/AFP; 27 – Patrick Eagar/Popperfoto; 28 – PA Images/Alamy Stock Photo; 29 – Jack Atley/Getty Images Sport; 30 – PA Images/Alamy Stock Photo; 31 – Getty Images/Hulton Archive; 32 – Associated Press/Alamy Stock Photo; 33 – Adrien Murrell/Getty Images Sport Classic; 34 – PA Images/Alamy Stock Photo; 35 – Tom Shaw/Getty Images Sport; 36 – Gareth Copley/Getty Images Sport; 37 – Patrick Hamilton/AFP; 38 – Alex Davidson/Getty Images Sport.

INDEX

Abbas, Zaheer 226
Abed, Dik 165
Achrekar, Ramakant 299
Adams, Andre 428
Adams, Jimmy 448
Adams, Paul 408
Adiga, Aravind 469
Afghan Cricket Club 514
Afghan Cricket Federation 515
Afghanistan 509, 514–17, 519–21
Afghanistan Cricket Board 517
Afridi, Shaheen Shah 501
Afridi, Shahid 259, 516
Agarwal, Mayank 464
Ahmed, Imtiaz 346
Ahmed, Mushtaq 258, 292
Ahmed, Niaz 409
Ahmed, Tauseef 228
Ahmun, Rob 479
Ajmal, Saeed 327, 439–40
Akhtar, Shoaib 315, 382
Akmal, Kamran 352
Akram, Wasim 227, 229, 292, 304–5, 376
   reverse swing 237–8, 239, 240–1
Alam, Fawad 501, 502
Alderman, Terry 211–12, 215
Alderson, Professor Jacqueline 326
Alexander, Gerry 128, 136, 137
Ali, Azhar 437, 440, 441, 444
Ali, Syed Abid 172, 173
Ali, Syed Mushtaq 62
Allen, Gubby 83, 84, 145, 160
allrounders 213–30
   Botham 213, 214–16, 217, 227, 230
   Dev 213, 218–21, 227, 230

   Hadlee 221–5, 227, 230
   Khan 213, 225–30
Allsop, G. 26
Altham, H.S. 33
Amarnath, Lala 65, 115, 119
Amarnath, Mohinder 177
Ambrose, Curtly 188–9, 190, 262, 263, 281, 378, 448
   on Akram 239
   bowling to Tendulkar 491
   on county cricket 195–6
   on Waugh 264, 265
   on the WICB's failures 450
Ames, Les 344, 345–6
Amir, Mohammad 294–5, 295–6, 297, 437
Amiss, Dennis 204
Amla, Hashim 393, 394–5, 402, 406–7
Anderson, James 337, 386, 387, 390–2
apartheid 152–65, 280, 281
   boycotts 162, 164
   cricket during 154–5
   D'Oliveira affair 157–62
   non-racial South African team 155, 156
   policies 153
   rebel tours 206–7, 208–11, 280
   Test matches 153–4
   vs. Australia 162–4
Archer, Jofra 527
Argentina 41–3
Arlott, John 91–2, 101, 108, 151, 156, 159, 266
Armstrong, Warwick 38, 46, 47, 48, 78
Arnold, Russel 428
Aronstam, Marlon 287, 288
Ashes Tests 46, 98–9, 108
   (1877) 7, 9–10

INDEX

Ashes Tests – *Cont'd.*
  (1882) 1–3
  (1891/92) 14
  (1894/95) 14–16
  (1902) 28–9, 33–4
  (1921) 46–7
  (1926) 48–9, 52
  (1928/29) 52–3, 54, 344–5
  (1932/33) 82–7
  (1936/37) 88
  (1946/47) 90
  (1948) 90–2
  (1953) 99–102
  (1954/55) 104–7
  (1956) 109–11
  (1961) 149–51
  (1981) 214, 215–17
  (2005) 368–74
  (2010/11) 386–9
  (2019) 523–4, 526
Ashes, the 3, 14
Ashraf, Faheem 502
Ashraful, Mohammad 415–16
Ashwin, Ravichandran 431–2, 461, 474–6, 476, 505, 506
  on Bazball 534
Asia Cup 412
Asian Cricket Council 412
Asian Cricket Council Trophy 515
Asif, Mohammad 294–5, 296, 297, 387, 437, 490
Atherton, Mike 288, 376, 377, 379, 380
  on Australian cricket 271
  central contracts 375, 376
  cricketers' earnings 451, 452
  facing Donald 492–3
  fine 241
Atkinson, Eric 236
Austin, Richard 211
The Australasian 12
Australia 97–8
  aggressive approach 273–4
  captaincy of 144, 147–51
  club system 266
  domestic cricket 457
  growth of cricket 11
  players' earnings 198–9, 271
  playing for money 12, 13
  professionalism 270–1
  rebel tours 209–10, 211–12
  Test history success 266–7, 275
  tours to England 9, 10–13
  vs. England *see* Ashes Tests
  vs. India 276–8
  vs. Pakistan 341
  vs. West Indies 126–31, 181, 262–3, 264–5
  see also Packer, Kerry
Australian Board of Control for International Cricket 13, 198, 202
Australian Cricket Board 38, 89, 202, 291
Australian Cricketers' Association 271
Australian Imperial Forces 45
Australian Institute of Sport 269
Australian Services XI 97–8
Azharuddin, Mohammad 292–3, 303–4

Bacher, Dr Ali 206, 282, 285, 408
Badrinath, Subramaniam 402
Bailey, Abe 26–7, 43
Bailey, Trevor 99, 100
Bairstow, Jonny 350, 523, 528, 529
Baksh, Vaneisa 126, 135
ball-tampering 239–42
Baloo, Palwankar 62–3
Bancroft, Cameron 242, 525
Bangladesh 409–22
  Asia Cup 412
  Associate membership of ICC 411
  bid for Test status 413–14
  early Test results 415–17
  facilities 416
  ICC KnockOut (1998) 412–13
  independence 409, 410–11
  MCC tour (1976/77) 411
  National Sports Control Board 412
  student protests 421
  Test wins 419–20, 421–2
  vs. Australia 419–20
  vs. England 418–19
  vs. India 415
  vs. Pakistan 421–2
  vs. Zimbabwe 416–17
  World Cups 412, 413
Bangladesh Cricket Control Board 411

INDEX

Bannerman, Charles 10
Barbados 131–3
Barbados Cricket Association (BCA) 132
Barbados Cricket League (BCL) 132
Bardsley, Warren 40
Barlow, Eddie 163
Barnes, Alan 199
Barnes, Sydney 36–7, 38, 111
Barrington, Ken 103–4, 173
Bashar, Habibul 417
Basil D'Oliveira Trophy 162
batting
    left-handed 432–4
    top-hand dominant 433
batting averages, decline 489
Bavuma, Temba 407
Bazball 528–34
Beauclerk, Lord Frederick 8
Beckett, Samuel 512
Beckles, Hilary 68, 70, 135, 137
Bedi, Bishan 169, 171, 174, 180, 241, 430–1
Bedser, Alec 106, 214, 215, 352
Beginner, Lord 134–5
Beldam, George 29
Bell, Ian 439
Benaud, Richie 101, 126–7, 128, 131, 137, 199
    captaincy 147, 149–51
Benjamin, Winston 228, 229
Bishop, Ian 188, 262
Blackham, Jack 344
Bligh, Ivo 3, 14
Blythe, Colin 20, 45
Board of Control for Cricket in India (BCCI) 63, 301–2, 465
Board of Control for Cricket in Pakistan 116
Bobby, Ahmed Sajjadul Alam 411
Bodyline series (1932/33) 82–7
Boer War 25
Boland, Scott 532
Bombay Gymkhana 61
Bombay School of Batsmanship 66, 176, 301
Border, Allan 217, 223, 256, 261, 263, 329, 425
Border-Gavaskar Trophy 462
Bosanquet, Bernard 17–18

Bose, Mihir 60–1, 171, 290
Botham, Ian 213, 214–16, 217, 227, 230, 249, 382
Boucher, Mark 406, 492
Boult, Trent 502, 503, 505, 528
bouncers 191, 238, 483, 485, 487
bowling 4, 17–18, 19, 20–1, 36–7
Boycott, Geoffrey 177, 206
Bracewell, Michael 530
Bradman, Sir Donald 93, 96, 126, 127, 163–4, 297
    Bodyline series (1932/33) 83–4, 86–7
    on bowler-captains 148
    captaincy 90–1
    childhood 77
    earnings 88–9
    on England 86
    lifestyle 80
    physique 79
    on politics and sport 163–4
    retirement 92
    self-taught batting technique 78–9, 80–1
    on Sobers 139
    team meeting 323
    on Tendulkar 298
    Test batting average 77, 91–2
    Test debut 77–8
    vs. England 77–8, 83–4, 86–7, 88, 90–2
    whistlestops 244
Brathwaite, Kraigg 539
Brearley, Mike 160, 214–15, 216
Brettig, Daniel 323
Briggs, Aaron 233, 238
Bright, Ray 216, 217
Bripumyarrimin 'King Cole' 9
Broad, Chris 436
Broad, Stuart 385, 388, 391–2, 429
Brookes, Nicholas 211, 246
Brooks, Reginald Shirley 3, 14
Brown, Bill 67
Brown, Freddie 145, 146, 152–3
Brown, John 15–16
Brukner, Peter 485, 486
Buchanan, John 273, 277–8
Bucknor, Steve 379
Buenos Aires Cricket Club 41, 42
Bulawayo 356

563

INDEX

Bulawayo African Cricket Association 356
Bumrah, Jasprit 473, 489
Burton, Tommy 70
Butcher, Mark 320, 374
Butt, Salman 294, 295, 296, 437

Caddick, Andy 378, 380
Cadwallader, Harry 24
Calcutta Cricket Club 60, 117
Calthorpe, Frederick 56
Campbell, R.H. 47, 50, 86
Campbell, Sherwin 446
captaincy
   of Australia 144, 147–51
   batsmen 148
   bowlers 148–9
   class in England 143–7
   race in the West Indies 136–8
Cardus, Neville 31, 33, 34, 95–6
Caribbean *see* West Indies
Caribbean Community's Cricket Governance Subcommittee 449, 450
Caribbean Premier League 458
Carr, Arthur 48, 81
Carr, Donald 160, 161
carrom ball 475
Carter, Bob 494
Carter, Hanson 31
Cartwright, Tom 161
central contracts 208, 295, 375, 376, 392, 469
Ceylon 243–4
   advantageous geographical location 243–4
   bid for Test status 246–7, 248
   later Sri Lanka *see* Sri Lanka
   origins of cricket 244–5
   schedule 245
   schools 244–5
   unofficial tests 246
   Westernization 245
   whistlestops *see* whistlestops
Challenor, George 74
Chandrasekhar, B.S. 170, 172, 173, 174
Chang, Herbert 211
Channel Nine 198, 202
Chappell, Greg 203, 219

Chappell, Ian 168, 174, 199, 236, 273
   on Australia's club system 266
   on bowler-captains 148
   on facing fast bowling 482, 483
   on front-foot batsmen 485–6
   on helmets 204
   on Lillee and Thomson 181, 182
   on Sobers 140–1
   on the WSC 202
Chappell, Trevor 216–17
Chatfield, Ewen 223, 485
Chawla, Sanjay 285
Chester, Frank 49
Chowdhury et al 427
Chowdhury, Saber Hossain 414
Churchill, Winston 27
Clark, Stuart 490
Clarke, Sylvester 186
Clinton, Hillary 515
Close, Brian 151, 184
Cobham, Lord 157
Cockermouth Cricket Club 522
Collins, Herbie 49
Collins, Jack 424
Colombo Cricket Club 243, 244, 245
Coltart, David 365
Compton, Denis 55, 91, 97, 112, 156
   appeal of 95–6
   football career 94–5
   partnership with Edrich 94
   partnership with Hutton 102–3
   style of play 95
concussion substitutes 486
Condon, Sir Paul 293
Coney, Jeremy 222–3, 224
Connolly, Alan 235
Constantine, Learie 71–2, 73–4, 96, 142, 161, 194
   on biased umpiring 424
   on Hutton's appointment 146
   on white captains 137, 138
Contractor, Nari 168
conventional swing 232–3, 234, 238
Conway, Devon 506
Cook, Alistair 386, 388, 389, 390, 418
Cork, Dominic 379
County Championship 35, 375, 377

INDEX

overseas players 195
solvency of clubs 38
Covid-19 pandemic 427, 457, 459
Cowdrey, Colin 103, 104, 107, 158, 160, 430
Cozier, Tony 446
Crawley, John 320
Crawley, Zak 531
cricket
  amateurs 32
  broadcasting revenue 452, 453
  commercial potential 88–9
  corruption 8, 285–97, 437
  day-night matches 201, 203
  deaths and injuries 485, 486
  dismissals backing up 67
  earnings of cricketers 198–9
  exported from England 8–9
  governance *see* International Cricket Council (ICC)
  growth in England 8
  influx of revenue 451–2
  live radio broadcasting 100–1
  minimum wage 456
  players' strikes 13
  political and security crises 436
  professionals 32, 54
  roots and development of 3–4, 10–11, 41–2
  structural changes 454–5
  underpaid cricketers 198
  as a way of life 26
  widening rich/poor gap 452–3
  during World War II 97
  see also Test matches/cricket; World Series Cricket (WSC)
Cricket South Africa 408, 535, 536
CricViz 257, 329, 353, 484, 490
Crocker, Gary 354
Croft, Colin 187, 209
Cronje, Frans 289
Cronje, Hansie 283, 284
  match-fixing 285–9, 293
Crowe, Martin 222, 224, 496–7, 501
Cullinan, Daryll 258
Cummins, Pat 462, 464, 523–4, 532
  on Bazball 533, 534
  on financial inequality 456–7

  fitness 487–8
  on pain 480
  wobble seam 490–1
Curran, Kevin 357
Currie Cup 356, 357

Dacca 410
Dalmiya, Jagmohan 302, 413, 510
Daniel, Wayne 186
Darling, Joe 29, 144, 432
Das, Litton 421
Davidson, Alan 127, 150
Decision Review System (DRS) 428, 429, 430–2, 433, 434
Dempster, Stewie 59
Denness, Mike 181
Dev, Kapil 170–1, 213, 218–21, 227, 230, 424, 466
Dexter, Ted 150, 151, 246
Dhoni, M.S. 470–1
Dilley, Graham 215, 216, 217
Dilshan, Tillakaratne 435
Dissanayake, Gamini 211
Dolan, Steve 512
D'Oliveira, Basil 155–62, 165, 356–7
Donald, Allan 'White Lightning' 207, 281, 282–3, 284, 480
  bowling to Atherton 492–3
Donnelly, Martin 59
Doordarshan 301–2
doosra 305, 321, 325, 329
Douglas, J.W.H.T. 241
Dravid, Rahul 304, 308–10, 312–14, 316, 402
  domestic pitches 467–8
  infrastructure 469–70
  U-19 selection process 467
Duckett, Ben 418, 531
Duckworth, George 344, 345
Duleepsinhji, Kumar Shri 39–40, 64
Duminy, J.P. 396, 401
Durani, Salim 171, 172
Durban High School 407

East Pakistan 409–10
  later Bangladesh *see* Bangladesh
Eden Gardens 307, 308, 310
Edrich, Bill 94, 100

INDEX

Edrich, John 172, 184
Emburey, John 212, 217, 248
Engineer, Farokh 173, 346
England 97–8
  in the 1980s 382
  in the 1990s 382
  amateurs (gentlemen) and
    professionals 13, 143–7
  Bazball approach 528–34
  bottom of *Wisden* rankings 374
  captaincy 143–7
  central contracts 295, 376, 392
  decline 382, 389–90
  earnings of cricketers 198
  Oxbridge influence 146–7
  rebel tours 206, 210, 212
  revenue from ICC 454
  run rate in the 1950s 104
  simultaneous Tests 56–7
  Test record 382–4, 391–2
  two divisions of County
    Championship 375–7
  vs. Australia *see* Ashes Tests
  vs. India 389, 390–1, 538
  vs. New Zealand 374
  vs. Pakistan 379–80
  vs. Sri Lanka 380
  vs. West Indies 378–9
England and Wales Cricket Board 382
Eranga, Shaminda 337
Evans, Godfrey 105, 106, 113, 156, 346, 352

Farbrace, Paul 436
fast bowling 47, 478–93
  back stress factors 479, 488
  ball-tracking 483–4
  batsmen's cues 483–4
  batsmen's reaction times 482–3, 484
  bloody-mindedness 480
  fitness and speed of bowlers 487–8
  improved bowling methods 488–9
  India 218, 466–8
  intimidation of batsmen 481
  judgement of batsmen 482–4
  pain 479–80
  physical demands of 479–80
  South Africa 399, 400
  West Indies 180–1, 186–90
  wobble seam 387, 489–91
Faulkner, Aubrey 19–20, 213
Felton, Paul 479
Fender, Percy 46, 80–1, 345
Fennex, William 8
Fernando, Andrew Fidel 334, 335
Fernando, Sunil 328–9
Fernando, Vishwa 339–40
Fingleton, Jack 31, 82
Finn, Steve 388
Fleming, Damien 269, 271, 376–7, 487
Fleming, Stephen 313
Fletcher, Duncan 342, 357, 369, 371, 372, 377–8
  technical eye 381
  using the sweep 381
Fletcher, Keith 172, 248, 410
Flintoff, Andrew 368, 370, 371, 372, 373–4, 428
flipper 226, 255, 260
Flower, Andy 349, 358–9, 360–1, 364, 390, 522
  England team meeting 384–5
  partnership with Olanga 364–5
  pie chart 361
  protests 365
  self-hypnosis 362
  Test record 362
  training plan 362
Flower, Grant 358–9
Foundation of Goodness 328
franchise competitions 456
Fraser, Angus 375
Fraser, Malcolm 279
Fredericks, Roy 183, 211
Frith, David 32, 324
Fry, C.B. 28, 34, 59, 250
Future Tours Programme 452, 498

Gaddafi Stadium 435, 436
Gaekwad, Anshuman 180
Gaelic Athletic Association (GAA) 512
gambling 7–8
  match-fixing 8, 285–97, 437
Gandhi, Indira 436

INDEX

Ganguly, Sourav 307, 311–12, 312, 314
Ganteaume, Andy 138
Gara, Tom 485, 486
Gardner, Ben 490
Garner, Joel 187, 190
Gatting, Mike 210, 253, 380, 425
Gavaskar, Sunil 219, 225, 236, 301, 424, 466
   batsmanship 177, 178
   childhood 176
   operational finger 175
   Test career 177, 178, 179
   Test debut 175–6
Gayle, Chris 456
Gentlemen of Philadelphia 41
Ghavri, Karsan 218
Gibbs, Herschelle 287, 397
Gibbs, Lance 130, 142, 180
Gibson, Clem 42
Gilbert, Eddie 81
Gilchrist, Adam 276, 277, 278, 310, 341–4, 349–51
   aggressive batting 274, 341, 342–3, 349–50
Giles, Ashley 369, 371, 379
Gill, Shubman 463, 505
Gillespie, Jason 274, 277, 436, 448
Gilligan, Arthur 56, 63
Gleneagles Agreement 205
Goddard, John 134, 135, 136
Golden Age 29, 31–3, 34, 35, 37, 39, 42
Gomes, Larry 192, 194
Gomez, Nicholas 447
Gooch, Graham 206, 212, 223, 382
goodwill series 314
Goodwin, Murray 360, 365
googly 17–18, 19, 20–1
Goonesena, Gamini 245
Gough, Darren 321, 375–6, 379, 380
Gould, Stephen Jay 92
Gower, David 210, 270, 382
Grace, W.G. 1, 2–3, 10, 30, 34, 37, 144
   dominance 5
   earnings 6–7
   family background 5
   intimidation of umpires 7
   memorial to 5–6
   preparation for matches 6
   testimonial 5
Grant, Jack 136
Graveney, Tom 98, 102, 160
Green, Cameron 539
Green Man and Still pub 8
Greenidge, Gordon 184, 191–2, 197, 228, 413
Gregory, Jack 46–7, 241
Greig, Tony 183–4, 185, 192, 199, 200
Griffin, Geoff 323
Griffith, Billy 157–8, 159
Griffith, Charlie 142, 168, 323, 430
Grimmett, Clarrie 58, 75, 87, 254, 255, 348
Grout, Wally 127, 128, 129, 150, 348
Guha, Keshava 469
Guha, Ramachandra 39, 62–3, 66, 120, 465
Gupta, Arvind 290
Gupta, Mukesh Kumar 286, 287, 288, 290, 291, 292

Hadlee, Richard 221–5, 227, 230, 254
Hadlee, Walter 59
Hafeez, Mohammad 439
Haigh, Gideon 31, 46, 203
Hair, Darrell 321–2
Hall, Wes 126, 127, 128–9, 130
Hambledon 4
Hammond, Wally 54–5, 88, 96, 145
Hampshire, John 354
Harare Sports Club 359, 367
Harmison, Steve 368, 369, 370, 371, 376
Harris, Lord 39, 61, 63, 464
Harris, Marcus 473, 524
Harris, Paul 402
Harris Shield 300
Hartley, Tom 538
Harvey, Neil 90, 99, 100, 105, 109, 150
Hasan, Raqibul 410–11
Hasan, Shakib Al 418, 419–21, 422
Hasina, Sheikh 421
Hassett, Lindsay 90, 99, 100
Hawke, Bob 163–4, 209
Hawke, Lord 25, 143, 355–6
Hayden, Matthew 272, 274
Haynes, Desmond 192, 208, 228, 264
Hayter, Reg 95

INDEX

Hayward, Tom 94
Hazare, Vijay 62, 66–7
Hazlewood, Josh 419, 462, 464, 539
Head, Travis 527, 539
Headley, George 56, 71, 74, 74–6, 136
Healy, Ian 264, 270, 274
helmets 180, 193, 204, 485, 486
Hemmings, Eddie 220
Hendricks, Krom 165
Hendricks Law 26
Hendricks, William Henry 23–4, 26
Henry, Matt 528
Henry, Omar 279–81, 281–2, 408
Herath, Rangana 337–8
Hesson, Mike 494, 504, 505
Hick, Graeme 320, 357, 376, 478
Hill, Clem 36–7, 432
Hirst, George 36
Hirwani, Narendra 220, 254
hit wicket decision 423
Hobbs, Jack 'The Master' 29–30, 48, 49–50, 52–3, 64
Hogg, Rodney 210
Hoggard, Matthew 370, 371, 372
Hohns, Trevor 212
Holder, Jason 455–6
Holding, Michael 'Whispering Death' 185, 189–90, 294, 425, 457, 479
  on biased umpiring 423
  on bowling fast 480–1
  on fees for away teams 452–3
  on injuries to batsmen
  on Packer 196
  responding to Greig's insult 183–4
  on Waight 196
  on the WICB's failures 450
  on winning in England 191
Holmes, Percy 65
Hood, John 503
Hookes, David 204
hooking 83, 193, 486
Horan, Tom 1
Hordern, Ranji 41
Houghton, David 354, 355, 357, 358, 360
Howard, Geoffrey 159
Howard, John 326
Howard, Nigel 145

Huddleston, Trevor 152–3
Huff, Nigel 364
Hughes, Kim 203, 209, 217
Hughes, Philip 485, 486
Hurlingham Club 41, 42
Hussain, Nasser 378, 379, 380, 396, 492–3
  captaincy 377, 381–2, 397, 399
  on Fletcher 381
  message to Cronje 288
Hutton, Len 75, 76, 96, 100, 485
  on Bradman 79
  captaincy 103, 145–6
  on Hammond 55
  partnership with Compton 102–3
  vs. Australia 105–6

Ibrahim, Dawood 292
Illingworth, Ray 146, 173
Illustrated Sporting and Dramatic News, The 12
Imperial Cricket Conference (ICC) 27, 42, 57, 116, 191, 323
  later International Cricket Conference (ICC) *see* International Cricket Conference (ICC)
India
  admission to Test cricket 57, 63
  All-India tour (1911) 62–3
  away Test record 311–12, 313, 316
  Bombay Pentangular 62
  cricket's coming of age 175
  democratisation of selection 468, 470
  expansion of cricket 61–2
  facilities 307
  fast bowling 218, 466–8
  financial investment 469–70
  gilli-danda 61
  independence 114–15
  investment in domestic pitches 467–8
  IPL 454–5, 468
  membership of the ICC 67
  National Cricket Academy 307
  opening batsmen 176–7
  origins of cricket 60–1
  partition 466
  revenue from ICC 454

INDEX

social acceptance 63–4
spin bowling 170–2, 174, 218
terrorist attack 317
transformation 465
vs. Australia 219–20, 307–11, 312–13, 459–64, 472–3
vs. England 63–5, 66, 170–1, 172–3, 175, 178, 220, 317–18
vs. New Zealand 171
vs. Pakistan 119, 120–2, 218–19, 304–6, 314–16, 316
vs. West Indies 171–2, 175–6, 178, 179–80, 220
World Test Championship (2021) 505–8
Inman, Clive 245
Insole, Doug 160
Intercontinental Cup 510, 516
International Cricket Conference (ICC) 200, 246–7
  Associate Members 247, 357
  later International Cricket Council (ICC) *see* International Cricket Council (ICC)
International Cricket Council (ICC) 242, 293
  Anti-Corruption Unit 293
  Associate Members 453, 454, 510
  Big Three takeover 454
  Elite Panel of Umpires 426
  failed plans 498–9
  financial inequality 453–7
  Full Members 279, 414, 453, 454, 510, 517
  neutral umpires 426
  opposition to expansion 509
  professionalisation 498
  rankings 498
  reforms 536–8
  revenue-distribution model 453–4, 535–6
  structure of Test cricket 497–9
Inzamam-ul-Haq 264, 291, 292, 382, 442
IPL 454–5, 468
Iqbal, Asif 121
Iqbal, Tamim 418
Ireland 509, 511–14, 517–19, 519–20, 521
Irish Cricket Union 512

Isam, Mohammad 417
Islam, Aminul 412, 413, 415, 416
Islamia College 118

Jackson, Archie 89–90
Jacobs, Ridley 446
Jadeja, Ravindra 431, 474, 476, 505, 506
James, C.L.R. 69–70, 74, 137, 195
Jamieson, Kyle 505, 506
Jardine, Douglas 73, 80–1, 87
  Bodyline 82–4, 85, 86
Jarman, Barry 159
Jayasinghe, Stanley 245
Jayasuriya, Sanath 252, 319–20, 321
Jayawardene, Mahela 331, 332, 333–5, 336, 339
Jenner, Terry 255–6, 373
Jessop, Gilbert 'Croucher' 33–4
Jinnah, Muhammad Ali 62
Johnson, Mitchell 481–2, 522
Johnston, Bill 90, 99, 100
Johnston, Brian 101
Jones, Ben 433
Jones, Ernie 324
Jones, Geraint 371
Jones, Simon 370, 371
Joseph, Alzarri 539
Joseph, Shamar 538–9
Joyce, Ed 513
Joyce, James 512
Jumadeen, Raphick 179

Kallis, Jacques 393, 395, 402, 403–5
Kaluwitharana, Romesh 349–50
Kambli, Vinod 300
Kanhai, Rohan 142
Kardar, Abdul 117, 120, 124, 248, 411
  captaincy 118–19
  on Pakistan's Test status 112
  vs. England 112, 113, 114
Karunatilaka, Shehan 339
Kasprowicz, Michael 277, 308, 371
Keating, Frank 94, 197, 210
Kenya 414
Kenyan Cricket Association 414
Khalil, Mohammad 435
Khan, Ayub 409–10

INDEX

Khan, Imran 147, 213, 225–30, 233, 425, 426
  on bowler-captaincy 148–9
  on Marshall 188
  reverse swing 232, 233, 235–6, 236–7, 238, 239, 240
Khan, Jahangir 362
Khan, Junaid 443
Khan, Rashid 516, 519, 521
Khan, Yahya 410
Khan, Younis 438, 440, 441–2, 444
Khan, Zaheer 467
Kidambi, Prashant 61
Kilkenny 511–12
King, Bart 41
King, Collis 208
Kinnock, Neil 206
Kirsten, Gary 283, 394, 397, 398, 471
Knott, Alan 173, 206, 347–8
Knox, Malcolm 13
Koertzen, Rudi 428
Kohli, Virat 353, 458, 460, 471–4, 506
Kumble, Anil 258, 259, 313

Labuschagne, Marnus 461, 462, 475
Laker, Jim 100, 109–11, 144–5, 152
Lal, Arun 237
Lamb, Allan 239, 282
Lambert, William 8
Lamming, George 76–7, 136
Lancashire League 59, 72
Langer, Justin 262, 272, 341, 368, 525
  on Buchanan 277–8
  concussions 486
  encouragement from Waugh 274
  facing fast bowling 485
  partnership with Hayden 275
Lara, Brian 378, 381, 445–9, 458
Larwood, Harold 79, 81–2, 83, 84–7
late cut shot 35
Latif, Rashid 291
Law, Stuart 272
Lawson, Geoff 216, 222, 423
Lawson, Sir Edward 5
Laxman, V.V.S. 308–10, 311, 312, 315
Leach, Jack 520, 524
Leamon, Nathan 352, 385–6, 389, 433
Lee, Brett 371, 372

left-handed batsmen 432–4
leg glance shot 34–5
leg spin 253–5, 256, 257–60
leg theory 82
  see also Bodyline series (1932/33)
Lehmann, Darren 272
Lillee, Dennis 181–2, 198, 215, 217, 224
  bowling style 182
  director of MRF Pace Foundation 466–7
  reverse swing 235–6
Lillywhite, James 7
Lindsay, Denis 348
Lindwall, Ray 66, 90, 99, 100, 104, 105, 150
Little, Josh 521
Llewellyn, Charlie 24–5, 281–2
Lloyd, Clive 179, 180, 183, 186, 192, 196
  players' earnings 207–8
Lloyd, David 182, 324, 376
Lock, Tony 100, 109, 323
Lockwood, Bill 29
Loehr, Dr Jim 362
Loffing, Florian 433
Lohmann, George 14
Lorgat, Haroon 408
Luckin, Maurice 23
Lyon, Nathan 395, 460, 462, 464, 524, 539
Lyttelton, Alfred 1

Macartney, Charlie 37
MacGill, Stuart 259, 272, 447, 448
MacKinnon, Donald 45
MacLaren, Archie 28, 40, 42
MacLaurin, Lord 382
Mahmood, Fazal 112–14, 115, 117, 119–20, 121, 122
Mahmood, Mazher 294
Mahmud, Hasan 422
Mahmud, Khaled 413
Mailey, Arthur 47–8, 49, 241, 254
Majeed, Mazhar 294–5
Malik, Saleem 229, 291, 292
Malik, Taj 514, 515
Malinga, Lasith 336
Mallett, Ashley 254

INDEX

Mammen, Ravi 466–7
Mandela, Nelson 210, 279, 281, 282, 284
Mankad, Vinoo 67
Manley, Michael 68, 74, 76, 281
Mann, David 482, 483, 484
Manthorp, Neil 404–5
Maple 69
Marlar, Robin 190, 411
Marsh, Jack 40, 81
Marsh, Rod 215, 269, 276, 348–9
Marsh, Shaun 473
Marshall, Malcolm 187–8, 190, 208, 228
Martindale, Manny 74
Martyn, Damien 272, 274–5, 277, 283
Marylebone Cricket Club (MCC)
   see MCC
Mascarenhas, Mark 302
match-fixing 8, 285–97, 437
Mathews, Angelo 336–7, 338
Matthews, Greg 223
Mayers, Kyle 457
May, Peter 104, 107, 146, 151, 430
May, Tim 262–3, 291
MCC 4, 11, 13, 16, 35–6, 498
   D'Oliveira affair 157–62
   laws of cricket 4
   vs. Argentina (1911/12) 42
McCabe, Stan 55, 83
McConnon, Jim 113–14
McCullum, Brendan 494–7, 503, 529
McDermott, Craig 263
McDonald, Colin 109, 110
McDonald, Ted 46–7, 241
McGrath, Glenn 264, 277, 370, 371
   bowling approach 267–8
   record 267, 271
Meckiff, Ian 128, 129, 322, 323
Mehta, Rabindra 233–4, 240
Melbourne Cricket Ground 7, 15, 139, 247, 321
   Boxing Day Tests 321, 386
Mello, Anthony de 64
Mendis, Ajantha 436
Mendis, Duleep 247, 248–9, 250
Merchant, Vijay 66, 176–7, 466
Merritt, Bill 59
Miandad, Javed 147, 226, 228–9, 237, 424

Midwinter, Billy 12–13
Midwinter, Eric 3, 43
Miller, Keith 66, 99, 100, 106, 110, 241
   on India 175
   on Richards 162
   talent 90, 98
Milton, William 'Joey' 22, 23–4
Miraz, Mehidy Hasan 418, 419, 421
Misbah-ul-Haq 437–8, 440, 441, 442, 443–4
Mitchell, Dr Keith 449
Mohammad family 123–4, 125
Mohammad, Hanif 113–14, 118–19, 120, 123, 124–5, 142
Mohammed, Sadiq 218
Monckton, Viscount 152
Moneyball 389
Moody, Clarence 10
Mooney, John 513
Moores, Peter 384, 385
Morgan, Eoin 513
Morkel, Morne 402
Morris, Arthur 90, 91, 99
Morris, Sam 40
Moseley, Ezra 211
MRF Pace Foundation 466–7
Mugabe, Robert 363, 364, 365
Mullally, Alan 374
Muralidaran, Muthiah 251, 319, 320–1, 324–33
   background 327–8
   bowling method 329
   doosra 325, 329
   spot bowling 329
   Test wickets record 330–3
   throwing incident 321–2, 324–5, 326
Murdoch, Billy 39
Murray, David 211
Murtagh, Tim 520
Mushtaq, Saqlain 305, 325, 413

Nabi, Mohammad 516
Nandy, Ashis 60
Natarajan, Thangarasu 468
National Cricket Academy 467
Nawaz, Sarfraz 231–2, 236, 240, 291
Nayudu, Cottari 63, 64, 65, 115

INDEX

Nehru, Jawaharlal 67, 119
Nelson 72, 73
New Zealand 171, 505–8
  admission to Test cricket 57
  changing culture 494–5
  cricketing struggles 60
  governance 503–4
  Hood Report 503
  loss of key players 58–9
  national contracts 504
  national team interests 505
  origins of cricket 57–8
  Plunket Shield 58
  vs. Australia 221–3
  vs. England 56, 57, 58, 223–4, 503
  vs. India 496–7
  vs. Pakistan 501–2, 503
  vs. West Indies 501
  warrant of fitness 504
  World Test Championship (2021) 500, 501–3
New Zealand Cricket Council 58, 503–4
New Zealand Cricket Players Association 504
Nichols, Stan 73
Nissar, Mohammad 65, 170
no-ball law 487
Noble, Monty 40
Noori, Allah Dad 515
Norris, Percy 436
Northern Ireland 512
Nourse, Arthur 19
Ntini, Makhaya 400, 408
Ntuta, Jean 356

Oakman, Alan 152
Oborne, Peter 115, 116, 157
O'Brien, Kevin 517–19
O'Brien, Niall 517–18
Odendaal, André 21, 25, 157
ODI World Cups *see* World Cups
Old, Chris 216, 217
Old Georgians 364
Old Winstonans (later Takashinga) 364
Oldfield, Bert 84, 87
Ollivierre, Charles 72–3, 195

Olonga, Henry 363–5
one-day cricket 247–8, 290
  see also World Cups
Ontong, Justin 408
Oosthuizen, Tienie 158, 159
O'Reilly, Bill 77, 86, 87, 254–5
Oriental Cricket Club 61
Outschoorn, Laddie 245
overarm bowling 4

pace bowling *see* fast bowling
Packer, Kerry 196, 198–205
  broadcasting deal 202–3
  contracts 199–200
  plan 198
  truce 202
  see also World Series Cricket
Pakistan 112–14, 115–16, 122
  boot camp 444
  curfews 437
  exile 443–4
  families of cricketers 122–4
  independence 115, 116
  neutral umpires 426
  origins of cricket 117–18
  Oxbridge Complex 147
  spin bowling 438–9
  spot-fixing scandal 294–7, 437
  terrorist attack 435–7
  Test status 116, 117, 118
  UAE base 438–9, 440, 443
  vs. Australia 440–1
  vs. England 112–14, 438–40, 444
  vs. India 119, 120–2, 237–8
  vs. MCC 116–17
  vs. West Indies 124–5, 227–30
  World Cup (2007) 511
Pakistan Cricket Board 443
Pall Mall Gazette 16
Panesar, Monty 317
Pant, Rishabh 353, 463, 464
Paranavitana, Tharanga 435, 436
Pardon, Sydney 38, 47
Parks, Jim 347
Parry, Richard 23, 25, 26, 157
Parsi community 61–3
Pataudi, Nawab of 64, 65, 83–4

INDEX

Pataudi, 'Tiger' (Nawab of Pataudi Jnr) 165–71, 466
  adapting to eye injury 167
  captaincy 168, 169–70
  car crash 166–7
  embracing spin bowling 170–1
  family background 168
  Test career 168–71
Patel, Brijesh 179, 180
Patiala, Maharajah of 64
Patterson, Patrick 188, 220
Pearson, Harry 72
Peate, Ted 2
Peel, Robert 15
Perera, Kusal 339–40
Peterson, Robin 405
Philander, Vernon 393, 402
Phillips, Jim 324
Pietersen, Kevin 375, 388, 439, 530
  aggressive batting 369, 370, 372–3, 390
  on DRS 432
  facing Johnson 481, 482
  facing spin bowling 390
  facing wobble seam 490
  loss of captaincy 384
  punishment 390
Plessis, Faf du 394
Plunket, William 58
Pollock, Graeme 162–3
Pollock, Shaun 275, 283, 293–4, 335, 396, 399, 405
Ponting, Ricky 259, 269, 275–6, 311, 371, 395, 403
Pooley, Ted 7–8
Porbandar, Maharajah of 64
Prasanna, Erapalli 169, 170, 171, 174, 469
Priestley, J.B. 141
Prince, Ashwell 407
Prior, Matt 388, 393, 429
Procter, Mike 163, 164, 357
Pujara, Cheteshwar 462, 463, 464, 473, 506
Punch 11
Puppala, Chandramohan 292
Pycroft, James 8

Qadir, Abdul 226, 228, 254
Qayyum Commission 291–2

Queen's Park Club 69
quick bowling *see* fast bowling

Rabada, Kagiso 339, 340, 407
racial divisions
  apartheid *see* apartheid
  in Australia 40
  in Ceylon 245
  in England 39–40, 191
  in South Africa 21, 24–5, 26, 39–40, 209, 279–80, 407–8
  in Southern Rhodesia/Zimbabwe 356, 364
  in the West Indies 126, 135–7, 138
  see also South Africa: rebel tours
Rafique, Mohammad 417
Rahane, Ajinkya 459–61, 462, 463
Rahim, Mushfiqur 418, 421
Rahman, Naimur 415
Rahman, Sheikh Mujibur 410
Ramadhin, Sonny 133–4, 135, 194
Ramprakash, Mark 257, 321, 375, 376
Rana, Nahid 422
Rana, Shakoor 425
Ranatunga, Arjuna 211, 250–1, 252, 319, 320, 322
Ranchi 470
Ranji Trophy 63, 97, 122
Ranjitsinhji, Kumar Shri 5–6, 34–5, 39
Raza, Ahsan 436
Rehman, Abdur 439, 440
Reiffel, Paul 264, 272
reverse sweep 124, 226
reverse swing 185, 225, 228, 231–42
  Akram 237–8, 239, 240–1
  ball tampering 239–42
  conditions for 233–4
  definition 234
  English cricketers 241–2
  Khan 236–7
  Nawaz 231–2, 236, 240
  origins of 231–2, 234–6
  Younis 237–8, 239
Rhodes, Jonty 407–8
Rhodes, Wilfred 29
Rhodesian Cricket Union 356
Rhodesian Indian Cricket Union 356

INDEX

Richards, Barry 162–3, 165, 202
Richards, Viv 184, 211, 229
  approach to batting 192–3, 196
  identification with black movements 193
  unpopular comments 193–4
Richardson, Arthur 49
Richardson, David (ICC) 453, 499
Richardson, David (wicketkeeper) 286
Richardson, Richie 188, 195
Richardson, Tom 15
Richardson, Vic 60
Ritchard, Cyril 83
Rizwan, Mohammad 501, 502
Roberts, Andy 184, 186–7, 189, 195, 204, 423–4
  bouncers 187
  Test debut 183
  on winning in England 191
Robertson-Glasgow, R.C. 54–5, 79, 80, 91
Robins, Derrick 205
Rogers, John 202–3
Root, Joe 418, 491, 531–3
Roro, Frank 165
Ross, Alan 103, 107, 110
Rouse, Paul 511
Rowe, Lawrence 208
Royal College Colombo 245, 250
Rudolph, Jacques 408
Russell, Jack 349
Ryan, Greg 57

S. Thomas' College 245, 250
Saha, Wriddhiman 353
Saini, Navdeep 462, 468
Salie, Taliep 165
Samaraweera, Thilan 436
Samiuddin, Osman 113, 118, 291
Sandle, Mike 494, 495
Sangakkara, Kumar 76, 330–1, 337, 339, 428, 435
  on batting 335
  on Gilchrist 350
  on Muralidaran 328
  partnership with Jayawardene 333–5, 336
Sangar, Tuba 517
Santner, Mitchell 502
Sardesai, Dilip 172, 173

Saunders, Jack 29
Sawle, Laurie 270, 271
Schwarz, Reggie 18–19, 27
seam bowling 490
Sehwag, Virender 277, 314–17
Sekhar, T.A. 466, 467
Sengupta, Arunabha 173
Shah, Ali 354
Shah, Yasir 441, 443, 444
shamateurs/shamateurism 6–7, 26, 144
Shami, Mohammed 473–4
Shamrock 69
Shannon 69
Sharma, Ajay 290
Sharma, Ishant 472, 473
Shastri, Ravi 462
Sheffield Shield 35, 266, 271
Sherwell, Percy 19
Shillinglaw, Tony 78, 79
Shiv Sena 304
short ball 478
Sibanda, Vusi 364
Simpson, Bob 130, 151, 203, 269–70
Sinclair, Jimmy 20
Sind Quadrangular 117–18
Singh, Harbhajan 310, 311, 331, 404
Singh, Manmohan 301
Singh, Yuvraj 318, 331
Sinhalese Sports Club (SSC) 251
Siraj, Mohammed 462, 467, 468
Slade, Justice 200
sledging 481
slider 255
Smith, Collie 141–2
Smith, Graeme 276, 393, 395, 396, 396–9, 408
  captaincy 396–8
  memorable innings 398–9
  school 396–7
Smith, Ian 356
Smith, Steve 79, 242, 461, 462, 475, 525–6, 539
  idiosyncratic technique 525
  sandpaper incident 525
  vs. England 525, 526–7
Smith, Sydney 73
Snooke, Tip 20

574

INDEX

Snow, John 410, 424
Sobers, Garry 126–7, 130, 138–42, 213, 356, 430
  County Championship 195
  on Sri Lanka 250
  Test record 403
Solkar, Eknath 172
Solomon, Joe 127, 129
South Africa 18–19
  Afrikaner cricketers 25–6
  apartheid era *see* apartheid
  Asian tours 284–5
  black batsmen 407
  black bowlers 407
  British military 21
  fast bowling 399, 400
  growth of cricket 21
  private tours 205
  Proteas 398
  racial divisions 21, 24–5, 26, 39–40, 209, 279–80, 407–8
  rebel tours 206–7, 208–11, 280
  return to Test cricket 281–2
  unequal distribution of wealth 407–8
  vs. Australia 283–4, 394–6, 401–2
  vs. England 19–20, 22–3, 393, 397, 398–9
  vs. India 402–3, 404–5
  vs. West Indies 281
South African Coloured Cricket Board 21
South African Cricket Association 21, 22, 25, 27, 161, 162
South African Cricket Board of Control 155
South African Cricket Union (SACU) 205–6
Southee, Tim 502, 503, 505
Southern Rhodesia 355–6
  later Zimbabwe *see* Zimbabwe
speed guns 487
Speed, Malcolm 452
spin bowling 17–18, 19, 20–1
Spofforth, Fred 'The Demon' 11, 81–2, 147–8, 324
  bowling variations 2
  on Grace 6
  vs. England (1882) 1–3

Sri Lanka (formerly Ceylon) 211
  Big Matches 250
  civil war 327–8
  domestic structure 339
  one-off Tests with England 319, 321
  school system 249–51
  team bus attack 435–6
  tsunami 328
  vs. Australia 330, 338
  vs. England 248, 249, 319–21, 336–7
  vs. India 248–9, 249, 330–2
  vs. South Africa 335–6, 339–40
  World Cups 247, 252, 319, 320
Srinath, Javagal 467
Srinivasan, Narayanaswami 454
Starc, Mitchell 462, 463, 538
Statham, Brian 106, 107, 151
Stewart, Alec 349, 350, 382
Stewart, Micky 239
Steyn, Dale 339, 340, 394, 395, 400–3, 481
  on managing pain 479–80
sticky wickets 30, 49, 53, 344
Stokes, Ben 522
  affray charge 522–3
  Bazball 528–34
  captaincy 527–8
  merging of red- and white-ball approach 529–30
  punishment 522
  vs. Australia 522, 523–4
Stollmeyer, Jeffrey 136
Strauss, Andrew 261, 372, 375, 390, 393, 399
  changing culture of players 384–5
  dinners with teammates 387
  on DRS reviews 429
  strategy 388, 389
  on Swann 387
  vs. Australia 261, 372, 386, 387, 388
Streak, Heath 360, 366
Strudwick, Herbert 344
Sundar, Washington 462, 464
Surendran, C.P. 302–3
Sutcliffe, Herbert 49–50, 51, 52–3, 64, 65
Suthar, Nihar 515
Swann, Graeme 317, 385, 387, 431
Swanton, Jim 104, 159–60, 200–1
sweep 381

INDEX

swing bowling 36, 490
   see also conventional swing; reverse swing
Sydney Cricket Ground 201

T20 competitions 399, 456, 457–8, 470, 498, 504, 509
   Caribbean Premier League 458
   IPL 454–5, 468
Taliban 514, 515, 516, 517
Tancred, Bernard 24
Tarapore, Keki 218, 312
Tate, Fred 29, 48
Tate, Maurice 48
Taufel, Simon 427, 429, 431
Tayfield, Hugh 154
Taylor, Lynton 535
Taylor, Mark 264
Taylor, Ross 506–7, 508
technology 427–32, 491
Tendulkar, Sachin 298–318, 389, 402, 491
   early Test career 300–1
   facing fast bowling 303
   maidans 298–300
   memorable innings 303–4, 305–6, 310, 313, 317–18
   method against Warne 306
   popularity of 302, 304
   pressure 302–3
   wealth 302
Test Cricket Fund 536
Test Match Special 101
Test matches/cricket 302–3
   awarded status of 10, 23
   batting performances 31–2, 36, 51
   bowler's run up 46–7
   bowling performances 36, 51
   conservatism 499
   exclusions from 42–3
   fears for future of 535
   home side advantage 489
   inaugural 7, 9–10
   matting wickets 19
   opening pair partnerships 52
   organisation of time 48
   scoring rates 534
   second chances 16

triangular tournament (1912) 43–4
uncovered pitches 30, 46–7, 49
Thakur, Shardul 462, 468
Thomson, Jeff 181–2, 198, 247
   bowling style 182–3
Thorpe, Graham 369, 376, 379, 380–1, 532
throwing 321–7
Tipperary 512
Tissera, Michael 246
top spin 58
Traicos, John 355
Transparency International 454
Tremlett, Chris 386, 388
Trescothick, Marcus 241–2, 370, 378
Trott, Albert 15
Trott, Jonathan 388, 482
Trueman, Fred 108, 151
Trumble, Hugh 29, 33, 34
Trumper, Victor 28, 29–31, 33, 37, 38
Tunga, Krishna 277, 278
Turner, Glenn 222
Tutu, Bishop Desmond 209–10
Twenty20 *see* T20
Twopeny, Robert 11
Tyldesley, Ernest 47
Tyson, Frank 104–5, 106, 107–8

U-19 World Cup 467
Ulyett, George 1
umpires
   bias 424–5
   complaints about 424–5
   contentious decisions 423–4
   disputes with 425
   DRS 428, 429, 430–2, 433, 434
   home umpires 426–7
   lbw decisions 424, 425, 426–7, 429–31, 432
   neutral 426, 434
   technology 427–32
   umpire's call 428–9
Underwood, Derek 248, 254, 348
Union of South Africa 26
United States of America (USA) 41, 42–3
Upington, Sir Thomas 22